T0348584

HANDBOOK OF
INTERNATIONAL ECONOMICS
VOLUME 2

HANDBOOKS IN ECONOMICS

3

Series Editors

KENNETH J. ARROW
MICHAEL D. INTRILIGATOR

ELSEVIER

Amsterdam • Boston • London • New York • Oxford • Paris
San Diego • San Francisco • Singapore • Sydney • Tokyo

HANDBOOK OF INTERNATIONAL ECONOMICS

VOLUME 2
INTERNATIONAL MONETARY ECONOMICS AND FINANCE

Edited by

RONALD W. JONES
University of Rochester

and

PETER B. KENEN
Princeton University

ELSEVIER

Amsterdam • Boston • London • New York • Oxford • Paris
San Diego • San Francisco • Singapore • Sydney • Tokyo

ELSEVIER SCIENCE B.V.
Sara Burgerhartstraat 25
P.O. Box 211, 1000 AE Amsterdam, The Netherlands

Hardbound edition 1985
Paperback edition 1988
Second impression 1988
Third impression 1990
Fourth impression 1996
Fifth impression 2003

Library of Congress Cataloging-in-Publication Data
A CIP record for this book is available from the Library of Congress

ISBN: 0-444-86793-7
ISSN: 0169-7218 (Handbooks in Economics Series)
⊗ The paper used in this publication meets the requirements of ANSI/NISO Z39.48-1992 (Permanence of Paper).

Transferred to Digital Printing 2009.

INTRODUCTION TO THE SERIES

The aim of the *Handbooks in Economics* series is to produce Handbooks for various branches of economics, each of which is a definitive source, reference, and teaching supplement for use by professional researchers and advanced graduate students. Each Handbook provides self-contained surveys of the current state of a branch of economics in the form of chapters prepared by leading specialists on various aspects of this branch of economics. These surveys summarize not only received results but also newer developments, from recent journal articles and discussion papers. Some original material is also included, but the main goal is to provide comprehensive and accessible surveys. The Handbooks are intended to provide not only useful reference volumes for professional collections but also possible supplementary readings for advanced courses for graduate students in economics.

KENNETH J. ARROW and MICHAEL D. INTRILIGATOR

PUBLISHER'S NOTE

For a complete overview of the Handbooks in Economics Series, please refer to the listing at the end of this volume.

CONTENTS OF THE HANDBOOK

VOLUME 1

PREFACE TO THE HANDBOOK

The scope of the Handbook

Very few economic problems can be analyzed completely without asking whether and to what degree an economy is open. Many problems are, of course, too intricate to analyze completely, and the implications of openness are therefore ignored to make room for other complications. But the international aspects of "domestic" problems are treated with increasing frequency and thoroughness in theoretical, empirical, and policy studies. In the United States, *The Annual Report of the Council of Economic Advisers* has almost always had an international chapter, but it was usually the last; in 1983, however, it moved from the back to the middle of the book.

Those of us who call ourselves international economists rejoice in the increasing importance attached to our subject; it is rewarding intellectually and may even have employment-creating effects. When it comes time to define our specialty, however, the trend is a bit perplexing. We cannot claim that our subject is coextensive with the whole of economics, but it is hard to draw defensible boundaries. Which problems should we claim as being intrinsically international? Which ones should we cede as being basically domestic? To organize this Handbook, we had first to define our subject carefully.

We have not included every subject and problem that has international aspects or ramifications. Instead, we have adopted a traditional definition of our subject, focusing primarily on the explanation of international transactions in goods, services, and assets, and on the main domestic effects of those transactions. We have done so for reasons of manageability, and for two other reasons as well. First, we believe that a traditional definition is least likely to disappoint or surprise those readers of this Handbook who approach it with expectations based on that sort of definition. Second, we expect other Handbooks to deal extensively with the international dimensions and ramifications of their own subjects.

The first volume of the Handbook deals with the "real side" of international economics. It is concerned with the explanation of trade and factor flows, with their main effects on goods and factor prices, on the allocation of resources and income distribution and on economic welfare, and with the effects of national policies designed explicitly to influence trade and factor flows. In other words, it deals chiefly with microeconomic issues and methods. The second volume deals with the "monetary side" of the subject. It is concerned with the balance-of-payments adjustment process under fixed exchange rates, with exchange-rate determination under flexible exchange rates, and with the domestic ramifications of these phenomena. Accordingly, it deals mainly with macroeconomic issues, although microeconomic methods are frequently utilized, especially in work on expectations, asset markets, and exchange-rate behavior.

Organization and objectives

Each volume of the Handbook is introduced by a pair of chapters which survey broadly the subjects covered by that volume. The chapters that follow supplement the introductions in one or more ways. Some chapters examine in detail subjects discussed briefly in the introduction; some chapters focus on new issues and approaches; some chapters complement the analytical surveys by reviewing empirical work. All of the chapters, however, attempt to integrate the results of recent research and to identify problems that call for more research.

The two chapters that introduce the first volume of the Handbook divide up their task analytically. In the first chapter, Jones and Neary present the "positive theory" of international trade, paying particular attention to the contributions and limitations of the Heckscher–Ohlin model that has been at the core of analytical work for about four decades. In the second chapter, Corden presents the "normative theory" of international trade, looking at the gains from trade and factor movements and at the various reasons for interfering with them. Subsequent chapters extend these surveys by looking more closely at trade and growth, international factor movements, trade in resource products, and other analytical issues. Other chapters review empirical work on the testing of trade models and on trade policies in developed and developing countries.

The two chapters that introduce the second volume of the Handbook divide up their task historically. In the first chapter, Kenen traces the evolution of international monetary theory through the three decades following the Second World War, paying particular attention to the Meade–Fleming–Mundell model, which played a role on the monetary side as important as that of the Heckscher–Ohlin model on the real side. In the second chapter, Frenkel and Mussa review more recent developments by assessing the contributions of monetary and asset-market models. Subsequent chapters examine in detail the modelling of asset markets and goods markets, the behavior and efficiency of foreign-exchange markets, aspects of policy interdependence, and the roles of reserves and reserve assets.

Some topics have fallen between the cracks, even though we have deliberately limited the scope of this Handbook. The activities of multinational firms are discussed in two chapters, but there is no comprehensive survey of research of their behavior or the broad economic implications of their activities. International capital movements are discussed extensively, but there is not much said about the Euromarkets, international bank lending, or the many issues related to them.

More generally, the chapters in the first volume of the Handbook fit together fairly well, but those in the second are not as well integrated. This testifies, however, to the state of the art rather than the success or failure of the editors and authors. The real side of trade theory is more cohesive than the monetary side, which reflects all too well the disintegration of professional consensus on macro-economic theory and policy.

Acknowledgements

We are deeply grateful to the authors of this volume for the care they took in preparing their chapters, the time they took to read and comment on other authors' drafts, and the attention they paid to the instructions and advice with which we assaulted them. We want also to thank the International Finance Section at Princeton University for sponsoring two conferences at which the authors presented first drafts of their papers, dealt with gaps and duplication, and gave the editors useful advice about the enterprise as a whole. Without those meetings, the Handbook would have taken longer to complete, and it would have had many more defects.

RONALD W. JONES
University of Rochester

PETER B. KENEN
Princeton University

CONTENTS OF VOLUME II

Chapter 13

MACROECONOMIC THEORY AND POLICY: HOW THE CLOSED ECONOMY WAS OPENED

PETER B. KENEN

Princeton University

Contents

Handbook of International Economics, vol. II, edited by R.W. Jones and P.B. Kenen
© *Elsevier Science Publishers B.V., 1985*

1. Introduction

This chapter is designed as background to those that follow, It shows how international transactions and relationships were introduced into macroeconomic models and policy in the twenty-five years following the Second World War. It does not trace each step in that complicated process or give credit to each contributor. It uses a simple model to show how issues were defined, how they were analyzed, and how well or badly the dominant approach reflected the realities of economic life.[1]

This chapter does not bring us up to date. That task has been left to Frenkel and Mussa, whose survey of recent developments in Chapter 14 starts shortly before this one ends, and to the authors of the specialized chapters that complete this volume. Nevertheless, there are three ways in which this introduction can cast light on current work and controversy.

First, it introduces tools of analysis that are (or ought to be) employed in current work. Modern models of exchange-rate determination focus sharply on money and bond markets. They cannot describe the path of the exchange rate, however, without showing what happens to the current-account balance, and the evolution of that balance is governed in part by the price elasticities and income propensities that were the main ingredients of older models. The Marshall–Lerner–Robinson condition, discussed later in this chapter, was developed to show how a change in the exchange rate affects the current-account balance. It is found in recent models too, but tucked away in stability conditions and equations dealing with the path of the economy. The Keynesian multiplier, adapted to the open economy by Metzler (1942a), Machlup (1943), and Meade (1951), was used to show how changes in domestic activity affect the balance of payments and to trace the propagation of business fluctuations. It is found in recent models too, but lurking alongside the elasticities conditions.

Second, the period on which this chapter concentrates was one in which there was widespread agreement about the aims and instruments of economic policy. Great weight was given to full employment and to fiscal policy. Less weight was given to price stability and to monetary policy. There were vigorous disagreements about the choice between fixed and flexible exchange rates, the contribution of "money illusion" to the success of fiscal and exchange-rate policies, and the conduct of monetary policy. These were the precursors of debates that rage

---

[1] The approach followed in this chapter owes much to the ideas and work of Ronald McKinnon; see especially McKinnon (1981). He and I had planned to write this chapter jointly and conferred extensively at an early stage. Unfortunately, he had to withdraw from the project in order to honor prior commitments. I am grateful to him for suggestions and advice, but I must bear all blame for defects in the chapter.

today. Yet there was less dissonance than we endure today. Debates were conducted by appealing to beliefs that were firmly held by most of the participants. They did not develop from deep disagreements about the way in which economies behave. No one had told us that "rational expectations" keep policies from having permanent effects on output or employment. No one had told us that currency markets are inhabited by hosts of risk-neutral speculators capable of gobbling up the central banks' reserves.

Arguments about fixed and flexible exchange rates dealt mainly with the best technique for altering rates promptly. Here is how I put the issue when I was younger and the world was simpler:

> The issue, in the end, is horribly subjective. Will it be easier to persuade the central banks that speculators are not gnomes and that they can be trusted to manage the exchange rates, or instead to convince them that their own self-esteem does not depend upon the preservation of a fixed parity, but rather on their skill in choosing a new rate? [Kenen (1969a, p. 364)].

Not much was said about the ways in which exchange-rate changes can influence wages and prices, nominal rates of return on financial instruments, or the demand for real balances.

Arguments about the use of monetary policy dealt mainly with the size and stability of lags in the influence of money on aggregate demand. The case for a "predictable" monetary policy was based on the belief that lags are long and changeable, so that "fine tuning" of the money supply or close concentration on the management of interest rates can amplify economic fluctuations. Little was said about the possibility emphasized so often now that nominal interest rates and money stocks can rise and fall together, rather than moving in opposite directions, because expectations about inflation are sensitive to monetary policy. The distinction between anticipated and unanticipated changes in the money supply had not made its appearance.

Finally, we need to be reminded frequently that models which appear to be very general are rooted shallowly in recent experience. The actors within any economic model base their own decisions on experience. The ways in which households, firms, and governments respond to information are conditioned by earlier successes and mistakes. They may be maximizing something or other, but their strategies are almost always based on imperfect information and imperfect methods for collecting and assessing it. The institutional framework within which they operate is itself a product of experience. Economic institutions and arrangements can change rapidly, and arrangements designed de novo by governments, because others have malfunctioned or broken down, reflect all too faithfully the dominant diagnosis of their predecessors' defects. Finally, economists design their own models to fit certain sets of facts, frequently subsets of "stylized facts" distilled from recollection and observation by methods that we do not articulate clearly, and the need to be "relevant" leads us to build models that fit the recent facts most closely. Theory is inspired by history, but good theorists do not always have long memories.

2. Stylized facts and economic analysis

In the period on which this chapter concentrates, two sets of stylized facts had enormous influence on theory and policy. International monetary relations were governed by the Bretton Woods Agreement of 1944, which reflected the dominant interpretation of international monetary history before the Second World War — of errors made in monetary reconstruction during the twenties and in monetary management during the thirties. The analysis and conduct of domestic policy were dominated by the stylized facts from which Keynes constructed *The General Theory* (1936).

2.1. The stylized facts of Bretton Woods

The architects of the Bretton Woods Agreement are often criticized for having insufficient faith in markets and excessive faith in governments. The criticism is half right.

Those who met at Bretton Woods did not believe that markets can regulate exchange rates in a satisfactory way. The dominant interpretation of experience was given by Nurkse in *International Currency Experience* (1944):

> The twenty years between the wars have furnished ample evidence concerning the question of fluctuating *versus* stable exchanges. A system of completely free and flexible exchange rates is conceivable and may have certain attractions in theory; and it might seem that in practice nothing would be easier than to leave international payments and receipts to adjust themselves through uncontrolled exchange variations in response to the play of demand and supply. Yet nothing would be more at variance with the lessons of the past.
>
> Freely fluctuating exchanges involve three serious disadvantages. In the first place, they create an element of risk which tends to discourage international trade. The risk may be covered by "hedging" operations where a forward exchange market exists; but such insurance, if obtainable at all, is obtainable only at a price and therefore generally adds to the cost of trading. ...
>
> Secondly, as a means of adjusting the balance of payments, exchange fluctuations involve constant shifts of labour and other resources between production for the home market and production for export. Such shifts may be costly and disturbing; they tend to create frictional unemployment, and are

obviously wasteful if the exchange-market conditions that call for them are temporary. ...

Thirdly, experience has shown that fluctuating exchanges cannot always be relied upon to promote adjustment. Any considerable or continuous movement of the exchange rate is liable to generate anticipations of a further movement in the same direction, thus giving rise to speculative capital transfers of a disequilibrating kind. ... Self-aggravating movements of this kind, instead of promoting adjustment in the balance of payments, are apt to intensify any initial disequilibrium and to produce what may be called "explosive" conditions of instability. We have observed such forces at work in several cases of freely variable exchange rates; we may recall in particular the example of the French franc during the years 1924–26 [Nurkse (1944, pp. 210–211)].

The architects of Bretton Woods, however, did not trust governments either. The dominant interpretation of experience gave three reasons for concern.

Governments had made serious mistakes in choosing new exchange rates after the First World War:

An exchange rate by definition concerns more currencies than one. Yet exchange stabilization was carried out as an act of national sovereignty in one country after another with little or no regard for the resulting interrelationship of currency values in comparison with cost and price levels. This was so even where help was received from financial centers abroad. Stabilization of a currency was conceived in terms of gold rather than of other currencies. ... From the very start, therefore, the system was subject to stresses and strains. The two most familiar but by no means the only sources of disequilibrium arose from the successive stabilization of the pound sterling and the French franc early in 1925 and late in 1926 respectively, the one at too high and the other at too low a level in relation to domestic costs and prices [Nurkse (1944, pp. 116–117)].

It was therefore decided at Bretton Woods that countries joining the International Monetary Fund would have to choose their parities in consultation with the Fund. (Unfortunately, this decision led to another problem. Countries had to choose their parities too soon, before they could assess, let alone correct, the economic damage done by the war.)

National sovereignty in exchange-rate policy is open to abuse. Exchange rates can be manipulated for "beggar-my-neighbor" purposes. This was the conventional interpretation of the devaluations that took place in the thirties:

In contemporary discussion much stress was laid on the competitive aspects of currency devaluation. In many quarters devaluation was regarded primarily as a means of improving a country's foreign trade balance and hence its volume of domestic employment — an effective means but one that operated necessarily at the expense of other countries and invited retaliation [Nurkse (1944, p. 129)].

Therefore, the Bretton Woods Agreement called on governments to notify the Fund before changing their exchange rates and prohibited them from making large exchange-rate changes without its consent. The only justification for an exchange-rate change, moreover, was a "fundamental disequilibrium." A country with a temporary deficit in its balance of payments was expected to finance it by drawing down reserves and drawing on the Fund.

Finally, governments could not be expected to deflate their economies in order to balance their external accounts. They had not followed the "rules of the game" during the 1920s and 1930s, and they should not be expected to do so in the future.[2] The theory of balance-of-payments adjustment under fixed exchange rates emphasized price changes. But these require changes in output and employment that may not be acceptable:

> Experience has shown that stability of exchange rates can no longer be achieved by domestic income adjustments if these involve depression and unemployment. Nor can it be achieved if such income adjustments involve a general inflation of prices which the country concerned is not prepared to endure. It is therefore only as a consequence of internal stability, above all in the major countries, that there can be any hope of securing a satisfactory degree of exchange stability as well [Nurkse (1944, p. 229)].

We come thus to a second set of stylized facts, having to do with internal stability.

2.2. The stylized facts of Keynesian macroeconomics

Keynes led the British delegation to Bretton Woods, and though the plan adopted there came mainly from American proposals, it owed much to his influence. And this was not his first appearance in the international monetary arena. The book that made him famous, *The Economic Consequences of the Peace* (1919), attacked the economic and financial clauses of the Versailles Treaty. Furthermore, the foreign-exchange markets held center stage in his first major book on monetary theory, *A Tract on Monetary Reform* (1923).

---

[2] The "rules" required contraction of the money supply when reserves were falling and expansion when they were rising. In most cases examined by Nurkse, however, the central banks' foreign and domestic assets moved in opposite directions, reducing or preventing money-supply changes. In some instances, "sterilization" took place automatically because of the ways in which central banks and governments financed their intervention in the foreign-exchange markets. In other cases, it was undertaken deliberately [Nurkse, (1944, pp. 68–88)]. Bloomfield (1963) found evidence of sterilization even before the First World War.

In *The General Theory* (1936), however, we find no discussion of exchange rates, international aspects of income determination, or the need for international cooperation to achieve national stability. "Keynesian macro theory focused on the national economy, and the national government was, explicitly or implicitly, asserted to be the natural form of organization for achieving macroeconomic stability" [Lindbeck (1979, p. 1)].

Keynes probably made the right tactical choice in focusing on the national economy. The concepts introduced in *The General Theory* were not easy to grasp. The policy implications were unorthodox. It was therefore sensible to concentrate on monetary and fiscal policies for a closed economy, not to deal at the same time with foreign repercussions, exchange rates, reserves, and the problem of protection — matters that Keynes had tackled before and would take up again. His choice had important consequences, however, for the way in which other economists would analyze international issues. They opened the Keynesian model of the national economy by adding international transactions, instead of revising the model systematically to allow for the effects of foreign trade and payments on the basic behavioral relationships.

This incremental approach was not harmful for a while. In the years right after the Second World War, foreign trade and payments were indeed additional. They had only marginal effects on domestic markets and behavior. As trade and payments grew, however, the approach became less helpful. Furthermore, some features of *The General Theory* were based on British experience in the 1920s and 1930s, which made it less than general.

In earlier debates about economy policy, Keynes had argued that wage rigidity was the main cause of Britain's economic plight. Money wage rates had fallen sharply in 1921–22, along with prices, but did not continue to fall thereafter, even though unemployment was very high. Keynes went farther. Money wage rates were not likely to rise sharply, he believed, in response to an increase in aggregate demand, a devaluation of the pound, or the use of import tariffs.[3] In *The General Theory*, he converted wage rigidity from a defect to a virtue, although he was careful to point out that he was describing a closed economy:

... I am now of the opinion that the maintenance of a stable general level of money-wages is, on a balance of considerations, the most advisable policy for a closed system; whilst the same conclusion will hold good for an open system, provided that equilibrium with the rest of the world can be secured by means of fluctuating exchanges. There are advantages in some degree of flexibility in the wages of particular industries so as to expedite transfers from those which are relatively declining to those which are relatively expanding. But the money-wage level as a whole should be maintained as stable as possible, at any rate in the short period [Keynes (1936, p. 270)].

[3] Keynes' views and the policy debate itself are summarized in Eichengreen (1981).

This opinion was based largely on another — that prices are determined by demand and supply conditions in domestic markets — so that stable wages can lead to stable prices:

> This policy will result in a fair degree of stability in the price-level. ... Apart from "administered" or monopoly prices, the price-level will only change in the short period in response to the extent that changes in the volume of employment affect marginal prime costs; whilst in the long period they will only change in response to changes in the cost of production due to new technique and new or increased equipment [Keynes (1936, pp. 270–271)].

These views animated the Keynesian approach to wages, prices and exchange rates. As domestic prices depend chiefly on domestic wages, and money wages tend to be rigid, a change in the exchange rate can alter real wages and the level of employment without undermining domestic price stability. It will change the home-currency prices of foreign goods and the foreign-currency prices of domestic goods. But it will not necessarily change the home-currency prices of domestic goods.

Here is how Meade put the matter in *The Balance of Payments* (1951), the most ambitious adaptation of Keynesian analysis to international economic problems:

> There is... no absolute criterion by which it can be decided whether there is sufficient wage flexibility to operate the gold-standard mechanism successfully. It depends upon the degree of wage rate adjustment which it is expected that the adoption of this mechanism will demand. ... If it were judged that there were insufficient flexibility of *money* wage rates to meet the demands which are likely to be put upon a gold-standard system, then some other method of adjustment (such as variable exchange rates) would have to be chosen in its place.
>
> But it would be useless to turn to the mechanism of variable exchange rates unless there were sufficient flexibility of *real* wage rates, because any spontaneous disturbance which, if a new equilibrium is to be found, requires a change in the real terms of trade between A and B is likely to require some change in real wage rates in A and B. For example, a shift of demand away from B's products on to A's products will... require a movement in the terms of trade against B to shift demand back again... and, therefore, in so far as imported products are consumed by wage earners it involves a fall in the real wage in B.
>
> Under the gold standard the necessary reduction in the real wage of labour will be brought about partly by the reduced demand for labour in B causing a reduction in the money wage rate in B, and partly by the increased demand for A's products leading to a rise in the money prices of A's products. ... With variable exchange rates the decline in the real wage rate in B will be brought about by the depreciation of B's currency which will make A's products more

expensive in terms of B's money. Money wage rates in B and the money prices of B's products will remain unchanged, but imports from A will be higher in price.

We may conclude, therefore, that for the gold-standard mechanism to work effectively there must be "sufficient" flexibility of money wage rates; and for the variable-exchange-rate mechanism to work effectively there must be "sufficient" divorce between movements in the cost of living and movements in money wage rates.... [Meade (1951, pp. 201–203)].

Many economists disagreed with Keynes about the rigidity of the money wage. Few were prepared to claim, however, that it is flexible enough to make the gold standard work effectively. It was for this very reason, indeed, that economists started to criticize the Bretton Woods system in the 1960s. The rules of the system, the attitudes of governments, and the freeing of capital movements, permitting speculative attacks on currencies whose rates might be expected to change, had combined to make exchange rates very rigid. The world had thus wandered into a "disequilibrium system" in which there was no way to change the terms of trade. Money wage rates were too rigid. So were exchange rates.[4]

To be consistent, of course, critics of the system had to hold strong views about the cost of living or the real wage. On the one hand, they could hold with Keynes that the prices which figure importantly in the cost of living are determined mainly in domestic markets, so that the cost of living is not affected substantially by a change in the exchange rate. This is the view implicit in the model that Keynesians developed from *The General Theory*. On the other hand, they could hold (or hope) with Meade that "money illusion" permeates the labor market, divorcing the money wage from the cost of living and imparting flexibility to the real wage.

Keynes himself was quite consistent in another way. Even as the prices of domestic goods are determined in his model by domestic markets, so too are the prices of domestic assets and, therefore, the interest rate. In *The General Theory*, the interest rate depends on its own future — on forecasts about interest rates conditioned by experience. (It should also depend on income and wealth, as Keynes' own followers were quick to note, but that is not the issue here.) In an open economy, however, the domestic interest rate depends in part on foreign interest rates and on expectations about exchange rates. Keynes was not unaware of this important point; he came close to making it explicitly in *A Tract on Monetary Reform* (1923), where he worked out the interest-parity condition for the forward exchange rate. But he chose to neglect it a decade later. Finally, the

---

[4] The phase "disequilibrium system" was used by Mundell (1961a), who had in mind one additional feature of the system — the tendency of governments to sterilize changes in reserves — which meant that there could be no changes in price levels even if wage rates were flexible.

money supply is determined domestically in Keynes' model by open-market operations in domestic bonds. There are no operations in foreign exchange.

This approach was not an auspicious starting point for those who sought to study international problems. Consciously or carelessly, they were too faithful to Keynes' model. They neglected the links between domestic and foreign interest rates, as well as the influence of exchange-rate expectations. They neglected the crucial problem of managing the money supply itself. In most Keynesian models of the open economy, including Meade's model, the domestic interest rate is the chief instrument of monetary policy. The central bank holds a stock of foreign currency large enough to peg the exchange rate and a stock of domestic securities large enough to sterilize changes in reserves. It controls the money supply, and it can use the money supply to control the interest rate.

2.3. The insular economy

The Keynesian model of the closed economy was too simple, and so was the open version. Nevertheless, the open version represented quite faithfully many characteristics of the national economies that emerged from the Second World War. McKinnon (1981) has described those economies as *insular*. Their international transactions did not impinge dramatically on their domestic markets, because those markets were not integrated closely with foreign markets. Opportunities for arbitrage in goods and assets were severely limited by the trade, capital, and currency countries put in place in the 1920s and 1930s and the additional barriers erected during the war.

Many new trade barriers were thrown up in the 1920s and 1930s. They were not dismantled until the sixties. The United States adopted the Smoot–Hawley Tariff, the highest in its history, in 1930. The United Kingdom opted for protection two years later. Some countries started to use quotas and other direct controls, and these were reinforced by strict exchange controls after the outbreak of the Second World War. Liberalization got under way soon after the war in the

Table 2.1
Average trade-to-income ratios

Period	U.K.	U.S.
1915–24	41.5	12.4
1925–34	35.4	7.7
1935–44	23.1	6.8
1945–54	32.3	7.4
1955–64	31.5	7.1
1965–74	35.2	10.2

Source: Grassman (1980).

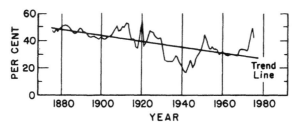

Figure 2.1. Sum of exports and imports as a percentage of gross national product, United Kingdom, 1875–1975. *Source*: Grassman (1980).

framework of the General Agreement of Tariffs and Trade (GATT) and in the Organization for European Economic Cooperation (OEEC), but progress was slow.

The effects of protection and other restrictions show up clearly in conventional measures of economic openness. Grassman (1980) has computed ten-year averages of trade-to-income ratios (sums of exports and imports as percentages of gross national product) for the United Kingdom and the United States (Table 2.1). The ratios drop steadily at first, recover in the first postwar decade, but fall back slightly in the next, even though trade liberalization had begun. Grassman traces the same process relative to trend, and his results for Britain are reproduced in Figure 2.1. The second quarter of this century shows up as the main aberration.[5]

Openness is an "average" concept. It cannot measure faithfully the extent to which foreign transactions impinge on domestic markets. But the change in openness that has taken place, most notably in the case of the United States, does serve to remind us of the difference between the world of the 1940s and 1950s and the world that we know today. American exports were but 5 percent of gross national product in 1950; they rose to 10 percent in 1980. Restrictions on capital flows were widespread and intensive thirty years ago; most of them have been dismantled, and those that remain are made much less effective by opportunities to lend and borrow in Eurocurrency markets. National economies were much more insular in the decades following the Second World War than they are today, and this fact was reflected by the typical model of the open economy. It was insular in three respects.

[5] These numbers tend to understate the recent increase in openness, because the rates of growth of GNP reflect in part rapid rates of growth of public-sector spending (i.e. spending on nontradables). The same point is made by Grassman (1980). The change in the situation of the United States is signaled by the numbers but is not described vividly enough. It would be hard to find an American industry that is not acutely sensitive today to foreign competition, whether it be competition in the domestic market or in export markets.

(1) The share of foreign trade in gross national product was relatively small and, more important, substantial trade barriers restricted the role of commodity arbitrage. In consequence, exchange rates could be changed without significant effects on domestic prices. Domestic prices were determined by domestic wages, and wages were determined by conditions in domestic labor markets. The Phillips curve was firmly anchored even before it was discovered.

(2) The international capital market did not function freely. Therefore, private capital movements could not automatically finance deficits and surpluses on current account. By implication, those deficits and surpluses could not raise or reduce asset stocks or wealth by enough to induce large changes in aggregate demand. (The private flows that did occur could also continue for long periods, because they were small in relation to the corresponding stocks.)

(3) The national monetary systems was insulated. On the one hand, official interventions in foreign-exchange markets were sterilized; they did not affect the monetary base. On the other hand, short-term interest rates could be controlled by monetary policy; they were not influenced by foreign interest rates or exchange-rate expectations.

In the review of theory undertaken below, I stress the roles of these assumptions. In the survey of subsequent developments at the end of this chapter, I show how they were challenged.

3. Incomes, prices, and the current account

Capital movements did not figure importantly in the models of the fifties. When comparing balance-of-payments adjustment under fixed and flexible exchange rates, Meade (1951, ch. 15) was careful to include them, but they could be deleted without altering his argument. (It is indeed better to remove them, because they appear asymmetrically in Meade's comparison. With fixed exchange rates, they occur on account of endogenous changes in interest rates, resulting from endogenous changes in money supplies. There is no sterilization. With flexible exchange rates, they occur on account of exogenous changes in interest rates, because monetary policies are adjusted to maintain internal balance.) Capital movements played more important roles in the models of the 1960s. In Metzler (1960), they reflected changes in saving and investment, which were in turn reflected in the current-account balance. In Fleming (1962) and Mundell (1962, 1963), they reflected changes in monetary policy similar to those in Meade's analysis, but these took place with fixed as well as flexible exchange rates.

The models of the fifties concentrated on the current-account balance and even more narrowly on the trade balance. (When capital movements are neglected, interest-income payments can be neglected too.) Most of the models, moreover, were ultra-Keynesian, in that they fixed the prices of domestic goods rather than the money wage.[6] Two types of models were popular: (1) those in which each country produces a single traded good and (2) those in which each country produces a nontraded good as well as a traded good. In models of the first type, exchange-rate changes induce substitution in consumption by altering the terms of trade (and the "real" exchange rate is thus measured by the terms of trade). In models of the second type, exchange-rate changes induce substitution in production and consumption by altering the relative price of the nontraded good (and the "real" exchange rate is measured by that relative price).[7] I use the first type of model in the rest of this chapter.

3.1. The basic model

There are two goods: x_1 is produced at home, and its home-currency price is p_1, while x_2 is produced abroad, and its foreign-currency price is p_2^*. The nominal exchange rate is π and is measured in units of home currency per unit of foreign currency.

As x_1 is the only good produced at home and x_2 the only one produced abroad, nominal incomes (gross national products) are given by

$$Y = p_1 x_1 \quad \text{and} \quad Y^* = p_2^* x_2. \tag{3.1}$$

As both goods are consumed in each country and nominal consumption is equal to disposable income *less* saving,

$$C = p_1 c_1 + \pi p_2^* c_2 = (Y - T) - S$$

and

$$C^* = \frac{p_1}{\pi} c_1^* + p_2^* c_2^* = (Y^* - T^*) - S^*, \tag{3.2}$$

---

[6]Fixed prices can be squared with fixed wages by imposing a Ricardian assumption (fixed labor requirements per unit of output). As many models of the fifties adopted another Ricardian assumption (complete specialization), they should perhaps be called Ricardian–Keynesian. Various labor-market specifications can be handled simultaneously with a device adopted by Allen and Kenen (1980). Changes in income are measured first in nominal terms. They become output changes when prices are fixed (the case considered in the text); they become price changes when employment is fixed (the classical case considered in most monetary models); they become combinations of output and price changes when the money wage is fixed (the typical Keynesian case). Labor-market specifications are examined thoroughly in Chapter 16 of this Handbook.

[7]This is the only form of substitution in most such models, because the country is deemed to be small in all foreign markets (its terms of trade are fixed). A few models, however, allow both sorts of substitution by making the country large in one foreign market. Meade (1951) deals with both sorts of substitution in his *Mathematical Supplement* but drops the nontraded good from the model used in most of his book, making it into the first type of model. Salter (1959) develops the small-country version of the second type. For more on goods-market specifications, see Chapter 16 of this Handbook.

where c_i ($i = 1, 2$) is the quantity of good i consumed at home, and c_i^* is the quantity consumed abroad, while T and T^* are lump-sum taxes, and S and S^* are private-sector savings.

The home government buys a fixed quantity, g_1, of the domestic good; the foreign government buys a fixed quantity, g_2^*, of the foreign good. Therefore, the budget deficits are

$$D = p_1 g_1 - T \quad \text{and} \quad D^* = p_2^* g_2^* - T^*. \tag{3.3}$$

As g_1 and g_2^* are fixed and their prices are fixed too, changes in T and T^* are reflected fully by D and D^*, and the latter are used as fiscal-policy variables throughout this section. Budget deficits are financed by issuing bonds.[8]

In some applications of the model, it will be important for the interest rate to influence aggregate demand. It could do so by affecting investment, but investment is omitted to keep the model simple. Accordingly, saving is made to depend on disposable income and on the local interest rate:

$$S = s(r, Y - T) \quad \text{and} \quad S^* = s^*(r^*, Y^* - T^*), \tag{3.4}$$

where $0 < s_Y < 1$, $0 < s_Y^* < 1$, and $s_r, s_r^* > 0$.

These are the market-clearing equations for the domestic and foreign goods:

$$c_1 + c_1^* + g_1 - x_1 = 0 \quad \text{and} \quad c_2 + c_2^* + g_2^* - x_2 = 0. \tag{3.5}$$

In the simplest Keynesian model, where prices are fixed, goods markets are cleared by output changes. In the simplest classical model, where outputs are fixed, goods markets are cleared by price changes.

The current-account balance can be obtained from either of the two market-clearing equations. Multiplying the equation for x_1 by p_1, using eqs. (3.1) and (3.2) to replace $p_1 c_1$ with $p_1 x_1 - \pi p_2^* c_2 - T - S$, and using eq. (3.3) to replace $p_1 g_1 - T$ with D,

$$p_1 c_1^* - \pi p_2^* c_2 = S - D. \tag{3.6}$$

As $p_1 c_1^*$ is the level of domestic exports expressed in domestic currency and $\pi p_2^* c_2$ is the level of domestic imports, the left-hand side of (3.6) is the trade balance and is equal in this model to the current-account balance. The right-hand side says that the current-account balance must be matched by the difference

---

[8] The inclusion of government bonds, however, introduces two complications. First, disposable income must be redefined. It becomes gross nation product *plus* interest income on the government bonds held by the public *less* the lump-sum tax. Second, the budget deficit must be redefined. It becomes expenditure *plus* interest payments to the public *less* the lump-sum tax. Both complications can be removed by dividing the lump-sum tax into two parts. The first part is determined exogenously. The second part is set equal at all times to the flow of interest payments and thus changes endogenously whenever there are changes in the interest rate or quantity of debt held by the public. It cancels interest income from the definition of the budget deficit. The first part is the one denoted by T (and T^*) in the text.

between saving and the budget deficit. (In a more general model, it would be matched by the difference between saving *less* investment and the budget deficit.)

Equation (3.6) can be used to explain the asset-market implications of budget deficits financed by issuing bonds. If the demand for money depends on the interest rate and income but not on wealth, saving does not raise it. Therefore, saving must show up as a flow demand for bonds, and bonds are the only other assets available. Under a flexible exchange rate, moreover, the current-account balance must always be zero, because there are no capital movements here. Therefore eq. (3.6) says that $D = S$. The flow supply of bonds produced by a budget deficit is equal to the flow demand for bonds produced by private saving. Under a fixed exchange rate, the current-account balance can differ from zero, but it is financed by reserve flows, and these are sterilized. Therefore, eq. (3.6) says that $D + \dot{R} = S$, where $\dot{R}$ is the rate of increase of reserves measured in domestic currency and it is matched by central-bank bond sales. The flow supply of bonds produced by a budget deficit is augmented or reduced by sterilizing reserve flows, and the adjusted flow supply forthcoming from this process is equal to the flow demand produced by private saving. The bond market remains in flow equilibrium at a constant interest rate whether the exchange rate is fixed or flexible.[9]

Goods are gross substitutes in private consumption, and the demand functions are homogeneous of degree zero in prices and consumption:

$$c_i = f_i\left(p_1, \pi p_2^*, C\right) \quad \text{and} \quad c_i^* = f_i^*\left(\frac{p_1}{\pi}, p_2, C^*\right), \tag{3.7}$$

where $f_{ii}, f_{ii}^* < 0$, and $f_{ij}, f_{ij}^* > 0$ for $i = 1, 2$. Furthermore, $m_1 + m_2 = 1$, and $m_1^* + m_2^* = 1$, where $m_i = p_i f_{ic}$, and $m_i^* = p_i^* f_{ic}^*$. Let demands be homothetic, so that $m_i C = p_i c_i$ and $m_i^* = p_i^* c_i^*$.[10]

As prices are constant here and hereafter, they can be set at unity, and the market-clearing equations can be rewritten:

$$f_1(1, \pi, C) + f_1^*\left(\frac{1}{\pi}, 1, C^*\right) + g_1 - Y = 0,$$

$$f_2(1, \pi, C) + f_2^*\left(\frac{1}{\pi}, 1, C^*\right) + g_2^* - Y^* = 0,$$

[9] An increase in income raises the demand for money and lowers the demand for bonds, but the central bank can satisfy these changes in demand by open-market purchases. It can maintain equilibrium in the money and bond markets at a constant interest rate. This is the assumption implicit in models that treat the interest rate as a policy instrument.

[10] When demand functions are homogeneous of degree zero in prices and nominal consumption and demands are homothetic, $e_{ij} = e_{ii} - 1$, where e_{ij} is the cross-price elasticity, $(p_j/c_i)f_{ij}$, and e_{ii} is the own-price elasticity, $-(p_i/c_i)f_{ii}$. With gross substitutability, $e_{ij} > 0$, so that $e_{ii} > 1$. Analogous properties attach to the foreign elasticities. These relationships are invoked below to show that the Marshall–Lerner–Robinson condition is satisfied automatically when goods are gross substitutes, demand functions are homogenous of degree zero, and demands are homothetic.

where

$$C = Y - T - s(r, Y - T) \quad \text{and} \quad C^* = Y^* - T^* - s^*(r^*, Y^* - T^*).$$

The left-hand side of the current-account equation can be rewritten as

$$B = f_1^*\left(\frac{1}{\pi}, 1, C^*\right) - \pi f_2(1, \pi, C),$$

where B is the current-account balance measured in home currency, and it is set equal to zero initially. I describe these hereafter as the basic equations of the model.

3.2. Income, imports, and the multiplier

The most Keynesian contribution to balance-of-payments analysis was the foreign-trade multiplier — the adaptation to an open economy of the basic Keynesian approach to income determination. It was used to show how economic fluctuations spread from country to country, how they affect the current-account balance, and how they should be countered by economic policies.[11]

The multiplier can be derived from the basic equations given above. Differentiate those equations totally (but hold g_1, g_2^*, and π constant); set $\pi = 1$, for simplicity, and solve for the income changes:

$$dY = \left(\frac{1}{K}\right)\left\{\left[m_1 s_Y^* + m_1^*(1 - s_Y^*)\right]\left[dA - (1 - s_Y)dT - s_r dr\right]\right.$$
$$\left. + m_1^*\left[dA^* - (1 - s_Y^*)dT^* - s_r^* dr^*\right] + s_Y^* dB^a\right\},$$

$$dY^* = \left(\frac{1}{K}\right)\left\{\left[m_2^* s_Y + m_2(1 - s_Y)\right]\left[dA^* - (1 - s_Y^*)dT^* - s_r^* dr^*\right]\right.$$
$$\left. + m_2\left[dA - (1 - s_Y)dT - s_r dr\right] - s_Y dB^a\right\},$$

where

$$K = m_1^*(1 - s_Y^*)s_Y + m_2(1 - s_Y)s_Y^* + s_Y s_Y^*,$$

where dA is a spontaneous increase in domestic consumption (absorption), dA^* is a spontaneous increase in foreign consumption, and dB^a is a spontaneous shift in domestic or foreign demand from the foreign to the home good.[12] In the

---

[11]It was also used to analyze the transfer problem debated by Keynes (1929) and Ohlin (1929). See Metzler (1942b), Samuelson (1952, 1971), and Johnson (1956).

[12]The shifts dA and dA^* correspond to parametric shifts in the savings functions. The shift dB^a corresponds to a parametric shift in the demand functions such that $dB^a = p_1(dc_1^a + dc_1^{*a})$, where $p_1 dc_1^a = -\pi p_2^* dc_2^a$, and $p_1 dc_1^{*a} = -\pi p_2^* dc_2^{*a}$. The term K looks unusually complicated but is actually identical to the most common formulation. Define $m = m_2(1 - s_Y)$ and $m^* = m_1^*(1 - s_Y^*)$, so that m and m^* are the marginal propensities to import. Then $K = m s_Y^* + m^* s_Y + s_Y s_Y^*$, which is the most common formulation.

language used by Johnson (1961), dA and dA^* are shifts in expenditure, and dB^a is a switch in expenditure. The change in the current-account balance follows directly:

$$dB = \left(\frac{1}{K}\right)\left\{ m_1^* s_Y \left[dA^* - \left(1 - s_Y^*\right)dT^* - s_r^* dr^*\right] \right.$$
$$\left. - m_2 s_T^* \left[dA - \left(1 - s_Y\right)dT - s_r dr\right] + s_Y s_Y^* dB^a \right\}.$$

The shift in domestic expenditure, the effect of a change in domestic fiscal policy, and the effect of a change in domestic monetary policy appear jointly in all three equations. So do their foreign counterparts. In the absence of capital movements, changes in fiscal and monetary policies are equivalent to spontaneous shifts in expenditure and are thus interchangeable, because they affect Y, Y^*, and B only by changing expenditure. The spontaneous switch in expenditure, by contrast, appears by itself in all three equations (and with opposite signs in the Y and Y^* equations). We have not yet come to its policy counterpart.

An increase in domestic expenditure, whether spontaneous or the result of a policy change, raises incomes in both countries and drives the home country's current account into deficit.[13] An increase in foreign expenditure raises income in both countries too but drives the current account into surplus. Finally, a spontaneous switch in expenditure from foreign to home goods raises domestic income, reduces foreign income, and drives the current account into surplus.

It is easy to show that income changes are equilibrating in their effects on the current-account balance. If an increase in domestic expenditure did not raise foreign income, the current-account deficit would be larger than the one above. By raising foreign income, it raises the foreign demand for imports and reduces the current-account deficit. If a switch in expenditure from foreign to home goods did not raise domestic income and reduce foreign income, the current-account surplus would equal the switch in expenditure and would likewise be larger than the one above. The increase in domestic income raises the domestic demand for imports, the decrease in foreign income reduces the foreign demand for imports, and the two together cut the current-account surplus.

But equilibration is incomplete. A permanent shift or switch in expenditure leads to a permanent surplus or deficit. This was the feature of the multiplier

---

[13] Without imposing additional restrictions on the model, we cannot know whether it raises Y by more than it raises Y^*. When demand conditions are *identical* (i.e. $s_Y = s_Y^*$ and $m_i = m_i^*$), then $(dY/dA) = (dY^*/dA^*)$, and $(dY^*/dA^*) = (dY^*/dA)$, but $(dY/dA) \gtrless (dY^*/dA^*)$ as $m_1 \gtrless m_2$. When demand conditions are *symmetrical* and each country's marginal propensity to consume its own good exceeds its marginal propensity to consume the other's good (i.e. $s_Y = s_Y^*$, as before, but $m_1 = m_2^*$ and $m_1 > m_2$), then $(dY/dA) = (dY^*/dA^*)$, and $(dY/dA^*) = (dY^*/dA)$, but $(dY/dA) > (dY^*/dA^*)$, and $(dY^*/dA^*) > (dY^*/dA)$. All "own" effects exceed the corresponding "cross" effects. (In this same case, the sum of the marginal propensities to import is necessarily smaller than unity, a condition that plays an important role in several applications of the model, including analyses of the transfer problem.)

model that drew most criticism. Imbalances cannot last forever. The deficit country's central bank must run out of reserves eventually. At some point, then, governments or central banks must act to eradicate imbalances or allow their countries' money stocks to change in response to those imbalances. This point was made early on. [See Meade (1951, ch. 15) and Tsiang (1961).] It did not come to the fore, however, until money itself came to the fore — until the emphasis in balance-of-payments analysis shifted from goods markets to money and bond markets, and therefore from flows to stocks.

Moving on from positive to normative conclusions, let us see what the multiplier model had to say about the theory of economic policy. Suppose that the domestic and foreign economies begin in "internal balance" (i.e. at levels of Y and Y^* that correspond to full employment and price stability) and in "external balance" (i.e. with $B = 0$). How can their governments defend these states against spontaneous disturbances?

Clearly, a spontaneous increase in domestic expenditure can be offset completely by an increase in domestic taxes, an increase in the domestic interest rate, or some combination of the two. Therefore, these are "optimal" responses. If they are not adopted, the foreign government faces a dilemma. It would have to raise its taxes or interest rate to maintain internal balance, but would then move farther from external balance. It would have to reduce its taxes or interest rate to maintain external balance, but would then drive its own economy farther from internal balance. Faced with these unsatisfactory options, the foreign government is sure to complain — much as surplus countries usually complain that it is the obligation of deficit countries to deal with these problems — and it would be justified in this instance.

The problem is more complicated, however, when there is a spontaneous switch in expenditure from foreign to home goods. No combination of fiscal and monetary policies can defend internal balance in both countries and defend external balance simultaneously. If both countries followed policies for internal balance, the external imbalance would get larger. If they followed policies for external balance, both would be driven farther from internal balance. This is the true "conflict" or "dilemma" case, and it calls for the use of policie: to switch expenditure rather than shift it. A change in the exchange rate is one such policy.

3.3. Exchange rates and elasticities

The methods used to study exchange-rate determination and the effects of changes in exchange rates were at first Marshallian rather than Keynesian. The exchange rate was treated as the price that clears the foreign-exchange market, and that market was treated like any other — as a flow market for foreign or domestic currency with well-defined demand and supply curves. The partial-equilibrium models in Machlup (1939) and Haberler (1949) are good examples. Furthermore, one can trace back to Marshall (1923) the sufficient condition for devaluation to improve the current-account balance, although it was discovered independently by Lerner (1944) and Robinson (1947). But the treatment was Keynesian in one important way. The typical analysis did not distinguish clearly between a change in the nominal exchange rate and a change in the real rate (the terms of trade in the model used here). As the prices of domestic goods are determined internally in an insular economy, a change in the nominal exchange rate was expected to produce an identical change in the real rate.

The Marshall–Lerner–Robinson condition can be derived directly from the basic equations set out above. Differentiating the equation for the current-account balance with respect to the nominal exchange rate, π, while holding Y, Y^*, T, T^*, g_1, g_2^*, r, and r^* constant,

$$\mathrm{d}B = \mathrm{d}B^a + m_1^* \, \mathrm{d}A^* - m_2 \, \mathrm{d}A + e_\pi \left(\frac{\mathrm{d}\pi}{\pi} \right),$$

where

$$e_\pi = \left(c_1^* \right) e_{11}^* + \left(\pi c_2 \right) e_{22} - \left(\pi c_2 \right).$$

Here, e_{11}^* is the own-price elasticity of foreign demand for the domestic good, and e_{22} is the own-price elasticity of domestic demand for the foreign good. When $B = 0$ initially, $c_1^* = \pi c_2$, so that $e_\pi = c_1^*(e_{11}^* + e_{22} - 1)$. A devaluation of the domestic currency ($\mathrm{d}\pi > 0$) improves the current-account balance when the sum of the two demand elasticities is larger than unity.[14]

---

[14] The definition of e_π in the text describes the effect of a change in π on the home-currency value of the current-account balance. The effect on the foreign-currency value is given by

$$e_\pi^* = \left(\frac{c_1^*}{\pi} \right) e_{11}^* + \left(c_2 \right) e_{22} - \left(\frac{c_1^*}{\pi} \right) = \left(\frac{c_1^*}{\pi} \right) \left[e_{11}^* + \left(\frac{\pi c_2}{c_1^*} \right) e_{22} - 1 \right].$$

As Robinson (1947) and Hirschman (1949) pointed out, this condition is less stringent when $B < 0$ than when $B > 0$. When $B < 0$ initially, $\pi c_2 > c_1^*$, so that the weight attached to e_{22} increases. When domestic prices are not constant, the condition is more complicated. With upward sloping supply curves (and $B = 0$ initially), it is

$$e_\pi' = c_1^* \left[\frac{e_{11}^*(n_1 + 1)}{e_{11}^* + n_1} + \frac{e_{22}\left(n_2^* + 1 \right)}{e_{22} + n_2^*} - 1 \right] > 0,$$

where n_1 is the own-price elasticity of the domestic supply curve and n_2^* is the own-price elasticity of the foreign supply curve. Clearly, $e_\pi > 0$ is sufficient (but not necessary) for $e_\pi' > 0$. Note that $e_\pi > 0$ in the basic equations of the model, because demand functions are homogeneous of degree zero in prices and consumption, demands are homothetic, and goods are gross substitutes in consumption. Using the relationships given in footnote 10, we can write $e_\pi = c_1^* + (c_1^*)e_{12}^* + (\pi c_2)e_{21}$, where e_{12}^* is the cross-price elasticity of foreign demand for the domestic good and e_{21} is the cross-price elasticity of domestic demand for the foreign good. As e_{12}^*, $e_{21} > 0$ with gross substitutability, $e_\pi > 0$. On this and related points, see Hahn (1959), Jones (1961), and Negishi (1968). Finally, $e_\pi > 0$ is a sufficient condition for local stability in the flow foreign-exchange market when trade flows are only sources of demand and supply in that market. See Haberler (1949) and Sohmen (1969, ch. 1).

The role of the Marshall–Lerner–Robinson condition is illustrated in Figure 3.1, adapted from Haberler (1949). The upper panels show demand and supply curves for exports and imports plotted against prices in domestic currency. The lower panels show them plotted against prices in foreign currency. (The prices p_1 and p_2^* are constant and were set at unity in the basic equations. They are shown explicitly in Figure 3.1 to clarify the presentation.)

Look first at the lower-left-hand panel. The foreign-currency price of the export goods begins at Oa, and the quantity demanded is Oc. Export receipts in foreign

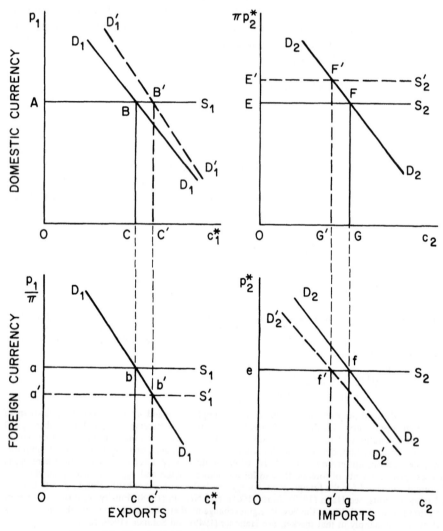

Figure 3.1. The elasticities approach to the analysis of devaluation.

currency are $Oabc$. A devaluation of the domestic currency has no effect on p_1 in an insular economy but reduces the foreign-currency price. Let it fall to Oa' and thus raise export volume to Oc'. Export receipts in foreign currency go to $Oa'b'c'$. This outcome is translated into domestic currency in the upper-left-hand panel. The export price remains at OA in domestic currency, but export volume rises to OC'. Seen from the standpoint of domestic firms, the outcome is a shift in the demand curve to $D_1'D_1'$ and an increase in export receipts to $OAB'C'$.

Look next at the upper-right-hand panel. The home-currency price of the import good begins at OE, and the quantity demanded is OG. Import payments in domestic currency are $OEFG$. A devaluation of the domestic currency has no effect on p_2^* but raises the domestic-currency price to OE' [i.e. $(E'E/OE) \approx (a'a/Oa)$]. Import volume falls to OG', and import payments in domestic currency go to $OE'F'G'$. This outcome is translated into foreign currency in the lower-right-hand panel. The import price remains at Oe in foreign currency, but import volume falls to Og'. Seen from the standpoint of foreign firms, the outcome is a shift in the demand curve to $D_2'D_2'$ and a decrease in import payments to $Oef'g'$.

Let the trade balance be zero initially, so that $OABC = OEFG$ and $Oabc = Oefg$. Suppose that e_{11}^* (the elasticity of D_1D_1) is unity in the neighborhood of b. Then $Oa'b'c' = Oabc$ and export receipts are unchanged in foreign currency. Suppose that e_{22} (the elasticity of D_2D_2) is greater than zero. Then $Oef'g' < Oefg$, and import payments fall in foreign currency. The values chosen for e_{11}^* and e_{22} satisfy the Marshall–Lerner–Robinson condition, and the devaluation improves the trade balance in foreign currency. When export proceeds are unchanged in foreign currency, their value in domestic currency must rise in proportion to the devaluation. When import payments fall in foreign currency, their value in domestic currency can rise or fall, but it cannot rise in proportion to the devaluation. Accordingly, $(OAB'C'/OABC) = (OE'/OE)$, but $(OE'F'G'/OEFG) < (OE'/OE)$, so that $OAB'C' > OE'F'G'$ and the trade balance improves in domestic currency.

This diagram can be used to work through other cases (the one, for instance, in which $e_{22} = 1$ and $e_{11}^* > 0$). I leave that to the reader, however, and turn instead to the main defect of the elasticities analysis illustrated in Figure 3.1.

We began by assuming that Y, Y^*, T, T^*, r, and R^* are constant. These assumptions hold C and C^* constant too, absent spontaneous shifts in consumption. When C and C^* are constant, however, Y and Y^* cannot be constant. If the Marshall–Lerner–Robinson condition is satisfied, the expenditure-switching effects of a devaluation must raise Y and lower Y^*.

Look first at the situation in the market for the home good. When domestic consumption is constant in domestic currency, a change in domestic spending on the imported good must be matched by an equal but opposite change in domestic spending on the home good. Therefore, domestic spending on the home good rises when $e_{22} > 1$ and falls when $e_{22} < 1$. Even when it falls, however, the decrease is smaller than the increase in foreign spending on the home good. An improvement in the current-account balance must raise aggregate demand for the home good.

Look next at the situation in the market for the foreign good. As foreign spending on the domestic good remains constant in foreign currency when $e_{11}^* = 1$, foreign spending on the foreign good remains constant too. Whenever $e_{22} > 0$, however, domestic spending on the foreign good falls in foreign currency. An improvement in the current-account balance must raise aggregate demand for the foreign good.

To get the story right, one must rework the elasticities analysis in a broader framework.

3.4. Exchange rates and absorption

The defect in the elasticities analysis illustrated in Figure 3.1 was known to its earliest exponents. In fact, the expenditure-switching effects of a devaluation were emphasized by Robinson (1947), because she was concerned to show how exchange-rate changes affect employment. The effects were modeled formally by several authors, including Harberger (1950), and can be replicated by differentiating the basic equations above with respect to π as well as other variables (i.e. by holding only g_1 and g_2^* constant).[15] Solving for the income changes,

$$dY = \left(\frac{1}{K}\right)\left\{\left[m_1 s_Y^* + m_1^*(1 - s_Y^*)\right](dA + dE) + m_1^*(dA^* + dE^*)\right.$$
$$\left. + s_Y^*\left[dB^a + (e_\pi)\left(\frac{d\pi}{\pi}\right)\right]\right\},$$

$$dY^* = \left(\frac{1}{K}\right)\left\{\left[m_2^* s_Y + m_2(1 - s_Y)\right](dA^* - dE^*) + m_2(dA - dE)\right.$$
$$\left. - s_Y\left[dB^a + (e_\pi)\left(\frac{d\pi}{\pi}\right)\right]\right\},$$

where $dE = -[(1 - s_Y)dT + s_r dr]$ and $dE^* = -[(1 - s_Y^*)dT^* + s_r^* dr^*]$, thus representing the expenditure-changing effects of monetary and fiscal policies. The change in the current-account balance is

$$dB = \left(\frac{1}{K}\right)\left\{m_1^* s_Y(dA^* + dE^*) - m_2 s_Y^*(dA + dE)\right.$$
$$\left. + s_Y s_Y^*\left[dB^a + (e_\pi)\left(\frac{d\pi}{\pi}\right)\right]\right\}.$$

[15] When the market-clearing equation for the domestic good is differentiated with respect to the exchange rate, the exchange-rate term appears as $(c_1 e_{12} + c_1^* e_{11}^*)(d\pi/\pi)$. But one can show that $c_1 e_{12} = \pi c_2 e_{21}$ [see Allen and Kenen, (1980, p. 36)], and I have shown in footnote 10 that $e_{21} = e_{11} - 1$. Thus, $(c_1 e_{12} + c_1^* e_{11}^*) = e_\pi$. Analogous substitutions are employed when differentiating the other market-clearing equation (along with the assumption that $B = 0$ initially). The appearance of e_π in the derivatives of the market-clearing equations recalls a statement made at the beginning of this chapter,

Note that the exchange-rate change is paired in each equation with the spontaneous switch in expenditure. It is therefore the expenditure-switching policy that was missing earlier.

Four propositions follow from these equations.

(1) A devaluation of the domestic currency raises domestic output but reduces foreign output.

(2) Because of its effects on Y and Y^* and their effects on trade flows, a devaluation improves the current-account balance by an amount smaller than the switch in expenditure defined by the Marshall–Lerner–Robinson condition.

(3) A change in the exchange rate is an optimal policy response to a spontaneous switch in expenditure, and it is also an optimal response for a country that faces a shift in foreign expenditure.

(4) If countries are at full employment, however, a change in the exchange rate by itself cannot be expected to improve the current-account balance.

The first proposition is the one anticipated in work with Figure 3.1. A devaluation of the domestic currency raises the demand for the domestic good, and domestic output must increase to clear the market for the domestic good. The devaluation reduces the demand for the foreign good, and foreign output must decrease to clear the market for the foreign good. By implication, devaluation is a "beggar-my-neighbor" remedy for unemployment.[16]

The second proposition follows from the first. An increase in domestic output raises domestic imports, and a decrease in foreign output reduces domestic exports. Therefore, the improvement in the current-account balance is smaller than the initial switch in expenditure. Nevertheless, the improvement is permanent, because equilibration is incomplete in the multiplier model and reserve flows are sterilized. In monetary models of the balance of payments, by contrast, a devaluation leads to a temporary surplus because there is no sterilization; reserve flows cause changes in money supplies that lead in turn to shifts in levels of expenditure. [See, for example, Dornbusch (1973)].

---

that the Marshall–Lerner–Robinson condition shows up in recent models as a condition for goods-market stability.

[16] Two qualifications are in order. Although a devaluation raises real output and thus raises real income measured in terms of the domestic good, it may not increase economic welfare. Using the term applied by Bhagwati (1958) to the welfare effects of economic growth, a devaluation can be "immiserizing" if it causes a large deterioration in the terms of trade. (This qualification also applies to the point made below, that an exchange-rate change can offset the output effects of a spontaneous switch in expenditure or shift in foreign expenditure.) Furthermore, one can build models in which a devaluation reduces domestic output. See, for example, Salop (1974), where the supply of labor depends on the real wage defined in terms of a price index containing the foreign good. By reducing the real wage, devaluation reduces the supply of labor and, therefore, domestic output. Alternatively, consider an economy that has debt-service payments denominated in foreign currency. A devaluation increases the amount of domestic currency that must be used to make those payments, and this can reduce domestic consumption. Possibilities of this sort led Cooper (1971) to warn against relying heavily on models that concentrate exclusively on trade flows and especially against assuming, as here, that trade is balanced initially.

The third proposition follows from an observation made above. The effects of a change in the exchange rate are paired with those of spontaneous switches in expenditure. Therefore, a change in the exchange rate is an optimal response to a spontaneous switch. It can maintain internal balance in both countries while maintaining external balance between them. Furthermore, a change in the exchange rate is the best response for a country that confronts the policy dilemma posed by a shift in foreign expenditure. (Return to a case considered earlier. An increase in domestic expenditure, whether due to a spontaneous increase in consumption or a change in domestic policy, raises income in the foreign country and saddles it with a current-account surplus. That country cannot deal with this situation by changing its fiscal or monetary policy. But it can solve its problem by revaluing its currency. This response will drive the domestic economy farther from internal balance, but that is the result of its own failure to stabilize expenditure by changing its fiscal or monetary policy.)

The fourth proposition takes us outside the basic equations of the model by introducing price changes, but I will pursue it briefly because of its importance for the theory of policy.

If the domestic economy begins at full employment, a devaluation of its currency cannot improve its current-account balance unless the devaluation is accompanied by a reduction in demand for the domestic good. It cannot increase domestic output to accommodate the increase in demand brought about by expenditure switching. If demand for the domestic good is not reduced, the market for that good will be cleared by a price increase — one that keeps the real exchange rate from changing and therefore precludes any switch in expenditure. This will happen even in an insular economy, where prices are determined internally. It will happen even under the assumption adopted by Keynes (1936) that prices depend mainly on the money wage. If labor is fully employed initially, excess demand for the domestic good will show up as excess demand for labor, raising the money wage.

The importance of this fourth proposition was widely recognized and became the basic postulate of the "absorption" approach to the analysis of devaluation. When resources are fully employed, a devaluation cannot improve the current-account balance unless domestic absorption (expenditure) is reduced to accommodate the expenditure-switching effect of the devaluation. But the postulate generated two lines of analysis. It led one group of economists, including Alexander (1952, 1959), to look for ways in which a devaluation could affect absorption endogenously. It led another group, including Meade (1951), to build it into the theory of economic policy.

Those who hunted for endogenous links between the nominal exchange rate and the level of absorption worked with the basic national-income identity

$$B = Y - A = (S - I) - D,$$

where A is total absorption (the sum of consumption, investment, and government spending). They sought ways in which a devaluation could affect saving, investment, or both.[17]

Alexander (1952) and Machlup (1956), among others, stressed effects on the demand for real cash balances. By raising the domestic price of the imported good, a devaluation raises the price level, increasing the demand for real cash balances. This raises saving (hoarding) and reduces absorption. Their argument was revived by Dornbusch (1973) in the context of a simple monetary model; he showed that a devaluation would improve the current-account balance even if it had no influence whatsoever on the real exchange rate (i.e. no expenditure-switching effect).

Laursen and Metzler (1950) stressed effects on saving that do not derive from the demand for real cash balances. In the absence of money illusion, nominal consumption is homogeneous of first degree in nominal income. But real consumption is not necessarily homogeneous of first degree in real income. In Keynes (1936), for example, the marginal propensity to consume is smaller than the average propensity, and this means that an increase in the price level reduces real consumption. By implication, the price-raising effect of a devaluation will cut back absorption endogenously and will thus improve the current-account balance.[18]

3.5. Exchange rates and optimal policy

To show how the basic postulate of the absorption approach was built into the theory of economic policy, let us examine a single small economy using the famous diagram introduced by Swan (1963).[19] The vertical axis of Figure 3.2

[17]Early advocates of the absorption approach went too far in this direction, arguing that one should concentrate on these effects to the exclusion of expenditure-switching (elasticity) effects. They were not wrong analytically in attempting to show that a devaluation can improve the current-account balance by raising saving or reducing investment (i.e. cutting back absorption), even when it does not switch expenditure. The same point was made by Dornbusch (1973), Johnson (1977), and other advocates of the monetary approach. If domestic prices are not flexible, however, a devaluation that does not switch expenditure can improve the current-account balance only by reducing domestic output and driving the economy away from internal balance. It is a roundabout way of shifting expenditure and not an optimal response to a spontaneous switch in expenditure. This was not always realized, even by those who tried to synthesize the absorption and elasticity approaches.

[18]For a simple proof, see Sohmen (1969, pp. 133–135). The Laursen–Metzler effect vanishes when the marginal and average propensities are equal (and operates perversely when the marginal propensity is larger than the average). Recent criticisms of the Laursen–Metzler argument, including those that come from models in which current consumption depends on wealth or on intertemporal utility maximization, can be treated as criticisms of the assumption that the marginal propensity is smaller than the average.

[19]To represent a small economy by the basic equations, it is convenient to assume that $m_2[(1 - s_Y)\,\mathrm{d}Y + (\mathrm{d}A + \mathrm{d}E)] \approx 0$ in the total derivative of the Y^* equation (i.e. that the effects of changes in domestic consumption are too small to disturb equilibrium in the market for the foreign good). On

shows expenditure policy, E, which can be either monetary or fiscal policy, as they are interchangeable at this stage. An upward movement, then, denotes a tax cut or reduction in the interest rate. The horizontal axis shows the nominal and real exchange rates. They must move together, because goods prices do not change when the economy stays in internal balance (and it will not be allowed to stray far from internal balance). A rightward movement denotes a devaluation or depreciation of the domestic currency.

The DD curve shows how the exchange rate can be combined with expenditure policy to maintain internal balance. It is downward sloping because a devaluation or depreciation of the domestic currency switches domestic and foreign demands to the domestic good and requires a more restrictive expenditure policy to maintain internal balance. (At points above the DD curve, there is inflationary pressure; at points below, there is unemployment.) The FF curve shows how the exchange rate can be combined with expenditure policy to maintain external balance. It is upward sloping because a devaluation or depreciation improves the current-account balance and requires a less restrictive expenditure policy to maintain external balance. (At points above the FF curve, the current account is in deficit; at points below, it is in surplus.) The intersection of DD and FF at P

---

this assumption,

$$dY = \left(\frac{1}{k}\right)\left[\left(\frac{s^*}{k^*}\right)e_\pi\left(\frac{d\pi}{\pi}\right) + m_1(dA + dE) + dQ\right],$$

$$dB = \left(\frac{1}{k}\right)\left[s_Y\left(\frac{s_Y^*}{k^*}\right)e_\pi\left(\frac{d\pi}{\pi}\right) - m_2(dA + dE) + s_Y dQ\right],$$

where $k = s_Y + m_2(1 - s_Y)$, $k^* = s_Y^* + m_1^*(1 - s_Y^*)$, and $dQ = (s_Y^*/k^*)dB^a + (m_1^*/k^*)(dA^* + dE^*)$. Note that a switch in expenditure and a shift in foreign expenditure look alike to the small economy and thus call for identical policy responses. (This point was anticipated in the text, where an exchange-rate change was shown to insulate an economy from a switch in expenditure *and* from a shift in foreign expenditure.) Denote by Y^t and B^t the target levels of Y and B, so that $Y = Y^t$ in internal balance and $B = B^t$ in external balance. The DD curve in Figure 3.2 can then be obtained from the income equation:

$$dE = -\left(\frac{1}{m_1}\right)\left[\left(\frac{s_Y^*}{k^*}\right)e_\pi\left(\frac{d\pi}{\pi}\right) + dQ - k\,dY^t\right] - dA.$$

It is negatively sloped. The FF curve can be obtained from the current-account equation:

$$dE = \left(\frac{s_Y}{m_2}\right)\left[\left(\frac{s_Y^*}{k^*}\right)e_\pi\left(\frac{d\pi}{\pi}\right) + dQ - \left(\frac{k}{s_Y}\right)dB^t\right] - dA.$$

It is positively sloped. Statements made in the text about shifts in the curves derive from these equations. Note that the FF curve is steeper absolutely than the DD curve when $(s_Y/m_2) > (1/m_1)$ or $s_Y[(1 - s_Y)/(1 + s_Y)] > m_2(1 - s_Y)$. This condition cannot hold unless s_Y, the marginal propensity to save, exceeds $m_2(1 - s_Y)$, the marginal propensity to import. It is the more likely to hold, the larger the marginal propensity to save and the smaller the marginal propensity to import (i.e. the less open the domestic economy).

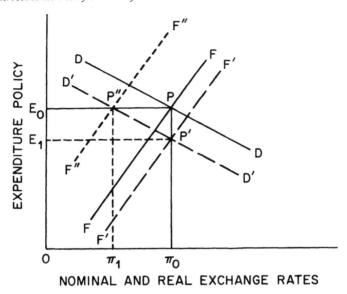

Figure 3.2. Policies for internal and external balance with a spontaneous increase in domestic expenditure and a spontaneous switch in expenditure.

defines an optimal policy combination — one that confers internal and external balance.

A spontaneous increase in domestic expenditure shifts DD downward, because a more restrictive expenditure policy is needed to maintain internal balance. It shifts FF downward too, because a more restrictive expenditure policy is needed to maintain external balance. In fact, the curves shift downward together, to $D'D'$ and $F'F'$, displacing P to P'. A change in expenditure policy from E_0 to E_1 can maintain internal and external balance without a change in the exchange rate.

A spontaneous switch in expenditure to the domestic good (or an increase in the level of foreign expenditure) shifts DD downward, because a more restrictive expenditure policy is needed to maintain internal balance. Let it shift to $D'D'$, just as it did in the previous example. This disturbance, however, shifts FF upward, because a less restrictive expenditure policy is needed to maintain external balance. It goes to $F''F''$, displacing P to P''. A change in the exchange rate from π_0 to π_1 (a revaluation or appreciation of the domestic currency) can maintain internal and external balance without a change in expenditure policy.

Both exercises illustrated in Figure 3.2 appear to violate a fundamental proposition in the theory of economic policy — that the number of policy instruments must be at least as large as the number of policy targets [Tinbergen (1952, ch. iv)]. Two policy targets were represented in Figure 3.2, internal and external balance. In each exercise, however, it was sufficient to change just one policy instrument — expenditure policy in the first and the exchange rate in the

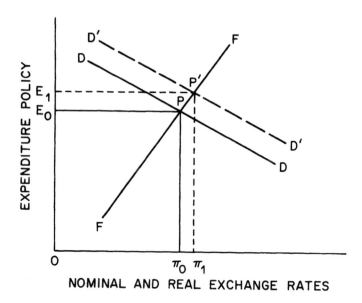

Figure 3.3. Policies for internal and external balance with an increase in the labor force.

second. But these were special cases. The economy began at an optimal policy point, and the disturbances that drove it from that point had properties that paired them with the policy instruments. The first was an increase in expenditure and could thus be offset by an expenditure-changing policy. The second was a switch in expenditure and could thus be offset by an expenditure-switching policy. When the disturbances do not have these properties, both policy instruments have to be adjusted. An illustration is supplied in Figure 3.3.

Suppose that the domestic labor force increases. Output must be raised to maintain full employment. The *DD* curve shifts upward to *D'D'*, because a less restrictive expenditure policy is needed for internal balance. The *FF* curve stays in place, however, so that the optimal policy combination is displaced from *P* to *P'*. Expenditure policy must be adjusted from E_0 to E_1, and the domestic currency must be devalued (or depreciate) from π_0 to π_1.

When working with Figure 3.2, we were able to pair disturbances with policies. When working with Figure 3.3, we are tempted to pair targets with instruments. With an increase in the labor force, for example, it seems natural to say that expenditure policy should be used to increase output and exchange-rate policy should be used to prevent a deterioration in the current-account balance. But the pairing of targets with instruments is a tricky business. It is the "assignment problem" and was studied by Mundell (1960) using what he called the "principle of effective market classification". Each instrument should be assigned to the policy target on which it has the greatest relative effect.

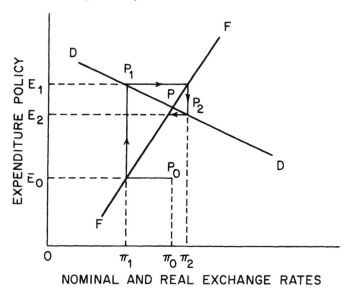

Figure 3.4. A stable assignment of instruments to targets.

The solution to the assignment problem is illustrated in Figure 3.4. Suppose that the domestic economy begins at P_0, with unemployment and a balance-of-payments surplus. Assign exchange-rate policy to external balance, assign expenditure policy to internal balance, and suppose that the managers of exchange-rate policy are the first to act. They will revalue the domestic currency from π_0 to π_1, taking the economy to the FF curve and achieving external balance. As there is still unemployment (more than there was to start), the managers of expenditure policy will adjust it from E_0 to E_1, taking the economy to the DD curve and achieving internal balance. At the new policy point P_1, however, there is a current-account deficit, because it lies above the FF curve. Accordingly, the domestic currency will be devalued from π_1 to π_2, which will trigger an additional adjustment of expenditure policy from E_1 to E_2. The next policy point is P_2. The policy path is described by the cobweb P_0, P_1, P_2, etc. and converges on the intersection of the DD and FF curves.[20]

This indirect decentralized procedure seems wasteful. The exchange rate goes up and down. So does expenditure policy. To move directly to the optimal point

---

[20] In this particular example, the managers of the policy instruments act sequentially and each instrument is adjusted by the full amount required to hit its policy target. In more general analyses of the assignment problem, instruments are altered simultaneously, and the size of each adjustment is a fraction of the one required to hit the policy target (i.e. a fraction of the gap between the current and desired values of the target variable). See, for example, Cooper (1969) and Patrick (1973).

P, however, policy makers must possess all of the information needed to construct the *DD* and *FF* curves and must know where those curves lie at all times. (Economists make assumptions of this sort when ascribing "rational expectations" to households and firms. But we all know that governments are dumber than private decision-makers!) The authorities, however, can recognize a balance-of-payments deficit or surplus, incipient unemployment, and incipient inflation. By pairing their policy instruments with these disorders, they can wend their way through the cobweb in Figure 3.4 without knowing much about the structure of the economy or the exogenous disturbances affecting it.

It is essential, however, to get the assignment right. In Figure 3.4, exchange-rate policy was assigned to external balance and expenditure policy to internal balance. This is the "conventional" assignment, but it is the right assignment only because the *FF* curve is steeper absolutely than the *DD* curve. If the sizes of slopes were reversed, the conventional assignment would be unstable; the policy point would move farther and farther from P. This would happen in a very open economy — one with a marginal propensity to import larger than its marginal propensity to save.[21] In such an economy, exchange-rate policy should be assigned to internal balance and expenditure policy to external balance.

3.6. The behavior of a flexible exchange rate

In the story told by Figure 3.4, the exchange rate was adjusted periodically, in the manner prescribed by the Bretton Woods Agreement. The same apparatus can be used to describe the behavior of a flexible exchange rate. In the underlying model, the exchange rate is the price that clears the foreign-exchange market, and the only flows that cross the market come from the current account and from exogenous capital flows of a sort introduced below. Furthermore, expectations are stationary, which means that traders will not lead or lag their foreign-exchange purchases in order to profit from exchange-rate fluctuations. Accordingly, the *FF* curve can be regarded as the market-clearing curve for the foreign-exchange market, and therefore the source of information about the behavior of a flexible exchange rate.[22]

The argument is illustrated in Figure 3.5. The economy begins at P_0, as in Figure 3.4, but P_0 has to lie on the initial *FF* curve. The economy cannot leave

---

[21] Strictly speaking, one in which $m_2(1 - s_Y) > s_Y[(1 - s_Y)/(1 + s_Y)]$; see footnote 19 above.

[22] Solving the current-account equation in footnote 19 for the change in π,

$$\left(\frac{d\pi}{\pi}\right) = \left(\frac{1}{e_\pi}\right)\left(\frac{k^*}{s_Y^*}\right)\left[\left(\frac{m_2}{s_Y}\right)(dA + dE) - dQ + \left(\frac{k}{s_Y}\right)dB^t\right],$$

where $B^t > 0$ can be taken to reflect the effect of an exogenous capital outflow requiring (and causing) a depreciation of the domestic currency. Note that $e_\pi > 0$ has become a condition for stability of the foreign-exchange market, a point made by Haberler (1949) and Sohmen (1969).

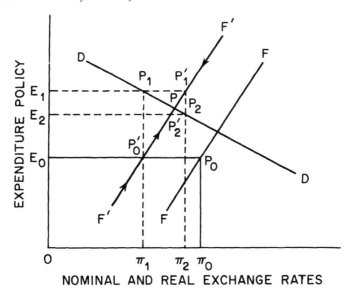

Figure 3.5. The behavior of a flexible exchange rate.

that curve, even momentarily, when the exchange rate is flexible. A spontaneous capital inflow begins and shifts FF to $F'F'$ because it requires an appreciation of the domestic currency to clear the foreign-exchange market. The exchange rate moves at once from π_0 to π_1. The foreign-exchange market does the job assigned heretofore to a policy-maker. But there is unemployment in the new situation, as P_0' lies below DD, and expenditure policy must be adjusted from E_0 to E_1 in order to achieve internal balance. The economy moves along $F'F'$ to P_1', because the domestic currency depreciates at once from π_1 to π_2. Unemployment is replaced by inflationary pressure, as P_1' lies above the DD curve, and expenditure policy must be adjusted from E_1 to E_2. The policy path is P_0, P_0', P_1', P_2', etc. rather than a cobweb. Nevertheless, the policy point converges on P, just as it did in Figure 3.4.

In Figure 3.5 the slopes of DD and FF show how the economy reacts to the way that expenditure policy is managed. If DD is flatter absolutely than FF, the economy will converge to P, even when expenditure policy is altered by large amounts (i.e. to achieve internal balance at the current exchange rate). The exchange rate will oscillate but not explosively. If DD is steeper than FF, the economy will not converge to P when expenditure policy is managed in this way. The exchange rate will oscillate explosively. But policy-makers are not as dumb as those who inhabit Figure 3.5. They can alter expenditure policy by smaller amounts and take explicit account of the exchange-rate changes produced by their decisions. (Matters become more difficult, however, when exchange-rate changes have lagged effects on trade flows and incomes.)

3.7. The choice between fixed and flexible exchange rates

The consensus favoring pegged exchange rates represented in the passages quoted from Nurkse (1944) began to break down rather quickly. Although Meade did not advocate flexible exchange rates in *The Balance of Payments* (1951), he did stress the need for adjustable exchange rates when the money wage is rigid, in order to deal with "conflict" situations. In 1953, however, Friedman published his celebrated case for flexible rates, and Meade came over two years later.[23] Many others crossed the aisle in the 1960s.

The growth of support for flexible exchange rates derived in part from disenchantment with the Bretton Woods regime. What some now remember nostalgically as exchange-rate stability was viewed at the time as exchange-rate rigidity. Furthermore, many economists had started to voice doubts about the compatibility of an adjustable peg with free capital movements. The issue had been raised by Meade some years earlier:

> ...an adjustable-peg mechanism can be successfully operated only if there is some direct control over speculative capital movements between the currencies concerned. And... this involves the maintenance of the apparatus of exchange control over all transactions and raises difficult problems in the decision as to what are, and what are not, speculative capital movements. This is undoubtedly a grave disadvantage of this mechanism of adjustment [Meade (1951, pp. 228–229)].

There was a more fundamental change in view, however, concerning the effect of private speculation on a flexible exchange rate. Nurkse (1944) said that it had been destabilizing. Meade (1951) said that it might be destabilizing.[24] But Friedman (1953) said that it should be stabilizing:

> People who argue that speculation is generally destabilizing seldom realize that this is largely equivalent to saying that speculators lose money, since speculation can be destabilizing in general only if speculators on the average sell when the currency is low in price and buy when it is high [Friedman (1953, p. 175)].

---

[23] See Friedman (1953) and Meade (1955).

[24] Central banks, he said, might have to intervene to counter "perverse" or "grossly excessive" speculation: "By such means, the monetary authorities can attempt to make the market for foreign exchange approximate toward what it would have been if there had been free competitive speculation with correct foresight of future movements. In this case all that the authorities have to do is to anticipate more correctly than private speculators the future course of exchange rates. And in so far as they do so they will make a profit at the expense of the private speculator" [Meade (1951, p. 224)]. Note that Meade anticipated the point made by Friedman (1953) concerning stability and profitability, and he also posed the issue about which we are still arguing — who can forecast exchange rates more accurately?

Friedman's assertion provoked a debate that has not yet ended.[25] But a growing number of economists, including Meade (1955), took positions closer to Friedman than to Nurkse. Private speculation would be forthcoming in directions and amounts sufficient to smooth exchange-rate fluctuations.[26] By implication, the advocates of flexible exchange rates rejected the elasticity pessimism that was another feature of earlier opinion — the fear that the Marshall–Lerner–Robinson condition would not be satisfied or would be barely satisfied.[27] Once private speculation had driven the nominal exchange rate to its "correct" level, the current-account balance would adjust rapidly, as producers and consumers responded to the new real exchange rate.

Friedman, Meade, and those who joined them disagreed among themselves on many major issues. Yet monetarists and Keynesians came to a common view concerning the exchange rate because they agreed tacitly on three propositions — that the typical economy is insular, that flexible exchange rates can therefore provide significant national autonomy in matters of macroeconomic policy, and that governments require that sort of autonomy because of differences in national objectives.

Recall the long passage from Meade (1951) in which he said that exchange-rate changes alter the domestic prices of imported goods but not those of domestic goods — an argument that drew on Keynesian assumptions about wage and price determination. Friedman made the same sort of statement:

A rise in the exchange rate produced by a tendency toward a surplus makes foreign goods cheaper in terms of domestic currency, even though their prices are unchanged in terms of their own currency, and domestic goods more expensive in terms of foreign currency, even though their prices are unchanged in terms of domestic currency [Friedman (1953, p. 162)].

Exceptions were recognized. Panama is too small and open to be an "optimum currency area" and should therefore maintain a fixed exchange rate with the U.S. dollar.[28] Belgium should maintain a fixed exchange rate with the deutsche mark. For larger and more insular economies, however, flexible rates seemed to make much sense.

---

[25] See the survey in Sohmen (1969, ch. III), where Friedman wins hands down. The debate has started up again, however, in the context of a larger debate about the usefulness of official intervention.

[26] The issue of sufficiency has come into question; see, for example, McKinnon (1979, ch. 7).

[27] On reasons for and answers to this earlier pessimism, see Orcutt (1950).

[28] The notion of an "optimum currency area" was introduced by Mundell (1961b), but he defined it differently than those who adopted it. In his paper, countries (regions) are exposed to real disturbances of the sort illustrated in our model by a spontaneous switch in expenditure. If factors of production moved freely between countries, endogenous factor flows could restore external balance, and there would be no need for changes in the terms of trade (the real exchange rate). Countries could afford to maintain fixed exchange rates. They would comprise an optimum currency area. As factors do not move freely enough and rigid money wages make for sticky prices, exchange-rate changes are required

We have already seen why a flexible exchange rate was thought to protect an economy from switches in demand and from fluctuations in foreign demand. In Figure 3.2, a spontaneous switch in expenditure displaced the internal-balance curve from DD to $D'D'$ and the external-balance curve from FF to $F''F''$. If the exchange rate is pegged at π_0, the authorities confront a policy conflict. There are inflationary pressures and a current-account surplus at the initial policy point (P is above $D'D'$ and below $F''F''$). Internal balance can be achieved by an expenditure policy that takes the economy to $D'D'$ at P', but this will make the current-account surplus bigger. External balance can be achieved by an expenditure policy that takes the economy to $F''F''$ at a point vertically above P, but this will exacerbate inflationary pressures. With a flexible exchange rate, however, the domestic currency will appreciate immediately from π_0 to π_1, taking the economy to P''. Internal balance will be maintained without any change in expenditure policy.

But belief in the need for national autonomy and its feasibility was perhaps the leading theme in the 1950s and 1960s. Johnson (1972a) put the point this way:

> The fundamental argument for flexible exchange rates is that they would allow countries autonomy with respect to their use of monetary, fiscal and other policy instruments, consistent with the maintenance of whatever degree of freedom in international transactions they choose to allow their citizens, by automatically ensuring the preservation of external equilibrium [Johnson (1972a, p. 199)].

With flexible exchange rates, for example, countries can choose different points on their Phillips curves:

> On the one hand, a great rift exists between nations like the United Kingdom and the United States, which are anxious to maintain high levels of employment and are prepared to pay a price for it in terms of domestic inflation, and other nations, notably the West German Federal Republic, which are strongly averse to inflation. Under the present fixed exchange-rate system, these nations are pitched against each other in a battle over the rate of inflation that is to prevail in the world economy, since the fixed rate system diffuses that rate to all the countries involved in it. Flexible exchange rates would allow each country to pursue the mixture of unemployment and price trend objectives it prefers, consistent with international equilibrium, equilibrium being secured by appreci-

---

to alter the terms of trade and restore external balance. Mundell's economies are insular in wage and price determination, but some are more open than others to capital and labor movements. In other papers on the subject, it is the insularity of wage and price determination that varies across countries. Fixed exchange rates were recommended for those that are not insular — whose money wages depend importantly on import prices — because changes in exchange rates can then lead to changes in domestic prices that undermine the quality of the domestic currency. See McKinnon (1963) and the surveys by Kenen (1969b) and Tower and Willett (1976).

ation of the currencies of "price-stability" countries relative to the currencies of "full-employment" countries [Johnson (1972a, p. 210)].

Although Friedman (1968) had already warned that the not-so-long-run Phillips curve is vertically sloped — that countries cannot choose between unemployment and inflation — Johnson's views were widely shared. Whitman (1972), for example, suggested that members of an optimum currency area ought to have similar policy preferences and similar "possibility surfaces" linking unemployment rates, inflation rates, and growth rates, and Corden (1972) cited differences in preferences and Phillips curves as the major obstacles to European monetary integration.

4. Interest rates and the capital account

Although the case for flexible exchange rates put forth in the 1950s was endorsed by many economists in the 1960s, it did not make much headway in official circles. Early debates on reform of the monetary system focused mainly on liquidity, not adjustment, and when they did turn to adjustment, they paid very little attention to exchange rates.[29] Even after the breakdown of the pegged-rate system, the negotiations on long-run reform sought to restore a system of "stable but adjustable" exchange rates. Floating was not sinful but was not to be permanent. It was a way for governments to ask for help from market forces when searching for new parities.

The breakdown of the pegged-rate system, however, was important in the history of exchange-rate theory. Even as it led to the adoption of flexible exchange rates by the major industrial countries, it demonstrated clearly the obsolescence of the macroeconomic model on which the case for flexibility was commonly based. The suggestion by Friedman (1968) that the Phillips curve is vertical had already challenged implicit assumptions about wage–price dynamics and raised doubts about the usefulness of national autonomy. The breakdown of pegged exchange rates reflected the increase of capital mobility, challenged explicit assumptions about insularity, and called into question the feasibility of national autonomy.

More realistic models of exchange-rate behavior began to appear soon after the advent of flexible exchange rates. Innovation took place very quickly, because of work done in the 1960s. The models of the 1970s are reviewed in Chapter 14 of this Handbook. I conclude this chapter by surveying briefly the innovations of the 1960s that made way for those models — the introduction of capital mobility into the flow models of the 1950s and the introduction of stock equilibrium, especially money-market equilibrium.

---

[29] The official debates and documents are reviewed in Solomon (1977, chs. iv, x, and xiv).

4.1. Capital flows and optimal policy

Capital movements appeared frequently in the models of the 1950s. They embel-
lished the description of the adjustment process given by Meade in *The Balance of
Payments* (1951). They played a more important role in the story told by Metzler
(1960). I concentrate here, however, on their role in the theory of economic policy
developed by Fleming (1962) and Mundell (1962, 1963).

Capital mobility was added to the model I have used thus far in the same way
that trade had been added to the Keynesian model of a closed economy. Two new
equations were tacked on without changing old ones:

$$\dot{F} = F(r, r^*), \qquad F_r > 0, \quad F_{r^*} < 0, \tag{4.1}$$

$$\dot{R} = B + \dot{F}, \tag{4.2}$$

where $\dot{F}$ is an inflow of capital, $\dot{R}$ is an inflow of reserves, and both are measured
in domestic currency. When $\dot{F} > 0$, foreigners are buying domestic government
debt, because government bonds are the only securities available in our basic
model. When $\dot{R} > 0$, the domestic economy has a balance-of-payment surplus, so
that the definition of external balance is $\dot{R} = 0$ rather than $B = 0$. The small-
country version of the model is one where r^* does not change. The limiting case
of "perfect" capital mobility is one where $F_r \to \infty$ and $r = r^*$ (the central bank
has no control over the domestic interest rate). One should, of course, make an
additional change in the model; an interest-income term should be added to the
current account. This amendment was usually neglected, however, because it
requires another amendment — the definition and inclusion of the integral of $\dot{F}$.[30]

In the absence of capital mobility, monetary and fiscal policies were interchangeable in their effects on the balance of payments, and they could be lumped
together as expenditure policies. With the introduction of capital mobility,
monetary policy acquires an additional influence on the balance of payments, by
way of its effect on the capital account, and we must distinguish carefully between
the two policies. The main implications come out clearly in the small-country
case.[31]

---

[30] This point was noted early on and one implication emphasized. An increase in r can worsen the
balance of payments. By raising interest payments to foreigners, it can weaken the current account by
more than it strengthens the capital account. The net effect of capital mobility on the balance of
payments is $\dot{F} - rF$, where $F = \int \dot{F}$, and its partial derivative with respect to r is $F_r - F$. Therefore, the
balance of payments improves if and only if $F_r > F$. See, for example, Gray (1964). When $F_r < F$,
incidentally, the model can become unstable.

[31] The equations in footnote 19 must be rewritten as

$$dY = \left(\frac{1}{k}\right)\left\{\left(\frac{s_Y^*}{k^*}\right)e_\pi\left(\frac{d\pi}{\pi}\right) + m_1[dA - (1 - s_Y)dT - s_r dr] + dQ\right\},$$

$$d\dot{R} = \left(\frac{1}{k}\right)\left\{s_Y\left(\frac{s_Y^*}{k^*}\right)e_\pi\left(\frac{d\pi}{\pi}\right) - m_2[dA - (1 - s_Y)dT - s_r dr] + s_Y dQ + kF_r dr\right\}.$$

In Figure 3.3 above, it was not possible to maintain internal and external balance without changing the exchange rate. In Figure 4.1, they can be maintained by exploiting the difference between the balance-of-payments effects of monetary and fiscal policies. Monetary policy (the interest rate) is shown on the vertical axis, and fiscal policy (the tax rate) is shown on the horizontal axis. Upward movements on the vertical axis and rightward movements on the horizontal axis denote increasingly restrictive policies (indications opposite to those employed in Figures 3.1 through 3.5).

The II curve shows how monetary and fiscal policies can be combined to maintain internal balance. It is downward sloping because an increase in T reduces domestic expenditure and requires a decrease in r to offset it. (At points above the II curve, there is unemployment; at points below it, there is inflationary pressure.) The XX curve shows how the two policies can be combined to maintain external balance. It is also downward sloping because an increase in T improves the balance of payments by reducing imports and requires a decrease in r to offset it. (At points above the XX curve, $\dot{R} > 0$; at points below it, $\dot{R} < 0$.) The XX curve is flatter than the II curve. The decrease in the interest rate required to maintain external balance is smaller than the one required to maintain internal balance. Its effect on the balance of payments includes an effect on the capital account (a decrease in inflows or increase in outflows), as well as an expenditure-increasing effect on imports.[32]

Suppose that the economy starts at P. Let its labor force grow, raising the income level required for internal balance. The internal-balance curve shifts from II to $I'I'$. Less restrictive policies are needed to maintain internal balance, and the policy point is displaced from P to P'. The tax rate must be reduced from T_0 to T_1 in order to raise income to the levels needed for internal balance, and the interest rate must be raised from r_0 to r_1 in order to produce the improvement in the capital account needed for external balance (the one needed to offset the increase in imports induced by the increase in income).

The assignment of instruments to targets implicit in the language of the previous paragraph is the right assignment. Tell the finance ministry to use the tax

---

[32] The income equation in the previous footnote gives the II curve:

$$ dr = -\left(\frac{1}{s_r}\right)(1 - s_Y)\, dT + \left(\frac{1}{m_1 s_r}\right)\left[\left(\frac{s_Y^*}{k^*}\right)e_\pi\left(\frac{d\pi}{\pi}\right) + m_1\, dA + dQ - k\, dY^t\right]. $$

The balance-of-payments equation gives the XX curve:

$$ dr = -\left(\frac{1}{u_r}\right)(1 - s_Y)\, dT - \left(\frac{1}{m_2 u_r}\right)\left[s_Y\left(\frac{s_Y^*}{k^*}\right)e_\pi\left(\frac{d\pi}{\pi}\right) - m_2\, dA + s_Y\, dQ - k\, d\dot{R}^t\right], $$

where $u_r = s_r + (k/m_2)F_r$, so that $u_r > s_r$ and $u_r \to \infty$ as $F_r \to \infty$. $\dot{R}^t$ is the target value of the balance of payments. The slopes of the II and XX curves do not depend on the size of the marginal propensity to import. The condition encountered earlier, that $s_Y[(1 - s_Y)/(1 + s_Y)] > m_2(1 - s_Y)$, does not determine the assignment of instruments to targets in the present case. (It is important, however, for the sizes of shifts in the II and XX curves.)

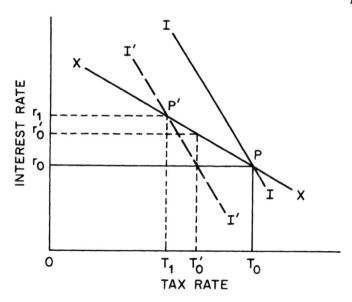

Figure 4.1. Monetary and fiscal policies for internal and external balance under a fixed exchange rate.

rate for internal balance. Tell the central bank to use the interest rate for external balance. The finance ministry will cut the tax rate from T_0 to T_0' in order to achieve internal balance, and this will cause a balance-of-payments deficit by putting the policy point below the XX curve. The central bank will raise the interest rate from r_0 to r_0' in order to achieve external balance, and this will cause unemployment by putting the policy point above the $I'I'$ curve. The finance ministry will cut the tax rate again, the central bank will raise the interest rate again, and the policy point will move gradually to P'. (Note that T and r move monotonically, instead of oscillating as they did in Figure 3.4.)

4.2. *Capital mobility and policy autonomy under fixed exchange rates*

Heretofore, the interest rate has been used as the instrument of monetary policy. With perfect capital mobility, however, the XX curve becomes horizontal, and the central bank loses control of the interest rate. Therefore, we must look more closely at the mechanics of monetary policy, and we must reexamine the relationship between monetary policy and fiscal policy.

Suppose that there is no capital mobility (so that $\dot{R} = B = S - D$, as before). When the finance ministry cuts taxes to stimulate demand, S and D rise, but S rises by less than D. The current account deteriorates, and there is an outflow of

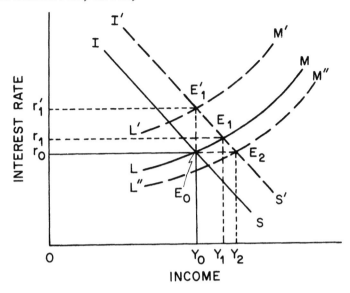

Figure 4.2. Fiscal policy and capital mobility under fixed exchange rates.

reserves. In earlier examples, the central bank sterilized that outflow. In this one, it will not. The short-run and long-run results are shown in Figure 4.2, using IS and LM curves.[33] A tax cut shifts the IS curve rightward to $I'S'$, displacing the equilibrium point from E_0 to E_1, raising the interest rate from r_0 to r_1, and raising income from Y_0 to Y_1. This is the permanent result for a closed economy, but it is the short-run result for an open economy with a fixed exchange rate. The outflow of reserves resulting from the current-account deficit reduces the money supply and shifts the LM curve. That curve must move leftward until $S = D$ so that $\dot{R} = 0$ and the money stock is stabilized. Therefore, it must move to $L'M'$, displacing the equilibrium point to E_1', raising the interest rate to r_1', and bringing income back to Y_0, its initial level. The money-supply effects of the current-account deficit "crowd out" enough consumption to offset completely the stimulus to spending afforded by the tax cut.[34]

Suppose that there is some capital mobility (so that $\dot{R} = B + \dot{F} = S - D + \dot{F}$). The tax cut raises S by less than it raises D, producing a current-account deficit,

---

[33] The IS curve is the goods–market relationship between income and the interest rate. It is downward sloping because an increase in the interest rate reduces income by raising saving and thus reducing consumption. Its position depends on the level of taxation and on the exchange rate. The LM curve is the money-market relationship between income and the interest rate. It is upward sloping because an increase in the interest rate is needed to clear the money market when an increase in income raises the demand for money. Its position depends on the size of the money stock.

[34] Return to the equations in footnote 31. When $\dot{R} = 0$ (and $F_r = 0$), then $(1 - s_Y)dT + s_r dr = 0$, and this means that $dY = 0$.

P.B. Kenen

but it does not necessarily cause an outflow of reserves. Let the interest rate rise to r_1, as before, but let it induce a capital inflow just large enough to take up the excess flow supply of bonds (i.e. let $\dot{F} = D - S$). Income rises to Y_1 and stays there indefinitely, because there is no shift in the LM curve. There may indeed be sufficient capital mobility to generate an inflow of reserves and drive the LM curve to the right. This is what happens with perfect capital mobility. The interest rate remains at r_0, the LM curve moves to $L''M''$, and income rises to Y_2. There is a larger current-account deficit here, but it serves to offset the capital inflow and therefore to terminate the increase in the money stock.

Consider, next, the use of monetary policy to influence aggregate demand. If there is no capital mobility, an open-market purchase of government bonds increases the money stock and decreases the interest rate. The short-run and long-run results are shown in Figure 4.3. The LM curve shifts to $L'M'$, displacing equilibrium from E_0 to E_1, reducing the interest rate from r_0 to r_1, and raising income from Y_0 to Y_1. This is the permanent result in a closed economy, but is again the short-run result in an open economy with a fixed exchange rate. The increase in income produces a current-account deficit and an outflow of reserves. If the central bank can sterilize that outflow, it can keep the economy at E_1. Otherwise, the money stock begins to fall, and it must go on falling until it has dropped back to its initial level. The LM curve drifts back to its starting point, the interest rate rises to r_0, and income returns to Y_0.

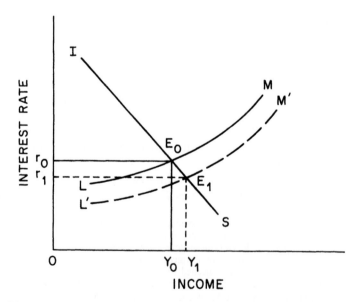

Figure 4.3. Monetary policy and capital mobility under fixed exchange rates.

The introduction of capital mobility makes matters worse. A reduction in the interest rates from r_0 to r_1 causes a capital outflow ($\dot{F} < 0$), adding to the outflow of reserves and reversing more rapidly the increase in income. There is, indeed, no increase whatsoever with perfect capital mobility. An open-market purchase of government bonds causes a capital outflow that is exactly equal to the open-market purchase, and there is no observable movement in the diagram — no shift in the *LM* curve, even temporarily, no change in the interest rate, and no change in income. The central bank has no control over the domestic interest rate. More important, it has no control over the money stock. The only effect of an open-market purchase is a change in the composition of its balance sheet; it loses reserve as rapidly as it buys bonds.

4.3. Capital mobility and policy autonomy under flexible exchange rates

Under a flexible exchange rate, there is no intervention in the foreign-exchange market. Therefore, the central bank can control the money stock, even with perfect capital mobility. This is the basic sense in which a flexible exchange rate furnishes autonomy. But capital mobility has important effects on the behavior of a flexible exchange rate and on the functioning of national policies.

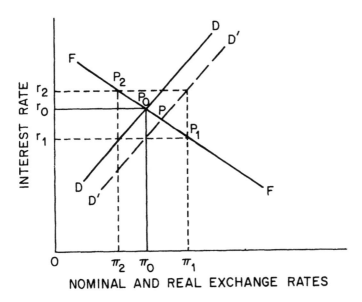

Figure 4.4. The behavior of a flexible exchange rate with high capital mobility.

The behavior of a flexible exchange rate is described in Figure 4.4, which is another version of the Swan (1963) diagram. The interest rate is shown on the vertical axis and is used to represent monetary policy. The nominal and real exchange rates are shown on the horizontal axis. Combinations of the interest rate and exchange rate that confer internal balance are given by the DD curve. It is upward sloping here because a depreciation of the domestic currency switches expenditure to the domestic good and must be offset by a more restrictive monetary policy. Combinations that confer external balance are shown by the FF curve. It is downward sloping because a depreciation of the domestic currency improves the current account and must be offset by a less restrictive monetary policy. (A less restrictive policy has two effects. It increases imports by raising expenditure, and it reduces the capital inflow or raises the capital outflow.) In earlier versions of this diagram, the FF curve was steeper absolutely than the DD curve. In Figure 4.4, the FF curve is flatter, reflecting the influence of high capital mobility. The higher the degree of capital mobility, the larger the exchange-rate change required to offset an interest-rate change. With perfect capital mobility, the FF curve is horizontal.[35]

As the foreign-exchange market determines the exchange rate, it is assigned implicitly to external balance, and monetary policy must be assigned to internal balance. When the FF curve is flatter than the DD curve, however, the central bank must be careful. If it does not make allowance for the change in the exchange rate resulting from a change in monetary policy, it can introduce explosive oscillations. Let there be growth in the labor force, introducing unemployment. The internal-balance curve shifts from DD to $D'D'$, because a lower interest rate is needed to raise output. If the interest rate is cut from r_0 to r_1, the reduction needed for internal balance at the current exchange rate, there will be a capital outflow (or smaller capital inflow), as well as an increase in imports. The policy point will move from P_0 to P_1, and the domestic currency will depreciate from π_0 to π_1. Unemployment will give way to inflation (P_1 lies below $D'D'$), and

---

[35] The equation for the DD curve is obtained by rearranging the equation for the II curve in footnote 32:

$$dr = \left(\frac{1}{m_1 s_r}\right)\left(\frac{s_Y^*}{k^*}\right)e_\pi\left(\frac{d\pi}{\pi}\right) + \left(\frac{1}{m_1 s_r}\right)\left[m_1\,dA - m_1(1 - s_Y)\,dT + dQ - k\,dY^t\right].$$

The equation for the FF curve is obtained by rearranging the equation for the XX curve (and omitting $\dot{R}^t$, the target value for the balance of payments):

$$dr = -\left(\frac{s_Y}{m_2 u_r}\right)\left(\frac{s_Y^*}{k^*}\right)e_\pi\left(\frac{d\pi}{\pi}\right) + \left(\frac{1}{m_2 u_r}\right)\left[m_2\,dA - m_2(1 - s_Y)\,dT - s_Y\,dQ\right].$$

The FF curve is flatter absolutely than the DD curve when $(s_Y/m_2 u_r) < (1/m_1 s_r)$, or $m_2(1 - s_Y) > [s_Y - k(F_r/s_r)][(1 - s_Y)/(1 + s_Y)]$, and this condition can obtain for large values of F_r (high capital mobility), even when the marginal propensity to import is much smaller than the marginal propensity to save.

the central bank will have to raise the interest rate. If the rate goes directly to r_2, as required for internal balance, the policy point will move to P_2, and the domestic currency will appreciate to π_2. Inflation will give way again to unemployment, but more than before, and the central bank will have to cut the interest rate. The path of the policy point is P_0, P_1, P_2, etc. and it does not converge on P.

The instability illustrated here does not condemn exchange-rate flexibility. It serves merely to remind us of the point made before, that the central bank cannot afford to ignore its own influence on the exchange rate, especially when capital mobility is high.

There are, of course, other ways to deal with the same problem. It would be possible, for instance, to use fiscal policy rather than monetary policy. When capital mobility is high, however, fiscal policy is not very powerful.

Under a fixed exchange rate, capital mobility enhanced the effectiveness of fiscal policy. Under a flexible exchange rate, capital mobility decreases its effectiveness. Figure 4.5 shows why. A tax cut shifts the *IS* curve rightward to $I'S'$, raising the interest rate from r_0 to r_1, and raising income from Y_0 to Y_1. This is the old outcome for a closed economy. But it is not the outcome for an open economy with a flexible exchange rate, not even in the short run. It does not allow for the change in the exchange rate. When capital mobility is low, the domestic currency depreciates; the increase in income raises imports by more than the

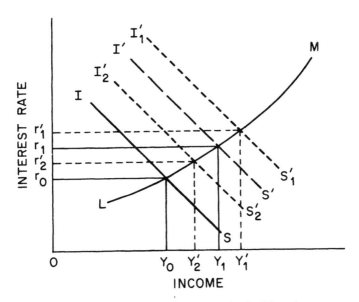

Figure 4.5. Fiscal policy and capital mobility under flexible exchange rates.

increase in the interest rate raises the capital inflow. The expenditure-switching effect of the depreciation shifts the *IS* curve from $I'S'$ to some position such as $I_1'S_1'$ and generates a bigger increase in income. It rises all the way to Y_1'. When capital mobility is high, however, the domestic currency appreciates; the increase in the interest rate raises the capital inflow by more than the increase in income raises imports. The expenditure-switching effect shifts the *IS* curve from $I'S'$ to some position such as $I_2'S_2'$ and generates a smaller increase in income. It drops only to Y_2'. With perfect capital mobility, the appreciation offsets the whole fiscal stimulus and keeps the *IS* curve from shifting. The interest rate remains at r_0, because it cannot change with perfect capital mobility, and income does not rise at all. Fiscal policy is completely ineffective.

Under a fixed exchange rate, the influence of monetary policy is transitory, and capital mobility reduces its effectiveness, diminishing its temporary influence on income. Under a flexible exchange rate, the influence of monetary policy is permanent, and capital mobility raises its effectiveness. In Figure 4.6, an open-market purchase of government bonds shifts the *LM* curve to $L'M'$, reducing the interest rate from r_0 to r_1 and raising income from Y_0 to Y_1. This is the old outcome for a closed economy. In an open economy with a flexible exchange rate, something more must happen. The domestic currency must depreciate, and the size of the depreciation must increase with capital mobility. Therefore, the *IS*

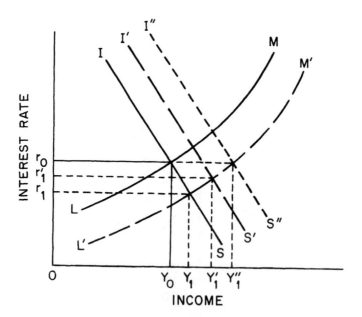

Figure 4.6. Monetary policy and capital mobility under flexible exchange rates.

curve shifts to some position such as $I'S'$, adding to the increase in income. It rises all the way to Y_1'. With perfect capital mobility, the increase in income is even larger. The domestic interest rate must stay at r_0, and this says that the IS curve must shift to $I''S'''$, driving income to Y_1''. (This conclusion is related to the point made in the discussion of Figure 4.4, that there is a risk of instability when capital mobility is high. The central bank must make adequate allowance for the large shifts in the IS curve that take place with large changes in the nominal exchange rate.)

4.4. Flows, stocks, and asset-market equilibrium

Most of the analysis just summarized is found in the papers by Fleming (1962) and Mundell (1962, 1963) that introduced capital mobility into the theory of economic policy. Related contributions are surveyed by Whitman (1970). At one important point, however, I drew on papers by McKinnon and Oates (1966) and McKinnon (1969). They were among the first to show that the Fleming–Mundell view of economic policy depended strategically on sterilizing reserve flows. If those flows are allowed to affect the money stock, they erode the influence of monetary policy, even in the absence of capital mobility, and they weaken the influence of fiscal policy unless capital mobility is high.

The link between reserve flows and the money stock, however, is only one of several links between flows and stocks that are missing from the Fleming–Mundell model. Consider the basic accounting relationship used so often earlier, rewritten and amended to include investment:

$$\dot{R} - \dot{F} - B = \dot{R} - \dot{F} + D - S + I = 0.$$

A balance-of-payments surplus (inflow of reserves) raises the money stock. A capital inflow raises stocks of debt to foreigners (or reduces stocks of claims on foreigners). A budget deficit financed by bond issues raises the stock of government securities. Private saving raises the stock of wealth. And investment raises the capital stock. A change in any stock, moreover, has effects on flows.

We have already seen how reserve flows alter the money stock, undermining the influence of monetary policy, and noted that this process can be deferred only for as long as central banks can sterilize reserve flows. The monetary approach to the balance of payments is built on this basic proposition.[36] It views a balance-of-

---

[36] The monetary approach has a long history, going back to David Hume. It was resurrected by Polak (1957) and Hahn (1959) but owes much of its influence to Mundell (1968, 1971) and Johnson (1972b), because they could connect it with monetarist models of the closed economy developed by Friedman (1956) and Patinkin (1956). One can take a monetary view of the balance of payments without using a monetarist model, but most monetary models are monetarist. Real income and the real interest rate are determined on the "real" side of the economy, and they in turn determine the demand for real balances. In a small (price-taking) country with a fixed exchange rate, then,

payments deficit as a manifestation of excess supply in the money market, which will be self-correcting in the long run. A balance-of-payments deficit cannot endure unless the central bank perpetuates the excess supply of money by sterilizing reserve losses. Here is Johnson's formulation:

> The central propositions of the monetary approach are, first, that the balance of payments is a monetary phenomenon and requires analysis with the tools of monetary theory and not barter or "real" trade theory; second, that money is a stock, whereas real theory traditionally deals with flows, so that an adequate balance-of-payments theory must integrate stocks and flows; and third, that the money stock can be changed in two alternative ways, through domestic credit creation or destruction and through international reserve flows, the policy choice being important for balance-of-payments analysis [Johnson (1977, p. 251)].

There are, he said, three implications:

> First, and as a fundamental proposition, balance-of-payments deficits and surpluses... are monetary symptoms of monetary disequilibria that will cure themselves in time without any inherent need for a government balance-of-payments policy. If the natural processes of adjustment cannot be allowed to work themselves out, because of inadequacy of international reserves, the policy indicated to speed the natural adjustment process is deliberate monetary contraction. Devaluation, or alternatively import restrictions and export-promoting policies, is a substitute for monetary contraction, logically having the same effect but achieving it by deflating the real stock of money backed by domestic credit through raising the domestic price level rather than by deflating the nominal stock of money through open market sales, and its effect is a transient one of accelerating the inherent natural process of adjustment to equilibrium. ...
>
> Second, on a fixed exchange rate system inflation is a world monetary phenomenon, which cannot be prevented by national monetary policy or its ineffective substitute, a national "wage–price policy," and can only be counteracted by any national policy if the currency is first freed to find its own level on the foreign exchange market (or the pegged rate is regularly and systematically altered to national anti-inflationary policy).
>
> Third, in a regime of floating exchange rates inflation is *not* a world but a national problem. ... Inflation does, however, remain a "world" or "externally-caused" problem to the extent that countries' exchange rate policies aim

---

the money market must be cleared by movements in reserves. See, for example, Dornbusch (1973). The monetary approach is developed more fully in Chapter 14 of this Handbook, and applied to the problem of exchange-rate determination. For earlier and more skeptical assessments, see Whitman (1975) and Hahn (1977).

at maintaining some conventional value or range of values of their currencies..., or more subtly the policy-makers aim at maintaining a conventional relation between the domestic and foreign interest rates. ... An important corollary of this proposition is that, contrary to widespread belief, a floating rate system yields little if any extra freedom for the independent exercise of national economic policy, if freedom means freedom from external influences and changes and is defined implicitly to mean independence exercised without cost in the form of disturbance [Johnson (1977, pp. 265–266)].

How different is this passage from the one quoted earlier, in which Johnson made the case for national autonomy and for a flexible exchange rate to achieve it! This one is an epitaph for insularity.

Another approach to the balance of payments originated in the 1960s. It is the portfolio-balance approach. Its origins and history, however, are different from those of the monetary approach. It was not set out all at once, in a group of formal models, and had no home comparable to the International Trade Workshop at Chicago, which nurtured the monetary approach. It was developed gradually by many contributors, who began to understand the importance of the links between certain flows and stocks and to build them, one by one, into their own models.[37]

The portfolio-balance approach grew out of the debates of the 1960s about the way to estimate capital-flow equations. The first efforts of the 1960s were based on the simple specifications in the Fleming–Mundell model, represented by eq. (4.1) above, which linked flows of capital with levels of interest rates. Critics pointed out that one should work with stocks, not flows. Capital movements should be treated as episodic stock adjustments, following the theory of portfolio selection developed by Markowitz (1959) and Tobin (1967, 1969). Formally, eq. (4.1) should be replaced by equations of this sort:

$$F^{\mathrm{d}} = F(r, r^*, W^*), \qquad F_r > 0, \quad F_{r^*} < 0 \quad \text{and} \quad F_W > 0, \tag{4.1a}$$

$$\dot{F} = \gamma(F^{\mathrm{d}} - F), \quad \gamma > 0, \tag{4.1b}$$

where F^{d} is the foreign (stock) demand for the domestic bond, F is the stock actually held, W^* is foreign wealth, and γ is the speed of adjustment (the rate at which foreigners adjust their portfolios).

---

[37]The paper by McKinnon and Oates (1966) did contain a formal model that anticipated in a number of respects the full-fledged portfolio-balance models of the 1970s. There was only one bond in that model, however, and thus one interest rate. In this sense, the model was closer to a monetary model with perfect capital mobility than to the typical portfolio-balance model with imperfect capital mobility. A number of recent papers have shown that the difference in assumptions about capital mobility is one of the most important differences between the two groups of models. See the discussion and citations in Chapter 15 of this Handbook.

Branson (1968) was among the first to put stock-adjustment terms into capital-flow equations, and they added greatly to the quality of his results.[38] He was likewise among the first to emphasize the implications for the Fleming–Mundell model. The policy combination shown in Figure 4.1, where the interest rate was assigned to external balance and the tax rate assigned to internal balance, will work for a while but cannot work permanently in a stationary model. An increase in the interest rate leads to a permanent shift in portfolios but does not produce a permanent improvement in the balance of payments. Foreigners start to buy domestic bonds as soon as the interest rate rises, but the capital inflow falls off as the portfolio shift is completed.[39]

The next major step in the evolution of the portfolio-balance approach was taken when eq. (4.1b) was replaced by instantaneous stock adjustment.[40] The third step was taken when a number of economists introduced *two* links between saving and the stock of wealth. Eq. (3.4) above was replaced by these assertions:

$$S = \dot{W} = s(r, Y - T, W), \tag{3.4a}$$

where $0 < s_Y < 1$, $s_r > 0$, and, most importantly, $s_W < 0$. Saving raises wealth, and an increase in wealth reduces saving.[41]

In a typical portfolio-balance model, portfolio shifts occur instantaneously, but capital flows take place too, whenever there is saving or dissaving. Capital flows are not permanent, however, because saving and dissaving are not permanent; saving goes to zero as it raises wealth, and dissaving goes to zero as it lowers wealth. Therefore, these models have a self-correcting mechanism, but it is different from the one in monetary models, and it focuses attention on the current-account balance. A current-account surplus has its counterpart in saving (in flow demands for bonds and money), but saving raises wealth, and that in turn reduces saving. When saving and the current-account surplus go to zero, moreover, the overall balance of payments must go to zero too. Flow demands for bonds and money vanish completely. Monetary models, by contrast, focus attention directly on the balance of payments. A balance-of-payments surplus has its counterpart in hoarding (a flow demand for money), but hoarding raises the supply of money, and that in turn reduces hoarding.

---

[38]Similar specifications were used by Willett and Forte (1969), Miller and Whitman (1970, 1972), Bryant and Henderschott (1972), Branson and Willett (1972), and Kouri and Porter (1974).

[39]See Branson and Willett (1972); also Whitman (1970) and the papers cited there. Fleming and Mundell (1964) had made the same sort of point in their paper on official intervention in the forward exchange market but did not see its general applicability. See also Kenen (1965), who criticized Tsiang (1959) for failing to distinguish between stock and flow effects of changes in the forward rate.

[40]See, for example, Branson (1975) and Girton and Henderson (1977).

[41]See, for example, Branson (1976), Kenen (1976), and Allen and Kenen (1980); the basic formulation goes back to Metzler (1951).

5. Conclusion

I have carried my story as far as I can without poaching on domains assigned to others. The story is brought up to date later in this Handbook, by Frenkel and Mussa in Chapter 14 and by the discussion of asset-market processes by Branson and Henderson in Chapter 15.

I have tried to show how stylized facts influenced the modeling of open economies in the 1950s and 1960s, paying particular attention to the way in which Keynesian models of the closed economy were opened to trade and capital flows. I have also tried to trace the origins of recent work — the monetary and portfolio approaches — paying particular attention to the ways in which they have introduced stock–flow relationships into models of the open economy. Those approaches made fundamental contributions and paved the way for further work — for introducing expectations into explanations of exchange-rate behavior and studying the problems of policy formation in interdependent national economies.

Those new approaches, however, may have had one detrimental influence. They have drawn our attention in two directions and thus drawn it away from the central issues of economic policy. The Keynesian models with which most economists worked in the 1950s and 1960s were designed to deal with the medium run — with the problems of achieving economic stability over an old-fashioned business cycle. The newer approaches have drawn attention to the very short run — to market processes determining exchange rates from day to day and week to week — and drawn attention to the very long run — to the never-never land of the stationary state where stocks of money, bonds, and wealth have adjusted fully. We may have to come back to the medium run of the typical Keynesian model if we are to deal in a useful way with the hardest problems of the world economy.

References

Alexander, S.S. (1952), "Effects of a devaluation on a trade balance", International Monetary Fund Staff Papers, 2:263–278. Reprinted in: R.E. Caves and H.G. Johnson, eds., Readings in international economics (Irwin, Homewood, 1968) 359–373.

Alexander, S.S. (1959), "Effects of a devaluation: A simplified synthesis of elasticities and absorption approaches", American Economic Review, 49:22–42.

Allen, P.R. and P.B. Kenen (1980), Asset markets, exchange rates, and economic integration (Cambridge University Press, London).

Bhagwati, J.N. (1958), "Immiserizing growth: A geometrical note", Review of Economic Studies, 25:201–205. Reprinted in: R.E. Caves and H.G. Johnson, eds., Readings in international economics (Irwin, Homewood, 1968) 300–305.

Bloomfield, A.I. (1963), Short-term capital movements under the pre-1914 gold standard (International Finance Section, Princeton University, Princeton).

Branson, W.H. (1968), Financial capital flows in the U.S. balance of payments (North-Holland, Amsterdam).

Branson, W.H. (1975), "Stocks and flows in international monetary analysis", in: A. Ando, R. Herring, and R. Marston, eds., International aspects of stabilization policies (Federal Reserve Bank of Boston and International Seminar in Public Economics, Boston) 27–50.

Branson, W.H. (1976), "Portfolio equilibrium and monetary policy with foreign and nontraded assets", in: E. Claassen and P. Salin, eds., Recent issues in international monetary economics (North-Holland, Amsterdam) 241–250.

Branson, W.H. and T.D. Willett (1972), "Policy toward short-term capital movements; some implications of the portfolio approach", in: F. Machlup, W.S. Salant, and L. Tarshis, eds., International mobility and movement of capital (National Bureau of Economic Research, New York) 287–310.

Bryant, R.C. and P.H. Hendershott (1972), "Empirical analysis of capital flows: Some consequences of alternative specifications", in: F. Machlup, W.S. Salant, and L. Tarshis, eds., International mobility and movement of capital (National Bureau of Economic Research, New York) 207–240.

Cooper, R.N. (1969), "Macroeconomic policy adjustment in interdependent economies", Quarterly Journal of Economics, 83:1–24.

Cooper, R.N. (1971), Currency devaluation in developing countries (International Finance Section, Princeton University, Princeton).

Corden, W.M. (1972), Monetary integration (International Finance Section, Princeton University, Princeton).

Dornbusch, R. (1973), "Currency depreciation, hoarding, and relative prices", Journal of Political Economy, 81:893–915.

Eichengreen, B.J. (1981), Sterling and the tariff, 1929–32. (International Finance Section, Princeton University, Princeton).

Fleming, J.M. (1962), "Domestic financial policies under fixed and under floating exchange rates", International Monetary Fund Staff Papers, 9:369–379.

Fleming, J.M. and R.A. Mundell (1964), "Official intervention on the forward exchange market", International Monetary Fund Staff Papers, 11:1–17.

Friedman, M. (1953), "The case for flexible exchange rates", in: M. Friedman, Essays in positive economics (University of Chicago Press, Chicago) 157–203. Reprinted in: R.E. Caves and H.G. Johnson, eds., Readings in international economics (Irwin, Homewood, 1968) 413–437.

Friedman, M. (1956), "The quantity theory of money – a restatement", in: M. Friedman, ed., Studies in the quantity theory of money (University of Chicago Press, Chicago) 3–21.

Friedman, M. (1968), "The role of monetary policy", American Economic Review, 58:1–17.

Girton, L. and D. Henderson (1977), "Central bank operations in foreign and domestic assets under fixed and flexible exchange rates", in: P.B. Clark, D.E. Logue, and R.J. Sweeney, eds., The effects of exchange rate adjustments (U.S. Treasury, Washington) 151–178.

Grassman, S. (1980), "Long-term trends in openness of national economies", Oxford Economic Papers, 32:123–133.

Gray, H.P. (1964), "Marginal cost of hot money", Journal of Political Economy, 72:189–192.

Haberler, G. (1949), "The market for foreign exchange and the stability of the balance of payments: A theoretical analysis", Kyklos, 3:193–218.

Hahn, F.H. (1959), "The balance of payments in a monetary economy", Review of Economic Studies, 26:110–125.

Hahn, F.H. (1977), "The monetary approach to the balance of payments", Journal of International Economics, 7:231–249.

Harberger, A.C. (1950), "Currency depreciation, income and the balance of trade", Journal of Political Economy, 58:47–60. Reprinted in: R.E. Caves and H.G. Johnson, eds., Readings in international economics (Irwin, Homewood, 1968) 341–358.

Hirschman, A.O. (1949), "Devaluation and the trade balance: A note", Review of Economics and Statistics, 31:50–53.

Johnson, H.G. (1956), "The transfer problem and exchange stability", Journal of Political Economy, 64:212–225. Reprinted in: R.E. Caves and H.G. Johnson, eds., Readings in international economics (Irwin, Homewood, 1968) 148–171.

Johnson, H.G. (1961), "Towards a general theory of the balance of payments", in H.G. Johnson, International trade and economic growth (Harvard University Press, Cambridge) 153–168. Reprinted in: R.E. Caves and H.G. Johnson, eds., Reading in international economics (Irwin, Homewood, 1968) 374–388.

Johnson, H.G. (1972a), "The case for flexible exchange rates", in: H.G. Johnson, Further essays in monetary economics (Allen and Unwin, London) 198–222.

Johnson, H.G. (1972b), "The monetary approach to balance-of-payments theory", Journal of Financial and Quantitative Analysis, 7:1555–1572. Reprinted in: J.A. Frenkel and H.G. Johnson, eds., The monetary approach to the balance of payments (University of Toronto Press, Toronto, 1976) 147–167.

Johnson, H.G. (1977), "The monetary approach to the balance of payments: A non-technical guide", Journal of International Economics, 7:251–268.

Jones, R.W. (1961), "Stability conditions in international trade: A general equilibrium analysis", International Economic Review, 2:199–209.

Kenen, P.B. (1965), "Trade, speculation, and the forward exchange rate", in: R.E. Baldwin, et al., Trade, growth and the balance of payments (Rand-McNally, Chicago) 143–169.

Kenen, P.B. (1969a), "The future of gold: A round table", American Economic Review, 59:362–364.

Kenen, P.B. (1969b), "The theory of optimum currency areas: An eclectic view", in: R.A. Mundell and A.K. Swoboda, eds., Monetary problems of the international economy (University of Chicago, Chicago) 41–60.

Kenen, P.B. (1976), Capital mobility and financial integration: A survey (International Finance Section, Princeton University, Princeton).

Keynes, J.M. (1919), The economic consequences of the peace (Macmillan, London).

Keynes, J.M. (1923), A tract on monetary reform (Cambridge University Press, London).

Keynes, J.M. (1929), "The German transfer problem", Economic Journal, 39:1–7.

Keynes, J.M. (1936), The general theory of employment, interest, and money (Macmillan, London).

Kouri, P.J.K. and M.G. Porter (1974), "International capital flows and portfolio equilibrium", Journal of Political Economy, 82:443–467.

Laursen, S. and L.A. Metzler (1950), "Flexible exchange rates and the theory of employment", Review of Economics and Statistics, 32:281–299.

Lerner, A.P. (1944), The economics of control (Macmillan, New York).

Lindbeck, A. (1979), Inflation and open economies (North-Holland, Amsterdam).

Machlup, F. (1939), "The theory of foreign exchanges", Economica, 6:375–397.

Machlup, F. (1943), International trade and the national income multiplier (Blakiston, Philadelphia).

Machlup, F. (1956), "The terms of trade effects of devaluation upon real income and the balance of trade", Kyklos, 9:417–452.

Markowitz, H.M. (1959), Portfolio selection (Wiley, New York).

Marshall, A. (1923), Money, credit, and commerce (Macmillan, London).

McKinnon, R.I. (1963), "Optimum currency areas", American Economic Review, 53:717–725.

McKinnon, R.I. (1969), "Portfolio balance and international payments adjustment", in: R.A. Mundell and A.K. Swoboda, eds., Monetary problems of the international economy (University of Chicago Press, Chicago) 199–234.

McKinnon, R.I. (1979), Money in international exchange: The convertible currency system (Oxford University Press, New York).

McKinnon, R.I. (1981), "The exchange rate and macroeconomic policy: Changing postwar perceptions", Journal of Economic Literature, 19:531–557.

McKinnon, R.I. and W.E. Oates (1966), The implications of international economic integration for monetary, fiscal, and exchange-rate policies (International Finance Section, Princeton University, Princeton).

Meade, J.E. (1951), The balance of payments (Oxford University Press, London).

Meade, J.E. (1955), "The case for variable exchange rates", Three Banks Review, 27:3–28.

Metzler, L.A. (1942a), "Underemployment equilibrium in international trade", Econometrica, 10:97–112.

Metzler, L.A. (1942b), "The transfer problem reconsidered", Journal of Political Economy, 50:397–414. Reprinted in: H.S. Ellis and L.A. Metzler, eds., Readings in the theory of international trade (Blakiston, Philadelphia, 1949) 179–197.

Metzler, L.A. (1951), "Wealth, saving and the rate of interest", Journal of Political Economy, 59:930–946.

Metzler, L.A. (1960), "The process of international adjustment under conditions of full employment: A Keynesian view", published in: R.E. Caves and H.G. Johnson, eds., Readings in international economics (Irwin, Homewood, 1968) 465–486.

Miller, N.C. and M.v.N. Whitman (1970), "A mean-variance analysis of United States long-term portfolio foreign investment", Quarterly Journal of Economics, 84:175–196.

Miller, N.C. and M.v.N. Whitman (1972), "The outflow of short-term funds from the United States: Adjustment of stocks and flows", in: F. Machlup, W.A. Salant, and L. Tarshis, eds., International mobility and movement of capital (National Bureau of Economic Research, New York) 253–286.

Mundell, R.A. (1960), "The monetary dynamics of international adjustment under fixed and flexible exchange rates", Quarterly Journal of Economics, 74:227–257.

Mundell, R.A. (1961a), "The international disequilibrium system", Kyklos, 14:154–172.

Mundell, R.A. (1961b), "A theory of optimum currency areas", American Economic Review, 51:657–665.

Mundell, R.A. (1962), "The appropriate use of monetary and fiscal policy for internal and external stability", International Monetary Fund Staff Papers, 9:70–77.

Mundell, R.A. (1963), "Capital mobility and stabilization policy under fixed and flexible exchange rates", Canadian Journal of Economics, 29:475–485. Reprinted in: R.E. Caves and H.G. Johnson, eds., Readings in international economics (Irwin, Homewood, 1968) 487–499.

Mundell, R.A. (1968), "Barter theory and the monetary mechanisms of adjustment", in: R.A. Mundell, International economics (Macmillan, New York) 111–139. Reprinted in: J.A. Frenkel and H.G. Johnson, eds., The monetary approach to the balance of payments (University of Toronto Press, Toronto, 1976) 64–91.

Mundell, R.A. (1971), "The international distribution of money in a growing world economy", in: R.A. Mundell, Monetary theory (Goodyear, Pacific Palisades) 147–169. Reprinted in: J.A. Frenkel and H.G. Johnson, eds., The monetary approach to the balance of payments (University of Toronto Press, Toronto, 1976) 92–108.

Negishi, T. (1968), "Approaches to the analysis of devaluation", International Economic Review, 9:218–227.

Nurkse, R. (1944), International currency experience (League of Nations, Geneva).

Ohlin, B. (1929), "The reparation problem: Transfer difficulties, real and imagined", Economic Journal, 39:172–173.

Orcutt, G.H. (1950), "Measurement of price elasticities in international trade", Review of Economics and Statistics, 32:117–132. Reprinted in: R.E. Caves and H.G. Johnson, eds., Readings in International Economics (Irwin, Homewood, 1968) 528–552.

Patinkin, D. (1956), Money, interest, and prices (Harper & Row, New York).

Patrick, J.D. (1973), "Establishing convergent decentralized policy assignment", Journal of International Economics, 3:37–52.

Polak, J.J. (1957), "Monetary analysis of income formation and payments problems", International Monetary Fund Staff Papers, 6:1–50.

Robinson, J. (1947), Essays in the theory of employment (Blackwell, Oxford).

Salop, J. (1974), "Devaluation and the balance of trade under flexible wages", in: G. Horwich and P.A. Samuelson, eds., Trade, stability, and macroeconomics (Academic Press, New York) 129–151.

Salter, W.E.G. (1959), "International and external balance: The role of price and expenditure effects", Economic Record, 35:226–238.

Samuelson, P.A. (1952), "The transfer problem and transport costs: The terms of trade when impediments are absent", Economic Journal, 62:278–304. Reprinted in: J.E. Stiglitz, ed., The collected scientific papers of Paul A. Samuelson, II (MIT Press, Cambridge, 1966) 985–1011.

Samuelson, P.A. (1971), "On the trail of conventional beliefs about the transfer problem", in: J.N. Bhagwati, et al., eds., Trade, balance of payments and growth (North-Holland, Amsterdam) 327–351. Reprinted in: R.C. Merton, ed., The collected scientific papers of Paul A Samuelson, III (MIT Press, Cambridge, 1972) 374–398.

Sohmen, E. (1969), Flexible exchange rates (University of Chicago Press, Chicago).

Solomon, R. (1977). The international monetary system, 1945–1976 (Harper & Row, New York).

Swan, T.W. (1963), "Longer-run problems of the balance of payments", in: H.W. Arndt and W.M. Corden, eds., The Australian economy: A volume of readings (Cheshire Press, Melbourne) 384–395. Reprinted in: R.E. Caves and H.G. Johnson, eds., Readings in international economics (Irwin, Homewood, 1968) 455–464.

Tinbergen, J. (1952), On the theory of economic policy (North-Holland, Amsterdam).

Tobin, J. (1967), "Liquidity preference as behavior toward risk", in: D.D. Hester and J. Tobin, eds., Risk aversion and portfolio choice (Wiley, New York) 1–26.

Tobin, J. (1969), "A general equilibrium approach to monetary theory", Journal of Money, Credit and Banking, 1:15–30.

Tower, E. and T.D. Willett (1976), "The theory of optimum currency areas" (International Finance Section, Princeton University, Princeton).

Tsiang, S.C. (1959), "The theory of forward exchange and effects of government intervention on the forward exchange market", International Monetary Fund Staff Papers, 7:75–106.

Tsiang, S.C. (1961), "The role of money in trade-balance stability: Synthesis of the elasticity and absorption approaches", American Economic Review, 51:912–936. Reprinted in: R.E. Caves and H.G. Johnson, eds., Readings in international economics (Irwin, Homewood, 1968) 389–412.

Whitman, M.v.N. (1970), Policies for internal and external balance (International Finance Section, Princeton University, Princeton).

Whitman, M.v.N. (1972), "Place prosperity and people prosperity: The delineation of optimum policy areas", in: M. Perlman and C.J. Levin, eds., Spatial, regional and population economics (Gordon and Breach, New York) 395–393.

Whitman, M.v.N. (1975), "Global monetarism and the monetary approach to the balance of payments", Brookings Papers on Economic Activity, 3:121–166.

Willett, T.D. and F. Forte (1969), "Interest rate policy and external balance", Quarterly Journal of Economics, 83:242–262.

Chapter 14

ASSET MARKETS, EXCHANGE RATES AND THE BALANCE OF PAYMENTS

JACOB A. FRENKEL and MICHAEL L. MUSSA*

University of Chicago and National Bureau of Economic Research

Contents

*We are grateful to Stanley Black, William Branson and Peter Kenen for helpful comments on an earlier draft of this paper. The research reported here is part of the NBER's research program in International Studies and Economic Fluctuations. Any opinions expressed are those of the authors and not necessarily those of the NBER.

Handbook of International Economics, vol. II, edited by R.W. Jones and P.B. Kenen
© *Elsevier Science Publishers B.V., 1985*

1. Introduction

This chapter reviews developments in international monetary economics from the late 1960s through the early 1980s. Since the world remained on a system of fixed exchange rates until 1973, most of the research in the earlier part of this period focused on monetary relationships and macroeconomic behavior of open economies under a system of fixed exchange rates. An issue of central importance in this research, including the extensive literature on the "monetary approach to the balance of payments", was the economic determinants of the behavior of the balance of payments, especially, the theoretical elaboration and empirical investigation of the dynamic mechanism of balance of payments adjustment. With the shift to a system of floating exchange rates among major currencies in 1973, there was a corresponding shift of research interests away from primary focus on the balance of payments and to principal concern with the economic determinants of the behavior of exchange rates. The unifying theme in much of this research was the "asset market approach to exchange rates" which emphasizes conditions for equilibrium in the markets for stocks of assets, especially national monies, as the proximate determinant of the behavior of exchange rates.

Three general features of the research surveyed in this chapter distinguish it, in general emphasis and broad outline, from the earlier work on international monetary economics surveyed in Chapter 13 of this Handbook by Kenen. First, in the policy approach to open economy macroeconomics developed most extensively by Meade (1951), and extended by the important work of Mundell (1968c) and Fleming (1962), it is usually assumed that the level of national income is controlled by government policy, and that maintenance of full employment (or internal balance) is the paramount objective of economic policy. In this approach, the balance of payments is a "problem" because maintenance of balance of payments equilibrium (or external balance) constrains the use of macroeconomic policy for purposes of maintaining full employment. This problem can be satisfactorily resolved provided that governments have an adequate number of independent and effective policy instruments. More recent research on macroeconomics, for both closed and open economies, expresses far less confidence in the ability of governments to systematically affect levels of national income and consistently maintain full employment through policy manipulation. This view is reflected in the more recent research on international monetary economics where the balance of payments and the exchange rate are regarded as important in their own right, rather than as subsidiary concerns of policy management.

Second, in much of the earlier work on international monetary economics, policy actions and economic disturbances were assumed to have essentially permanent effects on payments flows. It was recognized, of course, that the losses of foreign exchange reserves associated with official settlements deficits would imply a declining domestic money supply, unless the monetary effects of the reserve loss were sterilized by domestic credit expansion. It was also recognized that reserve losses sterilized by domestic credit expansion could not go on forever because a government would ultimately run out of reserves. However, relatively little attention was paid to the dynamic process that would operate if reserve losses (or gains) were allowed to affect the money supply, or to the long run equilibrium that would be established if this process were allowed to operate, or to the longer run consequences of changes in supplies of securities necessarily associated with policies of sterilizing reserve losses and gains. In contrast, in the research surveyed here, the dynamic interaction among asset stocks and payments flows is at the center stage of the analysis.

Third, in earlier work on exchange rate theory, the condition for equilibrium in the flow market for foreign exchange transactions (exports, imports, and capital flows) was usually regarded as the proximate determinant of the exchange rate. In some analyses, expectations of future exchange rates had an important influence on current exchange rates by affecting speculative capital flows. But, even in these analyses, expectations of future exchange rates were usually determined exogenously or by some ad hoc expectations mechanism. Recent research on the theory of exchange rates, in contrast, has focused more on the conditions for asset market equilibrium as the proximate determinant of equilibrium exchange rates, and has usually regarded expectations of future exchange rates as a critical factor affecting the conditions for equilibrium in the relevant asset markets. Moreover, by adopting the assumption of "rational expectations," many recent models of exchange rate behavior have allowed for endogenous determination of expectations of future exchange rates in a manner consistent with the structure of the economic system, and have thereby permitted explicit analysis of the role of information in forming and revising expectations critical to explaining the behavior of exchange rates.

Differences between the research surveyed in this chapter and earlier approaches to balance of payments analysis and exchange rate theory should not, however, be overemphasized. The theoretical models applied to balance of payments analysis in the late 1960s and early 1970s incorporate the same basic elements as earlier such models and, correspondingly, share many of the same properties and implications. This essential unity is emphasized in this survey by beginning our discussion, in Section 2, with a review of the operation of the monetary mechanism of balance of payments adjustment in the context of the Meade–Mundell–Fleming model of open economy macroeconomics. We then turn in Section 3 to the more modern analysis of the dynamics of balance of payments adjustment under fixed exchange rates beginning with a simple exposition of the key elements of the monetary mechanism of balance of payments adjustment. The simple model is then extended to incorporate sluggish wage and output adjustments, endogenous monetary policy and sterilization operations, multiplicity of tradable and non-tradable goods, the case of large countries with endogenously determined terms of trade and, finally, capital mobility and portfolio balance.

Section 4 deals with the theory of flexible exchange rates. The evolution of the international monetary system from a regime of pegged exchange rates into a regime of flexible rates resulted in a renewed interest in the theory of exchange rate determination. Analogously to the characteristics of the modern theory of the balance of payments under fixed exchange rates, the modern theory of exchange rate determination has shifted the emphasis from the circular flow approach (that gained popularity with the Keynesian revolution) to considerations of portfolio choice and stock equilibrium. A consequence of this shift has been the development of the asset-market approach to the determination of exchange rates. Models which belong to the general category of the asset-market approach differ in their emphasis on the role of money and the other assets but they all highlight the roles of expectations and of stock equilibrium.

Our exposition of exchange-rate theory starts with a simple exposition of the monetary approach to exchange-rate determination. In this context we highlight the roles of purchasing power parities, non-traded goods, the real exchange rate, currency substitution, as well as the interaction between real and monetary factors which determine the equilibrium exchange rate. We then present a more general framework that views the question of exchange-rate determination as part of the general theory of the determination of asset prices. The broader framework highlights the unique role of expectations. The general framework is then used to characterize the interaction between the balance of payments and the equilibrium real exchange rate. This model shows that the current exchange rate depends on the entire expected future time paths of the relevant exogenous variables. The section concludes with a brief discussion of some empirical issues for exchange-rate analysis.

2. The Mundell–Fleming model

The key development in the area of balance of payments analysis in the late 1960s and early 1970s was the theoretical elaboration and empirical investigation of the dynamic mechanism of balance of payments adjustment. The essential idea of this dynamic mechanism, which dates back to Hume's discussion of the price–specie-flow mechanism, is that changes in asset stocks (especially the money supply) associated with payments imbalances alter the instantaneous equilibrium position of the economy over time and ultimately drive it to a long-run equilibrium at which the payments imbalance is eliminated. In much of the literature on balance of payments theory and open economy macroeconomics of the 1950s and 1960s, this dynamic mechanism of balance of payments adjustment was either ignored or suppressed by assuming that the domestic monetary authority sterilized the monetary effects of foreign exchange reserve gains and loses. However, at least in Mundell's (1961) description of the international disequilibrium system, this dynamic mechanism was explicitly introduced into the standard model that represented the main line of development in this earlier literature.

As illustrated in Figure 2.1, Mundell's analysis is based on the open economy extension of the IS-LM model, frequently referred to as the Mundell–Fleming model. In this diagram, the positively sloped LM curves show combinations of national income, Y, and the domestic nominal interest rate, i, for which the real demand for domestic money, $L(Y, i)$ (where $\partial L / \partial Y > 0$ and $\partial L / \partial i < 0$), is equal to the real supply, M/P. The different LM curves are all drawn for the same, parametrically determined domestic price level, P, but for different levels of the domestic nominal money supply, M, with lower LM curves corresponding to larger domestic nominal money supplies. The negatively sloped IS curve indicates the combinations of Y and i for which the demand for national product is equal to national income. The demand for national product is the sum of

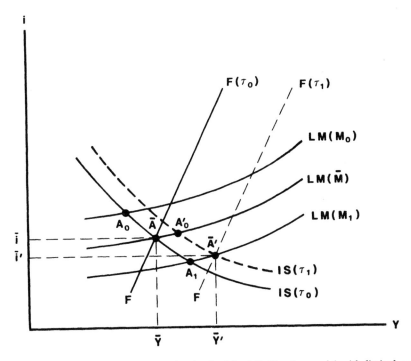

Figure 2.1. Monetary policy and devaluation in the Mundell–Fleming model with limited capital mobility

domestic demand for domestic product, $D(Y, i; \tau)$ (where $\partial D/\partial Y > 0$, $\partial D/\partial i <$ 0, and $\partial D/\partial \tau < 0$), plus foreign demand for domestic product, $I^*(\tau)$ (where $\partial I^*/\partial \tau < 0$); $\tau = P/S \cdot P^*$ is the terms of trade between domestic goods and foreign goods, where P^* denotes the foreign price of foreign goods and S denotes the exchange rate which is defined as the price of foreign exchange in terms of domestic currency. Alternatively, the demand for national product is the sum of total domestic expenditure, $E(Y, i)$ (where $1 > \partial E/\partial Y > \partial D/\partial Y > 0$, and $\partial E/\partial i < 0$) plus the trade balance surplus. In that alternative formulation, total domestic expenditure includes expenditure on imports, $I(Y, i; \tau) = E(Y, i) - D(Y, i; \tau)$, and, using this expression, the trade balance surplus is, $T(Y, i; \tau) = I^*(\tau) - I(Y, i; \tau)$, where $\partial T/\partial Y < 0$, $\partial T/\partial i > 0$, $\partial T/\partial \tau < 0$. The positively sloped FF curve shows combinations of Y and i for which the trade balance is zero.[1] The terms of trade, τ, is a parameter affecting the positions of the IS and FF curves.

At any moment of time, the instantaneous equilibrium position of the economy is determined by the intersection of the IS curve and the LM curve drawn for the current money supply. In particular, when the money supply is M_0 and the terms of trade is τ_0, the instantaneous equilibrium point is at A_0 in Figure 2.1. At this instantaneous equilibrium, the trade balance is in surplus, as indicated by the fact that A_0 is above and to the left of the FF curve. Since the present analysis assumes an absence of private capital flows, it follows that for the government to maintain a fixed exchange rate, it must purchase foreign exchange reserves at a rate equal to the trade surplus at A_0. If the government does not sterilize the monetary effects of this reserve accumulation, the domestic nominal money supply will grow at a rate equal to the rate of accumulation of foreign exchange reserves, valued in domestic money. Growth of M gradually shifts the LM curve in Figure 2.1 downward and to the right, moving the instantaneous equilibrium point along the IS curve away from A_0 and toward the point $\bar{A}$ determined by the intersection of the IS and FF curves. When the instantaneous equilibrium point (and the LM curve) reach $\bar{A}$, the trade balance is zero, accumulation of foreign exchange reserves ceases, and economy is in long-run equilibrium. The dynamic mechanism which drives the economy from A_0 (or any other initial instantaneous equilibrium position) to long-run equilibrium at $\bar{A}$ is the monetary mechanism of balance of payments adjustment. The total accumulation of foreign exchange reserve (the cumulative official settlements surplus) associated with the movement from A_0 to $\bar{A}$, valued in domestic money, is determined by the difference between the initial nominal money supply, M_0, and the long run equilibrium level of the money supply, $\bar{M} = P_0 \cdot L(\bar{Y}, i)$, where $\bar{Y}$ and i are the long-run equilibrium levels of Y and i that are associated with the long-run equilibrium point $\bar{A}$.

---

[1] In Figure 2.1 the FF curve is drawn steeper than the LM curve in order to emphasize that at this stage of the analysis we rule out private capital flows. This assumption is modified below.

Starting at the instantaneous equilibrium A_0, if the money supply were increased by a domestic credit expansion to the extent of the difference between M_0 and $\overline{M}$, the result would be an immediate shift of the LM curve to its long-run equilibrium position and an immediate jump of national income and the domestic interest rate to their respective long-run equilibrium values. As a consequence of this domestic credit expansion, therefore, the government would forgo the increase in foreign exchange reserves that would otherwise occur as a consequence of the natural adjustment process of the economy in moving from A_0 to $\overline{A}$, but would gain a more immediate increase in the level of national income. Alternatively, if the government expanded domestic credit starting from a situation of long-run equilibrium, it would temporarily shift the LM curve downward and to the right, creating an instantaneous equilibrium at a point like A_1 corresponding to the higher quantity of money, M_1. At A_1, there would be a balance of payments deficit, and the gradual adjustment of the domestic money supply implied by losses of foreign exchange reserves would ultimately drive the instantaneous equilibrium point back to $\overline{A}$. In the long run, therefore, the increase in the domestic credit component of the money supply would be fully offset by an equal loss of foreign exchange reserves, and the stimulative effect of the domestic credit expansion on national income would only be temporary. If the government attempted to maintain national income at a level above its long-run equilibrium level by sterilizing foreign exchange reserve losses through offsetting domestic credit expansions, it could do so for a while, but ultimately it would run out of reserves.

A devaluation from an initial equilibrium at $\overline{A}$ increases S and reduces τ from τ_0 to τ_1 (since in this analysis P and P^* are assumed to be given) shifting both the IS and FF curves to the right to $IS(\tau_1)$ and $FF(\tau_1)$, respectively. The new *long-run* equilibrium is at $\overline{A}'$, with a higher long run equilibrium level of national income, $\overline{Y}'$, and a lower long-run equilibrium level of the domestic interest rate, $\bar{i}'$.[2] If at the time of this devaluation, the money supply was at the long-run equilibrium level appropriate for the old exchange rate, the impact effect of the devaluation will be to move the instantaneous equilibrium point up along the LM curve passing through $\overline{A}$ to the intersection between this LM curve and the new IS curve as illustrated by point A_0'. The *impact* effect of devaluation, therefore, is to increase domestic income and the domestic interest rate and to create a balance of payments surplus. These impact effects of devaluation, however, are not the permanent, long-run effects of devaluation. Increases in the money supply resulting from payments surpluses that are the short-run consequence of the devaluation drive the economy to its new long-run equilibrium $\overline{A}'$ at which domestic income is higher and the domestic interest rate is lower than A_0' and at which the

---

[2] This result follows from the fact that the horizontal shift of the FF curve is larger than the corresponding shift of the IS curve since $\partial E/\partial Y < 1$. Both curves shift to the right since income must rise to offset the impact of the fall in τ on demand.

(flow) balance of payments surplus initially created by the devaluation is eliminated. With respect to the balance of payments, therefore, the long-run effect of devaluation is a permanent, cumulative change in the level of reserves equal to increase in the long run equilibrium size of the nominal money supply from $\overline{M} = L(\overline{Y}, i)$ to $M_1 = \overline{M}' = L(\overline{Y}', i')$, but not a permanent surplus in the flow magnitude of the balance of payments.

When privately held financial assets are internationally mobile, this analysis of the balance of payments adjustment mechanism needs to be modified to take account of the effects of capital movements on reserve holdings and national money supplies. Specifically, with perfect capital mobility, the *FF* curve indicating balance of payments equilibrium becomes a horizontal line at the level of the world interest rate, i^*, as indicated in Figure 2.2. In this situation an instantaneous equilibrium at a point like A_0, determined by the *IS* curve and the *LM* curve for a domestic money supply of M_0, is not sustainable as an instantaneous equilibrium because a domestic interest rate i_0 that is above the world interest rate i^* would induce a huge capital inflow. Domestic residents would sell securities to foreigners in order to increase their money balances to the level consistent with $i = i^*$. The increase in reserves implied by this capital inflow causes the *LM* curve to jump until it passes through the long-run equilibrium point $\overline{A}$ determined by the intersection of the *IS* curve with the *FF* curve. Thus,

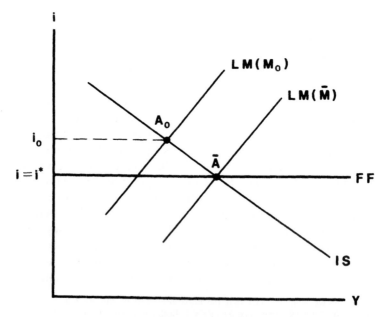

Figure 2.2. The Mundell–Fleming model with perfect capital mobility.

with perfect capital mobility, the balance of payments adjustment process is not a gradual process in which money supply gradually adjusts to reserve gains and losses associated with trade imbalances, but rather an instantaneous adjustment process in which the level of reserves adjusts immediately in response to international capital movements.

The essential elements in this analysis of the mechanism of balance of payments adjustment, including the analysis of the cumulative effects on the balance of payments of changes in domestic credit or the exchange rate and of the consequences of international capital mobility are also central in the literature on balance of payments theory that developed during the late 1960s and early 1970s. In this literature, however, less reliance is placed on the Keynesian assumptions of rigid domestic prices and demand determined output levels as the relevant assumptions for balance of payments analysis, and more attention is devoted to explicit modelling of the dynamics of the balance of payments adjustment process. The analysis in Section 3 focuses on these issues.

3. The dynamics of balance of payments adjustment under fixed exchange rates

3.1. Adjustment in a small open economy without capital mobility

To illustrate the monetary mechanism of balance of payments adjustment consider first a small open economy facing given world relative prices of all (tradable) goods produced and consumed by domestic residents. Using the Hicksian aggregation principle, domestic real income (equal to domestic output), Y, and domestic real expenditure, E, are measured in common units of a composite tradable good. Domestic real income is constant at the level determined by full employment of domestic resources. Domestic real expenditure depends on domestic real income, the domestic real interest rate, r, and the real value of privately held domestic assets, A/P:

$$E = E(Y, r, A/P), \qquad \partial E/\partial Y > 0, \qquad \partial E/\partial r < 0, \qquad \partial E/\partial (A/P) \geq 0.$$
$$(3.1)$$

Privately held domestic assets consist of domestic money, M, and domestic interest bearing securities, B, which are denominated in units of domestic money and have an infinitesimal maturity (like call loans):

$$A = M + B. \qquad (3.2)$$

In the absence of international mobility of capital, these assets are assumed to be non-tradable internationally. The real value of these assets depends on the domestic price level, P, which is equal to the foreign price, P^*, multiplied by the exchange rate, S:

$$P = S \cdot P^*. \tag{3.3}$$

The domestic money supply (under the simplifying assumption that the money multiplier is unity) is high powered money issued by the domestic central bank and is equal to the sum of the domestic money value of the foreign exchange reserves of the central bank, $S \cdot R$, domestic securities held by the central bank, B_g, and the fiat issue (the "net worth") of the central bank, J:

$$M = S \cdot R + B_g + J. \tag{3.4}$$

The fiat of the central bank designates a balance sheet entry which represents the "net worth" of the central bank — that is, the difference between the value of the central bank's monetary liabilities, M, and the value of its reserves and domestic security holdings, $S \cdot R + B_g$. An increase in the domestic currency value of foreign exchange reserves due to an increase in S that is not monetized by the central bank is offset by a corresponding decline in J.

Interest bearing securities and national monies are not internationally tradable. The total stock of domestic securities issued by the domestic government, $\bar{B}$, is held either by domestic residents or by the central bank:[3]

$$B + B_g = \bar{B}. \tag{3.5}$$

Since the asset demands of domestic residents for domestic money and domestic securities must satisfy the balance sheet constraint, the condition for asset-market equilibrium in this country can be expressed as the condition for money market equilibrium:

$$L(Y, i, A/P) = M/P, \qquad \partial L/\partial Y > 0,$$
$$\partial L/\partial i < 0, \qquad 1 > \partial L/\partial(A/P) > 0, \tag{3.6}$$

where $L(Y, i, A/P)$ is the real demand for domestic money, and where i denotes the domestic nominal interest rate that is equal to the real rate, r, plus the expected rate of inflation. In what follows we assume that the expected rate of inflation is zero and, therefore, we identify r with the nominal rate of interest. The condition of asset market equilibrium implicitly determines the equilibrium of the domestic interest rate so that

$$r = \tilde{r}(M/P, B/P, Y), \qquad \partial \tilde{r}/\partial(M/P) < 0,$$
$$\partial \tilde{r}/\partial(B/P) > 0, \qquad \partial \tilde{r}/\partial Y > 0. \tag{3.7}$$

Given the interest rate (which is implicitly determined by the requirement of asset

---

[3]Interest payments on government bonds outside of the central bank are assumed to be financed by lump-sum taxes so as to avoid issues associated with changes in the government budget and disposable income.

market equilibrium), the level of real domestic expenditure becomes a reduced form function of the real money supply, real private security holdings, and domestic real income:

$$E = \tilde{E}(M/P, B/P, Y) \equiv E(Y, \tilde{r}(M/P, B/P, Y), (M/P) + (B/P)). \quad (3.8)$$

An increase in M/P increases $\tilde{E}$ both because it reduces $\tilde{r}$ and because it increases A/P. An increase in B/P has an ambiguous effect on $\tilde{E}$ because the effect on $\tilde{r}$ works in the opposite direction of the effect on A/P. An increase in Y may be presumed to increase $\tilde{E}$ provided that the direct effect, $\partial E/\partial Y$, is stronger than indirect interest rate effect, $(\partial E/\partial r) \cdot (\partial \tilde{r}/\partial Y)$. The indirect interest rate effect, however, should be sufficient to insure that $\partial \tilde{E}/\partial Y < 1$, even if $\partial E/\partial Y > 1$.

In accord with the basic equation of the absorption approach to the balance of payments, the home country's real trade balance, T, must equal the excess of real income (equal to domestic output) over domestic real expenditure; that is, $T = Y - E$ [see Alexander (1952)]. Using the reduced form expenditure function $\tilde{E}$, it follows that

$$T = \tilde{T}(M/P, B/P, Y) \equiv Y - \tilde{E}(M/P, B/P, Y). \quad (3.9)$$

An increase in M/P raises spending and worsens the real trade balance since $\partial \tilde{T}/\partial(M/P) = -\partial \tilde{E}/\partial(M/P) < 0$. An increase in B/P has an ambiguous effect on the real trade balance because its influence on spending, i.e. the sign of $\partial \tilde{E}/\partial(B/P)$ is ambiguous. An increase in Y improves the real trade balance because it raises income by more than spending since $\partial \tilde{T}/\partial Y = 1 - \partial \tilde{E}/\partial Y$ is presumably positive.

Since, by assumption, trade imbalances cannot be financed by private capital flows or by changes in private holdings of foreign monies, they must be financed by a flow of international reserves which the domestic central bank is compelled to absorb or supply in order to maintain the fixed exchange rate. The magnitude of this reserve flow is given by

$$\dot{R} = P^* \cdot T, \quad (3.10)$$

where $\dot{R}$ denotes the rate of change of international reserves, i.e. $\dot{R} \equiv \mathrm{d}R/\mathrm{d}t$. Assuming that the central bank does not alter its domestic security holdings or fiat issue, either to sterilize the foreign exchange flow or for any other reason, the rate of change of the domestic nominal money supply, $\dot{M}$, must equal the nominal value of the trade balance:

$$\dot{M} = P \cdot \tilde{T}(M/P, B/P, Y). \quad (3.11)$$

This result captures four essential features of the monetary mechanism of balance of payments adjustment.

First, there is a natural equilibrating process through which foreign exchange reserve flows associated with trade imbalances adjust the domestic money supply

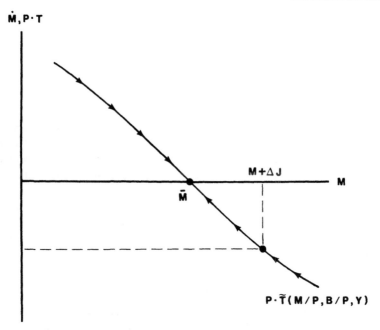

Figure 3.1. The dynamics of monetary adjustment.

to its long-run equilibrium level and simultaneously bring equilibrium to the trade balance. The nature of this equilibrating process is illustrated in Figure 3.1 where the $P \cdot \tilde{T}(M/P, B/P, Y)$ curve shows the relationship between the rate of change of the domestic money supply and the level of the domestic money supply, given constant values of B, Y and P. This $P \cdot \tilde{T}(M/P, B/P, Y)$ curve is negatively sloped because an increase in M reduces the trade balance surplus or increases the trade balance deficit. The unique intersection of this curve with the M axis occurs at the long-run equilibrium level of the domestic money demand, $\overline{M}(Y, B, P)$, which is determined implicitly by the requirement that

$$\tilde{T}(M/P, B/P, Y) = 0. \tag{3.12}$$

When M is less than $\overline{M}(Y, B, P)$, the relatively high level of the domestic interest rate and the relatively low level of privately held domestic assets induce a level domestic real expenditure that is less than domestic real income and, correspondingly, a trade balance surplus. The reserve inflow implied by this trade surplus gradually raises the domestic money supply and ultimately drives the economy to its long-run equilibrium where $M = \overline{M}(Y, B, P)$, and the trade balance is zero. The opposite process occurs if M is initially larger than $\overline{M}(Y, B, P)$.[4]

Second, any change in the supply of domestic money that is not offset by a change in the long-run equilibrium level of domestic money demand leads to an equivalent change in foreign exchange reserves and to a corresponding cumulative payments surplus (or deficit). This change in reserves and cumulative payments surplus must be measured relative to the long-run level of reserves and cumulative payments position that would have resulted in the absence of the initiating change in the money supply. For example, suppose that starting with a money supply of $\overline{M}$, there is an increase ΔJ in the fiat issue of the central bank. Immediately after this increase in fiat, M will exceed $\overline{M}$ by ΔJ and, as illustrated in Figure 3.1, there will be a trade deficit corresponding to the nominal value of the induced excess of domestic real expenditure over domestic real income. From the figure it is clear that the cumulative magnitude of nominal trade deficits during the process of convergence back to $\overline{M}$ must equal the initial fiat increase in the domestic money supply.[5]

Third, any change in the long-run equilibrium level of domestic money demand that is not offset by changes in the domestic assets component of the money supply ultimately leads to corresponding change in the foreign exchange reserve component of the money supply and to a corresponding cumulative payments surplus (or deficit). For example, suppose that economic growth increases domestic real income from Y_0 to Y_1, thereby increasing the long-run equilibrium level of money demand from $\overline{M}_0 = \overline{M}(Y_0, B, P)$ to $\overline{M}_1 = \overline{M}(Y_1, B, P)$.[6] If there are no changes in the other components of the money supply, then relative to what would have happened in the absence of the increase in domestic income, there must be net inflow of foreign exchange reserves and a corresponding cumulative payments surplus equal to $\overline{M}_1 - \overline{M}_0$.

---

[4]The concept of the "natural distribution" is one of the central propositions of the classical doctrine. Accordingly, "A Nation cannot retain more than its natural proportion of what is in the world, and the balance of trade must run against it" [Gervaise (1720, p. 12)]. Similar statements were made by Hume (1752, pp. 62–64), Ricardo (1821, p. 123) and Mill (1893, book III, p. 194–95). For further references see Frenkel (1976b) and Frenkel and Johnson (1976a).

[5]The loss of control over the money supply is central to the predictions of the monetary approach to the balance of payments. For examples see Johnson (1958), Mundell (1968c, 1971), Mussa (1974). This loss of control is, of course, the key message of Hume's (1752) famous experiments of sudden annihilation of four-fifths of the money supply. For expositions of analyses of the monetary mechanism of balance of payments adjustment see Collery (1971), Frenkel (1976b), Hahn (1959), Johnson (1976a), Mundel (1968a), Mussa (1974), Swoboda (1972, 1973), Swoboda and Dornbusch (1973), Frenkel and Johnson (1976a), International Monetary Fund (1977), Allen and Kenen (1980).

[6]For analyses of growth and the balance of payments see Mundell (1968b), Komiya (1969), Dornbusch (1971), Frenkel (1971, 1976b), Flood (1977), and Purvis (1972).

Another example is a devaluation that raises the exchange rate, S, and hence the domestic price level, $P = S \cdot P^*$. The elasticity of the long-run equilibrium level of money demand with respect to the domestic price level (and hence the exchange rate) is given by

$$(P/\overline{M}) \cdot \partial \overline{M}/\partial P = 1 + (B/\overline{M}) \cdot [\partial \tilde{T}/\partial(B/P)/\partial \tilde{T}/\partial(M/P)]. \qquad (3.13)$$

If $\partial \tilde{T}/\partial(B/P) = -\partial \tilde{E}/\partial(B/P) < 0$, then a devaluation will result in a more than proportional increase in the long-run equilibrium level of money demand and in a corresponding increase in foreign exchange reserves and cumulative payments surplus. If the effect of the rise in the rate of interest is sufficiently strong so as to result in $\partial \tilde{T}/\partial(B/P) > 0$, then (when the system is stable so that $(B/\overline{M}) \cdot [\partial \tilde{T}/\partial(B/P)/\partial \tilde{T}/\partial(M/P)] > -1$), a devaluation will result in a less than proportional increase in the long-run equilibrium level of money demand and in a correspondingly smaller increase in foreign exchange reserves and cumulative payments surplus. The reason why the long-run equilibrium level of money demand may not rise proportionately with the increase in the exchange rate (as it does in some simple monetary models of devaluation) is that the nominal stock of bonds, B, is a parameter affecting the long-run equilibrium level of money balances. This non-neutrality of exchange rate changes disappears if domestic bonds are denominated in real goods rather than in domestic money, or if private residents see through the government budget constraint and regard government debt as completely and perfectly offset by expected future tax liabilities.[7] An import tariff, in contrast to a devaluation, generally has non-neutral effects because a tariff alters relative commodity prices, in addition to affecting the general level of domestic prices, and this alteration of relative prices may influence the long run equilibrium level of real money balances.[8]

Fourth, the factors that influence the path of convergence of the money supply toward long-run equilibrium and hence the flow magnitude of payments surpluses and deficits are to a large extent distinct from the factors that influence the cumulative payments surplus or deficit that results from a change in the long-run equilibrium level of money demand or in the components of the money supply other than foreign exchange reserves. For example, the speed of convergence to long-run equilibrium and the magnitude of the payments flow resulting from an increase in the fiat issue of the central bank are determined by the slope of the

[7] For analyses of devaluations see Dornbusch (1973a, 1973b), Berglas (1974), Boyer (1975), Blejer (1977), Frenkel and Rodriguez (1975), Johnson (1976a, 1976b). For empirical evidence see Connolly and Taylor (1976), Miles (1979) and Craig (1981). On the role of government debt, future tax liabilities, and the capital market see Metzler (1951), Mundell (1971) and Barro (1974).

[8] On the balance of payments effects of tariffs and other commercial policies see Mussa (1976a), Johnson (1976b) and Hawtrey (1922).

$P \cdot \tilde{T}$ curve in Figure 3.1:

$$\frac{\partial \tilde{T}}{\partial (M/P)} = - \frac{\partial E}{\partial (A/P)} - \left(\frac{\partial E}{\partial r} \right) \cdot \left[\frac{1 - (\partial L / \partial (A/P))}{\partial L / \partial r} \right]. \tag{3.14}$$

High responsiveness of desired spending to the real value of privately held assets and to the interest rate, and low responsiveness of money demand to these same variables all contribute to produce a high speed of convergence to long-run equilibrium and hence a rapid loss of foreign exchange reserves in response to an increase in the fiat issue of the central bank. In contrast, the long-run, cumulative response of the balance of payments to an increase in the fiat issue of the central bank does not depend on any of these properties of the desired expenditure function and the money demand function, but only on the property that a change in the fiat issue does not alter the long-run equilibrium level of money demand.

3.2. Extensions of the simple model

The preceding analysis of the monetary mechanism of balance of payments adjustment for a small open economy employed a number of restrictive assumptions that have been the focus of much of the criticism of the monetary approach to the balance of payments.[9] Some of the critics of the monetary approach have argued that some of its simplifying assumptions lack realism. Among the assumptions that were singled out were (i) the reliance on some form of real balance effect, (ii) the assumption that commodity and factor prices adjust instantaneously to clear commodity and factor markets and maintain full employment, (iii) the assumption that central banks do not systematically offset foreign exchange reserve flows through sterilization operations, (iv) the assumption that all goods are internationally traded, (v) the small country assumption that implies that the economy takes the relative prices of all goods, or at least of all traded goods, as fixed by world conditions and (vi) the neglect of international capital mobility in many of the simple expositions of the monetary approach. In the following sections, it is shown that these simplifying assumptions can be relaxed without altering significantly the fundamental characteristics of the monetary mechanism of balance of payments adjustments.

3.2.1. The real balance effect

The model examined in the preceding section incorporates a "real balance effect" through the assumption that desired real spending depends positively on the real

---

[9]For criticism of the restrictive assumptions see Chipman (1978), Hahn (1977), Kreinin and Officer (1978), Tsiang (1977). For a survey of the issues see Whitman (1975).

value of assets, which includes the real value of money balances. This real balance effect, however, is not necessary to deriving the critical reduced form relationship $\dot{M} = P \cdot \tilde{T}$ of the type illustrated in Figure 3.1. The essential features of the monetary mechanism of balance of payments adjustment remain unchanged even if the real balance effect is absent. In that case the reduced form effect of an increase in M on $\dot{M}$ depends exclusively on the effect of the increase in M on the rates of interest and, thereby, on desired expenditure.

Alternatively, the model of the preceding section could be modified so that the only channel through which changes in M affect the trade balance and $\dot{M}$ is through a special form of the real balance effect known as the "hoarding function" [see Dornbusch (1973a, 1973b)]. If there are no domestic interest bearing securities (and financial capital is not internationally mobile), all saving and dissaving must take the form of accumulation and decumulation of money balances. Under these conditions, it is plausible to suppose that desired real saving, which equals the excess of domestic real income over domestic real expenditure, depends on the divergence between the long-run desired level of real money balances, $\bar{L}(Y)$, and the actual level of real money balances, M/P:

$$T = Y - E = H(L(Y) - (M/P)), \tag{3.15}$$

where $H(\cdot)$ is the "hoarding function" which has the properties that $H(0) = 0$ and $H' > 0$ [see Dornbusch and Mussa (1975)]. Since the trade surplus (or deficit) must be financed by an inflow (or outflow) of foreign exchange reserves, and since these reserve flows alter the domestic money supply in the absence of offsetting changes in other assets of the central bank, it follows that

$$\dot{M} = P \cdot T = P \cdot H(L(Y) - (M/P)). \tag{3.16}$$

The key point of this exercise is that the reduced form relationship $\dot{M} = P \cdot H(L(Y) - (M/P))$ has the same critical properties as the reduced form relationship $\dot{M} = P \cdot \tilde{T}(M/P, B/P, Y)$ examined in the preceding section. It follows that the specification of a hoarding function yields all of the essential features of the monetary mechanism of balance of payments adjustment discussed in the preceding section. But, neither this special form of the assumption of a real balance effect, nor any other form of that assumption is necessary to the derivation of the essential features of this adjustment mechanism.

3.2.2. Wage and output dynamics

The assumption of instantaneous adjustment of commodity and factor prices to clear all markets and maintain full employment is easily modified without altering the essential features of the monetary mechanism of balance of payments adjustment. A simple, alternative assumption is that the domestic nominal wage rate, W, is at least temporarily fixed, and that the level of employment is determined by the quantity of labor that domestic producers demand at this nominal wage rate [see Rodriguez (1976a) and Leiderman (1979)]. With this assumption about the labor market, domestic output is determined by an aggregate supply function:

$$Y = Y^s(P/W), \qquad \partial Y^s/\partial(P/W) > 0. \tag{3.17}$$

Allowing for the endogenous determination of domestic output modifies the reduced form relationship describing the rate of change of the domestic money supply:

$$\dot{M} = P \cdot \tilde{T}(M/P, B/P, Y^s(P/W)). \tag{3.18}$$

If the nominal wage rate is determined parametrically, rather than adjusted endogenously, the process of adjustment of the domestic money supply through reserve flows toward its long-run equilibrium level is exactly as described in Section 3.1. Moreover, changes in the fiat issue of the central bank, in private securities holdings, or in the long-run equilibrium level of money demand that do not involve changes in W or P have exactly the same long-run and short-run effects as in Section 3.1. A change in W, holding P constant, changes Y and has exactly the same long-run and short-run effects as a change in Y in Section 3.1. The only significant modification of previous results is with respect to the effects of a devaluation which raises, proportionately, the domestic price level. Previously, the long-run effect of devaluation on the stock of foreign reserves reflected the typical proportional effect of a rise in the price level on the long-run equilibrium level of money demand, supplemented by the effect of a reduction in the real value of privately held securities on the long-run equilibrium level of money demand. Allowing for the endogeneous determination of domestic output through the function $Y^s(P/W)$ and assuming that nominal wages are given, increases the effect of devaluation in expanding the stock of foreign exchange reserves because it introduces an additional channel, an increase in domestic output, through which a devaluation increases the long run equilibrium level of money demand.

If the nominal wage rate adjusts endogenously, modifications of the analysis of Section 3.1 are more substantial, but the essential features of the monetary mechanism of balance of payments adjustment remain intact. Abstracting from anticipated inflation and anticipated changes in productivity that would contribute a trend component to the rate of change of the nominal wage rate, suppose that W adjusts at a rate that is proportional to the divergence between its equilibrium value, $\overline{W}$, and its current value, W:

$$\dot{W} = \delta \cdot (\overline{W} - W), \qquad \delta > 0. \tag{3.19}$$

The equilibrium nominal wage rate is the value of W that would keep aggregate output at its full employment level, $\overline{Y}$; it is proportional to the domestic price level and is determined implicitly by the requirement that

$$Y^s(P/\overline{W}) = \overline{Y}. \tag{3.20}$$

The dynamic system that jointly determines the evolution of the domestic money supply (resulting from reserve flows) and the adjustment of the domestic nominal wage rate consists of the differential equations (3.18) and (3.19). The behavior of this dynamic system (for given values of the parameters B, P, $\overline{W}$, B_g and J) is illustrated in the phase diagram shown in Figure 3.2. The horizontal line along which $W = \overline{W}$ shows the combinations of M and W for which $\dot{W} = 0$. Above this line $\dot{W}$ is negative, and below this line $\dot{W}$ is positive. The negatively sloped schedule labeled $\dot{M} = 0$ shows the combinations of M and W for which $P \cdot \tilde{T}(M/P, B/P, Y^s(P/W)) = 0$, for the given values of B and P. This line is negatively sloped because an increase in M which makes $\dot{M} < 0$ needs to be offset by a decrease in W which makes $\dot{M} > 0$ in order to keep $\dot{M} = 0$. Above and to the right of the $\dot{M} = 0$ line $\dot{M}$ is negative, and below and to the left of this line $\dot{M}$ is positive. The intersection of the $\dot{W} = 0$ and $\dot{M} = 0$ schedules occurs at the long-run equilibrium point where $W = \overline{W}$, as determined by (3.20), and the nominal money supply is equal to the long-run equilibrium level of money demand, $\overline{M}(\overline{Y}, B, P)$ as determined by (3.12) with $Y = \overline{Y}$.

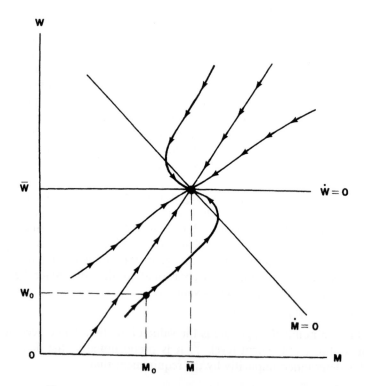

Figure 3.2. The dynamics of monetary and wage adjustment.

Since the dynamic system illustrated in Figure 3.2 is stable, for any positive speed of adjustment of the nominal wage rate, the domestic money supply will ultimately adjust to $\overline{M}$ through reserve flows associated with trade imbalances. Furthermore, given any initial divergence of the domestic money supply from the long-run equilibrium level of money demand, the cumulative payments surplus or deficit that occurs along the path of convergence to the long run equilibrium point in Figure 3.2 must entail a cumulative gain or loss of foreign exchange reserves just sufficient to bring the domestic money supply to equality with $\overline{M}$. This conclusion also applies to any divergence between M and $\overline{M}$ that is created by a change in the non-reserve assets of the central bank or in factors that determine the long run equilibrium level of money demand. Thus, the modifications of monetary mechanism of balance of payments adjustment implied by simultaneous endogenous adjustment of the domestic nominal wage rate do not affect the stability of this mechanism or the conclusions concerning the long run, cumulative effects of disturbances to the money supply or to the long-run equilibrium level of money demand.

These modifications affect only the details of the behavior of the money supply and the balance of payments along the path of convergence to long-run equilibrium. In particular, in the analysis of Section 3.1, convergence of the domestic money supply to the long-run equilibrium level of money demand was always monotonic. With endogenous adjustment of the domestic nominal wage rate, however, the money supply need not converge monotonically to its long-run equilibrium value. For example, if we start at the point (M_0, W_0) in Figure 3.2, with $M_0 < \overline{M}$ and W_0 well below $\overline{W}$, the path of convergence to long run equilibrium is one along which the money supply rises above its long-run equilibrium level through a series of trade surpluses and reserve inflows, and then falls back to $\overline{M}$ through a series of trade deficits and reserve outflows.[10]

3.2.3. Endogenous monetary policy and sterilization

Sterilization is a form of endogenous monetary policy in which a central bank offsets all or part of the changes in the money supply resulting from foreign exchange reserve flows by countervailing changes of its non-reserve assets. A simple form of sterilization policy is described by the rule:

$$\dot{J} = -\phi \cdot S \cdot \dot{R}, \qquad 0 < \phi < 1, \tag{3.21}$$

---

[10] This analysis of non-clearing of the labor market and gradual adjustment of the domestic nominal wage rate can be extended to other markets and other prices. Provided that the adjustment mechanisms that are assumed to operate in these other markets are specified in a consistent manner, the essential features of the monetary mechanism of balance of payments adjustment are preserved. The exact details of path of convergence of other variables, however, are likely to be critically affected by the precise forms of these adjustment mechanisms.

where the sterilization coefficient ϕ indicates the fraction of foreign exchange changes that the central bank offsets by varying its fiat issue, and where the rate of change in the domestic currency value of foreign exchange reserves, $S \cdot \dot{R}$, is determined by the nominal trade surplus, $P \cdot \tilde{T}(M/P, B/P, Y)$.

This form of sterilization policy does not affect the long-run equilibrium level of money demand, but it does slow down the convergence of the money supply to the long-run equilibrium level. Specifically, with the sterilization policy (3.22), we have

$$\dot{M} = S \cdot \dot{R} + \dot{J} = (1 - \phi) \cdot S \cdot \dot{R} = (1 - \phi) \cdot P \cdot \tilde{T}(M/P, B/P, Y). \qquad (3.22)$$

This slowdown in the speed of convergence to long-run equilibrium comes at the expense of a greater cumulative change in foreign exchange reserves. If the initial divergence between the long-run equilibrium level of money demand and the actual domestic money supply is ΔM, the cumulative change in foreign exchange reserves in the process of convergence to long-run equilibrium is

$$\Delta R = (\Delta M/S)/(1 - \phi), \qquad (3.23)$$

and it is apparent that a policy of complete sterilization is not feasible. If a central bank attempts to set $\phi = 1$, then any small divergence between M and $\overline{M}$ will ultimately lead either to an infinite gain in foreign exchange reserves or an infinite loss of such reserves.[11]

In addition to sterilization, it is possible to analyze other forms of endogenous monetary policy. One such policy might be directed at moderating movements in the domestic interest rate. If the only cause of interest rate fluctuations, other than variations in the domestic money supply, were changes in the long-run equilibrium level of money demand, then such a monetary policy might contribute to economic stability and reduce the need for variations in foreign exchange reserves. However, if fluctuations in interest rates were caused by disturbances other than fluctuations in the long-run equilibrium level of money demand, then an interest rate stabilization rule for monetary policy would probably exacerbate fluctuations in foreign exchange reserves and might destabilize the economic system [see Frenkel and Mussa (1981)].

3.2.4. Non-traded goods

The assumption that a small country produces and consumes only traded goods with relative prices determined in world markets is easily modified by allowing the country to produce and consume its own non-traded good.[12] Equilibrium in

---

[11] On the non-viability of long-run sterilization policies see Mundell (1968), Swoboda (1972). On empirical aspects see Kouri and Porter (1974), Magee (1976), and Obstfeld (1982).

[12] For analysis of the role of non-traded goods see Dornbusch (1973b, 1974), Mundell (1971), Berglas (1974).

the market for this non-traded good requires that

$$N^d(E,Q) = N^s(Q), \qquad \partial N^d/\partial E > 0, \qquad \partial N^d/\partial Q < 0, \qquad \partial N^s/\partial Q > 0,$$
$$(3.24)$$

where N^d is demand for the non-traded good, N^s is supply of the non-traded good, E is total real expenditure (measured in traded goods), and $Q = P_N/P_X$ is the relative price of non-traded goods (whose domestic nominal price is P_N) in terms of traded goods (whose domestic nominal price is P_X). The supply of non-traded goods, $N^s(Q)$, and the supply of traded goods, $X^s(Q)$, are determined by the point on the economy's transformation curve at which the slope of this curve, relative to the N-axis, is equal to Q. Domestic income (measured in traded goods) is given by

$$Y = Y^s(Q) = X^s(Q) + Q \cdot N^s(Q), \qquad \partial Y^s/\partial Q = N^s(Q) \geq 0. \qquad (3.25)$$

Domestic demand for traded goods, $X^d(E, Q)$, is related to domestic demand for non-traded goods through the expenditure constraint:

$$X^d(E, Q) = E - Q \cdot N^d(E, Q), \qquad \partial X^d/\partial E > 0, \qquad \partial X^d/\partial Q \gtrless 0. \quad (3.26)$$

Desired real expenditure (measured in traded goods) depends on domestic real income (measured in traded goods), Y, on the domestic interest rate, r, and on the real value of privately held assets (measured in traded goods), $(A/P_X) = (M/P_X) + (B/P_X)$ through an expenditure function $E(Y, r, A/P_X)$ with the same properties as the expenditure function introduced in Section 3.1. The condition of asset market equilibrium is expressed by the requirement

$$L(Y, r, Q, A/P_X) = M/P_X, \qquad \partial L/\partial Y > 0, \qquad \partial L/\partial r < 0,$$
$$\partial L/\partial Q > 0, \qquad 0 < \partial L/\partial(A/P_X) < 1, \qquad (3.27)$$

where L is the real demand for domestic money and M/P_X is the real supply, each measured in traded goods. The relative price of nontraded goods enters the money demand function because the general level of domestic prices, $P = P(P_X, P_N)$, is a linear homogeneous function of the domestic money prices of both traded and non-traded goods.

Replacing the variable Y with $Y^s(Q)$ in the real money demand function and substituting $E(Y^s(Q), r, A/P_X)$ for the variable E in the non-traded goods market equilibrium condition, yields equilibrium conditions for the asset market and the non-traded goods market that jointly determine the instantaneous equilibrium values of Q and r as functions of M/P_X and B/P_X:

$$Q = \hat{Q}(M/P_X, B/P_X), \qquad \partial\hat{Q}/\partial(M/P_X) > 0, \qquad \partial\hat{Q}/\partial(B/P_X) \gtrless 0,$$
$$(3.28)$$

$$r = \hat{r}(M/P_X, B/P_X), \qquad \partial\hat{r}/\partial(M/P_X) < 0, \qquad \partial\hat{r}/\partial(B/P_X) > 0. \quad (3.29)$$

The domestic nominal price of traded goods is determined by the fixed exchange rate, S, and the world market price for such goods, P_X^*, through the arbitrage condition

$$P_X = S \cdot P_X^*. \tag{3.30}$$

Given the domestic nominal price of traded goods, the domestic nominal price of non-traded goods and the general domestic price level are determined by

$$P_N = \hat{P}_N(M, B, P_X) = P_X \cdot \hat{Q}(M/P_X, B/P_X), \tag{3.31}$$

$$P = \hat{P}(M, B, P_X) = P(P_X, P_X \cdot \hat{Q}(M/P_X, B/P_X)). \tag{3.32}$$

At an instantaneous equilibrium, the domestic supply of traded goods need not equal the domestic demand for traded goods. The excess of supply over demand is the instantaneous equilibrium value of the trade balance, measured in traded goods:

$$T = \hat{T}(M/P_X, B/P_X) = X^s(\hat{Q}) - X^d(E(Y^s(\hat{Q}), \hat{r}, A/P_X), \hat{Q}),$$
$$\partial \hat{T}/\partial(M/P_X) < 0, \qquad \partial \hat{T}/\partial(B/P_X) < 0, \tag{3.33}$$

where $\hat{Q}$ and $\hat{r}$ are the functions of M/P_X and B/P_X that indicate the instantaneous equilibrium values of Q and r. Using (3.25) and (3.26) and the fact that $N^d = N^s$ at any instantaneous equilibrium, it is easily established that the trade balance at any instantaneous equilibrium is equal to the excess of domestic income over domestic expenditure, as required by the fundamental equation of the absorption approach to the balance of payments:

$$\hat{T}(M/P_X, B/P_X) = Y^s(\hat{Q}) - E(Y^s(\hat{Q}), \hat{r}, A/P_X). \tag{3.34}$$

Since neither monies nor securities are assumed to be internationally traded among private agents, trade imbalances occurring at any instantaneous equilibrium must be financed by a net flow of official foreign exchange reserves. Assuming no sterilization of the effects of such reserve flows on the domestic money supply, the rate of change of the domestic nominal money supply occurring at any instantaneous equilibrium is given by

$$\dot{M} = P_X \cdot \hat{T}(M/P_X, B/P_X). \tag{3.35}$$

The qualitative properties of the relationship between the rate of change of the money supply and the level of the money supply embodied in (3.35) are exactly the same as those embodied in (3.18) and illustrated in Figure 3.1. For given values of B and $P_X = SP_X^*$, there is a unique long-run equilibrium level of domestic nominal money supply, $\overline{M}$, determined by the condition

$$\hat{T}(M/P_X, B/P_X) = 0, \tag{3.36}$$

at which the trade balance and the rate of change of the money supply are both zero.[13] When M is less than $\overline{M}$, there is a trade surplus and $\dot{M}$ is positive. When M is greater than $\overline{M}$, there is a trade deficit and $\dot{M}$ is negative. Thus, there is a natural dynamic process through which monetary changes resulting from reserve flows associated with trade imbalances gradually drive the economy to its long-run equilibrium where the trade balance and the rate of change of the domestic money supply are both zero.

The positively sloped $N^d = N^s$ curve in the upper panel of Figure 3.3 shows the relationship between $\hat{Q}$ and M/P_X for a given value of B/P_X. This curve may also be interpreted as showing the relationship between $\hat{P}_N$ and M, for given values of B and P_X. Since the market for non-traded goods must clear, the instantaneous equilibrium position of the economy must always be at the point on the $N^d = N^s$ curve, corresponding to the actual value of M/P_X.

The market for traded goods need not clear domestically. Any excess supply of traded goods can be sold on the world market and any excess demand for traded goods can be purchased from the world market in exchange for flows of international reserves. The trade balance surplus measures the domestic excess supply of traded goods:

$$T = X^s(\hat{Q}(M/P_X, B/P_X)) - X^d[E(Y^s(\hat{Q}), \hat{r}, A/P_X), \hat{Q}]. \tag{3.37}$$

It is noteworthy that the function $\tilde{T}(M/P_X, B/P_X, Y)$ is similar to the function $\tilde{T}(M/P, B/P, Y)$ introduced in Section 3.1 and that the trade balance can also be expressed as the difference between domestic income and domestic expenditure; that is,

$$\tilde{T}(M/P_X, B/P_X, Y^s(Q)) \equiv Y^s(Q) - \tilde{E}(M/P_X, B/P_X, Y^s(Q)). \tag{3.38}$$

The combinations of Q and M/P_X for which $\tilde{T}(M/P_X, B/P_X, Y^s(Q)) = 0$, for a given value of B/P_X, are indicated by the negatively sloped $X^d = X^s$ curve in the upper panel of Figure 3.3. Alternatively, recognizing that P_X is fixed at $S \cdot P_X^*$, this curve may be regarded as representing the combinations of P_N and M for which $\tilde{T}(M/P_X, B/P_X, Y^s(P_N/P_X)) = 0$. In either case, above and to the right of this curve there is excess domestic demand for traded goods and a trade deficit; and below and to the left of this curve there is a trade surplus.

The intersection of the $N^d = N^s$ curve and the $X^d = X^s$ curve in the upper panel of Figure 3.3 occurs at the point where the relative price of non-traded goods equals its long-run equilibrium value $\overline{Q}$ and where the real domestic money supply is at its long-run equilibrium value $\overline{M}/P_X$. Alternatively, this intersection point indicates the long-run equilibrium nominal price of non-traded goods $\overline{P}_N = P_X \cdot \overline{Q}$ and the long-run equilibrium level of the nominal money supply $\overline{M}$.

---

[13] The level of income does not appear as a determinant of $\overline{M}$ in (3.36), while it does in (3.12), only because the transformation curve determining the economy's production possibilities for traded and non-traded goods has been assumed fixed.

When the domestic money supply differs from its long-run equilibrium value, the economy must be at the point in the upper panel of Figure 3.3 along the $N^d = N^s$ curve corresponding to the actual size of the domestic money supply. At such a point, the trade balance is given by

$$T = \hat{T}(M/P_X, B/P_X) \equiv \tilde{T}\left[M/P_X, B/P_X, Y^s\left(\hat{Q}(M/P_X, B/P_X)\right)\right]. \quad (3.39)$$

Corresponding to the trade balance there is a net flow of foreign exchange

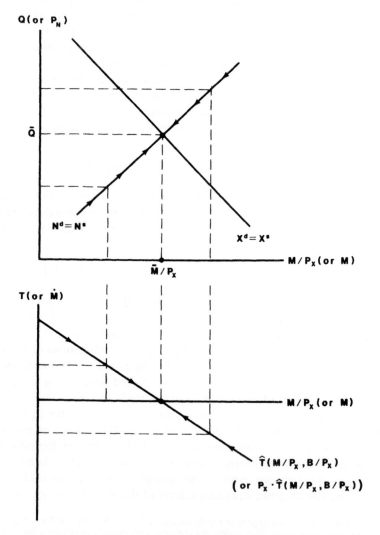

Figure 3.3. Instantaneous equilibrium and dynamics with non-traded goods.

reserves which, holding constant the other assets of the central bank, determines the rate of change of the domestic money supply:

$$\dot{M} = P_X \cdot \hat{T}(M/P_X, B/P_X). \tag{3.40}$$

In the lower panel of Figure 3.3, the curve labeled $\hat{T}(M/P_X, B/P_X)$ shows both the trade balance and the rate of change of domestic real money balances as a function of M/P_X, for a given value of B/P_X. Alternatively, if this curve is labeled as the $P_X \cdot \hat{T}(M/P_X, B/P_X)$ curve, it shows the rate of change of the domestic nominal money supply as a function of the level of the domestic nominal money supply, for given values of B and P_X. The intersection of the $\hat{T}(M/P_X, B/P_X)$ curve with the horizontal axis occurs at the long-run equilibrium level of real money balances, $\overline{M}/P_X$, where the value of $\overline{M}$ is determined implicitly by the condition

$$\hat{T}(\overline{M}/P_X, B/P_X) = 0. \tag{3.41}$$

Comparison of the lower panel of Figure 3.3 with Figure 3.1 and comparison of the condition (3.41) with the condition (3.12) reveals the close analogy between the monetary mechanism of balance of payments adjustment that operates with nontraded goods and the mechanism that operates when all goods are traded, and between the condition that determines the long-run equilibrium level of money demand with non-traded goods and the condition that is relevant when all goods are traded. Momentary reflection reveals that the four general features of the monetary mechanism of balance of payments adjustment that were discussed in Section 3.1, as well as many of the specific conclusions of that earlier analysis, carry over to the case where we have nontraded goods.

The major innovations resulting from the introduction of non-traded goods are that we allow for variations in the relative price of non-tradable goods and in the general domestic price level along the path of convergence to long-run equilibrium. As is apparent from the upper panel of Figure 3.3, if the domestic money supply is initially less than $\overline{M}$, the instantaneous equilibrium relative and nominal prices of non-traded goods determined by the point on the $N^d = N^s$ curve are less than their respective long-run equilibrium values, $\overline{Q}$ and $P_X \cdot \overline{Q}$. The general domestic price level, P, which is an index of the nominal prices of traded and non-traded goods, will also be less than its long-run equilibrium value. As the domestic money supply rises due to reserve inflows resulting from trade surpluses, the instantaneous equilibrium position of the economy moves up along the $N^d = N^s$ curve toward the long-run equilibrium point, implying an increase in the relative and nominal price level as the economy converges to long-run equilibrium. The opposite process occurs if the initial money supply exceeds $\overline{M}$. It follows immediately that an increase in the fiat issue of the central bank, starting from $M = \overline{M}$, would have the initial effect of raising the relative and nominal prices of non-traded goods and the general domestic price level above their long-run equilibrium values, and this would be followed by a period of adjustment during which the domestic money supply and these prices all returned to their respective long-run equilibrium levels. Starting from an initial position of long-run equilibrium, a devaluation would immediately result in an equiproportional increase in the domestic nominal price of traded goods and would increase (not necessarily proportionately) the long-run equilibrium value of the domestic nominal money supply. The nominal price of non-traded goods, however, would not rise immediately in proportion with the devaluation nor will it rise to its new long-run equilibrium level. The relative and nominal prices of non-traded goods and the general domestic price level immediately following devaluation would all be below their new long-run equilibrium values and would only gradually rise to these values as the domestic money supply rises to its new long-run equilibrium level.[14]

When we consider the effects of growth in an economy with non-traded goods, the modifications of the earlier analysis are more substantial. With only a composite traded good, the long-run, cumulative effect of growth in domestic output and income depended only on the effect of an increase in income on the demand for domestic money. With non-traded as well as traded goods, growth can affect the long-run equilibrium level of money demand both through the usual effect of an increase in income and through the effect of changes in the long-run equilibrium relative price of non-traded goods. For example, if the growth of domestic output (at constant relative prices) is biased toward traded goods, relative to the growth of domestic demand, then the long-run equilibrium relative price of non-traded goods will have to rise as growth occurs.[15] With the domestic nominal price of traded goods fixed by the exchange rate and by the given world prices of such goods, the increase in the long-run equilibrium relative price of non-traded goods requires an increase in the domestic nominal price of such goods and, hence, in the general price index. This increase in the general price index enhances the effect of growth in expanding the long-run demand for domestic money and, thereby, increases the cumulative payments surplus resulting from growth. The opposite holds if growth is biased towards the production of non-traded goods. It is still true, however, that the cumulative effect of growth on the balance of payments reflects the effects of growth on the long-run equilibrium level of money demand. With non-traded goods, there simply are more channels through which growth can effect the long-run equilibrium level of money demand.

---

[14] For analyses of the price dynamics see Dornbusch (1973b), Berglas (1974), and Blejer (1977).
[15] On the effect of the patterns of growth on relative prices see Balassa (1958).

3.2.5. Large countries

When the home country is not small relative to the rest of the world, it is necessary to modify the preceding analysis to account for the interaction between the home country and the rest of the world in determining the prices of tradable goods and the distribution of the world stock of foreign exchange reserves. To illustrate these modifications, it is useful to assume that the economic structure of the home country and the foreign country (identified with the rest of the world) is described by the model in the preceding section, with the two countries producing and consuming a common traded good, X, and with each country producing and consuming its own non-traded good, N. Variables for the foreign country are indicated by an asterisk ($*$).

The relative prices of non-traded goods that clear domestic markets in the two countries are given by $\hat{Q}(M/P_X, B/P_X)$ and $\hat{Q}^*(M^*/P_X^*, B^*/P_X^*)$. The trade balance surpluses for the two countries are given by $\hat{T}(M/P_X, B/P_X)$ and $\hat{T}^*(M^*/P_X^*, B^*/P_X^*)$. Nominal prices of traded goods in the two countries are linked by the fixed exchange rate through the relationship $P_X = S \cdot P_X^*$. The condition for equilibrium in the world market for traded goods is expressed by the requirement:

$$\hat{T}(M/P_X, B/P_X) + \hat{T}^*(M^*/P_X^*, B^*/P_X^*) = 0. \tag{3.42}$$

Given the domestic and foreign nominal money supplies and the parametrically fixed values of B, B^* and S, this equilibrium condition determines the instantaneous equilibrium value of the nominal price of traded goods in the two countries, as is illustrated in Figure 3.4. In this figure, P_X^* is plotted on the vertical axis and $P_X = S \cdot P_X^*$ is assumed to vary along with the foreign nominal price. The horizontal axis measures the trade surplus of the home country, T, and the trade deficit of the foreign country, $-T^*$. The positively sloped curves labeled T_i show the trade surplus of the home country, $T(M_i/S \cdot P_X^*, B/S \cdot P_X^*)$, as a function of P_X^*, for different levels of the domestic money supply. The negatively sloped curves labeled $-T_i^*$ show the trade deficit of the foreign country, $-T^*(M_i^*/P_X^*, B^*/P_X^*)$, as a function of P_X^*, for different levels of the foreign money supply. The levels of the domestic and foreign money supplies used in constructing these curves satisfy the condition

$$M_i/S + M_i^* = M_w, \tag{3.43}$$

where M_w is the constant level of the world money supply (measured in units of foreign money). This is consistent with the assumption that the non-reserve assets of both central banks are constant and that money supply changes occur only as a consequence of redistributions of a fixed world stock of international reserves. When the distribution of this stock of reserves is such that money supplies in the

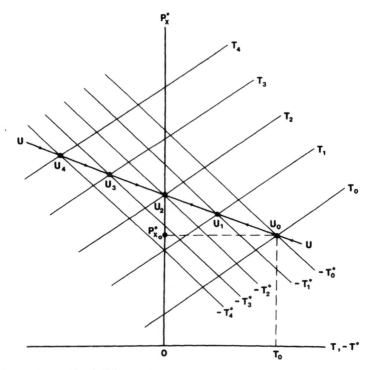

Figure 3.4. Instantaneous equilibrium and dynamics in the world market for traded goods.

two countries are M_0 and M_0^*, instantaneous equilibrium occurs at the point U_0 in Figure 3.4, with $P_X^* = P_{X_0}^*$ and $T = -T^* = T_0$. At this instantaneous equilibrium position, foreign exchange reserves are flowing from the foreign country to the home country at a rate consistent with the trade balances of these countries. As the home money supply rises and the foreign money supply declines due to this flow of reserves, the instantaneous equilibrium point gradually moves from U_0 to U_1, which is the instantaneous equilibrium position that is relevant when the domestic money supply is $M_1 > M_0$ and the foreign money supply is $M_1^* = M_0^* - ((M_1 - M_0)/S) < M_0^*$. This adjustment process continues until reserve flows have increased the domestic money supply to its long-run equilibrium level $M_2 = \overline{M}$ and have decreased the foreign money supply to its long-run equilibrium level $M_2^* = \overline{M}^*$. At this time the instantaneous equilibrium position is at U_2 on the P_X^*-axis, the trade balances of both countries are zero, and the world is in long-run equilibrium. Similarly, if the initial distribution of international reserves is such that $M = M_4 > \overline{M}$ and $M^* = M_4^* < \overline{M}^*$, the world starts out at the instantaneous equilibrium point U_4 and gradually moves to the right along the UU locus, with reserves flowing out of the home country and into the foreign country, until long-run equilibrium is achieved at U_2.

The behavior of the instantaneous equilibrium nominal price of traded goods (P_X^* and $P_X = S \cdot P_X^*$) reflects a version of the "transfer problem criterion". As we move from the instantaneous equilibrium U_0 along the UU locus toward long-run equilibrium, the nominal price of trade goods rises, as illustrated in Figure 3.4, if and only if $|\partial \hat{T}/\partial(M/P_X)| > |\partial \hat{T}^*/\partial(M^*/P_X^*)|$; that is, if and only if at constant nominal prices of the traded good, the effect of an increase in the domestic real money supply on excess demand for traded goods in the home country is larger than the effect of an equivalent reduction in the foreign money supply on the excess supply of traded goods in the foreign country. If so, then at the old nominal prices of traded goods and the new distribution of the world money supply, there will be an excess world demand of traded goods, and the nominal prices of traded goods will have to rise in both countries (reducing the real values of money and bond holdings) in order to restore equilibrium to the world market for traded goods.

While the monetary mechanism of balance of payments adjustment is more complicated for the two-country world than for the small country, the basic elements of this mechanism are essentially the same. Starting from a situation in which the domestic nominal money supply is below its long-run equilibrium level and, correspondingly, the foreign money supply is above its long-run equilibrium level, reserve flows associated with trade imbalances gradually move the economic system to long-run equilibrium by raising the domestic money supply and reducing the foreign money supply to their respective long-run equilibrium levels. As in the case of the small country, the essential ingredient underlying this adjustment process is the relationship through which a deficiency in a country's money supply relative to its long-run equilibrium level leads to an excess of domestic income over domestic expenditure which implies a trade surplus which brings an inflow of foreign exchange reserves and a gradual restoration of money balances to their long run equilibrium level.

In the two-country world, it remains true that a given initial divergence of a country's money supply (and a corresponding divergence with the opposite sign for the other country) will ultimately lead to a cumulative payments surplus and change in reserves just equal to this initial divergence (assuming there is no change in the non-reserve assets of central banks). The long-run cumulative effect of disturbances that affect money supplies and money demands, however, are somewhat different in the two-country world than they are for a small country. For example, in the small-country case, an increase in the fiat issue of the central bank does not alter the long-run equilibrium level of domestic money demand and, hence, ultimately leads to an equal loss of foreign exchange reserves. In the large-country case, an increase in the fiat issue of the home country increases the world money supply and thereby increases the long-run equilibrium level of the nominal price of traded goods in both countries. This increase in the nominal price of traded goods implies an increase in the long-run equilibrium level of nominal money demand in both countries, and hence a loss of foreign exchange reserves by the home country that is smaller than the increase in the fiat issue of its central bank. Similar reasoning leads to the conclusion that a devaluation by the home country raises the long-run nominal price of traded goods in that country while reducing the long-run nominal price of traded goods in the foreign country. Because part of the effect of devaluation is absorbed by a decline in the foreign price level, the long-run nominal demand for domestic money rises less as a consequence of devaluation than it would if the home country were small. Correspondingly, the cumulative gain in foreign exchange reserves for the home country due to devaluation is less than it would be if the country were small [see Dornbusch (1973b)]. Note, however, that these modifications of the small country results do not alter the basic principle that the cumulative effect of any disturbance on a country's balance of payments is equal to the effect of the disturbance on the divergence between the domestic money supply and the long-run equilibrium level of domestic money demand.

When two large countries produce and consume only a single traded good, in addition to their own non-traded goods, the stability of the mechanism of balance of payments adjustment is not critically affected by the relative price elasticities of demand or of excess demand for tradable or non-tradable goods. These elasticities do influence the extent of variations in the relative price of non-tradables as we move along the path of convergence to long-run equilibrium, and they do affect the speed of convergence to long-run equilibrium. But, low price elasticities of demand do not introduce the possibility of instability in the mechanism of balance of payments adjustment. The reason for this is that the price elasticity that is critical for the stability of this mechanism is the elasticity of demand for imports of tradables into a country with respect to the relative price of tradables between the two countries. The assumption that tradable goods for the two countries are perfect substitutes implies that this elasticity is infinite, and this removes any possibility of instability.

When large countries exchange two or more tradable goods, elasticities of import demands for these countries are important for the stability of the monetary mechanism of balance of payments adjustment. In the standard two-country, two-commodity model of the pure theory of international trade, it is well known that the Marshall–Lerner condition (the requirement that the sum of the absolute values of the import demand elasticities of the two countries be greater than one) is the necessary and sufficient condition for the existence of a unique equilibrium relative price of the two commodities [see Johnson (1956)]. In the monetary extension of this model, in which money supplies, bond supplies and interest rates affect only the level of spending in each country but not its distribution among commodities, the Marshall–Lerner condition becomes the condition for a unique long-run equilibrium in which the trade balance of each country is zero and there is no ongoing redistribution of the world money supply.

If for each distribution of the world money supply, the instantaneous equilibrium position of the world economy is unique, it may be shown that the monetary mechanism of balance of payments adjustment ultimately drives the world economy to this unique long-run equilibrium. Along the path of convergence to this long-run equilibrium, spending differs from income by equal and opposite amounts in the two countries, implying equal and opposite trade imbalances and an ongoing redistribution of the world money supply through flows of foreign exchange reserves. The adjustment of the relative commodity price along the path of convergence to long-run equilibrium is determined by application of the standard transfer problem analysis to the endogenously determined magnitude of the transfer corresponding to the trade imbalances of the two countries [see Dornbusch (1973a)].

If equilibrium is not unique in the standard two-country, two-commodity trade model, long-run equilibrium will not be unique in the monetary extension of this model. Corresponding to each real equilibrium, there will be a separate long-run monetary equilibrium. If for each distribution of the world money supply, there is a unique instantaneous equilibrium in the monetary model, the monetary mechanism of balance of payments adjustment will still be well defined. That is to say, there will be a well-defined differential equation that expresses the rate of change of the distribution of the world money supply as a function of that distribution. Moreover, it may be shown (not without some difficulty) that the stable nodes of this differential equation describing the monetary mechanism of balance of payments adjustment will correspond to the real trade equilibria at which the Marshall–Lerner condition is satisfied, and that the unstable nodes of this differential equation will correspond to the real trade equilibria where the Marshall–Lerner condition is not satisfied. Thus, as suggested by many earlier writers, sufficiently large elasticities of import demand are essential for stability of the mechanism of balance of payments adjustment. While this interpretation reflects different considerations, it rationalizes some of the statements made by proponents of the elasticity approach to the balance of payments [see Machlup (1939)].

3.2.6. Capital mobility

Two important modifications of the preceding analysis of the monetary mechanism of balance of payments adjustment are required when we allow for international mobility of privately held financial assets. First, the official settlements balance is no longer equal to trade balance but to the sum of the current account balance (which is the trade balance plus the flow of interest income that domestic residents earn on their net foreign securities holdings) and the capital account balance (which measures net sales of privately held financial assets by domestic residents to foreign residents). Second, we must allow for the possibility of swaps of stocks of privately held assets between domestic and foreign residents that occur at an instant of time. The possibility of asset swaps does not alter the principle that the current account balance is a flow magnitude, but, it does introduce the possibility of stock unit changes in a country's international reserves resulting from private attempts to swap domestic money for financial securities.[16]

The implications of capital mobility for the monetary mechanism of balance of payments adjustment are most easily illustrated by returning to the case of a small open economy that produces and consumes only traded goods. The model presented in Section 3.1 is modified by assuming that securities held by domestic residents, B, are perfect substitutes for securities issued in the rest of the world, and that the domestic interest rate, r, is equal to the (fixed) interest rate prevailing in the world capital market, r^*. Net foreign security holdings of domestic residents, V, are the excess of domestic private security holdings over the stock of government debt that is outside of the domestic central bank:

$$V = B - \left(\bar{B} - B_g \right). \tag{3.44}$$

Domestic real income, Y, is equal to the full employment level of domestic output, $\bar{Y}$, plus interest income from net foreign security holdings, $r^* \cdot V/P$:

$$Y = \bar{Y} + r^* \cdot V/P. \tag{3.45}$$

The condition for asset market equilibrium, $L(Y, r^*, A/P) = M/P$, no longer determines the domestic interest rate, but rather, the instantaneous equilibrium size of the domestic real money supply:

$$M/P = \tilde{m}\left(A/P, \bar{Y}, \left(\bar{B} - B_g \right)/P, r^* \right). \tag{3.46}$$

The effect of an increase in real private domestic assets on M/P,

$$\partial \tilde{m}/\partial (A/P) = \partial L/\partial (A/P) + r^* \cdot (\partial L/\partial Y)[1 - (\partial L/\partial (A/P))],$$

is assumed to be less than one.

The excess of domestic income over domestic expenditure determines the current account balance, $\Psi = Y - E$, where $E = E(Y, r, A/P)$. Setting $r = r^*$ and taking account of (3.44), (3.45) and (3.46), we arrive at a reduced form expression for the current account balance:

$$\Psi = \tilde{\Psi}\left(A/P, \bar{Y}, \left(\bar{B} - B_g \right)/P, r^* \right). \tag{3.47}$$

It is assumed that an increase in real private domestic assets worsens the current

---

[16]For analyses of portfolio equilibrium and the role of capital mobility see Branson (1970, 1976), Dornbusch (1975), Frenkel and Rodriguez (1975), McKinnon (1969), Henderson (1977), Allen and Kenen (1980), and Obstfeld (1980).

account balance; that is, we assume that

$$\partial \check{\Psi}/\partial(A/P) = -(\partial E/\partial(A/P)) + r^* \cdot [1 - \partial \tilde{L}/\partial(A/P)] \cdot [1 - \partial E/\partial Y]$$
$$< 0.$$

Given the domestic price level $P = S \cdot P^*$, and holding constant the non-reserve assets of the central bank, the current account balance determines the rate of change of real private asset holdings:

$$\dot{A}/P = \check{\Psi}\left(A/P, \overline{Y}, (\overline{B} - B_g)/P, r^*\right).\tag{3.48}$$

This differential equation characterizes the dynamic process through which the real stock of privately held assets is adjusted to its long-run equilibrium value, $\overline{A}/P$, which is determined implicitly by the condition

$$\check{\Psi}\left(\overline{A}/P, \overline{Y}, (\overline{B} - B_g)/P, r^*\right) = 0.\tag{3.49}$$

This adjustment process for private assets is illustrated in the middle panel of Figure 3.5, where the curve labeled $\check{\Psi}(A/P, \overline{Y}, (\overline{B} - B_g)/P, r^*)$ shows the relationship between $\dot{A}/P$ and A/P. In the top panel the curve labeled $\tilde{m}(A/P, \overline{Y}, (\overline{B} - B_g)/P, r^*)$ shows the reduced form relationship between the level of real private assets and the instantaneous equilibrium level of real money balances. Finally, in the bottom panel of Figure 3.5, the curve labeled $\check{\Psi} \cdot (\partial \tilde{m}/\partial(A/P))$ shows the relationship between the level of real private assets and the rate of change of domestic real money balances, $\dot{M}/P$, determined by

$$\dot{M}/P = (\partial \tilde{m}/\partial(A/P)) \cdot (\dot{A}/P)$$
$$= (\partial \tilde{m}/\partial(A/P)) \cdot \check{\Psi}\left(A/P, \overline{Y}, (\overline{B} - B_g)/P, r^*\right).\tag{3.50}$$

Three important principles concerning the mechanism of balance of payments adjustment when we allow for international capital mobility are reflected in Figure 3.5. First, the level of money balances in the economy adjusts immediately to the instantaneous equilibrium level associated with the actual level of privately held assets; that is, the economy always operates at the point on the $\tilde{m}$ curve in the top panel of Figure 3.5 corresponding to the actual level of A/P. Achievement of such an instantaneous equilibrium position subsequent to a disturbance that creates a stock unit divergence between the demand for domestic money and the existing supply requires a stock unit change in the central bank's holdings of international reserves as private asset holders buy or sell securities in order to achieve the desired composition of their assets between money and securities. Second, the process of adjustment of the stock of privately held assets that occurs as a counterpart of current account imbalances, as illustrated in the middle panel of Figure 3.5, is necessarily a gradual adjustment process in which the flow of net saving determined by the excess of domestic income over domestic expenditure accumulates over time into changes in the stock of privately held assets. Third, as

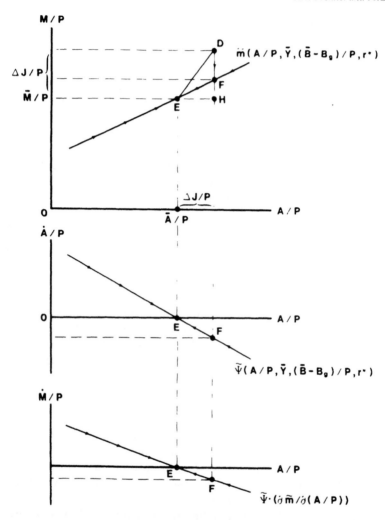

Figure 3.5. Portfolio balance, assets, and balance of payments adjustment with capital mobility.

illustrated in the bottom panel of Figure 3.5, changes in the stock of privately held assets resulting from current account imbalances cause gradual changes in the instantaneous equilibrium level of money balances and corresponding flows of foreign exchange reserves which are registered as official settlements surpluses or deficits. This mechanism of monetary adjustment is similar to the monetary mechanism of balance of payments adjustment that operates in the absence of international capital mobility. In the present case, however, reserve changes also occur in response to asset swaps motivated by the desire of domestic residents to adjust the actual level of money balances within their portfolio of assets to its desired level. Through reserve changes brought about by the operation of these two mechanisms, the level of the domestic money supply is ultimately adjusted to the long-run equilibrium level of domestic money demand that is associated with the long-run equilibrium level of privately held domestic assets and with long-run equilibrium of the current account balance.

These three principles all come into operation when we consider an increase ΔJ in the fiat issue of the domestic central bank. Starting from an initial situation of long-run equilibrium, domestic real assets exceed their long-run equilibrium value by the amount $\Delta J/P$. Since the entire increase $\Delta J/P$ in real privately held assets comes in the form of domestic money, the economy is tentatively at the point D in the top panel of Figure 3.5 which lies above the $\bar{m}$ curve as well as to the right of the long-run equilibrium level of A/P. To restore the desired composition of assets individuals sell money balances and purchase securities sufficient to move the economy downward from the point D in the top panel of Figure 3.5 to the point F that lies along the $\bar{m}$ curve. The additional securities are purchased from foreign residents who convert the domestic money they receive from their sales of securities into foreign money, with a consequent loss of foreign exchange reserves by the domestic central bank. This immediate, stock unit loss of foreign exchange reserves accounts for the reduction in the domestic money supply implied by the jump from the point D to the point F. At the point F, the real value of private domestic assets exceeds its long-run equilibrium value $\bar{A}/P$, resulting in an excess of domestic real expenditure over domestic real income and in a current account deficit, as indicated by the point F along the $\bar{\Psi}$ curve in the middle panel of Figure 3.5. Over time, downward adjustments in the real stock of privately held assets gradually reduce A/P to its long-run equilibrium level. The gradual reductions in A/P gradually reduce the instantaneous equilibrium level of real money balances, implying, as illustrated in the bottom panel of Figure 3.5, corresponding losses of foreign exchange reserves by the central bank. The total loss of reserves that results from this adjustment process, together with the initial swap of domestic money for foreign securities, exactly offsets the increase in the fiat issue of the central bank and restores domestic money balances to their long run equilibrium level [see Frenkel and Rodriguez (1975)].

The general features of this analysis extend to the effects of other types of disturbances. If the disturbance creates an incipient divergence between the actual level of money balances and their new instantaneous equilibrium level, there will be a swap of domestic money for foreign securities and a corresponding stock unit change in the central bank's holdings of international reserves. If after this asset swap the actual level of domestic privately held assets differs from the long-run equilibrium level, there will be a gradual process of adjustment of asset holdings through current account imbalances toward their long-run equilibrium level. Associated with these changes in the level of assets, there will be changes in the instantaneous equilibrium level of money balances which will induce changes in the central bank's holdings of foreign exchange reserves. The total change in reserves will equal the divergence that the initiating disturbance creates between the long-run equilibrium level of domestic money balances and the actual level of such balances.

The introduction of non-traded goods modifies the analysis of the mechanism of balance of payments adjustment with international capital mobility in essentially the same way as it modifies the analysis of this mechanism for the case in which capital is immobile. Starting from a level of A/P that is below $\bar{A}/P$, the domestic relative and nominal prices of non-tradables and the general domestic price level are all below their respective long-run equilibrium levels. As A/P rises due to current account surpluses, all of these prices rise toward their respective long-run equilibrium levels.

A modification that is in the same spirit as the introduction of non-traded goods is the introduction of a non-tradable asset that domestic residents hold in addition to domestic money and internationally tradable securities. The rate of return and the price of this non-tradable asset are determined by the requirement for equilibrium in the domestic market for this asset, in much the same way that the relative price of a non-tradable good is determined by the requirement for equilibrium in the domestic market for such a good. Starting from an initial value of A/P that is less than its long-run equilibrium value and assuming that asset demands are normal (in the sense that an increase in A/P increases the real demands for all assets), the instantaneous equilibrium price of the non-traded asset will be lower and the instantaneous equilibrium rate of return on this asset will be higher than their respective long-run equilibrium values. As A/P rises due to current account surpluses, the price of the non-traded asset will rise, and the rate of return on the non-traded asset will fall toward their respective long-run equilibrium values [see Dornbusch (1975) and Branson (1976); on the policy implications, see Frenkel and Mussa (1981)].

This analysis can be extended to the case of two large countries that trade a single good and exchange a single internationally mobile security. The results of this analysis are similar to those in Section 3.2.5, modified to reflect the implications of capital mobility. Prices of non-traded goods and yields on non-traded assets adjust to clear domestic markets for these goods and assets in each country, conditional on the world price of the tradable good, the world yield on the mobile security, and the prevailing distribution of world wealth. Instantaneous equilibrium requires that the world price of tradable goods and the world yield on the mobile security clear the world markets for these goods and securities, conditional on the distribution of world wealth. At such an instantaneous equilibrium, one country will generally spend more than its income and the other country will spend an equal amount less than its income, implying a corresponding current account deficit and current account surplus. The country with the surplus will be increasing its share of world wealth at the expense of the country with the deficit. The redistribution of world wealth that finances the trade imbalances will be accomplished partly by a flow of privately held securities and partly by a flow of official reserves (with effects on the money supplies of the two countries). If the balance of payments adjustment process is stable, as it should be in such a world, current account imbalances between the two countries will gradually decline as the wealth of the surplus country rises and the wealth of the deficit country declines, and the world will converge to a long-run equilibrium in which current account balances are zero and there is no further redistribution of world wealth [see Frenkel (1976b)].

In this type of model of the world economy, an increase in the fiat issue of the central bank of the home country results in an immediate loss of foreign exchange reserves as domestic asset owners rebalance their portfolios between money and securities. Foreign residents will accommodate this portfolio shift because the increase in the world price of traded goods and the adjustment of the world yield on internationally mobile securities induces them to swap securities for money. At the instantaneous equilibrium established immediately after the increase in the fiat issue of the home country's central bank, the wealth of home residents has risen and that of foreign residents has declined because the entire increase in the world money supply went initially to home residents while the increase in the world price level reduced the real value of the nominal assets of residents of both countries. During the process of adjustment subsequent to the establishment of this instantaneous equilibrium, the wealth of home residents will decline as they spend in excess of their income, and the wealth of foreign residents will rise as they spend less than their income. The central bank of the home country will suffer a further loss of foreign exchange reserves because the demand for money by home residents will decline along with their wealth. In the end, however, the total loss of foreign exchange reserves by the home central bank (both from the initial asset swap and from subsequent reserve flows) will be smaller than the increase in the fiat issue of this central bank. As in the case of no private capital mobility (Section 3.2.5), this is because the increase in the fiat issue of the home central bank has increased the world money supply, the long-run equilibrium level of all nominal prices and, hence, the long-run equilibrium level of the demand for domestic money.

An increase in the money supply of the home country brought about by an open market operation has somewhat different effects than an increase in the fiat issue of the home central bank because the open market operation affects the supplies of securities available to private asset holders. Moreover, the effects of such an open market operation depend on whether the securities purchased by the central bank are domestic non-tradable securities or internationally tradable securities. Under standard assumptions about substitutability among assets in private portfolio demands, a purchase of domestic non-tradable securities will decrease the long-run equilibrium yield on such securities both absolutely and relative to the yield on internationally mobile securities; whereas an open market purchase of the internationally mobile security will have a smaller effect in reducing the long-run equilibrium yield on this security and will reduce this yield relative to the yield on the domestic non-tradable security. The differential effect of these two policies on the long-run equilibrium world price level and on the distribution of international reserves depends on the degrees of substitution between national monies and different classes of securities [see Dornbusch (1975, 1977)].

Substitution relations among assets in portfolio demands are crucial in large countries models with two or more internationally tradable securities. Since the analysis of such models is provided by Branson and Henderson in Chapter 15 of this Handbook, together with an extended list of references, we conclude the present section by only highlighting one critical feature of these models — the effects of sterilized intervention in the foreign exchange market. If the central bank of the home country intervenes in the foreign exchange market by selling foreign securities in order to prevent depreciation of the foreign exchange value of domestic money and sterilizes the monetary effect of this intervention by buying domestic securities, the overall effect of the operation will be to increase the outstanding supply of foreign securities and decrease the outstanding supply of domestic securities while holding the money supply constant. Given standard assumptions about portfolio demands for different securities, this alteration of security supplies will increase the equilibrium yield on foreign securities and decrease the equilibrium yield on domestic securities. If each country's security is a closer substitute for its money than the security of the other country, then this alteration in yields will decrease the demand for home money and increase the demand for foreign money and, thereby, tend to alleviate the monetary disequilibrium that was the cause of the drain of foreign exchange reserves.

4. Flexible exchange rates

4.1. The monetary model of exchange rate determination

The move to floating exchange rates in the early 1970's occasioned a shift of research toward models of exchange rate behavior. To survey these developments, it is useful to begin with monetary models of the exchange rate.[17] An essential

---

[17]For theoretical developments and applications of the approach see, for example, Dornbusch (1976a, 1976b), Kouri (1976), Mussa (1976b), Frenkel (1976a), Frenkel and Johnson (1978), Bilson (1978a, 1978b), Hodrick (1978), Frankel (1979), and Frenkel and Clements (1982).

element of any monetary model is the assumption of money market equilibrium:

$$(p - p^*) = (m - m^*) + (l^* - l), \tag{4.1}$$

where l denotes the logarithm of the demand for domestic real balances, m denotes the logarithm of the nominal money supply, p denotes the logarithm of the price level and where an asterisk indicates a variable pertaining to the foreign country. A second essential element in a monetary model of exchange rate determination is a link between domestic and foreign prices through some form of the purchasing power parity, the simplest form of which is expressed by

$$p = e + p^*, \tag{4.2}$$

where e denotes the logarithm of the exchange rate, i.e. the price of foreign money in terms of domestic money. Using eq. (4.2) in (4.1) yields:

$$e = (m - m^*) + [l^* - l], \tag{4.3}$$

which expresses the exchange rate in terms of supplies of domestic and foreign monies and demands to hold these monies. Anything that increases the supply of domestic relative to foreign money or increases the demand for foreign relative to domestic money, raises the exchange rate (i.e. depreciates the domestic currency).

The assumption that the prices relevant for money market equilibrium are the same as those relevant for the purchasing power parities [eq. (4.2)] is easily relaxed by allowing the price level to be a weighted average of the prices of non-tradable goods and internationally traded goods:

$$p = \sigma p_N + (1 - \sigma) p_T, \tag{4.4}$$

$$p^* = \sigma^* p_N + (1 - \sigma^*) p_T^*, \tag{4.5}$$

where p_N and p_T denote, respectively, the logarithm of the prices of non-tradable and tradable goods, and σ denotes the weight of non-tradable goods in the price index. If purchasing power parity holds only for tradable goods, we replace eq. (4.2) by (4.6):

$$p_T = e + p_T^*. \tag{4.6}$$

Using (4.4)–(4.6) in (4.1) yields:

$$e = (m - m^*) + [l^* - l] + [\sigma(p_T - p_N) - \sigma^*(p_T^* - p_N^*)]. \tag{4.7}$$

This equation reveals a third important factor determining the exchange rate: relative price structures in the two economies. A rise in the domestic relative price of tradable goods (a loss of competitiveness), raises the exchange rate (i.e. depreciates the domestic currency).

Specification of the determinants of real money demand adds further content to the general monetary model of exchange rate determination. One such specification is given by

$$l = k + \eta y - \alpha i, \tag{4.8}$$

$$l^* = k^* + \eta^* y^* - \alpha^* i^*, \tag{4.9}$$

where y and i denote the logarithm of income and the rate of interest, respectively, and where η and α denote the income elasticity and the interest (semi) elasticity of the demand for money, respectively. Substituting this specification into (4.7) and assuming for simplicity of exposition that $\eta = \eta^*$, $\alpha = \alpha^*$, and $\sigma = \sigma^*$, we obtain:

$$e = (k^* - k) + (m - m^*) + \eta(y^* - y)$$
$$+ \alpha(i - i^*) + \sigma\left[(p_T - p_N) - (p_T^* - p_N^*)\right]. \tag{4.10}$$

Other things constant, a rise in the level of domestic relative to foreign income, appreciates the value of domestic currency (reduces e) and an increase in the domestic nominal interest relative to the foreign nominal interest rate depreciates the value of domestic currency (increases e).

The result (4.10) is further refined by incorporating the interest parity condition,

$$i - i^* = \pi, \tag{4.11}$$

where π denotes the forward premium on foreign exchange (i.e. the difference between the logarithms of the forward and the spot exchange rates). Substituting π for $(i - i^*)$ in eq. (4.10) yields the prediction that a rise in the forward premium on foreign exchange depreciates the currency (raises e).[18] This dependence of the current exchange rate on expectations concerning the future (as summarized by the forward premium) is a typical characteristic of price determination in asset markets. Thus, an expected future depreciation of the currency is reflected immediately in the current value of the currency.

In the above model we have not drawn the distinction between "the demand for domestic money" and "the domestic demand for money". Implicitly it has been assumed that domestic money is demanded only by domestic residents while foreign money is demanded only by foreign residents. Furthermore, the formulation of the demands for real cash balances [in eqs. (4.8)–(4.9)] included the domestic interest rate in the domestic demand, and the foreign interest rate in the foreign demand; it has been implicitly assumed that the only relevant alternative for holding domestic money is domestic securities while the only relevant alternative for holding foreign money is foreign securities. In principle, however, the alternatives to holding domestic money include domestic securities, foreign securities, inventories of domestic and foreign goods as well as foreign exchange. It

---

[18]See Frenkel (1976a) and Frenkel and Clements (1982).

follows that a richer formulation of the demand for money would recognize that, as an analytical matter, the spectrum of alternative assets and rates of return that are relevant for the specification of the demand for money is rather broad, including both rates of interest, i and i^*, expected domestic and foreign inflation, as well as the forward premium on foreign exchange, π. Furthermore, to the extent that under a flexible exchange rate system individuals might wish to diversify their currency holdings, the demand for domestic money would include a foreign component which depends on foreign income, while the demand for foreign money would include a domestic component which depends on domestic income.[19] These characteristics reflect the phenomenon of currency substitution which is likely to arise when the exchange rate is not pegged.[20] Under these circumstances the demand function l and l^* will be richer and, when substituted into eq. (4.7), the predictions of the effects of parametric changes in incomes or rates of interest will depend on the relative sensitivity of the demands for domestic and foreign monies to these parametric changes, which in turn may depend on the relative degrees of substitutions among assets in portfolios. The general principles which govern the effects of parametric changes on the relative demands for money are similar to those that govern the effects of international transfers on relative demands and resemble the "transfer problem criteria".

The monetary approach that was summarized in the preceding discussion differs from the elasticities approach to exchange rate determination in that concepts like exports, imports, and so forth, do not appear explicitly as being fundamentally relevant for the understanding of the evolution of the exchange rate. Rather, the relevant concepts relate to three groups of variables: first are those which are determined by the monetary authorities, second are those which affect the demands for domestic and foreign monies, and third are those which affect the relative price structures.[21]

The formulation of the link between domestic and foreign prices in eq. (4.6) assumed that purchasing power parity holds with respect to internationally traded goods. Implicitly it was assumed that there are no barriers to trade. This formulation can be easily extended so as to incorporate price differentials which stem from commercial policies. For example, when the domestic economy has

---

[19] For a discussion of the specifications of the demand for money under a flexible exchange rate regime see Frenkel (1977, 1979) and Abel, Dornbusch, Huizinga and Marcus (1979).

[20] For an analysis of the phenomenon of currency substitutions see Boyer (1973), Chen (1973), Chrystal (1977), Girton and Roper (1981), Stockman (1976), Calvo and Rodriguez (1977), Miles (1978) and Frenkel and Clements (1982).

[21] It should be noted that when *properly specified* other approaches to exchange rate determination would also yield a reduced form equation like (4.10) with money supplies, incomes, interest rates and relative prices appearing on the right-hand side. The virtue of the monetary approach in comparison with the elasticities approach is in bringing these variables to the foreground rather than leaving them in the "background".

tariffs on imports, eq. (4.6) becomes:

$$p_T = \kappa + e + p_T^*, \tag{4.12}$$

where κ denotes the logarithm of one plus the proportional tariff rate. Using (4.12) instead of (4.6) in the derivation of the exchange rate equation shows the negative dependence of e on κ. Accordingly, the imposition of a tariff results in an appreciation of the currency. In explaining this result the monetary approach does not emphasize the effect of the tariff on the *relative* price of imports along the lines of the "elasticity approach" but rather, it is argued that the currency appreciates because, ceteris paribus, a rise in the tariff rate raises the price level, induces a rise in the demand for nominal balances and results in a rise in the relative price of nominal balances. The monetary approach also provides for a mechanism by which a tariff may result in a depreciation of the currency. If subsequent increases in tariffs result in distortions which lower real income, the reduced real income reduces the demand for money and may outweigh the effect of the rise in the price level. In that case a rise in the tariff rate may weaken the currency [for further discussion see Kimbrough (1980)].

We turn now to a brief illustration of the working of the model under the assumption that capital is immobile internationally. As shown in eq. (4.10), the equilibrium exchange rate can be expressed in terms of variables pertaining to the demand and the supply of monies as well as to those which underlie the relative price structure. The equilibrium relative price structure is determined by the condition that the demands for traded and non-traded goods equal the corresponding supplies. Panel II of Figure 4.1 describes the determination of the equilibrium relative price $(p_T - p) = \sigma(p_T - p_N)$ for the domestic economy that is assumed to face a given foreign price of traded goods.[22] The NN and the TT schedules describe combinations of relative prices and interest rates that maintain equilibrium in the markets for non-traded and traded goods, respectively. The NN schedule is positively sloped since a rise in $(p_T - p)$ creates an excess demand for non-traded goods which can be eliminated by a higher interest rate. The higher interest rate restores the equilibrium since it lowers demand. The reduction in demand in turn is based on the assumption that aggregate spending depends negatively on the rate of interest. The TT schedule is negatively sloped since a rise in the relative price $(p_T - p)$ creates an excess supply of traded goods which can be eliminated by a fall in the rate of interest which induces a rise in spending. The equilibrium rate of interest and relative price are designated by point Q. Panel I of Figure 4.1 describes the condition for money market equilibrium. The horizontal axis represents the real value of cash balances as a function of the rate of interest. For subsequent use it is noted that, from eqs.

___

[22] This panel of Figure 4.1 is due to Dornbusch (1976b).

(4.4)–(4.6), the price level that is used in the computation of real balances can be written as

$$p = e + p^* + (p^*_T - p^*) - (p_T - p).\tag{4.13}$$

Consider a rise in spending that falls entirely on traded goods. As shown in panel II of Figure 4.1, this induces a rightward shift of the TT schedule to $T'T'$ and results in a new equilibrium at point Q' with a higher *relative* price of traded goods and a higher rate of interest. The higher rate of interest in turn lowers the demand for real balances and, as shown in panel I of Figure 4.1, results in a new equilibrium at point B. Inspection of eq. (4.13) helps to ascertain the effects of the change in spending on the exchange rate. Since, given the higher interest rate, the price *level* must rise (so as to reduce real balances) and since the rise in $(p_T - p)$ — which is induced by the decline in the nominal price of non-traded goods — contributes to a fall in the price level, it follows that the exchange rate, e, must rise so as to more than offset the price level effect of the relative price change.

Consider now the case where the rise in spending falls entirely on non-traded goods. In this case the NN schedule shifts to the left as in Figure 4.2 and the new equilibrium (point Q'') is characterized by a lower relative price of traded goods and a higher rate of interest. As before, the higher rate of interest induces a decline in the desired quantity of real balances (point C) and therefore, given the nominal quantity of money, necessitates a higher price level. In this case,

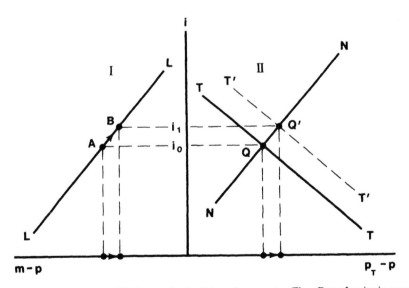

Figure 4.1. Stock and flow equilibrium under flexible exchange rates: The effect of a rise in spending on traded goods.

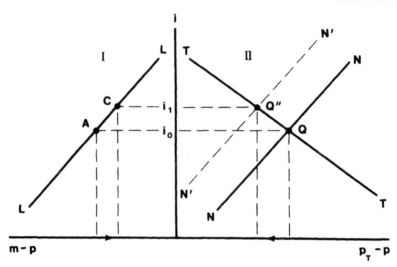

Figure 4.2. Stock and flow equilibrium under flexible exchange rates: The effect of a rise in spending on non-traded goods.

however, the change in the exchange rate is ambiguous. The fall of the relative price ($p_T - p$) raises the price level and therefore, depending on whether this rise in the price level exceeds or falls short of the rise that is necessary for money market equilibrium, the exchange rate will fall or rise. We conclude by noting that in contrast with the predictions of the "simple absorption" approach one may not conclude unambiguously that a rise in aggregate spending weakens the currency. Rather, the exchange rate effect may depend on whether the rise in spending falls on traded or non-traded goods.

The same model can be used to examine the effects of other changes like expenditure switching for which the rise in spending on one group of goods does not come at the expense of savings but rather corresponds to a decline in spending on the other group of goods. Likewise one could analyse the effects of economic expansion which originates in one of the sectors. In that case it can be shown that a rise in output originating in the traded goods sector, results in a fall in e (i.e. in an appreciation of the currency). On the other hand the exchange rate effects of a rise in output originating in the non-traded sector are ambiguous. As before, this ambiguity stems from the fact that the change in the equilibrium *relative* prices induces a change in the price *level* which may exceed or fall short of the change required by money market equilibrium at a given exchange rate.[23]

The above analysis which was intended to illustrate the working of the model was conducted under the assumption that capital was immobile internationally.

[23]See Dornbusch (1976b) and Kimbrough (1980).

Under these circumstances the balance of trade had to be balanced. The model can be extended to allow for capital mobility. In that case, flow equilibrium would require that in addition to a zero excess demand for non-traded goods, the trade balance surplus must equal the deficit on the capital account. The qualitative conclusions of the analysis remain unchanged except for the fact that the induced change in the rate of interest (and thereby the required change in the price level) would be smaller the higher the degree of capital mobility. In the extreme case, when capital is perfectly mobile, the interest rate and thus the desired level of real balances would not change. As can be seen from eq. (4.13), in this case to maintain a constant price level, the exchange rate would have to change by the same amount as the relative price (when both are measured logarithmically).

Finally, it is noteworthy that the model satisfies the homogeneity postulate. A once and for all rise in the domestic money supply results in a once and for all rise in the exchange rate and in the nominal price of non-traded goods while leaving all real variables (like real balances, relative prices, and the rate of interest) unchanged. Likewise, a once and for all equal rise in the domestic and the foreign money raises all nominal prices while leaving all real variables *and* the exchange rate unchanged.

The formulation in eqs. (4.9)–(4.10) presumed that money market equilibrium obtains continuously. The analytical framework could be modified easily to allow for a distinction between short-run and long-run demands for money. This formulation would imply the dynamics of adjustment. Likewise, the formulation in eq. (4.16) could be modified to allow for a gradual adjustment to purchasing power parities [see Bilson (1978a)]. While such modifications of the theoretical model do not introduce severe complexities, the implications for empirical estimates are much more involved and great care is required in the specification of the corresponding econometric model.

Further modifications of the model allow for legal restrictions on transactions in foreign currency which result in black markets [Blejer (1978)], as well as for government intervention in the determination of exchange rates which results in a crawling peg [Blejer and Leiderman (1981)]. An additional modification concerns the choice of the rate of interest that is included in the demand for money. The formulation that we have used included the nominal rate of interest as an argument without drawing a distinction between the real interest rate and inflationary expectations. Likewise, the specification assumed some form of purchasing power parity. This specification can be modified so as to allow for short-term price stickiness.[24] In that case a rise in the quantity of money lowers the real rate of interest for the short run and induces a depreciation of the currency.

The discussion of currency substitution suggested the possibility that the function characterizing the demand for money includes many alternative rates of

[24]See, for example, Frankel (1979) and Dornbusch (1978).

return corresponding to the many alternative assets. Again, as a theoretical matter this modification does not introduce severe complexities but the implications for empirical research may be severe since the various rates of return may be highly collinear. The degree of collinearity maybe very high if the alternative rates of return are linked to each other by various parity conditions. Among such parity conditions are the interest parity — linking the forward premium on foreign exchange to the difference between domestic and foreign rates of interest, the purchasing power parity — linking domestic and foreign prices, and the Fisher relations — linking the nominal rates of interest to the real rates of interest and to inflationary expectations.

The analysis of exchange rate determination within the monetary framework did not put much explicit emphasis on the stocks of other assets. According to the monetary model changes in the stocks of alternative assets result in exchange rate changes only to the extent that they alter the various rates of return which affect the demand for money. In contrast, the portfolio-balance model emphasizes the limited degree of substitutability among alternative assets. According to the portfolio-balance model the relative quantities of the various assets and of the rate of accumulation of these assets exert profound first-order effects on the exchange rate.[25] As an empirical matter, however, the implementation of this approach is made difficult due to limited availability of data on the various quantities of the assets that would be relevant for inclusion in the world portfolio model.

Since the rate of accumulation of assets equals the current account of the balance of payments, it provides for a dynamic linkage between the current account and the exchange rate. As a result, analyses of the portfolio-balance model have typically linked the exchange rate to the current account.[26] It is relevant to note, however, that such a linkage is not specific to the portfolio-balance model. Rather, it reflects the implications of the budget constraint by which the current account of the balance of payments equals the discrepancy between income and spending, and this constraint holds of course independent of the determinants of portfolio composition. Consequently, any model which allows for net savings, must imply a relationship between the exchange rate and the current account.[27]

Prior to concluding this section it might be useful to note that the monetary approach to the exchange rate does not claim that the exchange rate is "de-

---

[25]See for example Allen and Kenen (1980), Branson, Halttunen and Masson (1977), Branson (1977), Kouri (1976), Dooley and Isard (1978), de Macedo and Barga (1982), Frenkel (1984). For details see the analysis in Chapter 15 in this Handbook by Branson and Henderson.

[26]See, for example, Branson (1977) and Kouri (1976).

[27]For variety of additional models linking the exchange rate to the current account see Niehans (1977), Rodriguez (1980), Dornbusch and Fischer (1980), Mussa (1980, 1982), Kimbrough (1980), Shafer (1980) and Frenkel and Rodriguez (1982).

termined" only in the money or in the asset markets and that only stock rather than flow considerations are relevant for determining the equilibrium exchange rate. Obviously, general equilibrium relationships which are relevant for the determination of exchange rates include both stock and flow variables.[28] The money market equilibrium condition should be viewed as a reduced form that incorporates these general equilibrium relationships. Furthermore, the fact that the analysis of the exchange rate has been carried out in terms of the supplies and the demands for monies, does not imply that "only money matters" or that the exchange rate is determined only by the supply of domestic and foreign monies. On the contrary, in addition to the key role played by the intersectoral relative price structure, the demand for money plays a critical role and it depends on real variables like real income as well as on other real variables which underlie expectations. The rationale for concentrating on the relative supplies and demands for money is that they provide a convenient and a natural framework for organizing thoughts concerning the determinants of the relative price of monies. It is the same principle which has been used by proponents of the monetary approach to the balance of payments in justifying the use of the money demand–money supply framework for the analysis of the money account of the balance of payments under a pegged exchange rate system.[29]

The model that was discussed in this section included anticipatory variables, like the forward premium on foreign exchange, as one of the determinants of the current exchange rate. However, this formulation has not emphasized sufficiently the critical role that expectations play in affecting the exchange rate. This unique role is best exemplified within a more general framework that views the question of exchange rate determination as part of the more general theory of the determination of asset prices.

4.2. Exchange rates as asset prices

In the models of exchange rate determination examined in the preceding section, the dynamic behavior of the exchange rate is usually analyzed in terms of the

---

[28]It is noteworthy that the shift of emphasis from flow consideration to the requirement of stock equilibrium revived issues from the Bullionist controversy of the early 1800s which led to the competing "Balance of Payments Theory" and "Inflation Theory" of exchange rate determination; see Ricardo (1811) and Viner (1937). For an early modern formulation emphasizing stock equilibrium see Black (1973).

[29]See, for example, Mussa (1974) and Frenkel and Johnson (1976a); in the context of flexible exchange rates the same argument is made by Dornbusch (1976b) and Mussa (1976b). It should be noted that the money demand–money supply framework is not employed only for convenience; it reflects the hypotheses that money markets clear fast relative to goods markets, that the demands for real balances are relatively stable and that the supply of nominal balances is a policy instrument that is controlled by the monetary authorities.

response of the exchange rate to an exogenous disturbance (such as a permanent increase in the domestic money supply) and its subsequent path of convergence to its new long-run equilibrium. This general view of exchange rate determination, however, does not fully explain key empirical regularities that have been characteristic of the behavior of exchange rates during the 1970s and during earlier periods of generalized floating. As a statistical matter, the logarithms of spot exchange rates between the U.S. dollar and other major currencies (the British pound, the deutsche mark, the French franc, the Japanese yen and the Swiss franc) are generally well described as random walks in which month-to-month and quarter-to-quarter changes are almost entirely unpredictable. Changes in spot exchange rates are generally closely correlated with contemporaneous changes in forward exchange rates (especially for large changes), indicating that movements in spot rates are closely related to movements in the market's expectation of future spot rates. Monthly and quarterly changes in exchange rates are not, however, closely related to differentials in national inflation rates, implying that most short-run changes in nominal exchange rates correspond to changes in real exchange rates (i.e. to deviations from purchasing power parities). Moreover, monthly and quarterly changes in exchange rates are not closely related to differentials in rates of monetary expansion or to current account imbalances.[30]

These facts suggest that exchange rates should be viewed as prices of durable assets determined in organized markets (like stock and commodity exchanges) in which current prices reflect the market's expectation concerning present and future economic conditions relevant for determining the appropriate values of these durable assets, and in which price changes are largely unpredictable and reflect primarily new information that alters expectations concerning these present and future economic conditions. This general notion of exchange rates as "asset prices" can be represented in a skeletal model in which the logarithm of the equilibrium exchange rate in period t, denoted by $e(t)$, is determined by[31]

$$e(t) = X(t) + a \cdot \mathrm{E}[(e(t+1) - e(t)); t], \tag{4.14}$$

where $X(t)$ represents the basic economic conditions that affect the foreign exchange market in period t, $\mathrm{E}[(e(t+1) - e(t)); t]$ denotes the expected per-

---

[30]A number of empirical studies have reported results that are consistent with the empirical regularities discussed in this paragraph; see, for example, Mussa (1979b), Frenkel (1981a, 1981b) and, in particular, Chaper 19 by Levich in this Handbook. The implications of these regularities for the general approach to the theory of exchange rate determination are considered in Mussa (1979b, 1984), Frenkel and Mussa (1980), Frenkel (1981b) and Mussa (1982).

[31]The present exposition of the "asset-price" view of exchange rates draws on that given in Frenkel and Mussa (1980), Frenkel (1981b) and Mussa (1982, 1984). Key elements of this view are also contained in Mussa (1976b). It is also relevant to note that while our exposition presents a specific version of the "asset-price" view of exchange rates, there are also other versions that may be termed as "asset views"; see, for example, the version of the portfolio–balance model presented by Branson and Henderson in Chapter 15 of this Handbook.

centage rate of change of the exchange rate between t and $t+1$ conditional on information available at t, and the parameter a measures the sensitivity of the current exchange rate to its expected rate of change. To close the model, it is assumed that expectations are "rational" in the sense that they are consistent with the application of (4.14) in all future periods (and with a suitable boundary condition). By forward iteration, it follows that the exchange rate that is expected at any $t+j$, for $j \geq 0$, conditional on information available at t, depends on a discounted sum of expected future X's, starting at $t+j$; specifically:

$$E[e(t+j);t] = (1/(1+a)) \cdot \sum_{i=0}^{\infty} (a/(1+a))^i \cdot E[X(t+j+i);t]. \quad (4.15)$$

Setting $j = 0$, we obtain the "asset price" expression for the current exchange rate as a discounted sum of present and expected future X's.

Using (4.15), we also obtain a convenient decomposition of the change in the exchange rate, $D(e(t)) \equiv e(t+1) - e(t)$, into its expected change component,

$$D^e(e(t)) \equiv E[D(e(t));t] = E[(e(t+1) - e(t));t]$$

and its unexpected component,

$$D^u(e(t)) = e(t+1) - E[e(t+1);t].$$

The expected change in the exchange rate is a discounted sum of expected future changes in the X's:

$$D^e(e(t)) = (1/(1+a)) \cdot \sum_{i=0}^{\infty} (a/(1+a))^i \cdot E[D(X(t+i));t]. \quad (4.16)$$

Alternatively, the expected change in the exchange rate can be expressed as proportional to the difference between the discounted sum of all expected future X's that determines $E[e(t+1);t]$ and the current X:

$$D^e(e(t)) = (1/(1+a)) \cdot [E(e(t+1);t) - X(t)]. \quad (4.17)$$

The unexpected change in the exchange rate is a discounted sum of changes in expectations about future X's based on new information received between t and $t+1$:

$$D^u(e(t)) = (1/(1+a)) \cdot \sum_{i=0}^{\infty} (a/(1+a))$$

$$\cdot [E(X(t+j+1);t+1) - E(X(t+j+1);t)]. \quad (4.18)$$

These results provide a general rationale for many of the observed regularities in the dynamic behavior of exchange rates. The expected component of monthly changes in exchange rates between major industrial countries should usually be quite small because the factor of proportionality $1/(1+a)$ that appears in (4.17) is probably of the order of magnitude of $1/100$, implying that only very large differences between the current X and the discounted sum of all future X's could justify a substantial expected change in the exchange rate over a period of a month.[32] In contrast, the unexpected component of the monthly change in the exchange rate, which is necessarily unpredictable on the basis of information available at t, could be quite large. If new information received between t and $t+1$ leads to a substantial revision, in the same direction, of expectations, we should observe changes in expectations concerning future exchange rates that are in the same direction and are of similar magnitude as the unexpected change in the spot exchange rate.[33] This suggests a rationale for the observed relation between unexpected movements in spot and forward exchange rates, especially for large movements.

4.3. Balance of payments equilibrium and the real exchange rate

One procedure for introducing specific economic content into the general asset price model of exchange rates is to focus on the condition of balance of payments equilibrium as the fundamental determinant of the equilibrium exchange rate, and allowing for a suitable channel through which expected changes in the exchange rate influence the balance of payments. This procedure is reminiscent of traditional flow market models of the determination of exchange rates, and is also similar to a number of more recent analyses of the interaction between the exchange rate and the current account balance.[34] In implementing this procedure, it is convenient initially to deal with a real model of the determination of the real exchange rate, and only subsequently (in the next section) to introduce the monetary considerations centrally important in determining nominal exchange rates.[35]

---

[32]A value of $1/(1 + a)$ equal to $1/100$ means that an adjustment of about 1 percent in the annual expected rate of change of the exchange rate will offset a 10 percent divergence between the current month's expected X and the discounted sum of X's in all future months.

[33] The role of new information in inducing unexpected movements in exchange rates is emphasized by Dornbusch (1978), Frenkel (1981b), Frenkel and Mussa (1980), and Mussa (1976c, 1977, 1979b, 1980, and 1982).

[34] The "traditional approach" is the textbook approach in which the equilibrium exchange rate is determined by the intersection of the flow demand for foreign exchange arising from trade transactions with the speculative supply of foreign exchange provided by capital holders who are prepared to undertake risks in exchange for expected gains. More sophisticated versions of this approach are presented in the work of Black (1973) and Stein (1980). On the interaction between the exchange rate and the current account see Dornbusch and Fischer (1980), Rodriguez (1980), Mussa (1980, 1982), Sachs (1981) and Frenkel and Rodriguez (1982).

[35] The model considered in this section is developed in greater detail in Mussa (1984). Other models that emphasize the importance of real factors in determining the real exchange rate include those presented by Bruno and Sachs (1982), Buiter and Miller (1983), Neary and Purvis (1983), and Svennson and Razin (1983).

For a moderate size country, the real exchange rate, q, is identified with the logarithm of the relative price of domestic goods in terms of foreign goods. Domestic goods may either be exclusively non-traded goods or may be goods for which there is a less than infinitely elastic foreign demand. Consistent with either of these interpretations, it is plausible to assume that the current account surplus, b (measured in terms of imported goods), is determined by [36]

$$b = \beta \cdot (z - q) + r^* \cdot A, \qquad \beta > 0, \tag{4.19}$$

where z summarizes the exogenous real factors that affect domestic excess demand and foreign excess demand for domestic goods, β is a parameter that reflects the relative price elasticities of domestic and foreign excess demands for domestic goods, r^* is the (fixed) foreign real interest rate, and A is the net stock of foreign assets (denominated in foreign goods) held by domestic residents. Absent changes in official holdings of foreign assets, the current account surplus necessarily determines the rate of change of net private holdings of foreign assets:

$$D(A) = b = \beta \cdot (z - q) + r^* \cdot A. \tag{4.20}$$

The rest of the world, which is large relative to the home country, willingly absorbs changes in assets, A, in exchange for foreign goods, at the fixed foreign real interest rate, r^*. Hence, the capital account deficit of the home country (measured in terms of foreign goods), denoted by c, reflects the desired rate of accumulation of net foreign assets by domestic residents. Two factors are assumed to influence the desired rate of accumulation of net foreign assets: the divergence between the current "target level" of net foreign assets, $\hat{A}$, and their current actual level, A, and the expected rate of change of the real exchange rate; formally:

$$c = \mu \cdot (\hat{A} - A) - \alpha \cdot D^e(q), \qquad \mu, \alpha > 0. \tag{4.21}$$

The effect $D^e(q)$ on c may be thought of either as the influence of expected changes in the value of foreign assets (measured in terms of domestic goods) on desired accumulation of such assets, or as the influence of the domestic real interest rate (defined relative to a basket of both domestic and foreign goods) on desired saving.

Balance of payments equilibrium requires that the current account surplus, b, be matched by the capital account deficit, c; that is,

$$\beta \cdot (z - q) + r^* \cdot A = \mu \cdot (\hat{A} - A) - \alpha \cdot D^e(q). \tag{4.22}$$

---

[36] The equations of the present model are all assumed to be linear in the levels or logarithms of the endogenous and exogenous variables. This assumption allows for the explicit solution of the forward looking difference equation system that constitutes the reduced form of the model. The assumption that $\beta > 0$ implies that the Marshall–Lerner condition is satisfied; an increase in the relative price of domestic goods, holding other factors constant, worsens the current account.

This condition, together with (4.20), constitutes a simultaneous system of forward looking difference equations that may be solved for the expected future time paths of the endogenous variables, q and A, conditional on the current inherited stock of net foreign assets and on the expected future time paths (based on current information) of the exogenous forcing variables, z and $\hat{A}$. In particular, the solution for the current equilibrium real exchange rate is given by

$$q(t) = \bar{q}(t) + \gamma \cdot (A(t) - \bar{A}(t)), \tag{4.23}$$

where

$$\bar{q}(t) = \bar{z}(t) + (r^*/\beta) \cdot \bar{A}(t),$$

$$\bar{z}(t) = (1 - \Theta) \cdot \sum_{j=0}^{\infty} \Theta^j \cdot E[z(t+j); t],$$

$$\bar{A}(t) = (1 - \Theta) \cdot \sum_{j=0}^{\infty} \Theta^j \cdot E[A(t+j); t],$$

$$\Theta = (1/(1+\lambda)) \quad \text{and} \quad \gamma = (\lambda/\beta) - (1/\alpha) > 0,$$

$$\lambda = (1/2) \cdot \left[(r^* + (\beta/\alpha)) + \sqrt{(r^* + (\beta/\alpha))^2 + 4 \cdot (\mu\beta/\alpha)} \right] > (r^* + (\beta/\alpha)).$$

The result in (4.23) indicates that the current real exchange rate depends on (i) the current estimate of the long-run equilibrium real exchange rate, $\bar{q}(t)$, that is expected to be consistent with the requirement that on average (in present and future periods), the current account is balanced ($b = 0$), and (ii) on the divergence between current net foreign asset holdings and the current estimate of the long-run desired level of such holdings, $\bar{A}(t)$. The asset-price property of the real exchange rate is reflected in the dependence of $\bar{q}(t)$ on a discounted sum of present and expected future z's and in the dependence of $\bar{A}(t)$ on a discounted sum of present and expected future $\hat{A}$'s. The discount rate, λ, that is applied in determining both $\bar{q}(t)$ and $\bar{A}(t)$, reflects the sensitivity of the current account surplus to the level of q and the sensitivity of the capital account deficit both to expected rate of change of q and to the divergence of net foreign assets from their target level.

It is noteworthy that the asset price expression for the real exchange rate that is embodied in (4.23) is consistent with a sophisticated version of the traditional flow market model of exchange rate determination. As illustrated in Figure 4.3, the current real exchange rate may be thought of as being determined by the intersection of the b schedule, characterizing the flow of foreign exchange arising from current account transactions, $b = \beta \cdot (z - q) + r^* \cdot A$, and the c schedule, characterizing the flow of foreign exchange arising from capital account transactions, $c = \mu \cdot (\hat{A} - A) - \alpha \cdot (E[q(t+1); t] - q)$, where the expected future real exchange rate, $E[q(t+1); t]$, is treated as a parameter affecting the position of the

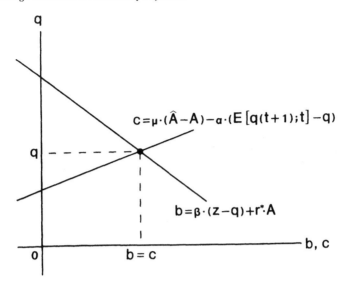

Figure 4.3. Balance of payments equilibrium and the real exchange rate.

c schedule.[37] The element of sophistication that transforms this traditional model into the asset pricing results expressed by (4.23) is the assumption that expectations concerning the future real exchange rate are consistent with the economic forces that will actually determine the future real exchange rate.

The present results are also consistent with recent models of the dynamic interaction between the exchange rate and the current account which view the current exchange rate as determined by the willingness of asset holders to hold existing stocks of foreign assets, and which view the rate of change of the exchange rate as determined by rate of change of foreign assets which is equal to the current account balance.[38] In particular, if we assume that the exogenous

---

[37]The c schedule is frequently identified with the activities of foreign exchange speculators. From a theoretical perspective, however, there is no good reason for such an identification; the c schedule represents desired behavior of all economic agents with respect to acquisition of foreign assets. For further discussion of this point, and of the meaning of the "balance of payments equilibrium condition" represented by eq. (4.22), see Mussa (1984).

[38]Kouri (1976) develops the idea that the current exchange rate, which depends primarily on the conditions of asset market equilibrium, affects the current account balance which determines the rate of change of foreign asset positions; change of these asset positions, in turn, feed back through the conditions of asset market equilibrium to determine the rate of change of the exchange rate. A similar view of the essential elements in the dynamic interaction between the exchange rate and the current account is embodied in the models developed by Branson (1977), Branson, Haltunen and Masson (1977), Calvo and Rodriguez (1977), Dornbusch and Fischer (1980), Flood (1981), Niehans (1977), and Rodriguez (1980).

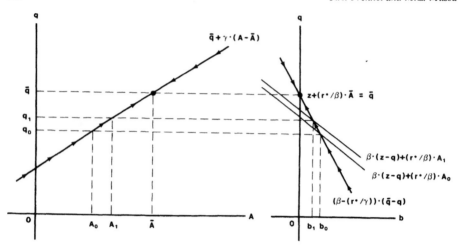

Figure 4.4. The dynamic interaction between the exchange rate, asset stocks and the current account.

factors affecting the current account (the z's) and the target levels of net foreign assets (the $\hat{A}$'s) are constant, then the current real exchange rate, $q(t)$, determined by (4.23) becomes a function of the inherited stock of net foreign assets, as illustrated in the left-hand panel of Figure 4.4. Also, as illustrated in the right-hand panel of Figure 4.4, the current account surplus, b, is determined by this value of $q(t)$ and by the interest received on the inherited stock of net foreign assets. When $A(t) = A_0$ is less than $\bar{A} = \hat{A}$, $q(t) = q_0 = \bar{q} + \gamma \cdot (A_0 - \bar{A})$ is less than $\bar{q} = z + (r^*/\beta) \cdot \bar{A}$, and the current account surplus is

$$b_0 = \beta \cdot (z - q_0) + (r^*/\beta) \cdot A_0 = (\beta \gamma - r^*) \cdot (\bar{A} - A_0)$$
$$= (\beta - (r^*/\gamma)) \cdot (\bar{q} - q_0) > 0.$$

This surplus adds to the stock of net foreign assets, and the new stock, $A_1 = A_0 + b_0$, determines a new real exchange rate, q_1, where $q_1 = \bar{q} + \gamma \cdot (A_1 - \bar{A}) = q_0 + \gamma \cdot b_0 > q_0$. The new real exchange rate, together with the new stock of net foreign assets, determine a new current account surplus, b_1, where

$$b_1 = \beta \cdot (z - q_1) + (r^*/\beta) \cdot A_1 = (\beta \gamma - r^*) \cdot (\bar{A} - A_1)$$
$$= (\beta - (r^*/\gamma)) \cdot (\bar{q} - q_1),$$

which is still positive but is smaller than b_0. This dynamic process continues, with ever smaller current account surpluses and ever smaller increases in q, until the current account is in balance and $q = \bar{q}$.

New elements enter into the analysis of exchange rate dynamics when we consider either expected changes in the z's and the $\hat{A}$'s or changes in expectations about the future paths of these exogenous forcing variables due to new information.[39] The general expression for the expected change in the exchange rate implied by (4.23) is given by

$$
\begin{aligned}
D^e(q(t)) = {}& (\beta\gamma - r^*) \cdot (\bar{A}(t) - A(t)) \\
& + (1 - \Theta - \beta\Theta) \cdot \mathrm{E}\big[(\bar{z}(t+1) - z(t)); t\big] \\
& - (\gamma - (r^*/\beta)) \cdot (1 - \Theta) \cdot \mathrm{E}\big[(\bar{A}(t+1) - \hat{A}(t)); t\big].
\end{aligned} \tag{4.24}
$$

The first term on the right-hand side of (4.24) captures the essential element of Figure 4.4, namely the effect of divergences between the current long-run desired level of net foreign assets and the current actual level of net foreign assets on the expected change in the real exchange rate. The second term on the right-hand side of (4.24) represents the effect on $D^e(q(t))$ of "temporary expected disturbances to the current account" associated with differences between the expected discounted sum of all future z's, $\mathrm{E}[\bar{z}(t+1); t]$, and the current expected values of z. The third term on the right-hand side of (4.24) reflects the effect of expected changes in the target level of net foreign assets, measured by $\mathrm{E}[(\bar{A}(t+1) - \hat{A}(t)); t]$, on the expected change in q. The general expression for the unexpected change in the real exchange rate implied by (4.23) is given by

$$
D^u(q(t)) = \gamma \cdot D^u(A(t)) + D^u(\bar{z}(t)) - (\gamma - (r^*/\beta)) \cdot D^u(\bar{A}(t)), \tag{4.25}
$$

where $D^u(A(t))$ is the unexpected change in net foreign assets associated with "innovations" in the current account, $D^u(\bar{z}(t))$ measures the effect of new information in revising expectations about future z's, and $D^u(\bar{A}(t))$ indicates the effect of new information in revising expectations about future target levels of A. The new information that leads to revisions of expectations about future z's and about future target levels of wealth may come from a variety of sources, including particularly the possible effect of innovations in the current account on expectations concerning the future behavior of the exogenous factors affecting the current account.

---

[39] The importance of these elements in understanding the dynamic behavior of the real exchange rate and its relation to the current account is emphasized in Mussa (1980). The "accounting framework" for the analysis of exchange rate dynamics developed by Dooley and Isard (1981) and Isard (1983) also incorporates these elements. Models developed by Marion (1981), Obstfeld (1981), Sachs (1981), and Helpman and Razin (1983) consider the effect of temporary expected disturbances in the current account of the behavior of the exchange rate.

4.4. Exchange rates and money in the general model of exchange rate determination

Models of the type examined in the preceding section are easily extended to incorporate monetary phenomena and to deal with the nominal exchange rate.[40] Let p denote the logarithm of the domestic money price of domestic goods, p^* denote the logarithm of the foreign money price of foreign goods, and e the logarithm of the domestic money price of foreign exchange. The logarithm of the relative price of domestic goods in terms of imported goods is given by

$$q = p - (e + p^*). \tag{4.26}$$

The logarithm of the general price level in the home country is given by

$$P = \sigma \cdot p + (1 - \sigma) \cdot (e + p^*) = e + p^* + \sigma \cdot q, \tag{4.27}$$

where σ is the weight of domestic goods in the domestic price index. The logarithm of the demand for domestic money is assumed to be given by

$$m^d = K + L \cdot P + J \cdot e + V \cdot q - N \cdot i - U \cdot D^e(e) + W \cdot A, \tag{4.28}$$

where K represents all exogenous factors (such as real income) affecting the demand for domestic money, $L > 0$, $J > 0$ and $V \gtrless 0$ are the elasticities of money demand with respect to the general price level, the nominal exchange rate and the relative price of domestic goods, and $N > 0$, $U > 0$ and $W > 0$ are the semi-elasticities of money demand with respect to the domestic nominal interest rate, i, the expected rate of change of the nominal exchange rate, $D^e(e)$, and the stock of net foreign assets. The domestic nominal interest rate is determined by the interest parity condition:

$$i = i^* + D^e(e) + \rho, \tag{4.29}$$

where i^* is the exogenous foreign nominal interest rate and ρ is an exogenous risk premium that accounts for differences between the forward premium on foreign exchange and the expected rate of change of the nominal exchange rate.[41]

---

[40] The analysis in this section is based on Mussa (1984). A similar approach to combining real and monetary factors in a model of the real and nominal exchange rate is adopted by Bruno and Sachs (1981), Buiter and Miller (1983) and Mussa (1977b). A different approach for incorporating real and monetary factors is motivated by a "finance constraint" (which is also referred to as the "Clower constraint") requiring goods to be purchased with currency accumulated in advance of the period in which trade takes place; see Stockman (1980), Helpman (1981) and Lucas (1982)

[41] The importance of a risk premium in influencing the relationship between the domestic and the foreign nominal interest rate is analyzed by Kouri (1976), Stockman (1978), Fama and Farber (1981), Hansen and Hodrich (1980, 1983), Frankel (1982) and Frenkel and Razin (1980). This risk premium could be allowed to be a function of any of the variables that appear in the money demand function (4.28) without significantly affecting the formal analysis carried out in this section.

The critical equilibrium condition for nominal variables is the requirement that the logarithm of demand for domestic money, m^d, must equal the logarithm of the supply of domestic money, m. Using eqs. (4.26)–(4.29), this equilibrium condition may be expressed in terms of the following "reduced form" condition for monetary equilibrium:

$$m = k + \zeta \cdot e - \eta \cdot D^e(e), \tag{4.30}$$

where $\zeta = L + J > 0$ and $\eta = N + U > 0$, and where k summarizes all of the factors other than e and $D^e(e)$ that influence the logarithm of demand for domestic money, i.e.

$$k = K + L \cdot p^* - N \cdot (i^* + \rho) + (V + \sigma L) \cdot q + W \cdot A. \tag{4.31}$$

If it is assumed that paths of the real variables q and A are determined independently of the behavior of the domestic money supply, as indicated by the analysis in the preceding section, then the expected path of the nominal exchange rate may be determined from the solution of the forward looking difference equation (4.30). As is seen from (4.32), the expected nominal exchange rate depends on a discounted sum of expected future differences between m and k:[42]

$$E[e(s); t] = (1/(\zeta + \eta)) \cdot \sum_{j=0}^{\infty} (\eta/(\zeta + \eta))^j \cdot E[(m(s+j) - k(s+j)); t]. \tag{4.32}$$

Setting $s = t$, we find that (the logarithm of) the current nominal exchange rate, $e(t) = E[e(t); t]$, depends on a discounted sum of present and expected future differences between m and k.

This result represents the "asset-price version" of the simple monetary model of exchange rate determination discussed in Section 4.1. Its advantage over this simpler model is that it indicates clearly dependence of the current exchange rate not only on current money supplies and money demands, but also on the entire expected future time paths of money supplies and money demands.[43] In accord with the general principles of the asset price view of exchange rates, the expected rate of change of the exchange rate is a discounted sum of expected future changes in $m - k$'s; and the unexpected change in the exchange rate is a discounted sum of revisions in expectations about future $m - k$'s brought about

---

[42] If there is no real balance effect on desired spending and if there is no other source of non-neutrality (such as fixed nominal contracts or incomplete information about the behavior of nominal variables), then the model of the real exchange rate discussed in the preceding section operates independently of the behavior of the domestic money supply. Even if these conditions are not satisfied (4.32) remains valid, but it is necessary to consider the effect of the behavior of the money supply and other nominal variables on the real exchange rate and the stock of net foreign assets.

[43] The reduced-form money market equilibrium condition (4.30) is used in Mussa (1976b) to derive the result (4.32). The present analysis shows that this reduced form is consistent with a fairly general model of goods and asset market equilibrium.

by new information received between t and $t + 1$. In general, these two components of the change in the exchange rate should reflect the stochastic process
generating $m - k$ and the information about this process that is available to
economic agents. For example, if $m - k$ is directly observable and is known to
follow a random walk, then the exchange rate, e, should also follow a random
walk in which all changes in e are unexpected and are proportional to the
observed unexpected changes in $m - k$. Alternatively, if k is unobservable (to
private agents) and is known to follow a random walk, and if the monetary
authority allows m to change to offset changes in k and adds an uncorrelated
error to changes in m, then e should still follow a random walk but, following the
rules of optimal forecast, the response of e to observed changes in m should
depend on the ratio of the variance of the pure error component of changes in m
to the variance of changes in k.

In (4.32) the influence of real factors on the expected path of the nominal
exchange rate comes through their effect on the expected paths of m, the money
supply variable, and k, the money demand variable. An alternative, analytically
equivalent expression for $E[e(s); t]$ brings the influence of these real factors into
sharper focus:

$$E[e(s); t] = E[P(s); t] - E[p^*(s); t] - \sigma \cdot E[q(s); t]. \tag{4.33}$$

where $E[P(s); t]$ is the expectation of (the logarithm of) the general level of
domestic prices, as determined by

$$E[P(s); t] = (1/(\zeta + \eta)) \cdot \sum_{j=0}^{\infty} (\eta/(\zeta + \eta))^j \cdot E[(m(s+j) - l(s+j)); t],$$

$$\tag{4.34}$$

where l is a measure of factors affecting (the logarithm of) the demand for
domestic money that is defined by

$$l = K - J \cdot p^* - N \cdot (i^* + \rho) + (V - \sigma J) \cdot q + \eta \cdot D^e(p^*)$$
$$+ \eta \sigma \cdot D^e(q) + W \cdot A. \tag{4.35}$$

The results (4.33)–(4.35) represent the asset-price version of the extended
monetary model of exchange rate determination considered before. From these
results, we find that a discounted sum of present and expected future money
supplies affects the nominal exchange rate by affecting the general level of all
domestic prices. Movements in the nominal exchange rate that are associated with
expected or unexpected changes in this discounted sum of present and future m's
are consistent with the maintenance of purchasing power parity. By the same
token, changes in the foreign price level, which are not associated with changes in
domestic money demand or supply or in the relative price of domestic goods in
terms of foreign goods, induce movements in the nominal exchange rate that are

consistent with purchasing power parity. Real economic factors influence the exchange rate through two channels: to the extent that such factors affect the discounted sum of present and future levels of demand for domestic money (measured by the l's), they induce movements in the nominal exchange rate that are consistent with purchasing power parity; however, to the extent that such real factors induce movements in the relative price of domestic goods in terms of foreign goods, they require movements in the nominal exchange rate and in prices that constitute divergences from purchasing power parity.

When we combine the model of the nominal exchange rate embodied in (4.33)–(4.35) with the model of the real exchange rate discussed in the preceding section, we arrive at a general model in which the exchange rate exhibits the essential properties of an "asset price", and that also incorporates the key ingredients both of monetary models and of balance of payments models in a general equilibrium model of exchange rate determination. This already general model of exchange rate determination can be further extended by introducing phenomena associated with macroeconomic disequilibria. The two modern approaches to the modelling of such phenomena are (i) the contracting models and (ii) the incomplete information models. Both share the common feature that stabilization policy (especially monetary policy) has no capacity to affect the long-run equilibrium behavior of national output, but they differ critically in their implications for the successful short-run use of stabilization policy. In the contracting models, changes in the money supply that were unanticipated at the time when existing nominal contracts were established can temporarily affect the level of national output, and the government can use its freedom to act with respect to monetary policy (while private agents are locked into existing nominal contracts) to improve the performance of national output [see Fischer (1977), Phelps and Taylor (1977), Taylor (1980)]. In contrast, in the incomplete information models, unanticipated changes in the money supply can temporarily affect national output, but stabilization policies linked to past values of variables observed by private agents have no capacity to improve the performance of national output [see Lucas (1972, 1975), Barro (1976)].

The key implications of these two approaches to modelling macroeconomic disequilibrium for the behavior of national output carry over from the closed economy setting in which they were originally developed to an open economy setting. In either approach, unanticipated money supply changes temporarily affect domestic output and, in general, have some effect on foreign output; but only in the contracting approach can stabilization policy be used successfully to improve the performance on national output.[44] In addition to these implications

---

[44] For applications of these approaches to modelling macroeconomic disequilibrium in an open economy setting see Flood (1979), Saidi (1980) and Stockman (1980).

with respect to national outputs, models that incorporate macroeconomic disequilibrium introduce the possibility that monetary disturbances may induce short-run price and exchange rate movements that diverge from purchasing power parity. In the incomplete information approach, such divergences are simply one of the manifestations of the real effects of unanticipated monetary changes, without any policy significance. In the contracting approach, stickiness of nominal prices resulting from existing nominal contracts may necessitate "overshooting" of the nominal exchange rate in response to unanticipated monetary changes and an associated temporary but persistent change in the real exchange rate.[45] This "overshooting" response to the nominal exchange rate may provide additional leverage for monetary policy to affect the short-run behavior of national output, and may increase the usefulness of exchange rates as indicators for the conduct of stabilization policy.

4.5. *Empirical issues in exchange rate analysis*

One of the significant developments characterizing research in international economics during the last decade has been the proliferation of empirical work.[46] In this section we only highlight some aspects of this research.

The empirical methodology followed three general lines. The first examined the characteristics of the foreign exchange market, the second examined the validity of basic parity conditions and the third examined the performance of specific models.

An example of the first line of research has been an examination of market efficiency. For an asset market to be "efficient" prices must appropriately reflect all available information and thus it should be impossible to make extraordinary profits by exploiting generally available information. Tests of foreign exchange market efficiency have focused on (i) the statistical properties of forward rates as predictors of future spot rates, (ii) the time-series properties of exchange rates and of deviations from forward rates, (iii) the relative degree of volatility of spot and forward rates, (iv) the ability to improve on market forecasts of future exchange rates by using past spot and forward exchange rates and other publicly available information, and (v) the capacity to make extraordinary profits by employing

---

[45]Exchange rate overshooting in response to a permanent increase in the money supply, due to slowness in the adjustment of the domestic price level, was initially considered by Dornbusch (1976c). Generalizations of Dornbusch's analysis have been considered by Wilson (1979), Rogoff (1979), Obstfeld (1981), Mussa (1982), Bhandari (1982) and Frenkel and Rodriguez (1982). For further analysis and references to the literature on exchange rate dynamics see Chapter 18 by Obstfeld and Stockman in this Handbook.

[46]Some of this work is included in Frenkel (1983). A detailed survey of the empirical studies of exchange rates is provided by Levich in Chapter 19 of this Handbook.

various trading rules. Different tests applied to different exchange rates in different time periods have not reached a unanimous consensus concerning the hypothesis of market efficiency.[47]

Tests of the various parity conditions examined the performance of the interest parity theory and the purchasing power parity doctrine. Tests of the interest parity have generally been favorable to the predictions of the theory at least when account is taken of the costs and timing of transactions in various markets [see, for example, Frenkel and Levich (1975, 1977)]. In contrast, tests of the purchasing power parity doctrine have not figured as well. The data, specifically during the 1970s, suggest that short-run changes in exchange rates bear little relationship to short-run differentials in national inflation rates, particularly as measured by consumer price indices. Further, changes in exchange rates over longer periods of time have frequently been associated with large cumulative divergences from relative purchasing power parities.[48] As an analytical matter, purchasing power parities can be expected to hold in the long run if most of the shocks to the system are of a monetary origin which do not require changes in relative prices. The evidence on the large cumulative deviations from purchasing power parities is consistent with prominence of "real" shocks. It is relevant to note that the short-run deviations from purchasing power parities reflect, in addition to the effects of real shocks, the intrinsic differences between the properties of exchange rates and those of national price levels. Exchange rates, like other asset prices, are likely to respond promptly to new information which alters expectations, while national price levels exhibit some "stickiness" reflecting the cost of price adjustment which result in nominal contracts of finite length. The resulting difference between the time-series properties of exchange rates and prices is reflected in the low correlation between the practically random month-to-month exchange rate changes and the serially correlated differences between national rates of inflation.

The third line of research has tested directly the performance of specific models. The monetary model was reasonably successful when applied to extreme episodes like the German hyperinflation of the 1920s where monetary shocks dominated the scene. However, when applied to more regular periods it yielded mixed results [see, for example, Frenkel (1976), Frenkel and Clements (1982), Bilson (1978a, 1978b) and Hodrick (1978)]. Modifications of the simple monetary model which included elements of the term structure of the interest rate and

---

[47] The relations between spot and lagged forward rates are examined in Poole (1967) and Giddy and Dufey (1975); the relations between spot and lagged forward rates are reported by Frenkel (1977, 1978, 1981b), Krugman (1977), Cornell (1977), Hsieh (1982), Bilson (1981), Hakkio (1979), Hansen and Hodrick (1980) and are surveyed by Levich (1979) and Kolhagen (1978); the relative degree of volatility of spot and forward rates is analysed by Meese and Singleton (1980) and Flood (1981). This is a very partial list of references. For a more complete list see Chapter 19 by Levich in this Handbook.

[48] For some evidence on Purchasing Power Parities see Genberg (1978), Isard (1977), Frenkel (1978, 1981a) and for surveys see Officer (1976) and Katseli-Papaefstratiou (1979).

which allowed for a trend in the income velocity have enjoyed limited success but have faced the difficulties arising from parameter instability [see, for example, Frenkel (1979, 1984), Dornbusch (1978)]. Likewise, tests of the portfolio-balance model yielded occasionally mixed success but further examination yielded poor results [see, for example, Branson, Halttunen and Masson (1977) and Frankel (1984)]. While the various models might have enjoyed some success in accounting for the variability of exchange rates during a specific sample period, all have performed poorly when applied to out-of-sample data [see, for example, Meese and Rogoff (1983)]. It seems that at the present stage the empirical evidence taken as a whole suggests the lack of a satisfactory structural model accounting for exchange rate behavior.

The analytical framework that was developed in Section 4.2 views the exchange rate as an asset price which is highly sensitive to new information that alters expectations. This general view implies that empirical research on the determinants of exchange rate changes should relate these changes to the "innovations" in the relevant variables.[49] The econometric modelling of these issues is, however, complex since it involves measurements of unanticipated events. Therefore, tests of these models are always joint tests of the specification of the model and of the decomposition of events into their anticipated and unanticipated components. Recent work on the relation between exchange rates and "news" measured "news" in a variety of ways and has produced evidence consistent with this general analytical view.[50] While this line of research is relatively new in exchange rate analysis, applications in other areas of economics show considerable promise.

References

Abel, A., R. Dornbusch, J. Huizinga, and M. Alan (1979), "Money demand during hyperinflation", Journal of Monetary Economics, 5:97–104.

Alexander, S.S. (1952), "Effects of a devaluation on the trade balance", International Monetary Fund Staff Papers, 2:263–278.

Aliber, R.Z. (1973), "The interest rate parity theorem: A reinterpretation", Journal of Political Economy, 81:1451–1459.

Allen, P.R. and P.B. Kenen (1980), Assets markets, exchange rates and economic integration (Cambridge University Press, Cambridge).

Balassa, B. (1964), "The purchasing-power-parity doctrine: A reappraisal", Journal of Political Economy, 72:584–596.

Barro, R.J. (1974), "Are government bonds net wealth?", Journal of Political Economy, 82:1095–1118

Barro, R.J. (1976), "Rational expectations and the role of monetary policy", Journal of Monetary Economics, 2:1–32.

Berglas, E. (1974), "Devaluation, monetary policy and border tax adjustment", Canadian Journal of Economics, 7:1–11.

[49]See Mussa (1977, 1979a), Dornbusch (1978), and Bilson (1978a).
[50]See Dornbusch (1980), Frenkel (1981b), Genberg (1984), Isard (1983) and Edwards (1983).

Bhandari, J. (1982), Exchange rate determination and adjustment (Preager, New York).

Bilson, J.F.O. (1978a), "Rational expectations and the exchange rate", in: J.A. Frenkel, and H.G. Johnson, eds., The economics of exchange rates: Selected studies (Addison-Wesley, Reading, Mass.) 75–96.

Bilson, J.F.O. (1978b), "The monetary approach to the exchange rate: Some empirical evidence", International Monetary Fund Staff Papers, 25:48–75.

Bilson, J.F.O. (1981), "The 'speculative efficiency' hypothesis", Journal of Business, 54:435–451.

Black, S.W. (1973), "International money markets and flexible exchange rates", Princeton Studies in International Finance, 32.

Blejer, M. (1977), "The short-run dynamics of prices and the balance of payments", American Economic Review, 67:419–428.

Blejer, M. (1978), "Exchange restrictions and the monetary approach to the exchange rate", in: J.A. Frenkel and H.G. Johnson, eds., The economics of exchange rates: Selected studies (Addison Wesley, Reading, Mass.) 117–128.

Blejer, M. and L. Leiderman (1981), "A monetary approach to the crawling peg system: Theory and evidence", Journal of Political Economy, 89:132–151.

Boyer, R.S. (1975), "Commodity markets and bond markets in a small, fixed-exchange-rate economy", Canadian Journal of Economics, 8:1–23.

Branson, W.H. (1970), "Monetary policy and the new view of international capital movements", Brookings Papers of Economic Activity, 235–262.

Branson, W.H. (1976), "Portfolio equilibrium and monetary policy with foreign and non-traded assets", in: E. Claassen and P. Salin, eds., Recent issues in international monetary economics (North-Holland, Amsterdam) 239–250.

Branson, W.H. (1977), "Assets markets and relative prices in exchange rate determination", Sozialwissenschaftliche Annalen, 1:69–89.

Branson, W.H., H. Halttunen and P. Masson (1977), "Exchange rates in the short-run: The dollar-deutschemark rate", European Economic Review, 10:303–324.

Bruno, M. and J. Sachs (1982), "Energy and resource allocation: A dynamic model of the 'Dutch disease'", National Bureau of Economic Research, working paper no. 852.

Buiter, W. and M. Miller (1983), "Real exchange rate overshooting and the output cost of bringing down inflation: Some further results", in: J.A. Frenkel, ed., Exchange rates and international macroeconomics (University of Chicago Press, Chicago) 317–358.

Chen, C. (1973), "Diversified currency holdings and flexible exchange rates", Quarterly Journal of Economics, 87:96–111.

Chipman, J.S. (1978), "A reconsideration of the 'elasticity approach' to balance of payments theory", in: J.S. Dreyer, ed., Breadth and depth in economics: Fritz Machlup — the man and his ideas (D.C. Heath and Company, Lexington, Mass.) 49–85.

Chrystal, K.A. (1977), "Demand for international media of exchange", American Economic Review, 67:840–850.

Clements, K.W. and J.A. Frenkel (1980), "Exchange rates, money and relative prices: The dollar-pound in the 1920's", Journal of International Economics, 10:249–262.

Collery, A. (1971), "International adjustment, open economies, and the quantity theory of money", Princeton Studies in International Finance, 28.

Connolly, M. and D. Taylor (1976), "Testing the monetary approach to devaluation in developing countries", Journal of Political Economy, 84:849–860.

Cornell, B. (1977), "Spot rates, forward rates and exchange market efficiency", Journal of Financial Economics, 5:55–65.

Craig, G.A. (1981), "A monetary approach to the balance of trade", American Economic Review, 71:460–466.

de Macedo, J.B. and J. Barga (1982), "Portfolio diversification across currencies", in: R.N. Cooper, P.B. Kenen, J.B. de Macedo and J. van Ypersele, eds., The international monetary system under flexible exchange rates (Ballinger, Cambridge, Mass.) 69–100.

Dooley, M. and P. Isard (1981), "A portfolio balance model of exchange rates", Washington, D.C.: Board of Governors of the Federal Reserve System, International Finance Discussion Paper no. 141 (revised).

Dornbusch, R. (1971), "Notes on growth and the balance of payments", Canadian Journal of

Economics, 4:389–395.

Dornbusch, R. (1973a), "Currency depreciation, hoarding and relative prices", Journal of Political Economy, 81:893–915.

Dornbusch, R. (1973b), "Devaluation, money and non-traded goods", American Economic Review, 63:871–883.

Dornbusch, R. (1974), "Real and monetary aspects of the effects of exchange rate changes", in: R.Z. Aliber, ed., National monetary policies and the international financial system (University of Chicago Press, Chicago) 64–81.

Dornbusch, R. (1975), "A portfolio balance model of the open economy", Journal of Monetary Economics, 1:3–20.

Dornbusch, R. (1976a), "Capital mobility, flexible exchange rates and macroeconomic equilibrium", in: E. Claassen and P. Salin, eds., Recent issues in international monetary economics (North-Holland, Amsterdam) 29–48.

Dornbusch, R. (1976b), "The theory of flexible exchange rate regimes and macroeconomic policy", Scandinavian Journal of Economics, 78:255–275. Reprinted in: J.A. Frenkel and H.G. Johnson, eds., The economics of exchange rate: Selected studies (Addison-Wesley, Reading, Mass.) 27–46.

Dornbusch, R. (1976c), "Expectations and exchange rate dynamics", Journal of Political Economy, 84:1161–1176.

Dornbusch, R. (1977), "Capital mobility and portfolio balance", in: R.Z. Aliber, ed., The political economy of monetary reform (Osmun and Co., Montclair, N.Y.) 106–125.

Dornbusch, R. (1978), "Monetary policy under exchange rate flexibility", in: Managed exchange-rate flexibility: The recent experience, Federal Reserve Bank of Boston Conference Series, No. 20.

Dornbusch, R. (1980), Open economy macroeconomics (Basic Books, New York).

Dornbusch, R. and S. Fischer (1980), "Exchange rates and the current account", American Economic Review, 70:960–971.

Dornbusch, R. and M. Mussa (1975), "Consumption, real balances and the hoarding function", International Economic Review, 16:415–421.

Edwards, S. (1983), "Comments on 'an accounting framework and some issues for modelling how exchange rates respond to the news'", in: J.A. Frenkel, ed., Exchange rates and international macroeconomics (University of Chicago Press, Chicago) 56–61.

Fischer, S. (1977), "Long term contracts, rational expectations and the optimal policy rule", Journal of Political Economy, 85:191–206.

Fleming, J.M. (1962), "Domestic financial policies under fixed and under flexible exchange rates", International Monetary Fund Staff Papers, 9:369–379.

Flood, R. (1977), "Growth, prices, and the balance of payments", Canadian Journal of Economics, 10:193–207.

Flood, R. (1979), "Capital mobility and the choice of exchange rate system", International Economic Review, 20:405–416.

Flood, R.P. (1981), "Explanations of exchange-rate volatility and other regularities in some popular models of the foreign exchange market", in: K. Brunner and A.H. Meltzer, eds., Carnegie-Rochester Series on Public Policy (North-Holland, Amsterdam) 15:219–250.

Frankel, J.A. (1979), "On the mark: A theory of floating exchange rates based on real interest differentials", American Economic Review, 69:610–622.

Frankel, J.A. (1982), "A test of perfect substitutability in the foreign exchange market", Southern Economic Journal, 49:406–416.

Frankel, J.A. (1984), "On the mark, pound, franc, yen and canadian dollar", in: J.F.O. Bilson and R. Marston, eds., Exchange rate theory and policy (University of Chicago Press, Chicago).

Frenkel, J.A. (1971), "A theory of money, trade and the balance of payments in a model of accumulation", Journal of International Economics, 1:159–187.

Frenkel, J.A. (1976a), "A monetary approach to the exchange rate: Doctrinal aspects and empirical evidence", Scandinavian Journal of Economics, 78:200–224. Reprinted in: J.A. Frenkel and H.G. Johnson, eds., The economics of exchange rates: Selected studies (Addison-Wesley, Reading, Mass., 1978) 1–25.

Frenkel, J.A. (1976b), "Adjustment mechanisms and the monetary approach to the balance of payments: A doctrinal perspective", in: E. Claassen and P. Salin, eds., Recent issues in international monetary economics (North-Holland, Amsterdam, 1976) 29–48.

Frenkel, J.A. (1976c), "A dynamic analysis of the balance of payments in a model of accumulation", in: J.A. Frenkel and H.G. Johnson, eds., The monetary approach to the balance of payments (Allen and Unwin, London, and University of Toronto Press, Toronto) 109–146.

Frenkel, J.A. (1977), "The forward exchange rate, expectations and the demand for money: The German hyperinflation", American Economic Review, 67:653–670.

Frenkel, J.A. (1978), "Purchasing power parity: Doctrinal perspective and evidence from the 1920's", Journal of International Economics, 8:169–191.

Frenkel, J.A. (1979), "Further evidence on expectations and the demand for money during the German hyperinflation", Journal of Monetary Economics, 5:81–96.

Frenkel, J.A. (1980a), "Exchange rates, prices and money: Lessons from the 1920's", American Economic Review, 70:235–242.

Frenkel, J.A. (1980b), "The forward premium on foreign exchange and currency depreciation during the German hyperinflation", American Economic Review, 70:771–775.

Frenkel, J.A. (1981a), "The collapse of purchasing power parities during the 1970's", European Economic Review, 7:145–165.

Frenkel, J.A. (1981b), "Flexible exchange rates, prices and the role of 'news': Lessons from the 1970's", Journal of Political Economy, 89:665–705.

Frenkel, J.A., ed., (1983), Exchange rates and international macroeconomics (University of Chicago Press, Chicago).

Frenkel, J.A. and Kenneth C. Clements (1982), "Exchange rates in the 1920's: A monetary approach", in: M. Flanders and A. Razin, eds., Development in an inflationary world (Academic Press, New York) 283–318.

Frenkel, J.A. and H.G. Johnson (1976a), "The monetary approach to the balance of payments: Essential concepts and historical origins", in: J.A. Frenkel and H.G. Johnson, eds., The monetary approach to the balance of payments (Allen & Unwin, London, and University of Toronto Press, Toronto) 21–45.

Frenkel, J.A. and H.G. Johnson, eds., (1976b), The monetary approach to the balance of payments (Allen & Unwin, London and University of Toronto Press, Toronto).

Frenkel, J.A. and H.G. Johnson, eds., (1978), The economics of exchange rates: Selected studies (Addison-Wesley, Reading, Mass.).

Frenkel, J.A. and R.M. Levich (1975), "Covered interest arbitrage: Unexploited profits?", Journal of Political Economy, 83:325–338.

Frenkel, J.A. and R.M. Levich (1977), "Transaction costs and interest arbitrage: Tranquil versus turbulent periods", Journal of Political Economy, 85:1209–1226.

Frenkel, J.A. and M.L. Mussa (1980), "The efficiency of foreign exchange markets and measures of turbulence", American Economic Review, 70:374–381.

Frenkel, J.A. and M.L. Mussa (1981), "Monetary and fiscal policies in an open economy", American Economic Review, 71:253–258.

Frenkel, J.A. and A. Razin (1980), "Stochastic prices and tests of efficiency of foreign exchange markets", Economics Letters, 6:165–170.

Frenkel, J.A. and C.A. Rodriguez (1975), "Portfolio equilibrium and the balance of payments: A monetary approach", American Economic Review, 65:674–688.

Frenkel, J.A. and C.A. Rodriguez (1982), "Exchange rate dynamics and the overshooting hypothesis", International Monetary Fund Staff Papers, 29:1–30.

Genberg, H. (1978), "Purchasing power parity under fixed and flexible exchange rates", Journal of International Economics, 8:247–276.

Genberg, H. (1984), "Properties of innovations in spot and forward exchange rates and the role of money supply processes", in: J.F.O. Bilson and R. Marston, eds., Exchange rate theory and policy (University of Chicago Press, Chicago).

Gervaise, I. (1720), The system or theory of the trade of the world. Reprinted in: Economic Tracts (Johns Hopkins Press, Baltimore, MD).

Giddy, I.H. and G. Dufey (1975), "The random behavior of flexible exchange rates", Journal of International Business Studies, 6:1–32.

Girton, L. and D. Roper (1977), "A monetary model of exchange market pressure applied to the postwar Canadian experience", American Economic Review, 67:537–548.

Girton, L. and D. Roper (1981), "Theory and implications of currency substitution", Journal of

Money, Credit and Banking, 13:12–30.

Hahn, F.H. (1959), "The balance of payments in a monetary economy", Review of Economic Studies, 26:110–125.

Hahn, F.H. (1977), "The monetary approach to the balance of payments", Journal of International Economics, 7:231–249.

Hakkio, C.S. (1979), "Expectations and the foreign exchange market", unpublished Ph.D. dissertation, University of Chicago.

Hansen, L.P. and R.S. Hodrick (1980), "Forward exchange rates as optimal predictors of future spot rates: An econometric analysis", Journal of Political Economy, 88:829–853.

Hansen, L.P. and R.S. Hodrick (1983), "Risk averse speculation in the forward foreign exchange market: An econometric analysis of linear models", in: J.A. Frenkel, ed., Exchange rates and international macroeconomics (University of Chicago Press, Chicago) 113–142.

Hawtrey, R.G. (1932), The art of central banking (Longmans, Green and Company, London).

Hawtrey, R.G. (1950), Currency and credit (Longmans, Green and Company, London) 1st edition, 1919; 4th edition, 1950.

Helpman, E. (1981), "An exploration in the theory of exchange rate regimes", Journal of Political Economy, 89:865–890.

Helpman, E. and A. Razin (1982), "Dynamics of floating exchange rate regime", Journal of Political Economy, 90:728–754.

Henderson, D. (1977), "Modeling the interdependence of national money and capital markets", American Economic Review, 67:190–199.

Hodrick, R.J. (1978), "An empirical analysis of the monetary approach to the determination of the exchange rate", in: J.A. Frenkel and J.G. Johnson, eds., The economics of exchange rates: Selected studies (Addison-Wesley, Reading, Mass.) 97–116.

Hsieh, D.A. (1982), "Tests of rational expectations and no risk premium in forward exchange markets", National Bureau of Economic Research, working paper no. 843.

Hume, D. (1752), Political Discourses. Reprinted in: E. Rotwein, David Hume: Writings on economics (Nelson, London, 1955).

International Monetary Fund (1977), The monetary approach to the balance of payments (International Monetary Fund, Washington, D.C.).

Isard, P. (1977), "How far can we push the 'law of one price'?", American Economic Review, 67:942–948.

Isard, P. (1978), "Exchange rate determination: A survey of popular views and recent models", Princeton Studies in International Finance, 42.

Isard, P. (1983), "An accounting framework and some issues for modelling how exchange rates respond to the news", in: J.A. Frenkel, ed., Exchange rates and international macroeconomics (University of Chicago Press, Chicago) 19–56.

Johnson, H.G. (1956), "The transfer problem and exchange stability", Journal of Political Economy, 59:212–225.

Johnson, H.G. (1958), "Towards a general theory of the balance of payments", in his International trade and economic growth (Harvard University Press, Cambridge) 153–168.

Johnson, H.G. (1976a), "The monetary approach to balance of payments theory", in: J.A. Frenkel and H.G. Johnson, eds., The monetary approach to the balance of payments (Allen and Unwin, London and University of Toronto Press, Toronto) 147–167.

Johnson, H.G. (1976b), "The monetary theory of balance of payment policies", in: J.A. Frenkel and H.G. Johnson, eds., The monetary approach to the balance of payments (Allen and Unwin, London and University of Toronto Press, Toronto) 262–284.

Katseli-Papaefstratiou, L.T. (1979), "The reemergence of the purchasing power parity doctrine in the 1970's", Special Papers in International Economics, No. 13, Princeton University.

Kimbrough, K.P. (1980), "Real aspects of the monetary approach to the exchange rate", unpublished Ph.D. dissertation, University of Chicago.

Kohlhagen, S.W. (1978), The behavior of foreign exchange markets—a critical survey of the empirical literature. Monograph-3, Monograph Series in Finance and Economics (Salomon Brothers Center, New York University).

Komiya, R. (1969), "Economic growth and the balance of payments: A monetary approach", Journal of Political Economy, 77:35–48.

Kouri, P. (1976), "The exchange rate and the balance of payments in the short run and in the long run: A monetary approach", Scandinavian Journal of Economics, 78:280–304.

Kouri, P. and M. Porter (1974), "International capital flows and portfolio equilibrium", Journal of Political Economy, 82:443–467.

Kreinin, E.M. and L. Officer (1978), "The monetary approach to the balance of payments: A survey", Princeton Studies in International Finance, 43.

Krugman, P. (1977), "The efficiency of the forward exchange market: Evidence from the twenties and the seventies", unpublished manuscript, Yale University.

Leiderman, L. (1979), "Expectations and output-inflation tradeoffs in a fixed exchange-rate economy", Journal of Political Economy, 87:1285–1306.

Levich, R.M. (1979), "The efficiency of markets for foreign exchange", in: J.A. Frenkel and R. Dornbusch, eds., International economic policy: Theory and evidence (Johns Hopkins University Press, Baltimore) 246–267.

Lucas, R.E., Jr. (1972), "Expectations and the neutrality of money", Journal of Economic Theory, 4:103–124.

Lucas, R.E., Jr. (1973), "Some international evidence on output-inflation tradeoffs", American Economic Review, 63:326–334.

Lucas, R.E., Jr. (1975), "An equilibrium model of the business cycle", Journal of Political Economy, 83:1113–1144.

Lucas, R.E., Jr. (1982), "Interest rates and currency prices in a two-country world", Journal of Monetary Economics, 10:335–359.

Machlup, F. (1949), "The theory of foreign exchanges", Economica, 6:375–397.

Magee, S.P. (1976), "The empirical evidence on the monetary approach to the balance of payments and exchange rates", American Economic Review, 66:163–170.

Marion, N.P. (1981), "Anticipated and unanticipated oil price increases", National Bureau of Economic Research, working paper no. 759.

McKinnon, R.I. (1969), "Portfolio balance and international payments adjustment", in: A.K. Swoboda and R.A. Mundell, eds., Monetary problems of the international economy (University of Chicago Press, Chicago) 199–234.

Meade, J.E. (1951), The theory of international economic policy, Vol. I: The balance of payments (Oxford University Press, London, New York, Toronto).

Meese, R. and K. Rogoff (1983), "The out-of-sample failure of empirical exchange rate models: Sampling error or misspecification", in: J.A. Frenkel, ed., Exchange rates and international macroeconomics (University of Chicago Press, Chicago) 67–105.

Meese, R. and K. Singleton (1980), "Rational expectations and the volatility of floating exchange rates", working paper, Board of Governors of the Federal Reserve, Washington, D.C.

Metzler, L.A. (1951), "Wealth savings and the rate of interest", Journal of Political Economy, 59:93–116.

Miles, M.A. (1978), "Currency substitution, flexible exchange rates and monetary independence", American Economic Review, 68:428–436.

Miles, M.A. (1979), "The effects of devaluation on the trade balance and the balance of payments: Some new results", Journal of Political Economy, 87:600–620.

Mill, J.S. (1893), Principles of political economy, 5th edition (Appleton and Company, New York).

Mundell, R.A. (1961), "The international disequilibrium system", Kyklos, 14:154–172. Reprinted in: R.A. Mundell, ed., International economics (Macmillan, New York, 1968) Chapter 15.

Mundell, R.A. (1963), "Capital mobility and stabilization policy under fixed and flexible exchange rates", Canadian Journal of Economics and Political Science, 29:472–485. Reprinted in: R.A. Mundell, ed., International economics (Macmillan, New York, 1968) Chapter 18.

Mundell, R.A. (1968a), "Barter theory and the monetary mechanism of adjustment", in: R.A. Mundell, ed., International economics (Macmillan, New York, 1968).

Mundell, R.A. (1968b), "Growth and the balance of payments", in: R.A. Mundell, ed., International economics (Macmillan, New York, 1968) Chapter 9.

Mundell, R.A. (1968c), International economics (Macmillan, New York).

Mundell, R.A. (1971), Monetary theory (Goodyear Publishing Company, Pacific Palisades, California).

Mussa, M. (1974), "A monetary approach to balance of payments analysis", Journal of Money, Credit and Banking, 6:333–351.

Mussa, M. (1976a), "Tariffs and the balance of payments", in: J.A. Frenkel and H.G. Johnson, eds., The monetary approach to the balance of payments (Allen and Unwin, London and University of Toronto Press, Toronto) 187–221.

Mussa, M. (1976b), "The exchange rate, the balance of payments and monetary and fiscal policy under a regime of controlled financing", Scandinavian Journal of Economics, 78:229–248. Reprinted in: J.A. Frenkel and H.G. Johnson, eds., The economics of exchange rates: Selected studies (Addison-Wesley, Reading, Mass.) 187–221.

Mussa, M. (1976c), "Our recent experience with fixed and flexible exchange rates: A comment", in: K. Brunner and A. Meltzer, eds., Institutional arrangements and the inflation problem, Vol. 3 of the Carnegie Rochester Conference Series on Public Policy, a supplementary series to the Journal of Monetary Economics, 123–141.

Mussa, M. (1977), "Exchange rate uncertainty: Causes, consequences and policy implications", unpublished manuscript, University of Chicago.

Mussa, M. (1979a), "Macroeconomic interdependence and the exchange rate regime", in: R. Dornbusch and J.A. Frenkel, eds., International economic policy: Theory and evidence (Johns Hopkins University Press, Baltimore) 160–204.

Mussa, M. (1979b), "Empirical regularities in the behavior of exchange rates and theories of the foreign exchange market", Vol. 11 of the Carnegie-Rochester Conference Series on Public Policy, a supplementary series to the Journal of Monetary Economics, 9–57.

Mussa, M. (1980), "The role of the current account in exchange rate dynamics", unpublished manuscript, University of Chicago.

Mussa, M. (1982), "A model of exchange rate dynamics", Journal of Political Economy, 90:74–104.

Mussa, M. (1984), "The theory of exchange rate determination", in: J.F.O. Bilson and R. Marston, eds., Exchange rate theory and policy (University of Chicago Press, Chicago).

Neary, P. and D.D. Purvis (1983), "Real adjustment and exchange rate dynamics", in: J.A. Frenkel, ed., Exchange rates and international macroeconomics (University of Chicago Press, Chicago) 285–308.

Niehans, J. (1977), "Exchange rate dynamics with stock/flow interaction", Journal of Political Economy, 85: 1245–1257.

Obstfeld, M. (1980), "Imperfect asset substitutability and monetary policy under fixed exchange rates", Journal of International Economics, 10:177–200.

Obstfeld, M. (1982), "Can we sterilize? Theory and evidence", American Economic Review, 72:45–50.

Officer, L.H. (1976), "The purchasing-power-parity theory of exchange rates: A review article", International Monetary Fund Staff Papers, 23:1–61.

Officer, L.H. and T.D. Willett (1970), "The covered-arbitrage schedule: A critical survey of recent developments", Journal of Money, Credit and Banking, 2:247–257.

Phelps, E.S. and J.B. Taylor (1977), "Stabilizing powers of monetary policy under rational expectations", Journal of Political Economy, 85:163–190.

Poole, W. (1967), "Speculative prices as random walks: An analysis of ten time series of flexible exchange rates", Southern Economic Journal, 33:468–478.

Purvis, D.D. (1972), "More on growth and the balance of payments: The adjustment process", Canadian Journal of Economics, 5:531–540.

Ricardo, D. (1811), The high price of bullion. London. Reprinted in: E.C. Connor, ed., Economic essays by David Ricardo (Kelley, New York, 1970).

Ricardo, D. (1821), Principles of political economy and taxation. E.C. Donner, ed. (G. Gell and Sons, London, 1911).

Rodriguez, C.A. (1976a), "Money and wealth in an open economy income-expenditure model", in: J.A. Frenkel and H.G. Johnson, eds., The monetary approach to the balance payments (Allen and Unwin, London and University of Toronto Press, Toronto) 222–236.

Rodriguez, C.A. (1976b), "The terms of trade and the balance of payments in the short-run", American Economic Review, 66:710–716.

Rodriguez, C.A. (1980), "The role of trade flows in exchange rate determination: A rational expectations approach", Journal of Political Economy, 88:1148–1158.

Sachs, J.D. (1981), "The current account and macroeconomic adjustment in the 1970's", Brookings Papers on Economic Activity, no. 1, 201–268.

Saidi, N.H. (1980), "Fluctuating exchange rates and the international transmission of economic disturbances", Journal of Money Credit and Banking, 12:575–591.

Shafer, J.R. (1980), "Flexible exchange rates, capital flows and current account adjustment", unpublished manuscript, Board of Governors of the Federal Reserve System, Washington, D.C.

Stockman, A.C. (1976), "Monetary cross-substitution and the international transmission of monetary shocks under floating exchange rates", unpublished manuscript, University of Chicago.

Stockman, A.C. (1978), "Risk, information and forward exchange rates", in: J.A. Frenkel and H.G. Johnson, eds., The economics of exchange rates: Selected studies (Addison-Wesley, Reading, Mass.) 159–178.

Stockman, A.C. (1980), "A theory of exchange rate determination", Journal of Political Economy, 88:673–698.

Svennsson, L.E.O. and A. Razin (1983), "The terms of trade and the current account: The Harberger Laursen–Metzler effect", Journal of Political Economy, 91:97–125.

Swoboda, A.K. (1972), "Equilibrium, quasi-equilibrium, and macroeconomic policy under fixed exchange rates", Quarterly Journal of Economics, 86:162–171.

Swoboda, A.K. (1973), "Monetary policy under fixed exchange rates: Effectiveness, the speed of adjustment, and proper use", Economica, 40:136–154.

Swoboda, A.K. and R. Dornbusch, "Adjustment, policy and monetary equilibrium in a two-country model", in: M.G. Connolly and A.K. Swoboda, eds., International trade and money (Allen and Unwin, London) 225–261.

Taylor, J.B. (1980a), "Aggregate dynamics and staggered contracts", Journal of Political Economy, 88:1–23.

Taylor, J.B. (1980b), "Recent developments in the theory of stabilization policy", in: Stabilization policies: Lessons from the 1970's and implications for the 1980's. Center for the Study of American Business, Washington University, St. Louis, Missouri.

Tsiang, S.C. (1977), "The monetary theoretic foundation of the modern monetary approach to the balance of payments", Oxford Economic Papers, 29:319–338.

Viner, J. (1937), Studies in the theory of international trade (Harper and Brothers, New York).

Whitman, M.V.N. (1975), "Global monetarism and the monetary approach to the balance of payments", Brookings Papers on Economic Activity, 3:491–555.

Wilson, C.A. (1979), "Anticipated shocks and exchange rate dynamics", Journal of Political Economy, 87:639–647.

Chapter 15

THE SPECIFICATION AND INFLUENCE OF ASSET MARKETS

WILLIAM H. BRANSON

Princeton University and National Bureau of Economic Research

and

DALE W. HENDERSON*

Board of Governors of the Federal Reserve System and Georgetown University

Contents

*The authors appreciate helpful comments made by Michael Adler, Shoichi Katayama, Rene Stulz, and participants at the conference held at Princeton University in May 1982 to discuss preliminary drafts of Chapters 13–23 of this Handbook, especially Peter Kenen, Jorge de Macedo, and the two discussants of this chapter, Jacob Frenkel and Tim Padmore. This paper represents the views of the authors and should not be interpreted as reflecting the views of the Board of Governors of the Federal Reserve System or other members of its staff.

Handbook of International Economics, vol. II, edited by R.W. Jones and P.B. Kenen
© *Elsevier Science Publishers B.V., 1985*

1. Introduction

This chapter is a discussion of two complementary approaches to the analysis of asset markets in open economies.[1] Section 2 is devoted to portfolio balance models with postulated asset demands, asset demands broadly consistent with but not directly implied by microeconomic theory. Some implications of the microeconomic theory of portfolio selection for asset demands are spelled out in Section 3. Section 4 contains some conclusions.

2. Portfolio balance models with postulated asset demands

2.1. Overview

During the 1970s and 1980s there has been a thorough reworking of macroeconomic theory for open economies using a portfolio balance approach.[2] According to this approach, equilibrium in financial markets occurs when the available stocks of national moneys and other financial assets are equal to the stock demands for these assets based on current wealth, and wealth accumulation continues only until current wealth is equal to desired wealth.

In this section we review some of the important results that have been obtained using portfolio balance models. Although these models were originally developed to study movements of financial capital, variations in interest rates, and changes in stocks of international reserves under fixed exchange rates, they were quickly adapted to study movements of financial capital, variations in interest rates, and changes in the exchange rate under flexible exchange rates. Our discussion reflects the emphasis placed on the case of flexible exchange rates in more recent applications of portfolio balance models.

The builders of portfolio balance models have employed "postulated" asset demand functions. By proceeding in this way, they have not denied the desirability of deriving asset demands from explicit utility maximizing behavior. Indeed, they have attempted to establish the plausibility of their asset demands by

---

[1]Almost all the contributions to the literature on asset markets in open economies in the references of this chapter were published in 1975 or later. Many important contributions were published before 1975. Bryant (1975) provides an excellent assessment of empirical research on financial capital flows up to the mid 1970s. He includes in his references most of the important theoretical and empirical analyses dealing specifically with asset markets in open economies that were available when he wrote.

[2] The portfolio balance approach to macroeconomic modeling was developed by Metzler (1951) and Tobin (1969).

appealing to microeconomic theory – in the case of non-monetary assets to the theory of portfolio selection and in the case of monetary assets to the theory of money demand. There is widespread agreement on the importance of exploring the implications of macroeconomic asset demand functions derived from explicit utility maximizing behavior. A new sense of urgency has been added by the argument that, in general, utility maximizing behavior leads to modifications in asset demands when the policy regime changes.[3] While this exploration proceeds, results derived using postulated asset demands can best be regarded as suggestive hypotheses to be subjected to close scrutiny using asset demand functions with firmer microeconomic foundations.

After laying out a general specification of asset markets (Section 2.2), we summarize the fundamental short-run results of portfolio balance models using a very basic specification of asset markets (Section 2.3). Then, we supply rudimentary specifications of a balance of payments equation and goods market equilibrium conditions (Section 2.4) so that we can trace out the dynamic distribution effects of the trade account under static and rational expectations with both fixed goods prices (Section 2.5) and flexible goods prices (Section 2.6).

2.2. The general specification of asset markets

The model contains four assets: home money, foreign money, home (currency) securities, and foreign (currency) securities.[4] In the general specification it is assumed that residents of both countries hold all four assets. Home net wealth (W) and foreign net wealth ($E\overset{*}{W}$), both measured in units of home currency are given by

$$W = M + B + E(N + F), \qquad E\overset{*}{W} = \overset{*}{M} + \overset{*}{B} + E(\overset{*}{N} + \overset{*}{F}), \tag{2.1}$$

where M, B, N and F ($\overset{*}{M}$, $\overset{*}{B}$, $\overset{*}{N}$, and $\overset{*}{F}$) represent home (foreign) net private holdings of home money, home securities, foreign money, and foreign securities. E is the exchange rate defined as the home currency price of foreign currency.

Home (foreign) net wealth is allocated among the four financial assets:

$$W \equiv m(\cdot) + n(\cdot) + b(\cdot) + f(\cdot), \qquad E\overset{*}{W} \equiv \overset{*}{m}(\cdot) + \overset{*}{n}(\cdot) + \overset{*}{b}(\cdot) + \overset{*}{f}(\cdot), \tag{2.2}$$

where m, n, b, and f ($\overset{*}{m}$, $\overset{*}{n}$, $\overset{*}{b}$, and $\overset{*}{f}$) represent home (foreign) residents'

---

[3] This argument is often referred to as the Lucas (1976) critique.

[4] Throughout the rest of this paper home currency securities and foreign currency securities are referred to as home securities and foreign securities, respectively. In order to simplify the analysis, we assume that there are no home and foreign capital stocks and, therefore, no equity claims on those capital stocks. Models with capital stocks and equity claims are discussed by Bruce and Purvis in Chapter 16 and by Obstfeld and Stockman in Chapter 17 of this Handbook.

demands for home money, foreign money, home securities, and foreign securities, all measured in units of home currency.

The home currency value of the stocks of home money ($\tilde{M}$), foreign money ($E\tilde{N}$), home securities ($\tilde{B}$), and foreign securities ($E\tilde{F}$) available for private agents to hold are assumed to be positive:

$$\tilde{M} = M + \overset{*}{M} > 0, \qquad E\tilde{N} = E(N + \overset{*}{N}) > 0,$$

$$\tilde{B} = B + \overset{*}{B} > 0, \qquad E\tilde{F} = E(F + \overset{*}{F}) > 0. \tag{2.3}$$

The equilibrium conditions for the four asset markets are given by

$$m\left(0, \overset{-}{\varepsilon}, \overset{-}{i}\,\overset{-}{i}+\varepsilon, \overset{+}{PX}, \overset{+}{Q}, \overset{+}{W}\right) + \overset{*}{m}\left(-\varepsilon, 0, i-\varepsilon, \overset{+}{i}, E\overset{+}{P}Y, E\overset{+}{Q}, E\overset{+}{W}\right) - \tilde{M} = 0, \tag{2.4a}$$

$$n\left(0, \overset{+}{\varepsilon}, \overset{-}{i}, \overset{-}{i}+\varepsilon, \overset{+}{PX}, \overset{+}{Q}, \overset{+}{W}\right) + \overset{*}{n}\left(-\overset{-}{\varepsilon}, 0, i-\varepsilon, \overset{-}{i}, E\overset{+}{P}Y, E\overset{+}{Q}, E\overset{+}{W}\right) - E\tilde{N} = 0, \tag{2.4b}$$

$$b\left(0, \overset{-}{\varepsilon}, \overset{+}{i}, \overset{-}{i}+\varepsilon, \overset{-}{PX}, \overset{-}{Q}, \overset{+}{W}\right) + \overset{*}{b}\left(-\varepsilon, 0, i-\varepsilon, \overset{+}{i}, E\overset{-}{P}Y, E\overset{-}{Q}, E\overset{+}{W}\right) - \tilde{B} = 0, \tag{2.4c}$$

$$f\left(0, \overset{-}{\varepsilon}, \overset{-}{i}, \overset{+}{i}+\varepsilon, \overset{-}{PX}, \overset{-}{Q}, \overset{+}{W}\right) + \overset{*}{f}\left(-\varepsilon, 0, i-\varepsilon, \overset{+}{i}, E\overset{-}{P}Y, E\overset{-}{Q}, E\overset{+}{W}\right) - E\tilde{F} = 0. \tag{2.4d}$$

The first four arguments in each home (foreign) asset demand function are the nominal returns associated with home money, foreign money, home securities, and foreign securities measured in home (foreign) currency.[5] ε is the expected rate of depreciation of the home currency; it is equal to zero under static expectations and to the actual rate of depreciation ($\dot{E}/E$) under rational expectations (perfect foresight).[6] The fifth argument in each home (foreign) asset demand function is

---

[5] We assume that the sum of the partial derivatives of each asset demand function with respect to its first four arguments is zero so that, for example $\Sigma_{k=0}^{4} m_k = 0$. Under this assumption expressing any asset demand as a function of nominal returns is equivalent to expressing it as a function of real returns since the expected rate of change of the price of a country's consumption bundle in terms of its currency can be subtracted from all nominal returns without changing the value of the asset demand.

[6] Precisely, the assumption that expectations are static implies that ε is exogenous. However, it is usual to specify paths for the exogenous variables other than ε that lead to a unique value for the steady state actual rate of depreciation, and it is natural to set ε equal to that value. Throughout this section it is assumed that the asset stocks available for the public to hold do not change continuously over time ($\dot{M} = \dot{N} = \dot{B} = \dot{F} = 0$). Steady states are stationary states in which the actual rate of

home (foreign) nominal output measured in home currency. P ($E\overset{*}{P}$) is the home currency price of the single good produced in the home (foreign) country. X (Y) is real output of the home (foreign) good. The sixth argument in each home (foreign) asset demand function is the price of the home (foreign) consumption bundle measured in home currency. Q and $E\overset{*}{Q}$ are given by

$$Q = P^h(E\overset{*}{P})^{1-h}, \qquad E\overset{*}{Q} = P^{\overset{*}{h}}(E\overset{*}{P})^{1-\overset{*}{h}}. \tag{2.5}$$

h ($\overset{*}{h}$) is the constant weight of the price of the home good in the price of the home (foreign) consumption bundle. The seventh argument in each home (foreign) asset demand function is home (foreign) wealth measured in home currency.

The signs of the responses of asset demands to changes in the variables on which they depend are indicated by the signs over those variables. The signs over the nominal rates of return reflect the assumption that residents of both countries regard all the assets they hold as strict gross substitutes. The signs over nominal incomes and price indices reflect the assumption that residents of both countries hold both moneys for transactions purposes. The signs over nominal wealths reflect the assumption that all assets are "normal" assets. In the special case considered below some variables do not affect some asset demands.

Equations (2.2) imply that the asset demand functions of equations (2.4) are subject to familiar restrictions:

$$m_k + n_k + b_k + f_k \equiv 0, \quad k = 1, \ldots, 6; \qquad m_7 + n_7 + b_7 + f_7 \equiv 1; \tag{2.6a}$$

$$\overset{*}{m}_k + \overset{*}{n}_k + \overset{*}{b}_k + \overset{*}{f}_k \equiv 0, \quad k = 1, \ldots, 6; \qquad \overset{*}{m}_7 + \overset{*}{n}_7 + \overset{*}{b}_7 + \overset{*}{f}_7 \equiv 1. \tag{2.6b}$$

The assumption that private agents do not have money illusion implies that all asset demands must be homogenous of degree one in all variables measured in home currency:

$$m \equiv m_5 PX + m_6 Q + m_7 W, \qquad \overset{*}{m} \equiv \overset{*}{m}_5 E\overset{*}{P}Y + \overset{*}{m}_6 E\overset{*}{Q} + \overset{*}{m}_7 E\overset{*}{W}, \tag{2.7a}$$

$$n \equiv n_5 PX + n_6 Q + n_7 W, \qquad \overset{*}{n} \equiv \overset{*}{n}_5 E\overset{*}{P}Y + \overset{*}{n}_6 E\overset{*}{Q} + \overset{*}{n}_7 E\overset{*}{W}, \tag{2.7b}$$

$$b \equiv b_5 PX + b_6 Q + b_7 W, \qquad \overset{*}{b} \equiv \overset{*}{b}_5 E\overset{*}{P}Y + \overset{*}{b}_6 E\overset{*}{Q} + \overset{*}{b}_7 E\overset{*}{W}, \tag{2.7c}$$

$$f \equiv f_5 PX + f_6 Q + f_7 W, \qquad \overset{*}{f} \equiv \overset{*}{f}_5 E\overset{*}{P}Y + \overset{*}{f}_6 E\overset{*}{Q} + \overset{*}{f}_7 E\overset{*}{W}. \tag{2.7d}$$

Only three of the four asset market equilibrium conditions are independent. Eqs. (2.3) together with eqs. (2.1) imply that world wealth measured in home currency is equal to the sum of the stocks of all financial assets available for

---

depreciation is equal to zero, so it makes sense to set ε equal to zero under static expectations. Kouri (1976) develops a model in which residents of the home country face a fixed foreign currency price of the single world good and allocate their wealth between home and foreign money. He sets the exogenous expected rate of depreciation equal to the exogenous positive rate of growth of home money under static expectations.

private agents to hold. Eqs. (2.2) imply that the sum of all asset demands is identically equal to world wealth. Thus, the sum of all the excess demands given by eqs. (2.4) is identically equal to zero. In the algebraic analysis below attention is focused on the markets for home money, foreign money, and home securities.

2.3. The basic asset market specification

Many of the results that have been derived from portfolio balance models with postulated asset demands can be illustrated using a basic asset market specification. The basic specification is obtained from the general specification by imposing five simplifying assumptions. First, residents of neither country hold the other country's money; that is, there is no "currency substitution" ($\dot{M} = N = \dot{m} = n = \dot{m}_k = n_k = 0$, $k = 1, \ldots, 7$; $m_2 = b_2 = f_2 = 0$; $\dot{n}_1 = \dot{b}_1 = \dot{f}_1 = 0$).[7] Second, in each country residents' demand for money is independent of the return on the security denominated in the other country's currency ($m_4 = \dot{n}_3 = 0$). Third, in each country all changes in residents' demand for money resulting from changes in their nominal income and the price of their consumption bundle are matched by changes in their demand for the security denominated in their country's currency ($b_5 = -m_5$, $b_6 = -m_6$, $\dot{f}_5 = -\dot{n}_5$, and $\dot{f}_6 = -\dot{n}_6$). Fourth, in each country residents' demand for money is independent of nominal wealth ($m_7 = \dot{n}_7 = 0$). Fifth, in each country residents' demand for money is unit elastic with respect to their nominal income ($m = m_5 PX$, $\dot{n} = \dot{n}_5 EPY$).

The first and second assumptions imply that in each country the responsivenesses of residents' demands for the two securities to changes in the return on the security denominated in the other country's currency are equal and opposite in sign ($f_4 = -b_4$ and $\dot{f}_3 = -\dot{b}_3$). The first and third assumptions imply that in each country residents' demand for the security denominated in the other country's currency is independent of their nominal income and the price of their consumption bundle ($\dot{f}_5 = \dot{f}_6 = \dot{b}_5 = \dot{b}_6 = 0$). The third and fourth assumptions taken together with the homogeneity assumption embodied in eqs. (2.7) imply that the fraction of any increase in wealth allocated by residents of each country to securities denominated in their country's currency is equal to the ratio of their total holdings of assets denominated in their country's currency to their wealth [$b_7 = (M + B)/W$ and $\dot{f}_7 = (\dot{N} + \dot{F})/\dot{W}$]. That is, in each country the sum of residents' demands for assets denominated in a given currency is homogeneous of

---

[7]Models that allow for currency substitution have been constructed by Girton and Roper (1981), Kareken and Wallace (1981), Lapan and Enders (1980), and Nickelsburg (1983) among others. In most contributions currency substitution is defined as substitution among national moneys defined as currency and coin plus deposits that bear nonmarket related or zero rates of interest. According to Girton and Roper, currency substitution warrants special study because moneys are the only financial assets that have their stated returns, if any, fixed in terms of themselves. Girton and Roper employ postulated money demand functions. Kareken and Wallace, Lapan and Enders, and Nickelsburg assume that moneys are the only stores of value in models with overlapping generations composed of individuals who maximize explicit utility functions.

degree one in nominal wealth. The third, fourth and fifth assumptions taken together with the homogeneity assumption embodied in eqs. (2.7) imply that in each country residents' demands for money and securities denominated in their country's currency are independent of the price of their consumption bundle ($m_6 = b_6 = \tilde{n}_6 = \tilde{f}_6 = 0$).

Under the assumptions of the basic specification, eqs. (2.1) become eqs. (2.8):

$$W = M + B + EF, \qquad E\dot{W} = \dot{B} + E(\dot{N} + \dot{F}), \tag{2.8}$$

and eqs. (2.4) becomes eqs. (2.9):

$$m(\overset{0}{0}, \overset{-}{\varepsilon}, \overset{0}{i}, \overset{+}{\dot{i}+\varepsilon}, \overset{0}{PX}, \overset{0}{0}, W) - \tilde{M} = 0, \tag{2.9a}$$

$$\dot{n}(\overset{0}{-\varepsilon}, \overset{0}{0}, \overset{-}{i-\varepsilon}, \overset{+}{\dot{i}}, \overset{0}{E\dot{P}Y}, \overset{0}{E\dot{Q}}, E\dot{W}) - E\tilde{N} = 0, \tag{2.9b}$$

$$b(\overset{0}{0}, \overset{+}{\varepsilon}, \overset{-}{i}, \overset{-}{\dot{i}+\varepsilon}, \overset{0}{PX}, \overset{+}{Q}, W) + \dot{b}(\overset{0}{-\varepsilon}, \overset{+}{0}, \overset{-}{i-\varepsilon}, \overset{0}{\dot{i}}, \overset{0}{E\dot{P}Y}, \overset{+}{E\dot{Q}}, E\dot{W}) - \tilde{B} = 0, \tag{2.9c}$$

$$f(\overset{0}{0}, \overset{-}{\varepsilon}, \overset{+}{i}, \overset{0}{\dot{i}+\varepsilon}, \overset{0}{PX}, \overset{+}{Q}, W) + \dot{f}(\overset{0}{-\varepsilon}, \overset{-}{0}, \overset{+}{i-\varepsilon}, \overset{-}{\dot{i}}, \overset{0}{E\dot{P}Y}, \overset{+}{E\dot{Q}}, E\dot{W}) - E\tilde{F} = 0. \tag{2.9d}$$

Appropriate modifications are made in eqs. (2.2), (2.3), (2.6), and (2.7).

The impact effects of asset exchanges under static expectations ($\varepsilon = 0$) are of some interest in themselves.[8] In any case the analysis of impact effects with expected depreciation exogenous is one step in a complete analysis under rational expectations ($\varepsilon = \dot{E}/E$).

An initial asset market equilibrium is represented by the intersection of $\tilde{M}_0\tilde{M}_0$, $\tilde{B}_0\tilde{B}_0$, $\tilde{N}_0\tilde{N}_0$, and $\tilde{F}_0\tilde{F}_0$ in Figure 2.1. The unique home (foreign) interest rate that clears the home (foreign) money market, i_0 ($\dot{i}_0$), is indicated by the horizontal $\tilde{M}_0\tilde{M}_0$ (vertical $\tilde{N}_0\tilde{N}_0$) schedule. The pairs of i and $\dot{i}$ that clear the market for home (foreign) securities are represented by the upward sloping $\tilde{B}_0\tilde{B}_0(\tilde{F}_0\tilde{F}_0)$ schedule. An increase in the foreign interest rate lowers (raises) the demand for home (foreign) securities, so an increase in the home interest rate is required to raise (lower) the demand for home (foreign) securities if equilibrium is to be reestablished.

---

[8]If goods prices, outputs, and initial asset holdings are taken as exogenous, the model of eqs. (2.9) is representative of short-run portfolio balance models of international financial markets. Other models of this type are employed by Black (1973), Dooley and Isard (1982), Frankel (1983), Freedman (1977), Girton and Henderson (1977, 1976a, 1976b), Henderson (1979), Herring and Marston (1977a, 1977b), Hewson and Sakakibara (1975), Kouri and Porter (1974), and Marston (1980). When short-run portfolio balance models are used to analyze a regime of flexible exchange rates, it is usually assumed that exchange rate expectations are static or regressive.

The assumption that residents of both countries regard the assets they hold as strict gross substitutes implies that the $\tilde{B}\tilde{B}$ schedule must be flatter than the $\tilde{F}\tilde{F}$ schedule, as shown in Figure 2.1. If the $\tilde{B}\tilde{B}$ schedule were steeper, there would be excess supply of all four assets in the region to the northwest of a_0 between the $\tilde{B}_0\tilde{B}_0$ and $\tilde{F}_0\tilde{F}_0$ schedules. However, it has been established above that the sum of the excess demands for all four assets must be zero.

Depreciation of the home currency shifts both the $\tilde{B}\tilde{B}$ and $\tilde{F}\tilde{F}$ schedules down without affecting the $\tilde{M}\tilde{M}$ and $\tilde{N}\tilde{N}$ schedules. It raises not only the home currency value of wealth in both countries but also the home currency value of the supply of foreign securities. Thus, it creates excess demand for home securities

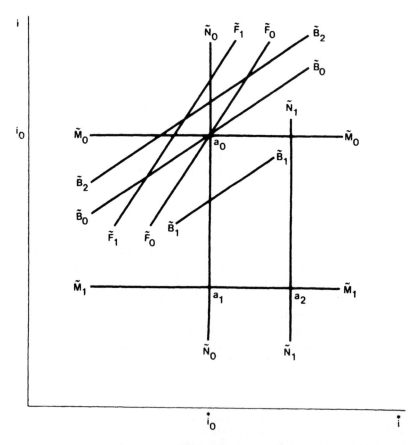

Figure 2.1

and excess supply of foreign securities.[9] A drop in i cuts (boosts) the demand for home (foreign) securities.

First consider an expansionary open market operation in the home country $(d\tilde{M} = -d\tilde{B} > 0)$. With the exchange rate fixed the $\tilde{M}\tilde{M}$ and $\tilde{B}\tilde{B}$ schedules shift down to $\tilde{M}_1\tilde{M}_1$ and $\tilde{B}_1\tilde{B}_1$. The shift in the $\tilde{B}\tilde{B}$ schedule is smaller; a reduction in the home interest rate not only reduces home residents' demand for home securities by more than it increases their demand for money because it simultaneously increases their demand for foreign securities but also reduces foreign residents' demand for home securities. The new equilibrium is at a_1 where i is lower and $\overset{*}{i}$ is unchanged. Depreciation of the home currency shifts the $\tilde{B}\tilde{B}$ and $\tilde{F}\tilde{F}$ schedules from $\tilde{B}_1\tilde{B}_1$ and $\tilde{F}_0\tilde{F}_0$ until they pass through a_1.

Now consider three types of intervention operations. Intervention of type I is an exchange of home money for foreign money $(d\tilde{M} = -d\tilde{N} > 0)$. This operation shifts the $\tilde{M}\tilde{M}$ and $\tilde{N}\tilde{N}$ schedules to $\tilde{M}_1\tilde{M}_1$ and $\tilde{N}_1\tilde{N}_1$. The new equilibrium is at a_2 where i is lower and $\overset{*}{i}$ is higher. Depreciation of the home currency shifts the $\tilde{B}\tilde{B}$ and $\tilde{F}\tilde{F}$ schedules down until they pass through a_2.

Intervention of type II is an exchange of home money for foreign securities $(d\tilde{M} = -d\tilde{F} > 0)$. This operation shifts $\tilde{M}\tilde{M}$ and $\tilde{F}\tilde{F}$ to $\tilde{M}_1\tilde{M}_1$ and $\tilde{F}_1\tilde{F}_1$. The new equilibrium is at a_1. The increase in the home money supply and the decline in the home interest rate are the same as they were in the case of an open market operation. Depreciation of the home currency shifts $\tilde{B}\tilde{B}$ and $\tilde{F}\tilde{F}$ down until they pass through a_1. The depreciation of the home currency is greater than it was in the case of an open market operation, since it must shift $\tilde{B}\tilde{B}$ from $\tilde{B}_0\tilde{B}_0$ to a_1 instead of from $\tilde{B}_1\tilde{B}_1$ to a_1.

Intervention of type III is an exchange of home currency securities for foreign currency securities $(d\tilde{B} = -d\tilde{F} > 0)$. Since this type of intervention leaves both money supplies unchanged, it has been called sterilized intervention. It shifts $\tilde{B}\tilde{B}$ and $\tilde{F}\tilde{F}$ to $\tilde{B}_2\tilde{B}_2$ and $\tilde{F}_1\tilde{F}_1$. The new equilibrium is at a_0 where i and $\overset{*}{i}$ are unchanged. Depreciation of the home currency shifts $\tilde{B}\tilde{B}$ and $\tilde{F}\tilde{F}$ down until they pass through a_0.

An exogenous increase in P operates exactly like an open market sale by the home authorities since it raises the excess demand for home money and lowers the excess demand for home securities by amounts that are equal in absolute value. Thus it causes i to rise and the home currency to appreciate. By analogy an exogenous increase in $\overset{*}{P}$ causes $\overset{*}{i}$ to rise and the home currency to depreciate.

We assume that there is "local asset preference"; home residents allocate a larger fraction of any increase in wealth to home securities than foreign residents

---

[9]Under the basic specification the derivative of the excess demand for foreign securities with respect to the exchange rate,

$$f_7 \overset{*}{F} + f_5 \overset{*}{P} Y + f_7 \left(\overset{*}{N} + \overset{*}{F} \right) - \overset{*}{F},$$

is negative if $0 < f_7, \overset{*}{f}_7 < 1$ since $\overset{*}{f}_5 \overset{*}{P} Y = -\overset{*}{n}_5 \overset{*}{P} Y = -\overset{*}{N}$.

$(b_7 > \overset{*}{b}_7)$. With local asset preference, a transfer of wealth from home residents to foreign residents ($dw < 0$) has effects which are identical to those of a sterilized intervention operation. It lowers the excess demand for home securities and raises the excess demand for foreign securities by amounts that are equal in absolute value.

The impact effects of the home authorities' policy instruments on two possible target variables are highlighted in Figure 2.2. The home authorities have two independent policy instruments, open market operations and intervention operations of type II, which they can use to achieve desired values for two target variables, the home money supply and the exchange rate, given a constant foreign money supply. Movements out the horizontal axis represent contractionary open market operations, increases in the stock of home securities ($\tilde{B}$) matched by decreases in the home money supply. Movements up the vertical axis represent contractionary intervention operations of type II, increases in the stock of foreign

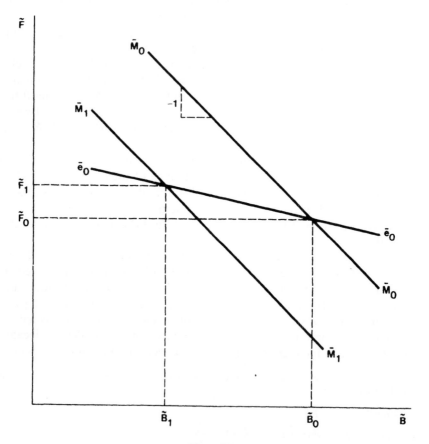

Figure 2.2

securities ($\tilde{F}$) matched by decreases in the home money supply. The $\overline{M}_0\overline{M}_0$ schedule shows the pairs of $\tilde{B}$ and $\tilde{F}$ that are compatible with a constant value of the home money supply. If currency units are defined so that the exchange rate varies in the neighborhood of unity, then the $\overline{MM}$ schedule has a slope of minus one. Under the basic specification, both interest rates are constant along the $\overline{MM}$ schedule because there is a one to one correspondence between the money supply and the interest rate in each country. The $\bar{e}_0\bar{e}_0$ schedule represents the pairs of $\tilde{B}$ and $\tilde{F}$ that are compatible with a constant exchange rate. The $\overline{ee}$ schedule must be flatter than the $\overline{MM}$ schedule since an intervention operation of type II has a greater effect on the exchange rate than an open market operation of equal size as shown above for the basic specification. It follows that movements down along the $\overline{ee}$ schedule lead to decreases in the home money supply and increases in the home interest rate. The home authorities can expand the home money supply from the level corresponding to $\overline{M}_0\overline{M}_0$ to the level corresponding to $\overline{M}_1\overline{M}_1$ without changing the exchange rate by conducting the open market purchase corresponding to $\tilde{B}_0\tilde{B}_1$ and the intervention operation of type II corresponding to $\tilde{F}_0\tilde{F}_1$.

As groundwork for the dynamic analysis below it is useful to provide an algebraic derivation of the results just arrived at graphically. We first select a state variable for the system and then express the asset market equilibrium conditions in terms of deviations of the variables from their stationary equilibrium values.

It will become clear below that it is convenient to define home (foreign) residents' wealth valued at the long-run equilibrium exchange rate, $\overline{E}$, as w ($\overline{E}\overset{*}{w}$):

$$w = M + B + \overline{E}F, \qquad \overline{E}\overset{*}{w} = \overset{*}{B} + \overline{E}(\overset{*}{N} + \overset{*}{F}), \tag{2.10}$$

and to choose w as the state variable of the system. The time derivative of w equals home residents' asset accumulation in the neighborhood of long-run equilibrium:

$$\dot{w} = \dot{M} + \dot{B} + \overline{E}\dot{F}. \tag{2.11}$$

The equilibrium conditions for the markets for home money, foreign money, and home securities in deviation form are given by

$$\tilde{m}_i\,di + \tilde{m}_p\,dp - d\tilde{M} = 0, \tag{2.12a}$$

$$\tilde{n}_i^*\,d\overset{*}{i} + \tilde{n}_p^*\,d\overset{*}{p} - d\tilde{N} = 0, \tag{2.12b}$$

$$\tilde{b}_i\,di + \tilde{b}_i^*\,d\overset{*}{i} + \tilde{b}_e\,de + \tilde{b}_\varepsilon\varepsilon + \tilde{b}_p\,dp + \tilde{b}_w\,dw - d\tilde{B} = 0, \tag{2.12c}$$

$$\tilde{m}_i = m_3, \qquad m_p = m_5X, \qquad \tilde{n}_i^* = \overset{*}{n}_4, \qquad \tilde{n}_p^* = \overset{*}{n}_5Y,$$

$$\tilde{b}_i = b_3 + \overset{*}{b}_3, \qquad \tilde{b}_i^* = b_4 + \overset{*}{b}_4, \qquad \tilde{b}_e = b_7F + \overset{*}{b}_7(\overset{*}{N} + \overset{*}{F}),$$

$$\tilde{b}_e = b_4 - \overset{*}{b}_3, \qquad \tilde{b}_w = b_7 - \overset{*}{b}_7, \qquad \tilde{b}_p = b_5X.$$

$\tilde{m}_k$, $\tilde{n}_k$, and $\tilde{b}_k$, represent the partial derivatives of the excess demands for home money, foreign money, and home securities with respect to the variables that appear as subscripts under the basic specification. A variable with a d in front of it represents the deviation of that variable from its stationary equilibrium value. e, p, and $\dot{p}$ are the natural logarithms of E, P, and $\dot{P}$ so that $de = dE/E$, $dp = dP/P$ and $d\dot{p} = d\dot{P}/\dot{P}$. In the neighborhood of stationary equilibrium $d\varepsilon = \varepsilon = 0$ under static expectations and $d\varepsilon = \varepsilon = \dot{e}$ under rational expectations. In deriving eqs. (2.12) we have set $E = P = \dot{P} = 1$ and have made use of the following relationships:

$$dW = dw + Fde, \qquad dE\dot{W} = d\dot{w} + (\dot{N} + \dot{F})de, \qquad (2.13a)$$

$$d\dot{w} = d\dot{B} + d\dot{N} + d\dot{F} = -dM - dB - dF = -dw. \qquad (2.13b)$$

To derive eq. (2.13b), sum the appropriately modified versions of eqs. (2.3) in deviation form to obtain:

$$d\tilde{M} + d\tilde{N} + d\tilde{B} + d\tilde{F} = d\dot{B} + d\dot{N} + d\dot{F} + dM + dB + dF. \qquad (2.14)$$

Eq. (2.14) implies the equality of the middle two terms in (2.13b) because world central bank intervention is governed by $d\tilde{M} + d\tilde{N} + d\tilde{B} + d\tilde{F} = 0$.

The effects of changes in the exogenous variables are given by

$$di = -\left(\tilde{m}_p/\tilde{m}_i\right)dp + \left(1/\tilde{m}_i\right)d\tilde{M}, \qquad (2.15a)$$

$$d\dot{i} = -\left(\tilde{n}_{\dot{p}}^{*}/\tilde{n}_{\dot{i}}\right)d\dot{p} + \left(1/\tilde{n}_{\dot{i}}\right)d\tilde{N}, \qquad (2.15b)$$

$$\tilde{b}_e de = \left[\left(\tilde{b}_i\tilde{m}_p - \tilde{b}_p\tilde{m}_i\right)/\tilde{m}_i\right]dp + \left(\tilde{b}_{\dot{i}}\tilde{n}_{\dot{p}}^{*}/\tilde{n}_{\dot{i}}\right)d\dot{p}$$
$$- \left(\tilde{b}_i/\tilde{m}_i\right)d\tilde{M} - \left(\tilde{b}_{\dot{i}}/\tilde{n}_{\dot{i}}\right)d\tilde{N} - \tilde{b}_\varepsilon \varepsilon - \tilde{b}_w dw + d\tilde{B}. \qquad (2.15c)$$

It is convenient not to divide through by the positive coefficient $\tilde{b}_e$ since eq. (2.15c) will be viewed in a different way in what follows.

2.4. The specification of the goods markets and the balance of payments

Even when the objective is to study the behavior of interest rates and the exchange rate at a point in time, it is not possible to conduct the analysis using just the asset market equilibrium conditions except under very restrictive assumptions. It was shown in the last section that if goods prices are fixed and expectations are static, then the conditions for asset market equilibrium are sufficient to determine interest rates and the exchange rate at a point in time. However, if goods prices are fixed and expectations are rational, then a balance of payments condition must be employed together with the asset market equilibrium conditions to jointly determine interest rates, the exchange rate, the percentage rate of change in the exchange rate, and the rate of transfer of wealth between home and foreign residents. Moreover, if goods prices are flexible, then under both static and rational expectations a complete model must include goods market equilibrium conditions. Of course, when the objective is to study the behavior of interest rates and the exchange rate over time, a balance of payments condition must be employed no matter whether expectations are static or rational.[10]

In this subsection we specify equilibrium conditions for the home and foreign goods markets and a balance of payments equation. Since the focus of this chapter is asset markets, we have deliberately kept the specification of the goods market equilibrium conditions and the balance of payments equation as simple as possible.[11]

Home (foreign) expenditure is allocated between home and foreign goods:

$$P(X - G) - s\left[P\left(X \overset{+}{-} G\right), \overline{W}\right] \equiv x(\cdot) + y(\cdot), \tag{2.16a}$$

$$E\dot{P}(Y - \dot{G}) - \dot{s}\left[E\dot{P}\left(Y \overset{+}{-} \dot{G}\right), \overline{E\dot{W}}\right] \equiv \dot{x}(\cdot) + \dot{y}(\cdot). \tag{2.16b}$$

$X - G$ $(Y - \dot{G})$ is home (foreign) real disposable income measured in the home (foreign) good.[12] G $(\dot{G})$ is home (foreign) real, balanced-budget governent spending measured in home (foreign) goods. s, x, and y $(\dot{s}$, $\dot{x}$, and $\dot{y})$ are home (foreign) saving, expenditure on the home good, and expenditure on the foreign good, all measured in home currency. Home (foreign) saving measured in home currency depends positively on home (foreign) nominal disposable income and negatively on home (foreign) nominal wealth, both measured in home currency.[13]

---

[10]A balance of payments condition or one or more goods market equilibrium condition or both are added to the asset market equilibrium conditions in the portfolio balance models of Allen and Kenen (1980), Boyer (1978, 1977, 1975), Branson (1977, 1974), Bryant (1980), Calvo and Rodriguez (1977), Dornbusch (1975), Enders (1977), Flood (1979), Frenkel and Rodriguez (1975), Henderson (1980, 1979), Henderson and Rogoff (1982), Kenen (1981, 1976), Kouri (1983a, 1983b), Kouri and de Macedo (1978), Masson (1981, 1980), McKinnon and Oates (1966), Melitz (1982), Myhrman (1975), Obstfeld (1982, 1980), Tobin and de Macedo (1981), and Wallace (1970).

[11]The implications of several alternative specifications of goods markets are considered by Bruce and Purvis in Chapter 16 of this Handbook.

[12]For simplicity we adopt the system of taxes and transfers under which interest payments do not enter the analysis suggested by Allen and Kenen (1980). Each government taxes away all the interest received by the residents of its country and transfers to the government of the other country an amount equal to the interest received by the residents of its country from the other country. Under this system, the current account surplus and trade account surplus of a country are equal, and if the budget of the government of a country is balanced, the disposable income of its residents is equal to output minus government spending.

[13]For simplicity we assume that saving in each country does not depend on the real returns on home and foreign securities. If this assumption were relaxed in the case of flexible prices and rational expectations, it would be necessary to analyze a system of four differential equations rather than a system of two differential equations.

The goods market equilibrium conditions and the balance of payments equation are given by

$$x\left[P\left(X - G\right), \overset{+}{W}, \overset{-}{P}, \overset{+}{EP}\right] + \overset{\cdot}{x}\left[E\overset{\cdot}{P}\left(Y - \overset{\cdot}{G}\right), E\overset{\cdot}{W}, \overset{-}{P}, \overset{+}{EP}\right] - P(X - G) = 0,$$

(2.17a)

$$y\left[P\left(X - G\right), \overset{+}{W}, \overset{+}{P}, \overset{-}{EP}\right] + \overset{\cdot}{y}\left[E\overset{\cdot}{P}\left(Y - \overset{+}{G}\right), E\overset{\cdot}{W}, \overset{+}{P}, \overset{-}{EP}\right] - E\overset{\cdot}{P}(Y - \overset{\cdot}{G}) = 0,$$

(2.17b)

$$\overset{\cdot}{x}\left[E\overset{\cdot}{P}\left(Y - \overset{+}{G}\right), E\overset{\cdot}{W}, \overset{-}{P}, \overset{+}{EP}\right] - y\left[P\left(X - G\right), \overset{+}{W}, \overset{+}{P}, \overset{-}{EP}\right] - \overset{\cdot}{w} - (E - \overline{E})\overset{\cdot}{F} = 0.$$

(2.17c)

Home (foreign) nominal spending on both home and foreign goods measured in home currency depends positively on home (foreign) nominal disposable income and nominal wealth, both measured in home currency. Increases in $P(E\overset{\cdot}{P})$ shift both home and foreign nominal spending from home (foreign) goods to foreign (home) goods. Therefore, increases in $P(E\overset{\cdot}{P})$ reduce (increase) the home trade surplus.[14] $\overset{\cdot}{w} + (E - \overline{E})\overset{\cdot}{F}$ is home residents' asset accumulation. $\overset{\cdot}{w}$ is defined by eq. (2.11).

Equations (2.16) imply that the expenditure functions of eqs. (2.17) are subject to familiar restrictions:

$$x_1 + y_1 \equiv 1 - s_1; \qquad x_2 + y_2 \equiv -s_2; \qquad x_k + y_k \equiv 0, \quad k = 3, 4; \qquad (2.18a)$$

$$\overset{\cdot}{x}_1 + \overset{\cdot}{y}_1 \equiv 1 - \overset{\cdot}{s}_1; \qquad \overset{\cdot}{x}_2 + \overset{\cdot}{y}_2 \equiv -\overset{\cdot}{s}_2; \qquad \overset{\cdot}{x}_k + \overset{\cdot}{y}_k \equiv 0, \quad k = 3, 4. \qquad (2.18b)$$

The assumption that private agents do not have money illusion implies that all expenditure functions are homogenous of degree one in all nominal variables:

$$x \equiv x_1 P(X - G) + x_2 W + x_3 P + x_4 E\overset{\cdot}{P},$$

$$\overset{\cdot}{x} \equiv \overset{\cdot}{x}_1 E\overset{\cdot}{P}(Y - \overset{\cdot}{G}) + \overset{\cdot}{x}_2 E\overset{\cdot}{W} + \overset{\cdot}{x}_3 P + \overset{\cdot}{x}_4 E\overset{\cdot}{P}, \qquad (2.19a)$$

$$y \equiv y_1 P(X - G) + y_2 W + y_3 P + y_4 E\overset{\cdot}{P},$$

$$\overset{\cdot}{y} \equiv \overset{\cdot}{y}_1 E\overset{\cdot}{P}(Y - \overset{\cdot}{G}) + \overset{\cdot}{y}_2 E\overset{\cdot}{W} + \overset{\cdot}{y}_3 P + \overset{\cdot}{y}_4 E\overset{\cdot}{P}, \qquad (2.19b)$$

$$s \equiv s_1 P(X - G) + s_2 W, \qquad \overset{\cdot}{s} = \overset{\cdot}{s}_1 E\overset{\cdot}{P}(Y - \overset{\cdot}{G}) + \overset{\cdot}{s}_2 E\overset{\cdot}{W}. \qquad (2.19c)$$

Below we consider two special cases of the goods market equilibrium conditions and the balance of payments equation. In both special cases real outputs in

---

[14] Our assumption about the effects of increases in P and $E\overset{\cdot}{P}$ on home and foreign spending on home and foreign goods is sufficient but not necessary to insure that increases in P reduce the home trade surplus and that increases in $E\overset{\cdot}{P}$ increase it. Of course, without our assumption it is possible that increases in P increase the home trade surplus and that increases in $E\overset{\cdot}{P}$ reduce it.

both countries are assumed to always be at their "full employment" or "natural" levels. In the first special case it is assumed that balanced budget fiscal policy is used in each country to fix the price of output in that country ($dp = d\overset{*}{p} = 0$). Furthermore, in each country the demand for the good produced in the other country is assumed to be independent of the level of nominal spending ($\overset{*}{x}_1 = \overset{*}{x}_2 = y_1 = y_2 = 0$). Therefore, the trade account of the home country is independent of nominal disposable incomes and nominal wealths. In deviation form the balance of payments equation is

$$\dot{w} = \eta \, de, \qquad \eta = \overset{*}{x}_4 - y_4 = \overset{*}{x}_4 + x_4 > 0, \tag{2.20}$$

where η is the effect of a depreciation of the home currency on the home trade surplus. In the neighborhood of stationary equilibrium $d\dot{w} = \dot{w}$ and $d(E - \bar{E})$ $\dot{F} = 0$.

In the second special case it is assumed that output prices are flexible and that $\overset{*}{G}$ and $\overset{*}{G}$ are equal to zero. In deviation form the goods market equilibrium conditions and the balance of payments equation are

$$\tilde{x}_p \, dp + \tilde{x}_p^* \, d\overset{*}{p} + \tilde{x}_e \, de + \tilde{x}_w \, dw = 0, \tag{2.21a}$$

$$\tilde{y}_p \, dp + \tilde{y}_p^* \, d\overset{*}{p} + \tilde{y}_e \, de + \tilde{y}_w \, dw = 0, \tag{2.21b}$$

$$t_p \, dp + t_p^* \, d\overset{*}{p} + t_e \, de + t_w \, dw - \dot{w} = 0, \tag{2.21c}$$

$$\tilde{x}_p = -\tilde{x}_p^* - x_2 W - \overset{*}{x}_2 \dot{W} < 0, \qquad \tilde{x}_e = \tilde{x}_p^* + x_2 F + \overset{*}{x}_2 (\dot{N} + \dot{F}) > 0,$$

$$\tilde{y}_p = y_1 X + \mu > 0, \qquad \tilde{y}_e = -\tilde{y}_p - y_2(B + M) - \overset{*}{y}_2 \dot{B} < 0,$$

$$t_p = -\tilde{y}_p < 0, \qquad t_e = \tilde{x}_p^* + \overset{*}{x}_2(\dot{N} + \dot{F}) - y_2 F \gtrless 0,$$

$$\tilde{x}_p^* = \overset{*}{x}_1 Y + \eta > 0, \qquad \tilde{x}_w = x_2 - \overset{*}{x}_2 > 0,$$

$$\tilde{y}_p^* = -\tilde{y}_p - y_2 W - \overset{*}{y}_2 \dot{W} < 0, \qquad \tilde{y}_w = y_2 - \overset{*}{y}_2 < 0,$$

$$t_p^* = \tilde{x}_p^* > 0, \qquad t_w = -\overset{*}{x}_2 - y_2 < 0,$$

where $\tilde{x}_k$, $\tilde{y}_k$, and t_k represent the derivatives of the excess demand for home goods, the excess demand for foreign goods, and the home trade surplus with respect to the variables which appear as subscripts.[15] $\mu = y_3 + \overset{*}{y}_3 > 0$ ($\eta = x_4 + \overset{*}{x}_4 > 0$) is the effect of an increase in the price of the home (foreign) good on excess demand for the foreign (home) good given that home (foreign) nominal income is held constant. $\tilde{x}_p$, $\tilde{x}_p^*$, $\tilde{y}_p$, $\tilde{y}_p^*$, t_p and t_p^* have the normal signs. The signs of $\tilde{x}_e$, $\tilde{y}_e$, t_e, and t_w reflect the assumptions that increases in wealth lead to increases in spending on both goods in both countries and that there are no negative net

---

[15] In the derivation of eqs. (2.21) we make use of the appropriately modified versions of eqs. (2.1) and eqs. (2.19).

foreign asset positions. We assume that there is "local good preference"; home residents allocate a larger fraction of increases in spending resulting from increases in wealth to home goods than foreign residents $(x_2 > \dot{x}_2)$, and foreign residents allocate a larger fraction of increases in spending resulting from increases in wealth to foreign goods than home residents $(y_2 < \dot{y}_2)$. With local good preference, a transfer of wealth to home residents $(dw > 0)$ increases demand for the home good and decrease demand for the foreign good $(\tilde{x}_w > 0,\ \tilde{y}_w < 0)$.

It is convenient for what follows to obtain expressions for dp, $d\dot{p}$, and $\dot{w}$ as functions of de and dw:

$$dp = C_1\,de + C_2\,dw, \tag{2.22a}$$

$$d\dot{p} = -C_3\,de - C_4\,dw, \tag{2.22b}$$

$$\dot{w} = C_5\,de - C_6\,dw, \tag{2.22c}$$

$$C_1 = \left\{\left[x_2 F + \dot{x}_2(\dot{N} + \dot{F})\right]\left[y_2 W + \dot{y}_2 \dot{W} + \tilde{y}_p\right]\right.$$
$$\left. +\left[y_2 F + \dot{y}_2(\dot{N} + \dot{F})\right]\tilde{x}_p^*\right\}/\Delta > 0,$$

$$C_2 = \left[(\dot{x}_2 - x_2)\dot{s}_2\dot{W} - (x_2 - \dot{s}_2)\tilde{x}_p^*\right]/\Delta > 0,$$

$$C_3 = \left\{\left[y_2(B + M) + \dot{y}_2\dot{B}\right]\left[x_2 W + \dot{x}_2\dot{W} + \tilde{x}_p^*\right]\right.$$
$$\left. +\left[x_2(B + M) + \dot{x}_2\dot{B}\right]\tilde{y}_p\right\}/\Delta > 0,$$

$$C_4 = \left[(y_2 - \dot{y}_2)s_2 W + (s_2 - \dot{s}_2)\tilde{y}_p\right]/\Delta > 0,$$

$$C_5 = s_2 W\dot{s}_2\dot{W}\left(\tilde{x}_p^* + \dot{x}_2\dot{W}\right)\left(b_7 - \dot{b}_7\right)/\Delta > 0,$$

$$C_6 = s_2\dot{s}_2(W + \dot{W})\left(\tilde{x}_p^* + \dot{x}_2\dot{W}\right)/\Delta > 0,$$

$$\Delta = \left(x_2 W + \dot{x}_2\dot{W}\right)\left(y_2 W + \dot{y}_2\dot{W}\right) + \left(y_2 W + \dot{y}_2\dot{W}\right)\tilde{x}_p^* + \left(x_2 W + \dot{x}_2\dot{W}\right)\tilde{y}_p > 0.$$

Assumptions imposed above imply that C_1, C_3, C_5 and C_6 are positive. We assume that responsivenesses of saving to wealth are the same in the two countries $(s_2 = \dot{s}_2)$ so that transfers of wealth between countries affect the distribution but not the level of world saving. Under this assumption C_2 and C_4 are positive. Since our assumptions imply that all the coefficients in eqs. (2.22) are positive, the signs preceding the coefficients indicate the signs of the effects of changes in the variables.[16]

[16] In the relatively lengthy and tedious derivation of eqs. (2.22) we make use of the appropriately modified versions of eqs. (2.1), eqs. (2.18), and eqs. (2.19). We approximate the goods market equilibrium conditions and the balance of payments equation around long-run equilibrium where home and foreign saving are zero. In the neighborhood of long-run equilibrium, eqs. (2.18) and (2.19) imply a key relationship:

$$\tilde{y}_p \equiv \tilde{x}_p^* + \dot{x}_2\dot{W} - y_2 W. \tag{2.23}$$

The relationships summarized by eqs. (2.22) are in accord with intuition. First, consider a transfer of wealth from foreign residents to home residents ($dw > 0$). Given that the responsivenesses of savings to wealth are the same in the two countries ($s_2 = \overset{*}{s}_2$) and that there is marginal local good preference ($x_2 - \overset{*}{x}_2 = \overset{*}{y}_2$ $- y_2 > 0$), the transfer raises demand for home goods and lowers demand for foreign goods by amounts that are equal in absolute value. An increase in the price of each good has an effect on excess demand for that good that is greater in absolute value than its effect on the excess demand for the other good ($|\tilde{x}_p| > |\tilde{y}_p|$, $|\tilde{y}_p^*| > |\tilde{x}_p^*|$).[17] For example, an increase in P reduces excess demand for home goods both by increasing savings and by reducing the home trade surplus; however, it increases excess demand for the foreign good only by increasing the foreign trade surplus which, of course, is the negative of the home trade surplus. Therefore, the transfer causes P to rise and $\overset{*}{P}$ to fall. The direct effect of the transfer on the home trade surplus is to reduce it since foreigners spend less on home goods and home residents spend more on foreign goods. The indirect effect resulting from the induced price changes reinforces the direct effect.[18]

Now consider a depreciation of the home currency ($de > 0$). Given that all security positions are positive (B, F, $\overset{*}{B}$, $\overset{*}{F} > 0$), the depreciation increases demand for home goods and decreases demand for foreign goods. A given percentage increase in the price of home goods has an effect on excess demand for home goods that is greater in absolute value than the effect of the same percentage depreciation ($|\tilde{x}_p| > |\tilde{x}_e|$) and an effect on the excess demand for foreign goods that is smaller in absolute value than the effect of the same percentage depreciation ($|\tilde{y}_p| < |\tilde{y}_e|$). For example, if eq. (2.17a) is divided by P, then E and P always enter as the ratio of E to P except in the terms for home and foreign real wealth measured in home goods. Equiproportionate changes in E and P lower real wealth. Similarly, a given percentage increase in the price of foreign goods has an effect on excess demand for foreign goods that is greater in absolute value than the effect of the same percentage depreciation ($|\tilde{y}_p^*| > |\tilde{y}_e|$) and an effect on excess demand for home goods that is smaller in absolute value than the effect of the same percentage depreciation ($|\tilde{x}_p^*| < |\tilde{x}_e|$). Therefore the depreciation causes p to rise and $\overset{*}{p}$ to fall.

A depreciation of the home currency increases the home trade surplus if there is local asset preference [$b_7 = (M + B)/W > \overset{*}{B}/\overset{*}{W} = \overset{*}{b}_7$], as shown in eq. (2.22c). Some intuition about this result can be gained by considering two special cases. Assume temporarily that there is no local asset preference [$(M + B)/W = \overset{*}{B}/\overset{*}{W}$]. Following a depreciation let P rise by enough to keep world wealth measured in home goods [$(W + E\overset{*}{W})/P$] constant and let $\overset{*}{P}$ fall by enough to keep world

---

[17]This assertion can be confirmed by substituting relationships implied by eqs. (2.18) and (2.19) into the definitions of $\tilde{x}$, $\tilde{y}_p$, $\tilde{x}_p^*$, and $\tilde{y}_p^*$.

[18]If s_2 is not equal to $\overset{*}{s}_2$, the indirect effect from the induced price changes does not necessarily reinforce the direct effect. However, the overall effect of the transfer on the trade surplus is always to reduce it; that is C_6 is always positive.

wealth measured in foreign goods $[(W + E\dot{W})/E\dot{P}]$ constant. Then the relative price of the foreign good (EP/P) remains constant, and there is no change in excess demand for either good or in the home trade surplus. Now assume again that there is local asset preference and assume temporarily that there is no local good preference $(x_2 = \dot{x}_2, \; y_2 = \dot{y}_2)$. In this case the changes in P and $\dot{P}$ considered above lower home real wealth measured in both goods and raise foreign real wealth measured in both goods. However, the goods markets remain in equilibrium since the redistribution of real wealth does not affect the excess demands for goods. Thus, there is no need for a change in the relative price of the foreign good and no need for further changes in P and $\dot{P}$. The home trade surplus increases since foreign spending on home goods increases and home spending on foreign goods falls. According to eq. (2.22c), the result that a depreciation increases the trade surplus when there is local asset preference is very general: it is independent of good preference and the signs of security positions.

2.5. The distribution effect of a trade surplus with goods prices fixed

If asset demands embody local asset preference, a transfer of wealth to home residents through a trade account surplus raises the demand for home securities and lowers the demand for foreign securities. In this subsection we spell out the implications of this distribution effect of a trade surplus with goods prices fixed. In this special case, our model is similar to what some have called a "partial equilibrium" model of exchange rate behavior.[19]

The first building block of the fixed price model is the balance of payments equation from the first special case of the goods market equilibrium conditions and the balance of payments equation. This equation is reproduced here for convenience:

$$\dot{w} = \eta \, de, \qquad \eta = x_4 - y_4 = \dot{x}_4 + x_4 > 0. \tag{2.20}$$

The $\dot{w}$ schedule in the left-hand panel of Figure 2.3 represents this relationship. It slopes upward because a depreciation of the home currency increases the home trade surplus and, therefore, increases home asset accumulation ($\dot{w}$). The long-run equilibrium exchange rate ($\bar{e}_0$) is the only value of e for which the trade surplus and, therefore, asset accumulation equal zero as indicated by the horizontal $\dot{w} = 0$ schedule in the right-hand panel of Figure 2.3. The horizontal arrows show the direction of motion of w. When the home currency price of foreign currency is too high ($e > \bar{e}_0$), the home country runs a trade surplus and accumulates assets ($\dot{w} > 0$).

---

[19]Kouri (1983a) uses this terminology.

The second building block of the fixed price model is the equation for the expected rate of change of the exchange rate (ε) implied by asset market equilibrium in the basic specification of asset markets. Solving eq. (2.15c) for ε with $dp = d\dot{p} = 0$ yields:

$$\varepsilon = \varepsilon_e de + \varepsilon_w dw - \varepsilon_{OMO} d\tilde{M}, \tag{2.24}$$

$$\varepsilon_e = -\tilde{b}_e/\tilde{b}_\varepsilon > 0,$$

$$\varepsilon_w = -\tilde{b}_w/\tilde{b}_\varepsilon > 0,$$

$$\varepsilon_{OMO} = (\tilde{b}_i + \tilde{m}_i)/\tilde{m}_i\tilde{b}_\varepsilon > 0.$$

The coefficient $-\varepsilon_{OMO}$ gives the effect of an expansionary open market operation ($d\tilde{M} = -d\tilde{B} > 0$) on ε.

The A_S schedule in the right-hand panel of Figure 2.3 is the asset market equilibrium schedule under static expectations. It represents the pairs of e and w that are compatible with asset market equilibrium given that ε is equal to zero. This schedule is downward sloping under the assumption of local asset preference ($b_7 - \dot{b}_7 > 0$). A transfer of wealth to home residents raises the demand for home

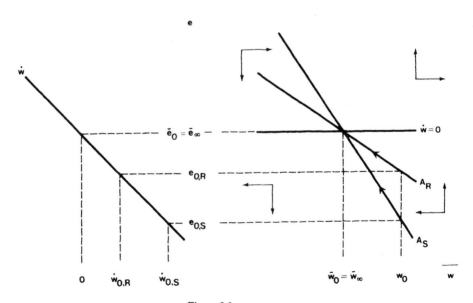

Figure 2.3

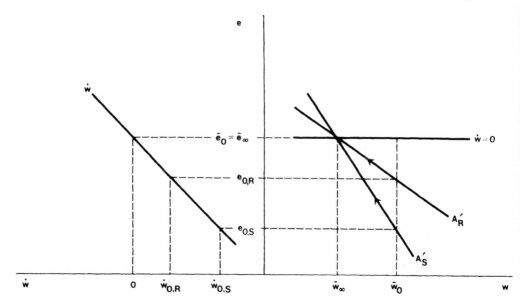

Figure 2.4

securities, so the home currency must appreciate to reequilibrate the asset markets if ε is to remain unchanged. The more pronounced is local asset preference, that is, the greater $b_7 - \bar{b}_7$, the steeper is A_S.

The A_R schedule is the asset market equilibrium schedule under rational expectations given that exchange rate expectations are compatible with the stability of long-run equilibrium. Under rational expectations the A_S schedule is simply the schedule along which $\varepsilon = \dot{e} = 0$. The vertical arrows show the direction of motion of e. Above A_S there is excess demand for home assets with $\dot{e} = 0$, so the home currency must be expected to depreciate ($\dot{e} > 0$) to equilibrate the asset markets. Long-run equilibrium is a saddle point under rational expectations as indicated by the arrows.[20] Following a disturbance the world economy will reach long-run equilibrium if and only if it moves along the unique saddle path represented by A_R.

The effects of an unanticipated transfer of wealth from foreign residents to home residents ($w_0 > \bar{w}_0 = \bar{w}_\infty$) are shown in Figure 2.3. This disturbance does not shift any of the schedules. Under static expectations the home currency appreciates ($e_{0,S} < \bar{e}_0$), and the home country begins to run a trade deficit ($\dot{w}_{0,S} < 0$). As

---

[20] The determinant of the differential equation system, made up of eq. (2.20) and eq. (2.24) with $\varepsilon = \dot{e}$, is $-\varepsilon_w \eta < 0$.

w falls, the home currency depreciates. The economy moves along A_S back to long-run equilibrium. Under rational expectations the home currency appreciates but not as much as under static expectations ($e_{0,S} < e_{0,R} < \bar{e}_0$), and the home country begins to run a trade account deficit but one which is smaller than under static expectations ($\dot{w}_{0,S} < \dot{w}_{0,R} < 0$). Once again, as w falls, the home currency depreciates. The economy moves along A_R back to long-run equilibrium. When agents take account of the future path of the exchange rate, the initial movement in this variable is damped.

The effects of an unanticipated contractionary open market operation are shown in Figure 2.4. This operation shifts the A_S and A_R schedules down to A_S' and A_R'. Under both static and rational expectations the home currency appreciates, and the home country begins to run a trade account deficit. In the new long-run equilibrium, home wealth is lower ($\bar{w}_\infty < \bar{w}_0$), but the exchange rate has the same value as in the initial long-run equilibrium ($\bar{e}_\infty = \bar{e}_0$). What happens is that the home interest rate rises by enough to clear the home money market. This increase is more than enough to re-equilibrate the market for home securities, so home wealth must decline to re-equilibrate that market.

The effects of an unanticipated shift in spending in either country from foreign to home goods is shown in Figure 2.5. This disturbance shifts the $\dot{w}$ schedule, the $\dot{w} = 0$ schedule, and the A_R schedule down to $\dot{w}'$, $(\dot{w} = 0)'$, and A_R'. Under static

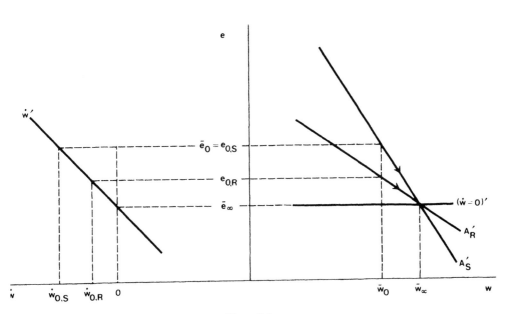

Figure 2.5

expectations there is no effect on the exchange rate initially $e_{0,S} = \bar{e}_0$, but under rational expectations the home currency appreciates at once ($e_{0,R} < \bar{e}_0$). Under both static and rational expectations the home country begins to run a trade account surplus. In the new long-run equilibrium, e is lower ($\bar{e}_\infty < \bar{e}_0$) and home wealth is higher ($\bar{w}_\infty > \bar{w}_0$). e must fall in order to reequilibrate the current account. With a lower e, w must be higher in order to reequilibrate the market for home currency securities.

2.6. Distribution effects of a trade surplus with goods prices flexible

If goods prices are flexible, not only local asset preference but also local good preference is sufficient to insure that a trade account surplus has a distribution effect. In this subsection we spell out the implications of the distribution effects of a trade surplus with goods prices flexible.

The first building block of the flexible price model is the reduced form asset accumulation equation (2.22c), which is reproduced here for convenience:

$$\dot{w} = C_5 \, de - C_6 \, dw, \tag{2.22c}$$

$$C_5 = s_2 W \dot{s}_2 \dot{W} \left(\tilde{x}_p^* + \dot{x}_2 \dot{W} \right) \left(b_7 - \dot{b}_7 \right) / \Delta > 0,$$

$$C_6 = s_2 \dot{s}_2 (W + \dot{W}) \left(\tilde{x}_p^* + \dot{x}_2 \dot{W} \right) / \Delta > 0.$$

The $\dot{w} = 0$ schedule in Figure 2.6 represents the pairs of e and w for which $\dot{w}$ equals zero. If there is local asset preference, it slopes upward. An increase in w lowers home asset accumulation, so the home currency must depreciate in order to increase it. If there is no local asset preference, the $\dot{w} = 0$ schedule is vertical since changes in the exchange rate do not affect asset accumulation. The horizontal arrows show the motion of w. Above the $\dot{w} = 0$ schedule the home country runs a trade surplus and accumulates assets.

The second building block of the flexible price model is the reduced form equation for the expected rate of change of the exchange rate (ε) derived by solving eq. (2.15c) for ε and eliminating dp and $d\dot{p}$ using eqs. (2.22a) and (2.22b):

$$\varepsilon = \varepsilon'_e \, de + \varepsilon'_w \, dw - \varepsilon'_{OMO} \, d\tilde{M}, \tag{2.25}$$

$$\varepsilon'_e = -(1/\tilde{b}_e)\left\{ \tilde{b}_e - \left[(\tilde{b}_i \tilde{m}_p - \tilde{b}_p \tilde{m}_i)/\tilde{m}_i \right] C_1 + \left(\tilde{b}_i \tilde{n}_p^* / \tilde{n}_i^* \right) C_3 \right\} > 0,$$

$$\varepsilon'_w = -(1/\tilde{b}_e)\left\{ \tilde{b}_w - \left[(\tilde{b}_i \tilde{m}_p - \tilde{b}_p \tilde{m}_i)/\tilde{m}_i \right] C_2 + \left(\tilde{b}_i \tilde{n}_p^* / \tilde{n}_i^* \right) C_4 \right\} > 0,$$

$$\varepsilon'_{OMO} = (\tilde{b}_i + \tilde{m}_i)/\tilde{m}_i \tilde{b}_e > 0.$$

The coefficient $-\varepsilon'_{OMO}$ gives the effect of an expansionary open market operation $(d\tilde{M} = -d\tilde{B} > 0)$ on ε.

The A_S schedule in Figure 2.6 is the asset market equilibrium schedule under static expectations. It represents the pairs of e and w that are compatible with asset market equilibrium given that ε is equal to zero. If there is either local asset preference or local good preference, the A_S schedule slopes downward. First consider the effect of an increase in w. If there is local asset preference, this increase in w raises the demand for home securities directly. If there is local good preference, the increase in w raises P and lowers $\tilde{P}$ as shown in eqs. (2.22a) and (2.22b). The net effect of these induced price changes is to increase the demand for home securities as shown in eq. (2.15c). Thus, either local asset preference or local good preference is a sufficient condition for an increase in w to raise the demand for home securities. Now consider the effect of an appreciation of the

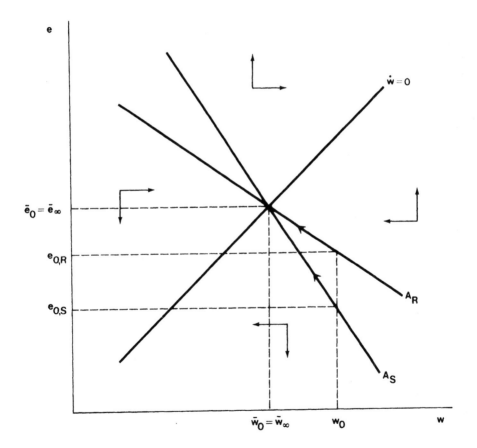

Figure 2.6

home currency, that is, a decrease in e. This decrease lowers the demand for home securities directly. It also lowers P and raises $\bar{P}$ as shown in eqs. (2.22a) and (2.22b). The net effect of these induced price changes is to lower the demand for home securities. Thus, a decrease in e unambiguously lowers the demand for home securities. If there is neither local asset preference nor local good preference, the A_S schedule is horizontal.

The A_R schedule is the asset market equilibrium schedule under rational expectations given that exchange rate expectations are compatible with the stability of long-run equilibrium. Under rational expectations, the A_S schedule is just the $\varepsilon = \dot{e} = 0$ schedule. The vertical arrows show the direction of motion of e. Above A_S there is excess demand for home assets with $\dot{e} = 0$, so the home currency must be expected to depreciate. Long-run equilibrium is a saddle point

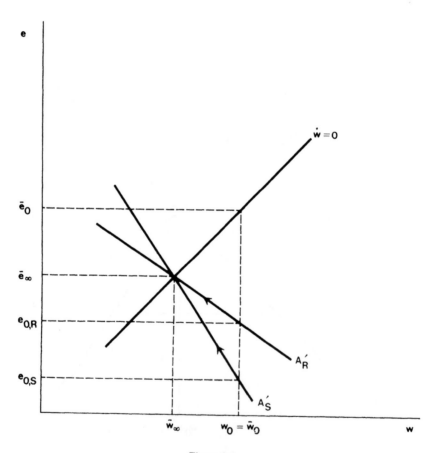

Figure 2.7

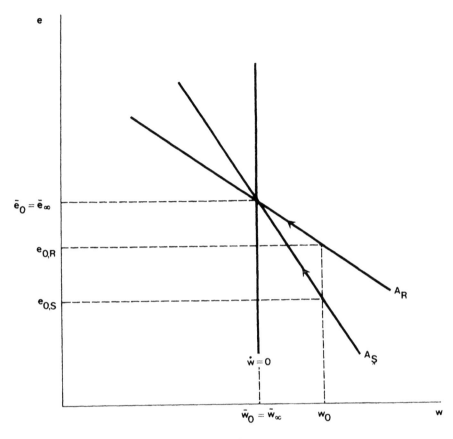

Figure 2.8

under rational expectations as indicated by the arrows.[21] A_R is the unique saddle path along which the economy must move following a disturbance in order to reach long-run equilibrium.

The qualitative effects of a transfer of wealth to home residents on e and w when there is local asset preference are the same whether or not there is local good preference. These effects are shown in Figure 2.6. This disturbance does not affect either of the schedules. Under both static and rational expectations the home currency appreciates ($e_{0,S} < e_{0,R} < \bar{e}_0$), and the home country begins to run a trade deficit. The economy moves along either A_S or A_R back to long-run equilibrium.

[21] The determinant of the differential equation system, made up of eq. (2.22c) and eq. (2.25) with $\varepsilon = \dot{e}$, is $-(\varepsilon'_e C_6 + \varepsilon'_w C_5) < 0$.

The qualitative effects of a contractionary open market operation on e and w when there is local asset preference are also the same whether or not there is local good preference. These effects are shown in Figure 2.7. The A_S and A_R schedules are shifted down to A_S' and A_R'. Under both static and rational expectations the home currency appreciates, and the home country begins to run a trade deficit. In contrast to the results obtained with goods prices fixed both home wealth and the exchange rate are lower in the long-run equilibrium. Since asset accumulation now depends on w as well as e and since w has declined, e need not return all the way to its initial value in order to raise asset accumulation to zero.

While the qualitative behavior of the nominal exchange rate is the same with local asset preference whether or not there is local good preference, the behavior of the terms of trade or real exchange rate (EP/P) differs in the two cases. We illustrate this result with the case of a transfer of wealth. At the outset note that

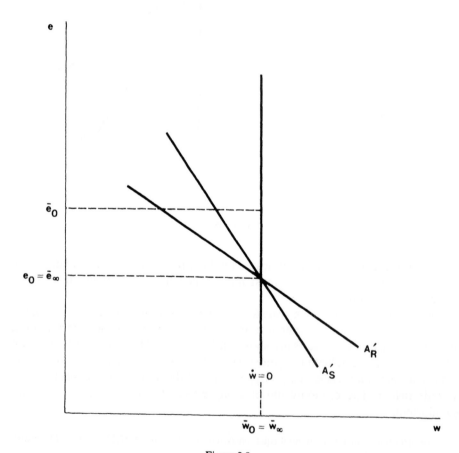

Figure 2.9

for this disturbance the real exchange rate is unaffected in the new long-run equilibrium. Then focus attention on the impact effects and the adjustment paths. First suppose that there is local good preference. It follows from eqs. (2.22a) and (2.22b) that an increase in w raises P and lowers $\dot{P}$. It also follows from these equations that an appreciation of the nominal exchange rate causes an appreciation of the real exchange rate:

$$d(e + \dot{p} - p)/de = (1/\varDelta)(x_2\dot{y}_2 - \dot{x}_2 y_2)(b_7 - \dot{b}_7)W\dot{W} > 0. \tag{2.26}$$

As a result the impact effect of the transfer of wealth must be an appreciation of the real exchange rate, so the real exchange rate must depreciate along the adjustment path. Now suppose there is no local good preference. Increases in w and changes in the nominal exchange rate have no effect on the real exchange

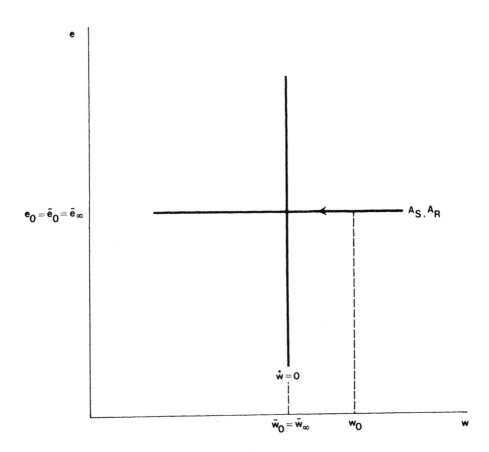

Figure 2.10

rate, so the real exchange rate remains unaffected by the transfer of wealth. This is a case of nominal exchange rate dynamics without real exchange rate dynamics.

The effects of a wealth transfer and an open market operation on e and w when there is local good preference but no local asset preference are shown in Figures 2.8 and 2.9. The only qualitative difference in the effects on e and w in this case is that the long-run equilibrium value of w is unchanged by an open market operation because asset accumulation is independent of the exchange rate.

An interesting special case arises when there is local good preference but no local asset preference and when open market operations are employed to peg nominal interest rates in both countries. In this special case movements in P and $\dot{P}$ do not affect asset market equilibrium. The effects of a wealth transfer are shown in Figure 2.10 in which the A_S and A_R schedules are horizontal. A transfer

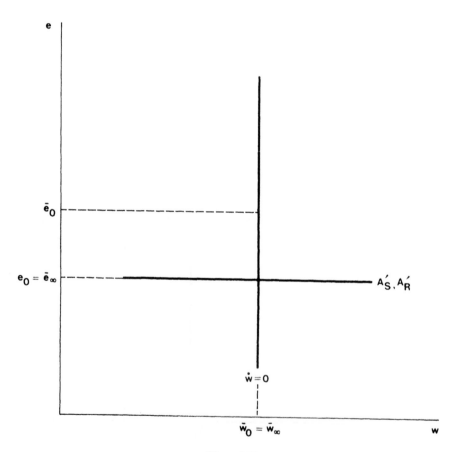

Figure 2.11

of wealth has no effect on the nominal exchange rate. However, it follows from eqs. (2.22a) and (2.22b) that it does affect the real exchange rate. The impact effect of the transfer is to raise P and lower $\overset{*}{P}$. These variables return to their original values as home residents decumulate wealth. This is a case of real exchange rate dynamics without nominal exchange rate dynamics.

The effects of a wealth transfer and an open market operation when there is neither local asset preference nor local good preference are shown in Figures 2.10 and 2.11. The A_S and A_R schedules are horizontal even though interest rates are not pegged. There are neither nominal nor real exchange rate dynamics. A transfer of wealth has no effect on the exchange rate, but the home country begins to run a trade account deficit. An open market operation causes the home currency to appreciate immediately to its new long-run equilibrium value and has no effect on the trade surplus of the home country.

2.7. Negative net foreign asset positions and stability

A negative net foreign asset position is a net debt of residents of one country denominated in the currency of the other country (F or $\overset{*}{B} < 0$). Several writers have suggested that negative net foreign asset positions alone can be a source of dynamic instability.[22] According to an alternative view presented in this subsection, negative net foreign asset positions are not an independent source of instability. Instability can arise only under nonrational expectations or because of destabilizing speculation.[23]

The exposition is simplified by retaining the assumption of local asset preference $[(M + B)/W > \overset{*}{B}/\overset{*}{W}$ and, therefore, $(\overset{*}{N} + \overset{*}{F})/\overset{*}{W} > F/W]$. This assumption taken together with our other assumptions implies that only net foreign asset positions can be negative: net domestic asset positions are always positive ($M + B, \overset{*}{N} + \overset{*}{F} > 0$). $W, \overset{*}{W}, \tilde{B}, \tilde{F}, \tilde{M} = M$ and $\tilde{N} = N$ are all positive. If $\overset{*}{B}$ and F are positive, B and $\overset{*}{F}$ may be negative. However, if there is local asset preference, $M + B$ and $\overset{*}{N} + \overset{*}{F}$ must still be positive. If $\overset{*}{B}$ and F are negative, B and $\overset{*}{F}$ and, therefore, $M + B$ and $\overset{*}{N} + \overset{*}{F}$ are positive.

---

[22] The instability problem associated with negative net foreign asset positions is a central issue in several recent papers: Boyer (1977); Branson, Halttunen, and Masson (1979); and Martin and Masson (1979). It is also discussed by Tobin and de Macedo (1981). Tobin (1980) summarizes a main conclusion reached in these papers. The problem is considered further by Henderson and Rogoff (1982), Kouri (1983a), Masson (1981), and Melitz (1982). The conclusions presented here are similar to those of Henderson and Rogoff, and Kouri but somewhat different from those of Masson. Melitz argues that the transactions demand for money is an important stabilizing influence.

[23] The negative net foreign asset case is not the only portfolio constellation that has led analysts to question the stability of open economy portfolio balance models. Enders (1977) and Masson (1980) discuss the possibility that instability might arise when positive net foreign asset positions are "too large". See footnotes 24, 26, 28, and 30.

Suppose goods prices are fixed. The $\dot{w}$ and $\dot{w} = 0$ schedules are the same as those shown in Figure 2.3 whether or not there are negative net foreign asset positions because net foreign asset positions do not enter the balance of payments equation.

In contrast, the slope of the asset market equilibrium schedule under static expectations (A_S) may be different when there are negative net foreign asset positions. A_S is downward sloping as in Figure 2.3 in the "normal" case. In this case, a depreciation of the home currency raises the value of ε required to clear the asset markets ($\varepsilon_e > 0$). As shown by (2.24), since $b_7 > \dot{b}_7$, an increase in w raises the value of ε required to clear the asset markets ($\varepsilon_w > 0$). Thus, an increase in w must be matched by an appreciation of the home currency if the asset markets are to remain in equilibrium. However, the A_S schedule is upward sloping as in Figure 2.12 in the "perverse" case. In this case, a depreciation of the home currency lowers the value of ε required to clear the asset markets ($\varepsilon_e < 0$). An increase in w must be matched by a depreciation of the home currency if the asset markets are to remain in equilibrium.

The restriction required for the normal case ($\varepsilon_e > 0$) is always satisfied if there

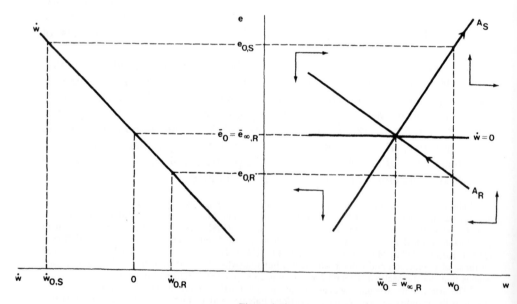

Figure 2.12

are no negative net foreign asset positions (F, $\dot{B} > 0$). When F and $\dot{B}$ are positive, a depreciation of the home currency unambiguously raises the demand for home securities ($\check{b}_e > 0$) because it raises home and foreign wealth. The restriction required for the normal case may be violated if either F or $\dot{B}$ is negative and is definitely violated if both are negative. If F is negative, a depreciation lowers home residents' wealth and, therefore, reduces their demand for home securities. If $\dot{B}$ is negative, a depreciation raises foreign residents' wealth. However, their demand for home securities falls as their wealth rises.

We investigate the stability of long-run equilibrium by analyzing an unanticipated transfer of wealth from foreign residents to home residents. Long-run equilibrium is stable under static expectations in the normal case. The analysis of a wealth transfer in Section 2.5, which is summarized in Figure 2.3, applies without modification. In the normal case negative net foreign asset positions do not alter the qualitative effects of wealth transfers and exchange rate changes on ε. Long-run equilibrium is definitely unstable under static expectations in the perverse case as shown in Figure 2.12. The transfer of wealth from foreign residents to home residents ($w_0 > \bar{w}_0$) raises demand for home securities. In the perverse case, asset market equilibrium is restored by a depreciation ($e_{0,S} > \bar{e}_0$) rather than an appreciation of the home currency, and the home country begins to run a trade surplus ($\dot{w}_{0,S} > 0$). As w rises, the home currency depreciates further. The economy moves along A_S away from long-run equilibrium.[24]

If speculation is stabilizing, long-run equilibrium is stable under rational expectations in both the normal and perverse cases.[25] As the arrows in Figures 2.3 and 2.12 indicate, long-run equilibria are saddle points under rational expectations. What is remarkable is that this result holds not only in the normal case but also in the perverse case. It is usual to find that if long-run equilibrium is stable under static expectations, it is a saddle point under rational expectations. However, here long-run equilibrium is a saddle point under rational expectations even if it is unstable under static expectations.

Under rational expectations the exchange rate jumps to clear the asset markets, just as it did under static expectations. Following a transfer, the world economy reaches long-run equilibrium if and only if it moves along the unique saddle path represented by A_R in Figure 2.3 in the normal case and by A_R in Figure 2.12 in

---

[24]If ε_e is positive but there is foreign asset preference ($b_7 < \dot{b}_7$), long-run equilibrium is definitely unstable under static expectations. With goods prices fixed, $b_7 < \dot{b}_7$ is a necessary and sufficient condition for ε_w to be negative. In this case, as in the perverse case of the text, the A_S schedule is upward sloping. It can be shown that if the assumption that in each country the demand for the good produced in the other country is independent of nominal spending is dropped, long-run equilibrium is stable for some, but not all, parameter values. Thus, with goods prices fixed, the Enders (1977) problem of instability caused by large net foreign asset positions can arise even if it is assumed that the home trade surplus depends on nominal spending in both countries.

[25]See footnote 20.

the perverse case. If the bidding of market participants causes the exchange rate to jump to $e_{0,R}$, the exchange rate on the A_R schedule corresponding to w_0, it will be said that speculation is stabilizing. When speculation is stabilizing, the home currency appreciates, and long-run equilibrium is stable no matter what the sign of ε_e. If the exchange rate remains unchanged at $\bar{e}_0$ or jumps to any value other than $e_{0,R}$, it will be said that speculation is destabilizing. When speculation is destabilizing, long-run equilibrium is unstable, as indicated by the arrows in Figures 2.3 and 2.12. Under rational expectations, instability can arise only because of destabilizing speculation and not because of perverse valuation effects associated with negative net foreign asset positions.[26]

Now suppose goods prices are flexible. The $\dot{w} = 0$ schedule is upward sloping as in Figure 2.6 whether or not there are negative net foreign asset positions. An increase in w reduces the home trade surplus. If the trade surplus is to be restored to its previous level, the home currency must depreciate under our assumption of local asset preference.

With goods prices flexible, just as with goods prices fixed, the slope of the asset market equilibrium schedule under static expectations (A_S) may be different when there are negative net foreign asset positions. A_S is downward sloping as in Figure 2.6 in the normal case. In this case, a depreciation of the home currency raises the value of ε required to clear the asset markets $(\varepsilon'_e > 0)$. As shown by (2.25), the net impact of the direct and indirect effects of an increase in w is to raise the value of ε required to clear the asset markets $(\varepsilon'_w > 0)$. Thus, an increase in w must be matched by an appreciation of the home currency if the asset markets are to remain in equilibrium. However, the A_S schedule is upward sloping as in Figure 2.13 in the perverse case. In this case, a depreciation of the home currency lowers the value of ε required to clear the asset markets $(\varepsilon'_e < 0)$. An increase in w must be matched by a depreciation of the home currency if the asset markets are to remain in equilibrium.

The restriction required for the normal case $(\varepsilon'_e > 0)$ is always satisfied if there are no negative net foreign asset positions $(F, B > 0)$. A depreciation of the home currency raises the demand for home securities directly by raising home and foreign wealth $(\tilde{b}_e > 0)$ and indirectly by raising the price of home goods thereby raising the home interest rate and by lowering the price of foreign goods thereby lowering the foreign interest rate. The restriction required for the normal case

---

[26]If $\varepsilon_e > 0$ but $b_7 < \dot{b}_7$ so that $\varepsilon_w < 0$, long-run equilibrium is definitely not a saddle point. The determinant of the differential equation system, made up of eq. (2.20) and eq. (2.24) with $\varepsilon = \dot{e}$, is $-\varepsilon_w \eta > 0$. It can be shown that either the two roots of the characteristic equation are real and positive or they are complex conjugates with positive real parts. It can also be shown that if the assumption that in each country the demand for the good produced in the other country is independent of nominal spending is dropped, long-run equilibrium is a saddle point under rational expectations if and only if it is stable under static expectations. Thus, with goods prices fixed, the Enders (1977) problem can arise under rational expectations even if it is assumed that the home trade surplus depends on nominal spending in both countries.

may be violated if either F or $\dot{B}$ is negative. It has been shown above that the direct effect of a depreciation on the demand for home securities may be perverse ($\tilde{b}_e < 0$) if F or $\dot{B}$ is negative and is definitely perverse if both are negative. The indirect effects may also be perverse: the price of home goods may fall if F is negative; the price of foreign goods may rise if $\dot{B}$ is negative. With goods prices fixed, a necessary and sufficient condition for the slope of A_S to be perverse is that the direct effect of a depreciation on the demand for home securities be perverse ($\tilde{b}_e < 0$). However, with goods prices flexible, $\tilde{b}_e < 0$ is neither a necessary nor a sufficient condition for the slope of A_S to be perverse. For example, suppose residents of both countries have negative net foreign asset positions ($F, \dot{B} < 0$) and that there is no local good preference ($x_2 = \dot{x}_2$ and $y_2 = \dot{y}_2$). Under those circumstances the direct effect of a depreciation is perverse ($\tilde{b}_e < 0$), but the indirect effects are normal, so the overall effect is indeterminate.

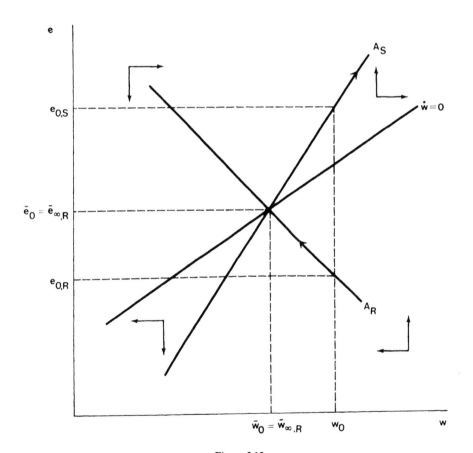

Figure 2.13

The results of stability analysis with goods prices flexible are similar to those with goods prices fixed. Long-run equilibrium is stable under static expectations in the normal case. The analysis of a wealth transfer in Section 2.6, which is summarized in Figure 2.6, applies without modification since in the normal case negative net foreign asset positions do not alter the qualitative effects of wealth transfers and exchange rate changes on ε. Long-run equilibrium is definitely unstable under static expectations in the perverse case, as shown in Figure 2.13, because the A_S schedule is steeper than the $\dot{w} = 0$ schedule.[27] The transfer of wealth to home residents ($w_0 > \bar{w}_0$) leads to a depreciation of the home currency ($e_{0,S} > \bar{e}_0$) and a trade surplus ($\dot{w}_{0,S} > 0$), and the economy moves along A_S away from equilibrium.[28] If speculation is stabilizing, long-run equilibrium is stable under rational expectations in both the normal and perverse cases.[29] As the arrows in Figures 2.6 and 2.13 indicate, long-run equilibria are saddle points under rational expectations. The unique saddle path is represented by A_R in Figure 2.6 in the normal case and by A_R in Figure 2.13 in the perverse case. When speculation is stabilizing, the exchange rate jumps to $e_{0,R}$. The home currency appreciates, and long-run equilibrium is stable no matter what the sign of ε'_e. When speculation is destabilizing, the exchange rate remains unchanged or jumps to some value other than $e_{0,R}$, and long-run equilibrium is unstable. No matter whether goods prices are fixed or flexible, under rational expectations instability can arise only because of destabilizing speculation and not because of perverse valuation effects associated with negative net foreign asset positions.[30]

3. The microeconomic foundations of asset demands in open economies

3.1. Overview

Demand equations for assets denominated in different currencies are based on the solution to a maximization problem faced by an individual investor. One specification of the problem is very common. The investor consumes a bundle of goods

---

[27] This assertion is proved in Appendix A.

[28] If ε_e is positive but there is foreign asset preferences ($b_7 < \dot{b}_7$), long-run equilibrium is definitely stable under static expectations. With goods prices flexible and $b_7 < \dot{b}_7$, ε'_w may be negative and C_5 is definitely negative. Thus, the A_S schedule may be upward sloping, and the $\dot{w} = 0$ schedule is definitely downward sloping. It is shown in Appendix A that if the A_S schedule is downward sloping, it is flatter than the $\dot{w} = 0$ schedule. Although the effect of a wealth transfer on the exchange rate depends on the slope of the A_S schedule, long-run equilibrium is stable whatever the slope of this schedule. Thus, with good prices flexible, the Enders (1977) problem cannot arise.

[29] It is shown in Appendix A that the determinant of the differential equation system, made up of eq. (2.22c) and eq. (2.25) with $\varepsilon = \dot{e}$, is always negative.

[30] If ε_e is positive but there is foreign asset preference ($b_7 < \dot{b}_7$), long-run equilibrium is definitely a saddle point under rational expectations. See footnote 21.

each of which is produced in a different country and priced in the currency of the country in which it is produced. In each currency denomination there is a security with a fixed nominal value and a certain nominal return. The investor has initial holdings of some or all of the securities and an uncertain stream of future labor income. Percentage changes in goods prices and exchange rates are assumed to follow "geometric Brownian motion". This assumption implies that successive percentage changes in these variables are independently distributed no matter how short the time interval and that the levels of the variables are log normally distributed. The investor maximizes the expected value of discounted lifetime utility.

In early analyses of portfolio selection in a closed economy, the specification of the investor's maximization problem was simplified by several assumptions.[31] First, it was assumed that the portfolio allocation decision in each period was separable from the saving decision. Under this assumption the optimal portfolio rule could be obtained by maximizing the expected utility of return in each period. Second, no distinction was made between nominal and real returns because the price level was assumed to be fixed. Third, it was assumed either that uncertain asset returns were normally distributed or that utility was quadratic in portfolio return. Fourth, it was assumed that there was an asset with a known return, the "safe" asset. These assumptions yielded the classic portfolio separation results.

More recent analyses of portfolio selection and saving in the closed economy have employed the tools of stochastic calculus.[32] An implicit solution for a general version of the investor's lifetime utility maximization problem has been obtained by applying the "Fundamental Theorem of Stochastic Dynamic Programming" and Ito's Lemma on stochastic differentials. In this general case the portfolio allocation problem is not separable from the saving decision and the classic portfolio separation results do not hold.

Recognizing the implications of some special assumptions in the more recent continuous time framework provides some perspective on earlier contributions. The assumption that the investor's instantaneous utility function exhibits constant relative risk aversion implies that the portfolio allocation decision is separable from the saving decision.[33] It is comforting to know that the separability of these decisions, which was simply assumed in earlier contributions, is implied by a class of utility functions. The assumption that the percentage changes in asset prices follow geometric Brownian motion so that the prices themselves are log-normally

---

[31] Markowitz (1959) and Tobin (1965) laid the foundations of portfolio selection theory.

[32] Merton (1971) pioneered this approach.

[33] Merton (1969) shows that the portfolio allocation decision is independent of the saving decision in a continuous time model. He assumes both that the investor's utility function exhibits constant relative risk aversion and that percentage changes in asset prices follow geometric Brownian motion. Samuelson (1969) derives the same result in a discrete time model. He assumes constant relative risk aversion but puts no restrictions on the distribution of returns.

distributed implies the classic portfolio separation results.[34] The very similar assumption that percentage returns are normally distributed yields these separation results in the earlier analyses.

The investor in the open economy must take account of both exchange rate and price index uncertainty.[35] Although a foreign security has a certain nominal return denominated in foreign currency, its nominal return in home currency is uncertain. Uncertainty about real returns arises not only because future values of exchanges rate are unknown but also because future values of the price index used to deflate nominal wealth are unknown. Exchange rate and price index changes are related in general, and the covariance between nominal returns inclusive of exchange rate changes and price index changes plays an important role in portfolio choice in an open economy. Changing the stochastic specification of the price index can have significant effects on this important covariance.

We begin by laying out in Section 3.2 a basic model with two assets: a home security and a foreign security. The implications of a popular specification of the price index are spelled out in Section 3.3. In Section 3.4 we show the effect of imposing relative purchasing power parity on this popular specification, and in Section 3.5 we trace out some consequences of violating the law of one price. Section 3.6 contains a three-asset model that is generalized in Section 3.7. Finally, in Section 3.8 we illustrate the integration of money into the open economy portfolio allocation problem.

3.2. Asset demands in a two-asset model with the exchange rate and the home price index stochastic

Analysis of demands for assets denominated in different currencies with the tools of stochastic calculus has usually proceeded under two simplifying assumptions. First, it has been assumed that percentage changes in prices follow geometric Brownian motion. Second, it has been assumed that the instantaneous utility function exhibits constant relative risk aversion $[U(\tilde{C}) = (1/\gamma)\tilde{C}^{\gamma}$, where $\tilde{C}$ is real consumption, and $\gamma < 1]$. Under these assumptions, the solution for optimal wealth allocation is the same as the one implied by maximization of an objective function that is linear in expected return and variance of return. Thus, the consumer can be viewed as deciding on the allocation of his wealth by maximizing the objective function:

$$V = E(d\tilde{W}/\tilde{W}) - (1/2)R[\text{var}(d\tilde{W}/\tilde{W})], \qquad (3.1)$$

---

[34] Merton (1971) proves this result.

[35] Solnik (1974) was the first to analyze portfolio selection in an open economy using stochastic calculus. He assumes that residents of each country consume only the good produced in that country and that goods prices are nonstochastic.

where $\tilde{W}$ is real wealth, and R is the coefficient of relative risk aversion $[-\tilde{C}U''(\tilde{C})/U'(\tilde{C}) = 1 - \gamma]$.

In the two-asset model, a home resident allocates a fraction λ of his nominal wealth W to foreign (currency) securities F and the remaining fraction $1 - \lambda$ to home (currency) securities B:

$$\lambda W = EF, \tag{3.2a}$$

$$(1 - \lambda)W = B. \tag{3.2b}$$

The exchange rate E is the home currency price of foreign currency. Home and foreign securities are short bonds and have certain nominal returns represented by i and $\overset{\bullet}{i}$ respectively:[36]

$$dB/B = i\,dt, \tag{3.3a}$$

$$dF/F = \overset{\bullet}{i}\,dt. \tag{3.3b}$$

Real wealth $\tilde{W}$ is nominal wealth deflated by the relevant price index Q:

$$\tilde{W} = W/Q = (B + EF)/Q. \tag{3.4}$$

Below we discuss the alternative assumptions about the stochastic properties of Q that have been made by different authors. For what follows it is useful to note that eqs. (3.2) and eq. (3.4) imply that

$$1/\tilde{W} = Q/W = \lambda Q/EF = (1 - \lambda)Q/B. \tag{3.5}$$

We begin by postulating stochastic processes for E and Q:[37]

$$dE/E = \varepsilon\,dt + \sigma_e\,dz_e, \tag{3.6}$$

$$dQ/Q = \pi_q\,dt + \sigma_q\,dz_q, \tag{3.7}$$

where ε and π_q are the means and σ_e^2 and σ_q^2 are the variances of the stochastic processes. z_e and z_q are standard normal random variables, so dz_e and dz_q are Wiener processes or Brownian motion often referred to in the literature as "Gaussian white noise". The covariance between the stochastic processes is denoted by ρ_{qe}. The investor's objective function depends on the mean and variance of the stochastic process followed by the percentage change in real wealth $d\tilde{W}/\tilde{W}$. In order to find $d\tilde{W}/\tilde{W}$, we make use of Ito's Lemma. Let $H = J(K_1, \ldots, K_n, t)$ be a twice continuously differentiable function defined on $R^n \times [0, \infty)$. Suppose the K_i follow geometric Brownian motion:

$$dK_i/K_i = \pi_i\,dt + \sigma_i\,dz_i, \qquad i = 1, \ldots, n. \tag{3.8}$$

---

[36] This is the approach followed by Adler and Dumas (1983).

[37] We assume that nominal interest rates are known in order to focus attention on exchange rate and price uncertainty. de Macedo, Goldstein, and Meerschwam (1983) allow for stochastic nominal returns in an N-country model.

According to Ito's Lemma the stochastic differential of H is given by

$$dH \equiv \sum_i (\partial J/\partial K_i)\, dK_i + (\partial J/\partial t)\, dt + (1/2)\sum_i \sum_j (\partial^2 J/\partial K_i \partial K_j)\, dK_i\, dK_j,$$

$$(3.9)$$

and the product $dK_i\, dK_j$ is defined by

$$dz_i\, dz_j = r_{ij}\, dt, \qquad i,j = 1,\dots,n, \tag{3.10a}$$

$$dz_i\, dt = 0, \qquad i = 1,\dots,n, \tag{3.10b}$$

where r_{ij} is the instantaneous correlation coefficient between the Wiener processes dz_i and dz_j.[38]

The stochastic differential of real wealth $d\tilde{W}$ is derived from the expression for real wealth $(B + EF)/Q$ in equation (3.4). $d\tilde{W}$ is equal to the conventional first differential of this expression plus one half times the conventional second differential:

$$d\tilde{W} = (1/Q)\, dB + (E/Q)\, dF + (F/Q)\, dE - (W/Q^2)\, dQ$$
$$+ (1/2)\big[-(1/Q^2)\, dQ\, dB + (1/Q)\, dE\, dF - (E/Q^2)\, dQ\, dF$$
$$+ (1/Q)\, dF\, dE - (F/Q^2)\, dQ\, dE - (1/Q^2)\, dB\, dQ$$
$$- (E/Q^2)\, dF\, dQ - (F/Q^2)\, dE\, dQ + (2W/Q^3)\, dQ^2 \big]. \tag{3.11}$$

Note that $\tilde{W}$ is not explicitly dependent on time, so there is no dt in the stochastic differential.

Multiplying eq. (3.11) by $1/\tilde{W}$, taking account of the relationships in (3.5), and combining terms yields an expression for $d\tilde{W}/\tilde{W}$:

$$d\tilde{W}/\tilde{W} = (1-\lambda)\, dB/B + \lambda\, dF/F + \lambda\, dE/E - dQ/Q$$
$$+ (1/2)\big[-2(1-\lambda)(dQ/Q)(dB/B) - 2\lambda(dQ/Q)(dF/F)$$
$$- 2\lambda(dE/E)(dF/F) - 2\lambda(dQ/Q)(dE/E) + 2(dQ/Q)^2 \big]. \tag{3.12}$$

Application of Ito's Lemma to the products of the stochastic processes yields:

$$(dQ/Q)(dB/B) = 0, \qquad (dQ/Q)(dF/F) = 0, \qquad (dE/E)(dF/F) = 0, \tag{3.13a}$$

$$(dQ/Q)(dE/E) = \rho_{qe}\, dt, \qquad (dQ/Q)^2 = \rho_{qq}\, dt, \tag{3.13b}$$

where ρ_{ij} is defined as $\sigma_i \sigma_j r_{ij}$ and is the covariance.

---

[38] For a more formal statement of Ito's Lemma and references to the mathematics literature on stochastic calculus, see Merton (1971).

The following example shows how the terms in (3.13) follow from Ito's Lemma. The product of (3.6) and (3.7) is

$$(dQ/Q)(dE/E) = \pi_q \varepsilon \, dt^2 + \pi_q \sigma_e \, dt \, dz_e + \varepsilon \sigma_q \, dt \, dz_q + \sigma_q \sigma_e \, dz_q \, dz_e. \quad (3.14)$$

The first term on the right-hand side is second order of magnitude, approximately zero. The product $dt \, dz_i$ is zero because dz_i is white noise. Therefore, the second and third terms disappear. Since the variance of a continuous time process is proportional to time, the standard deviation term dz_i is of the order of magnitude of the square root of dt.[39] Therefore, the last term becomes

$$\sigma_p \sigma_e \, dz_p \, dz_e = \sigma_p \sigma_e r_{pe} \, dt = \sigma_{pe} \, dt.$$

Thus (3.14) reduces to the expression for $(dQ/Q)(dE/E)$ in (3.13b).

The final expression for $d\tilde{W}/\tilde{W}$ is obtained by substituting eqs. (3.3), (3.6), (3.7), and (3.13) into eq. (3.12):

$$d\tilde{W}/\tilde{W} = \left[(1 - \lambda)i + \lambda \overset{*}{i} + \lambda \varepsilon - \pi_q - \lambda \rho_{qe} + \sigma_q^2 \right] dt$$
$$+ \lambda \sigma_e \, dz_e - \sigma_q \, dz_q. \quad (3.15)$$

The expected value of $d\tilde{W}/\tilde{W}$ is given by the coefficient of dt since the expected value of the dz_i terms is zero:

$$E(d\tilde{W}/\tilde{W}) = (1 - \lambda)i + \lambda \overset{*}{i} + \lambda \varepsilon - \pi_q - \lambda \rho_{qe} + \sigma_q^2. \quad (3.16)$$

Using Ito's Lemma to evaluate $(d\tilde{W}/\tilde{W})^2$ yields:

$$(d\tilde{W}/\tilde{W})^2 = \left(\lambda^2 \sigma_e^2 - 2\lambda \rho_{qe} + \sigma_q^2 \right) dt. \quad (3.17)$$

The variance of $d\tilde{W}/\tilde{W}$ is the coefficient of dt in (3.17):

$$\text{var}(d\tilde{W}/\tilde{W}) = \lambda^2 \sigma_e^2 - 2\lambda \rho_{qe} + \sigma_q^2. \quad (3.18)$$

The home consumer maximizes his objective function,

$$V = E(d\tilde{W}/\tilde{W}) - (1/2)R[\text{var}(d\tilde{W}/\tilde{W})], \quad (3.1)$$

with respect to his choice variable λ, the share of foreign securities in his portfolio. The optimal portfolio rule is

$$\lambda = \left(1/R\sigma_e^2\right)\left[\overset{*}{i} + \varepsilon - i + (R - 1)\rho_{qe} \right]. \quad (3.19)$$

The home investor's demands for foreign and home securities are given by eqs. (3.2) which are repeated here for convenience:

$$EF = \lambda W, \quad (3.2a)$$

$$B = (1 - \lambda)W, \quad (3.2b)$$

---

[39]See Chow (1979) for a precise derivation.

where λ is given by eq. (3.18). The partial derivatives of these demands for securities with respect to the expected return differential in favor of foreign securities are

$$\partial EF/\partial(\dot{i} + \varepsilon - i) = W/R\sigma_e^2 = -\partial B/\partial(\dot{i} + \varepsilon - i). \tag{3.20}$$

As risk aversion or the variance of the exchange rate increases, demands for securities become less sensitive to changes in the expected return differential.

In a model with two securities, the securities must be gross substitutes:

$$\partial EF/\partial(\dot{i} + \varepsilon) = W/R\sigma_e^2 = -\partial B/\partial(\dot{i} + \varepsilon), \tag{3.21a}$$

$$\partial EF/\partial i = -W/R\sigma_e^2 = -\partial B/\partial i. \tag{3.21b}$$

However, we show below that in a model with three securities, the securities need not be gross substitutes.

3.3. Implications of a popular specification of the home price index

Additional results can be obtained by assuming a particular specification of the home price index Q:[40]

$$Q = P^{1-\beta}(E\dot{P})^{\beta}. \tag{3.22}$$

P is the home currency price of home goods. $\dot{P}$ is the foreign currency price of foreign goods. The "law of one price" holds, so the domestic currency price of foreign goods is $E\dot{P}$. β is the share of expenditure devoted to foreign goods.

The exchange rate follows the stochastic process (3.6), and the prices of both goods follow geometric Brownian motion:[41]

$$dP/P = \pi_p dt + \sigma_p dz_p, \tag{3.23a}$$

$$d\dot{P}/\dot{P} = \pi_p^* dt + \sigma_p^* dz_p^*, \tag{3.23b}$$

where π_p and π_p^* are the means and σ_p^2 and σ_p^{*2} are the variances of the price processes. dz_p and dz_p^* are Brownian motion. The covariance between the two price processes is ρ_{pp}^*. The covariances of the exchange rate process with the two price processes are ρ_{pe} and ρ_{pe}^*. We note here in passing that eqs. (3.6) and (3.22) imply that purchasing power parity ($P = E\dot{P}$) does not hold in general. We return to this point in Section 3.4.

In Section 3.2 we specified a stochastic process for the domestic price index Q. In this section the stochastic process for Q is implied by the specification of the

---

[40] This specification is used by Kouri (1977) and de Macedo (1983, 1982).

[41] Kouri (1977) assumes that the price of one country's output is nonstochastic and uses the currency of that country as the numeraire currency.

price index given by eq. (3.21) and the stochastic processes for E, P, and $\dot{P}$ given by eqs. (3.6), (3.22), and (3.23), respectively. In Section 3.2 we showed that the only parameter of the stochastic process for Q that enters the optimal portfolio rule is the covariance of this process with the stochastic process for the exchange rate ρ_{qe}. The expression for ρ_{qe} implied by eqs. (3.21), (3.6), (3.22), and (3.23) is obtained by applying Ito's Lemma twice. First, it is used to find dQ/Q. Then, it is employed to evaluate the product $(dQ/Q)(dE/E)$:[42]

$$(dQ/Q)(dE/E) = \left[(1 - \beta)\rho_{pe} + \beta\sigma_e^2 + \beta\rho_{pe}^*\right]dt. \tag{3.24}$$

That is,

$$\rho_{qe} = (1 - \beta)\rho_{pe} + \beta\sigma_e^2 + \beta\rho_{pe}^*. \tag{3.25}$$

The specification of the home price index given by eq. (3.21) implies that the optimal portfolio rule depends on the share of expenditure devoted to the foreign good. Substituting (3.25) into (3.19) yields:

$$\lambda = (1/R\sigma_e^2)\left\{\dot{i} + \varepsilon - i + (R - 1)\left[(1 - \beta)\rho_{pe} + \beta\sigma_e^2 + \beta\rho_{pe}^*\right]\right\}. \tag{3.26}$$

In Section 2 it was shown that the properties of portfolio balance models with postulated asset demands depend critically on whether there is local asset preference. It seems clear that there is local asset preference in most countries. A widely accepted explanation for local asset preference is that foreigners allocate a larger share of their portfolios to foreign assets than home residents because they devote a larger share of their expenditure to foreign goods. Therefore, it is interesting to ask whether the portfolio rule of eq. (3.26) implies a positive association between the share of wealth devoted to foreign securities λ and the share of expenditure devoted to foreign goods β.

It turns out that λ does not necessarily rise when β increases. The derivative of λ with respect to β can be written as

$$\partial\lambda/\partial\beta = (\partial\lambda/\partial\rho_{qe})(\partial\rho_{qe}/\partial\beta), \tag{3.27}$$

where

$$\partial\lambda/\partial\rho_{qe} = (R - 1)/R\sigma_e^2, \tag{3.28}$$

$$\partial\rho_{qe}/\partial\beta = -\rho_{pe} + \sigma_e^2 + \rho_{pe}^*. \tag{3.29}$$

An increase in the correlation between the price index and the exchange rate ρ_{qe} raises λ if and only if the coefficient of relative risk aversion R is greater than one. If E is the only stochastic variable so that $\rho_{pe} = \rho_{pe}^* = 0$, then an increase in β definitely raises ρ_{qe}. In this case, $R > 1$ is a necessary and sufficient condition

---

[42] These calculations are performed in Appendix B.

for an increase in β to raise λ.[43] If E, P and $\dot{P}$ are all stochastic variables, the analysis is somewhat more complicated. In this case, $R > 1$ implies that an increase in β raises λ if and only if an increase in β raises ρ_{qe}. Presumably $\rho_{pe} > 0$ and $\rho_{pe}^{\bullet} < 0$, so $\partial \rho_{qe}/\partial \beta > 0$ if and only if the exchange rate variance σ_e^2 is larger than the sum of the absolute values of the covariances of the exchange rate with the two prices.[44] The result that $\partial \lambda/\partial \rho_{qe} > 0$ if and only if $R > 1$ arises because real wealth is the ratio of two stochastic variables, nominal wealth and the price index. Applying Ito's Lemma to this ratio yields an expression for the mean of the percentage change in wealth in eq. (3.16) which includes $-\lambda \rho_{qe}$. Therefore $-\rho_{qe}$ is included in the numerator of the portfolio rule.[45]

The portfolio rule (3.19) can be rewritten in two intuitively appealing forms whenever the exchange rate and the price index follow geometric Brownian motion. This rule can be written in a third intuitively appealing form in the special case of the popular specification of the price index in (3.22).

The optimal portfolio rule (3.19) can be viewed as a weighted average of the minimum variance portfolio rule and the logarithmic or "international investor's" portfolio rule.[46] The minimum variance portfolio rule (λ_M) is obtained by minimizing (3.17) with respect to λ:

$$\lambda_M = \rho_{qe}/\sigma_e^2. \tag{3.30}$$

If the investor's utility function is logarithmic $[U(\tilde{C}) = \ln \tilde{C}]$, then $R = 1$. The logarithmic portfolio rule (λ_L) is obtained by setting $R = 1$ in eq. (3.26):

$$\lambda_L = (1/\sigma_e^2)(\overset{?}{i} + \varepsilon - i). \tag{3.31}$$

This rule has often been referred to as the international investor's portfolio rule because it is independent of expenditure shares. The optimal portfolio rule can be

---

[43] This result was derived by Krugman (1981). Stulz (1983) shows that $R > 1$ is a necessary and sufficient condition only when the underlying utility function is homothetic in the goods consumed. In more general circumstances $R > 1$ is neither necessary nor sufficient.

[44] This result was derived by de Macedo (1982).

[45] Dornbusch (1983) does not use stochastic calculus. Instead he takes a short cut that has some surface appeal. First he finds the expression that would represent the percentage change in $\tilde{W}$ if $\tilde{W}$ were nonstochastic and calls this expression the real return on the portfolio. This expression is a weighted average of the expressions that would represent the percentage changes in the real values of the foreign and home securities. The component expressions contain nominal interest rates and percentage changes in the exchange rate and goods prices. Dornbusch assumes that the percentage changes in the exchange rate and goods prices are normally distributed. Dornbusch's short cut is invalid because of Jensen's inequality. He obtains incorrect expressions for the expected real returns on the assets. In terms of our model, Dornbusch's approach leads to omission of the $-\lambda \rho_{qe}$ term in the expression for the expected value of the change in real wealth. It is this omission which leads Dornbusch to the incorrect conclusion that increases in β increase λ for all values of R.

[46] Adler and Dumas (1983) emphasize this decomposition.

rewritten as a weighted average of λ_M and λ_L:

$$\lambda = [(R-1)/R]\left(\rho_{qe}/\sigma_e^2\right) + (1/R)\left[\left(1/\sigma_e^2\right)(\overset{*}{i} + \varepsilon - i)\right]. \tag{3.32}$$

As the coefficient of relative risk aversion R approaches infinity the optimal rule approaches the minimum variance rule. As R approaches one the optimal rule approaches the logarithmic rule. The covariance term ρ_{qe} enters only through the minimum variance portfolio, and the return differential enters only through the logarithmic portfolio.

The optimal portfolio can also be written as the sum of the minimum variance portfolio and a zero net worth "speculative" portfolio.[47] Writing the shares of the optimal portfolio in terms of deviations from the shares of minimum variance portfolio yields:

$$\lambda = \rho_{qe}/\sigma_e^2 + \left(1/R\sigma_e^2\right)\left(\overset{*}{i} + \varepsilon - i - \rho_{qe}\right), \tag{3.33a}$$

$$1 - \lambda = \left(1 - \rho_{qe}/\sigma_e^2\right) - \left(1/R\sigma_e^2\right)\left(\overset{*}{i} + \varepsilon - i - \rho_{qe}\right). \tag{3.33b}$$

The shares of the minimum variance portfolio, λ_M and $1 - \lambda_M$, sum to unity. Therefore, the shares of the speculative portfolio, λ_S and $-\lambda_S$, where

$$\lambda_S = \left(1/R\sigma_e^2\right)\left(\overset{*}{i} + \varepsilon - i - \rho_{qe}\right), \tag{3.34}$$

must sum to zero.

Finally, in the special case of the popular specification of the price index in (3.22), the optimal portfolio can be written as the sum of an "expenditure share" portfolio and two zero net worth portfolios. In this case ρ_{qe} is given by (3.25). Therefore, the minimum variance portfolio can be written as the sum of the expenditure share portfolio and a zero net worth "hedge" portfolio:

$$\lambda_M = \beta + \left(1/\sigma_e^2\right)\left[(1-\beta)\rho_{pe} + \beta\rho_{pe}^*\right], \tag{3.35a}$$

$$1 - \lambda_M = 1 - \beta - \left(1/\sigma_e^2\right)\left[(1-\beta)\rho_{pe} + \beta\rho_{pe}^*\right]. \tag{3.35b}$$

The expenditure shares sum to unity. Therefore, the shares of the hedge portfolio, λ_H and $-\lambda_H$, where

$$\lambda_H = \left(1/\sigma_e^2\right)\left[(1-\beta)\rho_{pe} + \beta\rho_{pe}^*\right], \tag{3.36}$$

must sum to zero. Note that if E is the only stochastic variable so that $\rho_{pe} = \rho_{pe}^* = 0$, then the minimum variance shares are simply the expenditure shares. If E, P, and $\overset{*}{P}$ are stochastic, the minimum variance shares deviate from the expenditure shares when exchange rate changes are associated with changes in goods prices. Substituting eqs. (3.35) into eqs. (3.33) confirms that the optimal

---

[47]Kouri (1977) and de Macedo (1982) emphasize this decomposition and the one that follows.

portfolio can be written as the sum of the expenditure share portfolio, the hedge portfolio, and the speculative portfolio. Of course, the hedge portfolio and the speculative portfolio could be added together so that the optimal portfolio could be expressed as the sum of the expenditure share portfolio and a single zero net worth portfolio.

3.4. Implications of relative purchasing power parity

When separate stochastic processes are specified for E, P, and $\dot{P}$ as in Section 3.3, the relative price of foreign goods (EP/P) is free to vary. Here we explore the implications of assuming that relative purchasing power parity (PPP) holds, i.e. that the relative price of the foreign good is constant $(E\dot{P}/P = k$, so $E = kP/\dot{P})$. Given relative PPP the stochastic differential of E is

$$\mathrm{d}E/E = (\mathrm{d}P/P) - \left(\mathrm{d}\dot{P}/\dot{P}\right) + \left(\mathrm{d}\dot{P}/\dot{P}\right)^2 - (\mathrm{d}P/P)\left(\mathrm{d}\dot{P}/\dot{P}\right). \tag{3.37}$$

Substituting in expressions for $\mathrm{d}P/P$, $\mathrm{d}\dot{P}/\dot{P}$, $(\mathrm{d}\dot{P}/\dot{P})^2$, and $(\mathrm{d}P/P)(\mathrm{d}\dot{P}/\dot{P})$ obtained using (3.22), (3.23) and Ito's Lemma yields:

$$\mathrm{d}E/E = \left(\pi_p - \pi_{\dot{p}} + \sigma_{\dot{p}}^2 - \rho_{p\dot{p}}\right)\mathrm{d}t + \sigma_p\,\mathrm{d}z_p - \sigma_{\dot{p}}\,\mathrm{d}z_{\dot{p}}. \tag{3.38}$$

Thus, the expected percentage change in the exchange rate is

$$\varepsilon = \pi_p - \pi_{\dot{p}} + \sigma_{\dot{p}}^2 - \rho_{p\dot{p}}. \tag{3.39}$$

Evaluating $(\mathrm{d}E/E)^2$, $(\mathrm{d}P/P)(\mathrm{d}E/E)$, and $(\mathrm{d}\dot{P}/\dot{P})(\mathrm{d}E/E)$ yields:

$$(\mathrm{d}E/E)^2 = \left(\sigma_p^2 + \sigma_{\dot{p}}^2 - 2\rho_{p\dot{p}}\right)\mathrm{d}t, \tag{3.40a}$$

$$(\mathrm{d}P/P)(\mathrm{d}E/E) = \left(\sigma_p^2 - \rho_{p\dot{p}}\right)\mathrm{d}t, \tag{3.40b}$$

$$\left(\mathrm{d}\dot{P}/\dot{P}\right)(\mathrm{d}E/E) = \left(-\sigma_{\dot{p}}^2 + \rho_{p\dot{p}}\right)\mathrm{d}t. \tag{3.40c}$$

Thus, the variance of the exchange rate and the covariances of the two prices with the exchange rate are

$$\sigma_e^2 = \sigma_p^2 + \sigma_{\dot{p}}^2 - 2\rho_{p\dot{p}}, \tag{3.41a}$$

$$\rho_{pe} = \sigma_p^2 - \rho_{p\dot{p}}, \tag{3.41b}$$

$$\rho_{\dot{p}e} = -\sigma_{\dot{p}}^2 + \rho_{p\dot{p}}. \tag{3.41c}$$

It has been argued that when relative PPP holds, the investor does not face exchange risk.[48] It is true that ε, σ_e^2, ρ_{pe}, and $\rho_{\dot{p}e}$ can be eliminated from the

[48] Grauer, Litzenberger, and Stehle (1976), Wihlborg (1978), and Fama and Farber (1979) make this argument.

optimal portfolio rule (3.26) with the use of the relationships in (3.39) and (3.41):

$$\lambda = \left[1/R\left(\sigma_p^2 + \sigma_{\tilde{p}}^2 - 2\rho_{p\tilde{p}}^*\right)\right]\left[\tilde{i} + \pi_p - \pi_{\tilde{p}}^* + \sigma_{\tilde{p}}^2 - \rho_{p\tilde{p}}^* - i + (R-1)\left(\sigma_p^2 - \rho_{p\tilde{p}}^*\right)\right].$$
(3.42)

However, whether this observation confirms the view that the investor does not face exchange risk is a question of semantics. Other expressions for the optimal portfolio besides (3.42) are consistent with relative PPP. For example, using the relationships in (3.41) to solve for $\rho_{\tilde{p}e}^*$ in terms of σ_e^2, σ_p^2, and ρ_{pe}; substituting the result into (3.26); and collecting terms yields:

$$\lambda = \left(1/R\sigma_e^2\right)\left[\tilde{i} + \varepsilon - i + (R-1)\rho_{pe}\right],$$
(3.43)

in which $\pi_{\tilde{p}}^*$, $\sigma_{\tilde{p}}^2$, $\rho_{\tilde{p}e}^*$, and $\rho_{p\tilde{p}}^*$ do not appear. All that relative PPP implies is that E, P, and $\tilde{P}$ are tied together so that specification of stochastic processes for any two of the three variables implies a stochastic process for the third.

3.5. Price index–exchange rate covariance and the law of one price

The optimal portfolio rule depends on the covariance between the price index and the exchange rate ρ_{qe} unless the coefficient of relative risk aversion equals one. In their survey of the literature on international portfolio diversification, Adler and Dumas (1983) report that for many countries the covariance between the consumer price index and the exchange rate is low in monthly data. This finding suggests that it is worth asking what might cause the covariance to be low.

In exploring for possible causes of a low price index–exchange rate covariance it is useful to adopt a general specification of the price index, one in which neither relative PPP nor the law of one price is imposed. Suppose that the home currency price of foreign goods P^f is equal to the product of the exchange rate E, the foreign currency price of foreign goods, and a variable representing the (proportional) deviation from the law of one price V:

$$P^f = E\tilde{P}V.$$
(3.44)

Then, the price index is given by

$$Q = P^{1-\beta}\left(E\tilde{P}V\right)^{\beta}.$$
(3.45)

The exchange rate, the price of home goods, and the price of foreign goods follow the stochastic processes (3.6), (3.22), and (3.23) respectively, and the deviation from the law of one price follows geometric Brownian motion:

$$dV/V = \pi_v dt + \sigma_v dz_v.$$
(3.46)

The expression for ρ_{qe} implied by eqs. (3.45), (3.6), (3.22), (3.23), and (3.46) is obtained by applying Ito's Lemma twice, first to find $\mathrm{d}Q/Q$ and then to evaluate $(\mathrm{d}Q/Q)(\mathrm{d}E/E)$:[49]

$$(\mathrm{d}Q/Q)(\mathrm{d}E/E) = \left[(1-\beta)\sigma_{pe} + \beta\sigma_e^2 + \beta\rho_{\dot{p}e}^* + \beta\rho_{ve}\right]\mathrm{d}t. \tag{3.47}$$

That is:

$$\rho_{qe} = (1-\beta)\sigma_{pe} + \beta\sigma_e^2 + \beta\rho_{\dot{p}e}^* + \beta\rho_{ve}. \tag{3.48}$$

Given that $\rho_{ij} = \sigma_i\sigma_j r_{ij}$, ρ_{qe} is equal to zero if and only if

$$0 = (1-\beta)\sigma_p r_{pe} + \beta\sigma_e + \beta\sigma_p r_{\dot{p}e}^* + \beta\sigma_v r_{ve}. \tag{3.49}$$

If goods prices are nonstochastic or if the correlations of E with P and $\dot{P}$ are zero, zero covariance between E and Q implies that the correlation between the exchange rate and the deviation from the law of one price must satisfy:

$$r_{ve} = -\sigma_e/\sigma_v. \tag{3.50}$$

If $\sigma_e = \sigma_v$, a perfect negative correlation between E and V makes the covariance between Q and E equal zero. If goods prices are nonstochastic or $r_{pe} = r_{\dot{p}e}^* = 0$, $\rho_{qe} = 0$ implies systematic deviations from the law of one price. In more general circumstances, condition (3.49) might be satisfied even if there were no deviations from the law of one price.

3.6. Asset demands in a three-asset model with exchange rates and the price index stochastic

In the two-asset model of Section 3.2 assets are gross substitutes as they are in all two asset models. However, in models with three or more assets, the possibility arises that some assets may be complements. Whether assets are substitutes or complements depends on the association between the returns on the assets. If the interest rate on the first asset rises and the returns on the second and third assets are highly correlated, the demand for the second asset may rise while the demand for the third asset falls, or vice versa.

In this subsection we spell out the conditions under which assets are complements in a three asset generalization of the two asset model of Section 3.2. The objective function V is given by eq. (3.1). The investor allocates a proportion λ_1 of his nominal wealth W to the first foreign security F_1, a proportion λ_2 to the

---

[49] These calculations are performed in Appendix B.

second foreign security F_2, and the remainder to the home security B:

$$\lambda_1 W = E_1 F_1, \tag{3.51a}$$

$$\lambda_2 W = E_2 F_2, \tag{3.51b}$$

$$(1 - \lambda_1 - \lambda_2)W = B. \tag{3.51c}$$

E_i, $i = 1, 2$, is the home currency price of foreign currency i. The first foreign security, the second foreign security, and the home security have certain nominal returns represented by $\overset{*}{i}_1$, $\overset{*}{i}_2$, and i, respectively:

$$d F_1/F_1 = \overset{*}{i}_1 dt, \tag{3.52a}$$

$$d F_2/F_2 = \overset{*}{i}_2 dt, \tag{3.52b}$$

$$d B/B = i \, dt. \tag{3.52c}$$

Real wealth $\tilde{W}$ is nominal wealth deflated by the price index:

$$\tilde{W} = W/Q = (B + E_1 F_1 + E_2 F_2)/Q. \tag{3.53}$$

Eqs. (3.51) and (3.53) imply:

$$1/\tilde{W} = Q/W = \lambda_1 Q/E_1 F_1 = \lambda_2 Q/E_2 F_2 = (1 - \lambda_1 - \lambda_2)Q/B. \tag{3.54}$$

The two exchange rates and the price index follow geometric Brownian motion:

$$d E_1/E_1 = \varepsilon_1 \, dt + \sigma_1 \, dz_1, \tag{3.55a}$$

$$d E_2/E_2 = \varepsilon_2 \, dt + \sigma_2 \, dz_2, \tag{3.55b}$$

$$dQ/Q = \pi_q \, dt + \sigma_q \, dz_q. \tag{3.55c}$$

The second-order terms utilized below are

$$(dQ/Q)^2 = \sigma_q^2 \, dt, \tag{3.56a}$$

$$(dQ/Q)(d E_1/E_1) = \rho_{q1} \, dt, \tag{3.56b}$$

$$(dQ/Q)(d E_2/E_2) = \rho_{q2} \, dt, \tag{3.56c}$$

$$(d E_1/E_1)(d E_2/E_2) = \rho_{12} \, dt. \tag{3.56d}$$

Calculating the stochastic differential of $\tilde{W}$ using Ito's Lemma, dividing through by $\tilde{W}$, and substituting in the expressions in (3.56) yields:

$$d\tilde{W}/\tilde{W} = \big[(1 - \lambda_1 - \lambda_2)i + \lambda_1 \overset{*}{i}_1 + \lambda_2 \overset{*}{i}_2 + \lambda_1 \varepsilon_1 + \lambda_2 \varepsilon_2 - \pi_q$$
$$+ \sigma_q^2 - \lambda_1 \rho_{q1} - \lambda_2 \rho_{q2}\big] \, dt$$
$$- \sigma_q \, dz_q + \lambda_1 \sigma_1 \, dz_1 + \lambda_2 \sigma_2 \, dz_2. \tag{3.57}$$

The expected value and variance of $d\tilde{W}/\tilde{W}$ are given by

$$E(d\tilde{W}/\tilde{W}) = (1 - \lambda_1 - \lambda_2)i + \lambda_1 \dot{i}_1 + \lambda_2 \dot{i}_2 + \lambda_1 \varepsilon_1 + \lambda_2 \varepsilon_2 - \pi_q$$

$$+ \sigma_q^2 - \lambda_1 \rho_{q1} - \lambda_2 \rho_{q2}, \tag{3.58a}$$

$$\text{var}(d\tilde{W}/\tilde{W}) = \sigma_q^2 + \lambda_1^2 \sigma_1^2 + \lambda_2^2 \sigma_2^2 - 2\lambda_1 \rho_{q1} - 2\lambda_2 \rho_{q2} + 2\lambda_1 \lambda_2 \rho_{12}. \tag{3.58b}$$

Substituting these expressions into the objective function (3.1) and setting the partial derivatives with respect to λ_1 and λ_2 equal to zero yields two equations in λ_1 and λ_2:

$$R(\sigma_1^2 \lambda_1 + \rho_{12} \lambda_2) = \dot{i}_1 + \varepsilon_1 - i + (R - 1)\rho_{q1}, \tag{3.59a}$$

$$R(\rho_{12} \lambda_1 + \sigma_2^2 \lambda_2) = \dot{i}_2 + \varepsilon_2 - i + (R - 1)\rho_{q2}. \tag{3.59b}$$

These equations can be rewritten in matrix form:

$$R\Omega\lambda = \delta + (R - 1)\rho, \tag{3.60}$$

where

$$\Omega = \begin{bmatrix} \sigma_1^2 & \rho_{12} \\ \rho_{12} & \sigma_2^2 \end{bmatrix}, \quad \lambda = \begin{bmatrix} \lambda_1 \\ \lambda_2 \end{bmatrix}, \quad \delta = \begin{bmatrix} \dot{i}_1 + \varepsilon_1 - i \\ \dot{i}_2 + \varepsilon_2 - i \end{bmatrix}, \quad \rho = \begin{bmatrix} \rho_{q1} \\ \rho_{q2} \end{bmatrix}.$$

Ω is the variance–covariance matrix for exchange rate changes; λ is the vector of the portfolio shares devoted to the first and second foreign securities; δ is the vector of differentials between the expected nominal returns on the first and second foreign securities and the home security; and ρ is the vector of covariances of the price index with the two exchange rates.

The portfolio rule can be obtained by inverting $R\Omega$:

$$\lambda = [(R - 1)/R]\Omega^{-1}\rho + (1/R)\Omega^{-1}\delta. \tag{3.61}$$

This rule is analogous to the rule obtained in the two-asset model. The share of wealth devoted to a single foreign security is replaced by a vector of shares. The inverse of the variance of exchange rate changes is replaced by the inverse of the variance–covariance matrix of changes in exchange rates. The single expected nominal return differential is replaced by the vector of expected nominal return differentials. The covariance of the price index with one exchange rate is replaced by a vector of covariances of the price index with exchange rates.

In eq. (3.60) the optimal portfolio shares are expressed as a weighted average of the shares of the minimum variance portfolio $\lambda_M = \Omega^{-1}\rho$ and the logarithmic portfolio $\lambda_L = \Omega^{-1}\delta$. The structure of the logarithmic and minimum variance portfolios in the three-asset model is analogous to the structure of those portfolios in the two-asset example: return differentials enter only the logarithmic portfolio and covariances of the price index with exchange rates enter only the minimum variance portfolio.

The portfolio rule can also be written as the sum of the minimum variance portfolio $\lambda_M = \Omega^{-1}\rho$ and a zero net worth speculative portfolio $\lambda_S = \Omega^{-1}(\delta - \rho)$:

$$\lambda = \Omega^{-1}\rho + (1/R)\Omega^{-1}(\delta - \rho), \tag{3.62}$$

where $\delta - \rho$ is a vector of expected real return differentials.

In a three-asset model it is possible for assets to be complements. The partial derivatives of the three security demand functions (3.51) with respect to $\overset{*}{i}$, are

$$\partial \lambda_1 W/\partial \overset{*}{i}_1 = W/R\sigma_1^2(1 - r_{12}^2), \tag{3.63a}$$

$$\partial \lambda_2 W/\partial \overset{*}{i}_1 = -\left[W(\sigma_1/\sigma_2)r_{12}\right]/R\sigma_1^2(1 - r_{12}^2), \tag{3.63b}$$

$$\partial(1 - \lambda_1 - \lambda_2)W/\partial \overset{*}{i}_1 = -W\left[1 - (\sigma_1/\sigma_2)r_{12}\right]/R\sigma_1^2(1 - r_{12}^2). \tag{3.63c}$$

An increase in the nominal return on the first foreign security raises the demand for that security, as always. The two other assets are gross substitutes for the first foreign security if both cross partials are negative, that is, if the correlation between the nominal returns on the two foreign securities, which is just the correlation between the two exchange rates, is positive but less than σ_2/σ_1. If the two exchange rates are positively correlated and have variances that are roughly equal, the three securities are definitely gross substitutes. Negative correlation between the two exchange rates implies that the two foreign securities are complements. Positive correlation and a large enough value of σ_1/σ_2 imply that the first foreign security and the home security are complements. Thus, in a three-asset model, making the assumption that the assets are gross substitutes is equivalent to imposing restrictions on the correlations between the nominal returns on assets.

3.7. Asset demands in a general model with exchange rates and the price index stochastic

The three-asset model can be easily generalized to the case in which there are N foreign securities and a home security. By analogy the optimal portfolio rule can be written in two ways:

$$\lambda = \left[(R - 1)/R\right]\Omega^{-1}\rho + (1/R)\Omega^{-1}\delta, \tag{3.64a}$$

$$\lambda = \Omega^{-1}\rho + (1/R)\Omega^{-1}(\delta - e), \tag{3.64b}$$

where $\lambda_M = \Omega^{-1}\rho$ is the minimum variance portfolio, $\lambda_L = \Omega^{-1}\delta$ is the logarithmic portfolio, and $\lambda_S = \Omega^{-1}(\delta - e)$ is the zero net worth speculative portfolio. λ is the N-dimensional column vector of the shares of the N foreign securities in the optimal portfolio. Ω is the $N \times N$ variance–covariance matrix for the changes in the N exchange rates, which are defined as foreign currency prices of the home currency. ρ is the N-dimensional vector of covariances of the price index with the

N exchange rates. δ is the N-dimensional vector of return differentials, $\overset{*}{i}_n + \varepsilon_n - i$, $n = 1, \ldots, N$. λ_M, λ_L, and λ_S are all N-dimensional vectors. For the rules λ, λ_M, and λ_L, the home security share is one minus the sum of the N foreign security shares; for the rule λ_S, the home security share is the negative of the sum of the N foreign security shares.

The basic structure of the general model is the same as that of the two- and three-asset models. The logarithmic portfolio is not sensitive to the choice of assumption regarding price index dynamics. However, the minimum variance portfolio is sensitive to this choice. Different assumptions about price index dynamics made by various analysts are reflected in different ρ vectors.

3.8. Integrating money into the microeconomic theory of asset demands

The portfolio rules of Sections 3.2–3.7 are rules for allocating nominal wealth among interest bearing securities. If the mean and variance of the change in real wealth are the only arguments in the objective function, noninterest bearing money is not held in portfolios because it is dominated by securities denominated in the same currency that pay a certain nominal return. Money has been integrated into the microeconomic theory of asset demands by assuming that real money balances enter the investor's objective function. Some analysts justify the procedure by arguing that real balances as well as goods are inputs into a "production function" for consumption, so utility can be expressed as a function of real balances and goods.[50] Others argue that an investor with higher real balances has more leisure because he need make fewer trips to the bank.[51] There is a lively debate about whether it is useful to assume that real balances enter the investor's objective function. We make no attempt to summarize that debate here.[52] Rather, we report some of the results that have been derived under the assumption that real balances enter the investor's objective function.

The investor's augmented objective function V^A is assumed to be the sum of V in eq. (3.1) and a function of real balances $Z(M/Q)$, where $Z' > 0$ and $Z'' < 0$:

$$V^A = \mathrm{E}(d\tilde{W}/W) - (1/2)R[\mathrm{var}(d\tilde{W}/\tilde{W})] + Z(M/Q). \tag{3.65}$$

The investor allocates a proportion λ of his nominal wealth to fore$\overset{.}{}$gn securities, a proportion μ to home money M, and the remainder to home securities:

$$\lambda W = EF, \tag{3.66a}$$
$$\mu W = M, \tag{3.66b}$$
$$(1 - \lambda - \mu)W = B. \tag{3.66c}$$

---

[50] Stulz (1981) makes this argument.
[51] McCallum (1983) makes this argument.
[52] McCallum (1983) provides a summary of this debate and argues strongly in the affirmative.

The expected value and variance of $d\tilde{W}/\tilde{W}$ become:

$$E(d\tilde{W}/\tilde{W}) = (1 - \lambda - \mu)i + \lambda\overset{*}{i} + \lambda\varepsilon - \pi_q - \lambda\rho_{qe} + \sigma_q^2, \tag{3.67a}$$

$$\text{var}(d\tilde{W}/\tilde{W}) = \lambda^2\sigma_e^2 - 2\lambda\rho_{qe} + \sigma_q^2. \tag{3.67b}$$

Substituting the expressions (3.67) into V^A, noting that $M/Q = \mu W/Q$, and setting the partial derivatives with respect to λ and μ equal to zero, yields:

$$\overset{*}{i} + \varepsilon - i - \rho_{qe} - R\left(\lambda\sigma_e^2 - \rho_{qe}\right) = 0, \tag{3.68a}$$

$$i - \left[Z'(\mu W/Q)\right](W/Q) = 0. \tag{3.68b}$$

Solving (3.68a) for the share of foreign securities λ yields exactly the same expression as the one in eq. (3.19), which is derived from the two-asset model with no money. Eq. (3.68b) implies a value for the share of money μ given values for W/Q and i. Below we assume some specific forms for the function $Z(M/Q)$ and solve explicitly for μ. The share of home securities is determined as a residual.

The optimal portfolio has some interesting properties. The investor can be viewed as making his portfolio allocation decision in two steps. First, he divides his portfolio between foreign securities and total home assets, money and securities, according to eq. (3.68a). Then, he expands his money holdings until eq. (3.68b) is satisfied. The rest of the portfolio goes into home securities. A change in wealth or the home interest rate alters the holdings of all assets, but a change in the foreign interest rate affects only holdings of home and foreign securities. Changes in the transactions demand for money are changes in Z'. Since these changes do not affect eq. (3.68a), the resulting adjustments in money holdings are matched one for one by adjustments in home security holdings. All of these properties are reflected in the basic specification of asset markets of Section 2, except that in the basic specification money demand does not depend on wealth.

Assuming specific forms for $Z(M/Q)$ makes it possible to solve explicitly for μ or the demand for real balances. First, suppose $Z(M/Q) = \alpha\ln(M/Q)$.[53] Then $Z' = \alpha/(M/Q)$, and according to (3.68b) the demand for real balances is

$$M/Q = (\alpha/i)(W/Q). \tag{3.69}$$

Now, suppose $Z(M/Q) = (M/Q)^\phi/\phi$. Then $Z' = (M/Q)^{\phi-1}$ and the demand for real balances is

$$M/Q = (W/iQ)^{1/(1-\phi)}. \tag{3.70}$$

If the underlying utility function displays constant relative risk aversion, $U(\tilde{C}) = \tilde{C}^\gamma/\gamma$, the solution of the lifetime consumption problem implies that optimal real

---

[53] Kouri (1977) uses this form.

consumption $\tilde{C}$ is a constant fraction of real wealth $\tilde{W}$ at every point in time.[54] In this case the demand for money can be written as

$$M/Q = (\tilde{C}/i)^{1/(1-\phi)},$$

with real consumption as the "activity" variable.

Under an alternative set of assumptions money demand depends on real income $\tilde{Y}$. Suppose that a measure of real transactions is given by $k\tilde{Y}$ and that the augmented objective function V^A is equal to the sum of V in eq. (3.1) and a function that is linear homogeneous in real balances $\tilde{M}$ and real transactions $Z = \tilde{M}^\psi (k\tilde{Y})^{1-\psi}$, where $0 < \psi < 1$. In this case $Z_{\tilde{M}} = \psi \tilde{M}^{\psi-1}(k\tilde{Y})^{1-\psi}\tilde{W}$ and money demand is given by

$$\tilde{M} = k\tilde{Y}(\psi\tilde{W}/i)^{1/(1-\psi)}.$$

The arguments of this money demand function are the same as those of the money demand function in the basic specification of asset markets of Section 2 except that the arguments of this money demand function include real wealth.

4. Conclusions

The microeconomic theory of asset demands discussed in Section 3 implies some but not all of the properties of the basic specification of asset markets in Section 2. Under the assumptions of Section 3 the demand for the sum of assets denominated in each currency is homogeneous of degree one in nominal wealth, and the demand for money in each country depends on the return on the security denominated in that country's currency but not on the return on securities denominated in other currencies. However, under these same assumptions the demand for money depends on real wealth. Since the conclusions of macroeconomic analysis often depend crucially on the form of asset demand functions, it is important to continue to explore the implications of the microeconomic theory of Section 3 and other microeconomic approaches.

The consumer of Section 3 arrives at his asset demands by maximizing his utility given interest rates and the parameters of the distributions of prices and exchange rates. Of course, the distributions of prices and exchange rates are not invariant to changes in the distributions of policy variables and stochastic components of tastes and technology. It has been recognized that a very important item on the research agenda is imbedding consumers' asset demands based on utility maximization in a general equilibrium model in which the distributions of prices and exchange rate are determined endogenously.[55]

---

[54] See Merton (1971).
[55] Cox, Ingersoll, and Ross (1984) and Walsh (1982) have constructed closed economy models in which the distribution of prices is endogenous. In the open economy model of Stulz (1981) the distributions of prices and the exchange rate are endogenous.

Appendix A

In this appendix it is shown that the determinant of the differential equation system made up of eq. (2.22c) and eq. (2.25) with $\varepsilon = \dot{e}$ is always negative. Thus, with flexible prices stationary equilibrium is always a saddle point. In the perverse case of Section 2.7 this result implies that the A_S schedule is steeper than the $\dot{w} = 0$ schedule.

Let G represent the matrix of coefficients of the differential equation system made up of eq. (2.22c) and eq. (2.25) with $\varepsilon = \dot{e}$. Then,

$$\det G = -\left(\varepsilon'_e C_6 + \varepsilon'_w C_5\right), \tag{A1.1}$$

where C_5 and C_6 are defined below eqs. (2.22) and ε'_e and ε'_w are defined below eq. (2.25). A lengthy and tedious derivation yields:

$$\begin{aligned}
\det G = H_1 \Big\{ &(M + B + \dot{B})(\dot{N} + \dot{F} + F)\Delta \\
&- H_2(\dot{N} + \dot{F} + F)\Big[\tilde{x}_p^*\big(s_2 W + \dot{s}_2 \dot{W}\big) + \dot{s}_2 \dot{W}\big(x_2 W + \dot{x}_2 \dot{W}\big)\Big] \\
&- H_3(M + B + \dot{B})\Big[\tilde{y}_p\big(s_2 W + \dot{s}_2 \dot{W}\big) + s_2 W\big(y_2 W + \dot{y}_2 \dot{W}\big)\Big]\Big\} < 0, \\
\end{aligned} \tag{A1.2}$$

$$H_1 = \left(s_2 \dot{s}_2 / \tilde{b}_e \Delta^2\right)\left(\tilde{x}_p^* + \dot{x}_2 \dot{W}\right) < 0,$$

$$H_2 = -\left(\tilde{b}_i \tilde{m}_p - \tilde{b}_p \tilde{m}_1\right)/\tilde{m}_1 > 0,$$

$$H_3 = \tilde{b}_i^* \tilde{n}_p^* / \tilde{n}_i^* > 0.$$

$\Delta > 0$ is defined below eqs. (2.22). In the derivation use is made of the relationship in footnote 8.

With flexible prices the difference between the slope of the A_S schedule and the slope of the $\dot{w} = 0$ schedule is given by

$$(\mathrm{d}e/\mathrm{d}w)_{A_S} - (\mathrm{d}e/\mathrm{d}w)_{\dot{w}=0} = -(1/\varepsilon'_e C_5)\left(\varepsilon'_e C_6 + \varepsilon'_w C_5\right),$$

$$= (1/\varepsilon'_e C_5)(\det G). \tag{A1.3}$$

If C_5, C_6, and $\varepsilon'_w > 0$ but $\varepsilon'_e < 0$, both $(\mathrm{d}e/\mathrm{d}w)_{A_S}$ and $(\mathrm{d}e/\mathrm{d}w)_{\dot{w}=0}$ are positive. A_S is steeper because $\det G$ is always negative. If C_6, ε'_e, and $\varepsilon'_w > 0$ but $C_5 < 0$, both $(\mathrm{d}e/\mathrm{d}w)_{A_S}$ and $(\mathrm{d}e/\mathrm{d}w)_{\dot{w}=0}$ are negative. A_S is flatter because $\det G$ is always negative.

Appendix B

In this appendix we derive an expression for the covariance of the stochastic processes for the domestic price index and the exchange rate ρ_{qe} when the exchange rate E, the home currency price of home goods P, the foreign currency price of foreign goods $\hat{P}$, and the deviation from the law of one price all follow geometric Brownian motion. The home price index is given by

$$Q = P^{1-\beta} \left(E \dot{P} V \right)^{\beta}.$$ (A2.1)

The stochastic processes for E, P, $\dot{P}$, and V are reproduced here for convenience:

$$dE/E = \varepsilon\, dt + \sigma_e\, dz_e,$$ (A2.2a)

$$dP/P = \pi_p\, dt + \sigma_p\, dz_p,$$ (A2.2b)

$$d\dot{P}/\dot{P} = \pi_p^*\, dt + \sigma_p^*\, dz_p^*,$$ (A2.2c)

$$dV/V = \pi_v\, dt + \sigma_v\, dz.$$ (A2.2d)

Calculating the stochastic differential dQ, multiplying it by $1/Q$, and collecting terms yields:

$$
\begin{aligned}
dQ/Q = {}& (1-\beta)\, dP/P + \beta\, dE/E + \beta\, d\dot{P}/\dot{P} + \beta\, dV/V \\
& + (1/2)\Big\{ -\beta(1-\beta)\Big[(dP/P)^2 + (dE/E)^2 + \big(d\dot{P}/\dot{P}\big)^2 + (dV/V)^2 \Big] \\
& + 2\beta(1-\beta)\Big[(dP/P)(dE/E) + (dP/P)\big(d\dot{P}/\dot{P}\big) + (dP/P)(dV/V) \Big] \\
& + 2\beta^2 \Big[\big(d\dot{P}/\dot{P}\big)(dE/E) + \big(d\dot{P}/\dot{P}\big)(dV/V) + (dE/E)(dV/V) \Big] \Big\}.
\end{aligned}
$$ (A2.3)

Substituting the processes (A2.2) into (A2.3) and using Ito's Lemma to evaluate the products of processes transforms (A2.3) into

$$
\begin{aligned}
dQ/Q = {}& \Big[(1-\beta)\pi_p + \beta\varepsilon + \beta\pi_p + \beta\pi_v - \beta(1-\beta)\big(\sigma_p^2 + \sigma_e^2 + \sigma_p^2 + \sigma_v^2 \big) \\
& + 2\beta(1-\beta)(\rho_{ep} + \rho_{pp} \cdot + \rho_{pv}) + 2\beta^2\big(\rho_{pe}^* + \rho_{pv}^* + \rho_{ev} \big) \Big]\, dt \\
& + (1-\beta)\sigma_p\, dz_p + \beta\sigma_e\, dz_e + \beta\sigma_p^*\, dz_p^* + \beta\sigma_v\, dz_v.
\end{aligned}
$$ (A2.4)

Using Ito's Lemma to evaluate the product $(dQ/Q)(dE/E)$ yields:

$$(dQ/Q)(dE/E) = \Big[(1-\beta)\rho_{pe} + \beta\sigma_e^2 + \beta\rho_{pe}^* + \beta\rho_{ve} \Big]\, dt.$$ (A2.5)

That is:

$$\rho_{qe} = (1-\beta)\rho_{pe} + \beta\sigma_e^2 + \beta\rho_{pe}^* + \beta\rho_{ve}.$$ (A2.6)

References

Adler, M. and B. Dumas (1983), "International portfolio choice and corporation finance: A survey", Journal of Finance, 38:925–984.

Allen, P.R. and P.B. Kenen (1980), Asset markets, exchange rates, and economic integration (Cambridge University Press, Cambridge).

Black, S.W. (1973), "International money markets and flexible exchange rates", Studies in International Finance No. 32 (Princeton University).

Boyer, R.S. (1975), "Commodity markets and bond markets in a small fixed-exchange rate economy", Canadian Journal of Economics, 8:1–23.

Boyer, R.S. (1977), "Devaluation and portfolio balance", American Economic Review, 67:54–63.

Boyer, R.S. (1978), "Financial policies in an open economy", Economica, 45:39–57.

Branson, W.H. (1974), "Stocks and flows in international monetary analysis", in: A. Ando, R. Herring, and R. Marston, eds., International aspects of stabilization policy, Federal Reserve Bank of Boston Conference Series No. 12 (Federal Reserve Bank of Boston) 27–50.

Branson, W.H. (1977), "Asset markets and relative prices in exchange rate determination", Sozialwissenschaftliche Annalen, 1:69–89.

Branson, W.H., H. Halttunen and P. Masson (1979), "Exchange rates in the short run: Some further results", European Economic Review, 12:395–402.

Bryant, R.C. (1975), "Empirical research on financial capital flows", in: P.B. Kenen, ed., International trade and finance: Frontiers for research (Cambridge University Press, Cambridge, England) 321–362.

Bryant, R.C. (1980), Money and monetary policy in interdependent nations (Brookings Institution, Washington).

Calvo, G. and C. Rodriguez (1977), "A model of exchange rate determination under currency substitution and rational expectations", Journal of Political Economy, 85:617–625.

Chow, G. (1979), "Optimum control of stochastic differential equation systems", Journal of Economic Dynamics and Control, 1:143–175.

Cox, J.C., J.E. Ingersoll, Jr., and S.A. Ross (1984), "A theory of the term structure of interest rates", Econometrica, forthcoming.

de Macedo, J.B. (1982), "Portfolio diversification across currencies", in: R.N. Cooper, P.B. Kenen, J.B. de Macedo, and J. van Ypersele, eds., The international monetary system under flexible exchange rates: Global regional, and national (Ballinger, Cambridge) 69–100.

de Macedo, J.B. (1983), "Optimal currency diversification for a class of risk-averse international investors", Journal of Economic Dynamics and Control, 5:173–185.

de Macedo, J.B., J.A. Goldstein, and D.M. Meerschwam (1984), "International portfolio diversification: Short-term financial assets and gold", in: J.F.O. Bilson and R.C. Marston, eds., Exchange rates: Theory and practice (University of Chicago Press, Chicago) forthcoming.

Dooley, M.P. and P. Isard (1982), "A portfolio-balance rational expectations model of the dollar-mark exchange rate", Journal of International Economics, 12:257–276.

Dornbusch, R. (1975), "A portfolio balance model of the open economy", Journal of Monetary Economics, 1:3–20.

Dornbusch, R. (1983), "Exchange rate risk and the macroeconomics of exchange rate determination", in: R.G. Hawkins, R.M. Levich, and C. Wihlborg, eds., The internationalization of financial markets and national economic policy (JAI Press, Greenwich) 3–27.

Enders, W. (1977), "Portfolio balance and exchange rate stability", Journal of Money, Credit and Banking, 9:491–499.

Fama, E.F. and A. Farber (1979), "Money, bonds, and foreign exchange", American Economic Review, 69:639–649.

Flood, R. (1979), "An example of exchange rate overshooting", Southern Economic Journal, 46:68–78.

Frankel, J.A. (1983), "Monetary and portfolio-balance models of exchange rate determination", in: J. Bhandari and B. Putnam, eds., Economic interdependence and flexible exchange rates (MIT Press, Cambridge) 84–115.

Freedman, C. (1977), "A model of the Eurodollar market", Journal of Monetary Economics, 3:139–161.

Frenkel, J. and C. Rodriguez (1975), "Portfolio equilibrium and the balance of payments: A monetary approach", American Economic Review, 65:674–88.

Girton, L. and D.W. Henderson (1976a), "Critical determinants of the effectiveness of monetary policy in the open economy", in: M. Fratiani and K. Tavernier, eds., Bank credit, money and inflation in open economies, Supplements to Kredit und Kapital Vol. 3, 231–283.

Girton, L. and D.W. Henderson (1976b), "Financial capital movements and central bank behavior in a two country, short-run portfolio balance model", Journal of Monetary Economics, 2:33–61.

Girton, L. and D.W. Henderson (1977), "Central bank operations in foreign and domestic assets under fixed and flexible exchange rates", in: P.B. Clark, D.E. Logue, and R.J. Sweeney, eds., The effects of exchange rate adjustments (U.S. Government Printing Office, Washington) 151-179.

Girton, L. and D. Roper (1981), "Theory and implications of currency substitutions", Journal of Money, Credit and Banking, 13:12-30.

Grauer, F.L.A., R.H. Litzenberger, and R. Stehle (1976), "Sharing rules and equilibrium in an international capital market with uncertainty," Journal of Financial Economics, 3:233-256.

Henderson, D.W. (1979), "Financial policies in open economies", American Economic Review Papers and Proceedings, 69:232-239.

Henderson, D.W. (1980), "The dynamic effects of exchange market intervention policy: Two extreme views and a synthesis", in: H. Frisch and G. Schwödiauer, eds., The economics of flexible exchange rates, Supplements to Kredit und Kapital Vol. 6, 156-209.

Henderson, D.W. and K. Rogoff (1982), "Negative net foreign asset positions and stability in a world portfolio balance model", Journal of International Economics, 13:85-104.

Herring, R.J. and R.C. Marston (1977a), National monetary policies and international financial markets (North-Holland Publishing Company, Amsterdam).

Herring, R.J. and R.C. Marston (1977b), "Sterilization policy: The trade-off between monetary autonomy and control over foreign exchange reserves", European Economic Review, 10:325-343.

Hewson, J. and E. Sakakibara (1975), The Eurocurrency markets and their implications (Lexington Books, Lexington).

Kareken, J. and N. Wallace (1981), "On the indeterminacy of equilibrium exchange rates", Quarterly Journal of Economics, 96:202-222.

Kenen, P.B. (1976), Capital mobility and financial integration: A survey, Studies in International Finance No. 39 (Princeton University).

Kenen, P.B. (1981), "Effects of intervention and sterilization in the short run and in the long run", in: R.N. Cooper, P.B. Kenen, J.B. de Macedo, and J. van Ypersele, eds., The international ¬onetary system under flexible exchange rates: Global, regional, and national (Ballinger, Cambridge) ɔ1-68.

Kouri, P.J.K. (1976), "The exchange rate and the balance of payments in the short run and in the long run: A monetary approach", Scandinavian Journal of Economics, 78:280-304.

Kouri, P.J.K. (1977), "International investment and interest rate linkages under flexible exchange rates", in: R.Z. Aliber, ed., The political economy of monetary reform (Macmillan, London) 74-96.

Kouri, P.J.K. (1983a), "The balance of payments and the foreign exchange market: A dynamic partial equilibrium model", in: J. Bhandari and B. Putnam, eds., Economic interdependence and flexible exchange rates (MIT Press, Cambridge) 116-156.

Kouri, P.J.K. (1983b), "The effect of risk on interest rates: A synthesis of the macroeconomic and financial views", in: R.G. Hawkins, R.M. Levich, and C. Wihlborg, eds., The internationalization of financial markets and national economic policy (JAI Press, Greenwich) 301-320.

Kouri, P.J.K. and J.B. de Macedo (1978), Exchange rates and the international adjustment process, Brookings Papers on Economic Activity, 1978, 111-150.

Kouri, P.J.K. and M.G. Porter (1974), "International capital flows and portfolio equilibrium", Journal of Political Economy, 82:443-467.

Krugman, P. (1981), "Consumption preferences, asset demands, and distribution effects in international financial markets", Working Paper No. 651, National Bureau of Economic Research.

Lapan, H.E. and W. Enders (1980), "Random disturbances and the choice of exchange regimes in an intergenerational model", Journal of International Economics, 10:263-283.

Lucas, R.E., Jr. (1976), "Econometric policy evaluation: A critique", in: K. Brunner and A.H. Meltzer, eds., The Phillips curve and labor markets, Carnegie-Rochester Conference Series on Public Policy No. 1 (North-Holland Publishing Company, Amsterdam) 19-46.

Markowitz, H.M. (1959), Portfolio selection: Efficient diversification of investments (John Wiley and Sons, New York).

Marston, R.C. (1980), "Cross country effects of sterilization, reserve currencies, and foreign exchange intervention", Journal of International Economics, 10:63-78.

Martin, J.P. and P. Masson (1979), "Exchange rates and portfolio balance", National Bureau of Economic Research Working Paper No. 377.

Masson, P.R. (1980), "Portfolio balance and exchange rate stability", Journal of Money, Credit and Banking, 11:228-230.

Masson, P.R. (1981), "Dynamic stability of portfolio balance models of the exchange rate", Journal of

International Economics, 11:467–477.

McCallum, B.T. (1983), "The role of overlapping-generations models in monetary economics", in: K. Brunner and A.H. Meltzer, eds., Money, monetary policy, and financial institutions, Carnegie-Rochester Conference Series on Public Policy No. 18 (North-Holland Publishing Company, Amsterdam) 9–44.

McKinnon, R. and W. Oates (1966), The implications of international economic integration for monetary, fiscal, and exchange rate policy, Studies in International Finance No. 16, Princeton University.

Melitz, J. (1982), "The stability of the spot price of foreign exchange in the absence of speculative influences", Journal of International Economics, 12:1–24.

Merton, R.C. (1969), "Lifetime portfolio selection under uncertainty: The continuous time case", Review of Economics and Statistics, 51:247–257.

Merton, R.C. (1971), "Optimum consumption and portfolio rules in a continuous time model", Journal of Economic Theory, 3:373–413.

Metzler, L.A. (1951), "Wealth, saving, and the rate of interest", Journal of Political Economy, 59:93–116.

Myhrman, J. (1975), Monetary policy in open economies, Monograph Series No. 5, Institute for International Economics, Stockholm.

Nickelsburg, G. (1983), "Dynamic exchange rate equilibria with uncertain government policy", MRG Working Paper No. 8032, University of Southern California.

Obstfeld, M. (1980), "Imperfect asset substitutability and monetary policy under fixed exchange rates", Journal of International Economics, 10:177–200.

Obstfeld, M. (1982), "The capitalization of income streams and the effects of open-market policy under fixed exchange rates", Journal of Monetary Economics, 9:87–98.

Samuelson, P.A. (1969), "Lifetime portfolio selection by dynamic stochastic programming", Review of Economics and Statistics, 51:239–246.

Sercu, P. (1980), "A generalization of the international asset pricing model", Revue de L'Association Francaise de Finance, 1:91–135.

Solnik, B.H. (1974), "An equilibrium model of the international capital market", Journal of Economic Theory, 8:500–524.

Stulz, R.M. (1983), "The demand for foreign bonds", Journal of International Economics, forthcoming.

Stulz, R.M. (1984), "Currency preferences, purchasing power risks and the determination of exchange rates in an optimizing model", Journal of Money, Credit and Banking, 16:302–316.

Tobin, J. (1965), "The theory of portfolio selection", in: F. Hahn and F.P.R. Brechling eds., The theory of interest rates (Macmillan, London) 3–51.

Tobin, J. (1969), "A general equilibrium approach to monetary theory", Journal of Money, Credit and Banking, 1:15–29.

Tobin, J. (1980), "Stabilization policy ten years after", Brookings Papers on Economic Activity, 1:19–78.

Tobin, J. and J.B. de Macedo (1981), "The short-run macroeconomics of floating exchange rates: An exposition", in: J. Chipman and C. Kindleberger, eds., Flexible exchange rates and the balance of payments: Essays in memory of Egon Sohmen (North-Holland, New York) 5–28.

Wallace, N. (1970), "The determination of the stock of reserves and the balance of payments in a neo-Keynesian model", Journal of Money, Credit and Banking, 2:269–290.

Walsh, Carl E. (1982), "The demand for money under uncertainty and the role of monetary policy", unpublished manuscript.

Wihlborg, C. (1978), Currency risks in international financial markets, Studies in International Finance No. 44, Princeton University.

Chapter 16

THE SPECIFICATION AND INFLUENCE OF GOODS AND FACTOR MARKETS IN OPEN-ECONOMY MACROECONOMIC MODELS

NEIL BRUCE and DOUGLAS D. PURVIS*

Queen's University, Canada

Contents

*This is a substantially revised version of our paper presented to the Handbook Conference at Princeton in May 1982. We would like to thank the participants at that conference, especially Morris Goldstein and John Helliwell who discussed our paper, Peter Kenen, Lars Svennson and our students Frank Barry, Michael Devereaux, Stuart Landon, Peter Sephton, and Connie Smith for helpful comments.

Handbook of International Economics, vol. II, edited by R.W. Jones and P.B. Kenen
© *Elsevier Science Publishers B.V., 1985*

1. Introduction

The art of macroeconomic model-building involves making strategic choices amongst a wide range of alternatives. Theoretical models range from the equation of exchange of the simple quantity theory to vast dynamic models involving many sectors and many agents and which defy analytical solutions. Quantitative models have an equally wide range, extending from single-equation St. Louis-type models to large-scale econometric models involving literally hundreds of equations. In this chapter we focus on a very small subset of the possibilities raised by this range of choices. We deal almost exclusively with theoretical models, and we restrict ourselves to consideration of the implications for open-economy models of alternative assumptions that can be made when specifying goods and factor markets.

Even within the context of this limited set of issues, a wide array of alternatives can be taken up. In order to focus our discussion, this chapter uses the following question as an organizing principle: "In macroeconomics, how does *openness* of the economy influence the treatment of model structure in terms of goods and factor markets?" Two key issues emerge.

(1) Multi-sectoral, multi-good considerations are important in open economy models, making it necessary to focus on at least one relative price, usually the terms of trade.

(2) The absorption/aggregate demand/capital mobility nexus leads to emphasis on intertemporal issues and the ability to "trade through time" via international capital markets.

One approach would be to look at macro models in an aggregate supply (AS) and aggregate demand (AD) framework, and to examine the implications of each of the two key issues for each of AS and AD. However, we eschew that purely taxonomic organization of the subject-matter. The relevant conclusions can be drawn from the various special cases that arise out of the model developed in the next section, which focuses on the two specific issues that we wish to address: To what extent are home goods substitutable for foreign goods? To what extent do markets for factors used in domestic production impinge on the determination of output, employment, prices, and the external balances?[1]

The plan of this chapter is as follows. We use the remainder of this section to set the stage by presenting two simple benchmark models: one which focuses completely on monetary factors at the expense of neglecting structural considerations entirely, and the other which focuses on structural factors but which fails to

---

[1] The latter can be thought of both in terms of market-clearing distinctions such as those that often separate monetarist from Keynesian analyses, and in terms of long-run versus short-run time frames where differences in results arise because of the role played by accumulation.

provide a complete model capable of determining the endogenous variables. In Section 2 we combine the two benchmark models under the assumption that real national output and income are constant. While the models so obtained are "complete", they abstract from output movements; accordingly, in Section 3 we introduce the role of the labor market and allow for the possibility of unemployment. In turn this creates room for output movements as part of the adjustment process, either as a result of changes in unemployment or as a result of endogenous changes in the equilibrium level of output due to changes in equilibrium relative prices. Section 4 then considers a couple of applications that clarify key issues which have arisen in the literature. The models to this point abstract from accumulation decisions; Section 5 extends the discussion to intertemporal models which focus on the long-run aspects of savings, investment and international capital movements. Summary remarks conclude the chapter in Section 6.

1.1. A benchmark monetary model

One extreme model which serves to highlight the importance of real structure in open-economy models is the simple monetary model. This model is parsimonious in the extreme in its specification of goods and factor markets.[2] Flexibility of factor prices ensures that factor markets clear instantaneously and that output remains at its full-employment level; constant technology and given terms of trade in turn ensure that full-employment real income is constant. The country is assumed to be small enough in world markets to take all prices as given; this is reflected in the given terms of trade. There are no non-traded goods.

Since all relative prices are fixed, all goods can be aggregated into a single Hicksian composite good. Hence, there is no distinction between goods which are exported and those which are imported; the focus instead is on the determination of *net exports*. The main insight of the approach stems from the fact that this lack of structure emphasizes the income-absorption nexus. Net exports do not depend on relative prices, comparative advantage, or any real, structural feature of the economy. They are determined by the difference between income and expenditure. This idea is central to all macro models of the open economy; Johnson (1956) presents an early discussion of some of its major implications. The monetary approach is a particular application that stresses the role of the real-balance effect in determining domestic expenditure.

In the simplest version of the monetary model, the difference between income and expenditure is proportional to the difference between the real stock of money

---

[2]See, for example, many of the papers included in Frenkel and Johnson (1976). The monetary approach is discussed in detail in Chapter 14 of this Handbook.

balances demanded, L (assumed constant), and the real stock of money balances supplied, M^S/P^I, where M^S is the nominal money stock and P^I is an index of domestic money prices. That is:

$$Y - E = \lambda(L - M^S/P^I),\qquad(1.1)$$

where Y is real national income, $E = C + I + G$ is the sum of real domestic expenditure on consumption (C), investment (I) and public goods (G), and $\lambda > 0$ is a coefficient denoting the rate at which money holders adjust actual money balances to those desired. We also have the national income identity:

$$Y = C + I + G + NX,\qquad(1.2)$$

where NX is net exports. Eq. (1.2) implies that $NX = Y - E$, so, from (1.1), net exports are proportional to the excess demand for money. The model is closed with the law of one price that states $P_i = eP_i^f$ for all goods i, where P_i is the domestic money price, e is the exchange rate and P_i^f is the exogenous foreign money price. Setting units so that $P_i^f = 1$ for all i, we have $P^I = e$.

Figure 1.1 illustrates the determination of the domestic money price level and the exchange rate in the flexible-exchange-rate case where there are two national moneys but agents in each country hold only their own country's currency. The 45° line labeled LOOP represents the law-of-one-price equality $P^I = e$. The horizontal line labeled $NX = 0$ represents eq. (1.1) solved for the value of P^I that sets $(Y - E)$, and hence NX, equal to zero. Since foreigners do not hold domestic money, the exchange rate must keep the economy on the $NX = 0$ locus. The

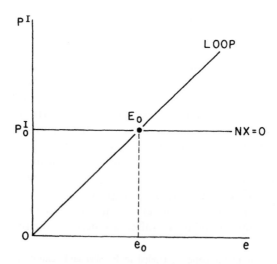

Figure 1.1. Flexible exchange rates and the benchmark monetary model.

equilibrium exchange rate e_0 and the price level P_0^I are determined at point E_0. Changes in the nominal money stock (or money demand) shift the $NX = 0$ locus, thus changing the price level and the exchange rate in proportion, as dictated by the law of one price.

With a sufficiently large stock of reserves, the domestic government can offer to buy and sell foreign exchange at a fixed rate e_0; it can, in effect, use its stock of foreign exchange to finance net exports. Figure 1.2 illustrates short-run and long-run equilibria for this case. The fixed exchange rate E_0 dictates the domestic money price level P_0^I as given by the vertical line labeled LOOP. The combinations of the nominal money stock and the domestic price level that maintain equality between the real money stocks demanded and supplied (and thus maintain $NX = 0$) are given by the ray labeled $NX = 0$ which has slope L. Above (below) this line $NX < 0$ ($NX > 0$). Given the predetermined money stock M_0, short-run equilibrium is at E_0 where $NX > 0$. As reserves accumulate, the domestic money stock rises and the short-run equilibrium travels up the LOOP line until the long-run equilibrium, E^*, is reached. Thus the long-run value of the nominal money stock M^* is endogenous.

The comparative statics are very simple. A change in the money stock has a transitory effect on the money stock itself and on NX. A change in the pegged exchange rate leads, on impact, to a change in NX and a proportionate change in P^I; in the long run M^* also changes proportionately and $NX = 0$ is restored. Monetary factors thus influence NX, but the influence is only transitory.

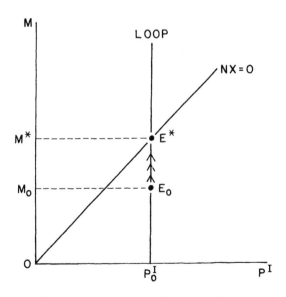

Figure 1.2. Fixed exchange rates and the benchmark monetary model.

The distinguishing feature of this benchmark monetary model is that relative prices are unaffected by domestic disturbances and play absolutely no role in the determination of equilibrium values or in the adjustment process. Perfectly elastic foreign excess demands and the law of one price serve to fix domestic relative prices from outside. Exchange-rate changes affect absolute price levels only. This is in sharp contrast to the so-called "elasticities" models which identify exchange-rate changes with changes in the terms of trade or in the relative price of traded to non-traded goods. We now consider a benchmark model of this type.

1.2. A benchmark real model

The second benchmark model we explore is the "elasticities" model which emphasizes the role of terms-of-trade changes in the external adjustment process. The distinguishing feature of the partial-equilibrium elasticities theory is that trade-balance or exchange-rate responses to various disturbances depend on certain supply and demand elasticities at home and abroad. The basic model is expressed as

$$Im^d(P_m) - Im^s(P_m/e) = 0,$$
$$X^d(P_x/e) - X^s(P_x) = 0, \qquad\qquad\qquad (1.3)$$
$$NX - (P_x^f X - P_m^f Im) = 0,$$

where Im^d (Im^s) is the volume of imports demanded (supplied) and $X^s(X^d)$ is the volume of exports supplied (demanded) by domestic residents (foreigners), P_i is the domestic money price of good i, and NX is the trade balance measured in units of foreign exchange.[3] Since the law of one price holds, the foreign money price of good i is P_i/e. The model can be closed either by specifying e as exogenous (fixed exchange rates) or by setting $NX = 0$ (flexible exchange rates). We will restrict our attention to the case of an exogenous exchange rate. We can differentiate the three equations around $NX = 0$ and normalize $e = P_m = P_x = 1$ to obtain:

$$\begin{bmatrix} -(\eta + \varepsilon^f) & 0 & 0 \\ 0 & -(\eta^f + \varepsilon) & 0 \\ Z(1-\eta) & -Z(1+\varepsilon) & 1 \end{bmatrix} \begin{bmatrix} dP_m \\ dP_x \\ dNX \end{bmatrix} = \begin{bmatrix} -\varepsilon^f de \\ -\eta^f de \\ 0 \end{bmatrix} \qquad (1.4)$$

In eqs. (1.4) η (η^f) is the elasticity of demand by domestic residents (foreigners) for imports (exports), ε (ε^f) is the supply elasticity of domestic residents (foreigners) for exports (imports), and Z is the initial trade volume. Eq. (1.4) can be

---

[3] In all cases the import and export goods are defined from the domestic economy's point of view.

solved for the famous Robinson–Metzler–Bickerdike "elasticities" equation (hereforth RMB equation) describing the effect of devaluation on the trade balance. That is,

$$\frac{\mathrm{d}NX}{\mathrm{d}e} = Z\left\{ \frac{\eta^f\eta(\varepsilon + \varepsilon^f + 1) + \varepsilon^f\varepsilon(\eta + \eta^f - 1)}{(\eta^f + \varepsilon)(\eta + \varepsilon^f)} \right\}. \qquad (1.5)$$

If the domestic economy is assumed to be a price-taker in the purchase of foreign goods, the RMB equation can be simplified. Finding the limit as ε^f tends to infinity and rearranging, we get:

$$\frac{\mathrm{d}NX}{\mathrm{d}e} = Z\left(\eta + \varepsilon\frac{(\eta^f - 1)}{(\eta^f + \varepsilon)} \right). \qquad (1.5')$$

These elasticities also determine the speed of adjustment if the monetary effects on domestic prices resulting from a trade imbalance are incorporated into the analysis, or they determine the responsiveness of the exchange rate to exogenous shocks if it is assumed that endogenous exchange-rate movements bring about trade balance.

This partial-equilibrium approach is misleading and can lead to incorrect conclusions (e.g. those of the elasticities pessimists) about the adjustment process because it is incomplete. It ignores the income and expenditure alterations that must be involved. In addition, it is obscure about what *relative* prices are involved since it assumes that domestic and foreign demand and supply functions depend on *money* prices.

Two special cases of the general elasticities model have been important in the development of some aspects of the modern theory, and we shall briefly treat each in turn.

1.2.1. The specialized domestic production model

In the first special case, the domestic economy is assumed to be specialized in the production of a single composite good which is distinct from goods produced abroad. Total domestic expenditure consists of expenditure on the domestic good $E^d(P/e)$, which is a negative function of its relative price P/e (recall that we fix $P^f = 1$ so that e is the money price of the composite foreign good) and expenditure on imports $E^m(e/P) = e/P\ Im(e/P)$. Imports are a negative function of their relative price e/P. Assuming that total expenditure does not depend on the relative price, we have

$$\eta^d = \frac{E^m}{E^d}(\eta - 1), \qquad (1.6)$$

where η^d is the elasticity of the domestic demand for the domestic product.

Exports of the domestic product equal total domestic output $Y(P/e)$ less $E^d(P/e)$. For reasons discussed in Section 3.3, domestic output may depend on the relative price P/e even though the economy is specialized in production. Thus:

$$\varepsilon = \frac{E^d}{X}\eta^d + \frac{Y}{X}\varepsilon^s, \tag{1.7}$$

where ε^s is the elasticity of domestic output. Combining (1.6) and (1.7) and assuming balanced trade so that $X = E^m$, we obtain:

$$\varepsilon = (\eta - 1) + \frac{Y}{X}\varepsilon^s \tag{1.8}$$

Two limiting cases arise. In the exogenous output case, with $\varepsilon^s = 0$, we have $\varepsilon = (\eta - 1)$. This can be substituted into the RMB eq. (1.5') to obtain:

$$\frac{dNX}{de} = Z\left(\eta + \frac{(\eta - 1)(\eta^f - 1)}{(\eta + \eta^f - 1)}\right). \tag{1.9}$$

The other simple case occurs when it is assumed that the domestic economy has a Keynesian aggregate supply curve which is perfectly elastic. In this case ε^s and hence ε become infinite. Assuming that the same thing holds in the foreign economy so $\varepsilon^* \to \infty$ and taking limits, the RMB eq. (1.5') becomes:

$$dNX/de = Z(\eta + \eta^f - 1) \tag{1.10}$$

Eq. (1.10) expresses the familiar Marshall–Lerner condition for a depreciation of the domestic currency to lead to an improvement in the trade balance in this model: that the sum of the domestic and foreign import demand elasticities exceed unity. Eq. (1.10) is expressed in terms of foreign goods. A rise in e leads to a fall in import volume and a rise in export volume; however, export value will fall if X^d is inelastic. The effects of such inelasticity on the behavior of the trade-account can be offset by a high elasticity of Im^d. (For a further discussion, including a diagrammatic treatment, see Chapter 13 of this Handbook.) This specification of the goods market can be "wedded" to the income–expenditure model [eq. (1.2)] and combined with asset-market equilibrium to yield the well-known Mundell–Fleming model discussed in Section 3.1.

1.2.2. The non-traded goods model

An alternative special case of the elasticities model has proved quite useful. Rather than producing a unique exportable in which it has price-making power, the country is assumed to be a price-taker for both the importable and exportable goods. In this case the external terms of trade are exogenous and independent of the exchange rate, so a composite "tradable" commodity can be defined. The foreign-currency price of this tradable can be fixed at unity and the exchange rate identified with its domestic money price.

Commodity market structure is introduced by assuming that some class of commodities cannot be traded externally because of, say, prohibitive transportation costs or tariffs. Thus, there is a composite non-traded good, often identified with the service sector, with money price P_N. The relative price of traded to non-traded goods, P_T/P_N, reduces to e when the foreign-currency price of the tradable is fixed at unity and the non-tradable is chosen as the numeraire. Because foreign demand and supply for tradables (X^d and Im^s, respectively) are perfectly elastic, the volume of trade depends on the domestic behavioral equations Im^d and X^s.

Letting η^f go to infinity in eq. (1.5') we can derive the effect of a devaluation on net exports:

$$dNX = Z(\eta + \varepsilon). \tag{1.11}$$

Since traded goods consumed at home are identical regardless of where they are produced, we have $\eta = (Z^T/Z)\eta^T$, where Z^T is the value of traded goods consumed and η^T is the demand elasticity of traded goods. Similarly, traded goods produced at home are identical regardless of where they are consumed, so $\varepsilon = (Z^T/Z)\varepsilon^T$, where Z^T is the value of domestic production of traded goods (equal to the value of traded goods consumed if trade is balanced) and ε^T is the elasticity of supply of traded goods. Hence, we can write (1.11) as

$$dNX/de = Z^T(\eta^T + \varepsilon^T). \tag{1.11'}$$

The implications of this special case are somewhat different from the import–export distinction that drives the Marshall–Lerner model. The value of Z^T is an important feature of the economy, ranging from very open economies where Z^T is large in relation to total national income to closed economies where Z^T is small. In addition, the relative substitutability of traded and non-traded goods in both demand and supply is highlighted; high values of η^T and/or ε^T result in a very "open" economy even if Z^T is small. These issues were argued by McKinnon (1963) to be very important in the optimal-currency-area issue.

An extension of the simple traded/non-traded good model is the so-called Scandanavian model which develops further linkages between traded and non-traded goods through wage adjustment. Prices in the traded-good sector are given when the exchange rate is pegged, so productivity in that sector determines the money wage for the whole economy and hence the factor cost of non-traded goods. As a result, the relative price of tradables to non-tradables does not depend on the exchange rate but instead is dependent on factors such as productivity.

These partial-equilibrium models with traded and non-traded goods encounter difficulties similar to those in the first special case considered. The income and expenditure changes that must underlie changes in net exports are ignored, which can only be "correct" if a special sort of accomodating demand policy is assumed.

Consider Figure 1.3, adapted from Dornbusch (1975). Output and consumption of the traded good are measured on the horizontal axis and the corresponding volumes for the non-traded good are measured on the vertical axis. VV is the production possibilities curve. The initial point P_0 is one of trade balance (as output and consumption of the traded good are equal), and the absolute slope of the tangent at P_0 is the relative price of the traded to nontraded good. A devaluation from e_0 to e_1 shifts production to P_1, causing a rise of $Z^T \varepsilon^T de$ in the output of traded goods. The consumption point shifts to C_1, causing a fall in consumption of traded goods of $Z^T \eta^T de$. The trade surplus created is $d(NX) = Z^T(\eta^T + \varepsilon^T) de$. The deficiency in the elasticities approach is immediately apparent; the devaluation also causes an excess demand for the non-traded good. According to the elasticities approach the effect of a devaluation is to cause output demanded to move to a non-feasible point B. Without some expenditure-reducing device the price of non-tradables must rise until the excess demand for them is eliminated. This occurs when P_N changes in the same proportion as e and restores the initial situation. Thus the elasticities model of traded and non-traded goods is very much like pre-Patinkin classical monetary theory; no means exists whereby the exchange-rate change can cause expenditure to change relative to

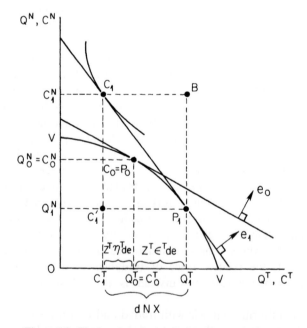

Figure 1.3. The benchmark real model: Non-traded goods.

income, and the relative price determined is that which clears both the traded and non-traded goods markets.

Dornbusch (1975) suggests that the expenditure-reducing device that is needed to rationalize the elasticities model is a fiscal authority that maintains internal balance by altering its expenditure on the non-traded good so as to fix its nominal price in response to a devaluation. In Figure 1.3, the fiscal authority would have to reduce domestic expenditures on the non-traded good until demand moves to C_1'. For example, the non-traded good could be a pure service and its nominal price would then be the money wage rate. A fiscal policy that alters expenditure on the service good so as to fix the money wage rate would validate the elasticities equation.

An alternative and more satisfactory approach is to make demands for traded and non-traded goods depend on total expenditure E which can differ from national income due to real-balance or wealth effects. This allows for an equilibrium determination of the adjustment process which involves both expenditure switching and expenditure reducing, as discussed in detail in Section 2.2 below.

2. Combining monetary and real factors in a full-employment context

The two benchmark models provide complementary rather than competing contributions to the theory of adjustment and exchange-rate determination. While the benchmark monetary model is complete in the theoretical sense, it gives the misleading impression that market structure plays no role in the adjustment process or in determining the impact effect of devaluation. The benchmark real model allows commodity-market structure to play a role through changes in the "real" exchange rate (the relative price of imports to exports in the specialized production case and the relative price of traded to non-traded goods in the non-traded good case). But it is theoretically deficient because no mechanism for altering expenditure relative to income (which *must* be present for NX to change) exists. Also, it gives the misleading impression that policies such as devaluation can create a permanent external surplus. Both of these problems can be solved by "marrying" the real and monetary models. We shall integrate each of the two special elasticities models with the monetary theory of expenditure determination.

2.1. Specialized production with a monetary sector

The distinguishing feature of the specialized production model is that goods produced domestically are distinct in demand from those produced abroad. Thus total domestic expenditure is divided into that on the domestic good and that on imports. Foreign demand for the domestic product is finite and depends on the relative price P/e. However, the partial theory does not explain how total expenditure E is determined. Since $NX = Y - E$, the partial model does not provide a theory of the external balance since E is unexplained and Y is either treated as exogenous or indeterminate (the Marshall–Lerner case). The simplest solution is to assume that total expenditure is a positive function of real money balances, $E(M/P)$, as implied by eq. (1.1), and that $E^d(\cdot)$ and $E^m(\cdot)$ depend on E as well as relative prices.[4] In this case we have:

$$E(M/P) = E^d(P/e, E) + E^m(e/P, E). \tag{2.1}$$

Adding the foreign demand for the domestic product $X^d(P/e)$, we can specify a complete model with the equations:

$$NX = X^d(P/e) - E^m(e/P, E(M/P)), \tag{2.2}$$

$$NX = Y - E(M/P), \tag{2.3}$$

where Y is exogenous. These equations can be solved for e and P under flexible exchange rates or for NX and P (M and P) under fixed exchange rates in the short (long) run.

In contrast to the simple benchmark monetary model, P/e is an endogenous variable; it is a relative price that can change in the face of real changes in the economy such as a change in the relative demand for domestic and imported goods. Also, this relative price and the associated demand elasticities play a role in the adjustment process and in determining the impact-effect of a devaluation. To see this, totally differentiate (2.2) and (2.3) to get:

$$\begin{bmatrix} 1 & Z(\eta^f + \eta - 1) - \delta^m \beta \\ 1 & -\beta \end{bmatrix} \begin{bmatrix} dNX \\ dP \end{bmatrix} = \begin{bmatrix} Z(\eta^f + \eta - 1)\,de - \delta^m \beta\, dM \\ \beta\, dM \end{bmatrix}. \tag{2.4}$$

In this expression all nominal variables have been normalized to unity, $\beta > 0$ is the effect of a change in real money balances on total expenditure, δ^m is the marginal propensity to spend on imports, and $\delta^D = 1 - \delta^m$. In the case of devaluation we can solve for:

$$dNX/de = \beta Z(\eta + \eta^f - 1)/(\beta\delta^D + Z(\eta + \eta^f - 1)). \tag{2.5}$$

Note that although the domestic and foreign elasticities of demand do play a role in determining the impact-effect of devaluation, a necessary condition for devaluation to increase net exports is that $\beta \neq 0$. A rise in the exchange rate must alter domestic expenditure through the real-balance effect. Finally, it can be observed

[4] In principle, real balances should be calculated by deflating the nominal money stock by an index of domestic and foreign prices. In this and the next section we adopt the common convention of measuring real balances in terms of the export price. For most purposes, this makes no substantial difference to the results; see however, footnote 8 below.

that as $(\eta^f + \eta)$ increases without bound, dNX/de approaches β, which is just the benchmark monetary model in which only the real-balance effect matters.[5]

2.2. Non-traded goods with a monetary sector

The partial non-traded goods model distinguished commodities, both in production and preferences (demand), according to whether they are traded or non-traded. A small-open-economy assumption permits all traded goods to be aggregated into a single composite traded good as in the benchmark monetary model. The partial model can be completed by "marrying" it to the monetary model of expenditure determination as done by Dornbusch (1973).

Let $p = P_N/e$ denote the relative price of non-traded goods and let the traded good be the numeraire. Total expenditure is the sum of the demand for traded goods $D^T(1/p, E)$ plus the value of non-traded goods demanded $pD^N(p, E)$. Demands are negative functions of their "own" relative price and each depends on total expenditure E. As in previous cases we can invoke the real-balance effect to make E a positive function of the stock of real money balances, M/e. (Again, real balances are measured in terms of the export good.) In addition, we have the supply functions of non-traded goods $Y^N(p)$ and $Y^T(1/p)$ as positive functions of the "own" relative price.

The complete model is now expressed in two equations:

$$Y^N(p) - D^N(p, E(M/e)) = 0, \tag{2.6}$$

$$Y^T(1/p) - D^T(1/p, E(M/e)) = NX. \tag{2.7}$$

Again we can determine e and p under flexible exchange rates, or instead solve for NX and p under fixed exchange rates in the short run (M and P in the long run). Let us focus on the fixed-rate case. Normalizing all nominal variables to unity and totally differentiating around the balanced-trade point we obtain the short-run solution:

$$\begin{bmatrix} 0 & Z^N(\varepsilon^N + \eta^N) \\ 1 & Z^T(\varepsilon^T + \eta^T) \end{bmatrix} \begin{bmatrix} dNX \\ dp \end{bmatrix} = \begin{bmatrix} \delta^N\beta(dM - de) \\ -\delta^T\beta(dM - de) \end{bmatrix}, \tag{2.8}$$

where δ^i is the marginal propensity to spend on good i, ε^i is the supply elasticity

---

[5]In this and other variable price models, the elasticity expression plays a role in the stability condition. For example, as can be checked from eq. (2.4), in the present model the Marshall–Lerner condition is sufficient, but necessary, to ensure that dNX/dM be less than zero.

of good i, η^i is the demand elasticity of good i, and Z^i is the value of output (expenditure) on good i. This can be rewritten as:[6]

$$\begin{bmatrix} 0 & Z^T(\eta^T + \varepsilon^T) + Z^N \\ 1 & -Z^T(\eta^T + \varepsilon^T) \end{bmatrix} \begin{bmatrix} \mathrm{d}NX \\ \mathrm{d}p \end{bmatrix} \begin{bmatrix} (1 - \delta^T)\beta(\mathrm{d}M - \mathrm{d}e) \\ \delta^T\beta(\mathrm{d}M - \mathrm{d}e) \end{bmatrix}. \tag{2.8'}$$

Solving for the effect of a devaluation we obtain:

$$\frac{\mathrm{d}NX}{\mathrm{d}e} = \beta \left(\frac{\varepsilon^T + \eta^T + \delta^T Z}{\varepsilon^T + \eta^T + Z} \right), \tag{2.9}$$

where Z is the ratio of non-traded to traded output, Z^N/Z^T. Again $\beta > 0$ is the sine qua non for devaluation to increase net exports. Also, the coefficient multiplying β is less than unity as long as $\delta^T < 1$. Therefore, the market structure underlying the traded and non-traded goods model reduces the impact-effect of devaluation as compared with the benchmark monetary model.[7]

In contrast to the specialized production model where market structure influenced the impact-effect of devaluation on net exports only through the substitutability of domestic and foreign goods, the traded and non-traded goods model introduces three senses in which the economy may be "very open" as in the benchmark monetary model. First, traded and non-traded goods may be close substitutes in demand so η^T (or $\eta^{T'}$) is large. Second, traded and non-traded goods may be close substitutes in supply so ε^T is very large. This is one possible interpretation of the Aukrust–Scandinavian model where the effect of changes in the price of traded goods feed through one-for-one (except for productivity growth differences) to those of non-traded goods via factor prices. Effectively this is equivalent to a linear production possibilities curve or $\varepsilon^T = \infty$ in (2.9) or (2.9'). Third, the economy may be very open in the sense that Z^N/Z^T is very small. In all three cases, the limiting value of $\mathrm{d}NX/\mathrm{d}e$ is β, the real balance effect of the monetary model.

A point made by Dornbusch that is relevant to both the monetary version of the traded and non-traded goods model and the monetary version of the special-

---

[6] In deriving (2.8'), we have made use of the following relationships. By the envelope theorem (assuming we are on the production-possibilities frontier), $Z^N\varepsilon^N = Z^T\varepsilon^T$. If total expenditure is independent of the relative price p, we also have $Z^T\eta^T - Z^N\eta^N + Z^N = 0$. Together, these imply that $Z^N(\varepsilon^N + \eta^N) = Z^T(\varepsilon^T + \eta^T) + Z^N$. Finally, we have $\delta^N + \delta^T = 1$.

[7] Using Slutsky's equation, $\eta^T = \eta^{T'} - \delta^T z$, where $\eta^{T'}$ is the compensated demand elasticity, we can express (2.9) as

$$\frac{\mathrm{d}NX}{\mathrm{d}e} = \beta \left(\frac{\varepsilon^T + \eta^{T'}}{\varepsilon^T + \eta^{T'} + \delta^N Z} \right), \tag{2.9'}$$

which is the expression derived by Dornbusch (1973).

ized production model is that the dNX/de expressions given by (2.9) and (2.5) capture only the impact-effect of exchange-rate changes. Over the long run, a positive trade balance created by devaluation from a balanced trade position would raise the money stock. This eventually would restore balanced trade along with the "natural" internal or external terms of trade. Consequently, the conclusions of the single-sector benchmark monetary model are replicated in the long run in two (or multi) sector models; this can be verified using the long-run solutions of the systems given by eqs. (2.2) and (2.3) or by eqs. (2.6) and (2.7) by setting $dNX = 0$ and letting dM be endogenous.

3. Unemployment: Keynesian specifications of open-economy macro models

While the marriage of the elasticities models with the monetary model of expenditure provides complete and consistent models of exchange-rate determination and of the adjustment process, the models differ from common textbook macroeconomic models in two respects. First, in the models of Section 2, the level of domestic income was assumed to be exogenous (typically supply determined) at its full-employment level. Second, the monetary-adjustment (or real balance) assumptions precluded a role for non-monetary, interest-bearing assets. That is, the asset side of the model presumed a single composite domestic asset. In this section we consider modifications of the specialized production and the traded and non-traded goods models that introduce unemployment and simple portfolio balance considerations into the analysis. (For a detailed discussion of portfolio balance in open economies, see Chapter 15 of this Handbook.)

Unemployment can be introduced by assuming a labor-market imperfection such as a rigid money wage. (In fact, this sort of modification could be introduced into the single-sector benchmark monetary model.) More commonly, one encounters Keynesian infinitely elastic supply functions. Such specifications can be justified in terms of quantity constrained dual-decision models of the type explored by Barro and Grossman (1971) and Malinvaud (1977). An analysis of such models in an open-economy context is undertaken for single-sector models by Dixit (1978) and for the non-traded-goods models by Neary (1980). In what follows, we restrict our discussion to the implications of such supply specifications and abstract from their underlying structural foundations.

On the asset side, we will utilize the familiar monetary equilibrium condition that

$$M/P = L(Y, i),$$

where i is the nominal interest rate on the non-monetary asset. With the further assumptions that the country is a small open economy in a world of perfect mobility for the non-monetary financial asset and that expectations about exchange-rate changes are static, we can peg the domestic interest rate to an exogenous foreign rate i^f, assumed constant in what follows. Finally, we can follow the convention of letting total expenditure (and expenditure on each commodity) depend on the level of income which is now an endogenous variable. We shall consider these sorts of modifications for both the specialized production and the traded and non-traded goods models.

3.1. The Mundell–Fleming model

The specialized production model coupled with the assumptions that domestic supply is infinitely elastic ($\varepsilon^s = \infty$) and that the domestic economy is a price-taker for import goods ($\varepsilon^f = \infty$), yields the so-called Marshall–Lerner model in terms of elasticities specification; see Section 1.2.1 above. This model is coupled with the *IS–LM* model of aggregate demand in the familiar open-economy macro model due to Mundell (1963) and Fleming (1962) (M–F model) which has been used extensively to examine the implications for monetary and fiscal policy under alternative exchange regimes. Although the original focus of the analysis was on the role of international capital mobility and the foreign exchange market, the model provides a useful framework for the examination of alternative specifications of goods and factor markets.

The basic framework is summarized by goods-market equilibrium given in eq. (1.2) and repeated below:

$$Y = C + I + G + NX. \tag{1.2}$$

Under fixed exchange rates, shifts in NX lead to the foreign-trade multiplier while domestic stabilization policies have effects that are mitigated by the presence of an additional "leakage" in the form of imports. Under flexible exchanges with zero capital mobility, NX is zero as a condition of equilibrium in the foreign-exchange market. As a result, eq. (1.2) reduces to the standard closed-economy goods-market equilibrium condition; unless the exchange rate enters one of the behavioral relations (as in the famous Laursen–Metzler–Harberger effect discussed in Section 5.1.3 below), an open economy under flexible exchange rates can, for all intents and purposes be treated as a closed economy. The important implication is that the foreign-trade multiplier "disappears" so that flexible exchange rates insulate the economy from foreign disturbances.

With international capital mobility, equilibrium in the foreign-exchange market does not require NX to be zero, and in the extreme case of perfect capital mobility, external equilibrium imposes *no* restrictions on the behavior of NX.

However that "degree of freedom" comes at the expense of linking domestic interest rates to foreign; this influences the fixed-exchange-rate results as well, once the condition for equilibrium in the monetary sector is added.

The M–F model is expressed in the two equations for equilibrium in the domestic goods and money markets:

$$Y = E(Y, i^f) + G + NX(\pi, Y, Y^f) \tag{3.1}$$

$$M^S = PL(Y, i^f). \tag{3.2}$$

Eq. (3.1) just restates eq. (1.2) by combining C and I into an aggregate expenditure function, $E(\cdot)$. The relative price term, π, is defined as eP^f/P, where e is the exchange rate, P^f is the foreign-currency price of imports, and P is the domestic-currency price of home goods. As shown in Section 1.2.1, the response of NX to a rise in π is given by $Z(\eta + \eta^f - 1)$, where Z is the import volume at the initial position of balanced trade, and where η and η^f are the domestic and foreign price elasticities of demand for imports. The condition that this response is positive is the familiar Marshall–Lerner condition; we shall assume henceforth that this condition is satisfied. (In fact, for simplicity we will have occasion to make the stronger assumption that the elasticity of the domestic demand for imports, η, exceeds unity.)

Equation (3.2) is the condition for equilibrium in the domestic money market. The money supply, defined to be the sum of foreign-exchange reserves plus domestic credit instruments held by the central bank ($M^S = F + C$), is deflated by the price of domestic goods, P. (Other variants measure real balances in terms of a price index, a point we take up in footnote 8 below.) For equilibrium, this must equal desired real balances, $L(\cdot)$, which depend on real domestic income Y and nominal interest rates.

Under fixed exchange rates, monetary and fiscal policy have impact effects similar to those that occur in a closed economy. However, capital mobility renders monetary policy impotent since the money supply becomes demand-determined; domestic credit creation is offset by outflows of foreign-exchange reserves. Capital mobility, however, reinforces the effects of fiscal policy; inflows of foreign exchange reserves lead to an *induced* monetary expansion which reinforces the initial fiscal stimulus.

With flexible exchange rates the relative effectiveness of the two policies is reversed. Independent control over the money supply is re-established so with a given money supply, fiscal policy can alter income only to the extent that it can alter interest rates; its ability to do that is limited by international capital mobility. "Crowding-out" is accomplished through appreciation of the domestic currency – equivalent to a rise in the terms of trade – and is evident in a reduction in NX that offsets any rise in G. Expansionary monetary policy stimulates potential capital outflows, hence requiring a rise in net exports via currency depreciation and thus further stimulating aggregate demand.[8]

Some controversy exists over the validity of these conclusions in the long-run because the capital flows are eventually reversed due to the repatriation of interest earnings. See, for example, Rodriquez (1976). However, the model ignores other considerations relevant in the long run, such as capital accumulation or adjustment of prices, so that the long-run impact of debt servicing is only of limited interest.

Under fixed exchange rates, export *volume* is taken as exogenous, determined by the level of foreign income. Relative prices play no role in the analysis. Since the price of the foreign good in terms of the foreign currency is also treated as fixed, relative prices or terms-of-trade changes are synonymous with exchange rate changes. (This association holds only in the special circumstances of this model; we return to this later.) Under flexible exchange rates, relative prices do play a role in this model, but it is a behind-the-scenes role operating entirely through the exchange rate.

Clearly the assumptions of perfectly elastic aggregate supply and, in the fixed-exchange-rate case, exogenous exports are extreme. In Section 3.3 we will consider a model that relaxes these assumptions; as we shall see this has the immediate benefit of identifying the terms of trade separately from the exchange rate.

3.2. The non-traded goods model with unemployment

The traded and non-traded goods model can also provide the underlying commodity-market structure in an *IS–LM* type aggregate-demand model. This makes possible a direct comparison of the traded and non-traded goods model to the familiar M–F model. The simplest approach is to assume that the non-traded good is a pure service that uses only labor in production. We can then identify P_N with the nominal wage W. Then Keynesian considerations can be introduced which imply that such services are supplied with infinite elasticity at an exogenous money price W_0. Output of non-traded goods will then be demand-determined so $Y^N = D^N(p, Y)$, where p, the relative price of services, is also the real wage in terms of traded goods, W_0/e. Income rather than expenditure is made an argument of demand so as to further conform with the usual Keynesian specification.

---

[8]A more detailed treatment of these issues is given in Chapters 13 and 17 of this Handbook. Note, however, the importance for the result that fiscal policy is impotent of deflating real balances only by the domestic price; if M were deflated by a price index involving e, then the appreciation following a fiscal expansion would "create room" in eq. (3.2) for some increase in output.

The output of traded goods must be supply-determined because of the small open economy assumption. This is made possible by assuming that traded goods are produced using both labor and capital, the latter being in fixed supply. Then, by the law of variable proportions, we have an upward sloping supply function of traded goods. The model is completed with a definition of national income, $Y = Y^{\mathrm{T}}(\cdot) + pD^{\mathrm{N}}(\cdot)$ and a portfolio-balance equation, $M^{\mathrm{S}} = L(Y).$[9] It should be noted that under the assumption of perfect capital mobility the domestic interest rate is fixed at the exogenous rate i^{f}. Thus the interest rate need not appear explicitly as an argument in $D^{\mathrm{T}}(\cdot)$, $D^{\mathrm{N}}(\cdot)$ and $L(\cdot)$.

The equations of the model are now summarized as:

$$NX = Q^{\mathrm{T}}(W_0/e) - D^{\mathrm{T}}(W_0/e, Y), \tag{3.3}$$

$$Y = Q^{\mathrm{T}}(W_0/e) + (W_0/e)D^{\mathrm{N}}(W_0/e, Y), \tag{3.4}$$

$$M^{\mathrm{S}} = L(Y). \tag{3.5}$$

In structure and conclusions this model is identical to the simplest M–F model discussed earlier. Under fixed exchange rates (3.4) is solved for Y, then (3.5) is solved for M^{S} and (3.3) solved for NX. An NX value different from zero can be maintained indefinitely by capital flows. An exogenous rise in domestic spending on services increases income and deteriorates the trade balance. A rise in M^{S} is offset immediately by capital flows. A devaluation increases output and NX. Under flexible exchange rates eq. (3.5) is solved for Y, (3.4) is solved for e and (3.3) is solved for NX. Again a value of NX different from zero can be sustained indefinitely by capital flows. A rise in exogenous spending on services is completely crowded out by an appreciation of the domestic currency and has no effect on Y. It does so, however, by reducing the relative price of the non-tradable good, thereby switching production away from these goods and domestic expenditure towards them. A rise in M^{S} increases output, reduces NX, and depreciates the home currency.

These results can be ascertained by totally differentiating eqs. (3.3), (3.4) and (3.5) and solving for the relevant endogenous variable.[10]

---

[9] Notice that in this model, real money balances have been defined in terms of the home (non-traded in this case) good. This is in order to conform as closely as possible with the M–F specification to facilitate comparison. In both cases the deflator in the real-balance calculation is a fixed domestic price which is normalized at unity. This specification thus departs from that used in the full-employment, non-traded goods model of Section 2 where the exchange-rate was used as the deflator. As with any of the models, this specification could be enriched by using a price index when calculating real money balances.

[10] We have also assumed that saving is independent of p so $D_p^{\mathrm{T}} + D_p^{\mathrm{N}} + D^{\mathrm{N}} = 0$, where the first two terms represent the responsiveness of D^{T} and D^{N}, respectively, to changes in p.

We will consider only the case of devaluation:

$$
\begin{bmatrix}
1 & \delta^T & 0 \\
0 & 1 - \delta^N & 0 \\
0 & l & -1
\end{bmatrix}
\begin{bmatrix}
\mathrm{d}NX \\
\mathrm{d}Y \\
\mathrm{d}M^S
\end{bmatrix}
=
\begin{bmatrix}
Z^T(\eta^T + \varepsilon^T)\,\mathrm{d}e \\
Z^T(\eta^T + \varepsilon^T)\,\mathrm{d}e \\
0
\end{bmatrix}
\tag{3.6}
$$

where the notation is as before, except δ^i now represents the marginal propensity to spend on good i out of *income* and l is the income responsiveness of the demand for money. We can solve (3.6) directly for the change in NX:

$$
\frac{\mathrm{d}NX}{\mathrm{d}e} = Z^T(\eta^T + \varepsilon^T)\left(\frac{s}{s+m}\right),
\tag{3.7}
$$

where $s = 1 - \delta^T - \delta^N$ is the marginal propensity to save and $m = \delta^T$ is the marginal propensity to import. Note that (3.7) only differs from the partial elasticities eq. (1.11') only by the last term. It is immediately apparent that for a devaluation to increase net exports it is necessary that the marginal propensity to save is positive. Moreover, since $m > 0$ in general, the coefficient multiplying the partial elasticities term $Z^T(\eta^T + \varepsilon^T)$ is less than unity. Only in the event that $m = 0$, so that all expenditure changes fall on non-tradable goods, will the partial-elasticities expression capture the impact effect of a devaluation on net exports. Finally, note that the expression in (3.7) only yields an impact effect since subsequent changes in the money stock will also affect net exports.

In conclusion, we have seen that the non-traded/traded good distinction yields the same sort of model structure and conclusions as does the home/foreign good distinction of the M–F model *provided that the models are specified similarily in other respects.* In each case there is a sheltered good for which the domestic economy is a price maker and an international good for which the domestic economy is a price-taker.[11]

One advantage of the non-traded goods model is that it permits substitution in supply as well as in demand, and therefore provides a richer representation of the real responses of the economy. Nevertheless, the particular specification in this section imposes a severe restriction which is analogous to the one in the M–F model of Section 3.1: in both models the supply of "the domestic good" is perfectly elastic. In the next section, we analyze an extended version of the M–F model which incorporates a richer specification of the supply side; a similar extension of the non-traded goods model allowing for an upward sloping supply

---

[11] One difference which may be important in some contexts is that only in the M–F model does the endogeneity of relative prices indicate some monopoly power. Failure to exploit this power leaves the economy in a second-best situation which may influence some comparative-statics exercises. In particular, there is in the M–F model a possibility of immiserization in response to certain policies.

function for the domestic service is also possible – see, for example, Prachowny (1982).[12]

3.3. An extended Mundell–Fleming model

Consider now a straightforward extension of the M–F model to include an aggregate supply relationship. Demand for labor depends on the real wage in terms of the home good while the supply of labor is sensitive to both domestic and foreign goods prices. [This distinction has been emphasized by Salop (1974), Casas (1975), Purvis (1976, 1979), and Leiderman (1979); Sachs (1980) and Marston (1982) develop similar models in terms of a wage indexation scheme. See also Chapter 17 of this Handbook.]

For symmetry we could also assume that the foreign country has an upward sloping aggregate supply curve. However, rather than move to a full two-country model, we maintain the small-economy assumption by making the foreign-currency price of imports parametric and hence independent of domestic demand for imports. However, the home economy is assumed to be "large" in the market for its export good so that it faces a less-than-perfectly elastic demand for its exports; export demand depends on the relative price π.

The supply of home goods is given by

$$Y = \tilde{S}(P/W), \qquad \tilde{S}' > 0, \tag{3.8}$$

where W is the nominal wage. The nominal wage might in turn respond to the prices of both home goods and imports. This response is approximated by

$$dW = \theta \left[\alpha_0 \, dP + (\alpha_1)(de + dP^f) \right]. \tag{3.9}$$

If nominal wages are rigid, $\theta = 0$. If nominal wages are variable there are two possible interpretations. One is the indexation or "real wage rigidity" version where $\theta = 1$, while $\alpha_0 \ (= 1 - \alpha_1)$ is the share of home goods in the price index. The other is the "market-clearing model" in which $\theta\alpha_0$ and $\theta\alpha_1$, both between 0 and 1 represent the interaction of price index shares and elasticities of labor demand and supply; furthermore, homogeneity requires that $\theta\alpha_0 = 1 - \theta\alpha_1$.

The labor market is illustrated in Figure 3.1 where the initial equilibrium is at E_0. A rise in the price of the home good shifts the demand for labor up to L_1^D. With rigid nominal wages the new equilibrium is at E_K with employment rising to L_K. An indexed or rigid real wage would cause the nominal wage to rise to W', so that the new equilibrium is at point E' with employment L'. In a market-clearing

---

[12] Of course, the non-traded goods model can also be expanded in the other directions that the M–F model has been developed; namely, wage adjustment, exchange rate expectations, intertemporal budget constraints and long-run stock-equilibrium conditions, etc.!

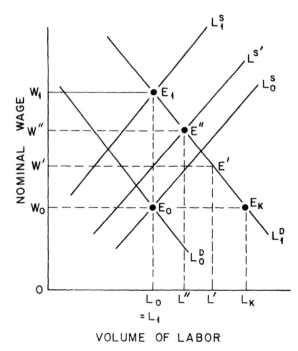

Figure 3.1. Labor market equilibrium and the terms of trade.

model the labor supply curve would shift vertically by $(W' - W_0)$ but the slope of the labor supply curve elicits a higher nominal wage, W'', and lower employment level, L''.

Now consider the effects of a rise in the import price eP^f proportional to the original rise in P. The demand for labor does not respond, so in the nominal-rigidity case equilibrium remains unchanged at point E_K with employment constant at L_K. However, the variable-wage cases both involve upward pressure on the nominal wage rate and in both cases homogeneity requires the new equilibrium to be at E_1 with employment returned to the original level L_0 and with nominal wage W_1 such that the real wage is also unchanged compared to that which prevailed at E_0.

These considerations mean that aggregate supply can be rewritten as

$$Y = S(P, eP^f). \tag{3.10}$$

In the Keynesian model where $dW = 0$, the aggregate supply function has the properties $S_1 > 0$ and $S_2 = 0$, where S_1 and S_2 indicate the partial derivatives of the supply function with respect to P and eP^f, respectively. In the variable nominal wage case, $S_1 = -S_2 > 0$. (Recall we have set the initial values of P, e, P^f, and W all equal to unity.)

The model now consists of eqs. (3.1), (3.2) and (3.10). Under fixed exchange rates, eqs. (3.1) and (3.10) can be solved for P and Y and eq. (3.2) then yields the equilibrium value for M^s in the standard recursive fashion. Under flexible exchange rates the three equations must be solved simultaneously for Y, P and e. [The endogeneity of P in eqs. (3.1) and (3.2) accounts for the fact that the flexible-exchange-rate model is no longer recursive as it was in the simple M–F model.]

3.3.1. Goods-market equilibrium

Differentiating the goods-market equilibrium condition (3.1), we get the traditional M–F expression:

$$dY = \left[Z(\eta + \eta^f - 1)\, d\pi + dG + m^f\, dY^f \right]/(1 - \delta), \tag{3.11}$$

where δ is the marginal propensity to spend out of income on domestic goods, equal to the sum of the partial derivatives of $E(\cdot)$ and $NX(\cdot)$ with respect to Y; that sum, in turn, is just one minus the sum of the domestic marginal propensities to save and import. The aggregate supply function can now be used to substitute for dY in eq. (3.11) to yield a solution for dP in terms of changes in the exogenous variables:

$$\gamma\, dP = \lambda(de + dP^f) + dG + m^f\, dY^f, \tag{3.12}$$

where m^f is the foreign marginal propensity to import, and where

$$\gamma = S_1(1 - \delta) + Z(\eta + \eta^f - 1)$$

is the excess supply of home goods caused by an increase in P, and

$$\lambda = -S_2(1 - \delta) + Z(\eta + \eta^f - 1)$$

is the excess demand created by a rise in e or P^f.

Consider γ. An increase in P creates an excess supply of home goods on two counts. First there is the increase in supply, S_1, multiplied by that fraction of the induced rise in income that is not spent on the home good, $(1 - \delta)$. Second there is a substitution away from home goods by both domestic residents and foreigners as indicated by the Marshall–Lerner condition given by $Z(\eta + \eta^f - 1)$. A similar explanation pertains to λ. Note that in the classical labor market case $\gamma = \lambda$ since $S_1 = -S_2$, while in the "Keynesian" labor market case γ is greater than λ since S_1 is greater than $-S_2 = 0$.

3.3.2. Fixed exchange rates

As noted above, monetary equilibrium does not impinge on the determination of output and prices under fixed exchange rates with perfect capital mobility. Hence eq. (3.12) is the reduced-form solution for P. The response of output to any given change can easily be found by substituting the results from (3.12) into the aggregate supply relationship, eq. (3.10).

However, in order to facilitate a diagramatic description of the model under fixed exchange rates it is useful to reorganize the goods-market equilibrium in eq. (3.1). This will also help expose the structure of the goods market. First we divide net exports into its two components:

$$NX(\pi, Y, Y^f) = X(\pi, Y^f) - \pi Im(\pi, Y),$$

where $X(\cdot)$ and $Im(\cdot)$ are export and import volumes. Next we define $D(\cdot)$ as the *domestic* demand for domestic goods:

$$D(Y, i^f, \pi) = E(Y, i^f) - \pi Im(\pi, Y). \tag{3.13}$$

Note that the response of $D(\cdot)$ to a rise in income is just given by ∂, defined above. Note also that in order for the domestic demand for home goods to decline with an increase in the relative price of home goods, the import demand function must be elastic, i.e. $\partial D/\partial \pi = Z(\eta - 1)$.[13]

The goods-market equilibrium can now be rewritten as:

$$Y = D(Y, i^f, \pi) + G + X(\pi, Y^f). \tag{3.1'}$$

It is illustrated in Figure 3.2. At price P' domestic demand for home goods, given by the sum of $D + G$, is just equal to domestic supply, given by eq. (3.10). For prices above P' domestic supply exceeds $D + G$; this difference is the amount available for export, and is drawn as the upward sloping export supply schedule, X^S, in the right-hand panel. Equilibrium occurs at P_0 where X^S equals X^D and hence eq. (3.1) is satisfied. The equilibrium pair (P_0, Y_0) shown in Figure 3.2 is, of course, contingent on the exogenous variables, e, P^f, Y^f, and G_0.

Equivalently the equilibrium response of P to changes in the various exogenous variables can be read directly from eq. (3.12), and the response of output can be derived from $S_1 dP + S_2(de + dP^f)$. The comparative-statics results are summarized in Table 3.1. As can readily be seen, an increase in any of Y^f, G, e, or P^f leads to an increase in P. As long as the country faces some elasticity in the foreign demand for its export good (so η^f, and hence γ, are finite), increases in foreign income or in domestic fiscal policy leads to an increase in domestic prices and hence in domestic output. In terms of the diagram, a rise in G shifts the X^S

---

[13] Substituting eq. (3.11) into (3.13) gives the following expression for the total response of domestic absorption to a change in π:

$$dD/d\pi = Z(\eta + \delta\eta^f - 1)/(1 - \delta).$$

We assume that the numerator is positive, a stronger assumption than that the Marshall–Lerner conditions hold since δ is less than one. A sufficient condition for the numerator to be positive is that the domestic demand for import be price elastic so that $(\eta - 1)$ is greater than zero; in what follows we shall assume that this condition is satisfied.

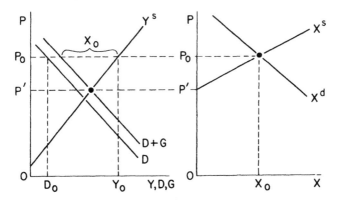

Figure 3.2. Fixed exchange rates and the extended Mundell–Fleming model.

curve up and to the left while a rise in Y^f shifts the X^D curve up and to the right. Both lead to a rise in P and induce a movement along the aggregate supply curve. As in the Mundell–Fleming model, fiscal policy is potent under fixed rates where fluctuations in foreign income are transmitted to the domestic economy (as long as η is finite). It follows, of course, that under fixed exchange rates the Keynesian prescription that fiscal policy be used to offset export fluctuations is preserved.

Note that these conclusions do *not* depend on the presence of nominal wage rigidities in the system. A rise in domestic prices alone will elicit an output

Table 3.1
Comparative statics under fixed exchange rates[a]

| | Rigid nominal wages $S_1 > 0,\ S_2 = 0,\ \gamma > \lambda$ | | | Variable nominal wages[b] $S_1 = S_2 > 0,\ \gamma = \lambda$ | | |
| | Response of: | | | Response of: | | |
	Price	Output	NX	Price	Output	NX
Fiscal policy dG	$\dfrac{1}{\gamma} > 0$	$\dfrac{S_1}{\gamma} > 0$	$< 0^{[d]}$	$\dfrac{1}{\gamma} > 0$	$\dfrac{S_1}{\gamma} > 0$	$< 0^{[d]}$
Foreign income dY^f	$\dfrac{m^f}{\gamma} > 0$	$\dfrac{S_1 m^f}{\gamma} > 0$	> 0	$\dfrac{m^f}{\gamma} > 0$	$\dfrac{S_1 m^f}{\gamma} > 0$	> 0
Foreign inflation[c]	$\dfrac{\lambda}{\gamma} < 1$	$S_1 \dfrac{\lambda}{\gamma} > 0$	$S_1(1-\delta)\dfrac{\lambda}{\gamma}$ > 0	$\dfrac{\lambda}{\gamma} = 1$	0	0

[a] Results for *SOE* can be found by letting $\lambda = \gamma \to \infty$.
[b] S_1 and hence γ are both lower here than in the rigid nominal wage case.
[c] Results for devaluation are identical.
[d] $dNX/dG = -[Z(\eta + \eta^f - 1) + mS_1]/\gamma < 0$, where m is the domestic propensity to import.

response even with labor-market clearing; since import prices are constant, an increase in labor supply or real-wage protection requires a less-than-proportionate increase in wages, and hence the real wage facing domestic producers falls. The implications for stabilisation policy of this relationship between aggregate demand, equilibrium output and the terms of trade are explored in more detail in Chapter 17 of this Handbook.

The effects of a devaluation are slightly more complicated since they (potentially) cause a shift in aggregate supply. From eq. (3.12) we see that

$$\mathrm{d}P/\mathrm{d}e = \lambda/\gamma \begin{cases} < 1, & \text{in the rigid wage case,} \\ = 1, & \text{in the variable wage case.} \end{cases} \tag{3.14}$$

Output response is positive in the rigid-nominal-wage case but zero in the variable wage case since in the latter case relative prices do not change. Note that the latter looks much like the "monetarist" Dornbusch (1972) results for a small open economy, but here the results come from the homogeneity of the system rather than from the exogeneity of the terms of trade. Further, the results differ substantially from the Dornbusch case since no improvement in NX occurs here; there would be a once-and-for-all portfolio shift to attain monetary equilibrium. Introduction of a wealth effect on expenditure would restore the Dornbusch result (i.e. that devaluation elicits a trade surplus) but would break the neutrality of devaluation on relative prices and output.

3.3.3. Flexible exchange rates

Under flexible exchange rates the goods-market and money-market equilibrium conditions must be solved simultaneously. Eq. (3.12) gives a restriction on movements in P and e imposed by goods-market equilibrium. In $P–e$ space this translates into a positively sloped line. In the case of a rigid nominal wage, the GG locus has a slope of $\mathrm{d}P/\mathrm{d}e = \lambda/\gamma$, which is between zero and one; movements up the GG curve are associated with increases in output. In the case of a variable nominal wage, the locus has a slope of unity, and output is constant along the locus. These two cases are illustrated by the two GG curves in Figures 3.3 and 3.4; in both cases, points above the line are associated with excess supply of home goods. An increase in G, Y^f, or P^f causes the GG curve to rotate up and to the left.

Money-market equilibrium comes from eq. (3.2); using the aggregate supply relation (3.10) to eliminate Y we have:

$$(M + lS_1)\,\mathrm{d}P = \mathrm{d}M^S - lS_2(\mathrm{d}e + \mathrm{d}P^f), \tag{3.15}$$

where l is again the income responsiveness of the demand for money. Hence, in $P–e$ space, the slope of the money-market equilibrium locus is:

$$\mathrm{d}P/\mathrm{d}e = -lS_2/(M + lS_1).$$

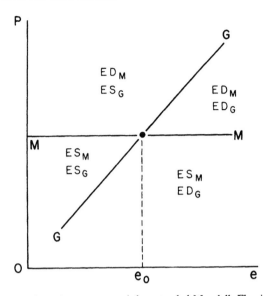

Figure 3.3. Flexible exchange rates and the extended Mundell–Fleming model (I).

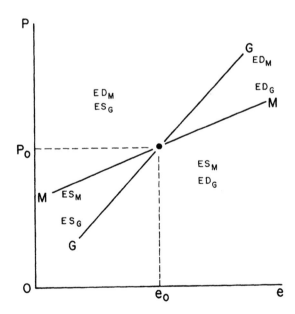

Figure 3.4. Flexible exchange rates and the extended Mundell–Fleming model (II).

With a rigid nominal wage, the slope is zero since S_2 is zero; income is constant along the locus. With a variable nominal wage the slope is positive but less than one; income falls for movements along the locus from left to right since P falls relative to eP^f. These two cases are shown by the MM curves in Figures 3.3 and 3.4, respectively; in both cases, points above the curve correspond to points of excess demand for money. Increases in M^S and P^f shift the MM locus to the left.

The comparative statics of the model are quite interesting. Under the assumption of a rigid nominal wage, shifts in the GG curve cause no movements in prices or output. Fiscal policy is impotent, and disturbances in foreign income or prices are insulated; a boom from any of these sources gives rise to an appreciation of the domestic currency thus crowding out private demand. Shifts in the MM curve elicit changes in both prices and domestic output; monetary policy is potent. These are the standard Mundell–Fleming results. However, in the variable-wage model these results are reversed. Shifts in the MM curve cause movements along the GG curve; although P is changed there is no change in domestic output. Fiscal policy and foreign disturbances shift the GG curve, eliciting changes in output associated with movements along MM.

These results can be verified algebraically. Solving eqs. (3.12) and (3.15) we get the following equilibrium expressions:

$$dP = (\lambda dM + lS_2 dG)/\Delta,$$

$$de = (\lambda dM - (lS_1 + M) dG)/\Delta,$$

where $\Delta = \gamma lS_2 + \lambda(lS_1 + M) > 0$. Output response can be calculated from the aggregate supply equation. Substituting the values $S_1 > -S_2 = 0$ and $\gamma > \lambda$ for the Keynesian case and $S_1 = -S_2 > 0$ and $\gamma = \lambda$ for the classical case gives the results depicted in Figures 3.3 and 3.4, and summarized in Table 3.2.

The variable-wage results are worth examining in some detail. Monetary policy is now rendered impotent via the homogeneity of the system and the merging of short- and long-run effects. Fiscal expansion still causes a nominal appreciation as in the Mundell–Fleming world. Although it also causes the domestic price to fall, the slope of MM shows that P falls less than e (if P and e fell by the same amount there would be excess supply of money). Thus P rises relative to e, though *both* fall. Fiscal expansion causes a *real appreciation* (i.e. a reduction in the manufacturing real wage) and hence elicits an increase in output.

3.3.4. Further extensions

One possible extension of the foregoing would be to allow exchange rates and foreign prices to influence real balances by using a price index to deflate the nominal money stock in eq. (1.8). A rise in e would create an excess demand for money. In the Keynesian case, the MM curve would be negatively sloped, since

Table 3.2
Comparative static results with flexible exchange rages [a,b]

	Rigid nominal wages $S_1 > 0, S_2 = 0, \gamma > \lambda$				Variable nominal wages $S_1 = -S_2 > 0, \gamma = \lambda$			
	Response of:				Response of			
	P	e	Y	NX	P	e	Y	NX
Fiscal policy dG	0	$\dfrac{-1}{\lambda} < 0$	0	-1	$\dfrac{-IS_1}{\lambda M} > 0$	$\dfrac{-(1+IS_1)}{\gamma} < 0$	$\dfrac{S_1}{\lambda} > 0$	?
Monetary policy[c] dM^S	$\dfrac{1}{D_K} > 0$	$\dfrac{\gamma}{\gamma D_K} > 0$	$\dfrac{S_1}{D_K} > 0$	$< 0^d$	$\dfrac{1}{M}$	$\dfrac{1}{M}$	0	0
Foreign inflation[e] dP^f	0	-1	0	0	0	-1	0	0

[a,b] See notes to Table 3.1.

[c] $D_K = (IS_1 + M)$.

[d] $\dfrac{dNX}{dM^S} = \dfrac{[Z(\eta + \eta^f - 1)(\lambda - \gamma - MS_1)]}{\lambda D_K} > 0$, for the rigid-wage case.

[e] The effects of a change of foreign income, dY^f, can be calculated by multiplying the coefficients in ιe dG row by m^f.

movements in e would have to be matched by opposing movements in P in order to preserve monetary equilibrium. In the classical case, a large enough weight of traded goods in the price index could offset the excess supply of money created by the income effect of a rise in e, so that the MM curve would be negatively sloped in this case too. Fiscal policy could have an effect on income even in a Keynesian world; the appreciation of the domestic currency would increase real balances and hence create room for an expansion of income. This, of course, would also be true in the simple M–F model if the effects of the appreciation on real balances were taken into account. Similarly, the expansionary effects of monetary policy would be somewhat reduced since depreciation would reduce the net expansion of the real money stock following a rise in the nominal money stock.

A second extension would be to incorporate wealth effects into the determination of expenditure. Aggregate domestic wealth is given by

$$A + M + B + eF,$$

where M is domestic money, B is other assets denominated in the domestic currency, and F is net foreign assets. Inclusion of such a variable in any of the behavioral relations would have one immediate important consequence: it would give a role for e separate from P^f. Until now e and P^f have always entered in product form; it followed trivially that fluctuations in P^f could be completely offset by fluctuations in e.

Suppose first that the wealth term were included in the money demand function. Increases in e would now give rise to excess demand for money in much the same manner as when e was included in the price index, and with much the same effects; see Purvis (1979).

If A, deflated by a price index, were included in the expenditure function, then the goods-market equilibrium condition would now become

$$\gamma dP = \lambda_1 de + \lambda_2 dP^f + dG + m^f dY^f. \tag{3.12'}$$

The response of the goods market to changes in e would differ from that to changes in P^f. If F were positive, λ_1 would exceed λ_2. If the wealth effect were strong enough it would also be possible for λ_2, and even λ_1, to be negative. Futhermore, there would no longer be any reason for γ to equal λ_1, or λ_2, even in the classical case, so that the neutrality of a devaluation would be lost. But the wealth effects would now elicit a change in NX. It is interesting to compare these results with the basic monetarist small open economy (SOE) analysis which imposes $\gamma = \lambda_1$ by letting η go to infinity, and which then *focuses* on the wealth-absorption nexus.

Finally, we note that the properties of the endogenous-wage or classical model are similar to those of a model incorporating an imported intermediate good; see, for example, Findlay and Rodriquez (1977).[14] A key feature of both models is that a change in the exchange rate leads to a change in domestic costs of production: this creates room, for example, for fiscal policy to be effective under flexible exchange rates, contrary to the usual M–F results. (On this, see also Chapter 17 in this Handbook.)

4. Open macroeconomic model specification: Some applications

In this section we highlight the importance of some of the issues raised above by considering two long-standing topics in the literature.

4.1. Specie flow and the automatic adjustment mechanism

A useful way of considering the subject-matter of this chapter is to look at its relevance for the automatic adjustment mechanism by which external imbalances are corrected under fixed exchange rates. This, of course, has been at the heart of the debate over the operation of the gold standard at least since the "specie-flow mechanism" was made famous by Hume.

---

[14] In fact, Findlay and Rodriguez derive a figure identical to Figure 2.4 above.

Consider an economy operating under a gold standard and experiencing a balance-of-payments surplus, i.e. experiencing a gold inflow. (The discussion below would hold equivalently for a gold outflow.) Further suppose that this economy is "obeying the rules of the game" so that the gold inflow translates into an increase in the domestic money supply. Will this inflow be self-correcting? For centuries economists have answered in the affirmative but have disagreed about the *mechanism* by which the automatic correction has been presumed to operate. These different conclusions have reflected different assumptions about the structure of goods and factor markets.[15]

The simplest case is that of a small open economy (SOE) which faces given international prices for all goods produced and consumed. Under the gold standard, the fixed international value of its own currency fixes the domestic prices of all goods. A gold inflow exerts no influence on domestic prices, but the increase in the domestic money supply increases the general level of demand in the economy. At the given domestic prices, the volume of export goods offered on world markets falls while the volume of imports demanded rises. Hence the external surplus falls.

The above automatic adjustment mechanism operates with no change in the domestic price level or in relative prices. This SOE structure gives rise to the ben chmark monetary model developed in Section 1.1 above and the automatic adjustment mechanism is the one illustrated in Figure 1.1.

An alternative scenario often considered is one where the domestic economy is large enough for changes in its excess demands to influence world prices. The gold ir ow represents a redistribution of purchasing power from the rest of the world to domestic residents. If domestic and foreign tastes are different, this will change relative prices; as is well known from the literature on the transfer problem, relative prices could go either way, depending in part upon the elasticity conditions discussed in Section 1.2 above. This scenario can be examined using the so-called Armington model, which has been particularly useful in macroeconomics; the domestic country is small (i.e. a price-taker) in the world markets for its imports, but it is specialized enough that it exerts an influence on the world price of its exports. Therefore the increased domestic absorption and subsequent reduction in the supply of exports to world markets resulting from a gold inflow drives up the relative price of domestic exports. This induces substitution of domestic and foreign consumption away from domestic exports. Whether or not it reduces the trade surplus depends upon the Marshall–Lerner conditions being met, as discussed in Section 1.2.1.

A third possible scenario arises when the SOE assumption is maintained in terms of the domestic economy's inability to influence foreign prices of traded

---

[15]See Samuelson (1969) for a detailed treatment. Frenkel (1971) discusses the role of relative price changes in the classical literature.

goods but consideration is given to a class of domestic goods not traded on international markets. The gold inflow again gives rise to an increase in imports and a decrease in exports, but it does so in part by bidding up the prices of non-tradable goods relative to the domestic prices of traded goods, which shifts production away from tradables and shifts consumption towards tradables, reinforcing the SOE automatic adjustment mechanism.

All three adjustment mechanisms outlined above ignore domestic income movements. If the increase in consumption demand resulting from the gold inflow also leads to an increase in domestic output and income, due to the existence of Keynesian unemployment, it will increase imports and again lead to an automatic decrease in the external surplus. This possibility was discussed in detail in Section 3.

4.2. *The purchasing power parity (PPP) doctrine*

The doctrine of purchasing power parity (*PPP*) holds that exchange rates and national price levels will adjust so as to maintain a given currency's purchasing power across national boundaries; at any moment of time the real value of a given currency will be the same in all countries. The doctrine has played a central role in open economy macroeconomic analysis and especially exchange-rate theory at least since Gustav Cassel introduced the term over sixty years ago. [*PPP* is also discussed in Chapter 18 of this Handbook where the distinction between absolute and relative *PPP* is introduced. The latter allows for different but constant relative prices at home and abroad (due, for example, to tariffs) so that only the percentage change over time of a currency's purchasing power is equalized.]

Purchasing power parity holds trivially in models where all goods are perfect substitutes (so relative prices are constant) and where commodity arbitrage is perfect so the law of one price holds. In these circumstances, which hold in most simple monetary models such as those described in Section 1.1 above, it is obvious that crossing borders and converting currencies involves no loss of purchasing power. A more contentious issue is whether purchasing power parity holds in more complicated models; it is useful to note at the outset of our discussion that in general *both* the constancy of relative prices and the operation of the law of one price are required for *PPP* to obtain.

There is, however, some tendency in recent literature to identify *PPP* only with the law of one price and to interpret observed deviations from *PPP* as either arbitrage failures or measurement errors. Such "deviations" from *PPP*, i.e. such differential changes in a currency's purchasing power, might instead reflect changes in equilibrium relative prices and hence reflect a failure of *PPP* to hold even though the law of one price prevails. The following discussion is intended to illustrate this point.[16]

Consider eq. (4.1), which can be used to summarize *PPP*:

$$P = keP^f. \tag{4.1}$$

In the absolute version of *PPP*, as embodied for example in the simple monetary model described above, k would be identically equal to one; the relative version of *PPP* allows k to differ from one in order to allow for the presence of tariffs and other distortions. If those distortions are constant (in percentage terms), k will be constant; hence, according to eq. (4.1), the positive association between P and eP^f will hold exactly in *rate-of-change form*.

While the precise theoretical basis for eq. (4.1) is contentious, it seems that the consensus view on *PPP* is that (*i*) *PPP* does not hold in the short run, but (*ii*) *PPP* is a good approximation in the long run. While evidence in support of (*i*) seem incontrovertible, the two statements together constitute a potentially misleading view.

If (*ii*) were true, of course, *PPP* would be a good basis for forming expectations, and, in fact, many forecasting models base their predictions on convergence towards a relationship like eq. (4.1). Yet traders betting on eq. (4.1) have tended to lose a lot of money over the past decade, as data from the 1970s have *not* shown strong tendencies for convergence towards *PPP*; "deviations" from *PPP* in the 1970s have tended to be not only substantial but persistent.[17]

The key problem with the position summarized in (*i*) and (*ii*) is that it tends to treat *PPP* as an arbitrage condition, even though eq. (4.1) is usually expressed in terms of price indexes relating to fairly broad aggregates of goods. In fact, *PPP* should be interpreted as a *comparative-statics* result arising from a monetary disturbance, embodying the essential feature of *monetary neutrality*. A neutral monetary disturbance alters no relative price; any change in domestic prices must be accompanied eventually by offsetting changes in the exchange rate so as to preserve the equilibrium relative prices of domestic goods in terms of foreign goods.

It seems useful to allow explicitly for the possibility that some nominal variables (prices or asset stocks) adjust only slowly; in this way we can emphasize the distinction between the short run and the long run. Therefore, we introduce k^* to denote the long-run equilibrium value for k, which obtains when all

---

[16]The discussion draws on Purvis (1982). Confusion concerning *PPP* was noted by Samuelson (1964) when he quipped that "to many analysts, *PPP* seems both a trivial truism of arbitrage and besides quite untrue".

[17]Even if eq. (4.1) did hold in the long run, it would not form a useful basis for *exchange-rate* forecasts unless one also had a sound basis for predicting relative inflation rates; convergence to eq. (4.1) can be achieved by an infinite number of paths of e, each accompanied by a different path of (P/P^f).

nominal variables have fully adjusted. In principle, it is now possible to distinguish movements in k that reflect movement in k^* from those that reflect deviations from k^*.

Systematic short-run non-neutralities of monetary policy, such as those emphasized by Dornbusch (1976), will create "deviations" from PPP, i.e. changes in k that are transitory.[18] But it is misleading to think of all variations in k as reflecting transitory deviations from PPP. Real disturbances give rise to changes in k^* and thus to deviations that are permanent, reflecting a change in the equilibrium relationship between the exchange rate and relative national price levels. Models such as the simple monetary model which do not allow for the possibility of a change in k^* give rise to a very naive and empirically ungrounded form of PPP.[19] In the next two sections we illustrate this point in the context of two specific models.

4.2.1. PPP and the non-traded goods model

Figure 4.1 illustrates the determination of the price of non-traded goods, P_N, and the exchange rate, e, in the model of Section 2.2; recall that e also represents the domestic price of traded goods and that all prices have been normalized to unity. The locus GG depicts the combinations of P_N and e which satisfy eq. (2.6), the equilibrium condition in the market for non-traded goods, given the quantity of money. The slope of GG is positive, indicating that for given M, P_N and e must move together, but it is less than one. A proportionate rise in P_N and e leaves the supply of non-traded goods unchanged but reduces demand via the real-balance effect. Therefore, if point A is a point of equilibrium (for a given value of M), point B must be a position of excess supply; equilibrium can be restored by a fall in the relative price of non-traded goods to eliminate the excess supply. Hence the GG locus, drawn for a given value of the money supply, must be flatter than a ray through the origin, passing from A through a point such as C.

Suppose that with the given initial money supply, the exchange rate e_0 was pegged so that $NX = 0$ and hence point A corresponded to a long-run equilibrium. Consider now the effects of a devaluation, a purely monetary disturbance, which raises the exchange rate from e_0 to e_1. Equilibrium in the market for non-traded goods requires that P_N rise less than proportionately; short-run equilibrium obtains at point C with the price of non-traded goods at P_N'. The fall in real balances requires some fall in the relative price p. In terms of the PPP eq. (4.1), k will have fallen.

---

[18] Whether such "deviations" are due to arbitrage failures, less than infinite substitution elasticities, or other causes such as different speeds of adjustment is not always clearly specified.

[19] In Purvis (1982), PPP is interpreted as holding when $k = k^*$. Models which specify that k^* is constant are referred to as *naive PPP* models.

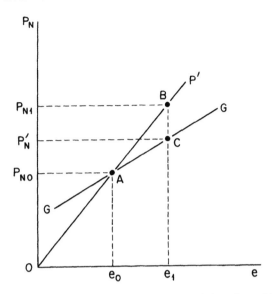

Figure 4.1. Monetary shocks and the non-traded goods model.

However, note that the new equilibrium at C is not stationary; the reduction in real balances will give rise to a reduction in absorption and hence elicit a trade surplus and an increase in the money stock. This, in turn, will shift the GG curve up and to the left, leading to further increases in P_N. It is easily verified from eqs. (2.6) and (2.7), by setting $dNX = 0$ and letting dM be endogenous, that in the long run $dp = 0$, or $dP_N = de$; long-run equilibrium is shown in Figure 4.1 as the ray through the origin, OP. The economy eventually moves to point B where all real variables are as at A. Monetary neutrality is re-established and, in particular, k in eq. (4.1) returns to its initial equilibrium value. PPP is preserved. Note that k^* never changes, but k "deviates" from k^* during the adjustment from short-run equilibrium at C to long-run equilibrium at A.[20]

This result is to be contrasted with the result of a real disturbance. There is a shift in the GG curve corresponding to any given value of the money supply, and the long-run value of p in eqs. (2.6) and (2.7) also changes. This means that not only will k diverge from k^* during the adjustment period, but the long-run value of k^* also changes. This is shown in Figure 4.2 where the initial equilibrium is again at A, the real shock shifts the economy to C in the short run but also causes

---

[20]Dornbusch (1976) presents a model of a flexible-exchange-rate economy where the price level is the sticky nominal variable that gives rise to the short-run/long-run distinction and to transitory deviations following a monetary shock. Nevertheless, in its implications for the discussion of PPP, the model is analogous to that outlined above.

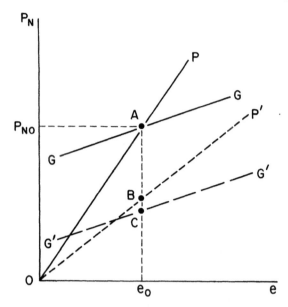

Figure 4.2. Real shocks and the non-traded goods model.

the long-run relative price relationship to rotate from OP to OP' so that the new long-run equilibrium is at B. In the case illustrated, k^* falls but k falls by even more on impact.

4.2.2. Middle products: PPP without direct arbitrage

The "middle-products model" due to Sanyal and Jones (1982) is also a useful vehicle for examining these issues, since it abstracts entirely from direct trade in final goods (see also Chapter 10 in this Handbook). Eq. (4.1), written in terms of final goods prices (e.g. the P's reflect consumer price indexes), is not subject to interpretation as an "arbitrage" condition but only as an equilibrium condition. Further, in the middle-products model, monetary changes are neutral and hence leave k (k^*) unchanged; however, k and k^* are subject to change in response to real factors.

A particularly simple version of the model can be described as follows. Let R and R^f be the domestic- and foreign-currency prices of the traded, middle product; assume that arbitrage is perfect and that there are no barriers to trade. Hence, we can write

$$R = eR^f.$$

$$(4.2)$$

Eq. (4.2) is just the law of one price for middle products. Consumer prices in the two countries, however, equal unit costs of producing final consumer goods, and unit costs in each country are a function of local nominal wage rates and the local price of the middle product:

$$P = a_L W + a_R R; \qquad P^f = a_L W^f + a_R R^f. \qquad (4.3)$$

We have assumed for simplicity that technology is common to the two countries. Solving eqs. (4.2) and (4.3) for e $(= R/R^f)$ yields:

$$e = \frac{P}{P^f} \frac{(a_L w^f + a_R)}{(a_L w + a_R)}, \qquad (4.4)$$

where w (w^f) is the real wage in terms of traded goods. It is clear that there is no reason to expect the second term, equivalent to k in eq. (4.1), to equal one or even to be constant. Furthermore, monetary factors which drive P/P^f can be offset by real wage movements so that the evolution of e does not reflect that of P/P^f; if the home country is inflating faster, for example, the home currency can nevertheless be appreciating (e falling) if real wages (net of productivity) grow faster at home than abroad (i.e. W/P is rising faster than W^f/P^f, given a_L).[21]

4.2.3. PPP: A summary

The foregoing discussion suggests the following general remarks concerning *PPP*. *PPP* obtains when the law-of-one-price holds *and* relative prices are constant; in terms of eq. (4.1), *PPP* holds when k (and k^*) is constant. Monetary disturbances leave k^* unchanged, but nominal rigidities can cause temporary deviations of observed k from k^*. Real disturbances in general lead to changes in k^* and can also cause actual k to deviate from the new value of k^*. The consensus view of *PPP* contained in statements (i) and (ii) in Section 4.2 is thus perfectly consistent with our view that *PPP* holds when $k = k^*$. It is only the interpretations which treat k^* as fixed that we take issue with.[22]

---

[21] Jones and Purvis (1981) explore the implications of eq. (4.4) using the middle-products model to determine the real wage. They show that structural differences between two countries confronted by a common external real shock – such as an oil-price increase – will cause their real wages and hence their exchange rates to respond differently; accordingly, the behavior of their bilateral exchange rate will not conform to *PPP*.

[22] The empirical task is to decompose movements in observed k into a component representing changes in k^* and a component representing temporary deviations from k^*. Stockman (1982) introduces the further complication caused by the effect of anticipated future disturbances on k^* and deviations from it.

5. Specification issues in dynamic open-economy models

We have emphasized throughout that the measurement of aggregate income and expenditure flows must satisfy certain accounting identities. These identities can be summarized as:

$$T = NX = Y - A = S' - I. \tag{5.1}$$

The external balance, measured as the current-account surplus or value of net exports (NX), is identically equal to the value of output (Y) less expenditure or absorption (A) and to the value of saving inclusive of the public sector surplus (S') less investment (I).

These identities are devoid of any theoretical content because they must be satisfied by double-entry bookkeeping conventions. However, they do illustrate that there are three equivalent measures of the external balance, and each has been the point of departure for a theory of the external balance. The benchmark real model of Section 1.2 focuses on NX and explains it in terms of the factors underlying the level of expenditure on distinct export and import goods. The benchmark monetary model of Section 1.1 ignores the composition of output and expenditure and focuses on the difference between the aggregate levels of output and expenditure as given by $Y - A$.

Recently attention has been focused on the third measure of external balance, which gives rise to a theory of the determination of NX based on factors underlying saving and/or investment behavior. As in the benchmark monetary model, the composition of exports and imports is ignored. However, the decisions underlying saving and investment are made by rational, forward-looking, optimizing economic agents, whereas decisions in the monetary model derive from a more or less static demand for real money balances. Households save so as to maximize utility over time, and firms invest so as to maximize the present value of future profits. Finally, the saving–investment approach to the external balance differs from the Mundell–Fleming model, which also includes saving and investment equations, by explicitly incorporating effects of stock accumulation. For example, the investment process raises the stock of productive capital and therefore the full-employment output of the domestic economy.

5.1. Private-sector accumulation and external balance

In this section it is assumed that all saving and investment are private and carried out by rational households and firms. The role of public-sector saving is ignored; a sufficient condition for this to be appropriate is that the public-sector budget be balanced; in Section 5.2 we consider other conditions under which this simplification might also be appropriate. In the next two sections we focus on private investment and private saving behavior, respectively.

5.1.1. Investment and portfolio balance in an open economy

Frenkel and Rodriguez (1975), drawing upon earlier work by Frenkel (1971) and Frenkel and Fischer (1972), explicitly incorporate the physical capital stock and investment into the benchmark monetary framework. Frenkel and Rodriguez maintain the assumption that there is a single world consumption good but follow Uzawa (1969) in allowing it to be transformed into domestic capital subject to adjustment costs. Specifically it is assumed that

$$\dot{k} + \delta k = h(I) < I; \qquad 0 < h'(\cdot) \le 1, \quad h'(0) = 1, \quad h''(\cdot) < 0. \tag{5.2}$$

In (5.2), k is the stock of physical capital located in the domestic economy (the capital–labor ratio, actually, but the labor supply is constant and can be set equal to unity), δ is the depreciation rate, an overdot denotes a time derivative, and I is the number of units of the consumption good absorbed in the investment process. The nominal price of a unit of installed capital P_k is the present value of the marginal product $f'(k)$ discounted at the interest rate i plus δ. The value of an installed unit of capital in units of consumption is given by:

$$p_k = P_k/P = f'(k)/(i + \delta). \tag{5.3}$$

Output $f(k)$ is produced subject to a concave production function with $f'(k) > 0$ and $f''(k) < 0$. Wealth, A, consists of nominal money balances M and the value of capital owned by domestic residents $P_k k^D$. It is important to recognize that in an open economy k^D need not equal k because of foreign ownership. Real wealth, $a = A/P$, is given by

$$a = m + p_k k^D, \tag{5.4}$$

where $m = M/P$. The demand for real money balances is assumed to be homogeneous of degree one in wealth, so that the value of claims on capital matters in financial markets (which was not the case in the M–F model); portfolio balance is represented by

$$m = L(i) p_k k^D; \qquad L'(i) < 0. \tag{5.5}$$

For a small open economy with a fixed exchange rate, P and i are exogenous, while k [and hence, by (5.3), p_k] is predetermined. Thus, eqs. (5.4) and (5.5) are sufficient to determine m and k^D.

Total spending in the economy consists of consumption and investment. As in the simple monetary models, consumption (and saving) is based on a wealth-adjustment process:

$$c = c(a), \qquad c'(\cdot) > 0. \tag{5.6}$$

Firms invest so as to maximize imputed profits, $f(k) - I + p^k k - ik$, subject to (5.2) which, assuming static expectations on p_k, implies $p_k = 1/h'(I)$. This can be inverted to yield the investment demand equation:

$$I = I(p_k); \qquad I'(\cdot) = -h'(\cdot)/h''(\cdot) > 0. \tag{5.7}$$

The trade balance, of course, is equal to output $f(k)$ less total expenditure, $c(a) + I(p_k)$. However, k^D need not equal k so that it is necessary to consider the service-account surplus $ip_k(k^D - k)_0$. This, added to the balance of trade, yields the current-account surplus:

$$b_c = f(k) - c(a) - I(p_k) + ip_k(k^D - k). \tag{5.8}$$

A further distinction must be drawn between b_c and the rate of wealth accumulation $\dot{a}$. By the balance of payments identity, the current account surplus must be financed by reserve inflows or reductions in net foreign liabilities:

$$b_c = \dot{m} + p_k(k^D - k). \tag{5.9}$$

Differentiating (5.4) yields $\dot{a} = \dot{m} + p_k k^D + k^D \dot{p}_k$, assuming that capital gains are unexpected and, in the first instance, absorbed into saving. Combined with (5.9), this yields:

$$\dot{a} = b_c + p_k \dot{k} + k^D \dot{p}_k. \tag{5.10}$$

It is clear from (5.10) that, even ignoring capital gains, wealth accumulation is not identical to the current account in an economy where net capital accumulation is going on.[23] The common identification of a current-account deficit with the dishoarding of wealth (or "living beyond one's means") fails to take into account domestic capital formation.

Frenkel and Rodriguez devote much of their analysis to demonstrating the equivalence of monetary policy and exchange-rate changes in this model. Because the value of the non-monetary asset is predetermined in real terms, a devaluation which raises the price level in the economy is equivalent to a tax on money balances. Frenkel and Rodriguez stress this money-neutrality aspect of their model. However, their model also makes clear that real disturbances in the capital-goods market can influence external balance (or the exchange rate in the case where it is not fixed).

Of course, in the long run following either a real or a monetary shock the economy will again be in a stationary state with zero net investment; this simply reflects the static nature of the model. The important thing is that phenomena influencing the long run desired capital stock and thus the rate of investment can and do have implications for external balance; these phenomena are distinct from

---

[23] Note that $b_c + p_k k$ is total capital formation in the economy and not just that domestically owned.

(and additional to) those arising from the desire to hoard or dishoard financial wealth. Current-account deficits may be the result of enlarged domestic investment opportunities rather than dishoarding or an excessive creation of money. In fact, Sachs (1981) marshalls evidence that different investment rates were a primary factor determining the configuration of current-account balances among *OECD* countries.

5.1.2. *Optimal savings decisions in an open economy*

While the Frenkel and Rodriguez analysis incorporates an investment decision grounded in rational choice, the saving–consumption decision is based on a mechanistic wealth-adjustment process. Recently, theories of the current account have incorporated a life-cycle saving theory based on intertemporal optimization. The life-cycle approach permits a more interesting analysis of the saving and investment theory of current-account determination. Sachs (1981*a*, 1981*b*), Obstfeld (1981) and Buiter (1981) have examined the determination of the current account (and/or exchange rate) in the context of optimal savings behavior.

The simplest case, adopted from Sachs (1981*b*), is the two-period model pictured in Figure 5.1. Current output is $Q_1 = {}_1F(K_1)$, where the current capital stock K_1 is given. The production function satisfies $F'(\cdot) > 0$ and $F''(\cdot) < 0$, and Ψ_1 is a shift parameter. Labor inputs are ignored for simplicity. Current output can be utilized for present consumption C_1 or as capital K_2 to be used in second-period production. Output in the second period is thus given by $\Psi_2 F(K_2)$. The above assumptions yield the convex production set with frontier $Q_1\Psi_2 F(K_1)$ with slope $-\Psi_2 F'(\cdot)$. The small open economy is assumed to be able to borrow and lend internationally at the fixed interest rate i^f. Profit-maximizing firms choose K_2 so as to maximize discounted future revenues less capital costs $\Psi_2 F(K_2)/(1 + i^f) - K_2$. This yields optimal investment K_2^*, determined by $\Psi_2 F'(K_2^*) = 1 + i^f$. Utility-maximizing households choose an intertemporal consumption plan C_1, C_2 so as to maximize $U(C_1, C_2)$ subject to the budget constraints $C_1 = Q_1 + B - K_2^*$ and $C_2 = \Psi_2 F(K_2^*) - (1 + i^f)B$, where B is first-period foreign borrowing (lending if negative). This yields the usual first-order condition $(U_1(\cdot)/U_2(\cdot)) = (1 + i^f)$ which, with the budget constraints, determines C_1^*, C_2^* and B^*. The first-period current-account surplus (capital-account deficit) is $Q_1 - C_1^* - K_2^* = -B^*$. The second-period current-account surplus is $\Psi_2 F(K_2^*) - i^f B^* - C_2^* = B^*$.[24] In the case pictured in Figure 5.1, the country borrows in the first period, running a current-account deficit in the first period followed by a surplus of equal present value in the second period.

---

[24] The distinction between the current account and the trade balance in a two-period model is arbitrary.

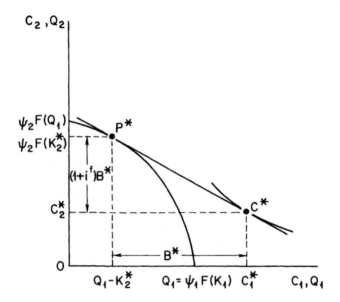

Figure 5.1. Intertemporal equilibrium in an open economy.

The effect of supply-side shocks in the form of actual or correctly anticipated changes in Ψ_1 and Ψ_2 can be analyzed. A rise in Ψ_1 raises current income but leaves the productivity of capital unchanged. This shifts the production-possibility curve out horizontally as shown in Figure 5.2. Part of the increased income will be saved to spend in the future; thus B^* falls to B' and the country runs a larger current-account surplus. An increase in Ψ_2 raises the productivity of capital and leaves current income unchanged. This shifts the production-possibility curve as shown in Figure 5.3, where $\Psi_2'(K)$ rises, increasing desired investment spending, and wealth rises too, increasing desired consumption; together, these raise B^* to B', and the current-account deficit is larger.

This simple framework can be extended to include an intermediate input (oil), fiscal policy, and exogenous changes in the terms of trade; see, for example, Djajic (1981). Also, the two-period framework can be extended to many or an infinite number of periods.[25] In these cases, one can define "permanent" or "perpetuity" equivalents for the values of the key variables. As in the two-period model, an exogenous shock influences the external balance by altering desired

---

[25] In the infinite-horizon model the intertemporal budget constraint must include a "feasibility" condition that the net worth of the economy be nonnegative. This "feasibility" condition does not alter the marginal conditions.

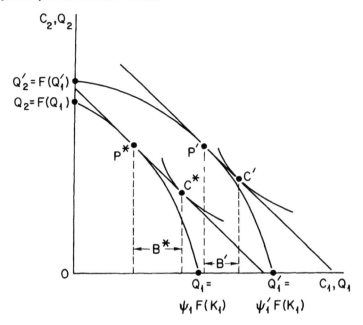

Figure 5.2. Output growth and the current account.

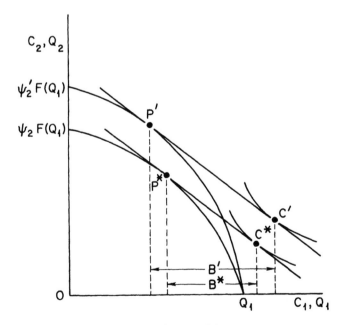

Figure 5.3. Technological change and the current account.

saving and investment. Since the models are "rational" and forward looking, the distinction between "permanent" and "transitory" shocks becomes important. For example, the effect of an oil-price increase that worsens the terms of trade of an oil-importing nation depends critically on whether such a shock is perceived as permanent or transitory. Similarly, fiscal-policy changes such as an income-tax cut or investment tax credit have quite different effects on the current account depending upon whether they are perceived as permanent or transitory. It should also be mentioned that the forward-looking behavior assumed in the model excludes "wealth illusion" with respect to the government debt. Households "internalize" the government's budget constraint so that the Ricardian equivalence theorem holds with regard to tax and debt financed government expenditures. This is discussed in further detail in Section 5.2.

While it is clear that the savings–investment approach to the current account is highly simplified, it has proved particularly useful for analyzing the implications of major real shocks such as the 1974 *OPEC* pricing agreement. The model also seems particularly useful for analyzing the current-account experiences and evaluating the external-balance policies of developing nations.

5.1.3. The Laursen–Metzler–Harberger effect

The savings–investment approach has also been used to establish rigorously the conditions under which the Laursen–Metzler–Harberger (L–M–H) effect holds.[26] The L–M–H effect states that a decrease in the terms of trade will decrease the amount saved out of a given domestic income and therefore reduce the external surplus. It was derived from the properties of the Keynesian saving function rather than rational saving behavior.

Obstfeld (1982) has examined the foundations of the L–M–H effect in the framework of intertemporal utility maximization and concludes that the effect will operate in the direction opposite to that postulated by L–M–H. Obstfeld maximizes an intertemporal utility function of the usual form except that the time preference rate is not constant but increases with the level of instantaneous utility (or "felicity"). A steady state requires that the economy attain a level of consumption such that the time preference rate is equal to the exogenous world interest rate and income is fully consumed. This condition uniquely determines the steady-state level of utility and also yields an extreme sort of target saving. No matter how poor (rich) the economy is made initially by a terms of trade change, it must save (dis-save) enough to achieve the fixed steady state utility level. Therefore, a deterioration in the terms of trade which reduces the economy's consumption opportunities will increase saving, not decrease it, as the economy is forced to restore utility to its steady-state level.

---

[26]See Laursen and Metzler (1949) and Harberger (1950).

Svensson and Razin (1983) also examine the $L-M-H$ effect in a utility-maximizing framework. They show that the effect on saving (and the external balance) of a deterioration in the terms of trade depends on whether the rate of time preference decreases or increases with the level of utility. While Obstfeld's assumption of an increasing rate of time preference is necessary and sufficient for a stable steady state, Svensson and Razin "do not regard stability of the stationary state more plausible than instability" (p. 30). In conclusion, it seems fair to say that the theoretical validity of the $L-M-H$ effect is still an open question, since the assumptions underlying Obstfeld's result are peculiar and the extreme target saving they imply seems rather implausible.

5.1.4. Further issues

The saving–investment approach has produced some other notable developments. In a model such as that of Sachs' (1981*a*) with infinitely lived households the life-cycle and intergenerational transfer (bequest) motives for saving are indistinct. Willem Buiter (1981) considers the life-cycle motive in isolation by constructing a two-country overlapping-generations model. Like Stiglitz (1970) he considers countries which differ only in "tastes", namely the rate of time preference, and shows that the country with the higher pure rate of time preference has a current-account deficit in the steady state. This is not necessarily true outside of the steady state. Also, since the overlapping-generations equilibrium is not Pareto efficient in autarky, the welfare implications of "intertemporal" trading through external surpluses and deficits are ambiguous.[27] This sort of model may be useful in examining how demographic features may influence a country's external balance. Given the same investment opportunities and other relevant factors, the country with a younger, growing population will save more than a country with a static, mature population and therefore run an external surplus. Yet the younger country may also have more profitable investment opportunities, so the overall effect will be ambiguous.

While the saving–investment approach has cast light on a number of interesting issues concerning the determination of the external balance, it does have a number of serious limitations. In contrast to the early elasticities theory, which stressed the ex ante behavioral specification of desired imports and exports to the exclusion of the savings and investment decision, the Sachs analysis assumes that NX adjust passively. This is only reasonable in a world with full employment and a single composite traded good. Short run endogeneity of output and the terms of trade are ruled out despite considerable evidence that such responses are important. By implication Sachs' analysis is most relevant to the long run. Another short run consideration is that at any point in time, measured variables need not

---

[27]See Fried (1980) and Dornbusch (1982) for further discussion.

equal their planned values. Furthermore, the scope for unplanned saving and investment is considerably greater than the scope for unplanned exports and imports. This has two implications. (i) In the short run, when ex ante and ex post values diverge, planned exports and imports are likely to be more important than planned saving and investment in determining the current account. (ii) There is likely to be more "noise" in measures of planned saving and investment than planned exports and imports, which has implications for testing the relative importance of the alternative theories.

Another shortcoming of Sachs' model is that it provides only a theory of the current account and not of the overall balance of payments. This could be rectified by introducing many assets plus some ad hoc portfolio balance behavior. Alternatively one could introduce a monetary asset that yields utility in the Patinkin–Sidrauski tradition. Obstfeld (1981) considers an economy where optimizing intertemporal decisions are made and wealth can be held in two forms – an internationally traded interest-bearing asset or domestic utility-yielding money. He then examines the impact and long-run effects of various macroeconomic disturbances. He finds, for example, that money creation through open-market operations is equivalent to helicopter-type money creation. This is because forward-looking agents capitalize the interest receipts on interest-bearing assets whether they are held by the government (which pays out the interest as transfers) or by themselves. Thus the open-market operation that shifts interest-bearing assets from private portfolios to the government has the same effect as a helicopter operation which drops money on the population.

5.2. Public-sector deficits and the external balances

A two-period model is also useful for analyzing the effects of government deficits on the external balance. In Figure 5.4, we consider a government which purchases goods in the amount G_1 and G_2, and raises taxes T_1 and T_2, in periods 1 and 2, respectively. The government's budget constraint requires that:

$$G_1 + \frac{G_2}{1 + i^f} = T_1 + \frac{T_2}{1 + i^f}. \tag{5.11}$$

For simplicity we assume the tax system is lump-sum and does not alter the after-tax interest rate. In this case, the locus of private-sector consumption opportunities is given by the line ZZ, and private consumption levels in the two periods are given by point C. Assume initially that government spending is positive and the government budget is balanced in both periods (i.e. $G_i = T_i > 0$ for $i = 1, 2$). In this case disposable outputs in the two periods are given by point A. The capital-account surplus (current-account deficit) for the first period is given by B, which is equal to $Q_1 - C_1 - K_2 - G_1$.

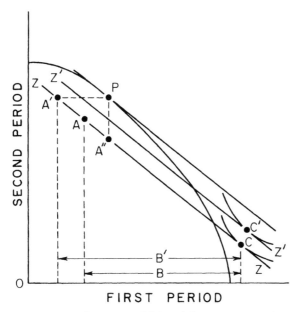

Figure 5.4. Government deficit and the current account.

We shall now consider increasing the first-period government deficit while holding the present value of total government spending [and, by (5.11), taxes] constant. This can be done by increasing government spending or reducing taxes in the first period. The effect on the external balance differs in each case.

First suppose that the government sets $G_2 = 0$ and increases G_1 accordingly. Disposable private product is given by point A' and the current-account deficit increases to B'. The increase in the current-account deficit is exactly equal to the increase in the public-sector deficit. Alternatively, consider the case where first-period government spending remains positive but the government collects all its tax revenue in the second period. In this case, disposable private product is given by A''. But households, foreseeing the higher second-period taxes, save more. In fact they save an amount exactly equal to the government deficit so the current-account balance remains unchanged at B.

The conclusion from the above discussion is that the current-account balance is not affected by the government deficit per se but instead by the level of government spending whether tax or deficit financed. This is because the perfect-foresight assumption implies an "Ricardian equivalence" between present and future taxation. Of course, in reality savers may not respond so rationally to government deficit finance.

Consider next the case where the government reduces taxes in the first period with savers anticipating that spending in both periods and taxes in the second are to be held constant. Such anticipations are irrational in the two-period model because they violate the government's budget constraint.[28] Nevertheless, under such incorrect expectations, households believe that the locus of consumption opportunities has shifted to $Z'Z'$ and increase their first-period spending accordingly. This causes the current-account deficit to rise. Of course next period's planned private consumption level C_2' cannot be realized (assuming no repudiation of foreign debt).

In summary, increases in the government deficit will raise current-account deficit in two cases. First, the increase of the deficit results from greater current-period public spending. Second, households do not fully foresee the future tax consequences of a current-period tax reduction.

6. Conclusions

It is apparent that a coherent theory of balance-of-payments adjustment and exchange-rate determination can be built on a foundation of output and expenditure determination with an extremely parsimonious specification of goods and factor markets. The benchmark monetary model is such a case. But such a theory would exclude the sectoral consequences of balance-of-payments adjustment and exchange-rate changes that are evident in the experience of most economies. It can be argued that external adjustment issues are of interest and concern precisely because relative prices as well as price levels are affected, at least in the short run. Of course, many shocks affect relative prices only in the short run, but the short run is not so short as to preclude these effects from showing up in the data that macro models attempt to explain.

While the early elasticities theories were incomplete because of their glaring omission of aggregate output and expenditure determination, they did focus attention on the relative-price effects of external adjustments that can play an important short-run role. The fact that they were not above reproach on macroeconomic grounds had the unfortunate consequence that they were made a "straw man" by the proponents of the so-called monetary approach, and the presence of relative-price effects in the adjustment process was ignored or even attacked.

We have seen in this chapter how special cases of the elasticities approach correspond to particular commodity-market and factor-market structures. The specialized product version focuses on the terms of trade and substitution between domestic and foreign products in demand. The non-traded goods model focuses on the "internal" terms of trade and the substitution between traded, and

---

[28] In a model with an infinite number of periods, such policies can be undertaken on a once-and-for-all basis without violating the government's budget constraint; it can borrow against the indefinite future.

non-traded goods in demand and supply. The Marshall–Lerner cum Mundell–Fleming analysis develops the specialized production model in the context of Keynesian unemployment; the model has also been generalized to cover other labor-market specifications. In all such models sectoral structure determines impact coefficients and speeds of adjustment. It also permits one to distinguish between the effects of real and nominal disturbances on long-run equilibria. Without such distinctions many issues, for example the validity of the purchasing-power-parity doctrine, would flounder in a sea of empirical contradictions.

Another issue raised by sectoral specification is the role of aggregate demand in the determination of output in a small open economy. Such an economy producing a single world good faces demand that is infinitely elastic at the prevailing world price so output must be "supply determined" in a meaningful sense. Keynesian-type notions that firms produce according to what they think they can sell, rather than what is profit maximizing, cannot be incorporated. Such demand-side factors can be analyzed by introducing a "sheltered good" in the form of a specialized domestic good, traded or non-traded. This specification permits a meaningful examination of the role of fiscal policy in a small open economy. It is this specification, rather than the asset-market specification that has received so much attention, that is the heart of the differences between the Mundell–Fleming and the monetarist approaches.

Until recently factor-market specification has been neglected in open-economy macro modeling. A richer specification of labor and capital markets shows that many of the conclusions of the simpler models which are driven only by aggregate demand *or* by aggregate supply are not robust. A major shortcoming has been the frequent practice of ignoring the effects of stocks of capital and financial assets on savings and investment decisions. Such effects are found to be rather important in determining the meaning and implications of external "imbalances". Such imbalances may no more reflect disequilibrium adjustment than does the observation that households may save or borrow in any given period.

Fruitful areas of future research will likely include more sophisticated analyses of price flexibility and inflexibility in goods and factor markets. More complete models of intemporal trading that integrate both savings–investment decisions and portfolio-balance considerations may cast further light on the equilibrium properties of external surplus and deficits. It does seem safe to conclude, in view of the developments reviewed in this chapter, that the fashion of a decade ago of ignoring sectoral structure when dealing with external adjustment has outlived its usefulness.

References

Barro, R. and H.I. Grossman (1971), "A general disequilibrium model of income and employment", American Economic Review, 61:82–93.

Buiter, W. (1981), "Time preference and international lending in an overlapping generations model", Journal of Political Economy, 89:769–797.

Buiter, W. and D. Purvis (1982), "Oil, disinflation and export competitiveness", in: J. Bhandari, ed., Economic interdependence under flexible exchange rates (M.I.T. Press, Cambridge, Mass.).

Casas, F. (1975), "Efficient macroeconomic stabilization policies under floating exchange rates", International Economic Review.

Dixit, A. (1978), "The balance of trade in a model of temporary equilibrium with rationing", Review of Economic Studies, 45:393–404.

Djajic, S. (1981), "Intermediate inputs and international trade: An analysis of the real and monetary aspects of an oil price shock", Queen's University Discussion Paper No. 394.

Dornbusch, R. (1973a), "Currency depreciation, hoarding, and relative prices", Journal of Political Economy, 81:893–915.

Dornbusch, R. (1973b), "Money, devaluation, and non-traded goods", American Economic Review, 63:871–880.

Dornbusch, R. (1975), "Exchange rates and fiscal policy in a popular model of international trade", American Economic Review, 65:859–871.

Dornbusch, R. (1976), "Expectations and exchange rate dynamics", Journal of Political Economy, 81:1161–1175.

Dornbusch, R. (1982), "Intergenerational and international trade", ms.

Findlay, R. and C. Rodriguez (1977), "Intermediate imports and macroeconomic policy under flexible exchange rates", Canadian Journal of Economics, 10:208–217.

Fleming, J.M. (1962), "Domestic financial policies under fixed and under floating exchange rates", International Monetary Staff Papers, 9:369–379.

Frenkel, J.A. (1971), "A theory of money, trade, and the balance of payments in a model of accumulation", Journal of International Economics, 1:159–187.

Frenkel, J.A. (1976), "A monetary approach to the exchange rate: Doctrinal aspects and empirical evidence", Scandinavian Journal of Economics, 78:200–224.

Frenkel, J.A. and S. Fischer (1972), "Investment, the two-sector model, and trade in debt and capital goods", Journal of International Economics, 2:211–233.

Frenkel, J.A. and H.G. Johnson, eds., (1976), The monetary approach to the balance of payments (Allen and Unwin, London).

Frenkel, J. and C. Rodriguez (1975), "Portfolio equilibrium and the balance of payments: A monetary approach", American Economic Review, 65:674–688.

Fried, J. (1980), "The intergenerational distribution of the gains from technical change and from international trade", Canadian Journal of Economics, 13:65–81.

Harberger, A.C. (1950), "Currency depreciation, income, and the balance of trade", Journal of Political Economy, 58:47–60.

Hume, D. (1752), "On the balance of trade". Reprinted as Chapter 1 in Richard N. Cooper, ed., International Finance Selected Readings (Penguin Books, Harmondsworth, England, 1969).

Johnson, H. (1956), "Towards a general theory of the balance of payments", in: International trade and economic growth (George Allen & Unwin, London).

Jones, R.W. and D.D. Purvis (1982), "International differences in response to common external shocks: The role of purchasing power parity", presented to Vth Paris–Dauphine conference on money and international monetary problems.

Laursen, S. and L.A. Metzler (1950), "Flexible exchange rates and the theory of employment", Review of Economics and Statistics, 32:251–299.

Leiderman, L. (1979), "Output supply in the open economy: Some international evidence", Discussion Paper #38, Boston University.

Malinvaud, E. (1977), "The theory of unemployment reconsidered" (Blackwell, Oxford).

Marston, R. (1982), "Wages, relative prices, and the choice between fixed and flexible exchange rates", Canadian Journal of Economics, 15:87–103.

McKinnon, R. (1979), Money in International Exchange, Oxford University Press.

Mundell, R.A. (1962), "The appropriate use of monetary and fiscal policy under fixed exchange rates", International Monetary Fund Staff Papers, 9:70–79. Reprinted as Ch. 18 in Mundell (1968).

Mundell, R.A. (1963), "Capital mobility and stabilization policy under fixed and flexible exchange rates", Canadian Journal of Economics and Political Science, 29:475–485. Reprinted as Ch. 18 in Mundell (1968).

Mundell, R.A. (1968), International Economics (Macmillan, New York).

Neary, P. (1980), "Non-traded goods and the balance of trade in a neo-Keynesian temporary equilibrium", Quarterly Journal of Economics, 95:403–429.

Neary, J.P. and D.D. Purvis (1981), "Real adjustment and exchange rate dynamics", in: J.A. Frenkel, ed., International Macroeconomics and Exchange Rates. University of Chicago Press, forthcoming.

Obstfeld, M. (1981), "Macroeconomic policy, exchange rate dynamics, and optimal asset accumulation", Journal of Political Economy, 89:1142–1161.

Obstfeld, M. (1982), "Aggregate spending and the terms of trade: Is there a Laursen–Meltzer effect"? Quarterly Journal of Economics, 97:251–270.

Prachowny, M.F.J. (1982), "Macroeconomic analysis for small open economies", Queen's University, Discussion Paper No. 445.

Purvis, D.D. (1976), "Wages, the terms of trade, and the exchange rate regime", Cowles Foundation Discussion Paper No. 438, Yale University.

Purvis, D.D. (1979), "Wage responsiveness and the insulation properties of a flexible exchange rate", in: Assar Lindbeck, ed., Inflation and Employment in Open Economies (North-Holland, Amsterdam).

Purvis, D.D. (1982), "Exchange rates: Real and monetary factors", Economic and Social Review, 13:303–314.

Rodriguez, C. (1979), "Short and long run effects of monetary and fiscal policy under flexible exchange rates and perfect capital mobility", American Economic Review, 69:176–182.

Sachs, J. (1980), "Wages, flexible exchange rates, and macroeconomic policy", Quarterly Journal of Economics, 94:731–747.

Sachs, J. (1981a), "The current account and macroeconomic adjustment in the 1970s", Brookings Papers on Economic Activity, 201–282.

Sachs, J. (1981b), "The current account in the macroeconomic adjustment process", Institute for International Economic Studies Discussion Paper 187, University of Stockholm.

Salop, J. (1974), "Devaluation and the balance of trade under flexible wages", in: G. Horwich and P.A. Samuelson, eds., Trade, Stability and Macroeconomics: Essays in Honour of Lloyd A. Metzler (Academic Press, New York).

Samuelson, P.A. (1964), "Theoretical notes on trade problems", Review of Economics and Statistics, 46:145–154.

Samuelson, P.Q. (1971), "An exact Hume–Ricardo–Marshall model of international trade", Journal of International Economics, 1:1–18.

Sanyal, K. and R.W. Jones (1982), "The theory of trade in middle products", American Economic Review, 72:16–31.

Stiglitz, J. (1970), "Factor price equalization in a dynamic economy", Journal of Political Economy, 78:456–488.

Stockman, Allan (1982), "Real disturbances and equilibrium models of exchange rates: An empirical investigation", ms.

Svennson, L. and A. Razin (1983), "The terms of trade, spending, and the current account: The Harberger–Laursen–Metzler effect", Journal of Political Economy, 91:97–125.

Uzawa, H. (1969), "Time preference and the Penrose effect in a two-class model of economic growth", Journal of Political Economy, 77:628–652.

Chapter 17

STABILIZATION POLICIES IN OPEN ECONOMIES

RICHARD C. MARSTON*

University of Pennsylvania and National Bureau of Economic Research

Contents

*The author would like to thank Joshua Aizenman, Richard Herring, Howard Kaufold, Stephen Turnovsky, Charles Wyplosz and the two discussants of the paper, Richard Cooper and Mohsin Khan, and other participants at a Princeton University Conference in May 1982 for their helpful comments on an earlier draft. Jean-Francois Dreyfus provided excellent research assistance. Financial support was provided by a German Marshall Fund Fellowship and a grant from the National Science Foundation (SES-8006414)

Handbook of International Economics, vol. II, edited by R.W. Jones and P.B. Kenen
© *Elsevier Science Publishers B.V., 1985*

1. Introduction

The modern open economy is not the one found in most macroeconomic textbooks, an economy that occasionally imports Bordeaux wine but which produces most of what it consumes at prices determined domestically. It is rather an economy integrated with those abroad through commodity and financial linkages which limit the scope for national stabilization policy. How that happens is the subject of this chapter.

Many of our ideas about stabilization policy can be traced to what McKinnon (1981) calls the "insular economy" which we discuss in Section 2. In such an economy, which was the paradigm most common in the 1950s and earlier, international capital mobility is low or non-existent, money supplies are controlled by the national authorities and price linkages across countries are limited. (Chapter 13 of this Handbook describes this economy in detail.) The literature on stabilization since the 1950s has modified this paradigm in several essential ways. The final product might not be recognized by its original craftsmen.

It is useful to classify these progressive modifications into three categories.

(1) *Capital mobility*. Mundell (1963) and Fleming (1962) showed the importance of international financial linkages in determining the effects of stabilization policy. Their work will be the focus of Section 3, but the propositions associated with Mundell and Fleming will be re-examined in the light of recent portfolio balance theories of the asset markets.

(2) *Wage and price flexibility*. Many recent studies, including those associated with the monetary approach to the balance of payments and with the new classical economics, have replaced the rigid wage assumption of Mundell and Fleming with various forms of wage flexibility. In Section 4 we introduce wage flexibility into the Mundell–Fleming model and show how much difference this makes in determining the effectiveness of government policy. When wages are flexible, wealth effects become of primary importance with the accumulation of wealth moving the economy from short-run equilibrium to a long-run steady state. We illustrate this wealth accumulation process using Dornbusch's (1973) version of the monetary approach to devaluation.

(3) *Rational expectations and the natural rate hypothesis*. No study of stabilization policy is complete without the "new classical macroeconomics". This literature combines the long-run wage and price flexibility of the classical model with an explicit treatment of expectations that includes assumptions about the availability of information which are crucial in determining the effectiveness of stabilization policy. In Section 5 we re-examine standard propositions about policy using rational expectations and a stochastic supply function; in Section 6 we use

the same model to re-examine the choice between exchange rate regimes and the insulating properties of flexible rates.

Throughout the chapter, one general model is used to interpret developments in the literature, with the model being progressively modified to include international financial linkages, wage flexibility and stochastic features. It focuses on a single national economy, although a foreign economy is added later in the chapter. This economy is assumed to produce its own (composite) good and to issue its own interest-bearing bond. In limiting cases commodity arbitrage pegs the price of the good at purchasing power parity and financial arbitrage pegs the interest rate at (uncovered) interest parity. The chapter will show how stabilization policy is affected by each of these linkages.

A chapter which treats such a broad range of issues must draw the line somewhere. We do not attempt to discuss the literature on non-traded goods or bonds. Nor do we discuss in detail the dynamic responses to policy changes that have been a dominant feature of some recent models. (Chapters 15 and 18 of this Handbook analyze this literature.) Even so, our general model will be required to span a wide range of recent developments. A single unifying framework will serve to place these developments in a clear perspective.

2. Stabilization policy in the insular economy

The balance of payments and exchange rate play very different roles in stabilization policy depending upon whether or not there is capital mobility. We begin the analysis of stabilization policy using a model without any capital account. This is the model of Harberger (1950), Tinbergen (1952), Tsiang (1961), and above all Meade (1951), which dominated the literature on international monetary economics until the 1960s.

The model varies from one study to another, but a number of characteristics are typical of most of the studies. First, the model is "Keynesian" in that nominal wages are fixed, at least over the time horizon relevant for policy. Second, the money supply is regarded as a policy instrument under the complete control of the authorities. (Alternatively, the interest rate may be controlled by the authorities.) All balance of payments flows are sterilized by open market sales or purchases of securities or by other policy actions. Third, the financial sector is simplified considerably by the immobility of capital. Usually, portfolios contain only one asset other than money, and the market for that asset is treated only implicitly. Finally, expectations are ignored.

We introduce below a model of a small country that illustrates all of these characteristics. The country is small in that it does not significantly affect foreign variables such as the price of foreign output.[1] Next we summarize some of the main conclusions about stabilization policy that can be derived from this model. Some of these conclusions are very sensitive to the precise specification of the model, so we conclude the section by discussing modifications of the model.

2.1. A model of trade and output

Since this model is a standard one in most respects, the description will be brief. The model consists of six equations:[2]

$$Y = Z + G_0 + B, \tag{2.1}$$

$$Z = Z'(Y, r, A/P), \qquad 0 < Z_Y' < 1, \quad Z_r' < 0, \quad Z_A' > 0, \tag{2.2}$$

$$B = B(Z, Z^f, P/P^fX), \qquad -1 < B_Z < 0, \quad B_f > 0, \quad B_P < 0, \tag{2.3}$$

$$Y = Q(P/\overline{W}), \qquad Q_P > 0, \tag{2.4}$$

$$M/P = m'(Y, r, A/P), \qquad m_Y' > 0, \quad m_r' < 0, \quad 0 \le (Am_A'/M) \le 1, \tag{2.5}$$

$$X\dot{F}^m = B. \tag{2.6}$$

Eq. (2.1) describes the demand for output in the home country; it must equal expenditure by domestic residents (Z), and the government (G_0) plus the trade balance (B), all measured in units of domestic output. Expenditure by residents (2.2) is a function of income (Y), the interest rate (r), and the real wealth of domestic residents; real wealth is the sum (A) of money and domestic bonds deflated by the domestic price (P).[3] The trade balance (2.3) is a function of domestic expenditure, foreign expenditure (Z^f), and the terms of trade, defined as P/P^fX, where P and P^f are the prices of domestic and foreign goods, respectively, and X is the domestic currency price of foreign currency. The trade balance is assumed to be negatively related to the terms of trade $(B_P < 0)$, which is the case if the Marshall–Lerner condition is satisfied.[4]

[1] The term "small country" often refers to a country producing the same good as other countries, but the country in this model is assumed to produce its own good except in the limiting case where domestic and foreign goods are perfect substitutes.

[2] The prime notation, Z' and m', is used to distinguish these functions from the corresponding ones in the next section. Restrictions on the partial derivatives are given directly following the function. The notation used for derivatives is straightforward; Z_Y', Z_r', Z_A' refer to the partial derivatives with respect to the three arguments of the function. To simplify the expressions, the derivatives are calculated at a stationary equilibrium where all prices (and the exchange rate) are equal to one.

[3] We assume that all bonds are issued by the government. We discuss below the issue of whether bonds can be included in wealth.

[4] That condition states that with initially balanced trade, a fall in the terms of trade improves the trade balance if the sum of the import and export demand elasticities exceeds unity. Note that the trade and current account balances are identical in this model since we ignore transfer payments and services.

The aggregate supply curve (2.4) describes the response of output (income) to an increase in the price of the domestic good, holding constant the nominal wage (W). Some models of this type fix the price of the good itself, but not much is gained by this further simplification of the model. The demand function for money (2.5) has a standard form familiar from models of the closed economy. The restriction on the wealth elasticity includes two limiting cases; the demand for money can be independent of wealth, as in the quantity theory, or can be homogeneous of degree one in wealth, as in some asset models. Eq. (2.6) is a balance of payments equation describing the accumulation of foreign exchange reserves (F^m).

The four equations jointly determine four variables: the domestic price, output, interest rate and either foreign exchange reserves or the exchange rate, depending upon the exchange rate regime. We begin by describing the flexible exchange rate regime.

2.2. Flexible exchange rates

With capital immobile, the exchange rate is determined entirely by flow conditions, as indicated by the balance of payments eq. (2.6). Since the balance of payments consists of the trade account only, the exchange rate must adjust to keep the trade balance at zero:

$$B(Z, Z^f, P/P^f X) = 0. \tag{2.3'}$$

This leads to very strong conclusions about domestic policy. Domestic output is determined as it would be in a closed economy:

$$Y = Z + G_0. \tag{2.1'}$$

The three equations determining domestic variables, (2.1'), (2.4), and (2.5), are now independent of the exchange rate and the parameters of the trade balance function, so monetary and fiscal policies have effects similar to those in a closed economy.

Without describing the full solution of the model, we can illustrate the effects of stabilization policy by calculating the multiplier for government spending. As is usually the case, it is obtained by assuming that the domestic price is constant (here we assume that Q_P is infinite) and that the domestic interest rate is pegged by monetary policy. Therefore,

$$\frac{dY}{dG_0} = \frac{1}{1 - Z'_Y} > 0. \tag{2.7}$$

The multiplier is identical to that of a closed economy; in particular, it is independent of the parameters of the trade balance.

A second striking conclusion is closely related to the first: domestic output and other domestic variables are independent of all foreign disturbances. The exchange rate completely insulates the economy from changes in foreign prices and foreign expenditure, the two foreign variables affecting the trade balance, so no foreign disturbance can affect the economy. This strong conclusion about insulation has often been used as an argument for flexible rates, even though it is very sensitive to assumptions about capital mobility.

2.3. Fixed exchange rates

With fixed exchange rates, the trade balance directly affects output in eq. (2.1), so the effects of domestic policy are modified by interaction with the foreign sector. Both monetary and fiscal policies are generally *less* effective in changing domestic output than under flexible rates, because of the leakage of expenditure onto imports. The multiplier for government spending, for example, is

$$\frac{dY}{dG_0} = \frac{1}{1 - Z'_Y(1 + B_Z)},$$

(2.8)

which is smaller than before, since $-1 < B_Z < 0$. A rise in government spending leads to a leakage of private expenditure onto imports, whereas there is no net effect on the trade balance under flexible rates.[5]

Foreign disturbances now affect the economy through the trade balance. An expansion abroad that raises foreign output, the foreign price, or both leads to an expansion of domestic output. The domestic economy becomes sensitive to foreign developments, including policies pursued by foreign governments.

Another much discussed result emerges from this same model. Under fixed exchange rates, there is a *conflict* between internal and external balance when a country is in one of two situations: with a balance of payments deficit and unemployment or a balance of payments surplus and full employment.[6] In either case, fiscal and monetary policies have undesirable effects on *either* internal or external balance. If there is a balance of payments deficit and unemployment, for example, an expansionary policy can eliminate unemployment, but it also leads to a deterioration of the trade balance. What is required in this situation, according

---

[5]In the general model where interest rates are variable, a rise in government spending could raise output more under fixed rates than under flexible rates if expenditure were sufficiently sensitive to the interest rate; a rise in the interest rate could reduce (crowd out) expenditure and thus reduce imports. The trade balance would improve under fixed rates, so the domestic currency would appreciate under flexible rates. This result is precluded in versions of the open economy model where the trade balance is expressed as a function of domestic output rather than expenditure.

[6]The second of these situations is usually described as a balance of payments surplus and "inflation", but models of this type are not well suited for describing inflationary situations.

to Johnson (1958), is an "expenditure switching" policy which is aimed at lowering the trade deficit at any given *level* of output. Corden (1960) examines various ways this policy could be carried out.

One such expenditure-switching policy is a devaluation. In this model, it unambiguously raises domestic output while improving the trade balance. In the simplest version, with fixed prices and a pegged interest rate, the multiplier for the change in the exchange rate is

$$\frac{dY}{dX} = \frac{-B_P}{1 - Z_Y'(1 + B_Z)} > 0,$$ (2.9)

while the change in the trade balance is

$$\frac{dB}{dX} = \frac{-B_P(1 - Z_Y')}{1 - Z_Y'(1 + B_Z)} > 0.$$ (2.10)

Using these expressions, we can interpret the two analytical approaches to devaluation often discussed in connection with models of this type, the elasticities and absorption approaches. [For the two approaches, see Robinson (1937) and Alexander (1952)]. According to the former, the trade balance improves following a devaluation if the Marshall–Lerner condition is satisfied, or $B_P < 0$. This condition is clearly based on a partial equilibrium analysis of the trade sector alone. The absorption approach is more concerned with the macroeconomic response to a devaluation; the trade balance is said to improve following a devaluation if output rises more than expenditure. That is the case in (2.10) provided the marginal propensity to spend is less than one. We discuss a more recent approach to devaluation, the monetary approach, in detail below.

2.4. Modifications of the model

Many results obtained above depend upon characteristics of the model which are more appropriate for a closed economy. Real domestic income, for example, is defined to be equivalent to real domestic output. But in an open economy real income is more appropriately defined as PY/I, where I is a general price index including foreign as well as domestic prices:

$$I = P^a(P^f X)^{1-a}.$$ (2.11)

Real expenditure should similarly be redefined as PZ/I and expressed as a function of real income. This respecification of the expenditure function leads to what is known as the Laursen–Metzler effect of a change in the terms of trade.[7] A fall in the terms of trade, which reduces P/I, leads to a fall in domestic

---

[7]See Laursen and Metzler (1950). Dornbusch (1980, pp.78–81) has a clear explanation of this effect.

expenditure measured in terms of the general price index but a rise in domestic expenditure measured in terms of the domestic good itself.

Other changes in specification might be made for similar reasons. All assets and wealth might be deflated by the general price index. Thus real money balances might be defined as M/I and treated as a function of real wealth, A/I, as well as real income. To the extent that expectations are explicitly modelled, the interest rate in the aggregate demand function might be specified in real terms as the nominal rate less the expected inflation rate of the general price index (the latter denoted by π_I). Finally, aggregate supply might be made a function of the price index, if wages vary at all. The first three of these changes will be adopted in the model introduced in the next section; wages will be made a function of the price index in a later section.

How much difference do all of these changes make? The answer certainly depends upon the actual magnitude of each effect. But notice that one dramatic result is overturned in the model used above once the general price level (and hence the exchange rate) is able to influence expenditure directly. Flexible rates no longer insulate the domestic economy from foreign disturbances. Indeed there are several channels through which the general price level, and therefore the exchange rate itself, can affect domestic variables.

3. Capital mobility and the Mundell–Fleming propositions

Few studies in international economics have had as much impact on the direction of research as those of Mundell (1963) and Fleming (1962). These studies showed how important capital mobility is to the conduct of stabilization policy, thus overturning many earlier propositions about policy, while redirecting attention towards the capital account and financial phenomena in general.

The two studies differed in their assumptions about the degree of capital mobility, Mundell assuming that there was perfect capital mobility between domestic and foreign countries. Their propositions about stabilization policy differed accordingly. Mundell's propositions were particularly dramatic. In a small open economy:

(1) monetary policy is ineffective in changing output under fixed exchange rates because capital flows offset a monetary expansion or contraction; and

(2) fiscal policy is ineffective in changing output under flexible rates because the exchange rate induces adjustments in the trade account which run counter to the fiscal policy.

In Fleming's model, where capital mobility was imperfect, each policy retained some effectiveness under both exchange rate regimes. His conclusions concerned the relative effectiveness of the two policies:

(1) monetary policy is more effective in changing output under flexible rates than under fixed rates; and

(2) fiscal policy is more effective in changing output under fixed exchange rates when capital is highly mobile, but this conclusion is reversed with low capital mobility.[8]

Both sets of propositions are modified in more general models, as we shall see below, but they have had a powerful influence on subsequent thinking about stabilization policy. Whitman (1970) has provided a concise summary of these and other studies in the same tradition.

We will review these propositions within the context of a model somewhat different from those used by Mundell and Fleming. We retain the fixed nominal wage assumption characteristic of Keynesian models but modify the expenditure function to incorporate terms of trade and wealth effects that may be particularly important when there is a flexible exchange rate. The most important change, however, is on the financial side. Fleming specified capital *flows* as a function of the *level* of the interest rate, but modern portfolio theory indicates that the *stock* of assets rather than the flow should be a function of the interest rate.[9] According to this latter view, capital flows occur as a result of more general portfolio adjustments encompassing money balances as well as domestic and foreign bond holdings. In place of the balance of payments flow (the time derivative of foreign exchange reserves), which was the center of attention in the Fleming model, we have an equation explaining the stock of foreign exchange reserves; it is one of the equations explaining asset market equilibrium.[10] Other differences between the model here and its antecedents are discussed below.

This section focuses on many of the issues that Mundell and Fleming emphasized and on which later authors expanded, including the offsetting effect of capital flows and the feasibility of sterilization. In addition, we compare the relative effectiveness of stabilization policies under fixed and flexible rates. The discussion draws on an excellent survey of these issues by Henderson (1977).

---

[8] Capital mobility is relatively low in his model if an increase in government spending leads to a trade deficit larger than the capital inflow induced by the corresponding increase in the interest rate. See Whitman (1970) for a full discussion.

[9] One implausible implication of the Fleming specification is that a rise in the domestic interest rate causes a continuing inflow of capital, whether portfolios are growing or not. Branson (1968) and Willett and Forte (1969) were among the first to formulate the portfolio balance approach to the capital account. In Mundell's (1963) model, with perfectly mobile capital, this question of specification does not arise.

[10] As is the case with most portfolio balance models, the model is specified in continuous time. It can be specified in discrete time, as in Henderson (1981) and Tobin and de Macedo (1980), and a balance of payments equation can be derived from the rest of the model, but such a model bears little resemblance to the earlier capital flow specification of Fleming and others.

3.1. A model with internationally mobile capital

The model introduced in this section will be used to describe stabilization policy in both this section and the next (where we consider a classical model with flexible wages). The model is complicated because it includes price and wealth effects and because domestic and foreign securities are treated as imperfect substitutes. Behavior in the model, however, can be summarized in a simple diagram which will be used to illustrate the effects of different stabilization policies.

We begin with the market for the domestic good:

$$Y = Z + G_0 + B, \tag{3.1}$$

$$\frac{PZ}{I} = Z\left[\frac{P(Y-T)}{I}, r - \pi_I, r^f + \pi_X - \pi_I, \frac{A}{I} \right], \tag{3.2}$$

$$0 < Z_Y < 1, \quad Z_r < 0, \quad Z_f < 0, \quad Z_A > 0,$$

$$B = B(Z, Z^f, P/(P^f X)), \qquad -1 < B_Z < 0, \quad B_f > 0, \quad B_P < 0, \tag{3.3}$$

$$Y = Q(P/\overline{W}), \qquad Q_P > 0. \tag{3.4}$$

The model is identical to the earlier one except for the expenditure equation (3.2), where expenditure and disposable income are deflated by the general price index, thus incorporating the Laursen–Metzler effect of a change in the terms of trade. Disposable income is defined as income less taxes, the latter being exogenous to the model.[11] Expenditure is also a function of real wealth, where wealth is now defined as the sum of money, domestic bonds and foreign bonds held by the domestic private sector: $A = M + H^d + XF^d$. Finally, expenditure is expressed as a function of the domestic and foreign *real* interest rates. The nominal return on the foreign bond is defined as the nominal foreign interest rate plus the expected appreciation of the foreign currency, π_X; both interest rates are then expressed in real terms by subtracting the expected rate of inflation of the general price index, π_I:

$$\pi_I = a\pi_p + (1-a)\pi_X,$$

$$\pi_p = e_P(\overline{P}/P - 1), \qquad 0 \le e_P \le 1,$$

$$\pi_X = e_X(\overline{X}/X - 1), \qquad 0 \le e_X \le 1.$$

For this part of the analysis, expectations are modeled in two alternative ways found frequently in the literature: *regressive* expectations (with e_P and e_X being

---

[11]Interest receipts and payments are ignored in the model. Alternatively, they could be explicitly introduced into the expressions for disposable income and the current account but neutralized by taxes and transfers. Allen and Kenen (1980, pp. 40–42) describe how this can be done.

positive constants less than or equal to one) where a rise in the current price or exchange rate leads to an expected fall in that variable towards some stationary value ($\bar{P}$, $\bar{X}$) and *static* expectations (with e_P and e_X being equal to zero) where the expected level of the price or exchange rate rises with the current level so that no further change is expected. We postpone until a later section a discussion of rational expectations.

The equations for the goods market contain four endogenous variables of interest to the analysis: Y, P, r, and either X or XF^m (the level of foreign exchange reserves). According to eq. (3.4), however, changes in P are always related to changes in Y as follows, $dP = dY/Q_P$, so that we can eliminate price from all expressions in the model and thus concentrate on only three variables.

The curve labelled GG in Figure 3.1 describes combinations of Y and r that give equilibrium in the goods market. The slope of this curve reflects the direct effects of output and the interest rate on expenditure (as well as the indirect effect of the domestic price). To obtain an expression for this slope, we first take the total differentials of eqs. (3.1)–(3.4) and combine them in the compact form shown in the first row of the matrix in Table 3.1. The matrix itself describes equilibrium under either flexible rates ($X dF^m = 0$) or fixed rates ($dX = 0$). The expression $G_Y + G_P/Q_P$ reflects the direct and indirect effects of higher output on the goods market, while G_r reflects the direct effect of a higher interest rate. Since increases in Y or r both raise the excess supply of the domestic good (i.e. $G_Y + G_P/Q_P$ and G_r are positive), the goods market curve GG must have a negative slope.

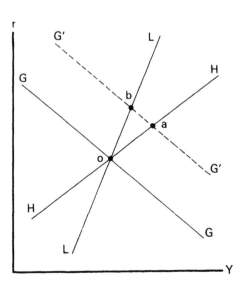

Figure 3.1. Increase in government spending.

Table 3.1
Modified Mundell–Fleming model

$$\begin{bmatrix} (G_Y + G_P/Q_P) & G_X & 0 & G_r \\ (L_Y + L_P/Q_P) & L_X & -(1+s) & L_r \\ (H_Y + H_P/Q_P) & H_X & s & H_r \end{bmatrix} \begin{bmatrix} dY \\ dX \\ XdF^m \\ dr \end{bmatrix} = \begin{bmatrix} dG_0 \\ dH_0^m \\ -dH_0^m \end{bmatrix}$$

$$G_Y = \left[1 - (1 + B_Z)Z_Y\right] > 0$$

$$G_P = (1 + B_Z)\left[\lambda - ae_P(Z_r + Z_f) + aZ_A A\right] - B_P > 0$$

$$\lambda = (1 - a)\left[Z - Z_Y(Y - T)\right] > 0$$

$$G_X = -(1 + B_Z)\left[\lambda + e_X\left(Z_r(1 - a) - Z_f(a)\right) + Z_A\left(F^d - A(1 - a)\right)\right] + B_P < 0$$

$$G_r = -(1 + B_Z)Z_r > 0$$

$$L_Y = m_Y > 0$$

$$L_r = m_r < 0$$

$$L_P = \left[m_Y Y(1 - a) + a(m(\cdot) - m_A A)\right] > 0$$

$$L_X = \left[(1 - a)(m(\cdot) - m_Y Y) - m_f e_X + m_A\left(F^d - A(1 - a)\right)\right] > 0$$

$$H_Y = h_Y < 0$$

$$H_r = h_r + h_r^f > 0$$

$$H_P = \left[h_Y Y(1 - a) + a(h(\cdot) - h_A A)\right] < 0$$

$$H_X = \left[(1 - a)(h(\cdot) - h_Y Y) + h^f(\cdot) + \left(h_r^f - h_f\right)e_X + h_A\left(F^d - A(1 - a)\right)\right] > 0$$

The definitions and signs of G_Y and all other coefficients are given in the table. (To simplify these expressions, we have assumed that all prices, including the exchange rate, are initially equal to one.) All of the signs follow directly from the earlier assumptions, with two exceptions: for λ to be positive, the elasticity of expenditure with respect to disposable income must be less than one. This condition ensures that the Laursen–Metzler effect obtains; a fall in the terms of trade raises expenditure measured in terms of the domestic good. The other exception concerns the sign of G_X. This model allows the exchange rate to affect the goods market through three channels: (a) relative price effects that work directly on the trade balance and through the Laursen–Metzler effect on expenditure; (b) exchange rate and inflationary expectations that drive the two real interest rates in different directions; and (c) the effect of the exchange rate on real wealth (which can either rise or fall in response to a rise in the exchange rate).[12] For G_X to be negative, the relative price effect must outweigh the latter two effects (if either or both are negative).[13] When G_X is negative, a rise in the exchange rate

[12]A rise in the exchange rate has two effects on real wealth: it raises the nominal value of wealth by $F^d dX$ (when F^d is positive), but it lowers the real value of any given amount of nominal wealth by $A dI = A(1 - a)dX$, since it raises the cost of imported goods in the price index.

[13]Under plausible conditions, these latter effects could both be equal to zero. The net effect of a change in the expected exchange rate is equal to zero when the partial derivatives of expenditure with respect to the two real interest rates are proportional to the shares of domestic and foreign goods in the consumption basket, $Z_r/Z_f = a/(1 - a)$. The wealth effect of an exchange rate change is equal to zero when the ratio of foreign assets to wealth is the same as the proportion of foreign goods in the consumption basket, $F^d/A = (1 - a)$. Such a diversification rule is given in Dornbusch (1982). But G_X could be negative under much weaker conditions.

(a devaluation or a depreciation of the domestic currency) shifts the GG schedule to the right.

The behavior of the financial markets is of central interest to the following discussion. The asset model described below is an open economy version of the Tobin–Brainard model as developed by Black (1973), Boyer (1975), Branson (1974), Girton and Henderson (1976, 1977) among others. Three assets are assumed to be available to domestic investors; money (M), domestic bonds (H^d) and foreign bonds (F^d), the latter available at an exogenous interest rate. There is no banking system in the model, so M also represents the monetary base. Foreign investors may hold domestic bonds but do not hold domestic money. The domestic demands for the two domestic assets are described by eqs. (3.5) and (3.7), the domestic demand for the foreign bond by (3.9), and the foreign demand for the domestic bond by (3.8):

$$M = m\left[\frac{PY}{I}, r, r^f + \pi_X, \frac{A}{I}\right]I = H^m + XF^m, \tag{3.5}$$

$$0 < Ym_Y/M \le 1, \quad m_r < 0, \quad m_f < 0, \quad 0 \le Am_A/M \le 1,$$

$$H^d + H^f = H_0 - H^m, \tag{3.6}$$

$$H^d = h\left[\frac{PY}{I}, r, r^f + \pi_X, \frac{A}{I}\right]I,$$

$$h_Y < 0, \quad h_r > 0, \quad h_f < 0, \quad 1 \le Ah_A/H^d, \tag{3.7}$$

$$H^f/X = h^f\left[Y^f, r - \pi_X, r^f, A^f/P^f\right]P^f,$$

$$h_Y^f < 0, \quad h_r^f > 0, \quad h_f^f < 0, \quad h_A^f > 0, \tag{3.8}$$

$$XF^d = f\left[\frac{PY}{I}, r, r^f + \pi_X, \frac{A}{I}\right]I,$$

$$f_Y < 0, \quad f_r < 0, \quad f_f > 0, \quad 1 \le Af_A/(XF^d). \tag{3.9}$$

The real demands for these assets are functions of real income, the expected returns on domestic and foreign bonds, and real wealth. The restrictions on the partial derivatives of the asset demands reflect the following assumptions: (a) all assets are assumed to be gross substitutes, i.e. a rise in the own (cross) return raises (lowers) the demand for that asset; (b) a rise in income raises the demand for money and lowers the demands for the other assets, but the income elasticity of money demand is assumed to be less than or equal to one; (c) a rise in wealth leads to an equal or more than proportionate rise in the demand for domestic and foreign bonds, and an equal or less than proportionate rise in the demand for money. These are all plausible assumptions that have been frequently adopted in the literature.[14]

The asset demands of domestic residents as well as the expenditure function introduced above are expressed as functions of real (domestic) wealth, where wealth includes bond holdings as well as money holdings. Barro (1974) has recently revived interest in the proposition that government bonds do not represent net wealth. The basic question at issue is whether individuals fully discount the future taxes implicit in any issue of government debt. Buiter and Tobin (1979) discuss the strong assumptions necessary for this proposition to hold, such as the absence of intergenerational distribution effects.[15] Here we adopt the conventional definition of financial wealth that ignores future taxes; this definition thus may overstate the magnitude of the real effects discussed below when there is at least partial capitalization of future taxes.[16]

Equations (3.5) and (3.6) equate the demands for money and domestic bonds, respectively, to their supplies. The supply of money is equal to the assets held by the central bank, which consist of domestic and foreign bonds. (We have omitted a balancing item which is needed to cancel capital gains earned by the monetary authority on changes in the foreign exchange rate.) The supply of domestic bonds consists of the total government issue less that held by the central bank. The supplies of these assets are related by sterilization policy. We consider below two possibilities, that the authorities sterilize all foreign exchange flows or do not sterilize any. In the former case, the domestic bonds held by the central bank become endogenous, so it is useful to describe the change in its domestic assets as the sum of two components:

$$dH^m = dH_0^m + sXdF^m. \tag{3.10}$$

The first term represents a discretionary change in domestic assets, independent of sterilization policy; the second term describes the endogenous response of domestic assets to a change in foreign exchange reserves. The parameter s is the sterilization coefficient, which is assumed to vary between zero and minus one. When no sterilization is carried out ($s = 0$), the supply of money is an endogenous variable under fixed exchange rates with the change in that supply given by $dH_0^m + XdF^m$. When full sterilization is practised ($s = -1$), the supply of bonds

---

[14]Gross substitutability is not a necessary consequence of expected utility maximization, although it is almost always assumed in asset market studies. Money demand is often assumed to be insensitive to wealth or to be homogeneous of degree one in wealth; these assumptions are limiting cases of the one adopted here.

[15]Voluntary intergenerational gifts can neutralize the real effects of involuntary redistribution by the government, but only under certain conditions. See Buiter and Tobin (1979).

[16]A related issue is whether exchange market intervention, which transfers ownership of foreign assets from the private sector to the government, can have any real effects. Obstfeld (1981) discusses the case where the private sector "sees through" these transactions; it capitalizes future transfers from the government financed by foreign interest payments (in effect regarding official foreign exchange holdings as its own).

available to the public becomes endogenous, with the change in that supply given by $-\mathrm{d} H_0^m + X \mathrm{d} F^m$.

In Figure 3.1, the curves labelled LL and HH describe combinations of Y and r that give equilibrium in the markets for money and domestic bonds.[17] The slopes of these curves can be obtained from the equilibrium conditions for the two asset markets summarized by the second and third rows of the matrix expression in Table 3.1. The signs of the asset coefficients follow from the earlier assumptions, with one exception. For L_X and H_X to be positive, the transactions and expectations effects must outweigh the wealth effect in cases where the latter is negative. (As discussed below, assumptions are frequently adopted which make $L_X = 0$.) The relative slopes of LL and HH depend upon the two assumptions adopted earlier regarding gross substitutability and wealth elasticities.[18]

One additional characteristic of the HH schedule is of special interest. It becomes infinitely elastic when domestic and foreign bonds are perfect substitutes. (HH becomes flat as $H_r = h_r + h_r^f$ goes to infinity.) This was the assumption adopted by Mundell (1963) as well as by many other authors since. We shall discuss its important implications below.

Before proceeding further, we should clarify the nature of the short-run equilibrium described in Table 3.1. All asset markets are assumed to be in continuous equilibrium in the sense that existing stocks of assets are willingly held. In this model, however, there is nothing to prevent asset stocks from changing continuously through time. In particular, a government deficit will generate a *flow supply* of government bonds: $\dot{H}_0 = P(G_0 - T)$, where $\dot{H}_0$ denotes the time derivative, $\mathrm{d} H_0 / \mathrm{d} t$. This flow supply is to be distinguished from a discrete change in the supply of bonds at one point in time associated, for example, with an open market operation, $\mathrm{d} H_0^m$. Similarly, a balance of payments surplus under fixed exchange rates will generate a flow supply of foreign exchange reserves: $X \dot{F}^m = PB + \dot{H}^f - X \dot{F}^d$. This flow supply is to be distinguished from the discrete change in foreign exchange reserves, $X \mathrm{d} F^m$, which occurs as a result of an instantaneous switch in portfolios or a single exchange market operation.

These flow supplies of assets, whether due to government deficits or payments imbalances, affect output and other variables in the model by altering gradually the *stock* of each asset, thereby moving the economy, in the words of Blinder and Solow (1973), from one instantaneous equilibrium to another.[19] Because the stocks of assets change through time, the cumulative effects of stabilization

---

[17]Stabilization policy has often been illustrated in a diagram with a balance of payments curve instead of a bond market curve. Most of the studies of the 1960s which specified capital flows as a function of the interest rate level used such a diagram. Henderson (1981) uses a balance of payments curve in a discrete time model based on asset demand functions like those presented here. The alternative diagram presented here was developed by Boyer (1978a) and Henderson (1979).

[18]The relative slopes of these curves can be established under weaker assumptions, as is evident from the expressions for $(H_Y + H_P/Q_P)$ and $(L_Y + L_P/Q_P)$.

policies vary with the time span over which policies are examined. (The longer the time span, however, the less tenable is the Keynesian assumption of fixed nominal wages.) To simplify the discussion below, we focus mostly on the *impact effects* of policies and thus ignore the effects of these flow supplies.[20] In Table 3.1, for example, only the impact effects of policies are shown. Readers interested in the longer run effects of the policies are referred to McKinnon and Oates (1966) and other studies.[21]

3.2. Stabilization policy under fixed exchange rates

Under fixed exchange rates, the equations of Table 3.1 determine domestic output and the interest rate on domestic bonds as well as foreign exchange reserves (XF^m). The system of equations, in fact, is recursive under two alternative assumptions regarding sterilization.

(1) With *no sterilization* ($s = 0$), the equations describing equilibrium in the goods and bond markets determine output and the interest rate, with the money market equation determining the (instantaneous) change in foreign exchange reserves. In terms of Figure 3.1, equilibrium is determined by the *GG* and *HH* schedules, with the *LL* schedule shifting in response to changes in foreign exchange reserves.

(2) With *full sterilization* ($s = -1$), the equations for the goods and money markets determine output and the interest rate, with the bond equation determining the change in foreign exchange reserves. Equilibrium is determined by the *GG* and *LL* schedules, with the *HH* schedule shifting in response to changes in foreign exchange reserves.

In this section we use this system of equations together with accompanying diagrams to interpret two types of stabilization policies: an increase in government spending and an open market expansion of the money supply. The role of sterilization will be discussed in connection with government spending where a geometric illustration of its effects is particularly simple.

The increase in government spending is assumed to fall exclusively on domestic goods. The spending is financed by the issue of government bonds rather than by

[19] Branson (1974) applied the closed economy analysis of Blinder and Solow to the case of an open economy under fixed exchange rates.

[20] With rational expectations or perfect foresight, however, future changes in stocks can affect endogenous variables immediately. Chapter 15 of this Handbook shows how, under perfect foresight, the eventual accumulation of wealth through the current account affects the current values of endogenous variables, including the exchange rate; Chapter 18 of this Handbook analyzes other dynamic models under perfect foresight. We discuss rational expectations in Section 5, but in models where the dynamics of asset accumulation are not essential to the analysis.

[21] McKinnon and Oates analyze a long-run (stationary state) equilibrium where wealth accumulation has ceased. Turnovsky (1976) examines the dynamics around such a stationary state equilibrium using flow equations such as those introduced above. See also Branson (1974) and Allen and Kenen (1980, especially Chs. 6 and 10).

taxes, with the government deficit generating a flow supply of bonds but no discrete change in the bond supply capable of affecting current variables. With no sterilization, an increase in spending leads to a rise in output and the interest rate. In Figure 3.1, point *a* is reached where the new $G'G'$ schedule intersects with a constant HH schedule. The effect of the policy on foreign exchange reserves is evident from the figure, since money market equilibrium requires a rightward shift (not shown) of the LL curve to point *a* and thus a rise in the money supply. The *magnitude* of the increase in foreign exchange reserves depends upon the degree of substitutability between domestic and foreign bonds, as reflected in the slope of HH. Since foreign exchange reserves increase under fixed exchange rates, we should expect the domestic currency to appreciate under flexible rates as discussed below.

Perfect substitution between domestic and foreign bonds (HH horizontal) leads to no qualitative differences in the effects of fiscal policy on output or foreign exchange reserves, although the interest rate would in that case remain constant. Perfect substitution between domestic and foreign goods, a limiting case where the *law of one price* holds, on the other hand, renders government spending *powerless* to affect output.[22] As the private sector is willing to exchange foreign for domestic goods at unchanged prices, government spending on domestic (or foreign) goods can have no effect on prices or output. (In this polar case, the GG schedule becomes a vertical line and shifts only in response to a change in the exchange rate or price of foreign output.)

Sterilization modifies the effects of fiscal policy, but output and the interest rate still increase. If there is complete sterilization, then the new equilibrium is found on an unchanged LL schedule at point *b*. The increase in the money supply associated with the influx of foreign exchange reserves is neutralized by the sale of bonds to the public. The bond supplies available to the public become endogenous, with HH shifting to the new equilibrium.

There is a serious problem with sterilization, however, when domestic and foreign bonds are highly substitutable. The more substitutable are the bonds, the greater is the change in foreign exchange reserves associated with the fiscal policy.[23] This can be seen by expressing the change in foreign exchange reserves given in Table 3.1 in terms of the changes in output and the interest rate:

$$X\mathrm{d}F^m = (H_Y + H_P/Q_P)\,\mathrm{d}Y + H_r\mathrm{d}r. \tag{3.11}$$

---

[22] For a description of the law of one price, see Katseli-Papaefstratiou (1979). She distinguishes between the law of one price, which is a commodity arbitrage relationship linking the prices of identical goods in different countries, and a more general form of purchasing power parity (*PPP*) reflecting a reduced form relationship between prices and exchange rates. For empirical evidence on *PPP*, see Isard (1977), Kravis and Lipsey (1978), and Frenkel (1981).

[23] In the case of an increase in government spending, foreign exchange reserves rise rather than fall, so the country is in no danger of running out of reserves as it might be in the case of a decline in government spending or an increase in the money supply. This is one aspect of a fundamental asymmetry between surplus and deficit countries under fixed exchange rates.

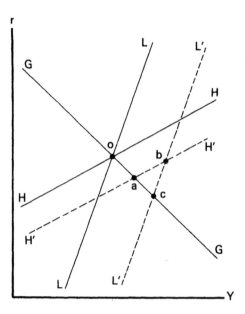

Figure 3.2. Open market operation.

Since the changes in Y and r (to point b in Figure 3.1) are the same whatever the degree of substitutability between bonds, the change in foreign exchange reserves must increase with higher substitutability (a larger H_r). In the limiting case of perfect substitution between assets, the problem of foreign exchange flows becomes overwhelming, as Mundell (1963) emphasized. In that case, sterilization implies an infinite gain of foreign exchange reserves.

During the 1950s, analyses of macroeconomic policy almost invariably assumed full sterilization of reserve flows, with monetary policy being characterized by a constant money supply or interest rate. In the early 1970s, the monetary approach to the balance of payments largely ignored sterilization or argued that sterilization was infeasible because of perfect substitution between assets. Since that time empirical evidence has accumulated showing that sterilization was indeed practised widely under the Bretton Woods system of fixed exchange rates.[24] But many of the same studies have also shown the empirical importance of the *offset* effect, a phenomenon which was central to the monetary approach to the balance of payments. It is to the offset effect that we now turn.

The subject of monetary policy under fixed rates has generated intense controversy, with many economists contending that monetary policy is powerless to

[24] For studies of sterilization in the 1960s, see Argy and Kouri (1974) and Herring and Marston (1977, ch. 5). Black (1982) and Obstfeld (1982) present evidence of sterilization in the more recent period of managed floating.

affect the domestic interest rate or output. That is because any expansionary open market operation by the central bank may be completely offset by a loss of foreign exchange reserves. (This offset controversy is distinct from the controversy associated with monetary policy under rational expectations to be discussed below.)

The monetary policy to be analyzed here is a simple open market purchase of domestic bonds by the central bank, which increases the supply of money and reduces the supply of bonds by dH_0^m. Figure 3.2 illustrates the effects of this operation: output rises while the domestic interest rate falls as *HH* shifts to the right to point *a*. Figure 3.2 also can be used to illustrate the offset to the monetary policy. In the *absence* of changes in foreign exchange reserves, the *LL* curve would shift to the right to $L'L'$ as a result of the open market purchase. This is the shift shown in the figure. With changes in reserves, however, the money supply is endogenous, and *LL* shifts back to point *a* in response to a loss in foreign exchange reserves. In Figure 3.2, the offset is negative, but it is smaller (in absolute value) than the open market purchase. Hence monetary policy still retains some effectiveness.

To determine under what conditions the offset is *complete*, we express the change in foreign exchange reserves as follows:[25]

$$\frac{X dF^m}{dH_0^m} = -1 - \frac{[L_r(G_Y + G_P/Q_P) - G_r(L_Y + L_P/Q_P)]}{[H_r(G_Y + G_P/Q_P) - G_r(H_Y + H_P/Q_P)]}. \tag{3.12}$$

It is clear from this expression that if there is perfect substitutability between assets (H_r infinite), the offset coefficient is equal to -1. In that case, monetary policy is powerless to affect output or the interest rate. In Figure 3.2, *HH* becomes horizontal and is unaffected by changes in bond supplies, so point *a* coincides with point *o*. Short of perfect substitutability, however, the offset is less than complete ($X dF^m/dH_0^m > -1$). Note that the offset could be positive rather than negative in the perhaps unlikely case where the increase in output (and price) causes a net shift out of foreign bonds to satisfy the demand for transactions balances.[26]

The empirical evidence on offset behavior suggests that the offset coefficient is negative and large, but significantly different from minus one. Kouri and Porter (1974), for example, estimated that the offset coefficient for Germany was -0.77

---

[25] This expression is obtained by solving the equations of Table 3.1 for the case of no sterilization.

[26] See Branson (1974) for a discussion of this case. Using (3.12), it can be shown that high substitutability between domestic and foreign bonds or low sensitivity of expenditure to real interest rates is sufficient to rule out a positive offset. Geometrically, a positive offset occurs when $L'L'$ and $H'H'$ intersect below the *GG* line.

based on evidence from the 1960s.[27] There are two ways of looking at such evidence. One is to say that the offset is less than complete, so the central bank retains control over the money supply. But there is another side to this good news. An offset as large as -0.77 implies a sizable change in foreign exchange reserves for any given (net) change in the money supply. The higher the degree of asset substitutability, in effect, the greater the change in foreign exchange reserves associated with any active monetary policy. For this very reason, countries such as Germany became increasingly disenchanted with fixed exchange rates during the late 1960s. Germany's attempts to pursue a tight monetary policy led to large surpluses in its overall balance of payments which in turn generated pressure from its trading partners for changes in its policies. Exchange rate flexibility seemed to provide a solution; the German money supply could then be under the full control of its authorities. Controlling one's money supply, however, is a necessary but not sufficient condition for an effective monetary policy, as we shall see below.

3.3. Stabilization policy under flexible exchange rates

Under flexible rates, the equations of Table 3.1 determine domestic output, the interest rate and the exchange rate. Foreign exchange reserves are exogenous. Figures 3.1 and 3.2 continue to describe the determination of output and the interest rate for any given exchange rate.[28] But changes in the exchange rate generally shift all three schedules.

The effect of exchange rate flexibility on an expansionary stabilization policy depends first of all upon whether the domestic currency appreciates or depreciates. An expansionary fiscal policy invariably leads to an appreciation in the model outlined, just as it unambiguously leads to an increase in foreign exchange reserves under fixed exchange rates. (In the Fleming analysis, by contrast, the exchange rate could appreciate or depreciate depending upon the relative effect of the policy on the capital and current accounts of the balance of payments.) The

---

[27]For the same period, Herring and Marston (1977, ch. 6) present estimates of a net offset coefficient which takes into account sterilization behavior. Most estimates of the offset effect are based on financial behavior only, whereas the general expression for the offset coefficient presented in eq. (3.12) also takes into account behavior in the goods market (which affects the size of the offset coefficient when $G_r \neq 0$). For an estimate of the offset effect based on an economy-wide econometric model, the $RDX2$ for Canada, see Helliwell and Lester (1976).

[28]We adopt the usual assumption that behavioral parameters are insensitive to the change in regimes, an assumption which has been criticized by Lucas (1972,1973) and others in a closed economy context. Cooper (1976) suggests that in comparing exchange rate regimes, we should take into account likely changes in both trade and financial behavior, but to do so would require the explicit modelling of the microeconomic behavior of trading firms and investors. In Section 5 we discuss the influence of policy rules on private behavior, and address more directly the Lucas critique.

effect of the rise in government spending and of the ensuing appreciation of the domestic currency are illustrated in Figure 3.1.[29]

The rise in the demand for the domestic good shifts the GG curve upward, but the appreciation *dampens* this movement. The appreciation also induces shifts in the asset schedules (not shown). As X falls, the demands for money and bonds both fall. (Recall that L_X and H_X are both positive because of the combined influence of price level changes, expectations and wealth effects on the demand for these assets.) As a result the LL curve shifts to the right and HH to the left. The economy ends up somewhere in the triangular area bounded by *abo*, with output and the domestic interest rate rising.

Under certain conditions, output remains fixed despite the government's increased demand for domestic goods; this is Mundell's well-known result that fiscal policy is powerless to change output under flexible rates. To show this, we follow Mundell in assuming that domestic and foreign bonds are perfect substitutes (H_r is infinite, so that HH is flat). But we also need to assume that the exchange rate has no net effect on the demand for money ($L_X = 0$, so that the LL schedule does not shift). The following are sufficient conditions for the demand for money to be independent of the exchange rate: (a) static expectations, (b) a zero wealth elasticity of the demand for money or an insensitivity of real wealth to exchange rate changes, and (c) a unitary income elasticity of the demand for money, which ensures that the fall in the general price level raises the transactions demand for money and real money balances by the same amount.[30] If money demand is independent of the exchange rate and if the domestic interest rate is tied to the foreign interest rate through perfect substitution, then only a constant output (and domestic price) are consistent with a constant money supply. Thus output remains at point o in Figure 3.1. Notice, however, how many assumptions are needed for this result. Under more general conditions, domestic output must rise.

The effect of monetary policy under flexible rates is shown in Figure 3.2, where we illustrate the normal case in which an open market purchase of domestic bonds leads to a depreciation of the domestic currency. The shifts of the asset market schedules illustrate the direct effect on asset supplies: the increase in the money supply shifts LL to the right to $L'L'$, while the reduction of the bond supply shifts HH to the right as well to $H'H'$. The depreciation itself then leads to an equilibrium somewhere in the triangle *abc*, with output increasing and the

---

[29] For a similar diagrammatic analysis of private sector disturbances see Henderson (1979).

[30] For a similar set of conditions, see Henderson (1981). Argy and Porter (1972) previously emphasized the importance of static expectations for Mundell's result. This assumption also implies that HH remains stationary as X changes. In the case of perfect substitutability between bonds, the position of HH is determined by the uncovered parity condition, $r = r^f + \pi_X$, which is unchanged if $\pi_X = 0$.

interest rate declining.[31] Under those conditions that produce a positive offset under fixed rates, an open market purchase can lead to an appreciation rather than a depreciation under flexible rates, but an appreciation is unlikely for the same reasons cited in connection with a positive offset.[32]

In the limiting case of perfect substitution between bonds, monetary policy is still effective in changing output, since there are no changes in foreign exchange reserves to offset the open market operation. Output and the domestic price still increase; the interest rate remains constant if expectations are static, and it falls if expectations are regressive (because HH shifts down by the change in the foreign interest return, $d\pi_X = -e_X dX$). In this limiting case, an open market operation and foreign exchange intervention are equivalent in effects, if the latter is defined as an exchange of foreign bonds for domestic money, since it cannot matter whether domestic or foreign bonds are exchanged for money. But *sterilized* foreign exchange intervention, involving an exchange of foreign for domestic bonds with no change in the money supply, must be totally ineffective in changing output, price or the interest rate.[33]

3.4. The relative effectiveness of policies and other issues

Having discussed fiscal and monetary policy in detail, we can briefly review the relative effectiveness of each policy in changing output under fixed and flexible rates. Fiscal policy is always less effective under flexible rates than under fixed rates, because an expansionary policy leads to an appreciation of the domestic currency, thereby dampening the rise in aggregate demand. Figure 3.1 illustrates this result clearly: with fixed exchange rates (and no sterilization) the economy reaches point a; with flexible rates, the economy ends up somewhere in the triangular area oab. Thus there is no ambiguity about the relative effectiveness of fiscal policy, a result which differs from Fleming's. The difference, of course, is that the movement of the exchange rate is governed by asset market behavior (the relative slopes of HH and LL) rather than by the trade and capital accounts of the balance of payments as in Fleming's study.

Fleming's conclusion with respect to the relative effectiveness of monetary policy is also modified in this model. Monetary policy is not necessarily more effective under flexible rates. But under the normal conditions in which the offset effect is negative, Fleming's conclusion is upheld. Figure 3.2 illustrates this result:

---

[31] The depreciation shifts $L'L'$ to the left, $H'H'$ and GG to the right, so the final equilibrium must be in the triangle bounded by $L'L'$, $H'H'$ and GG.

[32] If an appreciation occurs, the triangle is below the GG schedule, but output still increases and the interest rate declines.

[33] Girton and Henderson (1977) discuss both types of intervention. See also Kenen (1982) and Chapter 15 by Branson and Henderson in this Handbook.

under fixed exchange rates, an open market expansion of the money supply leaves the economy at point *a*, while under flexible rates the economy expands further to some point in the triangle *abc*. Only if the offset is positive is monetary policy less effective under flexible rates.

This type of analysis has often been used as a basis for comparing fixed and flexible rates. One regime is preferable to another if it makes a given policy instrument more effective in changing output. But the analysis has frequently been turned on its head. Instead of analyzing the effects of policy-induced changes in the money supply, some studies have analyzed the effects of monetary *disturbances*, unwanted changes in money demand or supply.[34] Similarly, aggregate demand disturbances originating in private behavior (e.g. shifts in demand from domestic to foreign goods) have often been analyzed in place of changes in government spending. The choice between exchange rate regimes then hinges on which regime *minimizes* the effects of the disturbances on output. This different perspective is commonly found in the new stochastic literature to be discussed in Sections 5 and 6. When it comes to analyzing foreign disturbances, however, it does not usually matter whether they are policy-induced or private in origin; in both cases we would normally choose the regime that best insulates the economy from those disturbances.[35] We shall discuss the insulating properties of exchange rate regimes in detail below.

Another important issue concerns the role of country size in determining the effectiveness of monetary and fiscal policies. The size of a country does make a difference, most particularly with respect to the strong conclusions reached by Mundell (1963) about monetary policy under fixed exchange rates and fiscal policy under flexible rates. We shall briefly review the modifications made to his analysis by drawing on his follow-up study, Mundell (1964).

If the domestic country is large enough to affect economic conditions in the rest of the world, monetary policy under fixed exchange rates regains its effectiveness. But with perfect substitutability between domestic and foreign bonds, the money supplies of different countries are fully linked through capital movements, and the domestic country can change its own money supply only by changing the money supply of the world as a whole. For the same reason, an open market operation abroad has as much effect on *domestic* output as an open market operation at home of equal magnitude.

---

[34] There could be unwanted changes in the money supply in any economy with a banking system if the authorities control bank reserves but not the money supply. Bryant (1980) analyzes several important issues involved in the conduct of monetary policy in such an economy.

[35] A specific policy initiative by a foreign government could very well be welcomed by the domestic country if it happened to have beneficial effects on the domestic economy, but in general countries prefer to be insulated from policy initiatives abroad. Domestic and foreign initiatives, however, might be coordinated by the governments concerned. Cooper (1969) and Bryant (1980) discuss problems of policy coordination.

As far as fiscal policy under flexible rates is concerned, this policy also regains its effectiveness, even under Mundell's assumptions, if the domestic country is large enough to influence foreign conditions. An increase in government spending in the domestic country leads to an appreciation of the domestic currency and a deterioration of the trade balance, as it did in the small country case. But the foreign country thereby experiences a boom, so that outputs and interest rates rise in both countries. Mundell considers an interesting special case where the two countries have identical income elasticities of the demand for money. In this case, the rise in government spending at home raises output at home relative to output abroad in proportion to the ratio of *domestic* to *foreign* output. Two countries of equal size, for example, would share equally in the expansion even though the increase in government spending fell solely on domestic goods. It is only when this ratio approaches zero that fiscal policy becomes ineffective in changing output. For further discussion of these and other results from two country models, the reader is referred to the excellent survey of macroeconomic interdependence by Mussa (1979).

Until this point we have evaluated fiscal and monetary policies separately and have judged each according to its effects on domestic output. We might also be concerned with the balance of payments or other external effects of the policies, however, and might therefore ask if it is possible to achieve both internal and external balance using fiscal and monetary policies together.[36] According to Tinbergen's (1952) famous rule, to achieve a given number of independent targets we must have as many independent instruments. Here we have two instruments, monetary and fiscal policy, and they can be varied to achieve two independent targets, since the policies generally differ in their relative impacts on output and external balance (defined in this model as a desired value of foreign exchange reserves).[37]

To the requirement that the number of instruments be as large as the number of targets, Mundell (1962) added another condition: that each policy instrument be directed toward that target for which it has relatively greater impact; he termed this the "principle of effective market classification".[38] In the flow models of the 1960s, monetary policy had a comparative advantage over fiscal policy in achieving balance of payments equilibrium under fixed exchange rates. In the model specified here, however, that comparative advantage no longer holds in all

---

[36] We confine our discussion to fixed exchange rates, although similar issues arise under flexible rates.

[37] In the asset model specified here, it is more natural to define external balance in terms of a desired level of foreign exchange reserves rather than a desired value for their time derivative (the balance of payments).

[38] This condition was necessary for dynamic stability in Mundell's model, when two different authorities controlled monetary and fiscal policy. Note that in this study, unlike the other cited earlier, Mundell assumed imperfect substitutability between domestic and foreign bonds.

cases. If the substitutability between domestic and foreign bonds is low enough, for example, monetary policy may have no net effect on foreign exchange reserves (the razor's edge case between a negative and positive offset). With perfect substitutability between bonds, on the other hand, the *only* effect of monetary policy is on foreign exchange reserves, as discussed before. So the degree of asset substitutability is also crucial in determining the comparative advantage of the two policies.

Today, concern over the balance of payments (or the exchange rate under flexible rates) would probably be replaced by concern over the price level or inflation rate. And assumptions about decentralized decisionmaking that lay behind Mundell's analysis would probably be replaced with assumptions about information asymmetries between the government and private agents. We discuss price behavior in the next section and those following, while information asymmetries are discussed in Section 5.

4. Flexible wages and the monetary approach

The macroeconomic model introduced so far displays the rigid nominal wages characteristic of Keynesian models of the 1960s and earlier, even while it incorporates asset behavior reflecting portfolio theory as it has developed in the 1970s. With the rise in inflation in the late 1960s, the assumption of rigid wages became increasingly untenable. As a result, some form of wage flexibility has become a feature of many open economy models. In the next section we will discuss contract models of wage determination which fix wages only temporarily. But before doing so we will introduce a simple classical model with *perfectly flexible* wages. This model will help to clarify the role of wealth effects in the economy's adjustment to long-run equilibrium. In the monetary approach to the balance of payments, these wealth effects constitute the main channel through which a devaluation affects the real sector of the economy. In addition, the model will describe a full information equilibrium which will serve as a benchmark for the new classical models to be described in the next section.

4.1. A model with flexible wages

The behavior of the model introduced in earlier sections changes markedly when wages become flexible. In an open economy, however, output does not become exogenous under this classical assumption; instead, aggregate supply becomes a function of the *terms of trade*, $P/P^f X$. To see why this is true, first consider labor supply behavior in an open economy. If labor consumes both domestic and foreign goods, the supply of labor should be responsive to the nominal wage relative to the general price level, I, rather than the price of domestic goods, P:

$$N^s = N^s(W/I). \tag{4.1}$$

The domestic producer, on the other hand, measures wages relative to the price of the good which he produces, so the demand for labor should be of the form:

$$N^d = N^d(W/P). \tag{4.2}$$

W/I is often called *labor's* real wage, while W/P is called the *producer's* real wage.[39] If the supply and demand equations are solved for an equilibrium wage and quantity of labor, and if the production function (3.4) is used to determine output, the result is a new supply equation of the form:

$$Y = Q^s(P/P^fX), \qquad Q^s_P > 0. \tag{4.3}$$

Any disturbance that changes the terms of trade also changes output.

With the new aggregate supply equation replacing (3.4) in the original model, we still have a four equation system determining Y, P, r, and X or XF^m. This system is more difficult to describe, however, since the domestic price can no longer be easily eliminated from the system. To make the system more manageable, we replace the bond equation with an uncovered parity condition, $r = r^f + \pi_X$, by assuming that domestic and foreign bonds are perfect substitutes. This assumption, in fact, is almost always adopted in the monetary approach and in the stochastic models to be discussed shortly. In addition, we assume that all expectations are static, i.e. π_X is zero and so the domestic interest rate is equal to the exogenous foreign rate. We briefly discuss the more general case below.

The parity condition allows us to eliminate the domestic interest rate from the aggregate demand and aggregate supply equations and from the equilibrium conditions for the money market. We can write the aggregate demand and supply equations in differential form, solving for the change in the domestic price in order to show the adjustment of this price more clearly:

$$dP = dX + dY/Q^s_P, \tag{4.4}$$

$$dP = -\frac{G_X}{G_P}dX - \frac{G_Y}{G_P}dY + \frac{dG_0}{G_P}. \tag{4.5}$$

These two equations can be illustrated in Y–P space in Figure 4.1. Under fixed exchange rates, the two schedules alone determine domestic output and price. The money market equation determines the change in foreign exchange reserves recursively. The system of equations under fixed exchange rates is thus qualitatively similar to the Keynesian system outlined above, at least as long as the

---

[39]Chapter 16 of this Handbook by Bruce and Purvis discusses labor market behavior in more detail. For a similar description of the labor market, see Salop (1974), Purvis (1979), Branson and Rotemberg (1980) and Sachs (1980). Later we discuss models where labor's real wage is kept rigid by indexation.

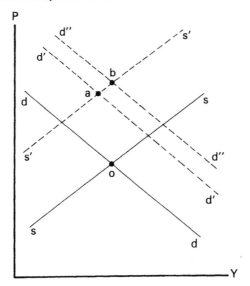

Figure 4.1. Devaluation or depreciation in the classical model.

foreign price is constant. If the exchange rate changes, however, both schedules in Figure 4.1 are affected. [For a similar diagrammatic analysis in a stochastic model, see Marston (1982b).]

4.2. Effects of a devaluation with flexible wages

How much difference the new aggregate supply equation makes to the behavior of the model can be seen by examining the effects of a devaluation. As in the Keynesian model, a devaluation leads to an increase in aggregate demand, which in Figure 4.1 is represented by an upward shift of the dd schedule. Whether this movement is proportional to the change in the exchange rate is crucial in determining the net effect of the devaluation, so we use eq. (4.5) and the definitions of Table 3.1 to express the (vertical) shift of the dd curve as follows:

$$\frac{\mathrm{d}P}{\mathrm{d}X} = 1 - \frac{(1 + B_Z)Z_A(A - F^d)}{G_P}. \tag{4.6}$$

The upward shift of the aggregate demand schedule is less than proportional if $Z_A > 0$, where Z_A is the derivative of expenditure with respect to real wealth. With money and domestic bonds fixed in nominal value at any point in time, the devaluation reduces the real value of domestic wealth (in proportion to $A - F^d =$

$M + H^d$); the sensitivity of aggregate demand to real wealth then holds down the increase in aggregate demand. Aggregate supply also adjusts upward because of the increase in nominal wages induced by the higher domestic price for the foreign good. In the case of the supply schedule, the upward shift is proportional because equal increases in X and P would raise wages proportionally and would leave output unchanged.

From Figure 4.1 it is evident that output actually *declines* and the domestic price rises less than proportionately in response to the devaluation (see point a). With changes in exchange rates affecting real wealth because some assets are fixed in nominal value, the devaluation has real effects despite the flexibility of wages. This is a familiar result in classical models.[40] The fall in output and the terms of trade generates a trade surplus for the devaluing country. As a result, the immediate impact of the devaluation on domestic prices and output is different from its long-run impact. That is because the trade surplus leads to a (flow) increase in wealth,

$$\dot{A} = PB > 0, \tag{4.7}$$

which moves the short-run asset market equilibrium continuously toward a long-run steady state. In that steady state, the trade account reaches equilibrium with total nominal assets increasing proportionally to the change in the exchange rate: $dA/A = dX/X$. Wages and prices also increase proportionally in the long run, so output returns to its initial level.

This process of wealth accumulation is an essential feature of the monetary approach to the balance of payments.[41] In many versions of this approach, money is the only asset so that *real money balances* rather than real wealth drive the accumulation process. As long as the domestic credit component of the monetary base is kept constant, moreover, foreign exchange reserves grow along with money balances so that the equation describing wealth accumulation explains the *balance of payments*.

Consider a simple version of this approach taken from Dornbusch's (1973) well-known study of devaluation:

$$M^d = kP\bar{Y} \tag{4.8}$$

$$P = \bar{P}^f X \tag{4.9}$$

$$\dot{M} = \gamma(kP\bar{Y} - M), \quad \text{where } M = H^m + XF^m. \tag{4.10}$$

The first equation is a quantity theory formulation for the demand for money.

---

[40] See Metzler's (1951) treatment of monetary policy in a closed economy.

[41] Frenkel and Johnson (1976) trace the origins of this approach back to the writings of Mill, Hume and other classical economists. Johnson (1972) provides one of the earliest formal descriptions of it. For references to the extensive literature that has emerged since, see Whitman (1975) and Chapter 14 in this Handbook by Frenkel and Mussa.

The second equation states the law of one price reflecting the assumption that domestic and foreign goods are perfect substitutes. The third equation specifies a wealth accumulation process that relates the rate of hoarding (income less expenditure) to the difference between money demand and supply.[42] According to this model, a devaluation has only temporary effects on the trade balance with the rate of asset accumulation being in proportion to the difference between the *stock* demand and supply of money. Through the accumulation of foreign exchange reserves the money supply in time reaches a new equilibrium with the money supply having risen in proportion to the exchange rate, $dM/M = dX/X$.

Results similar to Dornbusch's can be derived using the model with internationally mobile capital developed in this chapter. If we follow Dornbusch by assuming that the law of one price holds, then output is unaffected by the devaluation. [In the aggregate supply function (4.3), output is fixed by the constant terms of trade.] The price level rises in response to the devaluation, however, so the demand for money immediately rises. With bonds as well as money included in the menu of assets, there is no longer short-run disequilibrium between the stock demand and supply of money as in eq. (4.10). Instead, asset holders can instantaneously adjust their money holdings to the desired level by buying or selling bonds. If money balances are a positive function of wealth as in eq. (3.5), then money balances rise *immediately following* the devaluation, but less than proportionally to the exchange rate (and the price level):

$$\frac{dM}{M} = \left(1 - \frac{m_A}{M}(A - F^d)\right)\frac{dX}{X} \qquad (4.11)$$

The trade balance also rises as can be seen by solving the income–expenditure relationship (3.1):

$$dB = dY - dZ = Z_A(A - F^d)\,dX > 0. \qquad (4.12)$$

The improvement in the trade account is directly proportional to the change in real wealth rather than to the change in real money balances as in Dornbusch's model.[43] The trade account surplus, in turn, generates a flow increase in wealth as in (4.7). How that increase in wealth is divided between assets depends upon the sensitivity of money demand to real wealth (as reflected in m_A):

$$\dot{M}/P = m_A(\dot{A}/P). \qquad (4.13)$$

The wealth accumulation process ends when money balances as well as other

---

[42] In the same paper, Dornbusch extended his model to include non-traded goods and showed that a devaluation could have effects on the allocation of resources between sectors during the period when money balances are adjusting. In Chapter 14 of this Handbook, Frenkel and Mussa discuss a wider class of models showing how the monetary adjustment mechanism is affected by relaxing these assumptions.

[43] If domestic bonds did not represent net wealth, the wealth effect would be proportional to money balances only, $A - F^d = M$, just as in Dornbusch's model.

assets have increased in proportion to the devaluation just as in the simpler Dornbusch model.

This description of how an economy responds to a devaluation differs markedly from the earlier elasticity and absorption approaches.[44] In the elasticities approach, a devaluation improves the trade balance by changing the relative prices of imports and exports, but in the present model there is only one traded good. In the absorption approach, a devaluation works at least in part by increasing output relative to spending, but here output is fixed at full employment. The law of one price combined with flexible wages shuts off both of these traditional channels so that the devaluation must work through wealth effects alone.

If there are no real wealth effects in the aggregate demand function ($Z_A = 0$), then this dynamic accumulation process is eliminated. The devaluation then leads immediately to a proportionate rise in the domestic price even when domestic and foreign goods are imperfect substitutes. (Aggregate demand rises to point b in Figure 4.1.) The terms of trade are constant, and there is no change in output or employment. Furthermore, there is no change in the balance of trade, since it is a function of real expenditure and the terms of trade, both of which are constant under these conditions.

Regardless of the presence or absence of wealth effects, we must not lose sight of the vital role played by wage and price flexibility in obtaining these results. The contrast between the results obtained in this section (with or without wealth effects) and the results obtained with the Keynesian model could not be sharper. The Keynesian model predicts that a devaluation will raise output and improve the balance of trade, while the classical model predicts that its main if not exclusive effect will be on domestic prices. When the trade balance improves because of wealth effects, moreover, the classical model predicts a decline in output rather than the expansion associated with Keynesian models.

In choosing between the two alternative models, the time frame becomes very important. If we believe that wages are sticky in the short run, then we should expect output to expand and the trade balance to improve following a devaluation, as the Keynesian model predicts. But once wages adjust, the classical model becomes relevant, with an improvement in the trade balance occuring only to the extent that there are wealth effects on expenditure. If we believe that wages adjust rapidly, whether through recontracting or indexation, we should expect the classical model to hold in the short run too so that the immediate effects of a devaluation may be primarily on nominal rather than real variables. The timing

---

[44] For a discussion of these approaches, see Section 2.3 above. Earlier studies of devaluation did not necessarily ignore monetary factors. In his paper on the absorption approach, Alexander (1952) included a real balance effect, while in his synthesis of the elasticity and absorption approaches Tsiang (1961) emphasized the importance of monetary policy in determining the effects of a devaluation. In both studies, however, the authors were more concerned with the impact effects of a devaluation than with the dynamic adjustment process which is central to the monetary approach.

of wage and price adjustments is evidently crucial, and that timing is likely to vary across countries depending upon the extent of indexation and other factors.

4.3. Effects of monetary and fiscal policy with flexible wages

In both Keynesian and classical models, the effects of monetary policy depend upon the exchange rate regime. In Section 3 we showed that in the Keynesian model monetary policy under fixed exchange rates is powerless to affect output as long as domestic and foreign bonds are perfect substitutes. That must also be the case in the classical model, since the offset effect is independent of wage conditions in this limiting case. Monetary policy can affect output, however, even in the classical model if there is imperfect substitutability in the asset markets.

The effects of monetary policy under flexible rates, by contrast, depend upon the specification of supply and demand behavior in the model. In general, the open market purchase of bonds causes the domestic currency to depreciate. The effects of this depreciation on the domestic price and output can be illustrated by Figure 4.1, the same figure used to illustrate the effects of a devaluation. As in the case of a devaluation, a monetary expansion leads to a rise in the domestic price but a fall in output (to point *a*), because the higher price of domestic output and the depreciation reduce real wealth. The trade account goes into surplus thereby generating a flow increase in wealth just like in the case of a devaluation. The long-run equilibrium similarly involves a return of real wealth to its original level.

If domestic and foreign goods are perfect substitutes, so that the law of one price links domestic and foreign prices at purchasing power parity, however, then output is unaffected even in the short run. The primary effect of the monetary expansion is to drive up prices in proportion to the depreciating exchange rate. This is a common result in many versions of the monetary approach to the exchange rate. Consider one version consisting of three so-called "building blocks" of the approach: a quantity theory equation for the demand for money (with real balances a function of the interest rate), the law of one price, and uncovered interest parity: [45]

$$M^{d} = k(r)P\overline{Y}, \tag{4.14}$$

$$P = \overline{P}^{f}X, \tag{4.15}$$

$$r = \overline{r}^{f} + \pi_{X}, \tag{4.16}$$

where $\pi_{X} = 0$ if expectations are static. According to this model, an increase in the money supply has no effect on output, but raises the domestic price and exchange

---

[45]Frenkel (1976) applies these three building blocks to explain the exchange rate during the German hyperinflation. For a more detailed discussion of the monetary approach to the exchange rate, see Chapter 14 in this Handbook by Frenkel and Mussa.

rate in proportion to the increase in the money supply: $dP/P = dX/X = dM/M$.[46] Even in this model, however, the monetary expansion causes a temporary trade imbalance if expenditure (not shown) is a function of real wealth.

In order for there to be no real effects of the monetary expansion, we need to assume that expenditure is unaffected by changes in real wealth. In that case the economy is driven to point *b* in Figure 4.1 just as in the case of a devaluation. Both output and the trade balance are unaffected by the monetary expansion as prices rise in proportion to the exchange rate.

Leaving aside the issue of wealth effects, we can ask how much difference flexible wages make to the effectiveness of monetary policy. The introduction of flexible wages into the Mundell model undermines his conclusions and those of similar studies about the relative effectiveness of monetary policy. Monetary policy is not more effective in raising output under flexible exchange rates. On the contrary, it loses all of its effectiveness when wages are flexible, and may even reduce output if expenditure is a function of real wealth. Its principal effect, in fact, is to raise domestic prices. Monetary policy under fixed rates, in contrast, leaves the economy at point *o*, where price and output are constant, just as in the Keynesian model.

Increases in government spending have very different effects than monetary policy if, as is traditionally assumed, the government spending falls entirely on domestic goods. Whether exchange rates are fixed or flexible, the rise in government spending causes a *rise* in the *terms of trade* between domestic and foreign goods. To the extent that labor supply is sensitive to real wages, this rise in the terms of trade increases domestic output. Thus fiscal policy has real effects even though wages are perfectly flexible.

Consider first the case of fixed exchange rates, using Figure 4.2. The increase in government spending leads to an upward shift in the aggregate demand schedule to $d'd'$, raising domestic output and price to point *a*. With the exchange rate constant, the necessary rise in the terms of trade is accomplished solely through a rise in the price of the domestic good.

Under flexible rates, by contrast, the exchange rate does most of the adjusting. As in the Keynesian model, an increase in government spending leads to an appreciation because of the increase in the demand for money. The appreciation causes both the aggregate demand and supply curves to shift down (relative to the fixed exchange rate equilibrium at point *a*).

Consider the case where there are no wealth effects on aggregate demand or on the demand for money. The appreciation then shifts the aggregate demand and supply schedules down *proportionately* from point *a* to point *b*.[47] The apprecia-

---

[46] Note that the depreciation of the domestic currency is less than proportional to the increase in the money supply if expectations are regressive rather than static.

[47] The $d''d''$ schedule can even shift down below its original position at dd depending upon the relative importance of income and price effects on expenditure, as well as other factors.

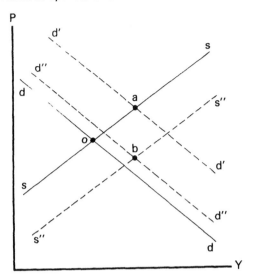

Figure 4.2. Government spending in the classical model.

tion has no net effect on output, so point *b* must be directly below point *a*. Thus, with perfect wage flexibility, perfect capital mobility and the absence of wealth effects, fiscal policy has identical effects on output in the two exchange rate systems. Output *does* change in both systems, but by the same amount. The price of domestic output, however, increases less under flexible rates; in fact, the appreciation of the domestic currency may be large enough to induce a fall in the domestic price (as illustrated by point *b*). Because of the appreciation, the general price level unambiguously falls under flexible rates. As to the *absolute* variation in prices in the two regimes, it is not possible to determine whether the price of domestic output varies more under fixed or flexible rates without further restrictions on the parameters The same is true of the variation in the general price level.

This analysis changes somewhat when real wealth effects are present. An appreciation of the domestic currency raises real wealth because the general price level falls, so output rises further under flexible rates than under fixed rates. The analysis changes more substantially, however, if domestic and foreign goods are perfect substitutes. Government spending raises output by changing the terms of trade between domestic and foreign goods; if those terms of trade are fixed by perfect substitutability, then government spending can have *no* effect on output.

To summarize the effects of monetary and fiscal policies, both are modified substantially by the flexibility of wages. In the Mundell–Fleming model monetary policy is more powerful in raising output under flexible rates and fiscal policy less powerful. In the classical model, any differences between output behavior in the two regimes depend upon wealth effects which are of secondary importance in the Mundell–Fleming model. If there are no wealth effects in the classical model, then monetary policy is equally powerless in each regime, while fiscal policy is as effective in a flexible regime as in a fixed regime.

Some of the new classical models bridge the gap between the wage assumptions of the monetary approach and Keynesian models by explicitly modeling the wage contracting process. In this new literature the distinction between the short and long runs becomes blurred because of the central role played by expectations. It is to this literature that we now turn.

5. The role of policy in the new classical macroeconomics

With many questions about stabilization policy still unresolved because of continuing controversies about asset substitutability, wage and price flexibility and other issues, economists were confronted in the 1970s with a new challenge associated with rational expectations and the new classical macroeconomics. A range of new propositions were put forward that redefine and severely limit the scope for an effective stabilization policy. Many of the basic insights of the earlier literature survive intact when rational expectations are introduced, but specific results about stabilization policy continue to hold only when disturbances in the economy, information flows and expectations take specific forms which were never adequately spelled out before.

The new classical macroeconomics has been developed mostly in the context of a closed economy in studies such as those of Lucas (1972, 1973), Sargent and Wallace (1975), and Barro (1976). The key propositions about stabilization policy can be summarized as follows.

(1) Anticipated changes in the money supply have no real effects. Unanticipated changes do affect output, but random variations of the money supply merely raise the variability of output.

(2) Monetary policy rules are ineffective in stabilizing output.
McCallum and Whitaker (1979) have extended these propositions to include changes in government spending. For surveys of this literature, which is too broad to be fully treated here, the reader is referred to Shiller (1978), Buiter (1980), and McCallum (1980).

This section will review some of the basic propositions of the new classical macroeconomics within the context of an open economy model. The same model will be used in the following section to investigate the choice between exchange rate regimes and insulation. Open economy versions of the new classical macroeconomics have been derived from their closed economy counterparts, but there are some important differences in the open economy versions which we will describe later.[48]

Before introducing a specific model, it is useful to point out several common characteristics found in many of the open economy models.

(1) Expectations are rational in the specific sense that the public knows the underlying economic model and forms expectations on the basis of that model.[49] The open economy studies concerned with stabilization policy, however, differ from their closed economy counterparts in their assumptions about what information is available when expectations are formed.

(2) In the stabilization literature of the 1960s and earlier, economic policy was commonly modeled in terms of discrete policy initiatives formulated on an ad hoc basis. In the new classical literature, policy usually takes the form of *rules* tying current policy instruments to past or current economic disturbances. These rules form part of the model, and the private sector is usually assumed to know them or at least be able to make inferences about them.

(3) Supply is responsive to *unanticipated* changes in prices, which drive the economy away from its "natural rate of unemployment" or its full information classical equilibrium. In the closed economy literature, the supply function is often explained in terms of a confusion between relative and absolute prices, as in the "island model" of Lucas (1973). As Flood (1979) has pointed out, however, this rationale is not appropriate for an open economy where contemporaneous international trading and intranational trading are permitted. Instead most studies base the supply function on a contract lag of the type specified by Gray (1976) and Fischer (1977c) for a closed economy.[50] In the open economy models, supply can also respond to *anticipated* changes in prices, as we will see below.

(4) Apart from the contract lag, almost all versions of the model exhibit classical neutrality. There are no wealth effects in the aggregate demand function, for example, and the supply function is homogeneous of degree zero in all prices.

---

[48]Among studies dealing directly with open economy stabilization policy under rational expectations are Eaton and Turnovsky (1982), Henderson (1982), Marion (1982), and Turnovsky (1980b, 1981). Other studies such as Flood (1979) and Flood and Marion (1981) use similar models to examine the choice between exchange rate regimes. Further references are given below.

[49]Black (1973) was one of the first to employ rational expectations in an open economy context. Later influential studies include Mussa (1976), Dornbusch (1976), Kouri (1976), the latter two employing non-stochastic models with perfect foresight.

[50]Recently Lucas (1981) has suggested that the two rationales for the supply function may turn out to be similar: "(*n*) one of these (contracting) models offers an explanation as to why people should choose to bind themselves to contracts which seem to be in no one's self-interest, and my conjecture is that when reasons for this are found they will reduce to the kind of informational difficulties already stressed in my 1972 article, for example". This passage is quoted in Canzoneri, Henderson and Rogoff (1981). Flood and Hodrick (1982) provide an alternative to the wage contract model which explains inventory as well as production behavior in an open economy.

An anticipated monetary disturbance, therefore, has no real effects, and an unanticipated disturbance has real effects only during the contract period.[51]

(5) Most of these models assume perfect substitutability between domestic and foreign securities. Notable exceptions are Eaton and Turnovsky (1982) and Henderson (1982). Many models also assume perfect substitutability between domestic and foreign goods, although this assumption is not necessary for most of the results.

5.1. A model of an open economy under rational expectations

In order to illustrate some of these characteristics and to discuss some of the more important results, we now introduce a model of a small open economy under flexible rates. The model, which is a simplified, stochastic version of the model used above, consists of three equations: aggregate demand and supply equations for the domestic good and an equation describing money market equilibrium.[52] All variables (except interest rates) are expressed in logarithms using small letters as follows $j = \log J$, where J is the corresponding level variable:

$$y_t = c\left(p_t - {}_{t-1}Ep_t\right) + \frac{c_1}{(1-a)}\,{}_{t-1}E\left(p_t - i_t\right) + c_0, \tag{5.1}$$

$$y_t = (1 - c')1_t^d = -c(w_t - p_t) + c\ln(1 - c'), \tag{5.2}$$

$$1_t^s = n(w_t - i_t) + n_0, \tag{5.3}$$

$$w_t' = \frac{{}_{t-1}E\left(p_t + nc'i_t\right)}{1 + nc'} + \frac{\ln(1 - c') - n_0c'}{1 + nc'}, \tag{5.4}$$

$$w_t = w_t', \tag{5.5}$$

---

[51] If expenditure were a function of wealth, monetary policy would be nonneutral in the short run if it changed the real value of wealth, as in the money–bond model introduced earlier. See Canzoneri (1980) for a discussion of wealth effects in stochastic models. Another source of non-neutrality is the Tobin effect of anticipated inflation which changes the real return on money balances. Fischer (1979) discusses this and other sources of non-neutrality. All statements about the effects of anticipated money below must be qualified if such non-neutralities are present.

[52] The main simplification is that wealth effects have been suppressed (as noted above). The new aggregate supply function with its contract specification, of course, is more complicated than the supply function used above. The model is written in logarithmic form as is most of the stochastic literature.

where

$$c = (1 - c')/c',$$

$$c_0 = (1 - c')[n \ln(1 - c') + n_0]/(1 + nc'),$$

$$c_1 = (1 - c')n(1 - a)/(1 + nc'),$$

$$y_t = g_p(p_t^f + x_t - p_t) - g_r[r_t - ({}_tEi_{t+1} - i_t)] + g_y y_t^f + g_0, \qquad (5.6)$$

$$m_t - i_t = (p_t + y_t - i_t) - k_1 r_t, \qquad (5.7)$$

$$r_t = r_t^f + {}_tEx_{t+1} - x_t. \qquad (5.8)$$

Equation (5.1) describes supply behavior, which is based on a contract lag of one period. As explained in the previous section, the supply equation takes a more complicated form than in a closed economy because there are two prices involved in supply decisions, the price of domestic output (p_t) and the general price level (i_t), the latter a weighted average of domestic and foreign prices,

$$i_t = ap_t + (1 - a)(p_t^f + x_t), \qquad (5.9)$$

where p_t^f is the price of the foreign good while x_t is the domestic currency price of foreign currency. Output is responsive to the nominal wage relative to the price of domestic output, but the nominal wage is fixed in period $t - 1$ in the light of expectations prevailing at that time.[53]

The supply equation (5.1) is derived from a Cobb–Douglas production function (5.2), from a labor demand equation based on the production function which is sensitive to the *producer*'s real wage, $w_t - p_t$, and from a labor supply equation (5.3) which is sensitive to *labor*'s real wage, $w_t - i_t$. The contract wage, w_t', is based on expectations of labor demand and supply formed at $t - 1$, as in eq. (5.4). If there is no wage indexation, the actual wage is equal to this contract wage, as in (5.5). With wages based on last period's expectations, output is a function of *unexpected* changes in the domestic price. In an open economy, however, output is also responsive to *anticipated* changes in the terms of trade,

$$_{t-1}E(p_t - i_t) = (1 - a)_{t-1}E(p_t - p_t^f - x_t),$$

for the same reason that output is a function of the terms of trade in the classical economy without contract lags described in the previous section.

This contracting approach to the aggregate supply function has been criticized by Barro (1977) who offers an alternative description of labor market behavior which gives Pareto optimal outcomes. Barro develops a model where wages are set in contracts but employment is made contingent upon shocks perceived after wages are set. Such contracts dominate the simple ones considered here, but bear

---

[53] $_{t-1}EJ_t$ denotes the expectation of J_t formed on the basis of information available at time $t - 1$.

little resemblance to actual contracts, as Fischer (1977a) observed in his comment on Barro's paper. The indexation of wages to prices is a common feature of labor contracts in some countries, but such schemes correct only imperfectly for the contract lags. We discuss indexation in detail in the next section.

Equation (5.6) describes aggregate demand for the domestic good as a function of the relative prices of foreign and domestic goods, the real interest rate, and foreign output (y_t^f). A rise in the foreign price relative to the domestic price (a fall in the terms of trade) increases aggregate demand, as does a rise in foreign output, while a rise in the real interest rate reduces aggregate demand. In the case of perfect substitution between domestic and foreign goods, g_p becomes infinite in size, and this aggregate demand equation reduces to the familiar purchasing power parity relationship.

There are three financial assets in the model as before, but domestic and foreign bonds are perfect substitutes in eq. (5.8). The demand for money (5.7) is expressed as a function of real income and the interest rate, but not real wealth; to further simplify the model, moreover, the income elasticity is set equal to one.[54]

In eqs. (5.6) and (5.8) expectations of changes in the general price level and the exchange rate are based on information available in period t, including knowledge of the current exchange rate and price levels at home and abroad. This expectations assumption is different from that in most of the closed economy literature, where expectations are based on knowledge of last period's price level. This difference is particularly important in determining the effectiveness of policy rules, so we will discuss it in detail below.

We begin by examining simple changes in the money supply which are alternatively unanticipated and anticipated by the general public. This will allow us to illustrate the crucial role played by expectations in determining the effectiveness of policy. The analysis draws most directly on a study by Turnovsky (1981), although other studies cited above are also relevant. Thereafter, we consider the role of policy rules which tie current policy to private sector disturbances.

5.2. Changes in the money supply

To examine several different types of changes in the money supply, we describe the money supply below as the sum of deterministic and stochastic terms:

$$m_t = m_0 + v_t, \qquad v_t = \alpha v_{t-1} + u_t^m.$$

---

[54] If this elasticity is not equal to one, a change in the general price level, and therefore the exchange rate, has an effect on the net demand for money proportional to one minus this elasticity.

The stochastic term has an autoregressive component, αv_{t-1}, in addition to the innovation in period t, u_t^m. If the innovation is temporary, $\alpha = 0$; if it is permanent, $\alpha = 1$. Substituting this expression for the money supply into eq. (5.7), we can solve the three-equation system for current values of x_t, p_t, y_t as functions of the money supply process:[55]

$$x_t - \bar{x} = m_0 + \frac{\alpha v_{t-1}}{A_2} + \frac{A_1(1 + k_1)u_t^m}{A_2 A_0},$$ (5.10)

$$p_t - \bar{p} = m_0 + \frac{\alpha v_{t-1}}{A_2} + \frac{(g_p + g_r a)(1 + k_1)}{A_2 A_0}u_t^m,$$ (5.11)

$$y_t - \bar{y} = \frac{c(g_p + g_r a)(1 + k_1)}{A_2 A_0}u_t^m,$$ (5.12)

where

$$A_1 = c + g_p + g_r a > 0,$$

$$A_2 = 1 + k_1(1 - \alpha) > 0,$$

and

$$A_0 = ck_1 + (g_p + g_r a)(1 + k_1 + c) > 0,$$

while $\bar{x}$, $\bar{p}$, and $\bar{y}$ are constants which are functions of the non-stochastic terms in eqs. (5.1)–(5.8). These expressions are used to interpret three different types of changes in the money supply as follows.

(1) *Unanticipated, temporary increase in the money supply* ($u_t^m > 0$, $\alpha = 0$). The immediate response to this type of change in the money supply is very similar to that discussed in the non-stochastic models with fixed nominal wages. The temporary expansion of the money supply induces a depreciation of the domestic currency. The depreciation is large enough to cause a fall in the terms of trade even though the price of domestic output rises. Therefore, the demand for the domestic good increases. With wages fixed during the contract period, the rise in the domestic price lowers the producer's real wage, so aggregate supply and output also rise. Thus, during the contract period at least, the change in the money supply has an expansionary effect on the economy. A temporary disturbance, however, has no effect on the economy beyond the current period; in the absence of further disturbances, the exchange rate, the domestic price and output return to their stationary values. For this reason, the rational expectation at t of any future value of a variable is the stationary value of that variable. The solution of the model is simple, a feature that is especially attractive if several

---

[55] The system can be solved by recursive substitution or by the method of undetermined coefficients [see Lucas (1972)]. To obtain a stable solution, we must assume the absence of speculative bubbles. Shiller (1978) discusses this assumption.

countries are to be analyzed at once. If there were no contract lag, or if information were complete at the time of the contract, then the monetary disturbance would have no effect on output even in the current period.

(2) *Unanticipated, permanent increase in the money supply* ($u_t^m > 0$, $\alpha = 1$). If the innovation is expected to be permanent, its effects in the current period differ markedly from its subsequent effects. In the current period, the economy responds much as it would to a temporary innovation. The domestic currency depreciates, while both domestic output and price rise.[56] (It can be shown that output rises somewhat more in the current period if the change in the money supply is permanent rather than temporary.) Since the information lag associated with the contracting process persists for only one period, the system reaches equilibrium in period $t + 1$. The effects of the innovation in that period are identical to those of any (other) anticipated change in the money supply. They are discussed immediately below.

(3) *Anticipated increase in the money supply.* Fully anticipated changes in the money supply leave output unchanged while increasing the domestic price and the exchange rate proportionately. Without further complicating the model introduced above, we can illustrate the effects of an anticipated increase in the money supply by focusing on v_{t-1} in eqs. (5.10)–(5.12); it represents the continuing effect of an earlier money supply innovation (which we assume to be permanent by setting $\alpha = 1$). Both x_t and p_t rise in proportion to v_{t-1}, demonstrating the homogeneity of the system in the absence of contract lags. Because the change in the money supply was anticipated at $t - 1$, it affects current wages, which are based on last period's expectations, so the only source of nominal rigidity in this system is removed. As a result, there are no effects on output in period t or beyond.[57] This result can also be interpreted in terms of the supply function (5.1) alone. Because the change in the money supply is anticipated, there is no unanticipated change in the domestic price to affect output, and the first term in (5.1) is zero. In addition, the second term in (5.1), which can be rewritten $c_{1t-1}E(p_t - x_t - p_t^f)$, is unaffected by the disturbance, because any anticipated monetary expansion leaves the *anticipated* terms of trade unaffected. Thus, we obtain the same result as in a closed economy despite a more complicated supply function. If there were real disturbances, however, supply *would* be affected through anticipated changes in the terms of trade.[58]

[56] Turnovsky (1981) has an interesting discussion of exchange rate overshooting in response to this disturbance. Overshooting is by no means necessary in this model, since output is endogenous. Whether overshooting occurs depends upon a condition involving price elasticities very similar to that presented by Dornbusch (1976), even though the nominal rigidities responsible for the overshooting are quite different in the two models.

[57] The announcement of an increase in the money supply does have an effect on output in the period of the announcement, although not in future periods. See Turnovsky (1981).

[58] Government spending, therefore, can have real effects even if it is anticipated since (as shown in Section 4) it changes the anticipated terms of trade between domestic and foreign goods. See Marion (1982) and Turnovsky (1980b). The effectiveness of government spending rules is discussed below.

The preceding analysis has illustrated the significant differences between the effects of anticipated and unanticipated changes in the money supply. When changes in the money supply are anticipated, we are essentially back in the classical world of Section 4 where changes in the money supply have no real effects. (Recall that the particular classical world described in this model is one where there are no real wealth effects on aggregate demand.) Unanticipated changes, however, do have real effects, although only during the contract period. But notice that such changes have no *stabilization role* thus far, since they are unrelated to those exogenous disturbances that stabilization policy is designed to control. In fact, as Sargent and Wallace (1975) have pointed out, these unanticipated changes in the money supply introduce unwanted noise into the system, raising the variance of output.

5.3. Policy rules

Stabilization policy is normally aimed at countering the effects of disturbances originating elsewhere in the economy or abroad. The question addressed in this section is whether *known* rules by which policy reacts to these disturbances can in fact counter them.

In the illustrative model introduced above, which is typical of most such studies of the open economy, policy rules *do* have an impact. To show how, we first modify the three-equation model introduced above by adding disturbances to the aggregate demand and money demand expressions as follows:

$$y_t = g_p \left(p_t^f + x_t - p_t \right) - g_r \left[r_t - \left({}_t E i_{t+1} - i_t \right) \right] + g_y y_t^f + g_0 + u_t^d, \quad (5.13)$$

$$m_t - i_t = p_t + y_t - i_t - k_1 r_t + u_t^n. \quad (5.14)$$

These disturbances represent random elements in private behavior, with a rise in $u_t^d (u_t^n)$ reflecting a rise in demand for the domestic good (money).[59]

What policy rule would be appropriate in this economy? Policy could respond currently to current disturbances, since the disturbances are part of the information set used in determining expectations. In that case, the disturbances could be perfectly offset. But suppose that only lagged responses are feasible. Then it is still possible, as Turnovsky (1980*a*) has shown in the context of a closed economy, for a policy rule to modify the effects of *current* disturbances.[60]

Suppose that the rule is of the form:

$$m_t = n_1 u_{t-1}^n + n_2 u_{t-1}^d + m_0; \quad (5.15)$$

---

[59] The disturbances have a mean of zero, are serially uncorrelated and uncorrelated with each other. We also could have considered a supply disturbance, but these two disturbances are sufficient to illustrate the effects of a policy rule.

[60] For a similar point, see Weiss (1980).

that is, the current money supply responds to *lagged* disturbances. In that case, output can be written as a function of the disturbances:

$$y_t - \bar{y} = \frac{-c(g_p + g_r a)}{A_0}\left[1 - \frac{k_1 n_1}{1 + k_1}\right]u_t^n + \frac{ck_1}{A_0}\left[1 + \frac{(g_p + g_r a)n_2}{1 + k_1}\right]u_t^d. \quad (5.16)$$

Notice that the parameters of the policy rule, n_1 and n_2, appear in the coefficients of both disturbances.

Consider the response to money demand disturbances as reflected in n_1. If the authorities choose $n_1 = (1 + k_1)/k_1$, then output is stabilized completely. The reason has to do with private expectations of *future* policy actions. The public is assumed to know the policy rule and to know all current information including the disturbances. So the public correctly anticipates the future movement of the money supply induced by today's disturbance: $m_{t+1} = m_0 + n_1 u_t^n$. It knows that the domestic currency will depreciate tomorrow, and the *expectation* of that depreciation raises the current interest rate, thus restoring equilibrium to the money market without any change in output.

In a similar way, we can compute the value of n_2 which will keep output constant in the presence of the aggregate demand disturbance, u_t^d. Keeping output constant, however, might be inappropriate. Barro (1976) has argued that policy rules should be aimed at stabilizing output relative to its value in a full information classical economy (i.e. one without contract lags) rather than stabilizing it absolutely.[61] And an aggregate demand disturbance does change output in a full information economy. If the supply function (5.1) for an economy with contract lags is replaced with a classical supply function of the form:

$$y_t^* = c_1(p_t^* - x_t^* - p_t^{f*}) + c_0, \quad (5.17)$$

then output in the full information economy (y_t^*) can be expressed as a function of the disturbance:[62]

$$(y_t^* - \bar{y}) = \frac{c_1}{c_1 + g_p + g_r a}u_t^d. \quad (5.18)$$

According to Barro, an appropriate rule for monetary policy would use the value of n_2 which minimizes ($y_t - y_t^*$). (This calculation is left to the reader.) Stabilizing output completely is appropriate only when the full information output is

---

[61] If the only inefficiencies in the model are those associated with labor being off its (ex ante) supply curve because of the contract lag, then our norm for assessing policy should be the output which would occur if labor were *on* its supply curve as in a full information economy.

[62] Note that output is not responsive to the monetary disturbance in this full information economy, for the reasons outlined in Section 4.

constant, which would be the case if c_1 were zero (i.e. labor supply were inelastic) or g_p were infinite (the terms of trade were constant).

Consider again why the monetary policy rule is effective in this open economy model. What would happen if we adopted the lagged dating of expectations commonly found in the *closed* economy (as opposed to the open economy) literature? The expected change in the exchange rate, for example, would be written $_{t-1}Ex_{t+1} - _{t-1}Ex_t$.[63] The answer is that the policy rule would become ineffective in modifying the impact of the disturbances. If the private sector cannot revise its expectations in response to current information, there is no lever by which such a policy rule can modify the output effect of a current disturbance. This is Sargent and Wallace's (1975) basic result showing the ineffectiveness of monetary policy. With lagged dating of expectations, a policy rule can be effective only if the government itself has an information advantage, and thus can respond to current disturbances even while the private sector cannot.[64]

The reason why policy is effective in one case and not in the other has to do with the *relative* amounts of information available to different agents in the economy. In the typical open economy model, wage earners' expectations are formed at $t - 1$ based on information available then, while the private sector forms all other expectations based on information at period t. (The government may or may not act on the basis of information at t.) If there were no contract lags, wage earners could set their wages based on current information, and a feedback rule would obviously be ineffective.[65] (We would be back in the classical world of Section 4.) In the typical closed economy model, by contrast, *all* expectations are formed at $t - 1$, so there is no lever for policy, whether acting through expectations or not. *Asymmetries* in information provide the leverage for policy rules.[66] And those asymmetries do *not* have to include superior knowledge

---

[63] Both assumptions about dating are subject to objections. Agents surely know the current interest rate and the current exchange rate, so expectations should be based at least partially on current information. But agents are unlikely to know other variables currently, such as the money supply and the price index for domestically produced goods. We discuss the use of partial information below.

[64] Sargent and Wallace (1975) and Barro (1976) both consider this case. Barro suggests that instead of pursuing stabilization policy in this case the government should make available any additional information it has.

[65] Contract lags, however, are not the only source of such information asymmetries. In the model specified by Bilson (1978b), there is a difference between the information sets of asset market and labor market participants not because of contract lags but because asset market participants have a greater incentive to acquire (costly) information.

[66] Turnovsky (1980b) studies government spending rules in an open economy with lagged dating (so that there are no asymmetries in information). A government spending rule based on past disturbances can affect output by changing the terms of trade as in a classical economy, an effect which is absent from a closed economy. But the rule cannot change output relative to its full information value (which changes by the same amount); according to Barro's criterion, then, government spending is ineffective even in an open economy. See Turnovsky (1980b).

on the part of the government as long as some private agents who have superior information know the government's policy rule.

Two other strands in the literature illustrate these points further. Contracts in the labor market which extend for more than one period provide a basis for effective policy rules. Fischer (1977b) shows that with two period contracts, for example, a policy rule tying the money supply to disturbances in period $t - 1$ can affect output in period t. In this case the authorities exploit an information asymmetry by setting the money supply in response to disturbances which, because of contract lags, are not simultaneously reflected in wages (or at least in some of the wages, since there are staggered contracts).[67] As in the earlier case, the information asymmetry is due to a contract lag, but neither the government nor the private sector need have information beyond that available in period $t - 1$.

Canzoneri, Henderson, and Rogoff (1981) have a one period contract lag, but adopt assumptions about information different from either the open or closed economy models. (Their model is of a closed economy, but the same point can be made in an open economy model.) They assume that some agents know the current interest rate in addition to lagged values of the price level and output.[68] Knowledge of the current interest rate allows agents to predict the current price level more accurately than would be possible with lagged information only. The study shows very clearly that the scope for policy rules depends on the existence of an asymmetry in information between wage earners, who set their wages in contracts based on information available in period $t - 1$, and other agents, who know the current interest rate. These other agents might consist of the government alone, the private sector alone (in its non-wage decisions) or both.

It is quite plausible to assume that most agents in the economy make use of current information on financial variables, probably more plausible than to assume that they use all current information or only lagged information. What is more controversial in this and other studies are the assumptions about labor market behavior – that wage earners set their wages based on expectations at $t - 1$ (or at $t - j$ in Fischer's model of multi-period contracts) with firms free to determine output on the basis of those wages. Until more research is done about labor contracts, these assumptions are likely to remain controversial. But so also are the assumptions underlying other versions of the supply function in models where policy is ineffective.

It is not surprising that assumptions about information are central to the discussion of policy ineffectiveness. In all versions of the new classical economics,

---

[67] Variations on this same theme are found in Phelps and Taylor (1977) and Taylor (1980).

[68] This is the same information assumption adopted by Poole (1970) in his well-known study of interest rate and money supply rules. The Canzoneri, Henderson and Rogoff study shows that many of Poole's results continue to hold when expectations are rational. Henderson (1982) extends Poole's analysis to an open economy where the government knows the current value of the interest rate and exchange rate.

supply functions are based on some form of imperfect information about prices. But with the effectiveness of policy rules depending so crucially on specific assumptions about information flows, it is difficult to draw any firm conclusions about stabilization policy until we are confident about the validity of those specific assumptions.

Apart from details about information flows, we need to know more about the ways that agents use information to form expectations. There is a large middle ground between the omniscience built into many versions of rational expectations, where agents have perfect knowledge of the economy, and the ignorance reflected in earlier expectations hypotheses. That middle ground needs to be more fully explored. It would be particularly useful to know how agents revise their expectations during the transition period following the adoption of a new policy. Indeed, McCallum (1980, p. 724) has described the new classical propositions as being relevant only to "stochastic steady states".

Further research clearly remains to be done in defining the scope for an effective stabilization policy – research on labor contracting and the behavior of firms, the gathering and efficient use of information, and the formation of expectations. Whatever the limitations of the current literature, however, it has had a profound effect on economists' views of macroeconomic policy. It has shown how crucial it is to distinguish between anticipated and unanticipated policies. The effectiveness of monetary policy, for example, is very much dependent upon whether or not the particular initiative is foreseen by the private sector. No description of a policy is complete without precise statements about what the private sector knows and when it knows it.

6. Exchange rate regimes

In this section we shift focus to another topic of central interest to stabilization policy. Instead of asking whether monetary or fiscal policy can help to stabilize output, we ask if fixed or flexible exchange rates can help to achieve this objective. We have already addressed this question briefly in discussing non-stochastic models but have reserved most of the discussion for this section where expectations can be treated more formally. In most of the models discussed in this section expectations are rational and supply is determined by a stochastic supply function of the same general form as (5.1).

As in the discussion of policy rules, the economy is assumed to be buffetted by real and financial disturbances, but now we include some disturbances that originate abroad. Flexible exchange rates are thought by some to insulate the economy from foreign disturbances, particularly if the disturbances are monetary in nature. We show that insulation is achieved only in special cases, although exchange rate flexibility does generally dampen the effects of foreign monetary disturbances.

One prominent feature of modern economies, especially those in Europe, is the indexation of wages to prices. Indexation helps to adjust wages to unforeseen shocks, but the adjustment takes a rigid form that can keep real wages constant even in the case of shocks that normally require adjustments in real wages. We show how indexation prevents the exchange rate from altering output and how it thus affects the relative advantages of fixed and flexible rates.

The section concludes with a brief discussion of intervention rules for managed floating and of exchange rate arrangements in a multi-country setting.

6.1. Domestic disturbances

Mundell's propositions about the relative effectiveness of stabilization policies under fixed and flexible rates can be readily transformed into statements about the effects of domestic monetary and aggregate demand disturbances. In the Mundell–Fleming model, fixed rates are preferable to flexible rates if domestic monetary disturbances are important, since such disturbances have no effect on output under fixed rates, but merely result in a change in foreign exchange reserves. This ranking of regimes is reversed when domestic aggregate demand disturbances are important. The present section shows that in rational expectations models of the type discussed above, with wages temporarily fixed due to contract lags, both propositions continue to hold as long as the disturbances are unanticipated. If wage indexation is introduced, however, then the exchange rate ceases to have any effect on real variables. For that reason, there is no difference in the response of output to these disturbances under fixed and flexible rates.

To illustrate each of these points, we employ the stochastic model of the previous section but with two changes to the supply function. First, we now allow wages to be indexed to the general price level:

$$w_t = w_t' + b(i_t - {}_{t-1}E i_t). \tag{6.1}$$

The actual wage, w_t, may differ from the contract wage, w_t', if the indexation parameter, b, is different from zero; this indexation parameter is assumed to vary between zero (no indexation) and one (full indexation).[69] Second, to simplify the analysis we assume that the (ex ante) labor supply function is inelastic, so that the supply of output is insensitive to anticipated changes in the terms of trade [$c_1 = 0$

---

[69]For studies of behavior with wage indexation, see Gray (1976), Fischer (1977c), and Modigliani and Padoa-Schioppa (1978). This analysis of domestic disturbances follows Marston (1982b), although Sachs (1980) and Flood and Marion (1982) present similar results in other models. Some features of the study by Flood and Marion are discussed below.

in eq. (5.1)].[70] We make this assumption so that full information output will be unaffected by the disturbances considered below; we are then left with a simple criterion for judging exchange rate regimes involving the variance of output alone. The aggregate supply equation takes the following form:

$$y_t = c(p_t - {}_{t-1}Ep_t) - cb(i_t - {}_{t-1}Ei_t) + c_0. \tag{6.2}$$

In the absence of indexation, only errors in predicting domestic prices affect aggregate supply, while with indexation errors in predicting the general price level also matter. With *full* wage indexation, an unanticipated change in the general price level can lead to a proportional adjustment of the domestic price with no change in output.

The equations of the model, now consisting of (5.13), (5.14), and (6.2), determine three variables: domestic output, the price of that output, and either the exchange rate or the money supply, depending on the exchange rate regime. If we assume that all foreign variables are constant, then we can express the three variables as functions of the domestic disturbances only. To facilitate comparison between the two exchange rate regimes, the aggregate demand and supply equations are first solved for y_t and p_t as functions of x_t and of the demand disturbance, u_t^d. The resulting expressions, eqs. (6.3) and (6.4) below, describe aggregate demand and supply behavior under *both* exchange rate regimes:[71]

$$y_t - \bar{y} = \frac{c(1 - ab)}{D_1} u_t^d + \frac{(g_p + g_r a)c(1 - b)}{D_1}(x_t - \bar{x}), \tag{6.3}$$

$$p_t - \bar{p} = \frac{u_t^d}{D_1} + \frac{(g_p + g_r a + cb(1 - a))}{D_1}(x_t - \bar{x}), \tag{6.4}$$

$$x_t - \bar{x} = -\frac{(1 + c(1 - ab))}{D} u_t^d - \frac{D_1}{D} u_t^n, \tag{6.5}$$

where

$$D_1 = g_p + g_r a + c(1 - ab) > 0,$$

$$D = (1 + k_1)D_1 + c(1 - b)(g_p + g_r a - 1) > 0.$$

Under fixed rates, x_t is kept equal to $\bar{x}$, with the money supply being determined recursively by (5.14). Under flexible rates, x_t can be expressed as in eq. (6.5) as a

---

[70] The ex ante labor supply function is inelastic ($n = 0$), but once the labor contract is signed the amount of labor supplied is determined by the demand for labor.

[71] All expectations in the model are assumed to be formed rationally, and the disturbances are unanticipated and serially uncorrelated. As was shown in the previous section, the rational expectation at t of p_{t+1} or x_{t+1} is therefore the stationary value of that variable (here denoted by $\bar{p}$ and $\bar{x}$, respectively).

function of both domestic disturbances, u_t^d and u_t^n, by solving all three equations (5.13), (5.14) and (6.2) for the reduced form.

We begin by examining the effects of the disturbances in the case where there is no wage indexation in the domestic economy, then we consider the effects of indexation. When there is no wage indexation, the effects of both disturbances correspond closely to those reported by Mundell (1963). A monetary disturbance, representing an increase in the money supply or decrease in money demand ($u_t^n < 0$), has no effect on output under fixed exchange rates; it results simply in an offsetting capital flow. With a flexible rate, in contrast, a monetary expansion leads to a depreciation of the domestic currency and to an increase in output as well as in the domestic price.[72] Similarly, as in Mundell's study, an aggregate demand disturbance leads to a greater change in output under fixed rates. An increase in aggregate demand raises both domestic output and the domestic price. Under flexible rates, the increase in the transactions demand for money leads to an appreciation of the domestic currency which *dampens* the overall increase in aggregate demand.[73] Thus, there is less output variation as well as less price variation under flexible rates. The similarity with Mundell's results should not be surprising since the labor contract fixes wages even if only temporarily.

In economies where wage indexation is important, however, these familiar results can break down. To understand why, notice that the effect of the exchange rate on domestic output is dependent on the degree of indexation in the domestic economy. As eq. (6.3) indicates, the effect is proportional to $c(1 - b)$, so that full indexation ($b = 1$) prevents the exchange rate from affecting domestic output at all. It allows the domestic wage and price to adjust currently to changes in the exchange rate. Therefore, the difference in output variation *between* the two regimes must be proportional to $c(1 - b)$. And with full indexation, each disturbance must have an *identical* effect on output in the two regimes.

In the case of a monetary disturbance under flexible rates, full indexation restores the classical result that changes in the money supply affect prices but not output; thus there is no output variation in either regime. In the case of an aggregate demand disturbance under flexible rates, the classical (full information) equilibrium is *not* generally restored since indexation cannot substitute for full wage flexibility.[74] But full indexation still results in output varying to the same

---

[72] The monetary disturbance affects output and the domestic price only through the exchange rate, as eqs. (6.3) and (6.4) indicate.

[73] Under flexible exchange rates, the direct (positive) impact of u_t^d on y_t in eq. (6.3) is dampened by the fall in x_t (which reduces y_t). In contrast to Mundell's study, however, output nonetheless increases even under flexible rates, because the appreciation leads to a rise in the domestic interest rate, thus allowing output to increase despite a constant money supply. (In the notation of Section 3, the coefficient L_x is not equal to zero since the exchange rate affects the demand for money through expectations.)

[74] With $c_1 = 0$, the aggregate demand disturbance has no effect on full information output, but raises current output as indicated by (6.3). Even in the general case where $c_1 \geq 0$, there is no particular reason for the two measures of output to coincide.

extent under flexible rates and fixed rates. With such indexation, therefore, the choice between regimes must be made not on the basis of output behavior but on other grounds such as price behavior.

For a non-indexed or partially indexed economy, the original Mundell results can be generalized in several respects, as a recent study by Henderson (1982) shows. Other types of disturbances can be considered, namely aggregate supply disturbances and financial disturbances involving shifts between domestic and foreign securities (at least if these securities are imperfect substitutes). Secondly, we can compare a "rates constant" policy, where the interest rate and exchange rate are held fixed, with an "aggregates constant" policy, where the domestic money and bond supplies are held fixed. The results cited above generalize as follows. When disturbances originate in the goods market, whether in the aggregate demand or supply equations, then an aggregates constant policy is preferable, because it permits adjustments in the interest rate and exchange rate that tend to dampen the output effects of the disturbances. When disturbances originate in the financial markets, a rates constant policy is preferable, because this policy confines the disturbances to the financial markets. The Henderson study will be discussed at greater length below in connection with optimal foreign exchange intervention.

One study which departs significantly from the Mundell framework is that of Fischer (1976); there is no capital mobility and output is independent of prices (and hence the exchange rate regime), being affected only by supply disturbances. To choose between regimes, Fischer adopts a criterion based on real consumption, where consumption is defined as $C_t = P_t Y_t - B_t$, nominal output less the trade balance (in levels). The ranking of regimes established above is reversed, with flexible rates being preferred when there are monetary disturbances and fixed rates when there are goods market disturbances.[75] Monetary disturbances affect real consumption under fixed rates, but not under flexible rates since the exchange rate adjusts to ensure that $B_t = 0$. Supply disturbances affect real consumption in both regimes (since Y_t changes) but by less under fixed rates, because the balance of payments plays a shock absorber role in that regime. As Fischer shows, however, these results may be overturned if output responds to price innovations, even if capital remains immobile.

6.2. Foreign disturbances and insulation

We turn now to foreign disturbances. Flexible rates are widely thought to insulate an economy from foreign disturbances, probably because of the insulation achieved in models without capital mobility. The analysis below shows that insulation applies only in special cases, and that in general flexible rates do not

---

[75]Frenkel and Aizenman (1981) use a similar model to analyze managed floating.

even insulate the economy from foreign monetary disturbances. This is the first of two central points that will emerge from the analysis. The second concerns the tendency in the literature to define foreign disturbances in terms of individual foreign variables such as foreign prices or interest rates. As Flood (1979) has emphasized, this can be highly misleading. Foreign disturbances almost always affect the domestic economy through a variety of channels. A foreign monetary disturbance, in particular, may raise the foreign price, lower the foreign interest rate and raise foreign output, with the combined effects of all these changes being very different from their individual effects. To analyze foreign disturbances, therefore, it is necessary to trace these disturbances through the foreign economy.

These points can be illustrated with a simple model of a foreign economy subject to monetary disturbances. The model consists of three equations paralleling those of the domestic model:[76]

$$y_t^f = c^f(1 - b^f)\big(p_t^f -_{t-1}\mathrm{E}p_t^f\big) + c_0^f, \tag{6.6}$$

$$y_t^f = -g_r^f\big(r_t^f - \big(_t\mathrm{E}p_{t+1}^f - p_t^f\big)\big) + g_0^f, \tag{6.7}$$

$$m_t^f = p_t^f + y_t^f - k_1 r_t^f + k_0 + u_t^{nf}. \tag{6.8}$$

The main difference is that only one good is involved, so there are no relative prices entering the foreign model. Aggregate supply, therefore, is a function of the price of the foreign good alone; output responds to unexpected changes in that price as long as there is less than complete indexation (b^f is less than one). Note that the monetary disturbance is defined as a money demand innovation but could be interpreted equally well as a (negative) money supply innovation.

The three equations can be solved for p_t^f, y_t^f, and r_t^f as functions of the foreign monetary disturbance, u_t^{nf}:

$$p_t^f - \bar{p}^f = -u_t^{nf}/F_1, \tag{6.9}$$

$$y_t^f - \bar{y}^f = -c^f(1 - b^f)u_t^{nf}/F_1, \tag{6.10}$$

$$r_t^f - \bar{r}^f = \big(1 + c^f(1 - b^f)/g_r^f\big)u_t^{nf}/F_1, \tag{6.11}$$

where

$$F_1 = 1 + k_1 + c^f(1 - b^f) + k_1 c^f(1 - b^f)/g_r^f > 0.$$

All three variables are affected by both foreign disturbances, although foreign output remains constant if there is full indexation abroad ($b^f = 1$).

---

[76] The model is described more fully in Marston (1982b). This is an example of what Flood (1979) terms an extended small country analysis; the two country model is recursive, so foreign disturbances can be studied first in the foreign model, then their effects can be traced through the domestic model.

Even with this simple model there are three channels through which a foreign monetary disturbance affects the domestic country: (a) the price channel, with the foreign price directly affecting domestic aggregate demand (and domestic aggregate supply as well if wages are indexed); (b) the output or income channel, also directly affecting aggregate demand; (c) the interest rate channel, affecting the real interest rate in the aggregate demand function and the nominal interest rate in the money equation.

Without formally solving the domestic model, we can summarize the main effects of a foreign monetary disturbance under flexible rates, where the disturbance represents a decrease in money demand or increase in money supply ($u_t^n < 0$). Although it originates as a monetary disturbance, it becomes both a real and nominal disturbance from the point of view of the domestic country. The real disturbance is represented by the change in foreign output and affects the domestic economy much as would a domestic aggregate demand disturbance. It *raises* demand for the domestic good, the increase being proportional to g_y in the domestic aggregate demand equation (5.13). The nominal disturbance is represented by the combined effect of a higher foreign price and an appreciating exchange rate (which is in turn influenced by the foreign interest rate as well as the foreign price and output). It *reduces* demand for the domestic good, because the appreciation is always large enough to ensure that the domestic currency price of the foreign good falls. The net result of a higher foreign output and an appreciating exchange rate can be either a rise or fall in domestic output.

With disturbances affecting the economy in so many ways, insulation is achieved only in special cases. Even if there is full wage indexation in the domestic country, for example, a flexible exchange rate does *not* generally insulate that country from a foreign monetary disturbance. Wage indexation can shield domestic output from an appreciating exchange rate, but it cannot prevent foreign income from directly raising aggregate demand, much as would a domestic aggregate demand disturbance.

Similarly, if there is perfect substitutability between domestic and foreign goods, a flexible rate does *not* insulate the economy from a foreign monetary disturbance. When the law of one price holds, the aggregate supply equation is modified as follows:

$$y_t = c(1 - b)(p_t - {}_{t-1}Ep_t) + c_0, \qquad (6.2)'$$

where $p_t = p_t^f + x_t$. As is evident from this equation, unexpected changes in the foreign price level lead to changes in domestic output and insulation is again not achieved.

In order for output to be insulated from this disturbance, the law of one price must be *combined* with full wage indexation in the domestic economy. Indexation shuts off the one remaining channel for foreign influence, unexpected changes in the foreign price. As these examples suggest, insulation is by no means a general feature of flexible rates.[77]

A study by Flood and Marion (1982) raises two further points about insulation and the choice between regimes. Exchange rate regimes have traditionally been compared under the assumption that behavioral parameters remain the same even when the regime changes. Flood and Marion argue, however, that the extent of wage indexation should adjust endogenously to the exchange rate regime. The appropriate comparison between exchange rate regimes, therefore, is one where the indexation parameter is at its optimal level (according to an output criterion) in each regime. The same point can be raised about other behavioral parameters such as the degree of asset substitutability. The second point they make is equally interesting: insulation may be an undesirable objective of exchange rate policy; it may be preferable to allow foreign disturbances to enter an economy if this helps to minimize the effects of other disturbances. The law of one price prevails in their model, so that full wage indexation provides insulation from foreign disturbances. They show, however, that under flexible rates it is better to have partial than full wage indexation, even though it prevents insulation from a foreign monetary disturbance, because partial indexation allows the exchange rate to dampen the output effects of a domestic supply disturbance.

6.3. Optimal foreign exchange intervention

Since neither fixed nor flexible rates stabilize output except in special cases, it is natural to ask if some limited form of exchange intervention, "managed floating", might be best. Intervention might follow a rule such as $m_t - \bar{m} = k(x_t - \bar{x})$, whereby the money supply is varied in response to current changes in the exchange rate. The polar cases of fixed and flexible rates correspond to infinite and zero values, respectively, of the intervention parameter, k.

Managed floating appears to be an attractive alternative to either fixed or flexible rates. This is the message of Boyer (1978), who examines optimal intervention in a small open economy. He shows that in the presence of domestic monetary and aggregate demand disturbances, a limited form of foreign exchange intervention is called for, with the degree of intervention determined by the relative importance of the two disturbances. Only in extreme cases are fixed or flexible rates warranted. If monetary disturbances alone affect the economy, then fixed rates are optimal. If aggregate demand disturbances alone affect the economy, then flexible rates are optimal, at least when money demand is independent

---

[77]Marston (1982b) shows that insulation can also be achieved if the foreign country is fully indexed. For another example of insulation, see Saidi (1980), who employs an aggregate supply function based on an intertemporal substitution effect rather than a contract lag to analyze the effects of foreign disturbances.

of the exchange rate. If money demand is positively related to the exchange rate, as with regressive expectations, then the authorities should "lean with the wind", exaggerating exchange rate movements to neutralize the aggregate demand disturbances. The results are analogous to those of Poole (1970) for optimal monetary policy in a closed economy.

The Boyer paper does not analyze the case where expectations are rational. Nor does it explain why private agents fail to utilize the same information that the authorities use in their managed intervention – the information provided by exchange rate movements. Yet we know from the earlier discussion how important information asymmetries are in determining the effectiveness of policy rules. Henderson (1982) analyzes intervention in a model with rational expectations, where assumptions about information are carefully set out.[78] Foreign exchange intervention is based on the authorities' knowledge of the current exchange rate and other financial variables, but private agents base wages on information available in period $t-1$. Henderson justifies this asymmetry by citing the relatively greater costs associated with renegotiating the nominal wage compared with adopting policy responses. His results are similar to those of Boyer and other studies, except that a wider range of disturbances is considered. He finds that fixed rates are called for if all disturbances are financial and that "leaning with the wind" is called for if there are either aggregate demand or aggregate supply disturbances. He also points out that a more complex financial policy, involving two policy instruments, would be necessary if the authorities had more than one objective or if the coefficients of the model were not known with certainty [as in Brainard (1967)].

Other recent studies have investigated exchange market intervention in a three-country or multiple-country setting. In such a setting, an analog of fixed exchange rates is an exchange-rate union which fixes exchange rates between two or more countries that float relative to the rest of the world. (European experiments with such unions, beginning with the Snake in 1972 and following with the European Monetary System in 1979, have heightened interest in the subject.) Corden (1972) discusses the different forms such a union can take, including the simplest "pseudo-exchange-rate union" involving no explicit integration of national economic policies beyond the commitment to fix bilateral exchange rates. A number of studies have investigated the desirability of such unions, including the classic studies of Mundell (1961) and McKinnon (1963).[79] Recently, Aoki (1982), Bhandari (1982) and Marston (1982*a*) have applied stochastic models similar to that outlined above to the union question. Marston, for example, shows how wage

---

[78] Roper and Turnovsky (1980) also analyze managed floating rules under rational expectations (as well as other expectations hypotheses). They have an interesting discussion of how "leaning with the wind" may put a country at odds with its neighbors to the extent that there are implicit international rules limiting intervention operations to dampen exchange rate movements. For a discussion of guidelines for managed floating, see Ethier and Bloomfield (1975).

[79] Tower and Willett (1975) provide a survey of this literature.

indexation, trade patterns, and the sources of economic disturbances influence the case for a union.

One alternative to an exchange rate union in the multiple-country setting is a basket rule tying a currency to a weighted average of exchange rates. Branson and Katseli-Papaefstratiou (1980), Flanders and Helpman (1979), and Lipschitz and Sundararajan (1980) have investigated alternative weighting schemes for the baskets. Branson and Katseli-Papaefstratiou, for example, show how weights based on market power in import and export markets can minimize the effects of exchange rate fluctuations on the terms of trade. Canzoneri (1981) analyzes basket rules within a macroeconomic model similar to that outlined above, showing that basket pegging is generally superior to exchange rate unions between subsets of countries. These studies point toward a fruitful area for future research which will go beyond the two country setting which previously dominated research on exchange market intervention.

References

Allen, P.R. and P.B. Kenen (1980), Asset markets, exchange rates and economic integration (Cambridge University Press, Cambridge).

Alexander, S.S. (1952), "Effects of a devaluation on a trade balance", International Monetary Fund Staff Papers, 2:263–278.

Aoki, M. (1982), "On existence of an exchange rate union in a three-country world model under flexible exchange rate regimes", unpublished.

Argy, V. and P. Kouri (1974), "Sterilization policies and the volatility in international reserves", in: R.Z. Aliber, ed., National monetary policies and the international financial system (University of Chicago Press, Chicago).

Argy, V. and M.G. Porter (1972), "The forward exchange market and the effects of domestic and external disturbances under alternative exchange rate systems", International Monetary Fund Staff Papers, 19:503–532.

Barro, R.J. (1974), "Are government bonds net wealth?", Journal of Political Economy, 82:1095–1117.

Barro, R.J. (1976), "Rational expectations and the role of monetary policy", Journal of Monetary Economics, 2:1–32.

Barro, R.J. (1977), "Long-term contracting, sticky prices, and monetary policy", Journal of Monetary Economics, 3:305–316.

Bhandari, J.S. (1982), "Determining the optimal currency composite", unpublished.

Bilson, J.F.O. (1978a), "The monetary approach to the exchange rate: Some empirical evidence", International Monetary Fund Staff Papers, 25:48–75.

Bilson, J.F.O. (1978b), "Rational expectations and the exchange rate", in: Jacob A. Frenkel and Harry G. Johnson, eds., The economics of exchange rates (Addison-Wesley, Reading, Mass.) 75–96.

Black, S.W. (1973), International money markets and flexible exchange rates, Studies in international finance, No. 32 (International Finance Section, Princeton).

Black, S.W. (1982), "The use of monetary policy for internal and external balance in ten industrial countries", in: J. Frenkel, ed., Exchange rates and international macroeconomics (N.B.E.R., Cambridge).

Blinder, A.S. and R.M. Solow (1973), "Does fiscal policy matter?", Journal of Public Economics, 2:319–337.

Boyer, R.S. (1975), "Commodity markets and bond markets in a small, fixed-exchange rate economy", Canadian Journal of Economics, 8:1–23.

Boyer, R.S. (1978a), "Financial policies in an open economy", Economica, 45:39–57.

Boyer, R.S. (1978b), "Optimal foreign exchange intervention", Journal of Political Economy, 86:1045–1055.

Brainard, W.C. (1967), "Uncertainty and the effectiveness of policy", American Economic Review, 57:411–425.

Branson, W.H. (1968), Financial Capital Flows in the U.S. Balance of Payments (North-Holland, Amsterdam).

Branson, W.H. (1974), "Stocks and flows in international monetary analysis", in: A. Ando, R.J. Herring, and R.C. Marston, eds., International aspects of stabilization policies (Federal Reserve Bank of Boston, Boston).

Branson, W.H. and L.T. Katseli-Papaefstratiou (1980), "Income instability, terms of trade, and the choice of exchange rate regime", Journal of Development Economics, 7:49–69.

Branson, W.H. and J.J. Rotemberg (1980), "International adjustment with wage rigidity", European Economic Review, 13:309–341.

Bryant, R.C. (1980), Money and monetary policy in interdependent nations (Brookings Institution, Washington, D.C.).

Buiter, W.H. (1980), "The macroeconomics of Dr. Pangloss: A critical survey of the new classical macroeconomics", Economic Journal, 90:34–50.

Buiter, W.H. and J. Tobin (1979), "Debt neutrality: A brief review of doctrine and evidence", in: G.M. v.Furstenberg, ed., Social Security versus Private Savings (Cambridge, Mass.) 39–63.

Canzoneri, M.B. (1980), "Wealth effects in the new neoclassical models", International Finance Discussion Papers, No. 158 (Federal Reserve Board, Washington).

Canzoneri, M.B. (1981), "Exchange intervention policy in a multiple country world", International Finance Discussion Paper, No. 174 (Board of Governors of the Federal Reserve System, Washington).

Canzoneri, M.B., D.W. Henderson, and K.S. Rogoff (1981), "The information content of the interest rate and optimal monetary policy", International Finance Discussion Papers, No. 192 (Federal Reserve Board, Washington)

Cooper, R.N. (1969), "Macro-economic policy adjustment in interdependent economies", Quarterly Journal of Economics, 83:1–24.

Cooper, N. (1976), "Monetary theory and policy in an open economy", Scandinavian Journal of Economics, 78:146–163.

Corden, W.M. (1960), "The geometric representation of policies to attain internal and external balance", Review of Economic Studies, 28:1–22.

Corden, W.M. (1972), "Monetary Integration, Essays in International Finance", No. 93 (International Finance Section, Princeton).

Dornbusch, R. (1973), "Devaluation, money, and nontraded goods", American Economic Review, 58:871–880.

Dornbusch, R. (1976), "Expectations and exchange rate dynamics", Journal of Political Economy, 84:1161–1176.

Dornbusch, R. (1980), Open economy macroeconomics (Basic Books, New York).

Dornbusch, R. (1982), "Exchange risk and the macroeconomics of exchange rate determination", in: R. Hawkins, R. Levich, and C. Wihlborg, eds., Internationalization of Financial Markets and National Economic Policy, forthcoming.

Eaton, J. and S.J. Turnovsky (1982), "Effects of monetary disturbances on exchange rates with risk averse speculation", Journal of International Money and Finance, 1.

Ethier, W. and A.I. Bloomfield (1975), "Managing the managed float", Essays in: International Finance, No. 112 (International Finance Section, Princeton).

Fischer, S. (1976), "Stability and exchange rate systems in a monetarist model of the balance of payments", in: R.Z. Aliber, ed., The political economy of monetary reform (Allanheld, Osmun and Co., Montclair, N.J.), 59–73.

Fischer, S. (1977a), "'Long-term contracting, sticky prices, and monetary policy': A comment", Journal of Monetary Economics, 3:317–323.

Fischer, S. (1977b), "Long-term contracts, rational expectations, and the optimal money supply rule", Journal of Political Economy, 85:191–205.

Fischer, S. (1977c), "Wage indexation and macroeconomic stability", in: K. Brunner and A.H. Meltzer, eds., Stabilization of the Domestic and International Economy (North-Holland, Amsterdam) 107–147.

Fischer, S. (1979), "Anticipations and the nonneutrality of money", Journal of Political Economy, 87:225–252.

Flanders, M.J. and E. Helpman (1979), "An optimal exchange rate peg in a world of general floating", Review of Economic Studies, 46:533–542.

Fleming, J.M. (1962), "Domestic financial policies under fixed and under floating exchange rates", International Monetary Fund Staff Papers, 9:369–379.

Flood, R.P. (1979), "Capital mobility and the choice of exchange rate system", International Economic Review, 20:405–416.

Flood, R.P. and R.J. Hodrick (1982), "Optimal price and inventory adjustment in an open-economy model of the business cycle", unpublished.

Flood, R.P. and N.P. Marion (1982), "The transmission of disturbances under alternative exchange-rate regimes with optimal indexing", Quarterly Journal of Economics, 97:43–66.

Frenkel, J.A. (1976), "A monetary approach to the exchange rate: Doctrinal aspects and empirical evidence", Scandinavian Journal of Economics, 78:200–224.

Frenkel, J.A. (1981), "The collapse of purchasing power parities during the 1970's", European Economic Review, 7:145–165.

Frenkel, J.A. and J. Aizenman (1981), "Aspects of the optimal management of exchange rates", NBER Working Paper, No. 748 (National Bureau of Economic Research, Cambridge).

Frenkel, J.A. and H.G. Johnson, eds. (1976), The monetary approach to the balance of payments (George Allen and Unwin, London) 21–45.

Girton, L. and D.W. Henderson (1976), "Financial capital movements and central bank behavior in a two-country, short-run portfolio balance model", Journal of Monetary Economics, 2:33–61.

Girton, L. and D.W. Henderson (1977), "Central bank operations in foreign and domestic assets under fixed and flexible exchange rates", in: P.B. Clark, D.E. Logue, and R.J. Sweeney, eds., The effects of exchange rate adjustments (Department of the Treasury, Washington, D.C.) 151–179.

Gray, J.A. (1976), "Wage indexation: A macroeconomic approach", Journal of Monetary Economics, 2:221–235.

Harberger, A. (1950), "Currency depreciation, income and the balance of trade", Journal of Political Economy, 1:47–60.

Helliwell, J.F. and J.M. Lester (1976), "External linkages of the Canadian monetary system", Canadian Journal of Economics, 9:646–667.

Henderson, D.W. (1977), "Modelling the interdependence of national money and capital markets", American Economic Review, 67:190–199.

Henderson, D.W. (1979), "Financial policies in open economies", American Economic Review, 69:232–239.

Henderson, D.W. (1981), "Balance of payments analysis, fiscal policy and the Boyer paper: A comment", forthcoming.

Henderson, D.W. (1982), "Exchange market intervention operations: Their effects and their role in financial policy", in: J.F.O. Bilson and R.C. Marston, eds., Exchange Rate Theory and Practice (N.B.E.R., Cambridge).

Herring, R.J. and R.C. Marston (1977), National monetary policies and international financial markets (North-Holland, Amsterdam).

Isard, P. (1977), "How far can we push the 'law of one price'?", American Economic Review, 67:942–948.

Johnson, H.G. (1972), "The monetary approach to balance of payments theory", in: Further Essays in Monetary Theory (George Allen and Unwin, London).

Katseli-Papaefstratiou, L.K. (1979), "The reemergence of the purchasing power parity doctrine in the 1970's", Special Papers in International Economics, No. 13 (International Finance Section, Princeton).

Kenen, P.B. (1982), "Effects of intervention and sterilization in the short run and the long run", in: R.C. Cooper et al., eds., The International Monetary System under Flexible Exchange Rates (Ballinger, Cambridge).

Kouri, P.J.K. (1976), "The exchange rate and the balance of payments in the short run and in the long run: A monetary approach", Scandinavian Journal of Economics, 78:280–304.

Kouri, P.J.K. and M. Porter (1974), "International capital flows and portfolio equilibrium", Journal of Political Economy, 82:443–467.

Kravis, I.B. and R.E. Lipsey (1978), "Price behavior in the light of balance of payments theories", Journal of International Economics, 8:193–246.

Laursen, S. and L. Metzler (1950), "Flexible exchange rates and the theory of employment", Review of Economics and Statistics, 32:281–299.

Lipschitz, L. and V. Sundararajan (1980), "The optimal basket in a world of generalized floating", IMF Staff Papers, 27:80–100.

Lucas, R.E., Jr. (1972), "Expectations and the neutrality of money", Journal of Economic Theory, 4:103–124.

Lucas, R.E., Jr. (1973), "Some international evidence on output-inflation tradeoffs", American Economic Review, 63:326–334.

Lucas, R.E., Jr. (1981), "Tobin and monetarism: A review article", Journal of Economic Literature, 19:558–567.

Marion, N.P. (1982), "The exchange-rate effects of real disturbances with rational expectations and variable terms of trade", Canadian Journal of Economics, 15:104–118.

Marston, R.C. (1982a), "Exchange rate unions as an alternative to flexible exchange rates", in: J.F.O. Bilson and R.C. Marston, eds., Exchange Rate Theory and Practice (N.B.E.R., Cambridge).

Marston, R.C. (1982b), "Wages, relative prices and the choice between fixed and flexible exchange rates", Canadian Journal of Economics, 15:87–103.

McCallum, B.T. (1980), "Rational expectations and macroeconomic stabilization policy", Journal of Money, Credit and Banking, 12:716–746.

McCallum, B.T. and J.K. Whitaker (1979), "The effectiveness of fiscal feedback rules and automatic stabilizers under rational expectations", Journal of Monetary Economics, 5:171–186.

McKinnon, R.I. (1963), "Optimum currency areas", American Economic Review, 53:717–725.

McKinnon, R.I. (1981), "The exchange rate and macroeconomic policy: Changing postwar perceptions", Journal of Economic Literature, 19:531–557.

McKinnon, R.I. and W. Oates (1966), "The implications of international economic integration for monetary, fiscal and exchange rate policy", Studies in International Finance, No. 16 (International Finance Section, Princeton).

Meade, J.W. (1951), The balance of payments (Oxford University Press, London).

Metzler, L.A. (1951), "Wealth, saving and the rate of interest", Journal of Political Economy, 59:93–116.

Mundell, R.A. (1961), "A theory of optimum currency areas", American Economic Review, 51:657–665.

Mundell, R.A. (1962), "The appropriate use of monetary and fiscal policy for internal and external stability", International Monetary Fund Staff Papers, 9:70–79.

Mundell, R.A. (1963), "Capital mobility and stabilization policy under fixed and flexible exchange rates", Canadian Journal of Economics and Political Science, 29:475–485.

Mundell, R.A. (1964), "A reply: Capital mobility and size", Canadian Journal of Economics and Political Science, 30:421–431.

Mundell, R.A. (1968), International Economics (Macmillan, New York).

Mussa, M. (1976), "The exchange rate, the balance of payments and monetary and fiscal policy under a regime of controlled floating", Scandinavian Journal of Economics, 78:229–248.

Mussa, M. (1979), "Macroeconomic interdependence and the exchange rate regime", in: R. Dornbusch and J.A. Frenkel, eds., International Economic Policy (Johns Hopkins University Press, Baltimore) 160–204.

Modigliani, F. and T. Padoa-Schioppa (1978), The management of an open economy with "100% plus" wage indexation, Essays in international finance, No. 130 (International Finance Section, Princeton).

Obstfeld, M. (1981), "Macroeconomic policy, exchange-rate dynamics, and optimal asset accumulation", Journal of Political Economy, 89:1142–1161.

Obstfeld, M. (1982), "Exchange rates, inflation, and the sterilization problem: Germany, 1975–1981", European Economic Review, forthcoming.

Phelps, E.S. and J.B. Taylor (1977), "Stabilizing powers of monetary policy under rational expectations", Journal of Political Economy, 85:163–190.

Poole, W. (1970), "Optimal choice of monetary policy instruments in a simple stochastic macro model", Quarterly Journal of Economics, 84:197–216.

Purvis, D.D. (1979), "Wage responsiveness and the insulation properties of a flexible exchange rate", in: A. Lindbeck, ed., Inflation and Employment in Open Economies (North-Holland, Amsterdam) 225–245.

Robinson, J. (1937), The foreign exchanges, Essays in the Theory of Employment (Macmillan, New York).

Roper, D.E. and S.J. Turnovsky (1980), "Optimal exchange market intervention in a simple stochastic macro model", Canadian Journal of Economics, 13:296–309.

Sachs, J. (1980), "Wage indexation, flexible exchange rates and macroeconomic policy", Quarterly Journal of Economics, 94:731–747.

Saidi, N.H. (1980), "Fluctuating exchange rates and the international transmission of economic disturbances", Journal of Money Credit and Banking, 12:575–591.

Salop, J. (1974), "Devaluation and the balance of trade under flexible wages", in: G. Horwich and P. Samuelson, eds., Trade, Stability and Macroeconomics (Academic Press, New York).

Sargent, T.J. and N. Wallace (1975), "'Rational' expectations, the optimal monetary instrument and the optimal money supply rule", Journal of Political Economy, 83:241–254.

Shiller, R.J. (1978), "Rational expectations and the dynamic structure of macroeconomic models: A critical review", Journal of Monetary Economics, 4:1–44.

Taylor, J.B. (1980), "Aggregate dynamics and staggered contracts", Journal of Political Economy, 88:1–23.

Tinbergen, J. (1952), On the theory of economic policy (North-Holland, Amsterdam).

Tobin, J. and J.B. de Macedo (1980), "The short-run macroeconomics of floating exchange rates: An exposition", in: J. Chipman and C.P. Kindleberger, eds., Flexible Exchange Rates and the Balance of Payments: Essays in Memory of Egon Sohmen (North-Holland, Amsterdam) 5–28.

Tower, E. and T.D. Willett (1976), "The theory of optimum currency areas and exchange rate flexibility", Special Papers in International Economics, No. 11 (International Finance Section, Princeton).

Tsiang, S.C. (1961), "The role of money in trade balance stability: Synthesis of the elasticity and absorption approaches", American Economic Review, 51:912–936.

Turnovsky, S.J. (1976), "The dynamics of fiscal policy in an open economy", Journal of International Economics, 6:115–142.

Turnovsky, S.J. (1980a), "The choice of monetary instrument under alternative forms of price expectations", Manchester School, 48:39–62.

Turnovsky, S.J. (1980b), "The effectiveness of monetary and fiscal policy rules in an open economy under rational expectations", unpublished.

Turnovsky, S.J. (1981), "Monetary policy and foreign price disturbances under flexible exchange rates", Journal of Money, Credit and Banking, 13:156–176.

Weiss, L. (1980), "The role of active monetary policy in a rational expectations model", Journal of Political Economy, 88:221–233.

Whitman, M.v.N. (1970), "Policies for internal and external balance", Special Papers in: International Economics, No. 9 (International Finance Section, Princeton).

Whitman, N.v.N. (1975), "Global monetarism and the monetary approach to the balance of payments", Brookings Papers on Economic Activity 3, 491–536.

Willett, T.D. and F. Forte (1969), "Interest rate policy and external balance", Quarterly Journal of Economics, 83:242–262.

Chapter 18

EXCHANGE-RATE DYNAMICS

MAURICE OBSTFELD

Columbia University and National Bureau of Economic Research

and

ALAN C. STOCKMAN*

University of Rochester and National Bureau of Economic Research

Contents

*We acknowledge with thanks the extremely helpful suggestions of the editors, Ronald Findlay, and Lars Svensson. Useful comments were made by participants in the National Bureau of Economic Research 1983 Summer Institute in International Studies. The research reported here was supported by grants from the National Science Foundation.

Handbook of International Economics, vol. II, edited by R.W. Jones and P.B. Kenen
© *Elsevier Science Publishers B.V., 1985*

1. Introduction

This chapter discusses the dynamic behavior of exchange rates. It focuses on both the exchange rate's response to exogenous disturbances and the relation between exchange-rate movements and movements in such endogenous variables as nominal and relative prices, interest rates, output, and the current account. These questions are addressed in a variety of models, some of which are based on postulated supply and demand functions for assets and goods, and some of which are based on an explicit utility-maximizing problem. Similar models are studied elsewhere in this Handbook (especially in Chapter 14 by Frenkel and Mussa, in Chapter 15 by Branson and Henderson, and in Chapter 17 by Marston), but the approach taken here is different. We do not attempt to present a single, unifying model that encompasses as special cases those discussed in the literature. Instead, we try to emphasize the common or unique features of the alternative models.

An ideal treatment of exchange-rate dynamics would begin by summarizing the relevant characteristics of the empirical record. All key features of the stochastic processes that appear to govern exchange rates and other statistically related economic variables would be catalogued. Then, a set of models that are compatible with at least some of the observed relationships would be presented. The discussion would point to features of the models that are consistent with the data and to features that are not; and it would highlight implications that might allow economists to distinguish among alternative models through future empirical research.

We have not attempted to attain this ideal, in large part because it would be premature to do so on the basis of our limited data on exchange-rate behavior. Only a few central banks have allowed more than intermittent floating, and the time series covering even extended periods of floating are relatively short. Thus, while high-frequency characteristics of exchange-rate changes have been studied with some success in recent years, studies of the lower-frequency characteristics of exchange-rate changes, corresponding to periodicities more common to macroeconomic phenomena, have proven less conclusive [Meese and Rogoff (1983), Shafer and Loopesko (1983)]. Another shortcoming of our data is the absence of quantifiable information about inherently unobservable market expectations. As the chapter illustrates, alternative expectational scenarios can give rise to very different empirical correlations between exchange-rate movements and changes in other observable variables.

In the face of limited data, economists have naturally concentrated their research on models consistent with what appear to be the stylized facts of the interwar and post-1973 experiences with floating. Earlier studies, which drew on the hyperinflationary episodes of the interwar period, emphasized the key role of monetary factors in exchange-rate determination [Frenkel (1976)]. The more moderate inflation and repeated real shocks of the post-1973 period highlight different empirical regularities, however. Among these are the strong correlations between exchange-rate movements and movements in terms of trade, the high variability of exchange rates compared to that of international price-level ratios, and the on-again, off-again relationship between the exchange rate and the current account [Genberg (1978), Frenkel and Mussa (1980), Flood (1981), Shafer and Loopesko (1983)]. All the models discussed in this chapter grew out of attempts to reconcile exchange-rate theory with at least some of these stylized facts.

Along with the empirical regularities, the rational-expectations "revolution" in macroeconomics has had an important impact on exchange-rate theory. The models reviewed below reflect that intellectual development in a number of ways. Following Black (1973), these models endow agents with rational expectations about the future. Some extend the recent closed-economy business-cycle literature by exploring channels through which money can exert a persistent influence on output in open economies. Finally, Lucas's (1976) celebrated critique of policy evaluation finds expression in the attempts described below to base dynamic exchange-rate theory on the explicit intertemporal optimization problems of individual agents.

A recurring theme of the chapter is the distinction we make between the *intrinsic* and *extrinsic* sources of an economy's dynamics. An intrinsic source of dynamics causes movement even when all exogenous variables that affect the economy are expected to remain constant forever. An example of intrinsic dynamic behavior is the adjustment of the capital stock to its steady-state level in a growth model. In contrast, extrinsic dynamics are associated exclusively with current or anticipated future changes in exogenous variables. A system with extrinsic dynamics only is stationary in the absence of such external shocks. Our distinction between intrinsic and extrinsic dynamics corresponds closely to Samuelson's (1947) distinction between "causal" and "historical" dynamic systems.

The chapter is organized as follows. Section 2 explores the simplest model in which the relation among the exchange rate, price levels, and the terms of trade can be addressed. This flexible-price, small-country model allows domestic and foreign consumption goods to be imperfect substitutes, but it includes no monetary non-neutralities and no intrinsic dynamics. Even so, the model predicts that current or anticipated future real shocks will induce simultaneous movements of the nominal exchange rate and the terms of trade. Furthermore, exchange rates may be more volatile than price levels when real shocks are dominant. While the exchange rate certainly displays asset-price characteristics, it also plays a role in accommodating required shifts in relative goods prices. The exchange rate's behavior is thus affected both by forces emphasized in the monetary approach to the exchange rate (see Frenkel and Mussa, Chapter 14 in this Handbook) and by forces emphasized in the older elasticities approach.

Section 3 introduces market frictions so that the role of endogenous output fluctuations can be studied. Section 3.1 alters the previous section's model by assuming that the money price of domestic goods is a predetermined or non-jumping variable that must adjust gradually in the face of goods-market disequilibrium. The assumption of domestic price stickiness reinforces both the correlation between exchange-rate and terms-of-trade changes and the high short-run variability of the exchange rate compared to that of international price-level ratios. Moreover, the price-adjustment process through which goods-market imbalance is gradually eliminated adds an intrinsic component to the economy's dynamics. These intrinsic dynamics are reflected in the persistent effects of disturbances on output, prices, and interest rates. Section 3.2 investigates alternative market frictions (and alternative sources of persistence) based on more detailed descriptions of the institutional or informational environment. Some of the models are stochastic, and their solution involves rules for inducing a probability distribution function on the exchange rate from the probability distributions of various exogenous variables. These solutions are different from those of the previous deterministic models, whose equilibria can be conveniently represented as solutions to systems of differential equations.

Section 4 returns to a setting of frictionless markets to study the links between asset accumulation and the exchange rate. The adjustment of foreign assets and domestic capital to their steady-state levels provide new sources of intrinsic dynamic behavior. Within this framework, it is shown that the relationship between the exchange rate and current account, even along paths converging to a fixed long-run equilibrium, is very loose. The models studied here reveal channels through which money can influence real variables even in the absence of market frictions.

Section 5 examines deterministic and stochastic models in which individual behavior is derived from an explicit intertemporal optimization problem. These models serve at least three related purposes. First, they are suggestive of assumptions under which the aggregate behavioral relations postulated in previous sections' models are consistent with individual maximizing behavior. Second, they provide a natural setting in which some welfare consequences of macroeconomic policies can be assessed. Third, because they are built up on the basis of preferences that are invariant with respect to policy change, they provide vehicles for policy analysis that are less vulnerable than models discussed earlier to Lucas's (1976) critique. Money is introduced into these optimizing models in rather ad hoc ways, however, so their immunity to Lucas's criticisms is less than total. Nonetheless, the approach discussed in this section leads to a deeper perspective on the possible causes of the observed empirical regularities.

Section 6 contains concluding remarks.

2. Expectations and the exchange rate in a simple flexible-price model

This section studies exchange-rate determination in a rational-expectations model with flexible prices. The model abstracts from the possible intrinsic sources of dynamics to be introduced in Sections 3 and 4 below, and thus highlights the extrinsic component of exchange-rate dynamics. As was noted in Section 1, intrinsic dynamics lead to changes in a model's endogenous variables that need not be associated with current or expected future changes in the levels of exogenous variables that impinge on the economy. Extrinsic dynamics, in contrast, arise exclusively in response to such exogenous events.

The model set out, which comes from Mussa (1977, 1982), displays some important channels through which current and anticipated future disturbances, both monetary and real, affect exchange rates. In addition, it illustrates the implications of rational expectations for exchange-rate dynamics. (The environment assumed in this section is non-stochastic, so "rational expectations" is equivalent to "perfect foresight" here.) The model also provides a useful benchmark for the analysis in later sections, particularly the discussion of exchange-rate dynamics under short-run price inflexibility in Section 3.

2.1. The model

Consider a small open economy specialized in the production of a good that is an imperfect substitute in consumption for an imported good.[1] Wealth may be held in the form of domestic fiat money (which is not held by foreigners) or in the form of interest-bearing bonds. Bonds denominated in either domestic or foreign currency are available, but these are perfect substitutes in portfolios. Thus, any difference between the nominal returns they offer is offset exactly by an expected change in the exchange rate.[2] The resulting (uncovered) interest-parity condition is written as

$$r_t = r_t^* + \dot{e}_t, \tag{2.1}$$

where r is the nominal interest rate on domestic-currency bonds, r^* is the rate on foreign-currency bonds, and e is the natural logarithm of the exchange rate,

---

[1] The economy is small in the sense that it faces a given foreign interest rate and a given foreign price of imports. However, the economy faces a downward-sloping demand curve for its export good. An alternative assumption, which yields a similar model, is that the economy produces both a traded good priced in the world market and a non-traded good priced at home [Dornbusch (1976a)]. Sections 3 and 5 below study models with non-traded goods.

[2] A number of recent econometric studies reject this hypothesis (see Chapter 19 by Levich in this Handbook). No alternative model of nominal interest differentials has received much statistical support, however, so it seems reasonable to entertain the perfect substitution hypothesis as a close empirical approximation for some applications.

defined as the price of foreign money in terms of domestic money. (A rise in e is a depreciation of the currency.) Unless otherwise noted, lower-case letters denote natural logarithms of the corresponding upper-case variables, except when representing rates of interest. A dot denotes a variable's (right-hand) time derivative.

Assume that agents have perfect foresight concerning all disturbances other than initial, unanticipated shocks that dislodge the economy from its previously expected trajectory. Perfect foresight is an assumption of convenience, and we could easily transplant the model explored here to an explicitly stochastic setting without changing its main implications [Mussa (1982)]. The perfect-foresight assumption permits us to identify the expected rate of change of the exchange rate with the actual rate of change.

Let m denote the nominal money supply (an exogenous variable under a floating exchange rate), p the home-currency price of domestic output, p^* the foreign-currency price of imports, γ the share of the home good in domestic consumption, and y domestic output. Equilibrium in the money market requires that

$$m_t - \gamma p_t - (1 - \gamma)(e_t + p_t^*) = \psi\left[p_t + y_t - \gamma p_t - (1 - \gamma)(e_t + p_t^*)\right] - \lambda r_t,$$

$$\psi \le 1. \qquad (2.2)$$

The left-hand side of (2.2) represents real money balances expressed in terms of the appropriate consumer-price index. Note that (2.2) can be rewritten as

$$m_t - \alpha p_t - (1 - \alpha)(e_t + p_t^*) = \psi y_t - \lambda r_t, \qquad (2.3)$$

where $\alpha \equiv \gamma + \psi(1 - \gamma)$.

We assume that aggregate (domestic plus foreign) demand for domestic output, d, is negatively related to the contemporaneous relative price of the domestic good in terms of the foreign good, $p - e - p^*$. If the relative price were constant over time, there would be a unique intertemporal price of consumption at time t_0 in terms of consumption at any other time t_1; and this relative price would depend only on the path of $r - \dot{p}$. If the contemporaneous relative price of domestic and foreign goods changes over time, however, there are two intertemporal relative prices between any two dates t_0 and t_1, one in terms of domestic goods and one in terms of foreign goods. For purposes of the present benchmark model, we assume that aggregate demand depends on an *average* intertemporal price expressed in terms of the home consumption bundle. We also assume that only the "instantaneous" average intertemporal relative price, the domestic real interest rate $r - \gamma\dot{p} - (1 - \gamma)(\dot{e} + \dot{p}^*)$, affects aggregate demand.[3]

---

[3] This assumption implies very strong restrictions on the form of any underlying optimization problem, as it severely limits the allowable substitutions between goods at different points in time. Note that the domestic real interest rate defined here can differ from the world real interest rate $r^* - \dot{p}^*$.

Under the foregoing assumptions, aggregate demand is given by

$$d_t = \phi\left(e_t + p_t^* - p_t\right) - \sigma\left[r_t - \gamma \dot{p}_t - (1 - \gamma)\left(\dot{e}_t + \dot{p}_t^*\right)\right] + g_t, \tag{2.4}$$

where g is a demand-shift factor such as government consumption. In this flexible-price model, aggregate demand must always equal the natural or full-employment level of output $\bar{y}$:

$$d_t = \bar{y}_t. \tag{2.5}$$

Note that the terms of trade between domestic and foreign goods are endogenously determined. In contrast, the paths of p^* and r^* are exogenously determined in world markets where the economy under study plays an insignificant part.

The model may be reduced to a system of two non-autonomous differential equations in e and p:

$$\dot{e}_t = \frac{1 - \alpha}{\lambda}\left(e_t + p_t^*\right) + \frac{\alpha}{\lambda} p_t - \frac{1}{\lambda} x_t - \dot{p}_t^*, \tag{2.6}$$

$$\dot{p}_t = \left(\frac{1 - \alpha}{\lambda} - \frac{\phi}{\sigma\gamma}\right)\left(e_t + p_t^*\right) + \left(\frac{\alpha}{\lambda} + \frac{\phi}{\sigma\gamma}\right) p_t - \frac{1}{\sigma\gamma} z_t - \frac{1}{\lambda} x_t, \tag{2.7}$$

where x and z are linear combinations of exogenous variables:

$$x_t \equiv m_t - \psi \bar{y}_t + \lambda\left(r_t^* - \dot{p}_t^*\right), \tag{2.8}$$

$$z_t \equiv g_t - \bar{y}_t - \sigma\left(r_t^* - \dot{p}_t^*\right). \tag{2.9}$$

Let $\omega = \phi/\sigma\gamma$. A general solution to the differential-equation system is:

$$e_t = k_1 \exp\left(\frac{t}{\lambda}\right) - \frac{k_2 \alpha \exp(\omega t)}{1 - \alpha - \lambda\omega} + \frac{1}{\lambda} \int_t^\infty \exp\left[\frac{(t - s)}{\lambda}\right] x_s \, ds$$

$$+ \frac{\alpha\omega}{1 - \lambda\omega} \int_t^\infty \left\{\exp\left[\frac{(t - s)}{\lambda}\right] - \exp[\omega(t - s)]\right\}\left(\frac{z_s}{\phi}\right) ds - p_t^*, \tag{2.10}$$

$$p_t = k_1 \exp\left(\frac{t}{\lambda}\right) + k_2 \exp(\omega t) + \frac{1}{\lambda} \int_t^\infty \exp\left[\frac{(t - s)}{\lambda}\right] x_s \, ds$$

$$+ \frac{\alpha\omega}{1 - \lambda\omega} \int_t^\infty \exp\left[\frac{(t - s)}{\lambda}\right]\left(\frac{z_s}{\phi}\right) ds$$

$$+ \frac{\omega(1 - \alpha - \lambda\omega)}{1 - \lambda\omega} \int_t^\infty \exp[\omega(t - s)]\left(\frac{z_s}{\phi}\right) ds, \tag{2.11}$$

where k_1 and k_2 are arbitrary constants [see, for example, Hirsch and Smale (1974)].

The arbitrary constants k_1 and k_2 reflect a fundamental indeterminacy in models assuming rational expectations or perfect foresight. The indeterminacy is a consequence of the self-fulfilling nature of those expectations. Returning to (2.1) and (2.3), we note that, given p, any level of the exchange rate is consistent with money-market equilibrium provided the perfectly-foreseen depreciation rate $\dot{e}$ satisfies (2.6). Similarly, (2.4) implies that any price p clears the goods market, given e and r, provided the rate of price increase $\dot{p}$, and hence the real interest rate, is appropriate. Because a higher e requires a higher $\dot{e}$, ceteris paribus, to clear the money market, and because a higher p calls for a higher $\dot{p}$, ceteris paribus, to clear the goods market, the characteristic roots λ^{-1} and ω of the differential-equation system given by (2.6) and (2.7) are positive. Because the constants k_1 and k_2 multiply time exponentials in those positive roots, any particular solution for e and p in which k_1 or k_2 differs from zero will entail explosive price behavior unrelated to market "fundamentals" – what might be called a "speculative bubble", since prices explode only because they are expected to do so [Sargent and Wallace (1973), Flood and Garber (1980)].

It has become standard in the exchange-rate literature to resolve this indeterminacy by identifying as *the* equilibrium of the economy the (hopefully) unique market-clearing price vector which excludes such speculative bubbles.[4] In the present context, this amounts to taking as the equilibrium exchange rate and domestic-goods price the particular solution to (2.6) and (2.7) incorporating the initial conditions $k_1 = k_2 = 0$. This choice of initial conditions is said to place the economy on its *saddle path*. The saddle-path assumption is an appealing one because it stipulates that prices depend only on current and expected future demand and supply conditions in markets; further, as we shall see, the assumption yields intuitively reasonable results.[5] The saddle-path solutions for the flexible-price equilibrium exchange rate and domestic-goods price, given by (2.6) and (2.7) with $k_1 = k_2 = 0$, are denoted by $\tilde{e}$ and $\tilde{p}$.

Denote the price of exports in terms of imports by $q = p - e - p^*$. We will refer to q as the terms of trade. (It is sometimes referred to as the real exchange rate, though we will reserve that term for its other common usage as the price of non-traded in terms of traded goods.) Along the saddle path

$$\tilde{q}_t = \omega \int_t^\infty \exp[\omega(t-s)] \left\{ \left[g_s - \bar{y}_s - \sigma(r_s^* - \dot{p}_s^*) \right] / \phi \right\} ds. \qquad (2.12)$$

Several features of these solutions are worthy of note. As (2.12) shows, the equilibrium terms of trade are independent of domestic and foreign monetary factors. $\tilde{q}$ depends exclusively on current and anticipated future shocks to real

---

[4]Sargent and Wallace (1973) proposed this convention for monetary perfect-foresight models. While the exclusion of bubbles typically results in a unique equilibrium (as in the present case), there exist "badly-behaved" models with multiple convergent equilibrium paths. [See Calvo (1979) for an example.] Such models possess multiple rational-expectations equilibria.

[5]Obstfeld and Rogoff (1983), building on work by Brock (1975), describe conditions under which the saddle path can be identified as the unique equilibrium path in an economy of infinitely-lived maximizing agents similar to the one studied in Section 5.1 below.

variables: aggregate demand, aggregate supply, and the world real interest rate, $r^* - \dot{p}^*$. In other words, purely *monetary* disturbances induce proportional movements in exchange rates and international price-level ratios, as purchasing power parity theory would predict. Because the domestic real interest rate can be written as $r^* - \gamma\dot{q} - \dot{p}^*$, it is also unaffected by monetary developments. Thus, the flexible-price model developed here implies a complete dichotomy between the real and monetary sectors.

Real as well as monetary disturbances can affect the exchange rate, however. In fact, any real disturbance requiring a movement in the equilibrium terms of trade must be accommodated in part through an exchange rate change and in part through a change in home goods prices, with the overall price *level* moving so as to maintain money-market equilibrium [Stockman (1980), Obstfeld (1980), Mussa (1982), Helpman and Razin (1982), Lucas (1982), Sachs (1983a)]. For example, (2.12) shows that a permanent shift in the path of aggregate demand from $\{g_s\}_{s=t}^\infty$ to $\{g_s + \Delta g\}_{s=t}^\infty$ causes the terms of trade to rise by $\Delta\tilde{q}_t = \Delta g/\phi$. To bring this rise about, the exchange rate $\tilde{e}_t$ falls (the domestic currency appreciates) by $\Delta\tilde{e}_t = -\alpha(\Delta g/\phi)$, while the output price $\tilde{p}_t$ rises by $\Delta\tilde{p}_t = (1-\alpha)(\Delta g/\phi)$. The corresponding change in the consumer price index is $\gamma\Delta\tilde{p}_t + (1-\gamma)\Delta\tilde{e}_t = -\psi(1 - \gamma)(\Delta g/\phi)$, while the change in the value of domestic output (in terms of the consumption bundle) is $(1-\gamma)(\Delta\tilde{p}_t - \Delta\tilde{e}_t) = (1-\gamma)(\Delta g/\phi)$. The increased demand for money (due to the increase in real income) exactly matches the fall in the consumer price index, so money-market equilibrium is maintained [see (2.2)]. The exchange rate's role in equilibrating the domestic goods market is reminiscent of the traditional elasticities approach to the exchange rate.

Note that if $\gamma = 1$ or $\psi = 0$, the consumer price index is unaffected even though the exchange rate falls. Also note that, depending on the value of α, the change in the exchange rate may be larger or smaller in absolute value than the change in the nominal price of domestic goods. Consequently, the model can be consistent with the empirical observation that exchange rates are often more volatile than the nominal prices of goods [Flood (1981)].

A corollary of the foregoing observations is that a negative correlation between movements in exchange rates and changes in the terms of trade need not imply any stickiness in domestic-goods prices. The demand shock Δg analyzed above forces the exchange rate to appreciate in real as well as nominal terms, but it does not induce goods-market disequilibrium. Nominal price rigidities can cause exchange rates and terms of trade to move in opposite directions even in response to monetary shocks, but the pattern may also emerge as the equilibrium response of the economy to real disturbances requiring adjustment in relative goods prices.

The saddle-path solutions for $\tilde{e}$ and $\tilde{p}$ imply that a change in p^*, given the paths of r^* and $\dot{p}^*$, is exactly offset by an equal and opposite change in e, so that p and q are unaffected. A flexible exchange rate therefore insulates the domestic economy against this disturbance. Similarly, the domestic economy is completely insulated against a change in the foreign inflation rate p^* if the foreign nominal interest rate fully reflects this change.[6]

The domestic economy is not insulated against foreign real disturbances, however. A change in the foreign real interest rate $r^* - p^*$ affects both p and q as well as e. A permanent, unanticipated increase in r^* alone, for example, causes the terms of trade to change by the amount $-\sigma/\phi$. This fall in the terms of trade is accommodated partly through a depreciation of the domestic currency ($\mathrm{d}\tilde{e}/\mathrm{d}r^* = \lambda + (\alpha\sigma/\phi)$) and partly through a change in the nominal price of the domestic good ($\mathrm{d}\tilde{p}/\mathrm{d}r^* = \lambda - [(1 - \alpha)\sigma/\phi]$).

2.2. Anticipated future disturbances

Although the model just described has no intrinsic dynamics, prices will move over in time in response to *anticipated* changes in exogenous variables. Only when the exogenous variables are expected to be constant forever will e and p be constant as well. To illustrate these extrinsic dynamics we consider the economy's response to a permanent increase in the money supply that is announced to the public in advance of its occurrence. The exercise [similar to those performed by Sargent and Wallace (1973) and Brock (1975) for closed economies] yields some important insights into exchange-rate and price behavior under rational expectations.

To fix ideas, it is assumed that, prior to the announcement at time $t = 0$ that the money stock will increase by an amount Δm at time $t = T > 0$, the money stock was expected to remain constant at level $\bar{m}$ forever. If we add the assumption that all other exogenous variables remain fixed throughout, then the economy is in a stationary state, prior to $t = 0$, with $\tilde{e} = \bar{x} - \alpha\bar{z}/\phi - \bar{p}^*$ and $\tilde{p} = \bar{x} + (1 - \alpha)\bar{z}/\phi$. Here, $\bar{x}$ and $\bar{z}$ are given by (2.8) and (2.9) evaluated at the constant levels of the exogenous variables (with $\dot{p}^* = 0$) and $\bar{p}^*$ is the fixed foreign-goods price. The announcement of the future policy action causes the exchange rate and domestic-goods price to jump upward immediately. The path of the economy from $t = 0$

---

[6]It can be verified that if r^* and $\dot{p}^*$ rise permanently by equal amounts, the paths of p and r are unaffected and the level of e does not change immediately. However, the currency begins to appreciate over time so as to offset rising foreign prices and the higher level of r^*. This result may seem strange: a rise in foreign trend inflation should be associated with a rise in foreign monetary growth and hence an appreciation of the domestic currency. The reason e does not jump immediately in the present model is the small country assumption, which artificially holds p^* constant when foreign inflation rises. In a two-country model, an increase in foreign money growth would move the exchange rate on impact.

onward is described by

$$\tilde{e}_t = \begin{cases} \bar{x} + \exp[(t-T)/\lambda]\,\Delta m - \alpha \bar{z}/\phi - \bar{p}^* & (0 \le t < T), \\ \bar{x} + \Delta m - \alpha \bar{z}/\phi - \bar{p}^* & (t \ge T), \end{cases} \tag{2.13}$$

$$\tilde{p}_t = \begin{cases} \bar{x} + \exp[(t-T)/\lambda]\,\Delta m + (1-\alpha)\bar{z}/\phi & (0 \le t < T), \\ \bar{x} + \Delta m + (1-\alpha)\bar{z}/\phi & (t \ge T). \end{cases} \tag{2.14}$$

Both e and p jump by $\exp(-T/\lambda)\Delta m$ at $t = 0$ and then rise smoothly until $t = T$, when their new stationary values are attained. The terms of trade are at no time affected by this purely monetary disturbance.

It is important to note that neither the exchange rate nor the price of domestic output jumps when the money stock jumps at time $t = T$. Between times 0 and T, the exchange rate depreciates at an accelerating pace, inducing a rising nominal interest rate that maintains money-market equilibrium as the price level rises and real balances shrink. At time T, when the money supply is increased, the depreciation rate drops to zero and the home interest rate drops back to the constant world level r^*. The interest rate's fall creates an increase in real money demand just equal to the increase in the real money supply at the current price level, removing any need for a discrete jump in e or p at that moment.

The economic explanation of this result is fundamental. The jump in prices at time $t = 0$ discounts to the present the expected future monetary expansion and thereby eliminates the possibility of an anticipated discrete jump in the exchange rate (and the price of domestic goods) along the economy's subsequent path. To see how the market discounts expected future events in this manner, suppose that a sharp jump in the exchange rate could occur at time T. Because such a jump would imply an instantaneously infinite real rate of capital loss on domestic-currency assets, investors would have an incentive to move into foreign exchange an instant before time T, causing e (and p) to jump earlier than expected. The contradiction is removed if prices jump only at time $t = 0$, when the news of the future disturbance first arrives.[7]

---

[7]Does the discrete, anticipated fall in the interest rate r at time T represents a violation of this principle? The answer is no, essentially because the short-term interest rate r is the nominal return on a bond of instantaneous maturity. What cannot jump, in the present setting, is the price of a long-term bond or consol. If P^C represents the price of a consol and C is the coupon payment, then, under perfect substitution, the short-term interest rate must satisfy the arbitrage condition $r = (C + \dot{P}^C)/P^C$ equating instantaneous returns on short- and long-term assets. The saddle-path solution for P^C as a function of the coupon C and expected future short rates is:

$$P_t^C = \int_t^\infty C \cdot \exp\left(-\int_t^s r_\tau \, d\tau\right) ds.$$

Thus, P^C does not jump when an anticipated discrete jump in r occurs. Rogoff (1979) studies the impact of anticipated monetary disturbances on the term structure of interest rates. For a more detailed discussion of the asset-price continuity condition, see Calvo (1977).

Another implication of the rational-expectations assumption deserves emphasis. In a world where prices move in anticipation of future events, one may not
observe any clear correlation between exchange-rate movements and *contemporaneous* movements in the exogenous determinants of the exchange rate. The
example given above shows that prices rise in advance of an expected money-
supply increase; if the increase is permanent, prices and money will have risen
proportionally by the time the money stock rises. There is an additional problem
in a world with uncertainty: the exchange rate may react sharply to heightened
probabilities of future policies which do not actually materialize, even though it
was reasonable ex ante to expect that they might. Partly for this reason, attempts
to explain historical exchange-rate movements in terms of observable "fundamentals" have often been unconvincing.

It is instructive to examine the features of the model that produce the dynamics
described above. The two key parameters that generate current responses to
anticipated future disturbances are the interest elasticity of the demand for money
(λ) and the interest elasticity of aggregate demand for domestic output (σ). It is
easy to see that if both λ and σ are zero, then neither e nor p responds to
anticipated future changes in any exogenous variable until those changes actually
occur.[8] The absence of any interest-rate sensitivity severs the link between the
present and the future in this section's model.

If the interest elasticity of money demand is negative ($\lambda > 0$) but $\sigma = 0$, the
model can be written as a single differential equation in e, together with an
equation for p:

$$\dot{e}_t = \frac{(e_t + p_t^*)}{\lambda} - \frac{1}{\lambda}\left(x_t - \frac{\alpha z_t}{\phi}\right) - \dot{p}_t^*, \tag{2.15}$$

$$\tilde{p}_t = \tilde{e}_t + p_t^* + z_t/\phi. \tag{2.16}$$

Here, z is given by (2.9) with $\sigma = 0$. Now anticipated future changes in m, $\bar{y}$, g,

---

It is apparent from (2.10) and the definitions of the forcing functions x and z that anticipated
discrete jumps in the foreign price level p^* have no impact on the exchange rate until the moment
they occur (provided the expected paths of the other exogenous variables are not simultaneously
affected). This fact does appear to contradict the asset-price continuity condition, since an anticipated
discrete jump in p^* then implies an equal and opposite anticipated discrete jump in e. The
small-country assumption is again responsible for this rather artificial violation of the continuity
condition (cf. footnote 6 above). Because anticipated discrete jumps in p^* would generally be
impossible in an explicit two-country model, the problem would not arise; and we therefore assume in
what follows that the path of p^* is expected to be continuous.
    [8]This is also a property of the Lucas (1982) model discussed in Section 5.2. When $\lambda = \sigma = 0$, $\tilde{e}$ and
$\tilde{p}$ are given by $\tilde{e}_t = m_t + [(\alpha - \psi\phi)/\phi]\bar{y}_t - (\alpha/\phi)g_t - p_t^*$ and $\tilde{p}_t = m_t - [(1 - \alpha + \psi\phi)/\phi]\bar{y}_t + [(1 - \alpha)/\phi]g_t$. It is important to keep in mind that many of the anticipated discrete price jumps possible in
the small-country case when $\sigma = 0$ or $\lambda = 0$ would be impossible in a two-country model if the
corresponding foreign interest elasticities differed from zero.

or $r^* - \dot{p}^*$ affect the current exchange rate and home-output price, since the saddle-path solution to (2.15) is

$$\tilde{e}_t = (1/\lambda) \int_t^\infty (x_s - \alpha z_s/\phi) \exp[(t-s)/\lambda] \, ds - p_t^*. \qquad (2.17)$$

However, it is obvious from (2.9) and (2.16) that the terms of trade $\tilde{q} = (g - \bar{y})/\phi$ are unaffected by these anticipated future changes (given the current values of $\bar{y}$ and g). Thus, while e cannot make anticipated discrete jumps, p and q can. Anticipated discrete terms-of-trade jumps imply instantaneously infinite expected domestic real interest rates. But when $\sigma = 0$, there is no incentive for the market to smooth such jumps through intertemporal substitution in consumption.

Although current real variables are unaffected by changes in anticipations of future variables in this case, current nominal variables are affected by changes in anticipations of both future nominal and future real variables. For example, the exchange-rate effect of an increase in anticipated future domestic output is ambiguous and works through two channels. First, by increasing the future demand for money and reducing the future price level and exchange rate, it increases the current demand for money and reduces the current price level and exchange rate. This effect is captured by the term x_s in (2.17). Second, a future increase in output reduces future q, partly through a rise in e. The expected fall in q is larger the smaller is ϕ, and the fraction of the fall in q that occurs as an increase in e is larger the larger is α. This second factor tends to raise the current price level and exchange rate by reducing current money demand. Its effect is captured by the term z_s in (2.17).

If the interest elasticity of aggregate demand is negative ($\sigma > 0$) but $\lambda = 0$, then the model becomes:

$$\dot{q}_t = \omega q_t + \left[\bar{y}_t - g_t + \sigma(r_t^* - \dot{p}_t^*) \right]/\sigma\gamma, \qquad (2.18)$$

$$\tilde{p}_t = m_t + (1 - \alpha)\tilde{q}_t - \psi\bar{y}_t. \qquad (2.19)$$

[Eq. (2.19) is an open-economy analogue of the monetary equilibrium condition postulated in the classical quantity theory of money.] The saddle-path solution to (2.18) is eq. (2.12); the exchange rate is given by

$$\tilde{e}_t = m_t - \alpha\tilde{q}_t - \psi\bar{y}_t - p_t^*. \qquad (2.20)$$

With intertemporal substitution in the goods market ($\sigma > 0$), the current terms of trade are naturally a function of future values of real variables. Discrete anticipated jumps in q are not possible. But while the exchange rate is a function of current and future values of the real variables in the model, it is not a function of future money supplies. When $\lambda = 0$, expected sharp jumps in e (and p) clearly can occur.

The influence of future real variables on e is greater for greater values of α, while the effect of future variables on p approaches zero as γ (and hence α) approaches one. Values of γ close to one are thus consistent with the idea that changes in expected future real variables have a large effect on the current exchange rate but a small effect on the current nominal price of domestic goods. (In a sense, $\gamma = 1$ means that both the exchange rate and terms of trade behave as "asset prices" – they depend on a whole time path of future real variables – while the nominal price of domestic goods does not.)

2.3. Expected regime change and exchange-rate dynamics

The discussion has so far neglected the possibility of drastic institutional or structural changes in the economy. This section is concerned with the influence of expected regime change on exchange-rate behavior. The problems involved are illustrated by the example of an anticipated future return to a fixed exchange rate. Future exchange-rate pegging implies an expected transition from a regime in which the money supply is exogenous and the exchange rate is endogenous to one in which the money supply is endogenously determined.

Models involving regime change have their roots in papers by Salant and Henderson (1978) and Salant (1983) describing the breakdown of government price-fixing schemes in natural resource markets. Salant and Henderson showed that under rational expectations, the timing of speculative attacks on government resource stockpiles can be uniquely determined by the familiar requirement (cf. Section 2.2) that the resource price not make an anticipated discrete jump as speculators acquire the government's reserves. Krugman (1979) extended their analysis to the foreign exchange market, demonstrating that the date at which a fixed exchange rate collapses in a sudden balance-of-payments crisis is also well defined in terms of official policies and private preferences. Flood and Garber (1983) use a stochastic model to study the problem that concerns us in this section, the influence of expected future fixing on the behavior of a currently floating exchange rate.[9]

A return to fixed exchange rates is analyzed in two steps. First, we ask what the value of the exchange rate must be just after the regime change occurs. Second,

---

[9]The analysis here differs from that in Flood and Garber (1983) because we assume agents know the date at which the return to fixed rates will take place. Flood and Garber allow that date to be endogenously determined as the date of the exchange rate's first passage through its new peg, but they are able to obtain a determinate solution to their problem only through the tacit assumption that central-bank foreign reserves are not expected to jump at the moment of pegging. No theoretical justification for such an assumption has been suggested, however.

we determine the extent to which the current exchange rate must discount the expected future event if there is to be no sharp jump in prices at the moment the event takes place.

Suppose that at time $t = 0$ the monetary authority announces its intention of fixing the exchange rate permanently at a time $t = T$ in the future. The level at which the exchange rate is to be pegged is denoted by $\bar{e}$. To focus on the effect of the announcement itself, we assume that the entire future path of g and the path of the money supply between times 0 and T are unaffected by the announcement.[10]

The analysis proceeds by deriving the equilibrium that will prevail under a fixed exchange rate regime and then "working backward" to time $t = 0$. When the exchange rate is fixed at $\bar{e}$, goods-market equilibrium can be written:

$$\bar{y}_t = \phi\left(\bar{e} + p_t^* - p_t\right) - \sigma\left[r_t^* - \gamma\dot{p}_t - (1 - \gamma)\dot{p}_t^*\right] + g_t, \tag{2.21}$$

where we have made use of the fact that $r = r^*$ when no change in the exchange rate is expected. The saddle-path solution to differential equation (2.21) is

$$p_t^f = \bar{e} + p_t^* + \omega\int_t^\infty \exp\left[\omega(t - s)\right](z_s/\phi)\,\mathrm{d}s. \tag{2.22}$$

An "f" superscript denotes a variable's equilibrium value under a fixed-rate regime.

The domestic money supply becomes an endogenous, jumping variable under fixed rates and capital mobility. Equations (2.3) and (2.22) imply that equilibrium nominal balances are given by

$$
\begin{aligned}
m_t^f &= \alpha p_t^f + (1 - \alpha)\left(\bar{e} + p_t^*\right) + \psi\bar{y}_t - \lambda r_t^* \\
&= \bar{e} + p_t^* + \alpha\omega\int_t^\infty \exp\left[\omega(t - s)\right](z_s/\phi)\,\mathrm{d}s + \psi\bar{y}_t - \lambda r_t^*.
\end{aligned} \tag{2.23}
$$

Eq. (2.22) relates the equilibrium output price to the exchange rate, to the world price level, and to current and expected values of variables that disturb the terms of trade. Monetary factors play no role: changes in money demand or supply are accommodated or offset through the capital account. According to (2.23), devaluation is neutral in the present setting. A rise in $\bar{e}$ leads to equiproportionate increases in the home-goods price and the nominal money stock, but has no real effects.

Even though the exchange rate is to be pegged at time T, the behavior of prices during the interval between times 0 and T is governed by eqs. (2.6) and (2.7). Because these equations do not apply after T, it is convenient to write a general

---

[10] Other exogenous variables are unaffected, as always. We also assume that the monetary and fiscal policies pursued both before and after pegging do not result in a speculative attack on the central bank's reserves.

solution to the implied differential-equation system as

$$
e_t = k_1' \exp\left(\frac{t}{\lambda}\right) - \frac{k_2' \alpha \exp(\omega t)}{1 - \alpha - \lambda \omega} + \frac{1}{\lambda} \int_t^T \exp\left[\frac{(t-s)}{\lambda}\right] x_s \, ds
$$

$$
+ \frac{\alpha \omega}{1 - \lambda \omega} \int_t^T \left\{ \exp\left[\frac{(t-s)}{\lambda}\right] - \exp[\omega(t-s)] \right\} \left(\frac{z_s}{\phi}\right) ds - p_t^*, \qquad (2.24)
$$

$$
p_t = k_1' \exp\left(\frac{t}{\lambda}\right) + k_2' \exp(\omega t) + \frac{1}{\lambda} \int_t^T \exp\left[\frac{(t-s)}{\lambda}\right] x_s \, ds
$$

$$
+ \frac{\alpha \omega}{1 - \lambda \omega} \int_t^T \exp\left[\frac{(t-s)}{\lambda}\right] \left(\frac{z_s}{\phi}\right) ds
$$

$$
+ \frac{\omega(1 - \alpha - \lambda \omega)}{1 - \lambda \omega} \int_t^T \exp[\omega(t-s)] \left(\frac{z_s}{\phi}\right) ds \qquad (2.25)
$$

$(0 \le t < T)$, where k_1' and k_2' are arbitrary constants. (It is assumed that $\lambda \ne 0, \sigma \ne 0$.) To trace out the economy's path over the time interval $(0, T)$, we must determine appropriate values for k_1' and k_2'.

These values are determined by the requirements that the exchange rate and domestic-goods price not jump discretely at time T. In other words, the system's initial conditions must result in a path $\{\tilde{e}_t', \tilde{p}_t'\}_{t=0}^T$ for prices such that $\tilde{e}_T' = \bar{e}$ and $\tilde{p}_T' = p_T^f$, where the latter price is given by eq. (2.22). Setting $t = T$ in eqs. (2.24) and (2.25), we find that this continuity condition implies:

$$
k_1' = \left\{ \bar{e} + p_T^* + \frac{\alpha \omega}{1 - \lambda \omega} \int_T^\infty \exp[\omega(T-s)] \left(\frac{z_s}{\phi}\right) ds \right\} \exp\left(\frac{-T}{\lambda}\right), \qquad (2.26)
$$

$$
k_2' = \frac{\omega(1 - \alpha - \lambda \omega)}{1 - \lambda \omega} \int_T^\infty \exp(-\omega s) \left(\frac{z_s}{\phi}\right) ds. \qquad (2.27)
$$

Substitution of (2.26) and (2.27) into (2.24) and (2.25) yields the equilibrium prices prevailing between dates 0 and T.

It was assumed above that the only changes accompanying the announcement of future pegging are changes in the monetary policy pursued after the exchange rate is fixed. That assumption yields a compact and revealing representation of the effect of future pegging. Let $\{\tilde{e}_t, \tilde{p}_t\}_{t=0}^\infty$ denote the price path that would have prevailed *in the absence* of any move to fix the exchange rate; $\tilde{e}$ and $\tilde{p}$ are given by eqs. (2.10) and (2.11) with $k_1 = k_2 = 0$. The initial conditions (2.26) and (2.27) imply that the paths of the exchange rate and the domestic-goods price between times 0 and T can be written in the form:

$$
\tilde{e}_t' - \tilde{e}_t = (\bar{e} - \tilde{e}_T) \exp[(t - T)/\lambda], \qquad (2.28)
$$

$$
\tilde{p}_t' - \tilde{p}_t = (\bar{e} - \tilde{e}_T) \exp[(t - T)/\lambda]. \qquad (2.29)
$$

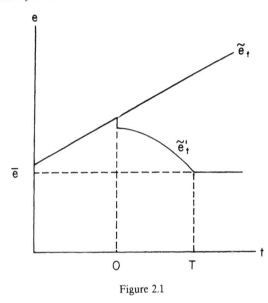

Figure 2.1

The foregoing expressions make clear that the change in the exchange rate's path (relative to its unperturbed level) depends on the relation between the new peg $\bar{e}$ and the exchange rate that would have prevailed at time T in the absence of the regime change. If $\bar{e} < \tilde{e}_T$, for example, the announcement of future pegging leads to an immediate appreciation of the currency relative to its previously anticipated path; $\tilde{e}'$ remains below $\tilde{e}$ for the balance of the floating-rate period, and the divergence between the two grows exponentially at rate $1/\lambda$. As was assumed in the solution procedure, $\tilde{e}'$ reaches $\bar{e}$ at time T, so that pegging can take place with no discrete movement of the exchange rate. Figure 2.1 illustrates a path such as the one just described.

The evolution of the domestic goods price relative to its predisturbance path is identical to that of the exchange rate. This is not surprising: because the regime change is a change only in the process determining nominal magnitudes, it has no effect on the path of the terms of trade. It is noteworthy that as $T \to \infty$, the effect of future pegging on the economy's path becomes progressively smaller. Further, if the exchange rate is to be pegged at time T at the value that would have materialized in the absence of a regime change, the announcement does not alter the economy's path between times 0 and T in any way.

As Figure 2.1 suggests, pegging generally entails a change in the currency's depreciation rate, and hence a change in the domestic nominal interest rate. Because domestic real income does not jump at time T, a discrete change in the demand for real balances is implied. How is this change in demand accommodated when no jump in the price level is possible? To peg the exchange rate at time *T*, the central bank intervenes in the foreign exchange market: it sells domestic money and buys foreign reserves if pegging results in a rise in money demand, but buys money and loses reserves in the opposite case. Central-bank intervention thus facilitates the private-sector portfolio shift that may be necessary to maintain continuous money-market equilibrium. If the nominal interest rate falls at the instant of pegging, there is a momentary capital inflow, and if it rises, there is a capital outflow.

3. Market frictions and output fluctuations

The assumptions of perfect price flexibility and full information are now relaxed so that we may study how market frictions influence the exchange rate's dynamic response to official policy shifts and other exogenous disturbances. We first explore a stylized "sticky-price" model in which the nominal price of domestic output is constrained to be a slowly-adjusting variable. Then we consider more detailed models in which pre-negotiated contracts, imperfect information, or both lie behind the tendency of goods prices to appear sluggish when compared to the exchange rate.

Models of exchange rate dynamics with sticky prices are direct descendants of the open-economy IS–LM models developed by Fleming (1962) and Mundell (1968). This type of model is studied in Section 3.1, below. The Mundell–Fleming approach begins with a Keynesian economy characterized by rigid domestic prices and demand-determined output; that economy is "opened" by introducing international trade and capital movements. Shocks to the goods and asset markets lead to once-and-for-all adjustments of the exchange rate, rather than to a dynamic process of macroeconomic adjustment. These equilibrating exchange-rate movements are in fact terms-of-trade changes which are maintained indefinitely even when the initial shock is monetary.

The static Mundell–Fleming model of exchange-rate determination proved inadequate as an analytical tool in the inflationary environment of the 1970's. The dynamic Mundell–Fleming models, developed primarily by Dornbusch (1976b) and Mussa (1977, 1982), extended the earlier framework in two important respects. First, while retaining the assumption that the nominal price of domestic output is fixed (i.e. predetermined) at any moment in time, the dynamic models allow that price to adjust *over* time in response to deviations between aggregate demand and the full-employment level of output. A monetary expansion, for example, induces not only a temporary rise in output and fall in the terms of trade, but also an inflationary process in which the initial expansionary impact is dissipated and purchasing-power parity is restored. Second, the dynamic models endow market participants with rational expectations of exchange rate and price movements.

The foregoing discussion highlights two distinct sources of dynamics: the equilibrium adjustment of prices to current and anticipated future movements in exogenous variables, and the adjustment of prices and quantities as goods-market disequilibrium is eliminated over time. The first source of dynamics is extrinsic, and was contained in the flexible-price model presented in Section 2. The second source of dynamics is intrinsic to the sticky-price model.

The sticky-price assumption produces models mimicking the observed tendency of international price-level ratios to exhibit considerably less volatility than the corresponding exchange rates. Moreover, the intrinsic dynamics of such a system imply that monetary and other disturbances result in temporary yet persistent deviations of output, goods prices, and asset prices from the values they would assume in a frictionless equilibrium. But while the sticky-price model is useful as a descriptive tool, it does not analyze the institutional or informational features of the economy that might result in an apparently sluggish price level.

Because the precise source of market frictions is crucial for policy analysis, attention has recently been given to exchange-rate models in which contracts and informational asymmetries give rise to monetary non-neutrality. This type of model is the subject of Section 3.2. The policy implications of contracting models are of course very different from those of models based exclusively on imperfect information; however, all the models discussed in Section 3.2 predict that monetary shocks (at least when imperfectly perceived) will have persistent, but not permanent, effects on output. As is illustrated below, the intrinsic dynamics of these models can arise from such sources as inventory adjustment, multi-period contracts, and external asset accumulation. Because the last source of dynamics is properly the province of Section 4, it is touched on only briefly in this section.

3.1. Sticky domestic prices and overshooting

The sticky-price model retains the continuous asset-market equilibrium that was a feature of Section 2, but stipulates that the domestic output price is a predetermined or non-jumping variable that can adjust only over time. Both key features of the sticky-price model – instantaneous asset-market clearing and perfect short-run output-price rigidity – are surely extreme characterizations of actual market adjustment. Nonetheless, these polar extremes yield an analytically tractable model that highlights neatly the dynamic implications of different adjustment speeds between markets. [Niehans (1977) and Frenkel and Rodriguez (1982) study models in which some asset markets adjust slowly.] The most celebrated implication of this type of model is Dornbusch's (1976b) finding that when the price of home goods is sticky, the exchange rate may "overshoot" its eventual level in the short run in response to a permanent change in the money supply.

To introduce price stickiness into the exchange rate model of Section 2, we replace the goods-market equilibrium condition (2.5) with the assumption that domestic output y is identically equal to aggregate demand, d. Demand-determined output might be the result of pre-negotiated nominal wage contracts which require workers to supply all the labor demanded by firms at the contract wage. However, the labor market is not modeled explicitly (see Section 3.2, below). It is assumed that the price of domestic goods moves upward over time in response to both the excess of output y over its natural level $\bar{y}$ and a measure of "equilibrium" inflationary expectations. The expectational component of the price-adjustment rule is crucial. A rule omitting this component is analogous to a pre-Phelps–Friedman Phillips curve, and, as Mussa (1982) observes, yields a model in which constant monetary growth is inconsistent with an inflationary steady state unless output remains perpetually above its natural level.

To obtain the expectations term in the pricing rule, we define a price $\bar{\bar{p}}$ by

$$\bar{y}_t = \phi\left(e_t + p_t^* - \bar{\bar{p}}_t\right) - \sigma\left[r_t - \gamma\dot{p}_t - (1 - \gamma)\left(\dot{e}_t + \dot{p}_t^*\right)\right] + g_t. \tag{3.1}$$

Note that $\bar{\bar{p}}$ equates aggregate demand to the natural output level for current values of the other variables. We then assume the price-adjustment scheme postulated by Mussa (1977, 1982):

$$\dot{p}_t = \theta(y_t - \bar{y}_t) + \dot{\bar{\bar{p}}}_t = \theta(d_t - \bar{y}_t) + \dot{\bar{\bar{p}}}_t. \tag{3.2}$$

According to (3.2), producers adjust prices to reduce excess demand and to ensure that prices "keep up" with changes in their current equilibrium level.[11]

The model is described by (2.1)–(2.4), (3.1), and (3.2). We solve the model by steps [as in Obstfeld and Rogoff (1984)], first finding the equilibrium terms of trade and then using that solution to find the equilibrium exchange rate and home-goods price. To this end, it is convenient to formulate the model in terms of deviations from the flexible-price equilibrium studied in Section 2; thus, we define $\hat{q} \equiv q - \tilde{q}$, $\hat{e} \equiv e - \tilde{e}$, and $\hat{p} \equiv p - \tilde{p}$.

By (2.18), the flexible-price terms of trade $\tilde{q}$ obey the equation:

$$\dot{\tilde{q}}_t = \omega\tilde{q}_t + \left[\bar{y}_t - g_t + \sigma\left(r_t^* - \dot{p}_t^*\right)\right]/\sigma\gamma. \tag{3.3}$$

Differentiating (3.1) and (3.3) with respect to time and using (2.1), (3.2), and (3.3),

---

[11] The price $\bar{\bar{p}}$ can differ from $\tilde{p}$, the output price clearing the goods market in a full flexible-price equilibrium. Obstfeld and Rogoff (1984) show that the alternative pricing rule $\dot{p}_t = \zeta(y_t - \bar{y}_t) + \dot{\tilde{p}}_t$ leads to an observationally equivalent exchange-rate model (equivalent if ζ is chosen suitably). Dornbusch (1976b) implicitly adopts the latter pricing scheme. Frankel (1979), Liviatan (1980), and Buiter and Miller (1982) allow for an inflationary steady state by appending to the Phillips curve an expectations term equal to the current monetary growth rate. This formulation is consistent with rational expectations only if there are no anticipated changes in money growth or other exogenous variables [Obstfeld and Rogoff (1984)].

we obtain an autonomous second-order differential equation in $\hat{q}$:

$$\ddot{\hat{q}}_t = \omega(1 - \theta\sigma\gamma)\dot{\hat{q}}_t + \omega\phi\theta\hat{q}_t. \tag{3.4}$$

A general solution to (3.4) is $\hat{q}_t = k_1\exp(\omega t) + k_2\exp(-\theta\phi t)$, where k_1 and k_2 are constants. Saddle-path equilibrium again requires that the coefficient k_1 of the explosive exponential be set at zero. But (3.4) possesses a negative root, $-\theta\phi$, associated with the predetermined nominal price of domestic goods. (The negative sign of this root reflects the stabilizing effect of excess demand on prices.) Because the initial terms of trade q_0 will not generally coincide with the flexible-price value $\tilde{q}_0$ in this sticky-price model, the additional initial condition $k_2 = q_0 - \tilde{q}_0$ is required to obtain the saddle-path solution for q:

$$q_t = (q_0 - \tilde{q}_0)\exp(-\theta\phi t) + \tilde{q}_t. \tag{3.5}$$

As (3.5) shows, the price-adjustment scheme (3.2) drives the terms of trade toward their flexible-price value at an exponential rate.

Using the fact that $\tilde{e}$ and $\tilde{p}$ must satisfy (2.1)–(2.4), we derive the equation:

$$\dot{\hat{e}}_t = \left(\frac{1}{\lambda}\right)\hat{e}_t - \left(\frac{\psi\phi - \alpha}{\lambda}\right)\hat{q}_t + \left(\frac{\psi\sigma\gamma}{\lambda}\right)\dot{\hat{q}}_t. \tag{3.6}$$

Differentiation of (3.5) yields:

$$\dot{\hat{q}}_t = -\theta\phi\hat{q}_t, \tag{3.7}$$

which, when combined with (3.6), implies that

$$\dot{\hat{e}}_t = \left(\frac{1}{\lambda}\right)\hat{e}_t + \left[\frac{\alpha - \psi\phi(1 + \theta\sigma\gamma)}{\lambda}\right]\hat{q}_t. \tag{3.8}$$

Eqs. (3.7) and (3.8) constitute an autonomous system in $\hat{e}$ and $\hat{q}$. The saddle-path solution for $\hat{e}$ leads to the expression:

$$\begin{aligned}
e_t &= \frac{-(q_0 - \tilde{q}_0)[\alpha - \psi\phi(1 + \theta\sigma\gamma)]}{(1 + \lambda\theta\phi)}\exp(-\theta\phi t) + \tilde{e}_t \\
&= \frac{-(p_0 - \tilde{p}_0)[\alpha - \psi\phi(1 + \theta\sigma\gamma)]}{[(1 - \alpha) + \psi\phi(1 + \theta\sigma\gamma) + \lambda\theta\phi]}\exp(-\theta\phi t) + \tilde{e}_t. \tag{3.9}
\end{aligned}$$

From (3.5) and (3.9), the path of p is given by

$$p_t = (p_0 - \tilde{p}_0)\exp(-\theta\phi t) + \tilde{p}_t. \tag{3.10}$$

Expressions (3.9) and (3.10) show that the exchange rate and domestic-goods price will differ from their flexible-price equilibrium values whenever the predetermined initial output price p_0 differs from the value that would prevail in the hypothetical Walrasian equilibrium of the flexible-price model. The adjustment rule (3.2) drives the discrepancy $p - \tilde{p}$ to zero at rate $\theta\phi$. According to (3.9), e converges to $\tilde{e}$ at that rate.

As in the flexible price model of Section 2, current and anticipated changes in exogenous variables contribute to the system's dynamics. They do so by altering $\tilde{e}$ and $\tilde{p}$ over time, thus changing the long-run equilibrium toward which the economy converges. The process of convergence, however, is a second, intrinsic component of dynamics. Differentiation of (3.9) and (3.10) yields:

$$\dot{e}_t = -\theta\phi(e_t - \tilde{e}_t) + \dot{\tilde{e}}_t, \tag{3.11}$$

$$\dot{p}_t = -\theta\phi(p_t - \tilde{p}_t) + \dot{\tilde{p}}_t. \tag{3.12}$$

Eqs. (3.11) and (3.12) show that the motion of the system is in fact the *sum* of two sources of motion: the (extrinsic) movement in the system's flexible-price equilibrium and the (intrinsic) adjustment of prices to their current flexible-price values in response to goods-market disequilibrium.

We now consider an unanticipated, permanent shock to the money supply occurring at time $t = 0$, i.e. a shift in the anticipated path of the money supply from $\{m_t\}_{t=0}^{\infty}$ to $\{m_t + \Delta m\}_{t=0}^{\infty}$. To highlight the effects of this shock, we suppose that the economy is in full equilibrium before it occurs, with $p_0 = \tilde{p}_0$. As the analysis of the flexible-price model showed, both $\tilde{e}_0$ and $\tilde{p}_0$ jump immediately by the amount Δm; indeed, the paths of $\tilde{e}$ and $\tilde{p}$ jump uniformly by that amount. Because the price of domestic output is predetermined, however, it remains temporarily at p_0. As (3.12) shows, the divergence between p_0 and the new $\tilde{p}_0$ raises the rate of domestic price inflation.

An interesting aspect of the exchange rate's response to a monetary shock is the possibility that it may "overshoot" its new flexible-price or full-equilibrium level.[12] From (3.9), the initial depreciation Δe_0 exceeds or falls short of $\Delta\tilde{e}_0$ as

$$\alpha - \psi\phi(1 + \theta\sigma\gamma) \gtrless 0. \tag{3.13}$$

Intuitively, overshooting arises as follows. Because domestic prices are predetermined, the initial depreciation of the currency is a *real* depreciation that shifts demand from foreign toward domestic goods. Aggregate demand is stimulated further through a fall in the real interest rate, so output unambiguously rises. The concomitant increase in the demand for money reduces the initial excess supply occasioned by the monetary expansion, as does the rise in the overall price level implied by the currency's depreciation. But if an excess supply of money remains after these adjustments, the nominal domestic interest rate must fall to preserve asset-market equilibrium. Since a permanent increase in the level of the money supply does not affect the depreciation rate in the flexible-price model, (2.1) and (3.11) imply that the home interest rate can fall only if the currency depreciates so

---

[12] In general, one can say that the exchange rate overshoots in response to a shock if its impact change exceeds the change that would be necessary if all predetermined variables could move immediately to their long-run levels. Flood (1979) offers this definition of overshooting. In the present context, the "long-run" level of the predetermined domestic output price is its flexible-price value. But, as we shall see below, overshooting can arise even with flexible prices if behavior is influenced by predetermined asset stocks that adjust over time toward some long-run target.

far on impact that it is expected to *appreciate* thereafter toward its flexible-price value. In contrast, if the increase in output raises money demand sufficiently to produce excess demand at the initial nominal interest rate, then overshooting will not occur. The nominal interest rate must *rise* to clear the money market in this case, and the exchange rate will be expected to depreciate thereafter toward its long-run level $\tilde{e}$. This is the "undershooting" case, in which the impact depreciation of the currency falls short of the depreciation that would take place in a flexible-price economy.

The adjustment of the system after the shock at time $t = 0$ is determined endogenously through the workings of the price-adjustment rule (3.2). p rises gradually toward $\tilde{p}$ and e may fall or rise toward $\tilde{e}$ depending on whether over- or undershooting has occurred. The real rate of interest rises over time as the terms of trade return to the initial level and output falls. Monetary policy is neutral in the long run but sluggish price adjustment gives it the power to alter output and relative prices in the short run. In the sticky-price setting, therefore, deviations from purchasing power parity may result both from real disturbances and, temporarily, from monetary shocks.

We now consider an *anticipated* future permanent increase in the money stock announced at time $t = 0$. It is assumed, as in Section 2.2, that the money supply, previously expected to be constant at $\bar{m}$, is now expected to increase by the amount Δm at $t = T$. All else remains fixed. If the economy is initially at long-run equilibrium with $p_0 = \tilde{p}_0$, (3.9) and (3.10) imply that its subsequent path is

$$e_t = \frac{[\alpha - \psi\phi(1 + \theta\sigma\gamma)]\exp(-T/\lambda)\Delta m}{[(1 - \alpha) + \psi\phi(1 + \theta\sigma\gamma) + \lambda\theta\phi]}\exp(-\theta\phi t)$$

$$+ \begin{cases} \bar{x} + \exp[(t - T)/\lambda]\Delta m - \alpha\bar{z}/\phi - \bar{p}^* & (0 \le t < T), \\ \bar{x} + \Delta m - \alpha\bar{z}/\phi - \bar{p}^* & (t \ge T), \end{cases} \tag{3.14}$$

$$p_t = -\exp(-T/\lambda)\Delta m \cdot \exp(-\theta\phi t)$$

$$+ \begin{cases} \bar{x} + \exp[(t - T)/\lambda]\Delta m + (1 - \alpha)\bar{z}/\phi & (0 \le t < T), \\ \bar{x} + \Delta m + (1 - \alpha)\bar{z}/\phi & (t \ge T). \end{cases} \tag{3.15}$$

The announcement causes both the exchange rate and nominal interest rate to jump upward, with the impact depreciation smaller than in the case of an unanticipated occurrence of the same shock. The domestic-goods price is sticky and cannot jump in response to the announcement, but it begins to rise gradually in response to a rise in output and inflationary expectations. As in the flexible-price model, neither the exchange rate nor the price of domestic goods jumps at time T when the anticipated increase in money occurs. Rather, the nominal interest rate falls at T as the rate of currency depreciation falls. In the overshooting case, the exchange rate will abruptly begin to appreciate at T, but without a discrete change in its level.

Note that goods-market disequilibrium remains even after the increase in money has taken place. Because the price level is sluggish, nominal prices cannot adjust fully to the anticipated disturbance by time T, as they did in the flexible-price case. Therefore, the real effects of anticipated money persist until the flexible-price equilibrium is asymptotically attained.

A very useful diagrammatic rendition of the model is possible under the assumption that x, z, and p^* are expected to remain constant at $\bar{x}$, $\bar{z}$, and $\bar{p}^*$ forever. Because $\tilde{e} = \bar{x} - \alpha \bar{z}/\phi - \bar{p}^*$ and $\tilde{p} = \bar{x} + (1 - \alpha)\bar{z}/\phi$ are then constant, the diagram highlights the intrinsic dynamics of the system. As we shall see, however, it is also possible to use the diagram to analyze the effects of anticipated shocks. [An alternative diagram, in which real balances and the terms of trade appear on the axes, is sometimes used. See, for example, Buiter and Miller (1982).]

Equations (3.6) and (3.7) may be transformed to yield:

$$\dot{e}_t = \frac{[(1 - \alpha) + \psi\phi(1 + \theta\sigma\gamma)]}{\lambda}(e_t - \tilde{e}) + \frac{[\alpha - \psi\phi(1 + \theta\sigma\gamma)]}{\lambda}(p_t - \tilde{p}),$$

(3.16)

$$\dot{p}_t = \frac{[(1 - \alpha) + \psi\phi(1 + \theta\sigma\gamma) + \lambda\theta\phi]}{\lambda}(e_t - \tilde{e})$$

$$+ \frac{[\alpha - \psi\phi(1 + \theta\sigma\gamma) - \lambda\theta\phi]}{\lambda}(p_t - \tilde{p}).$$

(3.17)

The phase diagram for this system in the case

$$0 < \alpha - \psi\phi(1 + \theta\sigma\gamma) < \lambda\theta\phi$$

(3.18)

is shown in Figure 3.1.[13] The long-run equilibrium A is a saddle point. A unique path SS converges to that stationary position, and all other paths diverge explosively.

To interpret the diagram, consider the general solution to (3.16) and (3.17):

$$e_t - \tilde{e} = k_1 \exp\left(\frac{t}{\lambda}\right) - \frac{k_2[\alpha - \psi\phi(1 + \theta\sigma\gamma)]}{[(1 - \alpha) + \psi\phi(1 + \theta\sigma\gamma) + \lambda\theta\phi]}\exp(-\theta\phi t),$$

(3.19)

$$p_t - \tilde{p} = k_1 \exp(t/\lambda) + k_2 \exp(-\theta\phi t).$$

(3.20)

The trajectory emanating from any point in the phase plane can be obtained by

---

[13] The case shown in Figure 3.1 implies exchange-rate overshooting in response to an unanticipated money supply change. There are two other cases. If the first inequality in (3.18) is reversed, the same disturbance causes undershooting [cf. (3.13)]. If only the second inequality in (3.18) is reversed, there is overshooting and the $\dot{p} = 0$ locus is negatively, rather than positively, sloped. In all cases the long-run equilibrium is a saddle point, but when $\alpha - \psi\phi(1 + \theta\sigma\gamma) < 0$, the saddle path slopes upward.

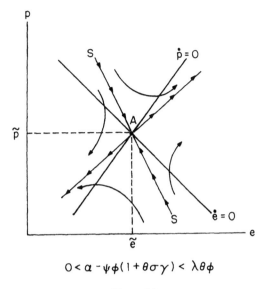

$$0 < \alpha - \psi\phi(1 + \theta\sigma\gamma) < \lambda\theta\phi$$

Figure 3.1

appropriate choice of the arbitrary initial conditions k_1 and k_2. Because the exponential $\exp(t/\lambda)$ induces explosive behavior, initial conditions with $k_1 \neq 0$ necessarily place the economy on one of the divergent paths. The saddle-path condition $k_1 = 0$, in contrast, places the economy on the convergent trajectory SS. Its position on that path is determined by the time that has elapsed since the last unanticipated shock and by the additional initial condition $k_2 = p_0 - \tilde{p}$. By setting $k_1 = 0$ in (3.19) and (3.20), we see that the equation for the saddle path SS is

$$p_t - \tilde{p} = \frac{-[(1-\alpha) + \psi\phi(1+\theta\sigma\gamma) + \lambda\theta\phi]}{[\alpha - \psi\phi(1+\theta\sigma\gamma)]}(e_t - \tilde{e}). \tag{3.21}$$

SS slopes downward or upward according to condition (3.13).

Figure 3.2 illustrates the effects of a permanent, unanticipated fiscal expansion when (3.18) holds. Initially, the system is at the long-run equilibrium A. The shift in policy moves the system's long-run equilibrium to the new point A' which, as (3.21) shows, is to the left of the original saddle path SS. Because the output price p cannot jump, the instantaneous post-disturbance equilibrium is at the point B' on the new convergent path $S'S'$. Thus, the currency appreciates, and the terms of trade and output rise. Because the currency is expected to appreciate further, the nominal interest rate falls, and because the terms of trade are expected to rise, the real interest rate falls. Over time, expectations are fulfilled: as the economy moves along $S'S'$ toward its new stationary position, the domestic currency

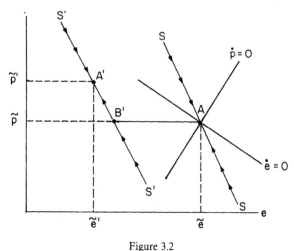

Figure 3.2

appreciates, the price of the home good rises, and output and interest rates return to their pre-disturbance levels. Note that while (3.18) implies exchange-rate overshooting in response to unanticipated, permanent monetary shocks, the present example shows that it does not imply overshooting in response to all shocks.

Although the diagrammatic analysis is predicated on the assumption that the exogenous variables are expected to remain constant, the apparatus may be rigorously used to study the effects of anticipated future disturbances [see Wilson (1979), Rogoff (1979), Gray and Turnovsky (1979), and Boyer and Hodrick (1982a)]. Consider again an anticipated, permanent increase Δm in the money supply. The long-run equilibrium after the increase in money is point A' in Figure 3.3. The path of the economy from the moment of the announcement on is described by (3.14) and (3.15). Between 0 and T, that path corresponds to the particular solution of (3.16) and (3.17) obtained by setting $k_1 = -k_2 = \exp(-T/\lambda)\Delta m$ in (3.19) and (3.20). Thus, the economy's motion over that time interval is described by one of the *unstable* paths of the system with steady state A, though because (3.14) and (3.15) incorporate the saddle-path assumption, the economy's path is in no sense a "bubble" path. After time T, however, the coefficient of $\exp(t/\lambda)$ in (3.14) and (3.15) is 0, and the economy may therefore be regarded as traveling along the convergent path $S'S'$ toward the long-run equilibrium A'. The additional information that the exchange rate cannot jump discretely at time T leads to the adjustment path depicted in Figure 3.3. When the future disturbance is announced, the exchange rate jumps immediately to e_0 (at point B), and then rises further to meet the new convergent path $S'S'$

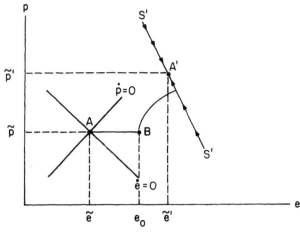

Figure 3.3

precisely at time T. Only one initial exchange rate e_0 places the economy on a trajectory hitting $S'S'$ at time T; e_0 is the equilibrium exchange rate because it alone is consistent with the absence of infinitely large expected arbitrage gains along the economy's path.

3.2. Exchange-rate dynamics with contracting and imperfect information

The sticky-price assumption of Section 3.1 resulted in short-run monetary non-neutrality and an intrinsic component of exchange-rate dynamics. Here we briefly discuss the predictions of some stochastic exchange-rate models in which monetary non-neutrality and intrinsic dynamics arise from other sources. For comparability with the main references on these models, we switch from the continuous time framework of previous sections to discrete time.

There are three channels through which a change in the money supply affects the exchange rate in the models discussed here. First, the exchange rate rises as other nominal variables rise in response to an increase in the money supply. Second, a change in money may affect output or aggregate demand and, by changing the demand for money, affect the exchange rate. Third, a change in money may change the *equilibrium* terms of trade or relative price of non-traded goods. As noted in Section 2, part of such a change will be accommodated by the exchange rate.

The first two of these channels were present in the sticky-price model of Section 3.1, and the first channel always dominates the second: an increase in money raises output (and money demand) only when the exchange rate rises. After its initial increase, the exchange rate falls or rises toward its long-run level depending on the sign of (3.13). Different exchange-rate dynamics are obtained by Flood and Hodrick (1983) in a model with "semi-sticky" prices. In that model, goods prices are determined simultaneously with the exchange rate and are sticky only in the sense of being set prior to the time when sales (which are stochastic) occur and output decisions are made. Unexpectedly high demand is met at the pre-set prices with an increase in output and a fall in inventories of final goods held by firms. An unperceived increase in the money supply causes asset-price movements that lead consumers and firms to the rational but mistaken inference that there has been a decrease in demand for the domestic good. As a result, domestic firms set a nominal price of goods that is consistent, given e and p^*, with a lower terms of trade. Because a fall in demand for the domestic good fails to materialize, the actual quantity demanded at the lower terms of trade is greater than firms had anticipated. Firms respond both by increasing output and reducing inventories.

Unlike in the model of Section 3.1, the fall in the terms of trade here is explicitly the result of an optimal choice made by firms with incomplete information. Furthermore, output responds only to monetary changes that are not fully perceived as such by firms. As usual, the fall in the terms of trade occurs partly through a rise in the exchange rate. Although the exchange rate initially rises in the Flood–Hodrick model as in the model of Section 3.1, and may overshoot its new long-run level, the subsequent dynamics are very different. The fall in inventories eventually causes an increase in the equilibrium terms of trade as firms re-build their goods stocks; and this increase occurs partly through a fall in the exchange rate. After its initial rise at the time of the monetary shock, the exchange rate therefore falls to a value below its new long-run equilibrium level and then rises monotonically to that level. In the Flood–Hodrick setup, the persistent real effects of monetary shocks reflect the intrinsic dynamics implied by the inventory adjustment process.

The Gray (1976) and Fischer (1977) models of nominal wage contracting are discussed in an open-economy context by Marston in Chapter 17, Section 5, of this Handbook.[14] In the model presented by Marston, the exchange rate initially rises in response to an unanticipated permanent increase in money, and subsequently rises or falls to its new long-run equilibrium. The intrinsic dynamics are similar to those in the sticky-price model of Section 3.1, but the speed of adjustment to the new long-run equilibrium now depends on how rapidly wages can move to eliminate labor-market imbalance. The degree of wage inertia is in general a function of contract lengths, indexation provisions, and the extent to which contract periods in different sectors of the economy overlap. Taylor (1980),

---

[14]Marston's chapter includes extensive references to the literature in this area.

for example, shows how staggered nominal wage contracts result in a persistent effect of disturbances on output. Burgstaller (1980), Sachs (1980), Obstfeld (1982), and Calvo (1983) study dynamic open-economy models assuming sluggish wage adjustment.

Models developed by Lucas (1975) and Barro (1980) ascribe the short-run non-neutrality of money entirely to incomplete information in decentralized markets: there is no role for pre-set prices. Koh (1984) extends this setup to the open economy. [See also Saidi (1980), Harris and Purvis (1981), Stockman and Koh (1984), and Kimbrough (1983).] In contrast to the other models discussed above, Koh's model predicts that the exchange rate may either rise or fall initially in response to an unperceived permanent increase in the money supply. There are several possible post-disturbance adjustment paths that reflect an intrinsic dynamic process powered by external asset accumulation.

To illustrate these results, we consider an "island" model of the type analyzed by Lucas and Barro. Each island in the small domestic economy can exchange a "traded" good with other islands in the domestic economy or with the outside world. This international good can be exchanged for domestic money or for an asset denominated in foreign currency. In addition, there is on each island a non-traded good that cannot be exchanged either with other islands or the outside world. Demand for and supply of the traded good (T) and the non-traded good (N) on each island z are functions of the relative price of the non-traded good on island z, $p^N(z) - p^T$; the stock of foreign assets held on island z, $f(z)$; and [as in Barro (1980)] a wealth term in unperceived nominal money, $m(z) - \mathbf{E}_z m$, where $m_t(z)$ is money held on island z at time t and $\mathbf{E}_z m_t$ is the expected per-island value of the aggregate domestic money stock, conditional on information available at time t on island z. These demand and supply functions are written as

$$y_t^{\mathrm{T},i}(z) = \gamma_1^i\big(p_t^N(z) - p_t^T\big) + \gamma_2^i f_t(z) + \gamma_3^i\big(m_t(z) - \mathbf{E}_z m_t\big) + \nu_t^i(z), \qquad (3.22)$$

$$y_t^{\mathrm{N},i}(z) = \beta_1^i\big(p_t^N(z) - p_t^T\big) + \beta_2^i f_t(z) + \beta_3^i\big(m_t(z) - \mathbf{E}_z m_t\big) + \varepsilon_t^i(z) \qquad (3.23)$$

($i = \mathrm{d,s}$). The parameters γ_1^d, γ_2^d, γ_3^d, β_1^d, β_2^d, and β_3^d are positive, while γ_1^s, γ_2^s, γ_3^s, β_1^d, β_2^s, and β_3^s are negative. Assume that $\nu^d(z)$ and $\varepsilon^s(z)$ are identically zero. $\nu^s(z)$ and $\varepsilon^d(z)$ are then random disturbances to the supply of traded goods and the demand for non-traded goods on island z.

Because money, like the foreign asset and the international good, can be traded across islands, there is an economy-wide money market in which aggregate money demand must equal the aggregate money supply. Let p^N, $y^{N,s}$, and $y^{T,s}$ be averages of all island-specific values of the corresponding prices and supplies. The money-market equilibrium condition is similar to (2.3), with $\lambda = 0$ for simplicity:

$$m_t - \alpha p_t^T - (1 - \alpha)p_t^N = \Omega y_t^{N,s} + (\eta - \Omega)y_t^{T,s}. \qquad (3.24)$$

It is also necessary for equilibrium that the demand for and supply of the non-traded good be equal on each individual island.

The exchange rate is given by

$$e_t = p_t^T - p_t^{T*}, \tag{3.25}$$

where p^{T*} is the exogenous foreign price of the traded good. Let $\mathbf{E}m$ and f denote the averages of $\mathbf{E}_z m$ and $f(z)$ over all islands, and define $\gamma_i \equiv \gamma_i^d - \gamma_i^s$ and $\beta_i \equiv \beta_i^d - \beta_i^s$. Then (3.22)–(3.25) and the goods-market equilibrium conditions imply:

$$e_t = m_t - v_t^s(\eta - \Omega) + \varepsilon_t^d \left[\Omega \frac{\beta_1^s}{\beta_1} + (\eta - \Omega) \frac{\gamma_1^s}{\beta_1} \right]$$

$$+ (m_t - \mathbf{E}m_t) \left[\frac{\beta_3}{\beta_1} (1 - \alpha + \Omega\beta_1^s + (\eta - \Omega)\gamma_1^s) - \Omega\beta_3^s - (\eta - \Omega)\gamma_3^s \right]$$

$$+ f_t \left[\frac{\beta_2}{\beta_1} (1 - \alpha + \Omega\beta_1^s + (\eta - \Omega)\gamma_1^s) - \Omega\beta_2^s - (\eta - \Omega)\gamma_2^s \right] - p_t^{T*}. \tag{3.26}$$

When consumers observe two prices – the exchange rate (or price of traded goods) and the price of non-traded goods on their own island – they are unable to infer the precise realized values of the three random variables m, v^s, and ε^d. Since the coefficient on unperceived money $m - \mathbf{E}m$ may be of either sign and may be arbitrarily large, an increase in m accompanied by a smaller increase in $\mathbf{E}m$ can either increase or decrease the exchange rate initially.[15]

The subsequent path of the exchange rate depends on the adjustment of the net stock of foreign assets in the economy, f. Because external assets adjust gradually, monetary shocks will have persistent real effects. It can be shown that an increase in m coupled with a smaller increase in $\mathbf{E}m$ raises $y^{T,d}$ and lowers $y^{T,s}$ in each island. The resulting trade deficit implies a reduction in next period's stock of foreign assets, and this reduction affects the exchange rate in subsequent periods. The role of foreign asset accumulation in exchange-rate dynamics has received considerable attention in the literature, and this is the subject to which we now turn.[16]

---

[15] The possibility of a temporary appreciation is due entirely to the effect of money on expenditure: if the relative price of non-traded goods is pushed sufficiently high, a currency appreciation may be required to restore money-market equilibrium in the short run. A similar result is derived by Kind (1982) in a sticky-price model incorporating external asset accumulation.

[16] In the present model, as in that of Flood and Hodrick (1983), only unperceived (or unanticipated) money has real effects. As we shall see in the next section, however, a fully understood change in trend inflation can have real effects in models with external asset accumulation. These real effects are absent in this particular model because money demand is insensitive to the nominal interest rate [eq. (3.24)] and expenditure depends, not on real money balances, but on the unperceived component of the nominal money supply.

4. Portfolio balance, wealth, and the exchange rate

The portfolio-balance approach introduces private wealth as an explicit determinant of the demands for both money and goods.[17] Stocks of external assets and domestic capital are predetermined variables that influence the rate at which new wealth is accumulated through current-account surpluses and investment; and changes in wealth, in turn, move the economy's short-run equilibrium over time. The introduction of wealth thus adds an intrinsic component to the economy's dynamics. In a rational-expectations context, the overall dynamics of the system will result from foreseen changes in exogenous variables as well as from the adjustment of external claims and capital to the long-run levels desired by firms and individuals. We simplify this section's discussion of the portfolio approach by assuming perfect price flexibility throughout.

Dynamic portfolio-balance models of exchange rate determination spring from two distinct sources in the closed-economy macrodynamic literature. The first source is the work on inflation and growth exemplified by models of Tobin (1965) and Foley and Sidrauski (1970). The second source is the work of Blinder and Solow (1973) and others on the long-run effects of policies in models where the government's budget constraint is taken into account.

Fixed exchange rates were assumed in the seminal studies of Branson (1974), Dornbusch (1975), and Frenkel and Rodriguez (1975), which applied the dynamic portfolio approach to the open economy. With the monetary base endogenous, asset markets adjusted to disturbances in part through stock-shift capital flows – instantaneous private portfolio shifts accommodated by the central bank's willingness to trade foreign bonds for money at the posted exchange rate. As wealth evolved over time through investment and external saving, a sequence of short-run portfolio equilibria was traced out, implying a path for the balance of payments.

The basic approach was easily applied to the study of floating exchange rates, as the papers of Dornbusch (1976c), Kouri (1976), and Calvo and Rodriguez (1977) demonstrated. The nominal money supply could no longer change over time to ensure continuous equilibrium as wealth changed, but the exchange rate did so, altering both the real money stock and, through its effect on expectations, the relative real yields on domestic and foreign assets.

4.1. Foreign bonds in a portfolio-balance model

The simplest possible model, due in its essentials to Kouri (1976), is used to develop the main elements of the portfolio approach. We consider a world in

---

[17]A satisfactory treatment of portfolio diversification naturally requires specification of both investors' preferences and the stochastic processes generating real returns. For a discussion of these topics, see Chapter 15 by Branson and Henderson in this Handbook.

which a single composite consumption good is available and examine a small economy whose residents may hold wealth in the form of domestic fiat money or bonds denominated in foreign currency and paying the fixed world interest rate r^*.[18] Foreigners do not hold domestic money, and because the central bank does not intervene in the foreign-exchange market, all net intertemporal trade between the home country and the rest of the world is accomplished through the private exchange of goods for foreign bonds.

On the assumption that the foreign-currency price P^* of the single consumption good is fixed and equal to 1, the domestic price level P may be identified with the exchange rate E and the domestic price inflation rate π with the proportional rate of increase of E. Output is perishable, with its home supply exogenous and equal to Y. When domestic investment is introduced explicitly below, home output of the consumption good will become an endogenous variable and the menu of available assets will expand by one.

The focus on external asset accumulation and wealth calls for a careful description of individuals' lifetime consumption possibilities. For simplicity, we assume throughout that an economy is inhabited by a single, representative agent. The typical individual's lifetime budget constraint limits the real present value of planned expenditure to total real wealth V, where wealth includes the present value of expected future output plus transfers from the government. Let M denote nominal money holdings, F the foreign-currency (and, because $P^* = 1$, real) value of external claims, and T real transfers. If an infinite planning horizon is assumed, the lifetime budget constraint takes the form:

$$\int_t^\infty \left[C_s + (r^* + \pi_s)(M_s/P_s) \right] \exp\left[-r^*(s-t) \right] ds$$

$$= (M_t/P_t) + F_t + \int_t^\infty (Y_s + T_s) \exp\left[-r^*(s-t) \right] ds \equiv V_t. \tag{4.1}$$

Constraint (4.1) reflects an expenditure concept that includes both spending on the consumption good and spending on the services of real balances, where the latter good is valued at the opportunity cost of holding money, $r^* + \pi$.

Consumption C is assumed to be an increasing function of both current disposable income Y^d and wealth V:[19]

$$C_t = C(Y_t^d, V_t), \qquad 1 > C_{Y^d} \geq 0, \quad C_V > 0. \tag{4.2}$$

---

[18] This model is more general than it seems to be, for it would be easy to introduce a domestic-currency bond paying an interest rate linked to the foreign rate by interest parity. Under perfect substitution, however, the fraction of domestic wealth held in the form of foreign-currency bonds is indeterminate, and so unanticipated shocks causing exchange-rate changes have indeterminate wealth effects. The problem does not arise in portfolio models assuming that bonds of different currency denomination are *imperfect* substitutes. In Chapter 15 of this Handbook, Branson and Henderson discuss portfolio-balance models that include imperfectly substitutable interest-bearing assets.

[19] In principle, consumption is also a function of the real interest rate r^*, as in previous sections. Because r^* is held constant, it does not appear explicitly in (4.2).

Disposable income is the sum of current output, real interest payments on foreign bond holdings, lump-sum transfers from the government, and real capital gains on asset holdings. Thus, $Y^d = Y + r^*F + T - \pi(M/P)$, where $\pi(M/P)$ is the inflation tax.

Instantaneous equilibrium in asset markets requires that the demand for real money balances equal the supply. The fraction of real wealth allocated to real money holdings is assumed to be a positive declining function $L(r^* + \pi)$ of the nominal interest rate. In equilibrium, therefore,

$$M_t/P_t = L(r^* + \pi_t)V_t, \qquad L' < 0. \tag{4.3}$$

If μ denotes the (positive) growth rate of the nominal money supply, $\dot{M}/M$, and l denotes desired real money balances (the level, not the logarithm), logarithmic differentiation of (4.3) shows that in equilibrium:

$$\dot{l}_t/l_t = \mu_t - \pi_t. \tag{4.4}$$

The model is closed by specification of the government's flow budget constraint. Real government consumption G and transfer payments must be financed through money creation; there is no government-issued interest-bearing debt.[20] This implies a public-sector finance constraint of the form

$$T_t + G_t = \dot{M}_t/P_t = \mu_t l_t. \tag{4.5}$$

Because the level of real balances l is an endogenous variable, the government cannot choose the paths of μ, T, and G independently while continuously satisfying (4.5). The analysis therefore takes μ and T to be the variables controlled by the government and assumes that government consumption adjusts passively according to the equation $G_t = \mu_t l_t - T_t$.

We now describe how expectations and asset stocks evolve over time in equilibrium.

The law of motion for real balances l is derived by combining equilibrium conditions (4.3) and (4.4) to obtain the relation

$$L[r^* + \mu_t - (\dot{l}_t/l_t)] = l_t/V_t = 1/\{1 + [(F_t + \tilde{Y}_t + \tilde{T}_t)/l_t]\}. \tag{4.6}$$

In (4.6),

$$\tilde{Y}_t = \int_t^\infty Y_s \exp[-r^*(s-t)] \, ds$$

and

$$\tilde{T}_t = \int_t^\infty T_s \exp[-r^*(s-t)] \, ds.$$

---

[20] There is an implicit assumption that the central bank does not hold interest-bearing foreign reserves. If these were held, the income they yielded could be used to help finance government outlays.

Inversion of (4.6) yields:

$$i_t = \{ r^* + \mu_t - \Phi[l_t/(F_t + \tilde{Y}_t + \tilde{T}_t)] \} l_t, \qquad \Phi' < 0. \tag{4.7}$$

Φ is a decreasing function because a higher portfolio share will be willingly allocated to money only if the inflation rate falls; and, given the monetary growth rate μ, a fall in inflation implies more rapid growth of real balances.

The system's second differential equation describes the motion of the foreign asset stock F. Because there is no domestic investment in the present model, the difference between disposable income and consumption equals the change in holdings of real money and real foreign bonds:

$$i_t + \dot{F}_t = Y_t^d - C_t = Y_t + r^* F_t + T_t - \pi_t l_t - C_t. \tag{4.8}$$

Eqs. (4.4) and (4.8) together give the equilibrium current-account balance $\dot{F}$ as

$$\dot{F}_t = Y_t + r^* F_t - C(Y_t + r^* F_t + T_t + i_t - \mu_t l_t, l_t + F_t + \tilde{Y}_t + \tilde{T}_t) + T_t - \mu_t l_t. \tag{4.9}$$

The public-sector budget constraint (4.5) implies that the current account equals the difference between national income, $Y + r^* F$, and national absorption, $C + G$.

If one is willing to consider a global linearization of the system consisting of (4.7) and (4.9) it is possible to study the economy's response to various expected trajectories for the forcing variables μ, T, and Y [see, for example, Barro (1978), Flood (1979), Rodriguez (1980), Boyer and Hodrick (1982b), and Mussa (1984)]. We assume instead that these variables are constant at levels $\bar{\mu}$, $\bar{T}$, and $\bar{Y}$ except for permanent unanticipated jumps; and we therefore focus on the intrinsic component of the system's dynamics fueled by the adjustment of foreign asset stocks to long-run desired levels. (As in the discussion of Section 3.1, however, the diagram we now develop to illustrate this adjustment process may be used also to study certain anticipated and transitory shocks.)

By requiring that the exogenous variables follow constant paths, we reduce (4.7) and (4.9) to an autonomous differential-equation system in l and F. That system is assumed to possess a unique stationary point $(\bar{l}, \bar{F})$ at which the growth rate of real balances l and the equilibrium current account $\dot{F}$ are simultaneously zero. The linear Taylor approximation to the system around $(\bar{l}, \bar{F})$ is

$$\begin{bmatrix} i_t \\ \dot{F}_t \end{bmatrix}$$

$$= \begin{bmatrix} -\phi' L/(1 - L) & \Phi' L^2/(1 - L)^2 \\ -\bar{\mu}(1 - C_{yd}) - C_V + [C_{yd}\phi' L/(1 - L)] & r^*(1 - C_{yd}) - C_V - [C_{yd}\phi' L^2/(1 - L)^2] \end{bmatrix}$$

$$\times \begin{bmatrix} l_t - \bar{l} \\ F_t - \bar{F} \end{bmatrix}, \tag{4.10}$$

where all functions are evaluated at long-run equilibrium. The determinant of the above matrix is assumed to be negative:

$$[\phi' L/(1-L)]\{C_V - r^*(1 - C_{Y^d}) + [L/(1-L)][C_V + \bar{\mu}(1 - C_{Y^d})]\} < 0.$$

(4.11)

Because the determinant is the product of the system's characteristic roots, the system must possess a negative root (associated with the predetermined variable F) and a positive root (associated with the jumping variable l, which varies inversely with E). Thus, the long-run equilibrium $(\bar{l}, \bar{F})$ is a saddle point.

Stability condition (4.11) requires that equilibrium public plus private absorption increase faster than income as foreign assets increase. Section 5 below shows that side conditions like (4.11) can sometimes be replaced by assumptions on preferences in models based on explicit intertemporal optimization: if a stationary position exists, the model's inherent logic will then imply saddle-path stability. As we shall see, however, there do exist optimizing models with no well-behaved long-run equilibrium, as well as optimizing models with multiple stationary points.

Figure 4.1 is the local phase diagram of the system described by eqs. (4.7) and (4.9). Differentiation of (4.7) shows that the locus of points along which $\dot{l} = 0$ is of slope $[F + (\bar{Y} + \bar{T})/r^*]/l$, which is a positive number if the stock of foreign claims never falls below $-(\bar{Y} + \bar{T})/r^*$.[21] The slope of the $\dot{F} = 0$ locus depends on the sign of $\partial \dot{F}/\partial F$ [given by the southeast entry of the matrix in (4.10)]. Figure 4.1 shows the case we will discuss: that in which $\partial \dot{F}/\partial F < 0$, so that the $\dot{F} = 0$ locus slopes downward.[22] Note that $\partial \dot{l}/\partial l$, given by the northwest entry of the matrix in (4.10), is always positive. As usual, the unique saddle path SS converging to long-run equilibrium at A is the rational-expectations equilibrium path of the economy provided no changes in exogenous variables are expected.

A salient feature of Figure 4.1 is the positive association between real balances and foreign assets along the saddle path. This translates into a relationship between the exchange rate and the current account, for when the current account is in surplus, the currency depreciates more slowly than its trend depreciation rate $\bar{\mu}$. Intuitively, the growing wealth implied by a current surplus leads to a growing

[21] Henderson and Rogoff (1982) study the stability properties of a two-country portfolio-balance model and allow for the possibility of negative net foreign asset stocks. Kouri (1983, appendix 3) discusses a small-country case. These authors conclude that saddle-path stability must always obtain under rational expectations. However, this result follows from their assumption that interest earnings on foreign assets do not affect the current account. As expression (4.11) shows, the present model always has the saddle-path property in the special case $r^* = 0$; but if $r^* > 0$, an otherwise well-behaved model can become completely unstable once the possibility that $1 - L < 0$ is admitted. Fortunately, this is never a problem in a model that incorporates an appropriate definition of wealth. As Section 5 below shows, the private intertemporal budget constraint (4.1) and the government constraint (4.5) imply that the present value of future private consumption is bounded from above by $F + (\bar{Y} + \bar{T})/r^*$ in equilibrium [see eq. (5.14)]. Accordingly, that quantity will normally be positive.

[22] In the case where $\partial \dot{F}/\partial F > 0$, the $\dot{F} = 0$ locus is positively sloped but steeper than the $\dot{l} = 0$ locus. The saddle path SS lies between these two loci and thus slopes upward as in Figure 4.1.

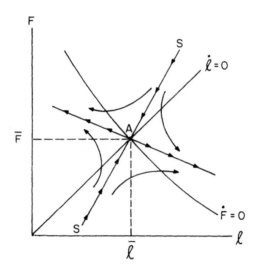

Figure 4.1

demand for real balances that prevents prices from rising to the full extent of the cumulative increase in the nominal money supply. We shall soon see that this surplus-appreciation, deficit-depreciation relationship, while characterizing the process of convergence to a fixed stationary state, need no longer hold once anticipated disturbances are considered. The relationship may break down also when non-monetary wealth can be held in the form of domestic capital as well as foreign claims.[23]

Assume now that the economy is initially in long-run equilibrium at point A. The first experiment to be considered is an unanticipated, permanent increase in the money stock – a discontinuous jump in M that leaves the growth rate of money unchanged. Equilibrium is restored if the currency depreciates immediately in proportion to the increase in money, leaving real balances at their

[23] We elaborate on this point in Section 4.2; see also Kouri and Macedo (1978). Another exception can occur when there are more than two countries [Krugman (1983)]. Two distinct alternative mechanisms can give rise to the familiar correlation between the exchange rate and current account along a convergent path. The pattern arises in models assuming imperfect asset substitutability when domestic residents have a greater marginal propensity to hold wealth in the form of domestic-currency bonds than do foreigners (see Chapter 15 by Branson and Henderson in this Handbook). Even when all bonds are perfect substitutes and wealth does not enter the money-demand function, the pattern will arise when domestic and foreign goods are imperfect substitutes in consumption, the terms of trade are endogenous, domestic residents have a relative preference for domestic goods, and the home goods market is stable in the Walrasian sense [see Calvo and Rodriguez (1977), Dornbusch and Fischer (1980) and Obstfeld (1980)]. The second case reflects the usual transfer mechanism whereby a current-account induced transfer of wealth from abroad raises demand for home goods, improving the terms of trade.

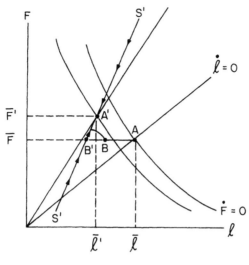

Figure 4.2

original level $\bar{l}$ and real wealth at its long-run desired level. Because prices are fully flexible and the system is homogeneous in all nominal variables, a monetary change of the type considered here has no real effects. In particular, it does not set into motion the intrinsic dynamics of the economy.[24]

An unanticipated permanent increase in the money growth rate $\bar{\mu}$, in contrast, can have a real impact on the economy. In other words, money is not superneutral, as it was in Section 2. Figure 4.2 illustrates the effects of this policy shift when the $\dot{F} = 0$ locus slopes downward.

As is easily verified, the $\dot{l} = 0$ and $\dot{F} = 0$ schedules both shift leftward near the steady state. While the long-run level of real balances falls unambiguously to $\bar{l}'$, the new long-run foreign asset stock $\bar{F}'$ may be greater or less than $\bar{F}$.[25] Figure 4.2 shows the case in which $\bar{F}' > \bar{F}$. When $\bar{\mu}$ is increased, the currency depreciates and a current surplus emerges as the economy jumps to point B' on the new saddle path $S'S'$. Real balances and foreign bonds subsequently rise together

---

[24]An anticipated increase in the money stock can induce current-account adjustment, however [Dornbusch and Fischer (1980)]. We have considered a "helicopter" monetary expansion rather than an expansion achieved through a central-bank purchase of bonds. The latter operation has the same effect as the helicopter expansion if individuals fully capitalize expected future transfer payments from the government (as they do here). Because the interest earnings on bonds purchased from the public are merely returned to the public in the form of transfers, there are no real effects [Obstfeld (1981) and Stockman (1983)]. If capitalization is incomplete, however, an official bond purchase will induce a current-account surplus, as in Kouri (1976, 1983).

[25]When $\partial \dot{F} / \partial F > 0$ (the case discussed in footnote 22), it is possible that long-run real balances rise in response to an increase in $\bar{\mu}$. Long-run foreign assets must also rise in this case. All one can say in general is that the ratio of real balances to other wealth must fall.

while the economy converges to its new long-run position A'. When $\bar{F}' < \bar{F}$, the increase in $\bar{\mu}$ naturally occasions a depreciation coupled with a deficit.[26]

These real effects of a change in monetary growth come from three related sources, none of which was present in the flexible-price model of Section 2. First, the concomitant increase in inflation reduces real wealth and hence private consumption by reducing desired real balances. Second, because real transfers $\bar{T}$ are held constant, there may be a change in the inflation tax that alters long-run disposable income. Third, a change in the product $\bar{\mu}l$ results in an equal change in government consumption, by (4.5). If the interest-rate elasticity of money demand exceeds 1, a rise in $\bar{\mu}$ lowers long-run government consumption and the long-run inflation tax. Because $C_{Y^d} < 1$, steady-state foreign assets must rise to ensure external balance. When money demand is inelastic with respect to the nominal interest rate, long-run foreign assets may fall.

Figure 4.2 may also be used to analyze an announced future increase in $\bar{\mu}$. As we have seen, the path of the economy between the announcement of the policy change and its implementation is described by an unstable trajectory of the autonomous system defined by (4.7) and (4.9). Furthermore, there can be no discrete jump in E at the moment $\bar{\mu}$ rises. Accordingly, the economy jumps immediately to a point like B and reaches $S'S'$ at the moment $\bar{\mu}$ is increased. It is noteworthy that as the economy travels between the momentary equilibrium B and $S'S'$, the currency depreciates at a rate exceeding $\bar{\mu}$ even though the current account is in surplus. The example shows that the surplus-appreciation, deficit-depreciation pattern, while characterizing the intrinsic component of the system's dynamics, need not dominate the response to anticipated exogenous disturbances.

Non-monetary disturbances can be studied as well. A permanent, unanticipated increase in $\bar{Y}$ leads to a fall $\Delta\bar{Y}/r^*$ in long-run external assets but to no change in long-run real balances $\bar{l}$. Accordingly, the currency appreciates in the short run and a current-account deficit emerges. Real balances and foreign assets both fall in the transition to the new stationary state.

4.2. Investment and the current account

It was noted above that the presence of domestic investment opportunities may alter the simple relation between the exchange rate and the current account characterizing convergent paths. Money demand depends on wealth in a portfolio setting, but wealth and foreign assets can move in opposite directions in a model with capital accumulation, even as the economy converges to a fixed long-run

[26] In the case shown in Figure 4.2, the exchange rate overshoots (in the sense discussed in footnote 12).

equilibrium. It therefore becomes possible that a current deficit will be accompanied by rising real balances and a current surplus by falling real balances.

We illustrate these possibilities by incorporating investment into the portfolio-balance model developed above [see Dornbusch (1980) and Hodrick (1980) for similar models]. The assumption of a single available consumption good is retained, but it is now assumed that the domestic supply of that good is endogenous and that the economy can produce, in addition, a non-traded investment good. The production technologies for the consumption and investment goods are described by constant-returns-to-scale, neo-classical production functions taking capital and labor as inputs. Because the investment good is not tradable, the output of the investment sector represents the (gross) capital accumulation of the economy. Labor is supplied inelastically at the fixed level N. Factors of production migrate freely between sectors.

Claims on domestic capital cannot be held by foreigners, but capital and foreign bonds are perfect substitutes from the standpoint of home investors.[27] Let ρ denote capital's real rental, the marginal product of capital in the consumption sector. If P^K is the price of a unit of capital in terms of the consumption good and ε is the rate of physical depreciation of capital, the perfect substitution assumption implies that

$$r^* = \frac{\rho_t + \dot{P}_t^K}{P_t^K} - \varepsilon, \tag{4.12}$$

so that the rate of physical return on capital plus the rate of capital gain equals the world bond rate.

On the assumptions that no factor-intensity reversals are possible, that the economy does not specialize in production, and that the investment good is relatively labor intensive, the Stolper–Samuelson reasoning allows us to write the rental ρ as a declining function of P^K and the real wage ω as an increasing function of P^K (see Chapter 1 by Jones and Neary in this Handbook). Arbitrage condition (4.12) then becomes a differential equation in the price of capital:

$$\dot{P}_t^K / P_t^K = \varepsilon + r^* - \left[\rho \left(P_t^K \right) / P_t^K \right], \qquad \rho' < 0. \tag{4.13}$$

The dynamic system in P^K described by (4.13) is unstable, with a single steady state at the unique capital price $\bar{P}^K$ such that $\varepsilon + r^* = \rho(\bar{P}^K)/\bar{P}^K$. The requirement of saddle-path stability allows us to conclude that the price of capital will always be constant at level $\bar{P}^K$, and, by implication, that the real rental and wage will also be constants. These are denoted by $\bar{\rho}$ and $\bar{\omega}$, respectively.

Given production possibilities (as summarized by the current capital stock K), output of the two goods depends on the relative price $\bar{P}^K$. The supply functions

---

[27] The model would not be altered if trade in equities were introduced, but the assumption in the text avoids some additional notation. If trade in capital goods were allowed, however, the rate of domestic investment would become indeterminate.

for the consumption good and the investment good may therefore be written as $Q^C(\bar{P}^K, K)$ and $Q^1(\bar{P}^K, K)$, respectively. By the Rybczynski theorem, $\partial Q^C / \partial K > 0$ and $\partial Q^1 / \partial K < 0$ (see Chapter 1 of this Handbook).[28]

Three differential equations summarize the dynamics of the system. Real net investment is given by

$$\bar{P}^K \dot{K}_t = \bar{P}^K Q^1(\bar{P}^K, K_t) - \varepsilon \bar{P}^K K_t. \tag{4.14}$$

External asset accumulation equals the difference between the economy's endowment of the consumption good and consumption spending, so that

$$\dot{F}_t = Q^C(\bar{P}^K, K_t) + r^* F_t - C(Y_t^d, V_t) + \bar{T} - \bar{\mu} l_t, \tag{4.15}$$

where now:

$$V_t = l_t + F_t + (\bar{\omega} N + \bar{T})/r^* + \bar{P}^K K_t. \tag{4.16}$$

The system's final equation is the analogue of (4.7):

$$\dot{l}_t = \left\{ r^* + \bar{\mu} - \Phi\left[l_t / (V_t - l_t)\right] \right\} l_t. \tag{4.17}$$

The stationary values of asset stocks are denoted by $\bar{K}$, $\bar{F}$, and $\bar{l}$.

For the present purpose, it is convenient to work with a representation of the model that differs from the one given by eqs. (4.14), (4.15), and (4.17). To derive this alternative (but equivalent) representation, note that by (4.4), (4.12), and (4.17), we may write disposable income as

$$Y_t^d = \bar{\omega} N + \left[(\bar{p}/\bar{P}^K) - \varepsilon\right] \bar{P}^K K_t + r^* F_t + \bar{T} - \pi_t l_t$$

$$= r^*(V_t - l_t) + \left\{ r^* - \Phi\left[l_t / (V_t - l_t)\right] \right\} l_t.$$

Similarly, by adding (4.14) and (4.15) we obtain:

$$\dot{V}_t - \dot{l}_t = r^*(V_t - l_t) - C\left[Y_t^d, (V_t - l_t) + l_t\right] - \bar{\mu} l_t. \tag{4.18}$$

Together, eqs. (4.17) and (4.18) constitute an autonomous differential-equation sub-system in real balances l and non-monetary wealth $V - l$. As before, eq. (4.14) describes the motion of domestic capital; but K does not appear explicitly in the dynamic sub-system defined by the two other equations.

The alternative representation implies that the economy's evolution does not depend on levels of capital and foreign claims separately, but only on their sum. (This would not be true if capital and bonds were imperfect substitutes in portfolios.) Thus, saving and equilibrium real balances are determined entirely by $V - l$: a lower capital stock, ceteris paribus, implies a higher investment level

---

[28] The factor intensity assumption is crucial, as it yields both the uniqueness of P^K [from eq. (4.13)] and the stability of the capital-accumulation process. It is also important that capital depreciates at a positive rate. If ε were zero, the economy would be specialized at the steady state and the Stolper–Samuelson and Rybczynski arguments would therefore not apply.

financed by an equal deterioration in the current account. What happens when the capital stock is initially at the stationary level $\bar{K}$ defined by $Q^1(\bar{P}^K, \bar{K}) = \varepsilon\bar{K}$? In this case capital and consumption-goods production remain constant through time, so that the model reduces to the simpler portfolio model discussed above in Section 4.1.

It is easy to derive the phase diagram for the sub-system consisting of (4.17) and (4.18); indeed, we have already done the work. Note that the system in l and $V - l$ described by (4.17) and (4.18) is identical to the system in l and F that equations (4.7) and (4.9) describe when μ, T, and Y are constant. Qualitatively, the dynamics of the present model can therefore be illustrated by Figure 4.1, with F replaced everywhere by $V - l$.[29]

The intrinsic dynamics of the extended model imply that increasing non-monetary wealth is accompanied by a rate of currency depreciation that falls short of the money growth rate $\bar{\mu}$, while decreasing wealth is accompanied by a depreciation rate exceeding $\bar{\mu}$. But no tight link between the exchange rate and the current account is implied, and a current deficit, say, may easily be accompanied by rising real balances. To see this, assume that non-monetary wealth is initially below its long-run level, that initial capital is lower than $\bar{K}$, and that initial foreign assets exceed $\bar{F}$. The stock of foreign claims cannot converge to its long-run level $\bar{F}$ unless the current account is in deficit along some portion of the subsequent transition path. As the diagram shows, however, real balances (and non-monetary wealth) will rise monotonically along that path, even during periods in which foreign assets are being run down.

We conclude that when the menu of assets is expanded, the current account, per se, may play no role in determining exchange-rate behavior along paths converging to a fixed long-run equilibrium. The linkage that does emerge is one between the exchange rate and the evolution of overall national wealth. Whether saving is external or internal is irrelevant in the present model.

5. Exchange-rate models based on individual intertemporal optimization

The exchange-rate dynamics highlighted in Section 4 were driven by external asset accumulation and domestic investment. Central to the analysis of that section were the assumed forms of the consumption function and the portfolio-balance schedule. We now turn to exchange-rate models in which the consumption function and asset demands are derived explicitly from individual preferences regarding alternative future expenditure paths. While the broad predictions of Section 4 can be replicated in some optimizing models, the results are quite sensitive to the assumptions one makes about intertemporal tastes.

---

[29]As footnote 22 suggests, there is an alternative configuration in which the $\dot{V} - l = 0$ locus slopes upward.

Models of optimal external borrowing developed by Bardhan (1967), Hamada (1969), and Bruno (1976) are the forerunners of optimizing exchange-rate models. While these models were concerned exclusively with real factors, the introduction of money yields a theory of exchange-rate dynamics in which the evolution of asset stocks results from optimal individual choices.

The proper role of money in an optimizing model is a controversial question, however, and results are sensitive to the way in which money is introduced. Why should maximizing agents hold money at all when it is dominated, in terms of both return and risk, by other assets? Below, we will discuss two methods of answering this question. The first, adopted by Sidrauski (1967) and Brock (1975), assumes that the level of real balances enters directly into agents' instantaneous utility functions. Thus, money offers a real "convenience yield" that may induce agents to hold it. The second device for introducing money, associated with Clower (1967), assumes that agents must acquire money and hold it for some time before purchasing consumption goods. In this sequential, "cash-in-advance" setup, money demand is closely linked to planned future purchases of consumption goods. It is clear that both approaches to money demand leave us far from a true theory of why money is held. Nonetheless, the models discussed below are both tractable and suggestive. Pending further developments in monetary theory, they represent the state of the art.[30]

5.1. A small-country, one-good model

We introduce individual optimization explicitly while retaining the assumptions and notation of Section 4. To simplify, we abstract from domestic investment throughout this section, although investment could be introduced along the lines of Section 4.2. Statements about the current account made below are predicated on the tacit assumption that the domestic capital stock is constant. If the assumption is relaxed, those statements must be interpreted as applying to the overall rate of accumulation of non-money assets. [Hodrick (1982) and Greenwood (1983) study versions of the present model. Sachs (1983b) introduces investment into a related two-country simulation model that includes two consumption goods and an intermediate good.]

A representative agent is now assumed to derive instantaneous utility $U(C, l)$ from his expenditure on the single consumption good and his holdings of real

---

[30]Another class of models introduces money through the assumption of finitely-lived, overlapping generations. See, for example, Kareken and Wallace (1981), Clarida (1982), Eaton (1982), and Lapan and Enders (1983). A related model is in Helpman and Razin (1979). Limited space precludes an adequate discussion of the interesting questions raised by these models.

money balances.[31] The consumer (who may also be thought of as a dynastic "family") is immortal and maximizes his lifetime welfare, W, subject to the lifetime budget constraint (4.1). It is assumed that W is a time-additive function of future instantaneous utilities:

$$W\left(\{C_t\}_{t=0}^{\infty}, \{l_t\}_{t=0}^{\infty}\right) = \int_0^{\infty} \exp(-\delta t) U(C_t, l_t) \, dt, \tag{5.1}$$

where δ is a constant rate of subjective time preference. (Alternative preference schemes are discussed later.) Let η_0 be the shadow price of real wealth at time 0. Given (5.1), the first-order conditions for the consumer's problem are

$$U_C(C_t, l_t) = \eta_0 \exp\left[(\delta - r^*)t\right], \tag{5.2}$$

$$U_l(C_t, l_t) = \left(r^* + \pi_t\right) \eta_0 \exp\left[(\delta - r^*)t\right]. \tag{5.3}$$

Conditions (5.2) and (5.3) define desired consumption and real balances as functions of the current inflation rate, the world interest rate, time, and η_0. The value of η_0 yielding an optimal program from the individual's standpoint is the unique value that allows the budget constraint (4.1) to hold with equality when planned consumption and real balances satisfy (5.2) and (5.3) at every point in the future.

It is instructive to compare the consumption and money demand functions implied by the constrained maximization of (5.1) with those assumed in Section 4. Closed-form behavioral functions cannot be obtained unless we specify a particular functional form for the utility function $U(C, l)$, so we assume that it is a member of the constant relative risk aversion family $(C^{\alpha} l^{1-\alpha})^{1-R}/1 - R$, where $R > 0$ and $0 < \alpha < 1$. (None of the results obtained below would be qualitatively altered if a wider class of utility functions was considered.) With this choice of utility function, (4.1), (5.2), and (5.3) imply that consumption and money demand are given by

$$C_t = \frac{\alpha V_t \left[\dfrac{\alpha(r^* + \pi_t)}{1 - \alpha}\right]^{-(1-\alpha)(1-R)/R}}{\displaystyle\int_t^{\infty} \exp\left\{\left[-r^* + \dfrac{(r^* + \delta)}{R}\right](s - t)\right\} \left[\dfrac{\alpha(r^* + \pi_s)}{1 - \alpha}\right]^{-(1-\alpha)(1-R)/R} \, ds}, \tag{5.4}$$

$$l_t = \left[\frac{\alpha(r^* + \pi_t)}{1 - \alpha}\right]^{-1} C_t, \tag{5.5}$$

where it is assumed that $-r^* + (r^* - \delta)/R < 0$ and that the integral in (5.4)

---

[31] The utility function is strictly concave and twice continuously differentiable. Also assumed are the standard Inada conditions. Both consumption and money services are normal goods.

converges. [See Obstfeld (1983) for the solution method.] As in (4.2) and (4.3), desired consumption and real balances are both increasing functions of wealth V, while money demand is a declining function of the current nominal interest rate $r^* + \pi$. But in addition, anticipated future inflation generally influences the demands for goods and assets; current inflation generally affects consumption; and current disposable income plays no role. An exception arises when $R = 1$, so that the utility function takes the separable form $\alpha \ln(C) + (1 - \alpha)\ln(l)$. In this special case, the consumption function takes the form given by (4.2) (with $C_{Y^d} = 0$) and the demand for real balances takes the form given by (4.3).

One source of monetary non-neutrality in the model of Section 4 was the assumption that government spending was a function of private real balances [see the discussion following eq. (4.5)]. To understand better the possible sources of non-neutrality in optimizing models, we now depart further from the assumptions of Section 4 and assume that it is the level of transfers, rather than government consumption, that adjusts passively to changes in inflation-tax revenue. With this assumption, transfers are given by

$$T_t = \mu_t l_t - G_t,\tag{5.6}$$

and the path of G is exogenous. Accordingly, changes in l can no longer affect an important real variable, the portion of national income consumed by the government.

To study the economy's perfect foresight equilibrium, we assume initially that the money growth rate is a positive constant, $\bar{\mu}$. Logarithmic differentiation of (5.5) shows that

$$\frac{\dot{l}_t}{l_t} = \frac{\dot{V}_t}{V_t} + \left[\frac{\alpha(1-R)-1}{R}\right]\frac{\dot{\pi}_t}{(r^* + \pi_t)} + \frac{(r^* - \delta)}{R} - \left[r^* - \left(\frac{C_t}{\alpha V_t}\right)\right],\tag{5.7}$$

where C is given by (5.4). Using the definition of V in (4.1) and eq. (4.8), we find that the planned change in wealth, $\dot{V}$, is given by $r^*V - C - (r^* + \pi)l$. (This relationship also appeared in Section 4.2.) Because $C + (r^* + \pi)l = C/\alpha$ (given the assumed form of the utility function), the first and last terms on the right-hand side of (5.7) cancel. Eq. (4.4) then implies that the equilibrium inflation rate must satisfy the non-linear differential equation:

$$\dot{\pi}_t = \frac{(r^* + \pi_t)}{[\alpha(1-R)-1]}\left[R(\bar{\mu} - \pi_t) + (\delta - r^*)\right].\tag{5.8}$$

Figure 5.1 shows the phase diagram for (5.8). The equation has two stationary points, one stable (at $\pi = -r^*$) · and one unstable (at $\pi = \bar{\mu} + (\delta - r^*)/R$). Because the marginal utility of money is always strictly positive, the stationary point at $\pi = -r^*$ is not an equilibrium, nor is any point to its left [cf. (5.3)]. Moreover, paths originating to the right of the unstable steady state imply that

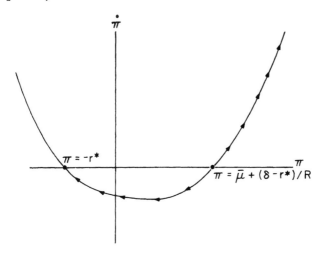

Figure 5.1

inflation explodes in spite of constant "fundamentals". Thus, the economy can reach its steady state equilibrium (the saddle path) only if inflation jumps immediately to the level,

$$\bar{\pi} = \bar{\mu} + (\delta - r^*)/R,$$ (5.9)

and remains there forever.

To find the equilibrium exchange rate, note that by (4.4) and (5.9):

$$l_s = l_t \exp[(r^* - \delta)(s - t)/R], \quad \text{for } s \geq t.$$ (5.10)

In equilibrium, therefore, the present value of future government transfer payments is

$$\tilde{T}_t = \int_t^\infty (\bar{\mu} l_s - G_s) \exp[-r^*(s-t)] \, ds = \frac{\bar{\mu} l_t}{[r^* + (\delta - r^*)/R]} - \tilde{G}_t,$$ (5.11)

where

$$\tilde{G}_t = \int_t^\infty G_s \exp[-r^*(s-t)] \, ds.$$

When combined, (5.4), (5.5), (5.9), and (5.11) imply that equilibrium real balances are

$$l_t = \frac{(1-\alpha)}{\alpha} \left[\frac{r^* + (\delta - r^*)/R}{\bar{\mu} + r^* + (\delta - r^*)/R} \right] (F_t + \tilde{Y}_t - \tilde{G}_t),$$ (5.12)

and that M_t/l_t is the equilibrium exchange rate. Equilibrium consumption is

$$C_t = [r^* + (\delta - r^*)/R](F_t + \tilde{Y}_t - \tilde{G}_t). \tag{5.13}$$

To interpret this equilibrium, return to the individual's lifetime budget constraint. By substituting (4.4) and (5.6) into (4.1) and integrating by parts, we obtain:[32]

$$\int_t^\infty C_s \exp[-r^*(s - t)] ds = F_t + \tilde{Y}_t - \tilde{G}_t. \tag{5.14}$$

Because money is a non-traded asset, the present value of domestic private consumption must equal the economy's non-monetary wealth, $F + \tilde{Y}$, net of the present value of future public consumption, $\tilde{G}$. In equilibrium, therefore, current consumption equals a fixed fraction of the present value of planned future consumption. If $\delta = r^*$, consumption equals "permanent" income, i.e.

$$C_t = r^*(F_t + \tilde{Y}_t - \tilde{G}_t) = r^* \int_t^\infty C_s \exp[-r^*(s - t)] ds,$$

so that $\dot{C} = 0$. If however, the consumer is less patient than the rest of the world ($\delta > r^*$), consumption will fall over time; and if he is more patient ($\delta < r^*$), consumption will rise. The current account is given by

$$\dot{F}_t = Y_t + r^* F_t - C_t - G_t$$
$$= [(Y_t - G_t) - r^*(\tilde{Y}_t - \tilde{G}_t)] - [(\delta - r^*)(F_t + \tilde{Y}_t - \tilde{G}_t)/R]. \tag{5.15}$$

The first term on the right-hand side of (5.15) shows that external borrowing and lending are used to smooth consumption in the face of deviations between disposable output, $Y - G$, and its "permanent" level, $r^*(\tilde{Y} - \tilde{G})$; this term is zero when the paths of Y and G are flat. The second term on the right-hand side of (5.15) reflects the discrepancy between the domestic and foreign time preference rates. If $\delta > r^*$, for example, the current account is perpetually in deficit if the paths of Y and G are flat.

The intrinsic dynamics of the economy are driven entirely by the discrepancy between δ and r^*. It is clear from (5.9) that the currency's depreciation rate exceeds or falls short of $\bar{\mu}$ as consumption falls or rises over time [see also Sachs (1983a)]. If $\delta > r^*$, however, the economy's wealth shrinks to zero asymptotically,

---

[32] The calculation leads to the equation:

$$\int_t^\infty C_s \exp[-r^*(s - t)] ds = F_t + \tilde{Y}_t - \tilde{G}_t + \lim_{s \to \infty} l_s \exp[-r^*(s - t)].$$

By (5.10), however:

$$\lim_{s \to \infty} l_s \exp[-r^*(s - t)] = l_t \left(\lim_{s \to \infty} \exp\{[-r^* + (r^* - \delta)/R](s - t)\} \right).$$

The last limit is zero because of the assumption that $-r^* + (r^* - \delta)/R < 0$.

while if $\delta < r^*$, the economy must grow until the small-country assumption is violated. Only if $\delta = r^*$ does the economy have a well-behaved steady state of the type assumed in Section 4. But that steady state is not unique: in equilibrium, the private sector chooses the highest constant consumption level consistent with the economy's non-monetary wealth, given the future path of government consumption. The currency depreciates at rate $\bar{\mu}$ in this case [by (5.9)], regardless of the current account's position. The system has no intrinsic dynamics.

Any previously unexpected increase in output or fall in government spending – whether permanent, transitory, or anticipated – causes a once-and-for-all rise in consumption and appreciation of the currency. An unanticipated increase in $\bar{\mu}$ or M, similarly, occasions a once-and-for-all depreciation, but does not influence consumption. It is noteworthy that anticipated monetary shocks need not be neutral, as (5.4) shows. Only when $R = 1$ (so that $U_{CI} = 0$) does anticipated monetary expansion have no impact on consumption and the current account. In general, the direction of the current-account effect is negative or positive as consumption and real balances are complements ($U_{CI} > 0$) or substitutes ($U_{CI} < 0$). The model of Section 4 also predicted a real dynamic response to an anticipated monetary shock, but the dynamics of the present system are entirely extrinsic when $\delta = r^*$.

The intrinsic dynamics caused by a divergence between the world interest rate and a constant time-preference rate are inconsistent with the existence of a well-behaved small-country steady state. Obstfeld (1981) studies a model in which the time-preference rate δ is endogenous and temporary discrepancies between δ and r^* drive the economy toward a conventional long-run equilibrium with $\delta = r^*$. Following Uzawa (1968), Obstfeld assumes that the subjective time preference rate is a monotonic function $\delta(U)$ of contemporaneous utility. The steady state is then characterized by a unique long-run utility level $\bar{U}$ satisfying $\delta(\bar{U}) = r^*$. Because expenditure is rising when $\delta(U) < r^*, \delta(U)$ can converge to r^* only if domestic residents become more impatient as utility increases, i.e. only if $\delta'(U) > 0$. This increasing impatience assumption plays the same role here that stability condition (4.11) played in Section 4: it ensures that when the current account is in surplus, say, consumption increases rapidly enough to eventually drive the surplus to zero.[33]

---

[33] The intertemporal welfare criterion with an endogenous time preference rate is no longer time additive, unlike the criterion W given by eq. (5.1). Lucas and Stokey (1984) study a general optimal growth model with heterogeneous consumers whose intertemporal preferences are not time additive. They, too, find that "the hypothesis of increasing marginal impatience...appears to be an essential component that any theory within the class considered in this paper must possess if it is to generate dynamics under which wealth distributions converge to determinate, stationary equilibria in which all agents have positive wealth and consumption levels". See also Epstein and Hynes (1983). If the constant time preference hypothesis is retained, the assumption that real bonds (as well as real money balances) yield direct utility leads to a model with a unique small-country steady state [Liviatan (1981)].

The resulting model is similar to that of Section 4. In particular, there is a unique small-country steady state with positive wealth, and a unique convergent saddle path along which foreign assets and real money balances rise together. Further, permanent changes in monetary growth cause movements along the economy's long-run utility contour $\overline{U}$ and thus alter the steady-state stock of foreign claims. This occurs even when the instantaneous utility function is separable in consumption and real balances ($U_{CI} = 0$).

5.2. *Models with two countries and two goods*

The previous sections of this chapter have studied small countries facing at least some prices that are determined outside the economy. We now turn to models of the world economy in which all prices are endogenously determined. As in Sections 2 and 3, it is assumed that two distinct consumption goods are available.

Lucas's (1982) model is a useful benchmark because there can be no intercountry wealth redistribution and all goods are traded. In addition, the "cash-in-advance" framework utilized in that model yields monetary equilibrium conditions that reduce to a simple quantity theory.

Consider a world of two countries, two goods, and two monies. All consumers in the world economy have identical tastes, and, as in Section 5.1, are risk averse and infinitely lived. A resident of the home country receives an exogenous stochastic endowment, Y, of a non-storable "home good" that can be traded with zero transport costs; a resident of the foreign country receives an exogenous stochastic endowment Y^* of a "foreign good" that can also be traded costlessly. The money supplies of each country, M and M^*, are determined exogenously by the respective governments. Monetary growth rates are stochastic: M increases via lump-sum transfer payments to domestic residents at the beginning of each period, and M^* increases via lump-sum transfers to foreign residents at the beginning of each period. Output levels and the growth rates of the two money supplies follow a joint first-order Markov process.

Let C and C^* denote consumption levels of the home and foreign goods. Consumers maximize the welfare criterion

$$W\left(\left\{C_t\right\}_{t=0}^{\infty}, \left\{C_t^*\right\}_{t=0}^{\infty}\right) = \mathbf{E}_0\left\{\sum_{t=0}^{\infty} \beta^t U\left(C_t, C_t^*\right)\right\}, \qquad 0 < \beta < 1, \qquad (5.16)$$

where $\mathbf{E}_0$ is an expected value conditional on $t = 0$ information, β is a constant subjective discount factor, and U is bounded. The maximization is subject to a budget constraint and to cash-in-advance constraints that provide an alternative to placing money directly into the instantaneous utility function. A typical consumer begins each trading "period" with a portfolio of assets that can include: domestic money, foreign money, claims to delivery of either money in any future period, and claims to shares of the nominal proceeds from future sales of either good (equities).

The sequence of events within each period is as follows. First, realized values of the stochastic endowments are revealed and the consumer receives a transfer payment of his country's money. After observing all current-period prices (including P, the home-currency price of the home good, and P^*, the foreign-currency price of the foreign good), the consumer visits an asset market in which monies and the other available assets are traded. Finally, the consumer visits a goods market where the two monies are used to purchase the consumption goods and endowments are sold. Only money held at the close of the current period's asset trading may be used to purchase current consumption. Money earned through the sale of endowments cannot be used in the same period, and thus enters the following period's pre-trade portfolio. Furthermore, it is assumed that all goods-market transactions involve the seller's money, implying that a domestic consumer receives PY units of domestic money in exchange for his endowment Y. [Helpman and Razin (1984) use a one-good framework to compare the dynamics of exchange rates when buyers' rather than sellers' currencies are used in transactions.] The consumer's choices are therefore subject to the cash-in-advance constraints

$$M_t^d \geq P_t C_t, \tag{5.17}$$

$$M_t^{*d} \geq P_t^* C_t^*, \tag{5.18}$$

where M^d and M^{*d} denote the quantities of the domestic and foreign monies that the consumer holds at the close of asset trading.

Although all consumers have the same tastes, the equilibrium of the model depends on the initial distribution of wealth. Lucas investigates a perfectly pooled, stationary equilibrium in which all consumers have the same wealth. Because tastes are identical and markets are complete, all choose the same portfolio and all consume the per capita world endowment of each good. As Section 5.1 showed, however, this perfectly-pooled equilibrium, while easy to analyze, need never be attained when the domestic and foreign time preference rates are fixed constants.

Lucas assumes that monetary policies are such that nominal interest rates are strictly positive. Because consumers would forgo interest payments by holding money balances exceeding planned consumptions, the monetary equilibrium conditions are

$$M_t = P_t Y_t, \tag{5.19}$$

$$M_t^* = P_t^* Y_t^*, \tag{5.20}$$

where quantities are now expressed in world per-capita terms. The necessary conditions for utility maximization include the standard requirement that the marginal rate of substitution between domestic and foreign goods equal their relative price:

$$P_t/E_t P_t^* = U_C(Y_t, Y_t^*)/U_{C^*}(Y_t, Y_t^*).\tag{5.21}$$

Together, (5.19)–(5.21) imply the exchange-rate equation:

$$E_t = (M_t/M_t^*)(Y_t^*/Y_t)[U_{C^*}(Y_t, Y_t^*)/U_C(Y_t, Y_t^*)].\tag{5.22}$$

Using (5.22) and the joint probability distribution for the exogenous variables Y, Y^*, M, and M^*, one can derive the probability distribution of the exchange rate.

This solution has several important characteristics. First, both changes in money supplies and changes in outputs of goods affect the exchange rate. Changes in tastes for goods (changes in the marginal rate of substitution function) also move the exchange rate. An increase in the output of the domestic good causes a fall in E, unless U_{C^*}/U_C rises with an elasticity greater than one when Y rises. The latter possibility would correspond to the usual condition for immiserizing growth, but immiserization can never occur here because the assumed perfect pooling prevents any agent's utility from falling when one country's endowment rises. The exchange rate is affected both by factors emphasized in the monetary approach to exchange rates and by factors emphasized in the elasticities approach.

Second, only current values of money supplies and outputs affect the exchange rate, even though prices of claims to future deliveries of goods or monies depend on the probability distributions of future money supplies and outputs. In a sense, therefore, the exchange rate is not really an "asset price" in this model, although the prices of claims clearly are. This characteristic of the model is not surprising given (a) the fixed velocity of money, (b) the intertemporally separable utility function that limits substitution over time in the goods market and prevents future or past levels of output from affecting the current marginal rate of substitution in equilibrium, and (c) the absence of real investment opportunities. [Barro and King (1983) discuss the roles of assumptions (b) and (c) in a closed-economy equilibrium.] These features yield a model resembling that of Section 2 in the special case $\lambda = \sigma = 0$. The condition $\lambda = 0$ has an exact analogue in the present setup because velocity is fixed. But consumption demands do respond to intertemporal relative prices here, so the condition $\sigma = 0$ has no counterpart. Rather, the insensitivity of the terms of trade to future real disturbances is a characteristic of the model's equilibrium.

Third (although Lucas does not discuss this), the volatility of exchange rates and price levels can differ in the model. A higher realized value of domestic output has an exchange-rate effect given by

$$\frac{de_t}{dy_t} = -\left[1 + \frac{(U_{CC}U_{C^*} - U_{CC^*}U_C)}{U_C U_{C^*}}Y_t\right]\tag{5.23}$$

(where small letters, as usual, denote logs). P falls in proportion to the rise in Y. If demand is sufficiently elastic that (5.23) is negative, then E and P both fall in response to an increase in Y, and the percentage change in E is smaller than that in P. If (5.23) is positive (the immiserizing-growth case), then E rises while P falls, and if demand is so inelastic the (5.23) exceeds unity, then the percentage change in E exceeds the percentage change in P. In this last case, real disturbances cause the exchange rate to have greater volatility than the price level.

The result that the exchange rate is unaffected by the probability distribution of future money supplies and outputs is eliminated if the model is altered so that velocity is variable. In the model of Stockman (1980), velocity is variable because households, when they visit asset markets, do not observe the nominal prices that they will subsequently face in the goods market. In Lucas's model, positive nominal interest rates lead households to leave the asset market with just enough money to finance planned consumption (and never more, since that would involve sacrificing interest): (5.17) and (5.18) hold as equalities, and aggregation yields (5.19) and (5.20) in equilibrium. But if goods prices are uncertain when households choose their portfolios, they must trade off forgone interest against the utility cost of the consumption forgone in the event that they have insufficient cash to finance desired consumption. This results in a "precautionary" demand for money as well as a "transactions" demand. Because velocities depend on interest rates, constraints (5.17) and (5.18) are not necessarily binding in equilibrium.

Consider a model in which households visit the goods-market at the beginning of each period and the asset market at the end of each period, as in Stockman (1980). The sequence of events now requires households to use money obtained in period $t - 1$, plus transfer payments at the beginning of period t, to buy goods in period t. The prices of goods in period t, however, are uncertain when portfolios are allocated among assets in period $t - 1$. Suppose also that the only assets available are the two monies and two one-period nominal bonds, B and F, which pay $1 + r$ and $1 + r^*$ units of domestic and foreign currency (respectively) after a period. The limited menu of assets implies that it is no longer feasible to perfectly pool risk and that the current account of the balance of payments is no longer identically zero, as in Lucas's model.

To simplify the analysis, we now assume that the representative agent's planning horizon is finite. A domestic consumer maximizes

$$W\left(\{C_t\}_{t=0}^{H}, \{C_t^*\}_{t=0}^{H}\right) = E_0\left\{\sum_{t=0}^{I} \beta^t U\left(C_t, C_t^*\right)\right\} \tag{5.24}$$

subject to the budget constraint,

$$P_t Y_t + M_{t-1} + P_t T_t + E_t M_{t-1}^* + (1 + r_{t-1}) B_{t-1} + (1 + r_{t-1}^*) E_t F_{t-1}$$
$$- P_t C_t - E_t P_t^* C_t^* - B_t - E_t F_t - M_t - E_t M_t^* = 0, \tag{5.25}$$

the cash-in-advance constraints,

$$M_{t-1} + P_t T_t \geq P_t C_t, \; E_t M^*_{t-1} \geq E_t P^*_t C^*_t, \tag{5.26}$$

initial conditions on asset stocks, and terminal conditions preventing debt at time $t = H$. A foreign representative household solves a similar problem but with income EP^*Y^* from selling the foreign good (instead of PY) and transfer payments EP^*T^* from the foreign government (instead of PT). Domestic and foreign outputs, Y and Y^*, and money supplies, M and M^*, are stochastic. Equilibrium requires that markets for all goods and assets clear.

The model can be solved by working backwards from time $t = H$. The necessary conditions for the optimization problem and the equilibrium conditions can be used to obtain the expression:

$$E_t = \mathbf{E}_t\left[U_{C^*}\left(C_{t+1}, C^*_{t+1}\right)/P^*_{t+1}\right]/\mathbf{E}_t\left[U_C\left(C_{t+1}, C^*_{t+1}\right)/P_{t+1}\right] \quad (t < H),$$
$$\tag{5.27}$$

where C and C^* are now the equilibrium levels of consumption in the domestic country (which depend on the international distribution of wealth). While it is not possible to obtain a simple reduced-form expression for the exchange rate in the general case, (5.27) restricts the relation between the exchange rate and other endogenous variables in a manner similar to consumption-based models of asset pricing [Hansen and Singleton (1983)]. This restriction does not depend heavily on the set of assets available to households. Svensson (1983), for example, obtains a similar result in a modified version of Lucas's model that permits variable velocities of money. As in the model of Section 2, with $\lambda > 0$ and $\sigma > 0$, anticipated future outputs and money supplies affect the exchange rate: (5.27) relates E_t to the probability distributions of Y_{t+1}, Y^*_{t+1}, P_{t+1}, and P^*_{t+1}.

Money is neutral in this model if nominal transfers are distributed in proportion to initial net nominal asset stocks.[34] But money is not superneutral because inflation in either currency acts as a tax on goods purchased with that currency. Thus, anticipated inflation affects the terms of trade and so the exchange rate.

If rates of time preference differ across countries, the model has no steady state in which all agents have positive wealth and consumption. Helpman and Razin (1982), assuming perfect foresight and an infinite horizon, discuss the exchange rate changes that occur in this case as wealth is redistributed across countries. The results are very similar to those derived in the model of Section 5.1.

---

[34] Helpman and Razin (1982) emphasize the real wealth-redistribution effects of unanticipated increases in money supplies when there are unindexed nominal bonds. Note that eq. (5.27) would still hold if bonds were indexed, as assumed in Section 5.3 below.

5.3. *The role of non-traded goods*

The previous sections of this chapter have focused mainly on models in which all goods are traded. But the exchange-rate effects of disturbances in the market for non-traded goods differ from those of disturbances in markets for traded goods. In all the models we have considered, an increase in domestic output raises the demand for money and tends to reduce all nominal prices including E. As we have seen, however, the reduction in E is mitigated or reversed if the rise in domestic output causes a fall in the terms of trade. Lucas's model implies that the exchange rate falls unless the condition for immiserizing growth is net. In contrast, the exchange-rate effect of an increase in the supply of non-tradables depends on the parameters of the demand for money. This will be illustrated by a two-country, finite-horizon model with a single traded good and a non-traded good in each country.

Assume that a representative domestic household maximizes

$$W\left(\left\{C_t^T\right\}_{t=0}^H, \left\{C_t^N\right\}_{t=0}^H, \{l_t\}_{t=0}^H\right) = \mathbf{E}_0\left\{\sum_{t=0}^H \beta^t U\left(C_t^T, C_t^N, l_t\right)\right\}, \qquad (5.28)$$

where C^T and C^N denote consumptions of traded and non-traded goods and real balances l are defined as nominal money M deflated by a price index Π. The latter is a weighted average of the money prices of traded and non-traded goods, P^T and P^N. Maximization of (5.28) is subject to initial and terminal conditions[35] and budget constraints of the form:

$$P_t^T\left(Y_t^T - C_t^T\right) + P_t^N\left(Y_t^N - C_t^N\right) + P_t^T\left(B_{t-1} - P_t^B B_t\right) + M_{t-1} + P_t T_t - M_t = 0, \qquad (5.29)$$

where Y^T and Y^N are endowments of traded and non-traded goods; B_{t-1} is the number of real bonds (claims to one unit of the traded good delivered at date t) purchased at date $t-1$ at price P_{t-1}^B; M_{t-1} denotes nominal money held before the period t transfer payment of money, $P_t T_t$; and M_t is the nominal money holding chosen by the household at date t. There is a similar maximization problem for the representative foreign household. (Foreign variables are marked with an asterisk.) We assume that rates of time preference are constant and equal in the two countries and that U and U^* are separable in their three arguments. Implicit in (5.29) is the assumption that national monies are not traded between countries.

The properties of the model can be analyzed by working backwards from the final period.

Equilibrium conditions require that the world market for tradables clear; that the two markets for non-tradables clear; and that all asset markets clear. These

---

[35] The terminal condition used here requires that all debts be paid at the end of the final period.

conditions can be combined with the necessary conditions for utility maximization to show the effect of changes in traded and non-traded outputs on the final period's exchange rate. Abstracting from any changes in money supplies or foreign output of either good, we can write

$$E_H = g^H(Y^T, Y^N). \tag{5.30}$$

Let Π_1 and Π_2 be the partial derivatives of the price index $\Pi = \Pi(P^T, P^N)$, and let J' be the derivative of $J(\cdot) = U_{C^T}^{-1}(\cdot)$.

$$K \equiv \frac{\Pi_1 P^N}{\Pi}[U_l + U_{ll}l] \bigg/ \left[U_l\left(1 - \frac{\Pi_2 P^N}{\Pi}\right) - U_{ll}l\frac{\Pi_2 P^N}{\Pi} \right].$$

Note that Π is homogeneous of degree one in P^T and P^N. The partial derivatives of the function $g^H(\cdot, \cdot)$ appearing in (5.30) are

$$g_{Y^T}^H = \left[\frac{-g^H\Pi}{J'P^TU_l} \right]\left[\frac{U_l}{lU_{ll}}\left(1 - \frac{\Pi_2 P^N}{\Pi}\right) - \frac{\Pi_2 P^N}{\Pi} \right], \tag{5.31}$$

$$g_{Y^N}^H = \frac{-U_{C^NC^N}\Pi_1^2 g^H(U_l + lU_{ll}}{lU_{ll}\Pi_2}. \tag{5.32}$$

Because $g_{Y^T}^H$ is negative, an increase in Y^T causes an appreciation of the domestic currency. But the sign of $g_{Y^N}^H$ depends on the sign of the term $U_l + U_{ll}l$. Denote the elasticity of the marginal utility of money by $\chi \equiv (MU_{ll}/\Pi U_l)$. Then an increase in the output of the non-traded good lowers (raises) the exchange rate, E, as $\chi \gtrless -1$. If the marginal utility of money is inelastic, then an increase in Y^N causes the domestic currency to appreciate, just as an increase in Y^T does. But if the marginal utility of money is elastic, then an increase in Y^N depreciates the domestic currency.[36] Note that a large elasticity of the marginal utility of money corresponds to a small income elasticity of money demand.

This result illustrates the different rules for obtaining a probability distribution on the exchange rate from the probability densities on outputs of traded and non-traded goods. Although the specific rule derived above applies only to the final period of the model, a recursive solution of the model shows how the dynamics of exchange rate changes over time are affected differently by disturbances in the two sectors. To conserve space, we discuss here the backward recursion in the intermediate case in which χ is constant and equal to -1.

The optimization problem of the representative domestic household in an $(H + 1)$-period model takes the form of maximizing

$$U\big(C_t^T, C_t^N, l_t\big) + \beta E_t V(M_t, B_t, H - t) \tag{5.33}$$

---

[36] Obviously a Cobb–Douglas utility function leads to the result that the exchange rate in the final period is independent of the supply of non-traded goods (though it is not independent of the supply of traded goods). See Stockman (1983).

subject to (5.29), where V is the value function or indirect utility function that shows the maximized value of utility from periods $t + 1$ through H. Let η_t be the time-t shadow value of a unit of domestic money. Standard techniques can be used to obtain the necessary conditions:

$$\eta_t = \frac{U_{C^T}}{P_t^T} = \frac{U_{C^N}}{P_t^N} = \frac{U_I}{\Pi_t} + \beta E_t(\eta_{t+1}) = \beta \frac{1}{P_t^T P_t^B} E_t[\eta_{t+1} P_{t+1}^T]. \qquad (5.34)$$

Similar conditions are obtained for the analogous maximization problem in the foreign country.

If the elasticity of the marginal utility of money is one, then $\eta_H \propto M_H^{-1}$, $\eta_{H-1} \propto M_{H-1}^{-1} + \beta E_{H-1}(1/M_H)$ and η_t is independent of the output of non-traded goods for all t [as long as the output of non-traded goods in t does not affect $E_t(1/M_{t+s})$ for $s > 0$, i.e. as long as it does not signal future changes in the money supply – a possibility from which we abstract in this discussion]. Since $\eta_H P_H^T = U_{C^T}(Y_H^T + B_{H-1})$ and $\eta_H^* P_H^{T^*} = U_{C^T}^*(Y_H^{T^*} - B_{H-1})$, the conditions

$$\eta_t = \frac{\beta}{P_t^T P_t^B} E_t(\eta_{t+1} P_{t+1}^T), \qquad \eta_t^* = \frac{\beta}{P_t^{T^*} P_t^B} E_t(\eta_{t+1}^* P_{t+1}^{T^*}), \qquad (5.35)$$

can be used to solve for P_{H-1}^B and B_{H-1}. The important property of the solution (used below) is that P^B and B are functions of P^T and P^{T^*} (as well as of η and η^*) but not (at least directly) functions of Y^N or Y^{N^*}. Let $J^*(\cdot) = U_{C^T}^{*-1}(\cdot)$. The equations

$$Y_t^T - J(\eta_t P_t^T) = -B_{t-1} + P_t^B B_t, \qquad Y_t^{T^*} - J^*(\eta_t^* P_t^{T^*}) = B_{t-1} - P_t^B B_t, \qquad (5.36)$$

allow us to define the functions:

$$P_t^T = h(B_{t-1}, \eta_t, \eta_t^*, Y_t^T, Y_t^{T^*}, H - t),$$
$$P_t^{T^*} = h^*(B_{t-1}, \eta_t, \eta_t^*, Y_t^T, Y_t^{T^*}, H - t). \qquad (5.37)$$

Then (5.35) and (5.37) constitute a four-equation system that can be solved for P^B, B, P^T, and P^{T^*} as functions of Y^T, Y^{T^*}, η, and η^*. But it was already shown that η and η^* are independent of current and expected future non-traded outputs. Thus the exchange rate $E = P^T/P^{T^*}$ depends on (current) outputs of traded goods in each country, but is independent of the outputs of non-traded goods when $\chi = -1$. By varying χ, one can change the rule that translates the dynamics of the output of both traded and non-traded goods into the dynamics of the exchange rate. The probability distribution on the exchange rate can be independent of the probability distribution on outputs of non-traded goods, as when $\chi = -1$, or (as in the analysis of $t = H$) the probability distribution induced on the exchange rate can respond in similar or in very different ways to the probability distributions on outputs of traded and non-traded goods.

This result that an increase in output of non-traded goods can push the value of the domestic currency upward or downward should not be surprising even if the precise condition was not initially obvious. On the one hand, an increase in Y^N reduces P^N and, for any given demand for money, requires a higher exchange rate to keep a weighted average of P^N and P^T fixed, as required for money-market equilibrium. On the other hand, an increase in Y^N raises aggregate output at the initial relative price and, given P^N, raises the demand for money and requires a lower exchange rate. The relative strengths of these effects turn on the elasticity of the marginal utility of money.

6. Conclusion

This chapter has reviewed a variety of dynamic exchange-rate models. These models have been developed to explain certain facts about floating rates, but they have other testable implications that can, perhaps, be used in the future to further limit the set of models that are consistent with the data. Existing empirical research on the models is inconclusive, however.

A common feature of all the models we have discussed is the assumption of rational expectations: individuals know the structure of the economy, and use all available information to make optimal forecasts of future variables. Most of the models reviewed can be analyzed under alternative expectational assumptions, as in Kouri (1976). But while the informational requirements of the rational-expectations hypothesis may appear extreme, we see two principal reasons for basing exchange-rate models on the assumption of rationality. First, the assumption yields results that arise entirely from the inherent logic of a model, not from arbitrary expectation-formation mechanisms that have been grafted onto it. Second, the assumption is probably much closer to the truth than simple alternatives like "static" or "adaptive" expectations. Exchange rates clearly do respond to anticipated future events, and while the rationality hypothesis may be incorrect in a literal sense, the qualitative correctness of its implications is difficult to deny. As the chapter has illustrated, expectations play a key role in exchange-rate determination, and little can be said about short- and medium-run exchange rate behavior unless some stand on the process generating expectations is taken. It is unfortunate, therefore, that formal empirical tests are unlikely to provide decisive evidence for or against rational expectations. As Levich argues in Chapter 19 of this Handbook, any test of rationality is a joint test of rationality *and* an underlying exchange-rate model which may itself be inappropriate.

The additional assumption of saddle-path stability was invoked repeatedly in the models studied above. That assumption requires more than just the efficient forecasting of future prices. There must also be market forces that prevent the emergence of self-fulfilling speculative bubbles, so that the exchange rate is tied to its fundamental determinants. Several simple theoretical models show how bubbles can be ruled out through considerations of intertemporal arbitrage or possible government interventions [see, for example, Obstfeld and Rogoff (1983)]. Casual empiricism reinforces these theoretical results, for it suggests that protracted bubbles have not been a feature of the recent experience with floating rates. Unfortunately, identification problems similar to those involved in testing rational expectations plague any attempt to detect speculative bubbles in actual data.

The question of which models and types of implications will be most useful in future attempts to understand exchange rates is open, and leads to deep philosophical and statistical questions that we will not try to resolve here. Nonetheless, it seems likely to us that as more data become available, progress will be made in serious attempts to develop and test new implications of models similar to those discussed above.

References

Bardhan, P.K. (1967), "Optimum foreign borrowing", in: K. Shell, ed., Essays in the theory of optimal economic growth (MIT Press, Cambridge, Mass.).

Barro, R.J. (1978), "A stochastic equilibrium model of an open economy under flexible exchange rates", Quarterly Journal of Economics, 92:149–164.

Barro, R.J. (1980), "A capital market in an equilibrium business cycle model", Econometrica, 48:1393–1417.

Barro, R.J. and R.G. King (1983), "Time-separable preferences and intertemporal substitution models of business cycles", Working Paper No. 888 (National Bureau of Economic Research, Cambridge, Mass.).

Black, S.W. (1973), International money markets and flexible exchange rates, Princeton studies in international finance, No. 32 (International Finance Section, Princeton University, Princeton).

Blinder, A.S. and R.M. Solow (1973), "Does fiscal policy matter?", Journal of Public Economics, 2:318–337.

Boyer, R.S. and R.J. Hodrick (1982a), "The dynamic adjustment path for perfectly foreseen changes in monetary policy", Journal of Monetary Economics, 9:185–201.

Boyer, R.S. and R.J. Hodrick (1982b), "Perfect foresight, financial policies, and exchange-rate dynamics", Canadian Journal of Economics, 15:143–164.

Branson, W.H. (1974), Stocks and flows in international monetary analysis, in: A. Ando, R. Herring, and R. Marston, eds., International aspects of stabilization policies (Federal Reserve Bank of Boston, Boston, Mass.).

Brock, W.A. (1975), "A simple perfect foresight monetary model", Journal of Monetary Economics, 1:133–150.

Bruno, M. (1976), "The two-sector open economy and the real exchange rate", American Economic Review, 66:566–577.

Buiter, W.H. and M. Miller (1982), "Real exchange rate overshooting and the output cost of bringing down inflation", European Economic Review, 18:85–123.

Burgstaller, A. (1980), "Flexible exchange rates, rational expectations, and the trade-off between inflation and unemployment", Discussion Paper No. 85 (Department of Economics, Columbia University, New York).

Calvo, G.A. (1977), "The stability of models of money and perfect foresight: A comment", Econometrica, 45:1737–1739.

Calvo, G.A. (1979), "On models of money and perfect foresight", International Economic Review, 20:83–103.

Calvo, G.A. (1983), "Staggered contracts and exchange rate policy", in: Jacob A. Frenkel, ed., Exchange rates and international macroeconomics (University of Chicago Press, Chicago).

Calvo, G.A. and C.A. Rodriguez (1977), "A model of exchange rate determination under currency substitution and rational expectations", Journal of Political Economy, 85:617–625.

Clarida, R.H. (1982) "Current account, exchange rate, and monetary dynamics in a stochastic equilibrium model", Working paper (Harvard University, Cambridge, Mass.).

Clower, R.W. (1967), "A reconsideration of the microfoundations of monetary theory", Western Economic Journal, 6:1–8.

Dornbusch, R. (1975), "A portfolio balance model of the open economy", Journal of Monetary Economics, 1:3–20.

Dornbusch, R (1976a), "The theory of flexible exchange rate regimes and macroeconomic policy", Scandinavian Journal of Economics, 78:255–275.

Dornbusch, R. (1976b), "Expectations and exchange rate dynamics", Journal of Political Economy, 84:1161–1176.

Dornbusch, R. (1976c), "Capital mobility, flexible exchange rates, and macro-economic equilibrium", in: E.-M. Claassen and P. Salin, eds., Recent issues in international monetary economics (North-Holland, Amsterdam).

Dornbusch, R. (1980), Open economy macroeconomics (Basic Books, New York).

Dornbusch, R. and S. Fischer (1980), "Exchange rates and the current account", American Economic Review, 70:960–971.

Eaton, J. (1982), "Optimal and time consistent exchange rate management in an overlapping generations economy", Discussion Paper no. 413 (Economic Growth Center, Yale University, New Haven). Journal of International Money and Finance, forthcoming.

Epstein, L.G. and J.A. Hynes (1983), "The rate of time preference and dynamic economic analysis", Journal of Political Economy, 91:611–635.

Fischer, S. (1977), "Wage indexation and macroeconomic stability", in: K. Brunner and A.H. Meltzer, eds., Stabilization of the domestic and international economy (North-Holland, Amsterdam).

Fleming, J.M. (1962), "Domestic financial policies under fixed and under floating exchange rates", International Monetary Fund Staff Papers, 9:369–379.

Flood, R.P. (1979), "An example of exchange rate overshooting", Southern Economic Journal, 46:168–178.

Flood, R.P. (1981), "Explanations of exchange-rate volatility and other empirical regularities in some popular models of the foreign exchange market", in: K. Brunner and A.H. Meltzer, eds., The costs and consequences of inflation (North-Holland, Amsterdam).

Flood, R.P. and P.M. Garber (1980), "Market fundamentals versus price-level bubbles: The first tests", Journal of Political Economy, 88:745–770.

Flood, R.P. and P.M. Garber (1983), "A model of stochastic process switching", Econometrica, 51:537–551.

Flood, R.P. and R.J. Hodrick (1983), "Optimal price and inventory adjustment in an open-economy model of the business cycle", Working paper No. 1089 (National Bureau of Economic Research, Cambridge, Mass.).

Foley, D.K. and M. Sidrauski (1970), "Portfolio choice, investment and growth", American Economic Review, 60:44–63.

Frankel, J.A. (1979), "On the mark: A theory of floating exchange rates based on real interest differentials", American Economic Review, 69:610–622.

Frenkel, J.A. (1976), "A monetary approach to the exchange rate: Doctrinal aspects and empirical evidence", Scandinavian Journal of Economics, 78:200–224.

Frenkel, J.A. and M. Mussa (1980), "The efficiency of foreign exchange markets and measures of turbulence", American Economic Review, 70:374–381.

Frenkel, J.A. and C.A. Rodriguez (1975), "Portfolio equilibrium and the balance of payments: A monetary approach", American Economic Review, 65:674–688.

Frenkel, J.A. and C.A. Rodriguez (1982), "Exchange rate dynamics and the overshooting hypothesis",

International Monetary Fund Staff Papers, 29:1–30.

Genberg, H. (1978), "Purchasing power parity under fixed and flexible exchange rates", Journal of International Economics, 8:247–276.

Gray, J.A. (1976), "Wage indexation: A macroeconomic approach", Journal of Monetary Economics, 2:221–235.

Gray, M.R. and S.J. Turnovsky (1979), "The stability of exchange rate dynamics under perfect myopic foresight", International Economic Review, 20:653–660.

Greenwood, J. (1983), "Expectations, the exchange rate, and the current account", Journal of Monetary Economics, 12:543–569.

Hamada, K. (1969), "Optimal capital accumulation by an economy facing an international capital market", Journal of Political Economy, 77:684–697.

Hansen, L.P. and K.J. Singleton (1983), "Stochastic consumption, risk aversion, and the temporal behavior of asset returns", Journal of Political Economy, 91:249–265.

Harris, R.G. and D.D. Purvis (1981), "Diverse information and market efficiency in a monetary model of the exchange rate", Economic Journal, 91:829–847.

Helpman, E. and A. Razin (1979), "Towards a consistent comparison of alternative exchange rate systems", Canadian Journal of Economics, 12:394–409.

Helpman, E. and A. Razin (1982), "Dynamics of a floating exchange rate regime", Journal of Political Economy, 90:728–754.

Helpman, E. and A. Razin (1984), "The role of saving and investment in exchange rate determination under alternative monetary mechanisms", Journal of Monetary Economics, 13:307–325.

Henderson, D.W. and K. Rogoff (1982), "Negative net foreign asset positions and stability in a world portfolio balance model", Journal of International Economics, 13:85–104.

Hirsch, M.W. and S. Smale (1974), Differential equations, dynamical systems, and linear algebra (Academic Press, New York).

Hodrick, R.J. (1980), "Dynamic effects of government policies in an open economy", Journal of Monetary Economics, 6:213–239.

Hodrick, R.J. (1982), "On the effects of macroeconomic policy in a maximizing model of a small open economy", Journal of Macroeconomics, 4:195–213.

Kareken, J. and N. Wallace (1981), "On the indeterminacy of equilibrium exchange rates", Quarterly Journal of Economics, 96:207–222.

Kimbrough, K.P. (1983), "The forward rate as a predictor of the future spot rate, the role of policy, and exchange rate regime choice", Working paper (Department of Economics, Duke University, Durham).

Kind, P. (1982), "On the robustness of models of exchange rate dynamics", Working Paper (Department of Economics, Columbia University, New York).

Koh, A.T. (1984), "Money shocks and deviations from purchasing power parity", Journal of Monetary Economics, 14:105–122.

Kouri, P.J.K. (1976), "The exchange rate and the balance of payments in the short run and in the long run: A monetary approach", Scandinavian Journal of Economics, 78:280–304.

Kouri, P.J.K. (1983), "Balance of payments and the foreign exchange market: A dynamic partial equilibrium model", in: J.S. Bhandari and B.H. Putnam, eds., Economic interdependence and flexible exchange rates (MIT Press, Cambridge, Mass.).

Kouri, P.J.K. and J.B. de Macedo (1978), "Exchange rates and the international adjustment process", Brookings Papers on Economic Activity, 9:111–150.

Krugman, P.R. (1979), "A theory of balance-of-payments crises", Journal of Money, Credit and Banking, 11:311–325.

Krugman, P.R. (1983), "Oil and the dollar", in: J.S. Bhandari and B.H. Putnam, eds., Economic interdependence and flexible exchange rates (MIT Press, Cambridge, Mass.).

Lapan, H. and W. Enders (1983), "Rational expectations, endogenous currency substitution, and exchange rate determination", Quarterly Journal of Economics, 98:427–439.

Liviatan, N. (1980), "Anti-inflationary monetary policy and the capital import tax", Warwick economic research paper, No. 171 (University of Warwick, Coventry).

Liviatan, N. (1981), "Monetary expansion and real exchange rate dynamics", Journal of Political Economy, 89:1218–1227.

Lucas, R.E., Jr. (1975), "An equilibrium model of the business cycle", Journal of Political Economy,

83:1113-1144.

Lucas, R.E., Jr. (1976), "Econometric policy evaluation: A critique", in: K. Brunner and A.H. Meltzer, eds., The Phillips curve and labor markets (North-Holland, Amsterdam).

Lucas, R.E., Jr. (1982), "Interest rates and currency prices in a two-country world", Journal of Monetary Economics, 10:335-359.

Lucas, R.E., Jr. and N.L. Stokey (1984), "Optimal growth with many consumers", Journal of Economic Theory, 32:139-171.

Meese, R.A. and K. Rogoff (1983), "Empirical exchange rate models of the seventies: Do they fit out of sample?", Journal of International Economics, 14:3-24.

Mundell, R.A. (1968), International economics (Macmillan, New York).

Mussa, M. (1977), "A dynamic theory of foreign exchange", in: M.J. Artis and A.R. Nobay, eds., Studies in modern economic analysis (Basil Blackwell, Oxford).

Mussa, M. (1982), "A model of exchange rate dynamics", Journal of Political Economy, 90:74-104.

Mussa, M. (1984), "The theory of exchange rate determination", in: J.F.O. Bilson and R.C. Marston, eds., Exchange rate theory and practice (University of Chicago Press, Chicago).

Niehans, J. (1977), "Exchange rate dynamics with stock/flow interaction", Journal of Political Economy, 85:1245-1257.

Obstfeld, M. (1980), "Intermediate imports, the terms of trade, and the dynamics of the exchange rate and current account", Journal of International Economics, 10:461-480.

Obstfeld, M. (1981), "Macroeconomic policy, exchange-rate dynamics, and optimal asset accumulation", Journal of Political Economy, 89:1142-1161.

Obstfeld, M. (1982), "Relative prices, employment, and the exchange rate in an economy with foresight", Econometrica, 50:1219-1242.

Obstfeld, M. (1983), "Intertemporal price speculation and the optimal current-account deficit", Journal of International Money and Finance, 2:135-145.

Obstfeld, M. and K. Rogoff (1983), "Speculative hyperinflations in maximizing models: Can we rule them out?", Journal of Political Economy, 91:675-687.

Obstfeld, M. and K. Rogoff (1984), "Exchange rate dynamics with sluggish prices under alternative price-adjustment rules", International Economic Review, 25:159-174.

Rodriguez, C.A. (1980), "The role of trade flows in exchange rate determination: A rational expectations approach", Journal of Political Economy, 88:1148-1158.

Rogoff, K. (1979), Essays on expectations and exchange rate volatility, Doctoral Disseration (Massachusetts Institute of Technology, Cambridge, Mass.).

Sachs, J. (1980), "Wage indexation, flexible exchange rates, and macroeconomic policy", Quarterly Journal of Economics, 94:731-747.

Sachs, J. (1983a), "Aspects of the current account behavior of OECD economies", in: E.-M. Claassen and P. Salin, eds., Recent issues in the theory of flexible exchange rates (North-Holland, Amsterdam).

Sachs, J. (1983b), "Energy and growth under flexible exchange rates: A simulation study", in: J.S. Bhandari and B.H. Putnam, eds., Economic interdependence and flexible exchange rates (MIT Press, Cambridge, Mass.).

Saidi, N. (1980), "Fluctuating exchange rates and the international transmission of economic disturbances", Journal of Money, Credit and Banking, 12:575-591.

Salant, S.W. (1983), "The vulnerability of price stabilization schemes to speculative attack", Journal of Political Economy, 91:1-38.

Salant, S.W. and D.W. Henderson (1978), "Market anticipations of government policies and the price of gold", Journal of Political Economy, 86:627-648.

Samuelson, P.A. (1947), Foundations of economic analysis (Harvard University Press, Cambridge, Mass.).

Sargent, T.J. and N. Wallace (1973), "The stability of models of money and growth with perfect foresight", Econometrica, 41:1043-1048.

Shafer, J.R. and B.E. Loopesko (1983), "Floating exchange rates after ten years", Brookings Papers on Economic Activity, 14:1-70.

Sidrauski, M. (1967), "Rational choice and patterns of growth in a monetary economy", American Economic Review, 57:534–544.

Stockman, A.C. (1980), "A theory of exchange rate determination", Journal of Political Economy, 88:673–698.

Stockman, A.C. (1983), "Real exchange rates under alternative nominal exchange-rate systems", Journal of International Money and Finance, 2:147–166.

Stockman, A.C. and A.T. Koh (1984). "Open-economy implications of two models of business fluctuations", Working paper (Department of Economics, University of Rochester, Rochester).

Svensson, L.E.O. (1983), "Currency prices, terms of trade, and interest rates: A general-equilibrium, asset-pricing, cash-in-advance approach", Working paper (University of Stockholm, Stockholm).

Taylor, J.B. (1980), "Aggregate dynamics and staggered contracts", Journal of Political Economy, 88:1–23.

Tobin, J. (1965), "Money and economic growth", Econometrica, 33:671–684.

Uzawa, H. (1968), "Time preference, the consumption function, and optimum asset holdings", in: J.N. Wolfe, ed., Value, capital and growth: Papers in honor of Sir John Hicks (Aldine, Chicago).

Wilson, C.A. (1979), "Anticipated shocks and exchange rate dynamics", Journal of Political Economy, 87:639–647.

Chapter 19

EMPIRICAL STUDIES OF EXCHANGE RATES: PRICE BEHAVIOR, RATE DETERMINATION AND MARKET EFFICIENCY

RICHARD M. LEVICH

New York University and National Bureau of Economic Research

Contents

Handbook of International Economics, vol. II, edited by R.W. Jones and P.B. Kenen
© *Elsevier Science Publishers B.V., 1985*

1. Introduction – historical setting

The introduction of floating exchange rates in the early 1970s marked a major systematic change for international financial markets. With the exception of the Canadian experiment (1950–1962), a system of pegged but adjustable exchange rates as specified under the Bretton Woods agreement dominated the post-Second World War experience of all industrialized countries. Exchange rate behavior under the Bretton Woods system was characterized by relatively large, discrete and infrequent exchange rate changes. Consequently, economists and market analysts concentrated their attention on balance of payments data and international reserves. Sustained payments imbalance along with a substantial shift in international reserve holdings would increase the probability that the central bank could no longer support the pegged rate. These pressures being slow to accumulate, analysts could be certain of the *direction* of exchange rate change. The *magnitude* of exchange rate change (i.e. the amount required to restore payments balance and to halt international reserve flows) could be estimated from a purchasing power parity (PPP) model or from other data. However, the ultimate decision to change the peg was fundamentally a political decision, and economic analysis was of little use in picking the breaking points of political officials.

Since the early 1970s, exchange rates have been determined largely by private market forces within a floating exchange rate system. However, central banks have continued to intervene in the market, so some would prefer the label *managed floating* system.[1] Exchange rate behavior under the current system can be characterized by relatively small and continuous price changes that occur quickly in response to new information. The search for a rational explanation of exchange rate behavior in the setting of an integrated international financial market has been the central thrust of empirical research over the last decade.

This broad research topic can be divided into three partially distinct categories. First, many empirical studies have examined the relationship between the spot exchange rate, S_t, and a set of independent variables. The purpose here, of course, is to test a particular model of exchange rate determination, in order to forecast exchange rates or to examine the effect of other economic policies on exchange rates and vice versa. Second, other studies have analyzed the statistical properties of variables constructed using S_t. For example, variables such as the percentage change in the spot rate, $\dot{S}_t = (S_t - S_{t-1})/S_{t-1}$, the forward premium, $\Pi_t = (F_t - $

---

[1] Giddy (1979) has estimated that the daily worldwide volume of foreign exchange trading increased from \$50 billion to nearly \$200 billion over the 1970s. With 250 trading days per year, the latter figure suggests a \$50 *trillion* annual trading volume. Direct intervention by central bank is small relative to this volume. But other economic policies and announcements by government officials can have a major indirect effect on exchange markets.

$S_t)/S_t$, and the forward rate forecasting error, $D_t = S_{t+n} - F_{t,n}$, provide information on the historical return and risk of particular currency trading strategies. Finally, empirical studies have sought to ascertain the efficiency of foreign exchange and international financial markets. As we will emphasize in Section 3, tests of market efficiency involve an implicit hypothesis concerning the equilibrium exchange rate or equilibrium returns. Because they involve joint hypotheses, the results of efficient market studies have been difficult to interpret.

The major insight to come from this decade of research is that foreign exchange is a financial asset. One implication of this conclusion is that the current spot exchange rate reflects expected values of future exogenous variables, discounted back to the present. This is, of course, analogous to the notion that a security's price reflects the present value of expected future cash flows. A second implication is that the price of a currency is determined by the demand for it as a financial asset relative to the demands for other currencies. This demand is based on the currency's utility as a medium of exchange, store of value and unit of account. The demand for foreign exchange, therefore, depends on a broader range of arguments than the demand for a typical security, which depends on return and risk relative to a market index.

The most recent modeling of exchange rate behavior reflects a combination of capital market theory and macroeconomics. The popular capital asset pricing models (CAPM) developed in the 1960s and 1970s solved for the prices of financial assets in a setting where returns are stochastic and investors are risk averse utility maximizers.[2] The CAPM framework incorporated two notable assumptions. First, assets were assumed to be in fixed supply. Consequently, the relative demands for securities, scaled by fixed supplies, were sufficient to determine prices. Trivial supply shocks, such as a stock split, had a direct effect on share prices but were easily incorporated by a change in scale. However, stochastic supply shocks (e.g. the exchange of convertible bonds for stocks and the exercise of warrents or executive stock options) have a much more complicated and ambiguous effect in a general equilibrium model of share prices. Second, the CAPM framework assumes that there are many securities and that the supply of each is small. Consequently, dramatic shocks affecting any individual security do not induce general wealth effects. Investors do not need to re-balance their portfolios so there are no feedback effects on the prices of other securities.

Asset models for exchange rate determination cannot make either of these assumptions and still hope to provide a realistic explanation of exchange rate behavior. Supplies of foreign currency and of government debt denominated in foreign currency are definitely not fixed and probably not predictable in any simple way. In turn, the private demands for foreign currency and for foreign

---

[2] The classic models are generally attributed to Sharpe (1964), Lintner (1965), Mossin (1966) and Black (1972).

currency denominated assets will depend on how well the currency contributes to private utility by providing services as a medium of exchange and store of value at low risk. Presumably, monetary discipline (i.e. slow and predictable money growth) and fiscal discipline (i.e. budget balance rather than deficits financed by issuing official debt) will have a positive impact on currency demand. Therefore, an asset framework for currency pricing ought to account for the simultaneous determination of demand and supply and the stochastic nature of supply. The original CAPM models used a partial equilibrium framework, and this puts obvious limitations on their application to foreign exchange.

Furthermore, while there may be thousands of traded securities and millions of investors, so that there is little need for portfolio re-balancing in response to security-specific shocks, this framework cannot be carried over to the foreign exchange market. More than 90 percent of world financial wealth is denominated in only six currencies and world financial wealth is similarly concentrated in a small number of countries. Therefore, a small change in the perceived risk and return properties of a particular currency may lead to portfolio re-balancing that has a significant impact on other currency prices. Similarly, current account imbalances can shift the international distribution of wealth among countries with different currency preferences affecting currency prices. Here, the popular examples are the current account surpluses of Japan and Germany, presumably with a preference for assets denominated in their domestic currencies, and the current account surpluses of OPEC countries, with an initial preference for U.S. dollar denominated assets. Finally, a shift in spending patterns from U.S. goods toward Japanese and German goods may cause risk averse currency managers to hold transaction balances in yen and DM rather than U.S. dollars.

The above discussion suggests that, at a conceptual level, macroeconomics must be combined with capital market theory to produce a fairly close approximation to the real world setting of foreign exchange markets and thus explain complex exchange rate movements. However, capital market theory places major emphasis on expectations, which are unobservable and may be difficult to approximate empirically. Therefore, it may still be extremely difficult to document exchange rate behavior empirically, especially short-run behavior, and to accept a particular model of exchange rate behavior while rejecting all others.

The empirical work completed over the last decade has dramatically increased our understanding of exchange rate behavior. For example, it has been amply demonstrated that the nominal exchange rate is a function of both nominal variables (e.g. current and anticipated values of the money supply and the inflation rate) and real variables (e.g. real income and current account balances). Empirical studies have been fairly successful in constructing models to explain cross-sectional exchange rate differences (e.g. 1300 Italian lira per U.S. dollar versus roughly 2 DM per U.S. dollar) and to explain exchange rate developments over the medium run and long run (e.g. quarter-to-quarter and year-to-year rate changes). Our ability to explain day-to-day or month-to-month exchange rate changes is much more limited. This is in part because many of the variables that play an important role in typical exchange rate models cannot be measured daily (e.g. the money supply or real income) and expected values of future exogenous variables cannot be observed directly.

The nature of the forward exchange rate – its determinants and relationship to the future spot rate – is an important empirical issue that is currently unresolved. While the forward rate may approximate the market's expectation of the future spot rate, it has been demonstrated clearly that the forward premium is a poor predictor of the future change in the spot exchange rate. However, the unanticipated portion of an exchange rate change does appear to be significantly correlated with "news" concerning fundamental macroeconomic variables.

The plan for the remainder of this chapter is as follows. Section 2 presents an overview of empirical results concerning recent exchange rate behavior. Alternative valuation measures, time series and distributional properties are covered, along with estimates of transaction costs in the foreign exchange market. Empirical tests of specific models of exchange rate determination are reviewed in Section 3. This section begins with the simple monetary approach, where exchange rates are determined by the relative demand for two moneys, and then proceeds to a portfolio balance approach which introduces bonds. A review of a generalized asset model and the role of news round out Section 3. Tests of foreign exchange market efficiency are presented in Section 4. It provides an overview of efficient market theory, a review of evidence on the efficiency of markets in removing risk-free opportunities and evidence of the efficiency of markets in removing risky profit opportunities. It includes evidence on the relationship between the forward rate and future spot rate.

2. Stylized empirical results about exchange rate behavior

2.1. Describing exchange rate movements

The purpose of this chapter is to present a critical review of methodological issues and empirical studies concerning exchange rates. Before we set about this task, however, it is essential to introduce basic terminology and to highlight particular institutional arrangements in the foreign exchange market.[3] In order to become more familiar with the dependent variable that is the subject of our analysis, we will also present simple plots of recent exchange rate behavior.

---

[3] Detailed descriptions of these institutional arrangements are presented in Kubarych (1978) and Levich (1981d).

2.1.1. Alternative measures of a currency's foreign exchange value

The most common notion of currency value is the *bilateral* exchange rate that is quoted by a foreign exchange trader or reported in a newspaper. This is a *nominal* exchange rate because it is the number of units of one currency that is offered in exchange for a unit of another (e.g. \$0.50/DM or \$2.00/£). The *spot* exchange rate, S_t (today's rate for an immediate exchange of currencies) and the *forward* exchange rate, $F_{t,n}$ (today's rate for an exchange of currencies n-periods in the future) are particular examples of nominal bilateral rates.[4] A nominal bilateral exchange rate is required to translate cash flows in one unit of account, say DM, into their equivalent in another unit, say U.S. dollars.

The *real* exchange rate expresses the value of a currency in terms of real purchasing power. The real exchange rate can be calculated on the basis of *absolute* purchasing power parity. For example, unrestricted goods arbitrage will establish that

$$S_t = C_t \cdot P_{\$,t}/P_{DM,t},$$ (19.1)

where $P_{\$}$ and P_{DM} represent the absolute prices of U.S. and German market baskets. The term C_t represents the real exchange rate in units of the U.S. market basket per unit of the German market basket. Very often, the real exchange rate is expressed as an index of the actual exchange rate relative to the PPP exchange rate

$$S_{real,t+n} = S_{t+n}/S_{PPP,t+n},$$ (19.2)

where

$$S_{PPP,t+n} = S_t \cdot \frac{P_{\$,t+n}/P_{DM,t+n}}{P_{\$,t}/P_{DM,t}}.$$

This formulation assumes that *relative* purchasing power parity will be maintained [i.e. that the factor C_t in expression (19.1) is constant] and that period t is an equilibrium base period. Values of S_{real} greater (less) than unity indicate real depreciation (appreciation) of the domestic currency, i.e. more (less) U.S. goods are required to purchase one unit of the German market basket. Values of S_{real} equal to unity indicate that the real exchange rate and relative purchasing power parity were maintained (i.e. that the nominal exchange rate change was exactly offset by the differential change in U.S. and German price indices). Consequently, the real exchange rate is a useful device for measuring the competitiveness of domestic goods in international markets, for predicting future changes in trade patterns and for evaluating long-term real investment projects.

---

[4] The exact delivery conditions for forward contracts are important for tests of market efficiency, as we shall see in Section 3.

The *effective exchange rate* is a multilateral rate that measures the overall nominal value of a currency in the foreign exchange market. For example, the effective U.S. dollar exchange rate combines many bilateral exchange rates using a weighting scheme that reflects the importance of each country's trade with the United States. Several institutions (International Monetary Fund, Federal Reserve Board, Morgan Guaranty Trust, and others) regularly calculate and report effective exchange rates. Each institution uses a slightly different weighting scheme. The effective exchange rate is a useful statistic for gauging the overall supply and demand for a currency on the foreign exchange market. By its nature, however, the effective exchange rate conceals price behavior in individual bilateral markets.

The *real effective exchange rate* is calculated by dividing the home country's nominal effective exchange rate by an index of the ratio of average foreign prices to home prices. The real effective exchange rate attempts to measure the overall competitiveness of home country goods in international markets. While it is important to gauge international competitiveness, a summary statistic such as the real effective exchange rate should be interpreted with caution.[5]

2.1.2. Recent exchange rate behavior

Prior to the early 1970s, most exchange rates were pegged to the U.S. dollar and their values were held within 1 percent of the parity or central rate through official intervention. In response to a fundamental disequilibrium, the central bank would make a discrete, step adjustment in the parity and then resume its official support. Since March 1973, the values of the currencies of major industrial countries have been determined primarily by free-market forces in a floating exchange rate system. (The Canadian dollar began floating in June 1970 and the British pound in June 1972.) From time to time, central banks have intervened, ostensibly to smooth "disorderly" market conditions, making the term managed floating more appropriate. This changeover from a pegged to floating exchange rate system has been associated with a dramatic increase in the volatility of exchange rates.

Figure 2.1 presents indexes of selected bilateral exchange rates in U.S. dollars per foreign unit. The graph clearly illustrates how the values of bilateral exchange rates, once pegged for long stretches of time, have strayed over a wide range since 1973. The Swiss franc, German mark and Japanese yen demonstrated a strong

[5] Hooper and Morton (1978) present detailed evidence on alternative multilateral exchange rates. In part, they concluded that "Any such aggregate measure is subject to problems due to incorrect measurement of prices, incorrect weighting system, and an inability to measure sectoral shifts in productivity. In addition, real exchange rate indexes are rough measures of price competitiveness only and do not measure important nonprice factors such as quality, dependability, and servicing, which have an important influence on trade patterns but may change relatively slowly" (p. 787).

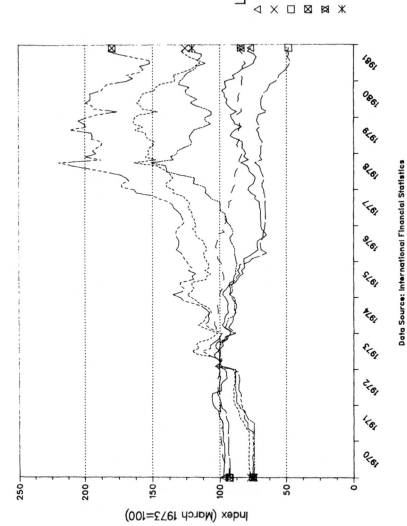

Figure 2.1. Selected nominal exchange rates, 1970–1981.

tendency to appreciate over the period, while the Canadian dollar and Italian lira generally weakened. The British pound depreciated sharply until late 1976, and appreciated thereafter. From 1973 through mid-1975, several currencies (noticeably the DM) demonstrated a cyclical pattern, leading observers to propose that exchange rates may overshoot their equilibrium values. From mid-1975 through mid-1977, exchange rate movements were relatively flat. But the strong appreciation of the Swiss franc, German mark and Japanese yen resumed in mid-1977, to be capped by the major U.S. intervention announced on 1 November 1978. The U.S. dollar appreciated during 1980 and 1981 against most currencies, with the exception of the British pound. Exchange rate volatility in this most recent period continued to be high, reflecting violent swings in U.S. interest rates.

The exchange rates in Figure 2.1 represent the typical dependent variables that we seek to model in Section 2. These series suggest that there is a substantial amount of variation to explain. However, visual inspection of Figure 2.1 suggests that exchange rates have not followed stationary time series processes the entire floating rate period. This may be the result of shifting volatility in the independent variables, erratic government intervention or highly complicated exchange rate determination process. The implication for empirical studies is that a fixed coefficient model without adjustments for government intervention is unlikely to provide an adequate explanation for the entire sample period. A further implication is that any fixed coefficient model that provides a good fit for a limited sample period, is unlikely to produce good forecasts for the post-sample period.

The record of effective exchange rates is illustrated in Figure 2.2.[6] Since most currencies will appreciate against those of some of their trading partners and depreciate against others, the pattern of effective exchange rates should be smoother than for bilateral exchange rates. The Swiss franc is an exception, since it appreciated vis-à-vis every currency and the appreciation against some currencies (notably the Italian lira and British pound) was considerably more than against the U.S. dollar. Analogously, the Italian lira depreciated against all other currencies, so that its effective depreciation (about 42 percent by 1980) exceeded its depreciation vis-à-vis the U.S. dollar (about 30 percent). Figure 2.2 also illustrates the effective value of the U.S. dollar. Even though the U.S. dollar depreciated substantially against the Swiss franc, German mark and Japanese yen, it appreciated against the Canadian dollar. And because the Canadian share of U.S. trade is large (roughly 40 percent), the effective value of the U.S. dollar has changed relatively little since 1973. At the end of 1980, the effective exchange rate for the U.S. dollar stood at 99.9 but climbed to 107.7 at the end of 1981.

---

[6] The data in Figures 2.2 and 2.3 are from *World Financial Markets*. Morgan Guaranty Trust Company which reports exchange rates in U.S. dollars per unit of local currency. Consequently, values greater (less) than 100 indicate local currency appreciation (depreciation).

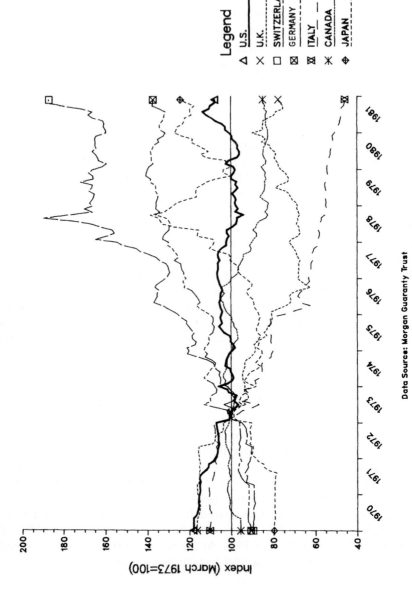

Figure 2.2. Effective exchange rates, 1970–1981.

Thus, the overall appreciation of the U.S. dollar of 7.7 percent since March 1973 throughly disguises the varied performance of the dollar against individual currencies.

A set of real effective exchange rates illustrated in Figure 2.3. They are generally less volatile than other series because relative inflation rates often move to offset exchange rate changes. Several individual currencies are interesting to examine more closely. The effective exchange rates for Germany and Switzerland at the end of 1981 were 137.1 and 186.6 respectively, reflecting the substantial appreciations of these currencies vis-à-vis most others. However, the real effective exchange rates for Germany and Switzerland stood at 98.7 and 112.7 suggesting that most, but not all, of the exchange rate change was offset by differential inflation rates. The figure for Switzerland implies the the real purchasing power of the Swiss franc was up by 12.7 percent on overage against its trading partners compared to its purchasing power in March 1973. This is a substantial *average* change.

The effective exchange rates for Canada and Italy were 84.9 and 46.0 respectively at the end of 1981. With inflation adjustments, however, their real effective exchange rates stood at 92.9 and 90.2, again suggesting that most, but not all, of the exchange rate change was offset by differential inflation rates. The United Kingdom presents an odd case. The effective exchange rate for the pound was 77.6 at the end of 1981 (a nominal depreciation), but the real effective exchange rate was 135.2 (a real appreciation). By way of comparison, the real effective exchange rate for the U.S. dollar hit its low (88.6) in October 1978, just before the Federal Reserve Bank intervened to offset the rate movement.[7]

2.2. Time series behavior, volatility and distributional properties

There are at least three reasons for examining the statistical properties of exchange rates. First, to many economists and policy-makers exchange rates seemed prone to "excessive" volatility and "prolonged" deviations from PPP. For some critics, this concern simply reflected a problem in positive economics (i.e. exchange rates may be too volatile to be consistent with existing models of exchange rate determination) rather than a normative problem (i.e. exchange rates may be too volatile to allow countries to reach their targets for internal and external balance). In either case, the extent of turbulence in the foreign exchange markets is an important part of the descriptive history of those markets.

---

[7]The real value of a currency can be computed using one of several price indexes. Real values for the U.S. dollar computed with export price indexes, wholesale price indexes, consumer price indexes, and unit labor cost indexes are reported in Hooper and Morton (1978).

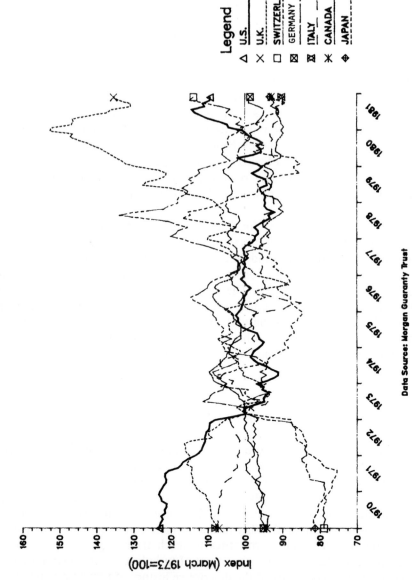

Figure 2.3. Real effective exchange rates, 1970–1981.

Second, some statistical properties of exchange rates bear on the efficiency of foreign exchange markets. In Section 3 [eq. (19.20)], we will show that the current spot rate is a function of current and expected values of future exogenous variables, so that

$$S_t = \frac{1}{1 + \varepsilon} \cdot \sum_{k=0}^{\infty} \left(\frac{\varepsilon}{1 + \varepsilon} \right)^k \mathrm{E}(Z_{t+k}) \qquad (19.3)$$

where ε is a constant, E is the expectations operator, and Z the vector of exogenous variables that determine the exchange rate. As a consequence, the variance of the exchange rate, σ_s^2, should reflect the variance–covariance structure of the variables in Z. It would be efficient for exchange rates to be highly volatile if the underlying economic variables are likewise highly volatile.

The efficiency principle can be introduced more directly. If exchange rates are excessively volatile, then unusual profit opportunities ought to exist for speculators who smooth exchange rate movements. Furthermore, efficiency requires that the exchange rate series not contain any patterns or signals that could be used to formulate a profitable trading strategy.

Finally, the statistical properties of exchange rates are important for assessing the riskiness of open foreign exchange positions. Many approaches to currency exposure management rely on estimates of exchange rate volatility. If a firm works with a portfolio model for currency exposure management, then the total risk (volatility) of a currency may exaggerate its contribution to overall portfolio risk. However, the total variance in currency prices does play a role in the pricing of currency option contracts.

2.2.1. Overview of theory

As Kohlhagen (1978) has commented, early empirical studies of floating exchange rates had a tendency to borrow techniques freely from studies of efficiency in other financial markets. One result of this tendency was a set of studies that tested for the random behavior of exchange rates as a criterion for market efficiency.[8] In his classic paper, Fama (1970) argued that efficiency requires that actual prices (or rates of return) follow a "fair game" process relative to expected equilibrium prices (or rates of return). Since expected equilibrium prices (or rates of return) need not be constant or display constant linear growth, efficiency does not require that prices (or rates of return) follow a random walk with zero or constant drift. Levich (1978) applied this argument to the foreign exchange market, noting that many equilibrium exchange rate models and scenarios are consistent with high

[8] Burt et al. (1977) comment that the purpose of their paper is "to test whether the price changes of the Canadian dollar, German mark and British pound conform to those which would be expected in an efficient market (i.e. a weak random walk model)" (p. 1325).

serial correlation in exchange rates. As a consequence, time series analysis is useful primarily as a descriptive technique, to measure the parameters of the exchange rate process, not to test for efficiency.

On the issue of excessive exchange rate volatility, theory suggests three important considerations.[9] First, expression (19.3) implies that volatility in the underlying variables contributes directly to exchange rate volatility. Certainly, the recent floating rate period has been marked by great real and monetary turbulence. Second, the process of expectation formation can contribute to exchange rate volatility. Bilson (1978b) has noted that if market participants classify a current innovation as permanent and extrapolate its impact into the future, an asset pricing framework such as (19.3) will result in current exchange rate changes that magnify the currently observed innovation. This extrapolative process may be irrational, however, because the innovations are not permanent. Finally, some exchange rate volatility may be the result of "overshooting" behavior rather than the arrival of unanticipated news. It has been argued correctly that if this overshooting reflects the failure of domestic prices to adjust quickly or of financial portfolios to rebalance quickly, then high exchange rate volatility need not testify to high adjustment costs.

With respect to the distribution of exchange rate changes, studies have generally used the normal distribution (for discrete time) or log-normal (for continuous time) as the null hypothesis. This is another example of methodology borrowed from stock market analysis. The use of the normal distribution can be defended on the assumption that any exchange rate change $S_n - S_1$ can be split into the summation of a sequence of changes $(S_n - S_{n-1}) + (S_{n-1} - S_{n-2}) + \cdots + (S_3 - S_2) + (S_2 - S_1)$. If each individual price change is drawn from a population with finite variance, then by the central limit theorem the aggregate price change $S_n - S_1$ should be normally distributed.

Because the normal distribution offered a poor fit to stock price changes, finance studies went on to consider other distributions (e.g. stable Paretian and Student-t) as well as compound processes and jump processes. As long as exchange markets are subject to periodic direct intervention and national monetary and fiscal policies are subject to abrupt changes, it seems unlikely that exchange rates will be stationary time series with stable parameters. As a corollary, it seems unlikely that a well-behaved normal distribution will provide a good fit to exchange rates over the entire floating period.

2.2.2. Empirical results

One of the first examinations of the time series properties of exchange rates was by Poole (1966, 1967), who analyzed the Canadian dollar rate during the 1950–1962 float and European rates during the 1920s. Poole found statistically

[9]Further details are provided in Section 3 and Chapter 18 of this Handbook

significant first-order serial correlation in many cases, but he concluded that the serial dependence was not great enough to result in economically significant profits. Levich (1979a) re-examined the Canadian dollar data using Box–Jenkins time series analysis. He concluded that the serial dependencies were significant only in the first and last years of the float. During the remainder of the sample, a simple random walk model was sufficient to describe the data. This finding is consistent with the notion that government intervention was greatest during the first and last years of the Canadian float. Giddy and Dufey (1975) applied Box–Jenkins techniques to the 1920s data and found that the simple random walk model was not adequate to describe the data. In a post-sample period, however, the Box–Jenkins forecasts performed worse (larger mean squared errors) than more naive forecasts such as the random walk. A common interpretation of these Box–Jenkins analyses is that the time series properties of exchange rates are not stable over long time periods, although the precise reasons for this phenomenon are not well understood.

Frenkel and Levich (1977) used Box–Jenkins procedures to analyze the similarities of exchange rate behavior across different currencies and time periods. They observed that the time series processes for spot and forward rates were remarkably more similar during two sample periods (1962–1967 and 1973–1975) than during a third, more turbulent sample period (1968–1969). This result is striking because the two similar time series processes pertained to different exchange rate regimes – pegged rates in the first and floating rates in the second. Frenkel and Levich interpreted their results to mean that the time series pattern of exchange rates depends principally on the behavior of underlying economic variables rather than on the formal exchange rate regime.

Quite naturally, the changeover to a floating rate system reawakened interest in the volatility of exchange rates. Figures 2.1, 2.2 and 2.3 describe the degree of medium-term volatility in both nominal and real rates. Figure 2.4 provides an illustration of daily exchange rate volatility.

It is not uncommon for exchange rates to change by 0.5 percent, 1.0 percent or even 2.0 percent in a single day. Many tests attempt to determine if this volatility is "excessive" relative to some benchmark standard. As Levich (1978) and others have emphasized, however, empirical tests of excessive volatility employ a joint null hypothesis and are, therefore, similar to efficient market tests. Accordingly, they are hard to interpret. And as Huang (1981) has added, any test for speculative excesses "should be judged on the basis of ex ante expectations rather than ex post occurrences".

Huang (1981) tests for excess volatility in line with the above comments. Huang's methodology is to compare actual exchange rate variability with the variance bounds implied by a monetary model of exchange rates under rational expectations. In an analysis of pound sterling and DM rates over the period 1973–1979, Huang finds that the implied variance bounds are often significantly violated. It follows either that the market is inefficient (i.e. excessively volatile) or that the rational expectations monetary model is incorrect, or both. As we will see in Section 3, other studies also suggest that PPP and simple monetary models are not adequate to explain exchange rate movements in the 1970s.

Another perspective on exchange rate volatility is offered by Frenkel and Mussa (1980). Their data, reported in Table 2.1, indicates that recent exchange rate volatility, measured as the mean absolute percentage change, is considerably greater than the volatility of relative cost-of-living indices. This suggests that other factors (e.g. volatility in incomes, government intervention or unanticipated news) may have contributed to exchange market volatility. Since exchange rates, like other asset prices, adjust more quickly than goods prices, these results do not seem very surprising. Table 2.1 also indicates that recent exchange rate behavior has been less volatile than stock market behavior. Yet most national stock markets are felt to be fairly efficient in the sense that price swings in these markets represent reasonably accurate assessments of changing real economic events and changing expectations. Frenkel and Mussa conclude that, by this standard, recent exchange rate volatility does not appear to be excessive or unprecedented.

The first empirical study on the underlying probability distribution of exchange rates was conducted by Westerfield (1977). In common with earlier stock price analysis, Westerfield tested the null hypothesis that exchange rate changes con-

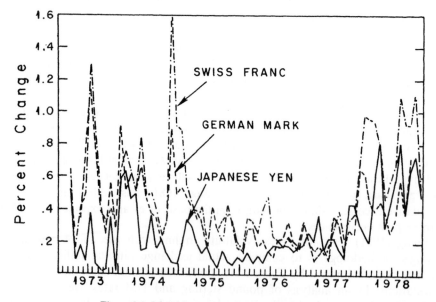

Figure 2.4. Monthly average of daily exchange rates.

Table 2.1
Mean absolute percentage changes in prices and exchange rates (monthly data:
June 1973–February 1979)

Variable Country	WPI	COL	Stock market	Exchange rate against the dollar	COL/COL US
U.S.	0.009	0.007	0.038	–	–
U.K.	0.014	0.012	0.066	0.020	0.007
France	0.011	0.008	0.054	0.020	0.003
Germany	0.004	0.004	0.031	0.024	0.004

Source: Frenkel and Mussa (1980).

form to a normal distribution. Her methodology considered the variable $R_t = \ln S_t - \ln S_{t-1}$ (the weekly percentage exchange rate change) for five major currencies during fixed rate and floating rate period (roughly 1962–1971 and 1973–1975). The alternative hypothesis was that exchange rate changes conform to a stable Paretian distribution with characteristic exponent $\alpha < 2.0$.[10] Westerfield concluded that the normal distribution is not adequate to describe the sample data and that the stable Paretian distribution, with α in the range roughly $1.3 - 1.7$, provides a superior fit for both the fixed and flexible rate periods.

Rogalski and Vinso (1978) re-examined Westerfield's data to consider an alternative non-normal distribution, the Student-t distribution with finite degrees of freedom.[11] Using likelihood ratio tests, Rogalski and Vinso confirm that a stable Paretian distribution is adequate to describe exchange rates during the pegged rate period, However a Student-t distribution (with degrees of freedom $d \approx 4.0$) provides a better description of rates during the floating rate period. The authors also note that the switch from pegged to floating rates was associated with a decline in the peakedness of the distribution of exchange rate changes and an increase in dispersion or variability. In broad terms, this finding is consistent with risk averse behavior in an efficient foreign exchange market.

2.2.3. Methodological issues and agenda

Empirical studies of volatility are an important part of the ongoing analysis of floating exchange rates. An important issue here is whether or not volatility is

[10] The normal distribution is equivalent to the stable Paretian distribution of $\alpha = 2.0$. The stable Paretian distribution represents a family of unimodal distributions. With $\alpha < 2.0$, the stable Paretian distribution is characterized by both (1) a greater probability of observations occurring in the tails of the distribution, i.e. "fat tails", and (2) a greater probability of observations in the intermediate ranges, i.e. "peakedness". In this case, variance is not defined and not appropriate as a measure of risk.

[11] With degrees of freedom $d = \infty$, the Student distribution is identical to the normal distribution. However, with $d > 2$, the first two moments of the Student distribution are known; therefore, Rogalski and Vinso argue that it is a superior framework for developing international portfolio risk measures.

"excessive". Tests are difficult to formulate and interpret because they reflect a joint hypothesis based on market efficiency and the normal volatility resulting from an equilibrium exchange rate model. Nevertheless, they are important since any claim of excessive volatility might provoke increased direct government intervention in the foreign exchange market, measures in aid of private speculation, or a move away from the floating rate system.

Another issue is whether volatility is influenced by the formal exchange rate regime. As an empirical matter, exchange rate volatility increased in the post-1973 period. However, there is also evidence to suggest that the time series properties of exchange rates may be very similar in pegged and floating rate periods and that some pegged rate periods (1968–1969) may be marked by extreme turbulence. Clearly, national economic policies and exogenous international economic events may be tranquil or turbulent, regardless of the legal exchange rate regime. It is still important, however, to determine whether the private demand for foreign exchange – either for transaction balances in international trade or for rebalancing financial portfolios in response to changes in expected returns and risk – is more volatile under a floating exchange rate regime.

Another important aspect of this topic is the impact of exchange rate volatility on other key macroeconomic variables – e.g. the prices and volume of international trade, the transmission of national economic disturbances and the independence of national economic policies. Studies by Hooper and Kohlhagen (1978) and Kreinin (1977) suggested that increased exchange rate volatility under floating rates had no measurable impact on the volume of international trade. Broadly speaking, this result is consistent with Friedman's (1953) claim that low-cost hedging services would become available to protect importers and exporters from unanticipated exchange rate swings. A recent study by Cushman (1983) considers the volatility in *real* exchange rates and, contrary to earlier studies, reports a significant impact on the prices *and* volume of international trade. This result seems more consistent with the implications of terms of trade volatility in standard trade theory models. The distinction between real and nominal magnitudes is a critical methodological issue to keep in mind in all aspects of international financial research. There is need for a companion study analyzing the impact of real exchange rate volatility on portfolio capital flows and direct foreign investment flows.[12]

Empirical studies on the distribution of exchange rate changes may not seem to be very useful, either for theoretical or practical purposes. As we will show in Section 4, the modern concept of exchange risk focuses more on the variability of a currency's real purchasing power or the covariability of an asset's real return with those of other assets in a well-diversified portfolio. However, the equilibrium

---

[12]Studies by Branson (1968), Kouri and Porter (1974) and Hodjera (1973) have examined the determinants of international capital flows. See also Chapter 15 of this Handbook.

pricing of currency option contracts will very likely depend on some measure of the own currency's dispersion or volatility.[13] Since currency option contracts began public trading on the Philadelphia Stock Exchange in December 1982, interest in estimating the volatility parameter has been renewed. In this regard, it may be important to keep in mind the distinction between transaction time and clock time. A little-referenced paper by Brada et al. (1966) hypothesized that non-normality in daily stock returns occurs because the volume of transactions is not uniform across the daily trading interval. When stock returns are calculated across a fixed number of transactions (say 50 or 100 trades), the distribution of returns is, in fact, normal. It is not clear whether this methodology can be replicated for currency price changes, since there is no central record of consecutive foreign exchange transactions.

2.3. Transaction costs in foreign exchange markets

Professional interest in transaction costs has increased over the last ten years. There are several reasons. First, if markets are efficient, transaction costs may be the only "true" cost of using the foreign exchange market. Foreign exchange risk management strategies sometimes use the forward premium as the "cost of hedging" or the differential between the forward rate and the expected future spot rate as an "opportunity cost" measure. In an efficient market, such alternative hedging opportunities are priced fairly, so that transaction costs capture all of the real costs involved.

Second, we would expect many international financial relationships (e.g. the covered interest rate parity condition) to hold exactly in the absence of transaction costs. The presence of transaction costs generally leads to a *neutral band*, within which deviations from the parity condition persist because they cannot be profitably exploited. One test of market efficiency in these cases is simply to count the percentage of observations falling within the neutral band. This procedure requires an independent estimate of transaction costs.

Finally, by most any measure, the cost of transacting has risen sharply over the floating rate period. On days when unexpected news reaches the market and uncertainty is high, transaction costs may increase dramatically and reduce or even completely halt the flow of trading. Therefore, transaction costs may be interpreted as a barometer for how well the floating exchange rate system is performing. Higher transaction costs are one component of the real resource costs of operating a floating exchange rate system rather than a pegged rate system.

---

[13]Pricing formulas for stock option and commodity option contracts include a measure of the variance of returns on the underlying asset. Models for currency option pricing remain to be fully developed. See Feiger and Jacquillat (1979) and Hoag (1981).

2.3.1. Concepts of transaction costs

The *liquidity theory* [Demsetz (1968)] argues that the bid–ask spread is only one component in the total cost of transacting. The spread ignores the costs of producing financial claims, the costs of being informed, etc. The spread represents the cost of making a quick exchange of a financial claim for money, i.e. the cost of liquidity services, and the theory suggests that the spread should decline as trading volume and the number of market-makers increases. More important, the liquidity theory assumes that prices are set at a fair or equilibrium level, so that the trader's major costs are associated with waiting for the arrival of buyers and sellers who want liquidity services. A transactor with inside information may be able to trade at a disequilibrium price and reduce his positioning cost below the quoted bid–ask spread.[14]

The *adversary theory* [Bagehot (1971)] explicitly considers the impact on transaction costs of having two groups of investors with different information. Adversary theory suggests that there are two such groups of traders. One group is "informed", trading to earn unusual profits based on an information advantage. The second group is "uninformed", expecting to trade at fair prices for liquidity purposes only. In theory, the trader or market-maker will respond differently to these two groups because he fears losing money to informed traders and expects to earn a fair profit from uninformed traders. Adversary theory also helps us to refine the relationship between risk and transaction costs. *Price risk* derives from the price volatility of the underlying asset while *liquidity risk* derives from the uncertainty of holding assets that are traded in small volume per unit of time. Transaction costs are positively related to both types of risk. According to this view, the percentage spread in spot gold prices should exceed the spread in U.S. treasury bill prices. Furthermore, the (per unit) cost of trading DM 1 000 000 should be smaller than for DM 1000 (because of scale economies). However, the (per unit) cost of trading DM 100 000 000 may *exceed* the cost of DM 1 000 000 because of liquidity risks.

2.3.2. Empirical measures

The bid–ask spread measures the cost of buying and then immediately selling an asset. Therefore, the percentage cost of one transaction equals $\frac{1}{2}$(ask price − bid price)/ask price. Estimates of transaction costs based on the bid–ask spread vary considerably across currencies and over time. Levich (1979a) reports that during the early 1960s, spreads were extraordinarily small, roughly 0.01 percent for sterling, 0.02 percent for DM and 0.03 percent for Canadian dollars. By the mid-1970s, these figures average 0.05 percent for spot contracts and 0.15 percent

---

[14]The possibility of a "negative trading cost" is suggested in Black and Scholes (1974). An empirical test for stock market transactions is in Cuneo and Wagner (1975).

for forward contracts. But a substantial number of spreads in the range 0.25–0.50 percent were observed.

Triangular arbitrage offers another opportunity to measure transaction costs. Frenkel and Levich (1975, 1977) argue that during a period when transaction costs are stationary, the upper limits of the deviation from triangular parity ($/DM = $/$C · $C/DM, for example) should equal the cost of the corresponding bilateral transaction. Estimates using the triangular arbitrage approach should be larger than those obtained from the bid–ask spread, since they include the costs of monitoring the deviations from triangular parity. Using the triangular approach Frenkel and Levich (1977) reported that transaction costs rose from roughly 0.05 percent in the 1962–1967 period to roughly 0.50 percent in the 1973–1975 period. McCormick (1979) argued that the triangular approach requires carefully collected, time-synchronous data. Based on a six-month sample of high quality data from 1976, McCormick estimated spot transaction costs in the range 0.09–0.18 percent.

A related study by Fieleke (1975) used regression analysis to test the relationship between bid–ask spreads and other macroeconomic variables. As hypothesized, the bid–ask spread was positively related to exchange rate volatility and a dummy variable reflecting government announcements likely to affect market uncertainty.

2.3.3. Methodological issues and agenda

As a boundary condition for many efficient market tests and general barometer on the functioning of foreign exchange markets, estimates of foreign exchange transaction costs should be of ongoing interest. The triangular arbitrage estimation procedure seems preferred, in that it represents a more inclusive measure of transaction costs. However, this approach has several major drawbacks: (1) it requires high-quality, time-synchronous data, (2) it requires a sample period with roughly stable transaction costs, and (3) the cross-rate, DM/$C in our example, must be set in a true, independent market. Since these conditions are not easily met, the bid–ask spread approach will continue to supply the most common estimates of transaction costs.

The concept of *price dispersion* – the variance of price quotations across market makers in a dispersed market – has been explored in some financial markets [Garbade and Silber (1976)] but not in the foreign exchange market. The cost of searching for the best execution prices across dispersed market-makers can be an

---

[15] Foreign exchange market practitioners seldom acknowlege attempts to minimize transaction costs, arguing that a momentary price swing can swamp the gain from lower transaction costs. However, one recent application of adversary theory is the so-called *discretionary order*. The U.S. corporate treasurer places an order for Japanese yen with a U.S. bank, whose traders use their discretion to execute the order during the next 24 hours at the most favorable price – probably within the Tokyo market. The discretionary order announces that the U.S. treasurer is both uninformed and willing to wait for best execution prices.

important part of transaction costs.[15] Although various electronic communication devices link the world-wide commercial bank trading operations, dispersed market-makers will simultaneously offer different quotations backed by different qualities of related services. These micro foundations of foreign exchange trading are poorly understood and worthy of further study. One practical result of such a study would be a better estimate of the "noise" inherent in a daily series of spot exchange rates and a new understanding of the risks in trading in a dispersed market.

3. Exchange rate determination – tests of specific models

The evidence presented in Section 1 demonstrates that exchange rates, both nominal and real, were substantially more volatile during the 1970s than during the earlier pegged rate period. The central question inspired by these data is clear: What is the model by which exchange rates are determined? The managed floating period offers a complex setting that presents a substantial challenge to the model-builder. It has been rich in economic disturbances (real and monetary, temporary and permanent, anticipated and unanticipated, economy-wide and industry-specific), and one must take account of many structural and institutional features (e.g. slow commodity price adjustment, heterogeneous expectations and differing risk preferences).

In Section 1 we introduced the notion that foreign exchange has many characteristics in common with other financial assets. The reader may be painfully aware of the difficulty of forecasting stock prices and the often aired views that certain stock are currently undervalued (or overvalued) in today's market. Consequently, we should expect exchange rate modeling, not to mention forecasting, to be a very difficult activity.[16] Our standards for adequate model performance reflect this view. No theory has been proposed seriously as a complete explanation for exchange rate behavior; therefore, we should not expect to explain all empirical exchange rate variation. In most cases, statistically significant parameter coefficients will be taken as support for a theory. Furthermore, we should expect models of exchange rate changes to have less explanatory power than models of exchange rate levels. This last result follows because exchange rates themselves are viewed as anticipatory prices which already incorporate expected future exchange rate changes.

The models in this section are developed roughly in chronological order and in order of complexity and richness.[17] We begin with the purchasing power parity

---

[16] In Section 3 I argue that exchange rate modeling and forecasting ought to be more difficult than stock price modeling.

[17] Theories of exchange rate determination are developed in more detail in Chapter 14 of this Handbook. Other useful survey articles are by Isard (1978) and Dornbusch (1980).

(PPP) view of exchange rates. Even though PPP is not a theory of exchange rate determination, it is an important building block and equilibrium condition for many international financial models. Evidence on the monetary approach to exchange rate determination is reviewed next. The monetary approach is a direct outgrowth of the PPP model but can be easily modified to accommodate additional assumptions – rational expectations of future exogenous variables, slow price adjustment in good markets, or the inclusion of long-term interest rates, wealth and other variables in the demand for money function. The monetary model can also be extended to allow individuals or firms to hold a portfolio of two or more currencies and to substitute among currencies. Among the potential problems with the monetary approach, we note that the demands for assets, beyond currency, is not considered; there is no portfolio-optimizing framework. Furthermore, from an empirical standpoint, it may not be efficient to introduce real disturbances in the only way that they can be introduced in the monetary model – through real income in the demand for money function. In order to model the impact on exchange rates of shifts in particular real variables – such as changes in the competitiveness of German goods, in consumer preferences for home goods or in the OPEC price of oil – it may be better to use a model that prescribes a less ambiguous role for these variables.[18]

The portfolio balance model or generalized asset approach attempts to rectify some of the above problems by specifying asset demand functions and providing an explicit role for the current account. While the portfolio balance model may seem to capture more realism, we will see that it is a difficult model to implement empirically.

We conclude Section 3 by commenting on empirical studies of exchange rate dynamics and the role of "news" – i.e. explanations for exchange rate changes not predicted by a standard, baseline model.

The most complex exchange rate models, simultaneous equation models developed by DRI, Chase Econometrics, Wharton Econometric Forecasting Associates and the Federal Reserve, are not reviewed here. The DRI, Chase and Wharton models are proprietary, and the Federal Reserve model has been tested primarily through simulation exercises.[19]

Any review of empirical studies of exchange rate determination can deteriorate into a "horse race" in which we see which model is "best". Our emphasis,

---

[18]Certain real disturbances, such as a change in the price ratio of traded to non-traded goods and in commercial policies, have been modeled within a monetary framework. See Frenkel (1981), Frenkel and Clements (1981) and footnote 23.

[19]The DRI, Chase Econometric and Wharton models utilize between 50 and 900 equations, depending on the company and currency. Levich (1981b) analyzed the forecasting performance of these companies over the period 1977–1980 and reported that Wharton and DRI significantly outperformed the forward rate in forecasting the spot rate. However, they did not significantly outperform other single equation or judgemental forecasts. Further information on the Federal Reserve's multi-country model is in Hernández-Catà, et al. (1978).

however, should be on selecting the appropriate model for the task at hand. For example, a simple monetary model may be adequate to describe exchange rate behavior during a hyperinflation dominated by monetary disturbances but inadequate to describe periods dominated by real disturbances. Similarly, if we want to analyze the impact of particular events (e.g. announced changes in future money supply policy, changes in spending patterns that alter the current account, or changes in the riskiness of foreign assets), we need a model that incorporates these variables in a consistent and efficient manner.

3.1. Purchasing power parity

3.1.1. Overview

Perhaps the most popular and intuitively appealing model of exchange rate behavior is represented by the theory of *purchasing power parity* (PPP).[20] The main thrust of purchasing power parity is that nominal exchange rates are set so that the real purchasing power of currencies is constant over time. As a result, PPP suggests that in the long run, the rate of change of the nominal bilateral exchange rate will tend to equal the differential in inflation rates between countries. Economists have long debated whether the PPP doctrine applies to the short run or the long run and whether the relevant inflation rate is on a narrow class of goods (e.g. only traded goods) or a broader class (e.g. the consumer price index). Frenkel (1976) has argued that much of the controversy over the usefulness of the PPP doctrine results from the fact that PPP specifies a final, equilibrium relationship between exchange rates and prices without specifying the precise linkages and details of the process. As prices and exchange rates are both determined endogenously in the real world, PPP represents an equilibrium relationship rather than a precise theory of exchange rate determination.

   An important building block of PPP doctrine is the *law of one price*, that is , perfect commodity market arbitrage of individual goods. For example, if the price of oil in New York is $40/barrel, we expect the price in London to be £20/barrel when the exchange rate is $2/£. The doctrine of PPP, however, usually pertains to fairly broad aggregates of goods. *Absolute purchasing power parity* requires that the exchange rate equalize the price of a market basket of goods in the two countries. Since the composition of market baskets and price indexes varies

---

[20] The term "purchasing power parity" is associated with Gustav Cassel who studied alternative approaches for selecting official exchange rates at the end of the First World War and the resumption of international trade. As Frenkel (1978) has pointed out, the intellectual origins of purchasing power parity can be traced to the early nineteenth century and the writings of Wheatley and Ricardo. For a recent overview and critique of theory and evidence on purchasing power parity, see Katseli-Papaefstratiou (1979).

substantially across countries, and because many goods are non-traded or subject to tariffs, it is unlikely that absolute PPP will hold in the real world.[21] *Relative purchasing power parity* requires merely that the *percentage change* in the exchange rate equal the difference between the *percentage changes* in the prices of the market baskets of goods in the two countries. If the factors that cause absolute PPP to fail (e.g. tariffs, some goods being non-traded) are constant over time, then relative PPP might hold even when absolute PPP does not.

It should be clear that when relative PPP holds, the real exchange rate [see expression (19.2)] is constant and the relative competitiveness of countries in foreign markets is unchanged. In this regard, Bruce and Purvis argue that "PPP should be interpreted as a *comparative-statics* result arising from a monetary disturbance, embodying the essential feature of *monetary neutrality*".[22] Consequently, short-run non-neutralities of monetary policy of the sort described by Dornbusch (1976) may lead to transitory deviations from PPP. Other real disturbances that are permanent may lead to permanent deviations from PPP. Since real disturbances are a common phenomenon, we cannot infer that deviations from PPP are the result of inefficient foreign exchange markets. On the other hand, arbitrage profit opportunities are available when deviations from the law of one price exceed transaction costs. This distinction between the law of one price and PPP should be kept in mind since, as we report next, deviations from the law of one price can be presented as prima facia evidence to explain deviations from PPP.

3.1.2. Empirical evidence

The empirical evidence on PPP is mixed. Moreover, the evidence may be sensitive to the countries, time periods and price indexes that we select. Over long time periods and during periods dominated by monetary disturbances, (such as hyperinflation), PPP offers a fairly good description of exchange rate behavior. However, over shorter time periods, say three to twelve months, it has not been uncommon to observe substantial exchange rate changes, say 10–20 percent, which are unrelated to commodity price changes.

We can describe three techniques for testing PPP. The first is regression analysis of the form

$$\ln S_t = a + b \ln \left(P/P^* \right)_t + U_t, \tag{19.4}$$

which corresponds to the absolute version of PPP, and

$$\Delta \ln S_t = b \Delta \ln \left(P/P^* \right)_t + v_t, \tag{19.5}$$

---

[21] McKinnon (1979, ch. 6) discusses the sufficient conditions for absolute PPP to hold.
[22] See Chapter 16 in this Handbook. Emphasis is in the original.

which corresponds to relative PPP. We use S_t to indicate the exchange rate (the domestic currency price of foreign currency) and $(P/P^*)_t$ to indicate the ratio of domestic to foreign price indices respectively. The term Δ is the first difference operator, and U_t and v_t denote classical error terms. Because prices and exchange rates are determined simultaneously, a two-stage least squares estimation procedure should be employed. The basic null hypothesis is that $a = 0$ in (19.4) and $b = 1$. Further empirical issues, such as the impact of alternative price indices and the equality of coefficients on domestic and foreign prices, might also be examined.

Frenkel (1980) reports results on eqs. (19.4) and (19.5) using monthly data drawn from the flexible exchange rate period of the 1920s. The sample includes four countries – Germany, which experienced hyperinflation, and France, Britain

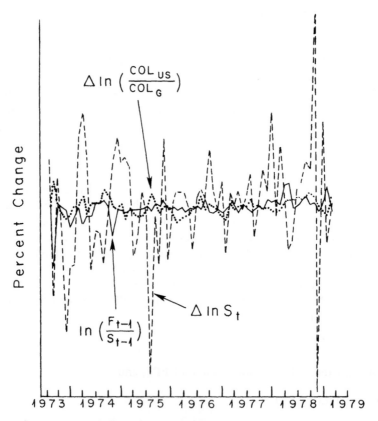

Figure 3.1. Consumer price indices, the spot exchange rate and forward premium – monthly percentage changes, U.S./Germany, July 1973–February 1979.

and the U.S. which experienced more normal economic conditions. Frenkel concludes that in most cases his data are consistent with the hypothesis that the elasticity of the exchange rate with respect to the price ratio is unity.

Frenkel (1981b) reports similar tests on data sampled from the 1970s floating exchange rate period. Here the results are extremely poor. The b coefficient is often far from the hypothesized value, has large standard errors and is unstable over time. Visual inspection of Figure 3.1 illustrates the weak correspondence between exchange rate changes and relative price changes in the 1970s. Frenkel explains the collapse of PPP (1) by changes in the ratio of the prices of traded to non-traded goods that occurred unevenly across countries and (2) by the very nature of exchange markets that react quickly to expectations of future events rather than reflect current and past circumstances that are captured in existing price contracts.[23]

A second technique for checking PPP is simply to calculate the exchange rate which satisfies PPP,

$$S_{\text{PPP},t+n} = S_t \cdot \frac{P_{t+n}/P_{t+n}^*}{P_t/P_t^*}, \tag{19.6}$$

and compare it to the prevailing exchange rate S_{t+n}. Figure 3.2 presents an example of the above calculation for Germany in the 1970s that happens to show substantial and ongoing deviations from PPP. In reference to this general phenomenon, McKinnon (1979, p. 133) observed that "Substantial and continually changing deviations from PPP are commonplace. For individual tradable commodities, violations in the 'law of one price' can be striking."

This last statement refers to a third method for checking PPP. A study by Isard (1977) compared the movements of the dollar prices of German goods relative to their American equivalents for specific goods selected at the two- and three-digit levels of the SITC classification. The results implied persistent violations of the

---

[23] To account for traded and non-traded goods, assume that the aggregate price level is a geometric average of the prices of traded goods, P_t, and non-traded goods, P_n, so that:

$$P = P_n^\alpha P_t^{1-\alpha}, \qquad P^* = P_n^{*\alpha^*} P_t^{*1-\alpha^*},$$

where α and α^* are the domestic and foreign expenditure shares on non-traded goods. Now assume that PPP applies only to traded goods so that:

$$S = \frac{P_t}{P_t^*} = \frac{(P_t/P_n)^\alpha}{(P_t^*/P_n^*)^{\alpha^*}} \cdot \frac{P}{P^*}.$$

Taking logarithms, we have:

$$\ln S_t = \alpha \ln(P_t/P_n) + \alpha^* \ln(P_t^*/P_n^*) + \ln(P/P^*),$$

which can be estimated in regression formats similar to eqs. (19.4) and (19.5). For an extensive and detailed study of international prices of traded and non-traded goods, see Kravis et al. (1975).

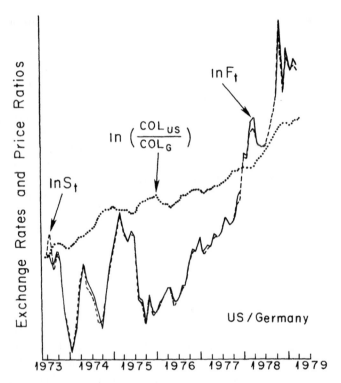

Figure 3.2. Consumer price ratios, the spot exchange rate and forward premium – monthly observations, U.S./Germany, July 1973–February 1979.

law of one price. Isard (1977, p. 942) concluded that "In reality the law of one price is flagrantly and systematically violated by empirical data.... Moreover, these relative price effects seem to persist for at least several years and cannot be shrugged off as transitory."

Notwithstanding the above, McKinnon (1979, p. 136) goes on to conclude that

> Until a more robust theory replaces it, I shall assume that purchasing power parity among tradable goods tends to hold in the long run in the absence of overt impediments to trade among countries with convertible currencies. But...because commodity arbitrage is so imperfect in the short run, it cannot be relied on to contain nominal exchange rate movements within the predictable and narrow limits suggested by the law of one price.

As a consequence, economists have turned to monetary and portfolio balance models of exchange rate determination which are discussed below.

3.2. Monetary theory and exchange rates

3.2.1. Overview

It is perhaps self-evident that whenever a voluntary foreign exchange transaction occurs, say between U.S. dollars and DM, it represents an excess demand for one currency (say DM) and an excess supply of the other. If we can identify the sources of this excess demand for DM (e.g. an increased transaction or speculative demand for DM or the expectation that DM balances will offer a more reliable store of real purchasing power), we have the basis for a monetary theory of exchange rates. The basic monetary approach to exchange rate determination is a direct outgrowth of purchasing power parity theory and of the quantity theory of money. While PPP concludes that the exchange rate is the relative price of goods in the two countries, monetary theory suggests that the exchange rate is the relative price of two moneys. In this context, it follows that exchange rate behavior reflects the evolution of the *relative demands* for two moneys.

Economists commonly represent the demand for real money balances, M/P, as some function, L, of real income, Y, interest rates, i, and other factors, K, so that

$$M/P = L(Y, i, K). \tag{19.7}$$

The relationship between real income and real money balances is direct since an increase in income raises the demand for transaction balances. The relationship between interest rates and real money balances is inverse since an increase in interest rates raises the opportunity cost of holding money balances and therefore lowers demand. Other factors, K, are included since, given Y and i, increasing sophistication among banking and financial institutions may increase the velocity of money and thus lower money demand.

According to the monetary approach, factors that increase the demand for domestic currency (i.e. the U.S. dollar) should increase the price of domestic currency on the foreign exchange market. As we just argued, two factors that would increase the demand for domestic currency balances are an increase in U.S. income and a fall in U.S. dollar interest rates. Therefore, these should cause the U.S. dollar to appreciate on the foreign exchange market. These predictions are contrary to those that come from more standard theories based on trade and capital flows.

Such models correctly argue that higher U.S. income will lead to greater demand for imports, and in turn an increased demand for foreign currency and a depreciation of the U.S. dollar. But this relationship reflects a partial equilibrium; it neglects capital flows that also respond to an increase in U.S. income. Monetary theory argues that in general equilibrium, the net effect of higher U.S. income should be a U.S. dollar appreciation because the increase in the demand for money and the corresponding improvement in the capital account exceeds the decline in the trade balance.

Capital flow models correctly argue that high *real* U.S. interest rates should attract foreign capital and thus cause the U.S. dollar to appreciate. Monetary theory, however, emphasizes that high *nominal* U.S. interest rates that incorporate a large inflation premium actually imply U.S. dollar depreciation via purchasing power parity. If a currency is expected to depreciate, the stock of currency is willingly held only if investors are compensated by higher interest rates. The data strongly confirm that currencies with high nominal interest rates (e.g. Brazil and Argentina) generally have been characterized by depreciation, while currencies with low nominal interest rates (e.g., Germany and Switzerland) generally have been characterized by appreciation.

3.2.2. Empirical evidence

To implement the monetary approach, we must first specify an explicit money demand function in place of (19.7). A popular specification is

$$M/P = K \cdot Y^\eta \cdot e^{-\varepsilon i}, \tag{19.8}$$

where η is the income elasticity of demand for real money balances and e is the interest rate semi-elasticity of demand. (A time subscript, t, is suppressed.) If we rearrange terms in (19.8) to isolate the price level, we have

$$P = M/(K \cdot Y^\eta \cdot e^{-\varepsilon i}). \tag{19.9}$$

Let us assume that the same specification of money demand also applies in the foreign country so that

$$P^* = M^*/(K^* \cdot Y^{*\eta} \cdot e^{-\varepsilon i^*}), \tag{19.10}$$

where, as before, an asterisk indicates the foreign country. For simplicity only we assume that the elasticities are identical in both countries. Substituting (19.9) and (19.10) into the purchasing power parity expression, $S = P/P^*$,

$$S = \frac{M^*}{M} \cdot \frac{(Y^*)^\eta}{(Y)^\eta} \cdot \frac{K^*}{K} \cdot e^\varepsilon (i - i^*). \tag{19.11}$$

Taking logarithms of (19.11), we obtain the linear expression:

$$s = (m - m^*) + \eta(y^* - y) + (k^* - k) + \varepsilon(i - i^*), \tag{19.12}$$

where a lower case letter represents the logarithm of a capital letter (e.g. $s = \ln S$).[24] Expression (19.12) can be refined further by setting $(i - i^*)$ equal to

---

[24]Again, if PPP applies only to traded goods, as in footnote 23, then eq. (19.12) contains terms that capture the relative price of traded to non-traded goods.

the forward rate premium, and then letting the forward rate reflect the future spot rate. These steps are taken in a later section.

In empirical tests, we expect the coefficient of $(m - m^*)$ to be unity, confirming the neutrality of money. The elasticity coefficient should be positive and significant, η should be in the neighborhood of 1.0 and ε should approximate the interest rate elasticity of the demand for money, in the neighborhood of 0.04 for monthly data. Naturally, the coefficients should be stable, the model should explain a large fraction of exchange rate variation, and the error terms should satisfy classical properties.

A large number of empirical studies have been conducted based on (19.12) and close variants. We will briefly review five different methodological styles based on the monetary approach.

(i) *Ordinary and two stage least squares regression.* Clearly, eq. (19.12) could be tested using simple OLS techniques. Frenkel (1976) reports one such test on monthly data for Germany in the 1920s, using the inflation rate as a proxy for exchange rate expectations. His results are fully consistent with the monetary approach; the homogeneity of money is confirmed and the proxy for ε is significant at a reasonable value. These results are also consistent with the view that monetary shocks dominated the sample period and purchasing power parity was maintained.

Dornbusch (1980) provides another test of eq. (19.12) based on quarterly data for the 1970s. These results are summarized in Table 3.1. They suggest that the estimated coefficients are generally insignificant and that the simple monetary approach offers a poor description of this period. Only the homogeneity postulate survives. Dornbusch goes on to consider other exchange rate theories. Other authors also report that they cannot accept the monetary approach for their sample data – Bilson (1978a) for a monthly sample of DM/£ rates in 1970s and Frenkel and Clements (1981) for a monthly sample of non-DM rates in the 1920s. However, these authors revise their empirical methodology instead of considering other theories.

(ii) *Mixed estimation.* A major problem cited in the studies mentioned above is imprecise parameter estimates. These imply that there is relatively little information in the sample data either to confirm or reject a particular theory. A Bayesian procedure for obtaining more precise parameter estimates is to supplement the sample information with prior information. In this case, prior information amounts to stochastic restrictions in the elasticities (i.e. regression coefficients) that are based on previous studies of the demand for money. The mixed estimation procedure, as applied by Bilson (1978b) and Frenkel and Clements (1981), produces coefficient estimates that are more precise and fully consistent with the monetary approach. However, the true test of this procedure is whether in a dynamic simulation the estimated model closely tracks the actual exchange rate over the sample period. In both studies, the authors report that the dynamic

Table 3.1
Equations explaining the monetary approach to exchange rate determination, using the dollar–mark exchange rate, 1973:2–1979:4 and subperiod*

Equation and sample period	Independent variable						Summary statistic			
	Constant	$(e + m^* - m)_{-1}$	$m - m^*$	$y - y^*$	$(i - i^*)_S$	$(i - i^*)_L$	R^2	Durbin–Watson	Standard error of estimate	Rho
2-1 1973:2–1979:4	5.76 (2.81)	⋯	−0.03 (−0.07)	−1.05 (−0.97)	0.01 (1.90)	0.04 (2.07)	0.33	1.83	0.05	0.88
2-2 1973:2–1978:1	4.82 (2.51)	⋯	1.00	−0.93 (−0.90)	−0.00 (−0.29)	0.07 (5.94)	0.66	1.69	0.04	0.06
2-3 1973:2–1979:4	4.63 (2.12)	⋯	1.00	−0.76 (−0.66)	0.01 (1.62)	0.04 (1.82)	0.08	1.80	0.05	0.99
2-4 1973:2–1979:4	0.23 (0.12)	0.83 (8.26)	1.00	0.16 (0.17)	0.01 (1.36)	0.01 (0.67)	0.88	1.85	0.05	⋯

Source: Dornbusch (1980).

Sources: Exchange rate—Board of Governors of the Federal Reserve System. *Federal Reserve Statistical Release*, G.5, "Foreign Exchange Rates," various issues; U.S. money supply—Board of Governors of the Federal Reserve System; German money supply—International Monetary Funds, *International Financial Statistics*, various issues, and Deutsche Bundesbank; real income—Organisation for Economic Co-operation and Development, *Main Economic Indicators*, various issues; and interest rates—Morgan Guaranty Trust Company of New York, *World Financial Markets*, various issues.

[a] The equations were estimated using quarterly data. The independent variables are: e—Logarithm of the dollar–mark exchange rate; m—logarithm of the money supply (M_1), seasonally adjusted; y—logarithm of gross national product at 1975 prices, seasonally adjusted at annual rates; is—yield on representative money-market instruments; and i_L—yield on domestic government bonds. An asterisk denotes a variable for Germany. The numbers in parentheses are t-statistics.

simulations track the data reasonably well. In other words, a monetary approach with coefficients estimated according to a Bayesian procedure does not produce results that are inconsistent with actual exchange rate behavior. It should be noted that Bilson's model includes a significant time drift term that might represent economic factors that could be modelled explicitly.

(iii) *Pooled time series and cross-section data.* Another procedure for increasing the precision of coefficient estimates is to increase the sample size and to increase the variance of the dependent variable. By combining sample data from many countries with a wide range of exchange rate experiences, pooled time series cross-section methodology accomplishes both objectives at once. Bilson (1976) applies this procedure to yearly data for 37 countries in the period 1956–1973. He incorporates a country specific term to take account of differences in velocity, the development of financial institutions, and other factors that differ across countries. Bilson's results offer strong evidence that the monetary approach explains a large fraction of cross-sectional exchange rate variation and that parameter estimates are in line with prior expectations. The mean absolute error in-sample is under 15 percent.

(iv) *Short-run and long-run interest rates.* The model proposed in eq. (19.12) assumes that real interest rate differentials are zero or constant. While this may be an adequate first approximation during a hyperinflation or a period dominated by monetary shocks, it is not a valid description of the 1970s. Frankel (1979b) modifies the simple monetary model to account for real interest rate differentials. His final estimating equation is

$$s = (m - m^*) + \eta(y - y^*) + \alpha(i - i^*) + \beta(\dot{p} - \dot{p}^*), \qquad (19.13)$$

where $\dot{p}$ and $\dot{p}^*$ are the current values of expected long-run inflation rates at home and in the foreign country, α is hypothesized to be negative and β is hypothesized to be positive and greater the α in absolute value. For econometric purposes, the opportunity cost of money balances (i and i^*) is represented by a short-run interest rate, while long-term interest rates are used to represent $\dot{p}$ and $\dot{p}^*$.

Frankel's original study used monthly data on the $/DM rate for the period July 1974–February 1978 and showed results very favorable to his hypothesis. However, the model gave signs of breakdown in the last few months of the sample. The results in Table 3.1, taken from Dornbusch (1980), confirm that this variation of the monetary model is not supported by the behavior of the $/DM rate in the 1970s. In a follow-up paper, Frankel (1982a) revises his model to include financial wealth as an argument in the demand for money function. This modification appears to correct the post-1978 deterioration of the baseline model. Frankel concludes that the monetary model with wealth as an argument succeeds in explaining the $/DM rate when alternative approaches fail.

(v) *In-sample and post-sample tests*. The final empirical methodology is represented by an ambitious paper by Meese and Rogoff (1983a). The authors estimate several competing exchange rate models, including a monetary approach, using a "rolling regression" format to estimate parameter coefficients from the most recent information available. Using these estimated models, Meese and Rogoff proceed to generate one to twelve month horizon forecasts in the post-sample period. The authors conclude that even when models perform well in-sample, they perform poorly in the post-sample period and fail to outperform the random walk model or the forward rate in forecasting the spot rate.[25]

In a subsequent paper, Meese and Rogoff (1983b) rule out parameter sampling error as a reason for poor post-sample performance. Instead, they suggest that model misspecification resulting from instability in the underlying money demand function and insufficient attention to risk factors and shifting real exchange rates may be at the heart of the problem.

3.2.3. Methodological issues

As was indicated earlier, parameter instability is one of the methodological issues affecting studies of the monetary approach. While this is a potential problem in any regression framework, monetary models applied to the 1970s may be particularly susceptible, because of the range of monetary conditions and financial innovations that characterized the period. Studies by Frankel (1979b, 1983) and Meese and Rogoff (1983a, 1983b) suggest that further studies on parameter instability may be rewarding.

Correcting possible model misspecification is another important avenue for research. The real side of the monetary model has been confined to real income and the relative price of traded versus non-traded goods. But other real factors – major changes in energy prices or major changes in current accounts that result from changes in tastes, international competitiveness, or the desire to re-balance portfolios – do not enter cleanly into the model. Equally important for short-run exchange rate determination is the specification of the money supply process. Traditional monetary models take the money supply as given, but the money supply should perhaps be made endogenous in the short run. For the long run, we might assume that central bank sterilization or intervention policies are of limited importance. The standard monetary approach disregards risk considerations, but it may be more logical to include these in a model where investors exercise portfolio choices.[26]

---

[25] The performance of professional currency forecasters, reviewed in Section 5, is likewise assessed using post-sample data.

[26] Dornbusch (1982) and Kouri (1982) develop models that add risk and portfolio optimizing behavior to the basic asset approach. See also Chapter 15 of this Handbook.

A final issue that applies to all empirical analyses of exchange rates is the degree of accuracy that we ought to expect from any stylized economic model. In Section 1 we noted that exchange rates often change by 1–2 percent in a day – conceivably a day when nothing an economist can measure has changed. Again, drawing an analogy to the stock market, we might argue that a model which describes monthly or quarterly exchange rate behavior within a tolerance of 5–15 percent is performing very well.

3.3. Currency substitution

An extension of the monetary approach allows domestic currency to be held by foreigners and vice versa.[27] Domestic residents might demand foreign currency because they seek to minimize transaction costs or reduce exchange risk by holding transaction balances or because they believe that foreign currency provides a more secure store of value. Significantly, even if both currencies are equal in terms of their own return and risk, risk averse individuals will hold portfolios containing both currencies as long as returns are not perfectly correlated (and ignoring transaction costs).

Frenkel and Clements (1981) develop a straightforward extension of the simple monetary approach in which the aggregate demand for money is the sum of domestic and foreign components. Demand for domestic money comes in part (λ) from domestic residents and in part ($1 - \lambda$) from abroad; demand for foreign money comes in part (λ^*) from foreign residents and in part ($1 - \lambda^*$) from abroad. The final exchange rate equation is similar to (19.12) except the two parameters λ and λ^* appear. When residents hold their local currency exclusively, $\lambda = \lambda^* = 1$ and the model reduces to (19.12). The authors do not present empirical evidence on the model.

Miles (1978) presents a model in which residents hold both domestic and foreign currencies because both contribute to the level of money services. The residents are assumed to maximize the production of monetary services subject to an asset constraint. Miles' empirical analysis is for Canada and the United States over the period 1960IV–1975IV. He reports that the elasticity of substitution between Canadian dollars and U.S. dollars is significant during floating rate periods. This suggests that portfolio considerations ought to be incorporated into exchange rate models of the Canadian dollar.

The major drawback of the currency substitution model is the limited menu of assets (i.e. currencies) under consideration. A portfolio balance framework expands the list of assets that may be substituted and therefore appears more realistic.

---

[27]Alternative theoretical formulations are presented in Girton and Roper (1976) and Calvo and Rodriguez (1977).

3.4. The portfolio balance approach

3.4.1. Overview

An extension of the monetary/currency substitution framework argues that individuals' excess demand is not for currency qua currency, rather individuals desire to shift from one set of financial assets (for example, dollar denominated) into another set of (DM denominated) financial assets. In the portfolio balance model, demand in the foreign exchange market for currencies is derived largely from demand for financial assets. As a consequence, if wealth accumulates (e.g. via current account surpluses) in a country that traditionally prefers DM assets, it is likely that the value of the DM will increase.

The essential building blocks of the model are domestic money, M; domestic bonds, B, that earn the interest rate r and are not internationally traded; and foreign-issued bonds, F, that earn the fixed interest rate $\bar{r}$.[28] Foreign bonds cannot be traded for M or B, so they can be accumulated only through a current account surplus. The asset market equilibrium conditions are given in the following equations:

$$M = m(r, \bar{r})W, \tag{19.14}$$

$$B = b(r, \bar{r})W, \tag{19.15}$$

$$eF = f(r, \bar{r})W, \tag{19.16}$$

$$W = B + M + eF. \tag{19.17}$$

The exchange rate is given by e, and W represents domestic financial wealth.

The portfolio balance approach is appealing because it presents a rich setting within which to analyze important real factors affecting exchange rates and yet maintain a tractable model. The model provides a clear link between real factors which affect the current account, the current account itself (i.e. flow changes in F) and the exchange rate. Furthermore, we can investigate the impact on the exchange rate of shifts in the distribution of financial wealth across currencies. Finally, the model is suited to analyzing the impact of risk and individual portfolio behavior on exchange rates.[29]

3.4.2. Empirical evidence and methodological issues

Empirical studies of the portfolio balance approach suffer from two important methodological problems. The first is a data problem; it is very difficult to track

---

[28] The notation follows Branson, Halttunen and Masson (1977).

[29] These theoretical relationships are developed in more detail in Allen and Kenen (1980), Branson (1977), Dornbusch (1982), Fama and Farber (1979), Kouri (1976). See also Chapter 15 of this Handbook.

the holdings of financial assets broken down by currency of denomination. In practice, most studies have started with a benchmark observation on the private stock of foreign assets held and have then accumulated current account balances for each country, less holdings of central banks. Necessarily, this method ignores capital gains on foreign assets, and it also assumes that domestic residents are the only holders of domestic assets and that all foreign assets are denominated in foreign currency. German corporations' Euro-dollar bonds and U.S. corporations' Euro–DM bonds are the counter-examples here.

The second methodological problem is specifying stable asset demand functions. Frankel (1982a) argues that while it may be appropriate to assume stationarity of expected returns in the context of a micro CAPM, it is inappropriate in a macro model since changes in expected returns are essential to the international adjustment process. Frankel contends that the stationarity assumption accounts for the sharp changes in "optimal" portfolio weights across currencies and the sometimes negative weights (for currencies in positive supply) that have been reported in the literature.

Perhaps because of these problems, empirical tests of the portfolio balance model have not met with great success. In a study of the $/DM rate in the 1970s, Branson, Halttunen and Masson (1977) report OLS coefficient estimates with the expected signs, but these are generally not significant, and some serial correlation remains in the residuals (see Table 3.2). However, using a two stage least squares procedure, the authors produce consistent parameter estimates that show greater significance and explanatory power.

A more recent study by Frankel (1982b) tests the portfolio balance model through mid-1981 for five countries. Single equation models are estimated using the Cochran–Orcutt technique. The results are dismal; many parameters are significant with the incorrect sign. As in Frankel (1982a), Frankel resorts to a synthesis of monetary and portfolio balance approaches. Coefficients of the portfolio balance parameters assume the correct sign and are generally significant, but the monetary variables remain insignificant.

3.5. Exchange rate dynamics

The general issue of exchange rate dynamics is covered in Chapter 18 of this Handbook. In this section, we focus on empirical studies of exchange rate overshooting.

3.5.1. Overview

The recent period of floating exchange rates has caused some market observers to wonder whether exchange rate volatility is excessive by some standards. The term

Table 3.2

Equations explaining the portfolio balance approach to exchange rate determination, the $/DM rate, monthly observations, August 1971–December 1976

Estimation Method	Constant	M1		Foreign assets		Rho	$\bar{R}^2$	D.W.
		Germany	U.S.	Germany	U.S.			
OLS	-94.3	-0.1034	0.1434	0.2495	-0.2899	n.a.	0.826	0.410
	(6.0)	(6.1)	(10.5)	(1.1)	(1.8)			
Cochrane–Orcutt	-8.8	-0.0571	0.0889	0.4563	-0.2934	0.8639	0.938	1.333
	(0.2)	(1.6)	(2.8)	(1.3)	(1.6)	(13.7)		
2 SLS	-4.9	-0.0618	0.0922	0.6758	-0.3976	0.8676	0.937	1.349
	(0.1)	(1.7)	(2.8)	(1.7)	(1.9)	(14.0)		

Source: Branson, Halttunen, and Masson (1977).

Note: Spot exchange rate is in $/DM, as an index 1970 = 100; money stock is in domestic currency: assets are private foreign asset stock expressed in dollars; $\bar{R}^2$ is squared coefficient of multiple determination, adjusted for degrees of freedom; and Rho is first-order serial correlation coefficient. *t*-ratios are in parentheses.

"overshooting" was coined to describe exchange rate changes in excess of such a standard. Interest in overshooting arises from two general concerns. First, exchange rate overshooting may signal that the market is inefficient and profit opportunities exist and/or some sort of government corrective action (not necessarily intervention) is required. Second, if the foreign exchange market is operating efficiently, overshooting may simply suggest that investing in foreign currency assets is somewhat riskier than is implied by simpler models.

Levich (1981c) proposes the following three definitions of overshooting.

(1) The current spot exchange rate (S_t) does not equal some long-run equilibrium rate ($\bar{S}$) that may be based on purchasing power parity or another long-run model.

(2) The equilibrium exchange rate change that occurs in the short-run (ΔS_{sr}) exceeds the equilibrium exchange rate change in the long-run (ΔS_{lr}).

(3) The actual exchange rate change that occurs in the market place (ΔS_t) exceeds the equilibrium exchange rate change ($\Delta S_t'$) that would occur if the market had full information about economic structure and disturbances.

The first definition reflects the conventional notion of overshooting as it is often reported in the press, such as: "The Swiss franc is currently overvalued relative to any reasonable standard." The third definition rests on the idea that agents may have heterogeneous or incomplete information about the world or be subject to severe trading constraints, leading them to place "unfair" prices on financial assets, i.e. prices that do not reflect *all* available information. This framework

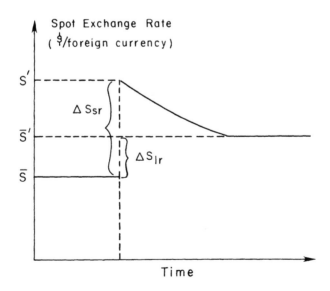

Figure 3.3. Exchange rate overshooting: definition (2).

posits that the actual exchange rate oscillates about the value that would be achieved if prices reflected *all* available information. Our purpose here is to consider definition (2).

That definition of overshooting draws a distinction between short-run and long-run equilibria while retaining the notion that the exchange rate is priced fairly at all times, a perfect reflection of all information. Overshooting of this type might be viewed as the result of forcing a given amount of international adjustment through a limited number of channels, because other potential adjustment channels are assumed to operate slowly or not to exist. Dornbush (1976) elegantly formalizes a monetary model of the exchange rate in which consumer price adjust very slowly relatively to the speed of adjustment in the foreign exchange market (see Figure 3.3). Within this framework, an unanticipated change in the money supply leads to exchange rate overshooting because consumer prices cannot move immediately to reflect the money supply change. A similar result can be illustrated with a portfolio balance model. In this case, a desired accumulation of foreign currency assets can proceed only slowly through cumulative current account surpluses. In the interim, the exchange rate overshoots to equate actual with desired holdings of that asset.[30]

3.5.2. Empirical evidence

The only direct test of the Dornbusch model of overshooting is by Driskill (1981) who analyzes the $/Swiss franc rate over the 1973–1979 period. Using regression analysis, Driskill reports that the elasticity of the exchange rate in response to an unanticipated monetary disturbance exceeds unity (its long-run value in a monetary model), i.e. overshooting is confirmed. For a one-unit monetary innovation, the exchange rate response is 2.30. However, contrary to theory, the empirical exchange rate adjustment path is non-monotonic.

Using vector-autoregression analysis, Bilson (1982) concludes that exchange rates and domestic interest rates exhibit significant negative contemporaneous correlation, as the Dornbusch model predicts. Finally, a study by Melhem (1982) reports that short-term forward rates are more volatile than long-term forward rates. This is consistent with Figure 2.3 and the notion that forward rates reflect the future spot rate. Therefore, the empirical evidence to date seems to be consistent with overshooting, even though by other measures (recall Table 2.1) exchange rate volatility may not be excessive.

---

[30] It seems intuitively clear that the more channels that exist and are free to operate, the less likely we are to observe overshooting behavior in exchange rates. Frenkel and Rodriguez (1982) formalize this idea. Specifically, they show that if prices are free to adjust somewhat (in the Dornbusch model) or if investors elect to spend some of their wealth on nontradable domestic goods (in the portfolio-balance model), then overshooting behavior need not occur.

3.6. The asset approach and the role of news

3.6.1. Overview

The monetary and portfolio balance approaches reviewed above suggest that the demand for currency depends on its qualities as a durable asset. If a currency is expected to continue offering services as a medium of exchange (i.e. transaction services) and as a store of value and unit of account (i.e. the choice for denominating portfolio wealth), then the currency will continue to be demanded. One additional property of financial assets that we associate with stocks and bonds is that their prices are forward looking, depending on future discounted cash flows. The same forward looking property should be expected of exchange rate pricing and that may be helpful in forecasting.

Refer to eq. (19.12) and note the interest rate differential term, $i - i^*$. Assuming covered interest parity, $(i - i^*) = f_t - s_t$. Assuming that forward rates are set equal to expected future spot rates, $f = E(s_{t+1})$. With these assumptions, we can now write (19.12) as

$$s_t = z_t + \varepsilon[E(s_{t+1}) - s_t], \tag{19.18}$$

where $z_t = (m - m^*) + \eta(y^* - y) + (k^* - k)$. If we collect terms:

$$s_t = \frac{1}{1+\varepsilon}z_t + \frac{\varepsilon}{1+\varepsilon}E(s_{t+1}). \tag{19.19}$$

Expression (19.19) shows that the log of today's spot rate depends on today's economic variables (the z_t) plus our expectation of the spot rate in the next period. But from (19.18), $E(s_{t+1})$ will depend on $E(s_{t+2})$. And $E(s_{t+2})$ will depend on $E(s_{t+3})$, etc. By this process of forward iteration,

$$s_t = \frac{1}{1+\varepsilon} \sum_{k=0}^{\infty} \left(\frac{\varepsilon}{1+\varepsilon}\right)^k E(z_{t+k}). \tag{19.20}$$

In other words, the current spot rate depends on our current expectation of all important driving variables (the z's), from now into the indefinite future.[31] The analogy with a security whose current price represents the discounted value of all future cash flows should be clear.

To put expression (19.20) as simply as possible, the current exchange rate reflects what is known or expected about the future. Without a model for the z's, this relationship is not useful for forecasting. However, the other implication of (19.20) is that exchange rates *change* only in response to *unanticipated* events (i.e. changes in the z_{t+k}). This brings us to the role of news.

---

[31] The derivation and algebraic form of (19.20) is adapted from Mussa (1976).

3.6.2. Empirical evidence

The implication of the asset market approach is that deviations between the forward rate (which, for now, we take as a proxy for the expected future spot rate) and the actual future spot rate are the result of news. In a regression format, we could write:

$$s_t = a + bf_{t-1} + \text{"news"} + w_t, \tag{19.21}$$

and test the joint hypothesis that $b = 1$ and that the coefficient of news is significant. Clearly, news can be modeled in a variety of ways.[32] Frenkel (1981) allows unanticipated changes in the term structure of interest rates to play the role of "news" and finds a significant relationship in the context of (19.21). Dornbusch (1980) represents news by unanticipated current account balances, unanticipated cyclical income movements and unanticipated interest rate changes. Again, the empirical evidence in Table 3.3 confirms that unanticipated changes in these important variables are significantly related to forward rate forecasting errors. This result is especially dramatic since, as Figure 3.1 suggests, forward rate errors tend to be large and serially uncorrelated.

The implication of these results is that analysts who can forecast one or two key variables better than the market as a whole may be able to outperform the forward rate forecast.

4. Tests of foreign exchange market efficiency[33]

Market efficiency is a major theme that has motivated numerous empirical studies of international financial markets. Tests of asset market efficiency, focusing on domestic equity and bond markets, began in the 1950s and gained increasing popularity and significance during the 1960s. With the establishment of floating exchange rates in the early 1970s (presumably dominated by free-market behavior), it was natural to begin the investigation of foreign exchange market efficiency. Some early studies relied too heavily on stock market techniques, and therefore were not testing appropriate hypotheses. By their nature, however, efficiency tests are difficult to formulate and subject to ambiguous interpretations. The reason for this, as we will explain in detail, is that efficiency tests implicitly require a joint null hypothesis.

---

[32] See Genberg (1983) for an empirical study of the relationship between the innovations in spot rate and forward rate series.

[33] Parts of this section rely heavily on earlier surveys by the author on this topic; see Levich (1978, 1979b).

Table 3.3

Equations explaining unanticipated depreciation of the nominal effective exchange rate of the dollar, second half of 1973 through second half of 1979.

Equation	Independent variable					Summary statistic			
	Constant	CAE	CYC	CYC*	INN	R^2	Durbin–Watson	Standard error of estimate	Rho
3-1	3.5 (1.88)	−0.49 (−2.62)	1.86 (1.35)	−1.86	...	0.41	2.13	6.2	...
3-2	2.7 (1.69)	−0.31 (−1.82)	0.47 (0.33)	−0.78 (0.57)	13.33 (1.99)	0.63	2.03	5.5	−0.24
3-3	3.1 (2.47)	−0.27 (−2.19)	...	...	13.79 (2.53)	0.61	2.13	5.1	−0.28

Source: Dornbusch (1980)

Sources: Forecast and actual current account balances and real output growth—Organisation for Economic Co-operation and Development, OECD *Economic Outlook*, various issues; exchange rate—same as Table 2.1; and interest rates—same as Table 3.1.
[a]The dependent variable, unanticipated depreciation of the dollar, is described in Figure 2.3, note a. *CYC* and *CYC** are unanticipated growth in real output of, respectively, the United States and a trade-weighted average of the five foreign countries in Table 2.1. Unanticipated growth is the difference between the OECD's six-month forecast and realized growth. The data are seasonally adjusted annual rates of growth. *CAE* is the forecast error for U.S. current account balances, using the OECD's forecasts. The data are measured in billions of dollars, seasonally adjusted. *INN* denotes the residuals from an autoregression of short-term interest differentials between the United States and a trade-weighted average of five foreign countries. Trade-weighted variables use the weights in Table 2.1, note a. The numbers in parentheses are *t*-statistics.

4.1. The efficient market hypothesis

The classic definition of an efficient market is a market where prices "fully reflect" all available information.[34] When this condition is satisfied, investors cannot earn an unusual profit by exploiting available information. The macroeconomic importance of market efficiency is derived from the role of prices as aggregators of structural information. When asset and commodity markets are efficient (in the above sense of reflecting information), economic agents who make decisions on the basis of observed prices will insure an efficient allocation of resources.

But the previous definition is too general to be tested empirically. We must posit a precise meaning for the term "fully reflect". Typically, this has been accomplished by assuming that market equilibrium can be stated in terms of equilibrium prices or equilibrium expected returns. If we choose the latter, then the excess market return on asset j is given by

$$Z_{j,t+1} = r_{j,t+1} - E(\tilde{r}_{j,t+1}|\Phi_t), \tag{19.22}$$

where $r_{j,t+1}$ is the actual one-period percentage return and Φ_t represents the information set that is assumed to be fully reflected in the price at time t. When the excess return sequence (Z_{jt}) is a "fair game" with respect to the information sequence (Φ_t), the market is efficient.[35]

The critical point of this discussion is that all tests of market efficiency are testing a joint hypothesis – first, the hypothesis that defines market equilibrium prices or expected returns as some function of the set Φ_t, and second, the hypothesis that economic agents can set actual prices or returns to conform to their expected values.[36]

For studies that reject this simultaneous test, it is impossible to determine whether an incorrect specification in equilibrium expected returns is responsible for the rejection or whether, in fact, investors were inefficient information processors. And for studies that cannot reject market efficiency, it can be argued

---

[34] This definition and the initial development of a formal theory of asset market efficiency is attributed to Fama (1970).

[35] If the sequence (Z_{jt}) is a fair game then $E(\tilde{Z}_{j,t+1}|\Phi_t) = 0$ and the Z_{jt} are serially uncorrelated. It follows that in an efficient market a few investors may occasionally make large gains or losses, but no group should make large gains or losses consistently.

[36] It is interesting that Fama organizes his 1970 survey according to the information set, Φ_t, which is being fully reflected. Information sets are classified as containing only historical prices (and testing what it called weak form efficiency), as containing public information (and testing semistrong form efficiency), or as containing all information including insider information (and testing strong form efficiency). However, Fama (1976) organizes the literature according to the underlying assumption about the equilibrium expected return. He considers four alternative equilibrium expected return processes: returns are positive, returns are constant, returns are generated by a market model, returns conform to a specific two-parameter model. The latter survey is more effective in highlighting the simultaneous nature of efficient market tests, because it stresses the problem of making operational the assumption about equilibrium returns.

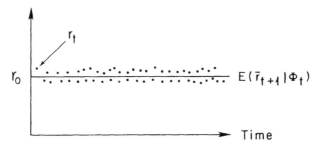

Figure 4.1. Efficient market behavior with the equilibrium expected return constant.

that the wrong equilibrium expected-return process was assumed. Relative to the "correct" standard, the market is really inefficient and unusual profit opportunities are available.

To illustrate the importance of this difficulty for empirical testing, consider Figures 4.1 and 4.2. In Figure 4.1 the equilibrium expected return is assumed to be constant at r_0. If actual returns vibrate randomly about r_0, the market is efficient. Generalizing, the market is efficient if actual returns follow a random walk with drift parameter r_0. In Figure 4.2 the equilibrium expected return is assumed to vary systematically. If actual returns vibrate randomly about the equilibrium, the market is efficient. In this case, however, equilibrium expected returns are serially correlated about their mean values and do not follow a random walk, which means that the market can be efficient even if actual returns do not follow a random walk.

Conditional on a constant equilibrium expected return or price, random price movement suggests market efficiency. But random price movement per se is neither a necessary nor sufficient condition for market efficiency. If the expected equilibrium return or price varies considerably, market efficiency requires non-random walk price movements. It seems obvious that, because of underlying

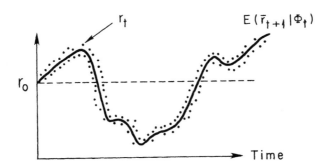

Figure 4.2. Efficient market behavior where the equilibrium expected return wanders substantially.

macroeconomic policies, both the level and the rate of change in equilibrium currency prices might vary systematically.

The early random walk studies of equity markets did not sufficiently recognize this point. However, several equilibrium return processes could be assumed and tested in respect of equity markets. First, we could assume that expected returns on equities are positive in every period, because utility maximizing, risk-averse investors would not willingly accept non-diversifiable equity risk without expecting a positive return. Second, we could assume that expected returns on equities are constant. Fama (1970) suggests that this assumption is plausible for equities, since over the typical differencing interval (one month or less) variation in equilibrium expected returns is small relative to other sources of variation in returns. Third, we could assume that expected returns on equities are generated by a market model or a specific capital asset pricing model.[37]

However, a convincing empirical test of efficiency in the foreign exchange market is made difficult because there is no general agreement on the appropriate model of equilibrium pricing comparable to that for equity markets.[38] Simply put, it is difficult to test whether investors efficiently set the actual spot exchange rate equal to its equilibrium value unless there is some agreement on what the equilibrium value is. Similarly, it is difficult to test whether risk-bearing is efficiently rewarded if there is no agreement on the fundamental nature of foreign exchange risk, no adequate measure of it, and no model that determines the equilibrium fair return for bearing it.

Equity markets and foreign exchange markets differ in another important respect. Firms might be characterized by their consistency – in terms of directors, product lines, financial strategy, customers, etc. This suggests that for firms operating in a stable environment with mature products, investors can learn the risk/return properties of equities. However, in the foreign exchange market, our confidence that underlying economic policies will be maintained is considerably less. The operation of monetary and fiscal policy is subject to sharp changes, because personnel in the Executive branch, Congress, or the Federal Reserve are replaced, or simply because existing personnel change their policies. Furthermore, under a managed floating system, the government may enter the market in a non-profit-maximizing and non-stationary manner. Therefore the equilibrium path of exchange rates can be expected to vary systematically and a model of equilibrium pricing of foreign exchange ought to include a role for government.[39]

---

[37] For a critical appraisal of empirical tests of asset pricing models, see Roll (1977).

[38] Once again, the reader is referred to Chapter 15 of this Handbook.

[39] It is important to note that government intervention per se does not imply exchange market inefficiency. To the extent that the intervention policy is known, it should be reflected in the price of foreign exchange (and in other financial markets). To the extent that intervention is unpredictable, increased uncertainty may reduce the willingness of traders to take positions. Such an increase in uncertainty may reduce the liquidity of markets and widen the bid-ask spread, but this is not a market inefficiency in the sense of Fama (1970).

To summarize, the efficient market hypothesis requires a simultaneous test of two hypotheses. A number of plausible hypothesis about equilibrium pricing or returns have been incorporated into efficient market tests for equities. However, in the case of foreign exchange there is no firm agreement on a model of equilibrium prices, and still less agreement on the stationarity of any model over time, especially in the presence of erratic macroeconomic policies or government intervention. In the absence of agreement on a hypothesis about the equilibrium exchange rate, it is not possible either to prove or disprove the efficiency hypothesis in the foreign exchange market.

4.2. Empirical evidence – certainty and risk-free investment

In the foreign exchange market, spatial, triangular and covered arbitrage are elementary investment opportunities that promise a certain return with no exposure to risks.[40] In an efficient market, prices of foreign exchange and interest-bearing assets should be set so that "unusual profits" from arbitrage are quickly eliminated. In theory, arbitrage is essentially risk-free and can be completed in a matter of seconds, so any profit in excess of transaction costs is unusual. In arbitrage, the equilibrium expected return is zero.

4.2.1. Currency Arbitrage.

The dispersion of quotations on individual currencies across market-makers is reduced by *spatial arbitrage*. Some price dispersion is consistent with market efficiency since there is a cost of searching for spatial arbitrage profits and some price risk associated with exploiting them. In addition, however, price dispersion that reflects quotations of different "quality" will persist. These issues have not been studied rigorously on data from the foreign exchange market.[41]

Price differences between interbank forward rate quotations and futures contract of similar maturity on Chicago's International Monetary Market have been examined by Cornell and Reinganum, (1981). While the futures contract and the forward contract are similar in many respects, the futures market convention of

---

[40] In the real world, arbitrage may involve a degree of price risk (i.e. risk of price change over the time required to complete arbitrage transactions), default risk on forward contracts, and varying degrees of bankruptcy risk or sovereign risk on assets. For a recent assessment of these risks, see Buiter (1983).

[41] A stark example of price dispersion due to quality differences comes from the Falkland Islands episode. Customers might require more favorable quotations on long-term forward contracts from affected British banks because there is a greater probability that these banks will default compared to unaffected U.S. banks. For a detailed study of price dispersion in the U.S. Treasury bill market, see Garbade and Silber (1976).

"marking-to-market" exposes the buyer to an interest rate risk as his funds are either deposited in or withdrawn from his margin account. Explicit margin requirements are not used with interbank forward contracts since only customers with prior credit approval are permitted to use the interbank market. Price differences, therefore, largely reflect differential risk.

A second profit opportunity in currency arbitrage is available through *triangular arbitrage* – the process which keeps cross-exchange rates (X_1/X_2) consistent with direct exchange rates ($\$/X_1$; $\$/X_2$) where X_1 and X_2 are arbitrary currencies. In most cases triangular parity, $\$/X_2 = \$/X_1 \cdot X_1/X_2$, holds by construction; traders use the formula to prepare quotations. For example, the Swiss franc/Mexican peso rate is simply the product of the $/peso, franc/$ rates. This reflects the fact that an independent franc/peso market does not exist and traders use the U.S. dollar as a vehicle currency. However, independent quotations for £ were offered in the 1960s, and independent DM/£ and DM/Yen markets developed in the 1970s. Triangular arbitrage, or the threat of it, is necessary to keep independent markets at parity. In this case, empirical studies [Frenkel and Levich (1975, 1977) and McCormick (1979)] have interpreted the upper limit of deviations from triangular parity as a measure of currency transaction costs. (See our earlier discussion in Section 2.3.)

4.2.2. Interest rate parity and covered interest arbitrage

One of the key building blocks for open economy macroeconomics is the interest rate parity theory which states that the forward premium and the interest differential are equal so that

$$\frac{F - S}{S} = \frac{i - i^*}{1 + i^*}. \tag{19.23}$$

When (19.23) holds, covered arbitrage profit opportunities are fully exploited. Numerous studies measure departures from interest rate parity [see Officer and Willett (1970) for a survey]. A variety of explanations are offered – less than infinite elasticities for foreign exchange and securities, transaction costs, non-comparable risk in securities, exchange controls (political risk) and taxes. Research suggests that all of these factors may play a role in explaining deviations from interest rate parity theory (IRPT). We proceed by raising a methodological issue.

Two natural ways to test (19.23) would be to (*a*) to regress the forward premium against the interest rate differential, expecting a 45° line, or (*b*) to calculate the deviations between the forward premium and the interest rate differential, expecting the mean deviation to be near zero. Frenkel and Levich (1975) argue that these procedures invite an incorrect inference when individual deviations are large but on average zero or when deviations are very small, but on average non-zero. The essence of market efficiency in these examples relies on the existence of a normal-profit boundary condition in every single period and not in some average sense. A calculation of the frequency with which covered arbitrage does not produce a significant profit allows us to make a direct inference about market efficiency. The higher this frequency, the greater the market efficiency.

Perhaps the most satisfactory studies of interest rate parity are those that analyze covered arbitrage opportunities between Eurocurrency assets. Since Eurocurrency deposits are comparable in terms of issuer, credit risk, maturity and all other respects *except* currency of denomination, they offer a proper test of IRPT. Studies by Clendenning (1970), Aliber (1973), Frenkel and Levich (1975, 1977) and others confirm that deviations from interest rate parity in the Eurocurrency markets are small and that a very high percentage of deviations are smaller than transaction costs. Therefore, the Eurocurrency market is efficient in that few opportunities for risk-free arbitrage exist.[42]

It is now well-understood [Deardorff (1979), Levich (1981d)] that bank traders *use* the interest rate parity theory to set forward rates. Traders observe a spot rate, S, and a swap rate [cost of a simultaneous borrowing and lending of Eurocurrency deposits in two currencies, $(1 + i)/(1 + i^*)$, and use these data to *construct* a forward rate $F = S(1 + i)/(1 + i^*)$]. The trader *must* follow interest rate parity or else customers will exploit the cheaper technique for establishing their forward positions. The implication is that arbitrage profit opportunities should never exist in a single trading room, but they could exist in a dispersed market which uses independent quotations on F, S, i, and i^*. Tests based on time-synchronous data from independent sources have not been reported.

A related issue that deserves further attention is the existence of deviations from interest rate parity for long-term securities. Hilley, Beidleman, and Greenleaf (1981) report that rates quoted by banks for three- to five-year forward contracts may be significantly worse than the implicit rates a customer might obtain by building his own forward position using a spot contract combined with long-term Eurocurrency borrowing and lending. The authors conclude that banks are playing more of a brokerage role and that the opportunity for a small arbitrage profit does not compensate them for the costs of keeping capital tied up for three to five years, for the adverse impact on balance sheet ratios, and for (possibly) substantial credit risks. Their finding and interpretation breathes new life into the old elasticities explanation for deviations from IRPT (see below).

The results for covered arbitrage between domestic or onshore assets are ambiguous. Frenkel and Levich (1975, 1977) and Levich (1979a) report that a much smaller fraction of observations are contained within the neutral band when arbitrage is between treasury bills or commercial paper traded in different

---

[42] For more on the institutional characteristics of the Eurocurrency markets and their impact on international financial relationships, see Dufey and Giddy (1978) and McKinnon (1979, ch. 9).

domestic markets. This apparent departure from market efficiency is more pronounced during turbulent periods on the foreign exchange market.

One way to explain the failure of interest parity between onshore markets is to introduce price elasticities in currency and security markets. Frenkel and Levich (1975, 1977) report that all apparent deviations from IRPT are explained if price elasticities are finite but still large enough to be consistent with a competitive environment. A second approach follows Aliber (1973) who noted that onshore markets differ in terms of political risk – i.e. the probability that the sovereign may interpose its authority between the investor and the market place.[43]

Dooley and Isard (1980) refine this concept by distinguishing between the cost of existing capital controls and the risk premium associated with prospective controls. They analyze German interbank and Eurocurrency interest rates over the period 1970–1974 and conclude that most of the interbank offshore interest rate differential, can be explained by the effective tax imposed by a sequence of known capital controls. However, they estimate that an expected return as high as 2 percent per annum may have been required to induce non-German residents to hold German outside debt in the face of potential capital controls.

Differential tax rates on capital gains and ordinary incomes can also affect covered arbitrage flows. Levi (1977) demonstrates that when forward contract gains are taxed at the capital gains rate, t_k, and interest rate gains are taxed as ordinary income, $t_y > t_k$, then the slope of the after-tax IRPT line is $(1 - t_y)/(1 - t_k)$, which is less than the 45° slope of the pre-tax IRPT line. When taxes are included, the normal incentives to exploit pre-tax arbitrage profits are changed considerably. Levi's model suggests that, ignoring transaction costs, elasticities, etc., a market that is efficient on a pre-tax basis, will not be efficient on an after-tax basis, and vice versa. No empirical study has fully considered the role of taxes in the IRPT model.

4.3. Empirical evidence – uncertainty and risky investments

Introducing uncertainty into single-period and multi-period investment models adds a degree of complexity, as well as realism, to tests of foreign exchange market efficiency. When the future spot exchange rate is a random variable, the dollar value of assets denominated in a foreign currency is uncertain. In this case,

---

[43] Interest parity holds in a single offshore center because the assets are exposed to the same political risks. Political risk is a fundamental argument behind the elasticity explanation for deviations from interest parity. Presumably, if there were no risks in arbitrage, the arbitrage supply schedule would be perfectly elastic. An alternative explanation for less than perfectly elastic arbitrage supply is that institutional constraints restrict the ability of banks to supply a sufficient number of forward contracts.

an investor who holds a net (asset or liability) position in foreign currency is exposed to foreign exchange risk.[44]

In an efficient market, prices (of spot and forward exchange, for example) should be set so that "unusual profits" from risky investment opportunities are quickly eliminated. Since a test of market efficiency tests a joint hypothesis, the specification of the expected equilibrium return for bearing foreign exchange risk is critical. We must have some standard for judging that profits from bearing such risk are "unusual".

There are basically two techniques for bearing foreign exchange risk – spot speculation and forward speculation. In spot speculation, the investor borrows domestic currency at interest rate i, buys foreign exchange in the spot market at the rate S_t, and invests in a foreign currency denominated asset at interest rate i^*. A forward speculator can establish a similar long position simply by buying foreign exchange in the forward market at the rate F_t. In either case, the profit depends on the expected future spot exchange rate, $\tilde{S}_{t+1}$, which is uncertain. It is easily shown that when the covered interest rate parity theorem holds, spot and forward speculation are equivalent investments in that they lead to the same time series of expected profits.

4.3.1. Spot market efficiency

Only two approaches have been proposed to test for spot market efficiency. One popular null hypothesis was that, under a regime of freely floating exchange rates, changes in spot exchange rates should be serially uncorrelated. Empirical tests of this hypothesis were reported by Poole (1967) and Burt, Kaen and Booth (1977). In general, this research concluded that there are significant departures from random behavior under floating exchange rates and therefore, the spot market was not efficient. However, as we suggested earlier, market efficiency requires a random behavior of returns only if the equilibrium expected return is constant. Therefore, only in the case where interest rates in the two countries differ by a constant and the equilibrium expected exchange rate thus follows a linear trend equal to that constant should we expect exchange rates to follow a random walk (with a drift term equal to the constant). By contrast, if the fundamental determinants of exchange rates are serially correlated, then equilibrium exchange rates will be also serially correlated.[45]

A second test of market efficiency in spot speculation has analyzed the performance of investment strategies that use *filter rules* as guides for picking

---

[44]Political risk was discussed in the previous footnote. Aliber (1973) argues that arbitragers bear political risk, while speculators bear exchange risk. For a model that considers default risk on forward contracts, see Adler and Dumas (1976).

[45]Equilibrium exchange rate models that allow for overshooting will also produce serially correlated exchange rate changes. See Chapters 14 and 18 of this Handbook and Section 2 of this chapter.

speculative positions. A filter rule is a mathematical rule that can be applied mechanically to produce buy signals and sell signals. An x percent filter rule leads to the following trading strategy: "Buy a currency whenever it rises x percent above its most recent trough; sell the currency and take a short position whenever the currency falls x percent below its most recent peak". A filter rule produces profits when momentum or "bandwagon" effects carry the exchange rate further in the direction indicated by the initial movement. However, the null hypothesis of efficiency suggests that Euro-currency traders should also recognize the expected momentum in the exchange market; Euro-currency traders should set relatively low interest rates on the appreciating currency and high interest rates on the depreciating currency, which should tend to offset the anticipated exchange rate change. This indeed summarizes the efficient market process – Euro-deposit interest rate differentials should exactly offset the expected exchange rate change, eliminating expected profits from the filter rule strategy.

An early study by Poole (1967) reports filter rule profits for the Canadian dollar during the floating rate period, 1950–1962, and for nine other series of flexible exchange rates in the post-First World War period. Poole finds evidence of statistically significant first-order serial correlation in exchange rate changes. In such circumstances, filter rule strategies tend to make large profits relative to a buy-and-hold strategy. Profits are not adjusted for the interest expense of a short position, the interest income of a long position, or the cost of transacting. Because of the last defect, Poole believes his results do not conclusively reject market efficiency.[46]

More comprehensive and rigorous studies of spot market efficiency have been conducted by Dooley and Shafer (1976, 1983). Dooley and Shafer report filter rule profits for nine currencies using daily spot rates over the 1970s floating rate period. Their calculations are adjusted to reflect the interest expense and income on short and long positions, and transaction costs are incorporated by using bid and asked foreign exchange quotations. Dooley and Shafer hypothesize that if the market is efficient, then filter rule profits adjusted to reflect the above costs should be a "fair game" (or martingale) process as in (19.22). Gross profits from the filter rule strategies imply net, abnormal profits and therefore reject market efficiency.

Dooley and Shafer's results indicate that small filters ($x = 1$, 3 or 5 percent) would have been profitable for all currencies over the entire sample period. However, there appears to be some element of riskiness in these trading rules,

---

[46]As a theoretical matter, adjusting for interest expense and interest income is critical. It is analogous to the importance of allowing for dividends in a filter rule analysis of equities. In the currency case, buying and holding Brazilian cruzerios in the 1970s surely would have resulted in losses. The correct null hypothesis is that the interest income on cruzerio assets just compensates for the expected exchange rate changes. Studies by Logue, Sweeney and Willett (1977) and Sweeney (1982) have maintained, incorrectly in our view, that the relevant alternative to the trading rule is holding the foreign currency. See Levich (1982) for further discussion.

since each filter would have generated losses in at least one currency during at least one subperiod. Furthermore, it is not clear that the size of the filter can be chosen ex ante to optimize or assure profits. Finally, because the filter rule actively switches the investor between currencies, the investor faces greater risk (i.e. loss of time diversification) than if he passively holds a portfolio with both currencies.

Since filter rule trading involves risk, the key question is whether unusual profit opportunities are available ex ante to spot speculators. Levich (1979b) suggests performance tests based on a mean–variance model, but these raise further problems concerning the appropriate market portfolio and risk aversion measure.

A recent paper by Goodman (1981) examines the performance of professional foreign exchange advisors that issue buy and sell signals based on technical analysis. Goodman reports that large profits in excess of the risk-free rate are generally available to users of these professional signals. There are also risks; the largest individual loss on one buy/sell signal was 2.4 times the initial 5 percent margin, and the largest stream of losses was 2.9 times the initial margin. Goodman suggests that these risks are small for investors who have enough capital to withstand intermittent losses and who use professional signals on a regular basis. To further bolster this case, Goodman reports that if investors use a composite signal based on two or more advisors, the risk/return trade-off improves.

4.3.2. Forward market efficiency

Tests of *forward market efficiency* have focused on the relationship between the *current n*-period forward rate, $F_{t,n}$, the *expected* future spot rate, $E(\tilde{S}_{t+n})$, and the *actual* future spot rate, S_{t+n}. Market efficiency requires that market agents are able to process available information and form rational expectations [i.e. $E(\tilde{S}_{t+n}) = S_{t+n}$]. However, market efficiency allows for the possibility that investors may demand a *risk premium* on forward contracts: therefore, it does not require that $F_{t,n} = E(\tilde{S}_{t+n})$. As a result, the relationship between the current forward rate, $F_{t,n}$, and the actual future spot rate, S_{t+n}, is ambiguous, *even in an efficient market*.

To restate these points, what we might call the *simple efficiency* hypothesis is that

$$F_{t,n} = E(\tilde{S}_{t+n}) \quad \text{and} \quad E(\tilde{S}_{t+n}) = S_{t+n}.$$

If this hypothesis is true, then deviations between $F_{t,n}$ and S_{t+n} should have mean zero and zero serial correlation. In a regression of the form

$$S_{t+n} = a + bF_{t,n} + cX_t + e_t, \tag{19.24}$$

our null hypothesis, given simple efficiency, is that $a = 0$, $b = 1$ and the coefficient of any other variable, X_t, is $c = 0$. The residuals, e_t, should of course be free of serial correlation.

A more *general efficiency hypothesis* that allows for a risk premium (RP) would say that:

$$F_{t,n} = \mathrm{E}(\tilde{S}_{t+n}) + \mathrm{RP}_{t,n} \quad \text{and} \quad \mathrm{E}(\tilde{S}_{t+n}) + S_{t+n}.$$

We can clearly see that in this case, the equality between $F_{t,n}$ and $\mathrm{E}(\tilde{S}_{t+n})$ is broken. Regression equations such as (19.24) that reject the $(a, b, c) = (0, 1, 0)$ hypothesis are subject to two interpretations.

(1) The simple efficiency hypothesis is rejected. The forward market is inefficient in reflecting exchange rate expectations. Expected profit opportunities through forward speculation exist.

(2) The general efficiency hypothesis cannot be rejected. A new forecast $S_{t+n} = a + bF_{t,n} + cX_t$ can be constructed which will be superior to the forward rate forecast. However, the profits we earn through forward speculation will be only the fair risk premium for the additional risk we incur.

Unfortunately, unless the variable X_t is a good proxy for risk (rather than a lagged forecast error or lagged forward rate), we are not on solid ground in accepting interpretation (2). And that is approximately where the frontier of research in this area stands today.

(i) *Foreign exchange risk premium.* As we have argued, whether or not the forward rate is an unbiased forecast depends on underlying economic factors; it is not an inherent property of any economic system, even one which is in equilibrium and processes information efficiently.[47] The theoretical case for forward rates as biased forecasters of future spot rates depends heavily on the existence of a risk premium. Under a pure floating rate system with no government intervention, small transaction costs, and efficient information processing, only the risk premium argument survives to explain a forward rate bias. Consequently, there has been renewed research interest in this topic.

In the modern theory of foreign exchange [Grubel (1966)] investors are assumed to be risk averse. The speculative demand for forward contracts is not infinitely elastic, because speculators will bear foreign exchange risk only if they are compensated with a risk premium. However, the determinants of the risk premium are not examined.

---

[47]Our special interest in unbiased forecasts is two-fold. First, if the forward rate is unbiased, no transformation of the forward rate is required to construct a forecast. Second, if the forward rate is unbiased, then any strategy for hedging foreign exchange risk or for speculating in forward contracts has the same long-run expected profit, namely zero.

Our interest in unbiased forecasts should not be construed to mean that this is the only property that matters for evaluating forecasts. Standard econometric methodology assumes implicitly that users of forecasts have quadratic utility functions and thus desire low variance of forecast errors as well as low average errors. In this setting, users choose the model that minimizes the mean squared forecasting error, even if it happens to yield a biased forecast. Nevertheless, the forward rate forecasting bias remains a fundamental property to analyze, especially for investors who seek to maximize expected profits without regard to variability.

Portfolio models offer a natural framework for analyzing foreign exchange risk. In general, portfolio models assume that agents acting as investors are free to purchase assets denominated in domestic and foreign currencies, that the risk of individual assets may differ and that returns are imperfectly correlated. Acting as consumers, moreover they choose among goods whose prices are denominated in a particular currencies and are imperfectly correlated with prices expressed in other currencies (i.e. that there are deviations from PPP). Exchange risk arises because the unit of account of an agent's cash inflows is imperfectly correlated with the unit of account of the agent's cash outflows.[48] Therefore, agents will hold assets denominated in foreign currency when the return is sufficient to compensate for the extra risk now associated with consuming domestic goods.

Models described in Frankel (1979a) and Dornbusch (1982) suggest that the risk premium is a function of the relative supplies of outside assets denominated in the two currencies. Fama and Farber (1979) emphasize the quality of money balances; in a PPP framework subject to uncertainty, agents will prefer the currency with lower inflation variance and less exposure to purchasing power risks. In general, the portfolio framework suggests that exchange risk premia are inversely correlated with greater monetary discipline, fewer debt-financed government expenditures, and perhaps less exposure to real disturbances. This framework suggests that risk premium can change signs over the short run, which makes it hard to measure the premium.[49]

Another model by Solnik (1973) relates the foreign exchange risk premium to relative international investment positions. For example U.S. investors may hold a net asset position in U.K. assets (i.e. U.S. investors own more U.K. assets than U.K. investors own of U.S. assets). If U.S. investors are risk averse, they may wish to hedge the returns on their investment consistently – even at forward rates less favorable than the expected future spot rate.[50]

(ii) *Empirical evidence.* Early studies examined the level of spot rates and lagged forward rates using (19.24) or simply calculated mean errors. These

---

[48] These risks are also present in a closed economy. For example, when an agents' wages are in nominal currency units and inflation is non-neutral, real consumption opportunities are uncertain. For more on exchange risk, see Wihlborg (1978).

[49] This concept of an exchange risk premium is fully consistent with the existence of liquidity or inflation risk premia in closed economy term structure theory. If both domestic rates, i, and foreign rates, i^*, reflect liquidity and inflation premia, then via interest parity, $F = S(1 + i)/(1 + i^*)$, and the forward rate reflects these relative risk factors.

[50] For example assume there is a U.S. firm in London that plans to repatriate a £1 million dividend in ninety days when the exchange rate is expected to be \$2.00/£. Unless there is a U.K. firm that wishes to repatriate \$2 million from New York to London in ninety days, the U.S. firm must locate someone who currently is in portfolio balance yet may be induced to exchange sterling for dollars in ninety days. Such a supplier of forward dollars may demand compensation for altering his currency portfolio and the U.S. firm, assuming risk aversion, will be willing to pay it. In this case, the U.S. firm may sell its sterling at \$1.98 even though it expects the price to be \$2.00 in ninety days. The \$.02 per pound is the compensation paid to the supplier of forward dollars for altering his initial currency portfolio thus and taking on additional risk. This framework seems less likely to lead to a risk premium that changes from positive to negative in the short run.

studies on exchange rates from the 1920s [Frenkel (1976, 1978, 1980)], the Bretton Woods system [Aliber (1974)], and the first few years of managed floating [Bilson (1976), Cornell (1977), Levich (1979b), Stockman (1978)] could not reject the simple efficiency hypothesis.

Later studies by Tryon (1979) and Levich (1980) reported that the percentage change version of (19.24),

$$\ln(S_{t+n}/S_t) = a + b \cdot \ln(F_{t,n}/S_t) + c \cdot \ln(X_t) + e_t, \qquad (19.25)$$

performed very poorly. Figure 3.1 illustrates that the forward premium is a relatively quiet series that explains very little of actual exchange rate changes.

A potential problem concerning eqs. (19.24) and (19.25) is the shortage of independent observations.[51] Since there are only four non-overlapping three-month periods per year, there are only four independent observations on three-month contracts per year; even fewer independent observations on longer-term contracts. This shortage of observations is regrettable; especially, if we also assume there may be a time-varying exchange risk premium or heteroscedastic errors because of erratic government intervention. Estimation is nearly hopeless with only nine years of floating rate data.

Two studies by Hansen and Hodrick (1980) and Hsieh (1982) solve the data shortage problem by a new generalized least squares estimation procedure. The technique allows the authors to use daily observations and increase the sample size by a factor of 20. Both studies find that lagged variables play a role in explaining forward rate forecast errors. Therefore, the authors reject the simple efficiency hypothesis.[52] The question remains whether this departure can be explained by a time varying risk premium, or whether the market is actually inefficient. Empirical studies by Meese and Singleton (1980) and Frankel (1982b) are not able to reject the hypothesis that a time-varying risk premium may be responsible for deviations between the forward rate and the future spot rate. However, Frankel admits that the tests probably have little statistical power.

The other avenue for testing forward market behavior is by comparing its forecasts with forecasts made by professional services. Levich (1980, 1981a, 1981b) reports that individual forecasting services do worse than the forward rate in terms of mean squared error. But the services exhibit significant expertise in predicting whether the spot rate will appreciate or depreciate relative to the

---

[51] Similar to the "data shortage" problem is the problem of infrequent exchange rate changes in a pegged rate system. Krasker (1980) argues that when there is a small probability of an event that would lead to a large exchange rate change, the standard tests for market efficiency are not necessarily valid. Krasker develops an alternative test procedure that focuses directly on the probability of the unusual event rather than the standard asymptotic distribution theory. These issues were raised during the 1976 Mexican peso devaluation; hence the literature sometimes refers to this as the "peso problem".

[52] Other studies that use different econometric techniques but draw the same conclusion are by Cumby and Obstfeld (1981), Hakkio (1981) and Longworth (1981).

forward rate – the key for corporate hedging strategies. Composite forecasts (i.e. weighted averages of individual forecasts) perform even better. This suggests further that professional forecasts can outperform forward rates, but there is no evidence that the corresponding speculative profits are unusually large in a risk adjusted sense.

Bilson (1981) uses a pooled time-series/cross-section technique to estimate a composite forecasting equation. In a post-sample period, the composite forecast significantly outperforms the forward rate and leads to positive profits.

4.4. Methodological issues and agenda

Empirical studies have clearly established the strong role that arbitrage plays in international financial markets. Certainly, within the Euro-markets, it has been demonstrated that covered arbitrage profit opportunities are not available. Future research opportunities fall into two groups.

At the micro level, the extent of price dispersion across market-makers has not been investigated. Continuing advances in communications technology and internationalization of markets makes this a relevant topic. Increasing importance of the DM and yen as independent currency markets may enhance possibilities for profitable triangular arbitrage. The development of new financial instruments – currency futures and currency option contracts – further suggests that the prices of these new instruments and traditional interbank contracts will have to be monitored to preclude arbitrage profit opportunities.

At the macro level, interest arbitrage between assets that are somewhat different in terms of risk or tax treatment deserves further attention. Arbitrage between long-term securities (in the Euro-market), between onshore securities, and the role of capital gains and ordinary income taxes could benefit from more detailed empirical study.

In a general sense, the efficiency studies suggest that the major foreign exchange markets exhibit behavior that is characteristic of other asset markets. Exchange rates react quickly to news; rates are volatile and difficult to forecast. Both spot and forward rates can be modeled as anticipatory prices, but the exact parameters of the models are unknown.

At a more microscopic level, empirical tests of spot market and forward market efficiency have often been based on small samples using techniques with low statistical power. Nonetheless, these studies have surrounded the simple efficiency hypothesis with substantial doubt. Rigorously tested academic models and performance studies of professional forecasters clearly demonstrate that speculative profit opportunities are available. Two questions are clear. Are these profits unusual in a risk-adjusted sense? Do existing portfolio theories adequately explain the time-varying risk premia in the market? What may seem like a short list is a very full agenda for future research.

References

Adler, M. and B. Dumas (1976), "Portfolio choice and the demand for forward exchange", American Economic Review, 66:332–339.

Aliber, R.Z. (1973), "The interest rate parity theorem: A reinterpretation", Journal of Political Economy, 81:1451–1459.

Aliber, R.Z. (1974), "Attributes of national monies and the independence of national monetary policies", in: R.Z. Aliber, ed., National monetary policies and the international system (University of Chicago Press, Chicago) 111–126.

Allen, P.R. and P.B. Kenen (1980), Asset markets, exchange rates, and economic integration (Cambridge University Press, New York).

Bagehot, W. (1971), "The only game in town", Financial Analysts Journal 27:No. 2, 12ff.

Bilson, J.F.O. (1976), "A monetary approach to the exchange rate", Unpublished Ph.D. dissertation, University of Chicago.

Bilson, J.F.O. (1978a), "The monetary approach to the exchange rate: Some empirical evidence", Staff Papers 25: No. 1, 25:48–75.

Bilson, J.F.O. (1978b), "Rational expectations and the exchange rate", in: J. Frenkel and H. Johnson, eds., The economics of exchange rates (Addison-Wesley, Reading, Mass.).

Bilson, J.F.O. (1981), "The 'speculative efficiency' hypothesis", Journal of Business, 54:435–451.

Bilson, J.F.O. (1982), "Exchange rate dynamics", Paper presented at NBER conference, Bellagio, Italy.

Black F. (1972), "Capital market equilibrium with restricted borrowing", Journal of Business, 45:444–445.

Black, F. and M. Scholes (1974), "From theory to a new financial product", Journal of Finance, 29:399–412.

Brada, J., H. Ernest and J. Van Tassel (1966), "The distribution of stock price differences: Gaussian after all?", Operations Research, 14:334–340.

Branson, W.H. (1968), Financial capital flows in the U.S. balance of payments (North-Holland, Amsterdam).

Branson, W.H. (1977), "Asset markets and relative prices in exchange rate determination", Sozialwissenschaftliche Annalen, 1:69–89.

Branson, W.H., H. Halttunenen and P. Masson (1977), "Exchange rates in the short run: The dollar deutschemark rate", European Economic Review, 10:303–324.

Buiter, W.H. (1983), "Implications for the adjustment process of international asset risks: Exchange controls, intervention and policy risk, and sovereign risk", in: R. Hawkins, R. Levich and C. Wihlborg, eds., Internationalization of financial markets and national economic policy (JAI Press, Greenwich, Conn.).

Burt, John, R. Kaen and G. Booth (1977), "Foreign exchange market efficiency under flexible exchange rates", Journal of Finance, 32:1325–1330.

Calvo, G.A. and C.A. Rodriguez (1977), "A model of exchange rate determination with currency substitution and rational expectations", Journal of Political Economy, 85:617–626.

Clendenning, E.W. (1970), The euro-dollar market (Clarendon Press, Oxford).

Cornell, B. (1977), "Spot rates, forward rates and exchange market efficiency", Journal of Financial Economics, 5:55–65.

Cornell, B. and M.R. Reinganum (1981), "Forward and futures prices: Evidence from the foreign exchange markets", Journal of Finance, 36:1035–1045.

Cumby, R.E. and M. Obstfeld (1981), "A note on exchange-rate expectations and nominal interest differentials: A test of the fisher hypothesis", Journal of Finance, 36:697–703.

Cuneo, L.J. and W.H. Wagner (1975), "Reducing the cost of stock trading", Financial Analysts Journal, 32: No. 6, 35–44.

Cushman, D.O. (1983), "The effects of real exchange rate risk on international trade", Journal of International Economics, 15:45–63.

Deardorff, A.V. (1979), "One-way arbitrage and its implications for the foreign exchange markets", Journal of Political Economy, 87:351–364.

Demsetz, H. (1968), "The cost of transacting", Quarterly Journal of Economics, 82:33–53.

Dooley, M.P. and P. Isard (1980), "Capital controls, political risk and deviations from interest rate parity", Journal of Political Economy, 88:370–384.

Dooley, M.P. and J.R. Shafer (1976), "Analysis of short-run exchange rate behavior: March, 1973 to September, 1975", International Finance Discussion Papers No. 76. (Federal Reserve System, Washington, D.C.).

Dooley, M.P. and J.R. Shafer (1983), Analysis of short-run exchange rate behavior: March, 1973 to November, 1981", in D. Bigman and T. Taya, eds., Exchange rate and trade instability (Ballinger, Cambridge, Mass.).

Dornbusch, R. (1976), "Expectations and exchange rate dynamics", Journal of Political Economy, 84:1161–1176.

Dornbusch, R. (1980), "Exchange rate economics: Where do we stand?", Brookings Papers on Economic Activity, No. 1:145–185.

Dornbusch, R. (1982), "Exchange rate risk and the macroeconomics of exchange rate determination", in: R. Hawkins, R. Levich and C. Wihlborg, eds., Internationalization of financial markets and national economic policy (JAI Press, Greenwich, Conn.).

Driskill, R.A. (1981), "Exchange-rate dynamics: An empirical investigation", Journal of Political Economy, 89:357–371.

Dufey, G. and I.H. Giddy (1978), The international money market (Prentice-Hall, Englewood Cliffs, N.J.).

Fama, E.F. (1970), "Efficient capital markets: A review of theory and empirical work", Journal of Finance, 25:383–417.

Fama, E.F. (1976), Foundations of finance (Basic Books, New York).

Fama, E.F. and A. Farber (1979), "Money, bonds and foreign exchange", American Economic Review, 69:639–649.

Feiger, G. and B. Jacquillat (1979), "Currency option bonds, puts and calls on spot exchange and the hedging of contingent foreign earnings", Journal of Finance, 34:1129–1139.

Fieleke, N.S. (1975), "Exchange rate flexibility and the efficiency of the foreign exchange markets", Journal of Financial and Quantitative Analysis, 10:409–426.

Frankel, J.A. (1979a), "The diversifiability of exchange risk", Journal of International Economics, 9:379–393.

Frankel, J.A. (1979b), "On the mark: A theory of floating exchange rates based on real interest differentials", American Economic Review, 69:610–622.

Frankel, J.A. (1982a), "The mystery of the multiplying marks: A modification of the monetary model", Review of Economics and Statistics, 64:515–519.

Frankel, J.A. (1982b), "In search of the exchange risk premium: A six-currency test assuming mean–variance optimization", Journal of International Money and Finance, 1:255–274.

Frankel, J.A. (1983), "On the mark, pound, franc, yen and Canadian dollar", in J. Bilson and R. Marston, eds., Exchange rate theory and practice (University of Chicago Press, Chicago).

Frenkel, J.A. (1976), "A monetary approach to the exchange rate: Doctrinal aspects and empirical evidence", Scandinavian Journal of Economics, 78:200–224.

Frenkel, J.A. (1978), "Purchasing power parity: Doctrinal perspectives and evidence from the 1920s", Journal of International Economics, 8:161–191.

Frenkel, J.A. (1980), "Exchange rates, prices and money: Lessons from the 1920s", American Economic Review, 70:235–242.

Frenkel, J.A. (1981), "Flexible exchange rates, prices and the role of 'news': Lessons from the 1970s", Journal of Political Economy, 89:665–705.

Frenkel, J.A. (1981b), "The collapse of purchasing power parity in the 1970s", European Economic Review, 16:145–165.

Frenkel, J.A. and K.W. Clements (1981), "Exchange rates in the 1920s: A monetary approach", in: Flanders and Razin, eds., Development in an inflationary world (Academic Press, New York) 283–318.

Frenkel, J.A. and R. M. Levich (1975), "Covered interest arbitrage: Unexploited profits?", Journal of

Political Economy, 83:325–338.

Frenkel, J.A. and R.M. Levich (1977), "Transaction costs and interest arbitrage: Tranquil versus turbulent periods", Journal of Political Economy, 86:1209–1226.

Frenkel, J.A. and M.L. Mussa (1980), "The efficiency of foreign exchange markets and measures of turbulence", American Economic Review, 70:374–381.

Frenkel, J.A. and C.A. Rodriguez (1982), "Exchange rate dynamics and the overshooting hypothesis", Staff Papers, 29:1–30.

Friedman, M. (1953), "The case for flexible exchange rates", in: M. Friedman, ed., Essays in positive economics (University of Chicago Press, Chicago).

Garbade, K.D. and W.L. Silber (1976), "Price dispersion in the government securities market", Journal of Political Economy, 84:721–740.

Genberg, H. (1983), "Properties of innovations in spot and forward exchange rates and the role of the money supply process", in J. Bilson and R. Marston, eds., Exchange rate theory and practice (University of Chicago Press, Chicago).

Giddy, I.H. (1979), "Measuring the world foreign exchange market", Columbia Journal of World Business, 14: No. 4, 36–48.

Giddy, I.H. and G. Dufey (1975), "The random behavior of flexible exchange rates", Journal of International Business Studies, 6: No. 1, 1–32.

Girton, L. and D. Roper (1976), "Theory and implications of currency substitution", International Finance Discussion Paper, No. 86, Federal Reserve Board of Governors.

Goodman, S. (1981), "Technical analysis still beats econometrics", Euromoney, August: 48–60.

Grubel, H.G. (1966), Forward exchange speculation and the international flow of capital (Stanford University Press, Stanford).

Hakkio, C.S. (1981), "Expectations and the forward exchange rate", International Economic Review, 22:663–678.

Hansen, L.P. and R.J. Hodrick (1980), "Forward exchange rates as optimal predictors of future spot rates: An econometric analysis", Journal of Political Economy, 88:829–853.

Hernández-Catá, E., et al. (1978), "Monetary policy under alternative exchange-rate regimes: Simulations with a multi-country model", in: Managed exchange-rate flexibility: The recent experience, Federal Reserve Bank of Boston, Conference Series, No. 20.

Hilley, J.R., C.R. Beidleman and J.A. Greenleaf (1981), "Why there is no long forward market in foreign exchange", Euromoney, January: 94–103.

Hoag, J.W. (1978), "An introduction to the valuation of commodity options", Columbia University Center for the Study of Futures Markets, Working Paper No. CSFM-19.

Hodjera, Z. (1973), "International short-term capital movements: A survey of theory and empirical analysis", Staff Papers, 20:683–740.

Hooper, P. and S.W. Kohlhagen (1978), "The effect of exchange rate uncertainty on the prices and volume of international trade", Journal of International Economics, 8:483–512.

Hooper, P. and J. Morton (1968), "Summary measures of the dollar's foreign exchange value", Federal Reserve Bulletin, 64:783–789.

Hsieh, D.A. (1982), "Tests of rational expectations and no risk premium in forward exchange markets", NBER Working Paper No. 843.

Huang, R.D. (1981), "The monetary approach to exchange rates in an efficient foreign exchange market: Tests based on volatility", Journal of Finance, 36:31–42.

Isard, P. (1977), "How for can we push the law of one price?", American Economic Review, 67:942–948.

Isard, P. (1978), "Exchange rate determination: A survey of popular view and recent models", Princeton Studies in International Finance, No. 42.

Katseli-Papaefstratiou, L.T. (1979), "The reemergence of the purchasing power parity doctrine in the 1970s", Princeton Special Papers in International Economics, No. 13.

Kohlhagen, S.W. (1978), The behavior of foreign exchange markets a critical survey of the empirical literature, New York University Monograph Series in Finance and Economics, No. 3 (Salomon Brothers Center).

Kouri, P.J.K. (1976), "The exchange rate and the balance of payments in the short run and in the long run: A monetary approach", Scandinavian Journal of Economics, 78:280–304.

Kouri, P.J.K. (1982), "The effect of risk on interest rates: A synthesis of the macroeconomic and financial views", in: R. Hawkins, R. Levich and C. Wihlborg, eds., Internationalization of financial markets and national economic policy (JAI Press, Greenwich, Conn.).

Kouri, P.J.K. and M.G. Porter (1974), "International capital flows and portfolio equilibrium", Journal of Political Economy, 82:443–467.

Krasker, W.S. (1980), "The 'peso problem' in testing the efficiency of forward exchange markets", Journal of Monetary Economics, 6:269–276.

Kravis, I., Z. Kennessey, A. Heston, and R. Summers (1975), A system of international comparisons of gross product and purchasing power (Johns Hopkins University Press, Baltimore).

Kreinin, M.E. (1977), "The effect of exchange rate changes on the prices and volume of foreign trade", Staff Papers, 24:297–329.

Kubarych, R.M. (1978), Foreign exchange markets in the United States (Federal Reserve Bank of New York, New York).

Levi, M.D. (1977), "Taxation and 'abnormal' international capital flows", Journal of Political Economy, 85:635–646.

Levich, R.M. (1978), "Further results on the efficiency of markets for foreign exchange ", in: Managed exchange-rate flexibility: The recent experience, Federal Reserve Bank of Boston, Conference Series, No. 20.

Levich, R.M. (1979a), "The international money market: An assessment of forecasting techniques and market efficiency (JAI Press, Greenwich, Conn.).

Levich, R.M. (1979b), "On the efficiency of markets for foreign exchange", in: R. Dornbusch and J. Frenkel, eds., International economic policy: An assessment of theory and evidence (Johns Hopkins University Press, Baltimore).

Levich, R.M. (1980), "Analyzing the accuracy of foreign exchange advisory services: Theory and evidence", in: R. Levich and C. Wihlborg, eds., Exchange risk and exposure (D.C. Heath and Co., Lexington, Mass.).

Levich, R.J. (1981a) "Maximizing the return on forex services", Euromoney Currency Report, February, 11:3.

Levich, R.M. (1981b), "How to compare chance with forecasting expertise", Euromoney, August: 61–78.

Levich, R.M. (1981c), "An examination of overshooting behavior in the foreign exchange market" Group of Thirty Occasional Studies, No. 3, New York.

Levich, R.M. (1981d), "Exchange rates and currency exposure", in: E. Altman, ed., Financial handbook (John Wiley, New York) Chapter 12.

Levich, R.M. (1982), "Comment on Sweeney", in: G. Haberler and T. Willett, eds., The international monetary system under stress (American Enterprise Institute, Washington, D.C.).

Lintner, J. (1965), "The valuation of risky assets and the selection of risky investments in stock portfolio and capital budgets", Review of Economics and Statistics, 47:13–37.

Logue, D.E., R.J. Sweeney and T.D. Willett (1978), "Speculative behavior of foreign exchange rates during the current float", Journal of Business Research, 6:159–174.

Longworth, D. (1981), "Testing the efficiency of the Canadian exchange market under the assumption of no risk premium", Journal of Finance, 36:43–50.

McCormick, F. (1979), "Covered interest arbitrage: Unexploited profits?: Comment", Journal of Political Economy, 87:411–417.

McKinnon, R.I. (1979), Money in international exchange (Oxford University Press, New York).

Meese, R. and K. Rogoff (1983a), " Empirical exchange rate models of the seventies: Do they fit out of sample?" Journal of International Economics, 14:3–24.

Meese, R. and K. Rogoff (1983b), "The out-of-sample failure of empirical exchange rate models: Sampling error or misspecification?" in J.A. Frenkel, ed., Exchange rates and international macroeconomics (University of Chicago Press, Chicago).

Meese, R.A. and K.J. Singleton (1980), "Rational expectations, risk premia, and the market for forward exchange", International Finance Discussion Paper, No. 165, Federal Reserve Board of Governors.

Melhem, M.F. (1982), "Money expectations and exchange rate dynamics", Unpublished Ph.D. dissertation, New York University.

Miles, M. (1978), "Currency substitution, flexible exchange rates and monetary independence", American Economic Review, 68:428–436.

Mossin, J. (1966), "Equilibrium in a capital asset market", Econometrica, 34:768–783.

Mussa, M. (1976), "The exchange rate, the balance of payments, and monetary policy under a regime of controlled floating", Scandinavian Journal of Economics, 78:229–248.

Officer, L.H. and T.D. Willet (1979), "The covered-arbitrage schedule: A critical survey of recent developments", Journal of Money, Credit and Banking, 2:247–257.

Poole, W. (1966), 'The Canadian experiment with flexible exchange rates", Unpublished Ph.D. dissertation, University of Chicago.

Poole, W. (1967), "Speculative prices as random walks: An analysis of ten time series of flexible exchange rates", Southern Economic Journal, 33:468–478.

Rogalski, R.J. and J.D. Vinso (1978), "Empirical properties of foreign exchange rates", Journal of International Business Studies, 9: No. 2, 69–79.

Roll, R. (1977), "A critique of the asset pricing theory's tests", Journal of Financial Economics, 4:129–176.

Sharpe, W.F. (1964), "Capital asset prices: A theory of market equilibrium under conditions of risk", Journal of Finance, 19:425–442.

Solnik, B.H. (1973), European capital markets (D.C. Heath, Lexington, Mass.).

Stockman, A.C. (1978), "Risk, information, and forward exchange rates", in: J. Frenkel and H. Johnson, eds., The economics of exchange rates (Addison-Wesley, Reading, Mass.).

Sweeney, R.J. (1982), "Intervention strategy: Implications of purchasing power parity and tests of spot market efficiency", in: G. Haberler and T. Willett, eds., The international monetary system under stress (American Enterprise Institute, Washington, D.C.).

Tryon, R. (1979), "Testing for rational expectations in foreign exchange markets", Board of Governors of the Federal Reserve System, International Finance Discussion Papers, No. 139.

Westerfield, J.M. (1977), "Empirical properties of foreign exchange rates under fixed and floating rate regimes", Journal of International Economics, 7:181–200.

Wihlborg, C.G. (1978), "Currency risks in international financial markets", Princeton Studies in International Finance, No. 44.

Chapter 20

INCOME AND PRICE EFFECTS IN FOREIGN TRADE

MORRIS GOLDSTEIN and MOHSIN S. KHAN*

International Monetary Fund

Contents

*The views expressed are the sole responsibility of the authors and do not necessarily reflect the views of the IMF. We are grateful to Jacques Artus,William Branson, Robert Cumby, Michael Dooley, David Folkerts–Landau, John Helliwell, William Hemphill, Peter Kenen, Malcolm Knight, Anne McGuirk, and Tim Padmore for helpful comments on an earlier draft.

Handbook of International Economics, vol. II, edited by R.W. Jones and P.B. Kenen
© *Elsevier Science Publishers B.V., 1985*

1. Introduction

Few areas in all of economics, and probably none within international economics itself, have been subject to as much empirical investigation over the past thirty five years as the behavior of foreign trade flows. Reasons for this unusual degree of attention are not hard to find. First, the data base is a rich one.[1] Statistics on the value of imports and exports extend over long time periods and can be disaggregated by commodity and by region of origin or destination to a relatively fine level.[2] Second, the underlying theoretical framework for the determination of trade volumes and prices is a familiar one from consumer demand and production theory, and can make do with relatively few explanatory variables, most of which have accessible empirical counterparts. Third, the estimated income and price elasticities of demand and supply have seemingly wide application to a host of important macro-economic policy issues, including but not limited to: the international transmission of changes in economic activity and prices, the impact of both expenditure-reducing (monetary and fiscal) policies and expenditure-switching (exchange rate, tariff, subsidy) policies on a country's trade balance, the welfare and employment implications of changes in own or partner-countries' trade restrictions, and the severity of external balance constraints on domestic policy choices.

In this chapter the aim is to identify, summarize, and evaluate the main methodological and policy issues that have surrounded the estimation of trade equations. By "trade equations" we mean equations for the time-series behavior of the quantities and prices of merchandise imports and exports,[3] and as the title of the chapter suggests, we focus explicitly on the role played by income and prices in the determination of these trade variables.

Our task is made easier by the admirable coverage of the early empirical literature and of many specific topics in trade modelling in previous survey papers. Indeed, trade surveys have appeared at least once every five years since

---

[1] The availability of trade data was surely a contributing factor to the advanced nature of the early empirical work on trade models. It is sufficient to note that by 1957 there already existed, inter alia: (i) at least 42 books and articles containing estimates of income and price elasticities for imports and exports [see Cheng's (1959) survey]; (ii) several superb methodological criticisms [Orcutt (1950), Harberger (1953)] that explained why estimated price elasticities could differ from the true elasticities; and (iii) at least one complete simultaneous model of import demand and supply [Morgan and Corlett (1951)], actually estimated by limited-information maximum likelihood methods, that displays the authors' awareness of many of the methodological issues that still entertain current research.

[2] Branson (1980), for example, in his paper on trends in U.S. international trade, presents data on U.S. trade balances by end-use commodity that extend back to 1925.

[3] Empirical work on international trade in services (or "invisibles") is still quite limited; see Bond (1980) and the references cited therein.

1959. Early (1936–57) estimates of income propensities and price elasticities have been surveyed and evaluated by Cheng (1959) and by Prais (1962). Early world trade models are discussed in Taplin (1973), and more recent multi-country models are compared and analyzed by Deardorff and Stern (1977) and by Fair (1979). Special mention should be made of the comprehensive trade surveys of Leamer and Stern (1970), Magee (1975), and Stern et al. (1976). The Leamer and Stern (1970) book has, among other things, a lucid discussion of the time-series estimation of import and export demand relationships. In this chapter we have tried to update and expand upon their analysis of methodological issues; in particular; we devote more attention to supply relationships.[4] Magee's (1975) trade survey is the broadest one available, encompassing methodological questions, empirical evidence, pure trade and monetary theory, and associated policy issues. We inevitably therefore cover some of the same ground but we have tried to minimize duplication.[5] Finally, Stern et al. (1976) have provided an exhaustive annotated bibliography of price elasticity studies in international trade spanning the 1960–1975 period, as well as summary tables of "median" price elasticities broken down by commodity group and by country. We offer our own updated "consensus" price and income elasticities which partially reflect Stern et al.'s (1976) findings but which also give higher weights to what we regard as the better quality estimates.[6]

The plan of the chapter is as follows. Section 2 addresses the main methodological issues in the specification of trade models. This is basically a discussion about what variables ought in theory to be included in demand and supply functions for imports and exports, what choices and compromises have to be made in the measurement of these variables, and what light existing evidence throws on the choice among competing specifications. Section 3 is concerned with what we call econometric issues in trade modelling. The subjects covered are the treatment of dynamics and time lags, aggregation, simultaneity, and stability of the relationships concerned. Section 4 turns to the empirical estimates of income and price elasticities themselves and to the policy implications of those estimates. Summary tables are constructed from recent empirical studies to illustrate the

---

[4] We have placed much less emphasis than Leamer and Stern (1970) on the theory and measurement of the elasticity of substitution in international trade and on index number problems associated with aggregation. Further, we do not deal at all with constant-market-share analysis of export growth.

[5] Specifically, we have provided only passing reference to Orcutt's (1950) criticisms of estimated price elasticities; to conflicts between Keynesian, absorption, and monetary approaches to the balance of payments; to estimates of the effects of tariff reductions on trade, and to earlier world trade models. Instead, we have substituted discussions of econometric issues involved with modelling of trade relationships, factors responsible for inter-country differences in price elasticities, feedback effects of exchange rate changes on domestic prices, and conflicts between specifications of demand and supply in trade models and those currently in vogue elsewhere in macroeconomics.

[6] Like the other trade surveys, our review of the empirical evidence concentrates on industrial-country trade. An up-to-date survey of empirical trade models for developing countries still waits to be written.

revealed "consensus", or lack of it, on (i) long-run price and income elasticities of demand for total merchandise imports and exports; (ii) the difference between short-run and long-run price elasticities of demand; (iii) price and activity elasticities for broad commodity classes of imports; (iv) supply price elasticities for exports, (v) the so-called "pass-through" of exchange rate changes onto the domestic currency prices of imports and exports; (vi) the elasticity of export prices with respect to domestic prices (or labor costs) and competitors' export prices; and (vii) the "feedback" effect of exchange rate changes on domestic prices. Drawing on this evidence, broad conclusions are advanced on the effectiveness of devaluation. Section 5 offers some concluding observations as well as suggestions for further research.

2. Specification issues in trade modelling

How should the time-series behavior of imports and exports be modelled? In our view, the appropriate model depends on, among other things, the type of good being traded (perfectly homogeneous primary commodities versus highly differentiated manufactured goods), on the end-use to which the traded commodity is being put (whether for final consumption or as a factor input), on the institutional framework under which trade takes place (an economy where resources are allocated via relative prices versus one where administrative controls play the predominant role in allocation), on the purpose of the modelling exercise (forecasting versus hypothesis testing), and sometimes even on the availability of data (e.g. if reliable data exist on trade values but not on volumes).

Nevertheless, it still makes sense as a framework for the discussion of particular specification issues to set out the two general models of trade that have dominated the empirical literature, namely, the imperfect substitutes model and the perfect substitutes model. Since most trade studies have dealt with aggregate imports (exports), the two models have often been viewed as competitors. Once disaggregation is admitted, however, there is no reason why the two models should not be seen as complements – one dealing with trade for differentiated goods, and the other with trade for close – if not perfect – substitutes.[7]

2.1. The imperfect substitutes model

The key underlying assumption of the imperfect substitutes model is that neither imports nor exports are perfect substitutes for domestic goods. Support for this assumption comes from two sources. First, there is the (debating) argument that *if*

---

[7]Clark (1977) is one of the few studies that actually follows this guideline.

domestic and foreign goods were perfect substitutes, then one should observe: (i) either the domestic or foreign good swallowing up the whole market when each is produced under constant (or decreasing) costs [Magee (1975)]; and (ii) each country as an exporter or importer of a traded good but not both [Rhomberg (1973)]. Since both of these predictions are counter to fact at both the aggregate and disaggregated level, i.e. one normally observes the coexistence of imports and domestic output and the flourishing of two-way trade, the perfect substitutes hypothesis can be rejected. The second bit of evidence is more direct. A large number of empirical studies [Kreinen and Officer (1978), Isard (1977b), Kravis and Lipsey (1978)] have shown that, even at the most disaggregated level for which comparable data can be gathered, there are significant and nontransitory price differences for the "same" product in different countries (after translation into a common currency), as well as between the domestic and export prices of a given product in the same country. In short, the "law of one price" does *not* seem to hold either across or within countries, except perhaps for standard commodities such as wheat or copper that are sold on international commodity exchanges.[8] It would appear therefore that finite price elasticities of demand and supply can in fact be estimated for most traded goods.

In eqs. (2.1)–(2.8) below, we present a "bare-bones" imperfect substitutes model of country i's imports from, and exports to, the rest of the world (*):

$$I_i^d = f(Y_i, PI_i, P_i), \qquad f_1, f_3 > 0, \quad f_2 < 0, \tag{2.1}$$

$$X_i^d = g(Y^*e, PX_i, P^*e), \qquad g_1, g_3 > 0, \quad g_2 < 0, \tag{2.2}$$

$$I_i^s = h[PI^*(1 + S^*), P^*], \qquad h_1 > 0, \quad h_2 < 0, \tag{2.3}$$

$$X_i^s = j[PX_i(1 + S_i), P_i], \qquad j_1 > 0, \quad j_2 < 0, \tag{2.4}$$

$$PI_i = PX^*(1 + T_i)e, \tag{2.5}$$

$$PI^* = PX_i(1 + T^*)/e, \tag{2.6}$$

$$I_i^d = I_i^s e, \tag{2.7}$$

$$X_i^d = X_i^s. \tag{2.8}$$

These eight equations determine the quantity of imports demanded in country i (I_i^d), the quantity of country i's exports demanded by the rest of the world (X_i^d), the quantity of imports supplied to country i from the rest of the world (I_i^s),[9] the quantity of exports supplied from country i to the rest of the world (X_i^s), the domestic currency prices paid by importers in the two regions (PI_i and PI^*), and

---

[8] The validity of the law of one price (net of transport costs and other impediments to trade) for these primary commodities is usually assumed rather than tested; see however McCloskey and Zecher (1976) who found support for it in price movements during the period 1870–1913.

[9] This is, of course, the supply of exports of the rest of the world to country i.

the domestic currency prices received by exporters in two regions (PX_i, PX^*). The exogenous variables are the levels of nominal income in the two regions (Y_i, Y^*), the price of (all) domestically produced goods in the two regions (P_i, P^*), the proportional tariff (T_i, T^*) and subsidy rates (S_i, S^*) applied to imports and exports in the two regions, and the exchange rate (e) linking the two currencies (expressed in units of country i's currency per unit of the rest-of-the world's currency).

The main characteristics of the imperfect substitutes model can be summarized as follows. In accordance with conventional demand theory, the consumer is postulated to maximize utility subject to a budget constraint.[10] The resulting demand functions for imports and exports thus represent the quantity demanded as a function of the level of (money) income in the importing region, the imported good's own price, and the price of domestic substitutes. For aggregate imports or exports, the possibilities of inferior goods and of domestic complements for imports are typically excluded, so that income elasticities (f_1 and g_1) and cross-price elasticities of demand (f_3 and g_3) are assumed to be positive,[11] whereas the own-price elasticities of demand (f_2 and g_2) are of course expected to be negative. Most often, the additional assumption is made that the consumer has no money illusion, so that a doubling of money income and all prices leaves demand constant, i.e. $f_1 + f_2 + f_3 = 0$, $g_1 + g_2 + g_3 = 0$. In its most common form, such homogeneity of the demand function is expressed by dividing the right-hand-side of eq. (2.1) by P_i so that the two arguments of the demand function become the level of *real* income (Y_i/P_i) and the relative price of imports (PI_i/P_i). In this simple model, only current income matters for import (export) demand, and no distinction is made between secular or cyclical income movements or between transitory and permanent income. Also note from eqs. (2.5) and (2.6) that the price of imports relevant for import demand is the landed domestic-currency price inclusive of all charges (tariffs, transportation, etc.) actually paid by the purchaser.

When we leave the two-country model for the n-country real world, the symmetry between the import demand eq. (2.1) and the export demand eq. (2.2) disappears. This is because a country's total imports face competition only from domestic producers, whereas a country's total exports face competition not only from domestic producers in the importing region but also from "third country"

---

[10] When the importer is a producer and when imports are intermediate goods that are inputs to the domestic technology, the demand for imports can analogously be derived by maximizing production subject to the producer's cost constraint. In that case, the resulting import demand function will have as its arguments the price of imports, the price of the domestic (composite) input, and the level of domestic gross output; for example, see Burgess (1974), and Kohli (1982).

[11] Less assurance about the signs of the income elasticity and cross-price elasticities is warranted when the demand equations are disaggregated by commodity or by region of origin or destination of the trade flow; see Magee (1975, p. 179).

exporters to that region. Indeed, the conventional practice in specifying export demand equations is to assume that the dominant relative price competition occurs among exporters. Thus, the only relative-price term that typically appears is the ratio of the export price to competitors' export prices (PX_c) adjusted for exchange rate change, i.e. ($PX_i/PX_c \cdot e$).[12] In much of the empirical literature, the estimation of price effects on export demand has in fact been carried out within an "elasticity of substitution" framework. The demand equation then takes the form:

$$X_i^{\mathrm{d}}/X^{\mathrm{d}*} = v(PX_i/PX^*e), \qquad v' < 0, \tag{2.2'}$$

where $X^{\mathrm{d}*}$ is the demand for exports to the rest of the world from third countries. One deficiency of eq. (2.2') compared to eq. (2.2), especially as regards aggregate exports, is that the former implicitly assumes that the income elasticities of demand for exports from country i and for those from third countries are the same in the rest of the world.[13] As there is no a priori reason for this to hold, imposing such a restriction without first testing it is likely to involve some misspecification.

The specification of the two supply eqs. (2.3) and (2.4) are identical, with the quantity supplied assumed to be a positive function of the own price and a negative function of the price of domestic goods in the exporting country. Imposition of homogeneity on the supply function is equivalent to the restriction that $-h_1 = h_2$ in eq. (2.3), and $-j_1 = j_2$ in eq. (2.4). Although the theory of export supply is still very much a contested and unresolved subject in empirical trade work, the basic idea behind eqs. (2.3) and (2.4) is a simple one. The supply of exports will increase with the profitability of producing and selling exports. Therefore, the domestic price index (P) serves a dual role in the supply functions. First, for a given level of the export price, the profitability of producing exports falls when factor costs in the export industries increase. As these factor costs are likely to move with the general level of domestic prices, P serves as a proxy for them. Second, to the extent that resources involved in exportables production can be transferred to other uses or that the export price of a given good can be kept different from the domestic price, the relative profitability of selling exports falls with an increase in domestic prices.[14] At the aggregate level, the domestic price index includes prices of tradable goods (PT) sold at home as well as the price of

---

[12] This restriction is often rationalized by the fact that industrial countries are their own principal competitors, so that PX_i/PX_c and PX_i/P_i will move together so long as domestic prices (P) and export prices (PX) are linked within countries.

[13] See Leamer and Stern (1970). For further analysis of the concept of "elasticity of substitution," see Richardson (1973).

[14] The model described by eqs. (2.1)–(2.8) does not really explain *why* domestic prices should not equal export prices. In the literature, the three main explanations for such a divergence are different demand elasticities in the home and export market, different cost structures for home and export production, or simply distortions in the market.

nontradables (PNT), i.e. $P = xPT + (1 - x)PNT$, where x is the weight of tradables in domestic consumption. Thus, the aggregate export supply functions (2.3) and (2.4) accommodate supply substitution between the home and export market for a given tradable good in the manner of the price-discriminating monopolist, as well as substitution between production of all tradables and nontradables.

Note that the relevant own price in the export supply functions is the price actually received by the exporter, inclusive of any subsidies (S) or other incentives or penalties for exporting, and that the price is expressed in domestic currency terms. This latter seemingly innocuous point carries one significant implication. Even if the country is "small" in the sense that it cannot affect the *foreign* currency prices of either its imports or its exports, it can still affect its export volume to the extent that it can affect the *internal* profitability of producing and/or selling exportables. For example, even in a situation where import demand is very price inelastic $(f_2, f_3 \approx 0)$, where exports must carry the same foreign currency price everywhere $(PX_i/PX_c e = 1)$, and where the export price cannot be separated from the domestic price of tradables $(PX/PT = 1)$, a devaluation can nevertheless have some potency (aside from expenditure-reducing effects) via its impact on the internal terms of trade between exports and nontradables (PX/PNT).

An advantage of presenting the supply side as well as the demand side of the imperfect substitutes model is to make it plain that the relationship between quantities and prices is, at least in theory, simultaneous. Despite this fundamental point, strongly emphasized in the trade literature of the 1950s [Orcutt (1950), Harberger (1953)], the bulk of the time-series work on import and export equations has addressed the supply side only by assumption. Specifically, the prevailing practice has been to assume that the supply-price elasticities for imports and exports [i.e. h_1 in eq. (2.3) and j_1 in eq. (2.4), respectively] are infinite. The great allure of such an assumption is that it permits satisfactory estimation of the import and export demand eqs. (2.1) and (2.2) by single-equation methods, since PI_i and PX_i can then be viewed as exogenous; conversely, if the supply elasticities are less than infinite, one should either estimate the full structural simultaneous model or solve for and estimate the reduced-form expressions for quantities and prices as functions of only the exogenous variables in the system. We shall have more to say on the simultaneity issue later. For now, it is sufficient to argue that the infinite supply-elasticity assumption is more defensible for a country's imports than for its exports. The rest of the world may well be able to increase its supply of exports to a single country without an increase in price, but it is less likely that even a large single country can increase its total export supply at a constant price unless there exists a large pool of unemployed resources in the export industry itself or elsewhere in the economy.

Our final comments on the imperfect substitutes model are caveats about the true "exogeneity" of at least one key exogenous variable (namely, domestic prices), about the legitimacy of an export supply function under conditions of less than perfect competition, and about the "equilibrium" or market-clearing property of the model.

On the first point, there is by now a considerable body of empirical evidence [see Goldstein (1980), Kenen and Pack (1979), and Section 4] that suggests that domestic prices (P_i), export prices in domestic currency terms (PX_i) and money wages rates are each strongly influenced by exchange rate changes (Δe) and by changes in foreign export prices (ΔPX^*), especially in small, highly-open economies with wage indexation schemes. The implication of such domestic price "feedback" effects, i.e. lack of exogeneity for P_i in eqs. (2.1)–(2.4), is that high price elasticities offer no guarantee that devaluation or other expenditure-switching policies will actually be effective in altering a country's trade balance.[15] If P_i rises by close to, or equal to, the same proportion as PI_i and PX_i in eqs. (2.1) and (2.4) respectively, then the *relative* price changes induced by such policy actions will be small.

A second caveat is that export supply functions, like eqs. (2.3) and (2.4), can in theory exist independently of the demand functions only under conditions of perfect competition [Basevi (1973)]. Only under perfect competition is it legitimate to regard the export price as exogenous, that is as beyond the influence of the quantity supplied by any individual exporting country. For this reason, many trade researchers have chosen instead to work with reduced-form export price equations where the quantity of exports does not appear at all. Following the empirical literature on domestic pricing under imperfect competition [e.g. Eckstein and Fromm (1968)], some such as Clark (1977) have assumed that the export price is set as a "markup" (λ) on the level of normal unit labor cost (Z),[16] with the size of the markup varying positively with the state of excess demand at home ($Y_i/\overline{Y}_i$) and abroad ($Y^*/\overline{Y}^*$), and with the level of competitors' export prices (PX_c):[17]

$$PX_i = \lambda\big(Z, Y_i/\overline{Y}_i, Y^*/\overline{Y}^*, PX_c\big), \qquad \lambda_1, \lambda_2, \lambda_3, \lambda_4 > 0. \tag{2.4'}$$

Note that eq. (2.4') has many similarities to the reduced-form equation that would emerge from solving the *structural* demand and supply eqs. (2.2) and (2.4) for PX_i in terms of only the exogenous variables. This also explains why there has often been some confusion about whether the explanatory variables in export price equations like eq. (2.4') represent supply or demand influences.

---

[15] We abstract here from the expenditure-reducing role of exchange rates or tariffs via their effect on the real value of money balances; on this latter role, see Frenkel and Johnson (1976).

[16] Normal unit labor cost is usually defined as the wage rate divided by the trend or normal level of real output per man hour.

[17] Another route is to derive the export price from the profit-maximizing conditions for a discriminating monopolist [see Artus (1977)]. The resulting estimating equation for PX, however, is usually quite similar to the one obtained from the markup model.

Turning to the equilibrium characteristic of the imperfect substitutes model as represented in eqs. (2.7) and (2.8), the implicit assumption is that prices move to equate supply and demand in each time period. This assumption, however, can be viewed as inconsistent with much of modern pricing theory, which argues that there are costs to changing prices in imperfectly competitive markets and that firms consequently will want to balance the costs of changing prices against the costs of other adjustment measures, such as changing inventories (stocks), unfilled orders (queues), and output itself [e.g. Hay (1970)].[18] This literature on "sticky prices" carries two suggestions for the specification of the imperfect substitutes trade model. One is that if the market-clearing property of the model is to be retained, then nonprice rationing variables should be included in both the demand and supply equations so that price changes alone are not responsible for market-clearing and the "full" or "effective" price actually faced by buyers and sellers governs demand and supply.[19] A second alternative solution is to postulate that observed trade quantities and prices reflect markets in "disequilibrium" and accordingly, then to specify what the adjustment mechanisms are. For example, one can postulate that export prices respond to excess demand while export quantities respond to excess supply, or vice versa [Goldstein and Khan (1978)]; alternatively, one can argue that observed quantities and prices represent the lower of export demand or supply and then use recent econometric techniques [Fair and Kelejian (1974), Minford (1978)] to identify which observations correspond to periods of excess supply and which to excess demand. In short, the equilibrium characterization of the imperfect substitutes model is only one of several possibilities.

2.2. The perfect substitutes model

Even though the imperfect substitutes model has been the mainstay of empirical work on trade equations, there are at least three reasons for examining the perfect substitutes model as well. First, despite many man-made impediments to arbitrage such as tariffs, quotas, and special preferential trading relationships, there is no denying that there are homogeneous commodities (wheat, copper, sugar, etc.) that are traded on organized international commodity markets at a common price (net of transportation and interest costs and expressed in terms of a common currency). For such "standard" commodities, a framework is needed where demands and supplies do not depend on price differentials between domestic and

---

[18]Such price stickiness is regarded as a key factor in recent explanations of both exchange rate "overshooting" and the failure of purchasing power parity to work in the short run [see Dornbusch and Jaffee (1978)].

[19]By the "full" or "effective" price, we mean the observed price plus other implicit costs (e.g. waiting times, storage costs) paid by buyers and sellers.

foreign goods. Second, it is possible that international differences in the methodology of constructing price statistics (e.g. weighting patterns, survey methods, index number formulae) can lead to observed international price differences for a given good or bundle of goods that understate the true degree of substitutability. In other words, some traded industrial goods may be closer substitutes than the (imperfect) price statistics would suggest. Third and finally, there may be insights about price and income elasticities for imports and exports that emerge from a perfect substitutes framework that do not when goods are assumed to be imperfect substitutes.

Equations (2.9)–(2.16) below constitute a simple perfect substitutes model of trade for our representative country i:

$$D_i = 1(P_i, Y_i), \qquad 1_1 < 0, \quad 1_2 > 0 \tag{2.9}$$

$$S_i = n(P_i, F_i), \qquad n_1 > 0, \quad n_2 < 0 \tag{2.10}$$

$$I_i = D_i - S_i, \tag{2.11}$$

$$X_i = S_i - D_i, \tag{2.12}$$

$$PI_i = P_i = PX_i = e \cdot P_w, \tag{2.13}$$

$$D_w = \sum_{i=1}^{m} D_i, \tag{2.14}$$

$$S_w = \sum_{i=1}^{m} S_i, \tag{2.15}$$

$$D_w = S_w. \tag{2.16}$$

In this perfect substitutes model, D_i is the total quantity of traded goods demanded in country i; S_i is the supply of traded goods produced in country i; I_i and X_i are the quantities of country i's imports and exports; PI_i, PX_i, P_i, and P_w are the import, export, domestic, and world prices of traded goods; D_w and S_w are the world demand and supply of traded goods; and Y_i and F_i are money income and factor costs in country i.

For the purposes of this paper, there are three main features of the perfect substitutes model. First, contrary to the imperfect substitutes model, there are no separate import demand or export supply functions. Instead, the demand for imports and the supply of exports represent the "excess" demand and "excess" supply respectively for domestic goods; see eqs. (2.11) and (2.12). This means that estimating or forecasting import demand or export supply for a perfectly substitutable good is really a matter of forecasting domestic demand and domestic supply, with imports or exports emerging as the residual. In practice, this often turns out to be more difficult than it sounds because estimates of domestic demand and supply elasticities are usually harder to obtain than those for imports or exports, and because the primary commodities that best fit the perfect substitutes mold are usually subject to "stock" as well as "flow" demand (with the former requiring specifications of price expectation schemes). Second, and again in contrast to the imperfect substitutes model, once we abstract from transportation costs and other trade barriers (e.g. tariffs) and express all prices in a common currency, then there is only one traded goods price in the perfect substitutes model (i.e. $P_i = PI_i = PX_i = P_w$); furthermore, this (world) price is determined by the interaction of *world* supply and *world* demand for the traded good.[20] Put in other words, country i will only be able to affect the world price of the traded good to the extent that it can affect either world supply or world demand. In general, it can be shown [Isard (1977a), Clark (1977)] that in the absence of inventory and backlog changes, a country's ability to influence the world price of a homogeneous good will depend (positively) on both its share of world consumption (imports) and world production (exports) and on the value of its own price elasticities of demand and supply for that good.[21] If the country is too "small" to affect the world price of the traded good, then an increase in domestic supply will reduce import demand directly (without any change in price). In contrast, the same increase in domestic supply in the imperfect substitutes model would reduce import demand via its effect on P_i and hence on the relative price of imports, PI_i/P_i; see eq. (2.1)

Yet a third noteworthy feature of the perfect substitutes model is that it yields several implications for inter-country differences in price elasticities of supply and demand for imports and exports that do not emerge from the imperfect substitutes model. Specifically, using eqs. (2.12) and (2.13) and employing standard definitions of price elasticities of demand and supply, it is possible to relate the price elasticity of demand for imports (ε_I^d) and the price elasticity of supply for exports (ε_x^s) to the domestic demand ($1_1 < 0$) and supply-price elasticities ($n_1 > 0$) of eqs. (2.9) and (2.10) as follows:[22,23]

$$\varepsilon_I^d = \frac{D_i}{I_i} \cdot 1_1 - \frac{S_i}{I_i} n_1, \tag{2.17}$$

$$\varepsilon_x^s = \frac{S_i}{X_i} n_1 - \frac{D_i}{X_i} 1_1. \tag{2.18}$$

---

[20] Once nontraded goods are admitted, however, their prices (PNT) would enter the aggregate demand equation (2.9) with a positive sign. Similarly, once disaggregation is permitted, prices of "other" traded goods may enter the demand equation. Still, the essence of the model is that the same product, as long as it is freely traded, should carry the same price everywhere.

[21] To see this, take the total differentials of eqs. (2.15) and (2.16), set $D_w = S_w$, and solve for dP_w.

[22] These derivations can be found in most international economics textbooks; for example, see Kreinin (1979).

[23] If an income term is added to the supply eq. (2.10), it is similarly possible to relate the income elasticity of demand for imports to income elasticities of demand and supply for domestic goods and to the shares of imports in domestic demand and in total supply; see Magee (1975, p. 189).

Equation (2.17) states that the price elasticity of demand for imports (ε_I^d) of a homogeneous good will be positively related to the (absolute) values of the domestic demand and supply price elasticities, and negatively related to the shares of imports in domestic demand and in domestic production of the good. This proposition has often been advanced by "elasticity optimists" to support the claim that import price elasticities of demand can be high even for relatively inelastic products, and the more so the more closed the economy, namely when the ratios I_i/D_i and I_i/S_i are low. As noted by Magee (1975), at least the former implication of eq. (2.17) seems to be consistent with empirical evidence in the sense that estimated import price elasticities of demand typically exceed estimated domestic price elasticities of demand.[24]

Turning to eq. (2.18), it similarly suggests that the export supply elasticity (ε_x^s) will be positively related to the (absolute) value of the domestic demand price elasticity and negatively to the supply price elasticity and the shares of exports in domestic demand and in total supply of the good. Unfortunately, comparable estimates of domestic and export supply elasticities simply do not exist, so it is not possible to draw any conclusions as to whether the latter are larger than the former.

Finally, if we let the quantity of world exports (X_w) equal the sum of country i's exports (X_i) and the exports of the rest of the world (X^*), country i's export price elasticity of demand $(\varepsilon_x^d)_i$ can be related to the export price elasticity of demand $(\varepsilon_x^d)_w$ and to the export price elasticity of supply $(\varepsilon_x^s)^*$ in the rest of the world:

$$\left(\varepsilon_x^d\right)_i = \left(X_w/X_i\right)\left(\varepsilon_x^d\right)_w - \left(X^*/X_i\right)\left(\varepsilon_x^s\right)^* \tag{2.19}$$

The implication of eq. (2.19) is again on the side of the "elasticity optimists", for even if the global export price elasticity of demand for a homogeneous good is relatively small, a single country's export price elasticity of demand can be high if it has a small share in world exports. Note, however, that if one views eqs. (2.17), (2.18) and (2.19) as a group, then a country cannot simultaneously have (relatively) large demand price elasticities for imports and exports and a large supply price elasticity for exports unless it is both relatively closed to imports and exports *and* maintains a relatively small share of world exports.[25] The United States, for example, would meet the first criterion but not the second, while the smaller European countries such as Belgium and the Netherlands would meet the second criterion but not the first.

---

[24] Compare the domestic price elasticities of demand in Houthakker and Taylor (1970) with the import price elasticities for the United States in Houthakker and Magee (1969), Stern et al. (1976), and Clark (1977).

[25] The question of inter-country differences in price and income elasticities is discussed at greater length in Section 4.

2.3. Choice of variables

With the general outlines of the imperfect and perfect substitutes models in mind, we next consider the empirical variables that have been used as the appropriate counterparts to the theoretical ones. The discussion is selective rather than exhaustive, concentrating upon what we regard as the most important issues.

2.3.1. Dependent variables

As indicated earlier, conventional trade models, like the demand and production theories on which they are based, treat import (export) quantities or prices but not their product as the dependent variables. Trade data, however, are oblivious to this theoretical nicety and are most readily available in value terms. This means that an appropriate deflator has to be found to convert the value data back into its quantity and price components. This problem takes on considerable difficulty and complexity when dealing with the large number of products that comprise a country's aggregate imports and exports. One encounters all the usual problems associated with constructing price indices, namely those related to current or base period weights, quality change, changing composition of products within broader goods categories, etc. along with the additional requirement of reasonable comparability across countries.

The best deflator would of course be the actual transactions or contractual prices for imports (PI) and exports (PX) themselves. Indices based on such international transactions prices do exist but their country, product, and time-period coverage are as yet quite limited.[26] In brief, these price data are restricted to only a few major industrial countries, the time-series seldom extends beyond a ten year period, only some manufactured goods are included, and exports are much better represented than imports.

Faced with the absence of comprehensive data on PI and PX, empirical trade researchers have relied on two second-best but more widely available price deflators, namely unit value indices (PUV) and wholesale price indices (PWH).[27] Unit value indices are calculated by dividing the value of imports (exports) by the

---

[26] The NBER export price series constructed by Kravis and Lipsey (1971, 1974, 1978) cover machinery, transport equipment, metals, and metal products for the time periods 1957–53, 1961–57, 1962–61, 1963–62, and 1964–63. The indices were calculated for the United States, the United Kingdom, Germany, and on a more partial basis for Japan and the Common Market as a whole. Official export price series are also produced by Germany and Japan, but Kravis and Lipsey (1974) raise some doubts about their quality. Finally, trade price indices for the United States have recently become available [Bureau of Labor Statistics (1980)] for some manufactured products over the 1970–79 period.

[27] Unit value indices are published in the IMF's *International Financial Statistics* (IFS) for practically all IMF member countries. They typically extend back to the early 1950s, and cover total imports and total exports. The coverage and availability of domestic wholesale price indices are similar to those of unit value indices.

physical quantities of imports (exports). While perfectly legitimate for a single product, this procedure yields spurious price indices when quite different products are combined in one index. For example, when the commodity composition of imports changes, a unit value index will change even if all "true" prices of the component import products remain unchanged. Similarly, because unit value indices are not fixed-weight indices, a price increase accompanied by a decrease in quantity demanded automatically lowers that good's weight in the index. Wholesale prices escape this latter problem but include some goods often regarded as nontradables, use domestic rather than international weights for the tradable goods, and refer to list rather than transaction prices.[28] Also, as suggested earlier, the domestic and export price for a given product can diverge for nontrivial time periods reflecting various types of market imperfections.

If PWH and PUV are conceded to have drawbacks as representations of true import and export prices, how significant are these drawbacks likely to be? Kravis and Lipsey (1974) have provided some answers to this question by comparing movements of PWH and of PUV with their series on international transactions prices for manufactured exports (PX). In short, they found that: (i) there was a statistically significant positive relationship between PX and PWH and between PX and PUV but that this relationship was considerably closer ($R^2 = 0.47$) in the first case than in the second ($R^2 = 0.06$); (ii) the relationship between PX and PWH was much closer for some countries (the United States, the United Kingdom), than for others (Germany, Japan); and (iii) the relationship between PX and PWH was not noticeably closer for time spans longer than one year than for one-year periods.

A related but perhaps more central question for this paper is how poor measures of PI and PX will affect the estimated price elasticities of demand and supply. Two cases need to be distinguished. The first case is where the dependent variable (I or X) is correctly measured but there is measurement error in the import or export price data. In this situation, we have a standard errors in variables problem [Kmenta (1971)], and we get the standard results, namely, the estimated coefficient on PI or PX will be biased toward zero.[29] Consistent with this diagnosis, Kravis and Lipsey (1974) found that replacement of PWH with PX in a conventional export elasticity-of-substitution equation [like eq. (2.2′) above] led to estimated elasticities that were roughly twice as high, as well as to significantly higher explanatory power for the equation itself. The second case, which is probably the predominant one in practice, is where an improperly measured PI or PX series is used to deflate an error-free import or export *value* variable, as well as for the explanatory price variable. Here, negative correlation

---

[28] The consumer price index and the gross domestic product deflator also have serious deficiencies as proxies for traded goods prices; see Goldstein and Officer (1979).

[29] This was one of the arguments used by Orcutt (1950) to support his position that true price elasticities of demand for imports exceeded the estimated ones.

will be introduced between the errors in the dependent variable and the errors in the explanatory price variable, with the result that the estimated price elasticity will be biased toward minus one [Kemp (1962a), Kravis and Lipsey (1974), Magee (1975)]. It therefore suggests some suspicion of unitary price elasticity estimates from studies where both the dependent and independent variables are derived using PWH or PUV.

The next relevant question is what options are available to the empirical trade researcher facing poor import and export price data. At one extreme, trade equations can be specified with the value of imports (exports) as the dependent variable [e.g. Branson (1968)]. Since the volume price elasticity of demand is equal to the value elasticity minus one, this procedure still permits estimation of the former. Also, if the purpose of the exercise is to estimate or forecast only the value of imports, this procedure has obvious advantages over trying to explain two component series of poor quality. Its main disadvantage is that the determinants of price and volume are different, and a single equation therefore carries the danger that the estimated coefficients will represent some unknown interaction of supply and demand influences. At the other end of the spectrum, one can work with the widely available price proxies (PUV, PWH), accept the danger of biased estimates, and exercise due caution on the ranges of the true elasticities. This has been the route followed in the most of the studies on total imports (exports) simply because the better quality export or import price data are not available at high levels of aggregation; also, some researchers [Beenstock and Minford (1976)] have argued that component measurement errors may at least partially cancel out at high levels of aggregation. Intermediate options include restricting hypothesis-testing on demand and supply elasticities to goods for which the better quality price data are available [e.g. Artus and Sosa (1978)]; replacing import unit values with a weighted index of exporters' domestic wholesale prices [e.g. Clark (1977)]; relaxing the homogeneity restriction on relative import (export) prices as a concrete response to the larger assumed measurement error in import or export prices than in either the domestic price index or the exchange rate [e.g. Ahluwalia and Hernandez–Cata (1975)]; and using the exchange rate and the tariff rate to generate the local-currency price of imports as a substitute for the unit value index [e.g. Mutti (1977)].

2.3.2. Income and other scale variables

In our exposition of the imperfect substitutes model, the demands for imports and exports were treated as positive functions of the level of real income in the importing regions. While this has overwhelmingly been the conventional practice in empirical work, alternative and/or additional "scale" variables have frequently been proposed for both aggregate and disaggregated demand functions. In addition, scale variables have also found their way into the export supply function.

2.3.2.1. Import demand. There are at least three conscious choices to be made in the specification of the scale variable in the aggregate import demand equation:[30] (i) should one use real income or real expenditure; (ii) if real income is chosen, should cyclical and secular movements in real income be treated separately; and (iii) how should "life-cycle" or "permanent/transitory" consumption patterns be handled in import demand.

(i) *Real income versus real expenditure.* The issue here is whether domestic demand for foreign goods (imports) should properly be related to domestic demand for all goods, i.e. to expenditure, or rather to the sum of domestic demand for domestic goods and the foreign demand for domestic goods (exports), i.e. to income. Micro demand theory offers little guidance since it typically constrains expenditure to equal income. In the empirical literature, the choice between these two scale variables has usually been made on grounds of consistency with the implicit or explicit overall model of balance-of-payments adjustment. Specifically, real expenditure has been favored in a monetary-oriented framework because it can be related to the difference between actual and real money balances, thereby assuring a direct role for money in trade and balance-of-payments adjustment [see, for example, Aghevli and Khan (1980)]. In contrast, the Keynesian preference for real income follows naturally from the foreign-trade multiplier, income-driven view of balance-of-payments adjustment.[31] Rather surprisingly, there has been practically no attempt to choose between these two alternative scale variables on empirical grounds (e.g. goodness-of-fit criterion).[32]

(ii) *Secular versus cyclical real income.* In our prototype import demand eq. (2.1), movements in real income (Y_i/P_i) were assumed to have the same effect on the quantity of imports demanded regardless of whether these movements repre-

[30] When the dependent variable in the import demand function is disaggregated by type of commodity, prevailing practice is to make an accommodating disaggregation adjustment in the scale variable so as to get a better fix on the particular component of aggregate income or expenditure that shifts the demand for that commodity. For example, Deppler and Ripley (1978) use real consumption expenditure as the scale variable in the import volume equation for foods and beverages, an average of output in manufacturing and real final domestic demand for manufactures in the equation for manufactures, etc. If the existing disaggregated import functions can be criticized it is not for failing to select an appropriate scale variable for a particular type of imports but rather for doing only that. Thus, import demand functions for primary products seldom distinguish between flow and stock demand; functions for investment goods make little effort to model expected output or to specify longer lag structures appropriate to capital goods; import functions for durable goods typically find no place for habit formation, etc. For discussion and estimates of disaggregated trade equations, see Kreinin (1967), Stone (1979), Deppler and Ripley (1978), and Rhomberg and Boissonneault (1965).
[31] Prevailing practice treats the monetary and Keynesian (cum elasticity) models of balance-of-payments adjustment as alternatives, but they can clearly be reconciled in a more general model of balance-of-payments adjustment; see Chapter 14 of this Handbook.
[32] An exception is the study by Brillembourg (1975) for three Latin American countries – Colombia, Ecuador, and Venezuela. He found that real expenditure, along with relative prices and quantitative rationing variables, produced a better explanation of import demand than did an analogous specification using real income.

sented trend (secular) or cyclical variations about that trend. This assumption has been challenged in empirical work. First, there is the argument alluded to earlier, that prices do not act to clear markets, especially during periods of excess demand. Instead, periods of excess demand are said to be characterized by longer domestic waiting times, less availability and higher costs of credit, and less vigorous pursuit of new orders by suppliers – a consequence of which is that consumers increasingly turn to foreign suppliers [Gregory (1971)]. For these reasons, the cyclical income elasticity of demand for imports is expected to exceed the secular elasticity. The second challenge, which complements the first one, is that the secular income elasticity of demand for imports is best viewed within a perfect substitutes framework as equal to the difference between the domestic production and consumption of importables [Johnson (1958), Magee (1975)]. This suggests not only that the secular elasticity may be less than the cyclical income elasticity but also that the secular elasticity might even be *negative* under certain conditions.[33]

Our reading of the empirical evidence on cyclical versus secular income elasticities can be summarized as follows. First, when trend (or potential) real income and cyclical real income are included in the import demand equation at the same time, both usually appear with positive and statistically significant coefficients [Clark (1977), Lawrence (1978)]; the same verdict applies to import demand equations where real income and capacity utilization appear jointly [Branson (1968), Hooper (1976, 1978)]. Second, there is some tendency for the estimated cyclical elasticities to exceed the secular elasticities [Deppler and Ripley (1978)], but there are enough exceptions [Khan and Ross (1975), Geraci and Prewo (1980)] to cast serious doubt on the final outcome. Third, since Magee's (1975) reluctant conclusion that he could not find any negative estimates of secular income elasticities for total imports, some have appeared [e.g. Khan and Ross (1975)], but it is by no means clear how these should be interpreted since they presumably mix together import substitution, tastes, and other structural factors. Fourth, if one grants the case that nonprice rationing of imports occurs during cyclical upswings, it is still an open question as to whether cyclical income variables are the best way to measure these effects [e.g. Gregory (1971) prefers estimated waiting times as a rationing proxy]. Fifth, more recent studies [e.g. Hooper (1976, 1978)] have moved in the desirable direction of including cyclical income abroad as well as at home in the demand equation to capture *relative* nonprice rationing costs. If prices do not clear markets at home, they probably do not abroad either.

(iii) *Permanent and transitory income.* As is well known, the distinction between current income and "permanent" or "life-cycle income" is at the core of modern

---

[33]As indicated in Magee (1975, p. 189), the condition for a negative income elasticity is $(DI/SI) < (E_Y^s/E_Y^d)$, where E_Y^s and E_Y^d are the domestic income elasticities of supply and demand respectively, and DI and SI are the domestic demand for and supply of importables, respectively.

consumption theory [see Dornbusch and Fisher (1978) for a lucid summary]. Since imports represent consumption by domestic residents of foreign goods, it is surprising that so little attention has been given to this distinction in the specification of the aggregate import demand function.[34]

Potential application of permanent income or life-cycle concepts to the aggregate import demand function raises the following points and puzzles. To begin, one motivation for the permanent income and life-cycle models was to explain the greater slope of the long-run consumption function in the United States, compared to the short-run function. As indicated earlier, however, most empirical trade studies find a higher income elasticity for imports from cyclical income than from potential or trend income. This suggests that cyclical non-price rationing effects predominate over permanent/transitory consumption differences. Second, it needs to be acknowledged that the key operational problem central to testing of both the permanent and life-cycle income hypotheses – how best to relate expected future income to current and past observed income – still seems to be unresolved in the literature. In addition to the econometric problems associated with generating permanent income via use of fixed distributed lags [see Lucas (1976)], there is the additional problem in import functions that one may not want to impose the same lag distribution on all the explanatory variables.[35] Third, and operating in the opposite direction, the joint finding that only current income is usually significant in import demand functions and that there is an apparent structural instability in the behavior of income elasticities of demand for imports [Hooper (1978), Stern et al. (1979)] is suggestive of some pay-off from trying alternative representations of real income. Similarly, one can note the considerable measure of success achieved by Sachs (1981) in using an inter-temporal life-cycle savings/investment framework to explain the pattern of current account positions after the oil shocks of the 1970s. In sum, there would seem to be plenty of room and reason for experimenting with other specifications of real income in the aggregate import demand function to bring it closer into line with the treatment of aggregate consumption in the domestic empirical literature.

[34]A notable exception is the recent study by Geraci and Prewo (1980) where cyclical and trend components of real income are given transitory and permanent income interpretations and where the estimated permanent income elasticity exceeds the transitory income elasticity in four out of the five sample countries. Also, note that the case for making permanent/transitory income distinctions does not apply to "separable" or "allocative" import functions where the decision of how much to consume is treated separately from the decision of how to allocate total consumption between imports and domestic goods.

[35]Hall (1978) has offered a way around these problems by proposing tests of the permanent income and life-cycle models that concede from the outset that none of the right-hand-side variables is exogenous; specifically, the test involves determining whether all variables other than consumption lagged one period have nonzero coefficients in a regression equation for current consumption. The rub is that this approach may reveal little about the true structural relation between consumption and its determinants.

2.3.2.2. Export supply. The application of income and other scale variables in work on export supply (or pricing) has been less intensive, but two issues merit discussion: (i) the roles of trend income and trend exports in export supply, and (ii) the effects of cyclical income or demand changes on the supply of exports.

(i) *Trend income.* The basic argument for including trend income in the export supply function is that a country or industry's ability and willingness to supply exports will not be fully captured by the ratio of export prices to domestic prices (or factor costs) but will depend also on the output capacity of the economy as a whole. Put in other words, secular changes in the level of aggregate real output will be accompanied by advances in factor supplies, infrastructure, and total factor productivity that will lead to an increase in export supply at any given level of export prices. When such a trend output variable has been added to a conventional total export supply function [like eq. (2.4)], the results have been encouraging. Goldstein and Khan (1978) found that trend income appeared with the expected positive sign and was statistically significant in their equations for total exports in all eight industrial countries in their sample. Similarly, Geraci and Prewo (1980) found a significant positive effect for potential output in all five of their country export–supply equations.

(ii) *Trend exports.* This is a variable that has not been considered in the empirical export–supply literature but one that should be if export supply functions are to be compatible with some of the recent theoretical literature on aggregate supply. At the center of this new neoclassical supply literature [see Lucas (1973), Sargent (1976)] is the so-called "surprise" supply function. The basic idea is that actual supply (Y) will exceed normal or trend supply $(\overline{Y})$ only to the extent that current price (P) exceeds the expected price (P^e).[36]

Application of the "surprise" supply function to exports is attractive for at least three reasons. First, it does not stretch the imagination unduly to think of the domestic price as a reasonable measure of the expected export price. Exporters know from experience that there will be *temporary* periods for which export prices will depart from domestic prices, but $PX = P_i$ in the long run and on average; hence P_i can serve as good predictor of PX.[37] Second, when $P^e = P$ (i.e. $P = PX$), where P^e is the expected price level, then the surprise supply function implies that actual (current) export supply will equal trend exports. This seems preferable to the implication of the standard supply function (2.4) that export supply will be constant when $PX = P$. Third, if trend exports and trend

---

[36]A stochastic (error) term is usually included in the supply function, but it need not concern us here.

[37]In cases where the data contradict the hypothesis that $PX = P$ on average, one could still retain the surprise supply function by: (i) using a time-series model to generate the "expected" ratio of PX to P; (ii) by using deviation of the actual from the expected ratio to measure "surprises" in relative export prices; and (iii) by relating export quantity surprises to relative export price surprises.

real output move closely together, then those empirical results that find a significant positive role for trend output in total export supply would likewise be consistent with a positive significant role for trend exports. In any case, this strikes us as a promising area for future research.

(iii) *Cyclical income effects.* Most of the empirical work in this area is based on the twin premises that when domestic demand pressure increases, selling in the home market becomes more profitable than selling abroad, and that this increased profitability is *not* fully captured by movements in the ratio of domestic to export prices. This cyclical tilt toward the domestic market might reflect the better quality of domestic customers (e.g. larger purchase volume, stronger brand allegiance) or a perceived higher risk associated with export sales. In any event, the prediction is that the quantity of resources devoted to export production and the quantity of goods offered to the export market will decline when domestic income rises above trend. Operationally, the implication is that a cyclical income or other scale variable ought to be added to the export supply equation

Review of the existing empirical evidence on the export supply effects of domestic demand pressure prompts the following conclusions and observations. First, Mintz's (1967) finding, based on non-econometric tests for the United States, that cyclical upturns are associated with decreases in export quantities and increases in export prices has been supported by later econometric studies for the United States and other industrial countries [Artus (1973) (1977), Clark (1977), Hooper (1976) (1978), Winters (1976), Dunlevy (1979)]. Second, no consensus has yet emerged on whether the positive export price effect of domestic demand expansions is larger or smaller than the negative export quantity effect. Ballpark estimates are that a 10 percent increase in the capacity utilization rate would in the long run reduce the quantity of exports supplied by 3–5 percent [Artus (1973), Dunlevy (1979)] and increase the export price by a similar percentage [Artus (1977)]; there are wide inter-country differences, however, around these central quantity and price elasticities. Third, one of the main channels by which domestic demand pressure reduces the quantity of exports is via the former's effect on lengthening delivery delays and hence on weakening the exporting country's nonprice competitive position [Ball et al. (1966), Artus (1973)]; this is sometimes referred to as the "pull" effect of domestic demand pressure and it suggests that domestic cyclical income variables play a role in the foreign demand for exports as well.

2.3.3. Relative prices

Whereas the choice for scale variables is usually which *one* among many to pick, the problem for relative prices is rather which *ones* to exclude so as to keep the number of price terms small enough for estimation purposes while still capturing the dominant sources of demand or supply substitution.

2.3.3.1. Aggregate import demand. A country's total imports face potential competition from two broad categories of domestically produced goods, namely
tradables and nontradables.[38] This means that an unrestricted demand equation
for imports would have three prices – import prices (PI_i), domestic tradable
prices (PT_i), and domestic nontradable prices (PNT_i). In the empirical literature,
the typical practice has been to *assume* that the demand for imports is independent of the price of nontradables, and the rationale is that the consumer engages
in a two-step decision process. In step one, he allocates his expenditure between
all tradable and nontradable goods on the basis on his income and the relative
price of tradables to nontradables. In the second step, he allocates his expenditure
on tradable goods (given at step one) between imports and domestic tradables. By
virtue of such "separability" in consumption, only one relative price – namely
that between imports and domestic tradables – need appear in the import demand
equation. *PNT* is relevant therefore only for the demand for all tradables. In
short, combining such separability with homogeneity, the import demand function takes the form

$$I_i^d = \gamma(Y_i/PT_i, PI_i/PT_i), \qquad \gamma_1' > 0, \quad \gamma_2' < 0. \tag{2.1'}$$

The problem is that when the researcher moves to estimate eq. (2.1'), he
immediately faces the problem that price indices for domestic tradables as such
do not exist. Conventional procedure is therefore to use one of two readily
available proxies, namely the wholesale price index (PWH) or the implicit
deflator of gross domestic product $(PGDP)$. However, both these indices contain
nontrivial shares of products that might reasonably be considered as nontradables
[Goldstein and Officer (1979)]. The consequence is that, in actual estimation of eq.
(2.1'), the cross-price elasticity of demand for imports is constrained to be
identical as between domestic tradable and nontradable goods. Thus, the *PNT*
that was excluded by theory comes in by the back door of data availability.

Goldstein et al. [1980], using price indices for tradable and nontradable goods
constructed from data on current and constant dollar *GDP* by industry of
origin,[39] found that the price of nontradable goods was not a significant determinant of the demand for total imports in the majority of industrial countries in
their sample. This finding supports the "separability" assumption typically made
in aggregate import demand studies. Second, both Goldstein et al. (1980) and
Murray and Ginman (1976), the latter working only with U.S. data, report that
the cross-price elasticity of demand for imports is higher, as expected, with
respect to the price of domestic tradables than the price of nontradables.

---

[38] If exports and domestic tradables carry different prices, then exports constitute a third separate
source of competition for imports.
[39] The tradable sector consists of agriculture, mining, and manufacturing. All other industries in
which GDP originates are classified as nontradables; see Goldstein and Officer (1979) for a more
detailed discussion of this data base on tradable/nontradable prices and real output.

Similarly, the estimated price elasticities of demand for imports generally turn out to be larger and more significant when the price of tradables is used as the denominator of the relative price variable than when a general domestic price index inclusive of nontradables ($PGDP$) is employed.[40]

2.3.3.2. Disaggregated import demand. Once imports or exports are disaggregated by type of commodity and/or by country of origin or destination, the number of potential competitors for imports of type i from country j increases dramatically. Therefore, some more systematic and explicit scheme has to be adopted to permit estimation or derivation of the own- and cross-price elasticities of demand.

The most popular solution to this problem, reflected in most recent world trade models [Samuelson (1973), Hickman and Lau (1973), Deppler and Ripley (1978), Artus and McGuirk (1981), Geraci and Prewo (1980)], is due to a pioneering contribution by Armington (1969). The building blocks of the Armington model can be summarized as follows.[41]

First, all commodities are distinguished by kind and by place of production. Types of commodities (called "goods") correspond to rather broad commodity classifications, such as nontradables, manufactures, raw materials, etc. Goods produced by different countries are called "products". Thus French and German manufactures are the same good but are different products. Products are assumed to be imperfect substitutes for one another.

Second, the import demand for a product is determined in a "separable" two-step manner. In step one, the consumer determines his demand for the goods family to which a product belongs on the basis of his income, the good's price, and the prices of other goods. In step two, he determines his demand for that product on the basis of his overall demand for that good (given at step one) and of the ratio of the product's price to the weighted average of the prices of other products in that same goods family.

Third, by assuming that the elasticities of substitution between all pairs of products in the same goods family are identical and constant in any market, it is possible to characterize the allocative or distribution function in step two as

$$I_{1ij}^{d}/I_{1i}^{d} = b_{ij}^{\phi_{ij}}\left(P_{1ij}/P_{1i}\right)^{-\phi_{ij}}, \tag{2.20}$$

---

[40] Turning from the domestic to the import price, it is important to note that tariffs should be included in the domestic-currency price of imports. Unhappily, inclusion of tariff rates is still the exception rather than the rule in the empirical literature, despite the fact that the average ad-valorem tariff on industrial-country imports has been changing (falling) over the past few decades [IBRD (1981)] and the evidence [e.g. Kreinin (1961)] that tariff changes do have sizeable effects on import demand. Quantitative restrictions on imports should similarly be taken into account in import demand although there is no obvious method of measuring them. See Brillembourg (1975), Khan (1974), Hemphill (1974), and Weisskoff (1979) for alternative approaches to measuring the effect of price and quantity restrictions on imports.

[41] Our description of the Armington model follows Branson (1972), Rhomberg (1973), and Artus and McGuirk (1981), but in a much more condensed form.

where I_{1ij}^d is the quantity of imports demanded in country i of good 1 exported by country j (that is of product ij), I_{1i}^d is the quantity of good 1 demanded in country i from all sources of supply, b_{ij} is the base period quantity share of country j in total imports of good 1 by country i, P_{ij} is the price of product ij, P_{1i} is the price of good 1 in country i (equal to a weighted average of product prices within good 1), and ϕ_{ij} is the elasticity of substitution for product ij.

Fourth, and most important, this framework permits the derivation of formulae for both the direct (d_{ij}) and cross price (c_{ij}) elasticities of demand for imports of any product into country i from any exporting country j using only three pieces of information: (i) the share of each exporter in the importing country's total demand for that good (S_{ij}); (ii) the elasticity of substitution for products within that goods family (ϕ_{ij}); and (iii) the own-price elasticity of demand in the importing country for that good (n_{i1}).[42] Trade share parameters $(S_{ij}\text{'s})$ can be readily obtained from published *OECD* or *IMF* sources on the direction of trade. The elasticities of substitution (ϕ_{ij}) and price elasticities of demand (n_{1j}) are less straightforward to acquire but usual practice is to base them on available published studies.

The Armington methodology has at least three appealing features. It provides an extremely economical and consistent method for estimating *all* the bilateral and multilateral direct and cross-price effects of a single or simultaneous set of traded goods price changes. For this reason, the methodology has been extensively used to estimate the trade balance effects of a hypothetical or actual set of currency realignments [Armington (1970), Branson (1972), Artus and Rhomberg (1973), Artus and McGuirk (1981)]. Furthermore, the methodology itself is quite flexible, as evidenced by its subsequent application to export supply functions [Geraci and Prewo (1980)] and to trade in intermediate goods [Clements and Theil (1978)]. Finally, the model yields some interesting implications for inter-country differences in price elasticities. Specifically, in the usual case when the elasticity of substitution (ϕ_{ij}) is larger in absolute value than the price elasticity of demand for the respective goods class (n_{1i}), the model implies that countries with larger market shares should have a relatively low own-price elasticities of demand for their goods and a relatively high cross-price elasticities of demand [Branson (1972), Tables 4 and 5, and eqs. (2.20a) and (2.20b)]. The rationale is that if a country has a small market share, a decrease in its relative price increases its sales principally by taking away business from other exporters; but if it already has a major share of the market, price declines increase its sales only if the size of the market itself grows.

---

[42]Following Branson (1972, p. 29), the direct (d_{ij}) and cross-price elasticities of demand (c_{ij}) by country i for product ij can be expressed as:

$$d_{ij} = -\left[\phi_{ij} - S_{ij}\left(\phi_{ij} - n_{i1}\right)\right], \tag{2.20a}$$

$$c_{ij} = S_{ij}\left(\phi_{ij} - n_{i1}\right). \tag{2.20b}$$

At the same time, it is also clear that the Armington model is not without problems. One is in choosing the right level of aggregation for the goods categories. If these are defined too narrowly, the separability assumption is likely to be violated; if they are very broadly defined, the assumptions governing estimates of the elasticity of substitution (i.e. identical income elasticities) are likely to be violated. Another caveat is that the Armington model is just a methodology for computing direct and cross-price elasticities of demand, and the estimates derived from it will only be as good as the estimates of ϕ_{ij} and n_{1i} on which the former are based. Estimates of elasticities of substitution abound in the literature, but much less is known about the price elasticities for broad goods classes.

3. Econometric issues in trade modelling

In proceeding from the theoretical models outlined in the previous section to actual estimation of trade relationships, several important econometric issues have to be addressed. The particular issues we consider in this section are: dynamics and the treatment of lags, aggregation, simultaneity, and the stability of the relationships over time.[43] While this list by no means exhausts all the econometric issues, it nevertheless covers the major ones. Careful attention to these issues is a prerequisite for doing quantitative work on the subject.[44]

For expositional convenience, the analysis here is conducted only for the case of the import demand function. It is a simple matter to translate the discussion to the case of export demand, and in general to the supply functions for imports and exports as well. Specific issues relating to the latter are dealt with separately as the analysis requires.

---

[43] Two particular issues which we do not cover here are homogeneity and the appropriate functional form of the estimating equation. The subject of homogeneity of demand and supply equations has been discussed by Leamer and Stern (1970) and tests of the postulate that the functions are homogeneous of degree zero in prices have been performed by Murray and Ginman (1976), Mutti (1977), and Goldstein et al. (1980), among others. In the last study, it is shown that the homogeneity postulate is generally accepted for import demand equations of most industrial countries. Insofar as the functional form is concerned, Khan and Ross (1977) provide a description of the Box and Cox (1964) methodology that can be used to determine empirically whether the function should be specified in linear or log-linear terms, and further show that log-linear specification is preferable for import demand equations in the cases of Canada, Japan and the United States. This finding was confirmed by Boylan, Cuddy, and O'Muircheartaigh (1980) for three smaller European countries – Ireland, Denmark and Belgium. An interesting recent paper by Honda and Ohtani (1980) jointly tests for homogeneity and the appropriate functional form by generalizing the procedure adopted by Khan and Ross (1977).

[44] It is probably fair to argue that researchers in the international trade sphere have been more conscious of econometric problems and pitfalls than those in most other areas of applied economics. This sensitivity can be traced back to the seminal paper of Orcutt (1950) which highlighted the various methodological issues involved in estimating import and export equations, and which still serves as a continuing guide and conscience to anyone engaged in empirical research on trade.

3.1. Dynamics and time lags

Thus far, the basic demand and supply equations for imports and exports have been presented as "equilibrium" relationships, without any reference to time units. In the real world, however, the presence of adjustment costs and of incomplete information implies that the adjustment of dependent variables to explanatory ones will not be instantaneous, i.e. importers and exporters will not always be on their long-run demand and supply schedules. Gauging the pattern and length of such time lags is important not only for obtaining forecasts of imports and exports but also for evaluating many policy issues related, for example, to changes in tariffs, exchange rates, and so on.

What is at issue, then, is not whether lags ought to be incorporated in trade equations but rather how best to do so. A simple approach to the modelling of dynamic trade behavior is to specify the equation within the framework of a general distributed-lag model with geometrically declining weights. This has come to be known popularly as the "Koyck" model, which for the specific case of import demand is written as: [45]

$$I_t = \beta \sum_{j=0}^{\infty} (1 - \beta)^j I_{t-j}^d. \qquad (3.1)$$

The parameter β measures the response of actual imports to the demand for imports and is bounded $(0,1)$. If actual imports are equal to the desired level, β will equal unity; in contrast, a value of zero for the β implies that equilibrium is never reached. The average or mean-time lag in adjustment can be calculated as $(1 - \beta)/\beta$.

There are two particular variants of the general function (3.1) that are typically employed in trade studies. First, the partial-adjustment model which states that imports adjust to the difference between the demand for imports and actual imports in the previous period:

$$\Delta I_t = \beta \left[I_t^d - I_{t-1} \right]. \qquad (3.2)$$

By substituting for I_t^d one obtains a reduced form equation that differs from the equilibrium model of eq. (2.1) simply by the addition of a lagged imports term. A second variant of the Koyck model is one where demand and supply depend not on actual prices but rather on some notion of "expected" prices. If expectations are formed according to the adaptive-expectations model of Cagan (1956), one obtains an equation fairly similar to that yielded by the partial-adjustment model (3.2).

---

[45] While we write the model in linear terms, it should be remembered that it could be defined in log-linear terms.

Estimates of import and export equations using some type of Koyck formulation have been made by Houthakker and Magee (1969), Magee (1970), and Goldstein and Khan (1976). These have shown that while adjustment is not instantaneous, the lags are fairly short, with most of the effect occurring within four quarters or so. For example, Goldstein and Khan (1976) estimated the average lag in total import demand to be between two and four quarters for a group of seven industrial countries; while in another study [Goldstein and Khan (1978)], the same authors found that the average lag for total exports ranged between one and five quarters.

Provided due care is paid to the error structure in the estimation equations, geometric lag models are relatively straightforward to estimate and the results are easily interpreted. However, such specifications do have certain fundamental features which may not be fully acceptable. First, and by definition, these models assume that the largest effect of any change in the explanatory variables occurs in the initial period. In contrast, it could be argued that the true lag effect builds up gradually over time and declines after that. In other words, the appropriate lag pattern could be an inverted "*v*" shape (or even a more complicated distribution) rather than the steadily declining lag pattern emerging from the Koyck-lag models. Some adjustment can be made to the general geometric distributed-lag model to allow for this, for example by permitting the first few lagged terms to be unrestricted, but in doing so one loses the theoretical rationales of the partial-adjustment and adaptive expectations models.

Another more serious problem with such models is that the lag in the response of the dependent variable is assumed to be the *same* irrespective of whether the change in imports is due to variation in prices or in the scale variable. It has been argued [for example by Magee (1975)] that there is no reason for the time response to be the same for all explanatory variables. Further, the lag that is estimated could be a combination of different lag patterns on the different explanatory variables. In this connection, the relatively short average lag that has been found in empirical studies using Koyck lags could primarily reflect a short real income lag that is not really valid for prices. A number of writers have argued that the delayed response of imports and exports due to recognition lags, decision lags, delivery lags, replacement lags, and production lags,[46] is likely to be quite different depending on the explanatory variable that initiates the response. While there appears to be some agreement that the effect of real income or other scale variables is largest in the initial period and declines rapidly thereafter, there is much less of a consensus on the proper distributed-lag pattern for price changes. For this reason, it is generally not appropriate to impose a geometrically declining pattern a priori.

---

[46]See Junz and Rhomberg (1973) for a discussion of these different types of lags.

These problems with Koyck lags have led to the wide use of polynomial (Almon) lag models in estimating trade equations. Such formulations avoid the imposition of a uniform lag pattern on all the explanatory variables and permit less stringent restrictions on the shape of that lag distribution. The results from such experiments have been, to say the least, quite mixed. In general, the lag pattern associated with the scale variable has been quite similar to that yielded by the geometric lag model, but the responses of imports and exports to price changes have displayed a variety of lag patterns. Some writers [e.g. Heien (1968) and Samuelson (1973)] have found that the effect on imports of a relative price change decays steadily over time, with about 75 percent of the effect taking place in the first year and the remainder occurring in the following year. Others [e.g Buckler and Almon (1972), Clark (1977)] found a bell-shaped or inverted "v" pattern for relative price changes. Applying the polynomial lag approach to aggregate import equations for twelve industrial countries, Goldstein and Khan (1976) discovered that the weights of the lag structure declined steadily in half the cases and either increased over time or took on the inverted bell shape in the other half. Interestingly, it was also found that the statistical significance of the relative price term was substantially lower than when a geometric lag structure was imposed.

Since polynomial lags allow for more flexibility than Koyck lags, they are perhaps better able to represent the reaction of the dependent variable to changes in the exogenous variables. However, the shape and form of the lag pattern is dependent on the degree of the polynomial, on whether end-point constraints are imposed and if so in what way, and on the number of lags included. Naturally, the researcher cannot be expected to go through all possible permutations so that some degree of subjective prefiltering is invariably present in the lag forms selected. This makes it difficult to determine whether the reported lag structure is the result of a number of preliminary tests with the selection based on some criteria of goodness-of-fit, or whether it simply reflects the priors of the researcher. Furthermore, one often finds such lag structures, particularly those from models utilizing higher-order polynomials and a large number of lags, yielding signs on the coefficients for some of the lagged values that are clearly at variance with theoretical expectations [Minford (1978)]. While some rationalization of such results is typically provided, the arguments seem somewhat strained, since sign-switching of the coefficients of lagged values of the variables is extremely difficult to justify theoretically.

Some compromise between the geometric and polynomial lag models can be made by incorporating the main advantages of the two, although to our knowledge this has not yet been done in trade equations. Hall and Sutch (1967), for example, suggest that the initial part of the lag distribution be represented by a low-order polynomial and the latter part by a Koyck distribution. In the more general case, separate low-order polynomials could be applied to the scale and price variables, with a common geometric lag structure being applied after some point in time. This would yield a model that was more flexible than the Koyck-type model, yet at the same time avoid many of the problems associated with polynomial lags.

Another worrisome problem is that the estimated lag distributions in trade equations do not seem to be independent of the unit of observation. In other words, one can obtain strikingly different results for the same model depending on whether the unit observation of the data is monthly, quarterly, or annual. This is the familiar time-aggregation problem in econometrics. It is possible, for example, that the very long lags (up to six years) on relative prices reported by some researchers [Junz and Rhomberg (1973)] are simply a consequence of their use of pooled time-series cross-section data. Some relief from this time-aggregation problem could perhaps be obtained by considering the methods of estimation proposed by Sims (1971) and Wymer (1972). These methods, which essentially involve the discrete-time approximation of continuous-time models, yield estimates of lags that are apparently independent of the unit of observation. As far as we can ascertain, there has again as yet been no effort made in this direction.

Finally, it would seem that there is also considerable potential in the application of the techniques of time series analysis to trade relationships. This methodology, associated with the names of Box and Jenkins (1970), is very powerful in identifying and estimating general distributed-lag relationships. The techniques of *ARIMA* models and transfer functions are now widely available and thus can be readily applied. The principal advantage of such an approach is that it involves a minimum of arbitrariness in the choice of the lag distribution, as the data itself is allowed to determine the form and length of the lag process.

In sum, the issue of timing is clearly a very crucial one in the estimation of trade relationships and has received a great deal of attention. Unfortunately, despite the energy expended on the topic, the issue is far from settled. We do not know the length of the lags involved and we are as yet unclear on how lag patterns ought to be modelled. Additional work in this area should still pay large positive marginal returns.

3.2. Aggregation

Since trade data are available on a disaggregated basis for most countries, it is relevant to ask two related questions.[47] First, is it necessary to estimate disaggre-

---

[47]We deal here only with disaggregation over commodities, not over regions. The latter form of disaggregation can be viewed as another way of disaggregating by commodities, since certain regions trade in certain types of commodities. The other main rationale for regional disaggregation is to give expression to the assumed particular import demand behavior of developing countries; see, for example Rhomberg and Boissoneault (1965).

gated relationships and then combine them to obtain an aggregate estimate? Second, if the answer to the first question is in the affirmative, how should the aggregate values for the elasticities be derived from the estimates of the components?

The general guideline for disaggregation is quite simple. If the effect of the determining variables is exactly the same as between the aggregate and disaggregated groups, or if the relationship between the components and aggregate explanatory variables is a stable one, then one can be indifferent between the aggregate and disaggregated equations.[48] If these basic preconditions are not satisfied, however, and they are unlikely to be satisfied in any realistic situation, disaggregation is always better, as the estimates obtained directly from the aggregate relationship are likely to be biased. This point was made persuasively by Orcutt (1950) for the case of price elasticities. In aggregate trade equations, goods with relatively low price elasticities can display the largest variation in prices and therefore exert a dominant effect on the estimated aggregate price elasticity, thereby biasing the estimate downwards. The same problem can in principle arise with respect to the scale variable, although here it is typically less serious.

The relationship between the parameters obtained from estimates of disaggregated equations and those from the aggregate equation has been defined rigorously by Theil (1954). In the case of the aggregate import-demand equation, for example, the parameters of real income and prices will depend not only on the corresponding parameters of the disaggregated relationship but also on the parameters of the other included variables. In other words, the aggregate real income coefficient will be a weighted average of the disaggregated real income coefficients and the weighted average of the disaggregated price coefficients. Unless all the disaggregated coefficients are equal, estimation of the aggregate relationship, by ignoring this interaction, will result in specification bias.

Concern with the issue of aggregation bias has led to a number of empirical studies that use disaggregated import and export data. In most such studies, the disaggregation tends to be limited to a standard one-digit *SITC* classification, although some studies [Kreinin (1967), Khan (1975), and Stone (1979)] have been able to disaggregate more finely. Estimates of income and price elasticities for disaggregated commodity categories are examined in Section 4, and it is sufficient here to note that these elasticities differ across commodity groups, with price elasticities higher for manufactures than for nonmanufactures. The activity or income elasticity of demand for manufactures also appears to be higher than those for the other groups, but perhaps less markedly.

If one accepts the view that disaggregation is usually warranted, how should one proceed to obtain aggregate elasticities from the disaggregated estimates? For

---

[48]See Madalla (1977).

a linear functional form of the equation, this is a relatively simple matter of taking the weighted average of the disaggregated estimates, with the weights being the shares of the components in the total. In the log-linear case, it has been demonstrated by Barker (1970) that one has to adjust the component elasticities by the variation in the component real incomes and prices relative to the variation in their respective aggregates. This ratio is generally referred to as the "distribution" factor. Thus, in the log-linear specification, a weighted average of the disaggregated import elasticities would equal the "true" elasticities only if the distribution factors were equal to one or if they were uncorrelated with the other terms. While it may be plausible to assume that these distribution factors for real income approximate unity, there is less reason to suppose that component price indices move exactly in proportion to the total price index. Both Magee (1975) and Khan (1975) found that import price elasticities calculated after adjusting for the distribution factor turned out to be significantly *lower* than those obtained utilizing the simple weighted average method.

Finally, it should be mentioned that while disaggregation may be preferable in principle, there has been some controversy on its merits in practice. If the disaggregated data are accurate and the component equations well specified, then disaggregation always results in more information. But Grunfeld and Griliches (1960) and Aigner and Goldfeld (1974) make the point that disaggregated data are generally subject to larger measurement errors than are aggregate data, and further that disaggregated functions are more likely to be misspecified than aggregate relationships. In such a case, it may be advisable to estimate the aggregate relationship. Essentially, the argument revolves around predictability, that is, whether predictions from a model using aggregate data are more accurate than those derived from disaggregated data. If the forecast errors from the disaggregated estimates cancel each other out, then disaggregation makes no difference. If such cancelling-out does not occur, the sum of forecast errors may be larger than those obtained from the aggregate relationship. Edwards and Orcutt (1969) show via simulation experiments that predictions from disaggregated data are much better than those from aggregated data, but this finding is challenged by Aigner and Goldfeld (1973) who show that this supposed superiority of disaggregated models cannot be generalized.

3.3. Simultaneity

As demonstrated by Orcutt (1950) and Prais (1962) among others, price elasticities in trade relationships can be seriously biased by simultaneity between quantities and prices. Thus, single-equation estimates of the price elasticities of demand and supply can be weighted averages of the "true" demand and supply elasticities and consequently can be biased downward. More formally, simultaneity implies correlation between the determining variables in an equation and the error term, which violates one of the conditions for the use of classical least squares analysis [Orcutt (1950), Harberger (1953), Kmenta (1971)]. The basic conditions under which one can proceed to estimate, say, a demand equation that would be free of such bias are either that the price elasticity of supply is infinite, or that the demand function is stable while the supply function shifts around.[49]

When such assumptions cannot be made, there are basically two options. The first is to solve the model to obtain the reduced form, and then estimate that by ordinary least squares. Provided that the model is just identified, one can recover the price and income elasticities of demand and supply from the estimates of the reduced-form equations. However, one seldom has the luxury of having a just-identified model to work with, so that the latter step is often not possible. For example, Amano's (1974) study of export behavior of industrial countries eliminates the problems created by simultaneity, but the over-identified nature of the model prevents one from calculating either the demand *or* supply price elasticities. An alternative approach is to estimate the model using simultaneous equation methods. The earliest attempt at simultaneous estimation of trade equations is contained in the impressive study by Morgan and Corlett (1951), who estimated import demand and supply functions for various commodities by limited-information maximum-likelihood methods. While the results were quite poor, their approach was correct conceptually, and it has properly served as a model for later research. More recent studies, using techniques such as two-stage least squares or instrumental variables, include those by Rhomberg and Boissoneault (1965), Basevi (1973), Khan (1974), Artus (1975) and Gylfason (1978). It is not possible in many of these cases to derive the supply-price elasticity, but the procedure adopted does correct for simultaneity.

Explicit export-supply functions have been incorporated into export demand models by Magee (1970), Gylfason (1978) and Goldstein and Khan (1978).[50] The last study formulates a two-equation model of exports and estimates the complete model simultaneously by full-information maximum-likelihood methods. All three studies introducing a supply function for exports found that this extension tended to raise the estimated price elasticity of demand (vis-à-vis the OLS estimates), a result that can be explained by the less-than-infinite supply-price elasticities found in these studies. Goldstein and Khan (1978), for example, report the latter as ranging from 1.1 to 6.6 for a group of seven industrial countries.

Given the accumulated evidence, it would seem that simultaneity is not a problem that can be dealt with by assumption, particularly in relation to exports.

[49]For a formal analysis, see Madalla (1977) and Leamer (1981).

[50]Simultaneous estimation of import relationships has rarely been undertaken, although here one would probably be justified in assuming that, in all but a few large countries, the price of imports is unaffected by variations in an individual country's demand. For two such attempts to estimate import supply equations, see Magee (1970) and Gylfason (1978).

Rather, the correct procedure is to formulate a complete model, test it, and then decide whether the price variable in the demand equation can be treated as exogenous. It needs to be recognized, however, that this procedure is laborious and there is always a risk of misspecification attached to the construction of complete models. Fortunately, there are certain statistical tests, such as the regression specification error test (RESET) due to Ramsey (1969), and the specification tests developed by Hausmann (1978), that can be applied in a single-equation context. These tests are quite powerful in detecting a nonzero mean disturbance that may be caused by omitted variables, incorrect functional form, or simultaneous-equation bias. Another option that has not been explored in the trade literature is to utilize the so-called "causality tests" due to Granger (1969) and Sims (1972), which enable one to test for feedback relations between variables.[51]

3.4. Stability of trade relationships

Whether a regression relationship varies or is stable over time is obviously important from both a predictive and an analytical point of view. Forecasts can be accurate only if the underlying equation on which they are based is unchanging. Similarly, determining the effects of changes of exogenous variables with any degree of confidence also requires that the parameters of the function be invariant over time. Changes in the basic relationship can be either gradual or sudden, and in either case the resulting parameters will be biased and inconsistent if allowance is not made for such shifts. There are in fact good reasons for expecting that trade relationships are subject to both types of changes. Gradual changes in the elasticities can come about as the pattern of trade changes during the process of economic development or as the result of changes in govenment trade policies. Sudden shocks such as changes in the exchange rate or exchange rate regime, or large oil price increases can also fundamentally alter the basic demand or supply relationships.

Yet another potential reason for instability of the parameters is the so called "quantum effect", originally suggested by Orcutt (1950). It is argued that the price elasticity of demand for imports will be larger for large price changes than for small price changes. The rationalization for this quantum effect is that the price change must be large enough to overcome buyer inertia and the costs related to switching suppliers [see, for example, Liu (1954)]. Its chief implication is that estimates of elasticities based on a sample containing both large and small price changes will not be equally applicable in other situations where large or small price changes predominate.

---

[51] In other words, if there were no contemporaneous relationship between the variables in question one could be justified in estimating the model by classical least squares methods.

The statistical procedures used to test for stability have typically involved the introduction of dummy variables to isolate the point at which the structural shift is suspected of taking place, and/or splitting the sample at this point and estimating the relevant functions for the two sub-periods. The latter approach was adopted by Kemp (1962b) for the case of Canadian imports. Estimating the import equation for sub-periods 1929–1939 and 1947–1955, Kemp (1962b) found that the income elasticity doubled in size. Magee (1972) used a similar approach on a bilateral model for U.S. imports and exports, and reported significant changes in both the price and income elasiticities as between the periods 1951–1960 and 1961–1969. Stability tests of a similar type have also been performed by Rhomberg and Boissoneault (1965) and Ahluwalia and Hernandez–Cata (1975) for U.S. exports and imports, respectively, and by Heien (1968) on import equations for a group of industrial countries.

More formal test to determine the constancy of the regression relationship over time have been conducted by Hooper (1978) and Stern et al. (1979). Hooper (1978) applied the standard approach of splitting the sample at the point where the shift is assumed to have occurred, and then proceeded to test whether the shift was statistically significant by using the *F*-test developed by Chow (1960).[52] The results of that exercise indicated that the demand for U.S. nonagricultural exports had been relatively stable for the period under consideration, but that the U.S. nonoil import demand function had been unstable. Hooper (1978) then introduced additional variables into the import demand function in a (partially successful) attempt to reduce the instability. This latter step, namely correcting in some way for the shift in the relationship, is rarely undertaken, so that the effort is to be commended.[53]

Identifying the point where a break in the relationship occurs is almost always a difficult task. Recently, however, new tests of stability have been developed, principally by Brown et al. (1975), that require no more information than is already contained in the data. Such tests have recently been applied to the case of the demand for aggregate U.S. imports and exports by Stern et al. (1979) over the period 1956–1976. The set of tests chosen, however, while powerful in detecting haphazard or nonsystematic shifts in the function, are not really suitable for the testing of gradual or secular changes. Brown et al. (1975) consider other tests

---

[52]An interesting search procedure was adopted by Hooper (1978) to determine the point of change in the relationship. It basically involves the estimation of export and import volume equations for the U.S. over a 24-quarter segment, then moving this segment along the overall sample (1957–77) year by year and repeating the estimation. Changes in the elasticities can be visually identified and the equations re-estimated for the sub-periods determined by this search procedure.

[53]Some other work has also been done on introducing the suspected cause of instability directly into the regression relationship. For example, Hooper and Kohlhagen (1978) introduce an exchange rate uncertainty variable into trade equations. A time trend to capture secular changes is also frequently employed.

more appropriate for the latter case, and it is advisable to employ the complete battery of tests instead of choosing a particular sub-set of such tests.[54]

The evidence on the quantum effect is somewhat mixed. The initial test of this hypothesis, conducted by Liu (1954), found the coefficient on a squared relative price-change variable in a equation for U.S. imports to be significantly different from zero and therefore concluded that the large/small price change distinction was a valid one, with large changes tending to raise the price elasticity. Goldstein and Khan (1976) tested the same quantum effect hypothesis for 12 industrial countries by allowing alternatively the import price elasticity and the speed of adjustment to vary with the size of the relative price change. They found no evidence that the price elasticity of demand for imports varied with the size of the price change, or that importers adjusted faster when faced with larger than "normal" price changes. These results, which held up when the tests were conducted at a lower level of disaggregation and with alternative lag structures, supported the more indirect tests reported by Magee (1975). In sum, notwithstanding Liu's (1954) results, there does not seem to be strong empirical support at this point for the quantum effect.

4. Estimates of price and income elasticities and related policy issues

In this section we turn from questions of methodology to a presentation of the actual econometric estimates of price, income (activity), pass-through, and feedback elasticities, and to the policy issues associated with the size and time patterns of those elasticities. In order of appearance, we consider: (i) price and income elasticities of demand for imports and exports; (ii) the price elasticity of supply for exports, the pass-through of exchange rate changes onto local-currency prices of imports and exports, and the elasticities of export price with respect to domestic costs and competitors' export prices; and (iii) the (feedback) elasticity of domestic prices with respect to changes in import prices and exchange rates. Following that, we offer some observations on the effectiveness of devaluation in improving a country's balance of payments.

To aid in the presentation of the empirical evidence, we have constructed summary tables of estimates for each of the elasicity parameters mentioned above. In selecting the entries for these tables, we have been guided by three considerations. First, because many interesting policy questions relate to inter-country differences in elasticities, we have given priority to multi-country studies since they usually use the same equation specification across countries. Second, to minimize duplication with earlier trade surveys [Magee (1975), Stern et al. (1976)],

---

[54] The reason for using several tests in combination is because departures from constancy of parameters may show up in different ways and the various tests may not be equally powerful in detecting the particular kind of departure encountered.

we have emphasized recent contributions (post 1973) and have seldom included estimates made prior to 1969. Third, we make no pretense of having compiled an exhaustive list of estimates but we have tried to cover the studies most frequently cited in the literature as well as those recent studies that, in our view, rest on the most solid methodological ground.

4.1. Price and income elasticities of demand for imports and exports

As indicated earlier, most of empirical trade work has been confined to the estimation of demand functions for imports and exports that closely resemble eqs. (2.1) and (2.2) of the imperfect substitutes model. Tables 4.1–4.4 provide a condensed picture of the relative price and income elasticities that have emerged from these empirical studies.

Four broad conclusions stand out. First, the sum of the long-run (greater or equal to 2 years) price elasticities of demand for imports and exports invariably exceeds one for industrial countries (Table 4.1).[55] Thus, if the Marshall–Lerner condition (together with infinite supply elasticities) is regarded as the dividing line between elasticity optimists and pessimists, we read Table 4.1 as firmly in the camp of the elasticity optimists. On the import side, Harberger's (1957) judgment of 25 years ago that the price elasticity of import demand for a typical country "...lies in or above the range of -0.5 to -1.0" still seems on the mark; his corresponding consensus export price elasticity of "...near or above -2" appears somewhat on the high side (a range of -1.25 to -2.50 would be our consensus estimate) but would be consistent with those studies that either estimate export price elasticities of demand in a simultaneous framework [e.g. Goldstein and Khan (1978)] or employ long lag distributions on the export price variable [e.g. Beenstock and Minford (1976)]. In short, the estimates in Table 4.1 suggest that over a period of two to three years, relative prices do play a powerful role in the demand for total imports and exports.[56] As such, the potential contribution of

---

[55] The only borderline case in Table 4.1 is the United Kingdom; here however, the results of other econometric studies [Barker (1976), Winters (1976)] strongly suggest that when U.K. imports and exports are disaggregated by commodity class, the aggregate price elasticities of demand increase significantly, suggesting that aggregation bias is perhaps a more serious problem in trade equations for the United Kingdom than in those for other countries.

The low estimated export price elasticities obtained in the recent study by Amano et al. (1981) for the seven major industrial countries are not so easy to dismiss. Until further work is done, we will not be able to tell whether these reflect some unusual features of their sample period (1971–1977), or specification and estimation differences, or a true secular decline in the price elasticities themselves.

[56] The range of estimated price elasticities in Table 4.1 is quite wide, and Kohli (1982) has shown how large differences in price elasticities can result from seemingly small differences in the definition of the scale and domestic price variables (e.g. real national income versus real national product) even when derived form the *same* structural model; further these differences in elasticities across alternative definitions of the right-hand-side variables increase with the size of the country's foreign trade sector.

expenditure-switching policy instruments (the exchange rate, tariffs and subsidies) to trade balance adjustment is a strong one.

The second conclusion, brought out forcefully in Table 4.2, is that *short-run* (0–6 months) price elasticities of demand for imports and exports are considerably smaller than the long-run elasticities. The considerable variation across studies in the estimated shape and length of the lag distribution on relative prices makes it hazardous to offer specific estimates of the relationship between short-run and long-run elasticities.[57] Nevertheless, the evidence in Table 4.2 would not be inconsistent with the judgment that long-run price elasticities are roughly twice as high as short-run ones, and that about 50 percent of the final relative price adjustment takes place within a one-year period.

This marked difference between short-run and long-run price elasticities of demand carries at least two policy implications.[58] One is that the trade balance response to devaluation can follow a pattern described by the "*J* curve". The value of the trade balance can worsen in the short run in response to devaluation because of low short-run price elasticities of demand and the tendency for import prices to rise more rapidly in local currency terms than export prices. Over time, the price elasticities of demand grow larger and export prices catch-up with import prices, with the result that the initial deterioration in the trade balance is halted and then reversed. Nevertheless, the preverse initial response of the trade balance can frequently last for say four to five quarters and it can amount to as much as 10 percent of the local-currency value of imports [Spitaeller (1980)].

The second and most significant implication of low short-run price elasticities is that short-run changes in countries' trade balances will then be dominated by real income movements at home and abroad. A comparison of the short-run price elasticities in Table 4.2 with the income elasticities of demand in Table 4 3, reveals that for periods up to one year in length, the sum of income elasticities for imports and exports is anywhere from two to four times larger than the respective sum of price elasticities. Consistent with this conclusion, most detailed analyses of short to medium-term changes in current account positions among major industrial countries [e.g. Wallich (1978), Truman (1978)] point to differential real income movements across countries as the key explanatory factor.

Our third broad conclusion, based on the estimates shown in Table 4.3, is that income elasticities of demand for a representative industrial country fall in the range of 1 to 2 on both the import and export sides. This carries two implications. The first is that in the absence of secular increases in the relative price of imports,

---

[57]As illustrated in Table 4.2, three of the troubling aspects of the estimates of time lags on relative prices are: (i) the tendency for the estimated long-run price elasticities to vary positively with the *assumed* length of the lag distribution; (ii) the tendency for studies based on pooled time-series and cross-section data [e.g. Junz and Rhomberg (1973)] to yield much longer lags than those based on time-series data for single countries; and (iii) the tendency for the polynomial lags to yield longer average lags than either the Koyck or discrete unconstrained distributed lag formulations.

[58]This subsection draws heavily on arguments presented in Goldstein (1980).

Table 4.1
Long-run price elasticities of demand for total exports and imports:
Representative estimates from recent studies

Country	Total exports									
	Houthakker–Magee (1969)	Goldstein–Khan (1978)	Hickman–Lau (1973)	Beenstock–Minford (1976)	Amano et al.[a] (1981)	Basevi (1973)	Samuelson (1973)	Adams et al. (1969)	Gylfason (1978)	Stern et al. (1976)
Austria	n.a.	n.a.	-0.93	n.a.	n.a.	n.a.	-1.21	n.a.	⋯	-0.93
Belgium	⋯	-1.57	-1.02	-0.84	n.a.	n.a.	-1.14	⋯	⋯	-1.02
Canada	-0.59	n.a.	-0.84	-1.00	-0.33	-0.59	-1.10	-0.23	⋯	-0.79
Denmark	-0.56	n.a.	-1.28	n.a.	n.a.	n.a.	-1.06	n.a.	n.a.	-1.28
France	-2.27	-1.33	-1.09	-1.59	-0.34	n.a.	-1.28	-1.06	⋯	-1.31
Germany	-1.25	-0.83	-1.04	-1.90	-0.29	-1.68	-1.12	-0.65	-0.38	-1.11
Italy	-1.12	-3.29	-0.93	-1.91	-0.30	-0.72	-1.29	-0.25	-1.91	-0.93
Japan	-0.80	⋮	-0.50	-3.00	-0.81	-2.38	-1.04	-0.71	-2.13	-1.25
Netherlands	⋮	-2.72	-0.95	-2.10	n.a.	-2.39	-1.07	-0.59	-0.88	-0.95
Norway	⋮	n.a.	-0.80	n.a.	n.a.	n.a.	-1.16	n.a.	n.a.	-0.81
Sweden	-0.47	n.a.	-1.99	n.a.	n.a.	-1.92	n.a.	n.a.	n.a.	-1.96
Switzerland	-0.58	n.a.	-1.01	n.a.	n.a.	n.a.	-1.51	n.a.	n.a.	-1.01
United Kingdom	-1.24	-1.32	-1.27	-1.47	-0.08	-0.71	-1.28	-0.48	-0.32	-0.48
United States	-1.51	-2.32	-1.38	n.a.	-0.32	-1.44	-1.13	-0.60	-0.62	-1.41

Country	Total imports									
	Houthakker-Magee (1969)	Adams et al. (1969)	Taplin (1973)	Goldstein-Khan (1980)	Beenstock Minford (1976)	Samuelson (1973)	Gylfason (1978)	Stern et al. (1976)	Armington (1970)	Geraci and Prewo (1980)
Austria	n.a.	n.a.	n.a.	-0.82	n.a.	-1.42	-1.21	-1.32	-1.37	n.a.
Belgium	-1.02	-0.61	-0.65	-0.48	-2.90	...	-2.57	-0.83	-1.11	n.a.
Canada	-1.46	-0.62	-1.59	-0.20	-2.50	-1.29		-1.30	-1.30	n.a.
Denmark	-1.66	n.a.	-0.85	-0.42	n.a.	-0.23	...	-1.05	-1.26	n.a.
France	...	-0.81	-0.39	n.a.	-1.31	-0.79	n.a.	-1.80	-1.53	-0.33
Germany	-0.24	-0.85	-0.61	-0.25	-0.74	-0.92	-0.46	-0.88	-1.48	-0.60
Italy	-0.13	...	-1.03	-0.45	-0.88	-1.01	-1.36	-1.03	-1.42	n.a.
Japan	-0.72		-0.81	n.a.	-1.21		-0.32	-0.78	-1.47	-0.72
Netherlands	...	-0.24	-0.02	n.a.		...	...	-0.68	-1.13	n.a.
Norway		n.a.	-1.20	n.a.	n.a.	...	-1.65	-1.19	-1.19	n.a.
Sweden	-0.79	n.a.	-0.76	-0.84	n.a.	-0.80	n.a.	-0.79	-1.30	n.a.
Switzerland	-0.84	n.a.	-1.10	n.a.	n.a.	...	n.a.	-1.22	-1.35	n.a.
United Kingdom	-0.21	...	-0.22	...		...	...	-0.65	-1.38	-0.79
United States	-1.03	-1.16	-1.05	-1.12	-1.04	...	-1.12	-1.66	-1.73	-1.23

[a]Unweighted average of (correctly-signed) estimates in Table I-2.
...indicates zero or wrong-signed coefficient on relative prices.

Table 4.2
Short-run versus long-run price elasticities of demand for imports and exports:
Representative estimates

Investigator	(1) Short-run (0–6 months) price elasticity	(2) Long-run (> 2 years) price elasticity	(3) Ratio of long-run to short-run elasticity	(4) Time period (in years) for 50% of final price effect
(1) Hooper (1976)	− 0.42	− 0.54	1.3	< 0.25
	− 0.17	− 0.79	4.6	1.00
(2) Lawrence (1978)	− 0.14	− 1.52	10.8	1–1.5
	− 0.17	− 1.85	10.8	1–1.5
(3) Deppler and Ripley (1978)	− 0.50	− 0.97	1.9	≈ 1.0
	− 0.80	− 1.40	1.7	≈ 1.0
(4) Beenstock and Minford (1976)	− 0.50	− 1.18	2.4	0.5–1.0
	− 0.70	− 1.73	2.5	0.5–1.0
(5) Goldstein and Khan (1978)	− 0.76	− 1.35	1.8	< 0.25
(6) Taplin (1973)	− 0.32	− 1.33	4.2	> 5.0
(7) Heien (1968)	− 0.77	− 0.93	1.2	< 1
(8) Junz and Rhomberg (1973)	− 1.52	− 3.88	2.5	2
(9) Artus and Sosa (1978)	− 0.07	− 0.77	11.0	n.a.
(10) Hickman and Lau (1973)	− 0.63	− 0.95	1.5	—

(5)	(6)	(7)	(8)
Total length (in years) of lag distribution	Type of distributed lag	Level of aggregation	Type of equation
2	Polynomial	U.S. nonfuel imports	Standard import demand
2	Polynomial	U.S. nonagricultural exports	Standard export demand
2	Polynomial	U.S. imports of manufactures	Standard import demand
2	Polynomial	U.S. exports of manufactures	Standard export demand
3.5	Discrete	Imports of manufactures (unweighted average, 14 industrial countries)	Standard import demand
3.5	Discrete	Exports of manufactures (unweighted average, 14 industrial countries)	Standard export demand
up to 5	Polynomial	Total imports unweighted average, 9 industrial countries	Standard import demand
up to 5	Polynomial	Total exports, unweighted average, 8 industrial countries	Standard export demand
∞	Koyck	Total exports, unweighted average, 8 industrial countries	Standard export demand
∞	Koyck	Total exports, pooled, cross-section for industrial countries	Elasticity of substitution framework
3	Variety	Total imports,unweighted average, 11 industrial countries	Standard import demand
5	Discrete	Manufactured exports pooled, cross-section 13 industrial countries	Elasticity of substitution framework
3	Discrete	13 industrial countries Exports of nonelectrical machinery (3 industrial countries)	Elasticity of substitution framework
—		Total exports of 25 industrial countries	Elasticity of substitution framework

Table 4.3
Long-run activity elasticities for total exports and total imports

Country	Total exports					
	(1) Houthakker– Magee (1969)	(2) Basevi (1973)	(3) Goldstein– Khan (1978)	(4) Deppler– Ripley (1978)[a,b]	(5) Balassa (1979)[c]	(6) Wilson– Takacs (1979)
Austria	n.a.	n.a.	n.a.	1.08	2.04	n.a.
Belgium	1.87	1.29	1.68	1.03	1.98	n.a.
Canada	1.41	1.15	n.a.	0.69	1.89	1.97
Denmark	1.69	n.a.	n.a.	1.08	1.82	n.a.
France	1.53	n.a.	1.69	0.70	2.04	2.14
Germany	0.91	1.33	1.80	1.11	2.27	1.59
Italy	2.68	1.18	1.96	1.12	2.07	n.a.
Japan	3.55	1.62	4.22	1.45	2.00	n.a.
Netherlands	1.88	0.85	1.91	0.65	1.91	n.a.
Norway	1.59	n.a.	n.a.	0.75	1.82	n.a.
Sweden	1.75	1.22	n.a.	1.14	1.93	n.a.
Switzerland	1.47	n.a.	n.a.	0.82	n.a.	n.a.
United Kingdom	1.00	0.61	0.92	0.90	2.20	1.75
United States	0.99	0.92	1.01	1.32	2.02	2.15

Country	Total Imports						
	(1) Houthakker– Magee (1969)	(2) Taplin (1973)	(3) Goldstein– Khan (1976)	(4) Samuelson (1973)	(5) Adams et al. (1969)	(6) Geraci– Prewo (1980)	(7) Wilson– Takacs (1979)
Austria	n.a.	1.04	n.a.	1.08	n.a.	n.a.	n.a.
Belgium	1.94	1.27	1.75	1.38	1.21	n.a.	n.a.
Canada	1.20	1.18	n.a.	0.95	0.90	n.a.	1.87
Denmark	1.31	1.08	0.84	1.38	n.a.	n.a.	n.a.
France	1.66	1.30	1.28	1.45	1.32	1.57	1.07
Germany	1.85	1.35	1.52	1.17	1.34	1.42	1.46
Italy	2.19	1.26	1.83	1.86	1.35	n.a.	n.a.
Japan	1.23	1.12	1.30	1.26	0.93	0.77	1.69
Netherlands	1.89	1.27	2.04	1.56	1.35	n.a.	n.a.
Norway	1.40	0.90	1.01	1.63	n.a.	n.a.	n.a.
Sweden	1.42	1.02	1.33	1.13	n.a.	n.a.	n.a.
Switzerland	2.05	1.25	n.a.	1.46	1.07	n.a.	n.a.
United Kingdom	1.45	1.24	1.78	1.46	1.07	2.24	2.57
United States	1.68	1.81	1.84	1.89	0.76	1.53	4.03

[a] Refers to manufactured exports only.
[b] Refers to cyclical changes in real income.
[c] Refers to trend (permanent) real income.

one should expect the shares of imports and exports in GNP (in real terms) to be rising over time. Evidence collected by Salant (1977, Tables 2 and 3) shows that this is just what has been happening, at least for industrial countries as a group since the late 1940s. The second implication is more controversial and relates to differences across countries in the relationship between income elasticities of demand for exports versus imports. If the income elasticity of demand for a country's imports is significantly larger than that for its exports, then the country confronts an unpalatable choice: either grow at the same rate as its trading partners and accept a secular deterioration in its balance, or to opt for external balance and accept a slower growth rate than its trading partners.[59]

This issue of unequal income elasticities first attracted attention in the empirical literature in the paper by Houthakker and Magee (1969), where the authors found that the income elasticity for Japan's exports was substantially higher than that for its imports, whereas the United Kingdom and the United States were in the opposite category – a finding that seemed to be consistent with the strong trade account performance of Japan and the weak performances of the United Kingdom and the United States during much of the 1960s. As shown in Table 4.3, subsequent multi-country econometric studies have on balance replicated this inter-country pattern of income elasticities.[60] Still, serious questions have been raised about both the existence and interpretation of the Houthakker–Magee income-elasticity effect. On the first count, Hooper (1978) has advanced the argument that the observed high estimated income-elasticity of demand for U.S. imports reflects the positive correlation between U.S. income growth and a relevant omitted variable, namely, supply capacity in the exporting countries, particularly the newly-industrialized developing countries. Under normal circumstances, such increases in supply capacity would be reflected in export prices and hence in U.S. import prices. In this case however, so Hooper (1978) argues, these exports contained many new products with zero or unduly low weights in the standard price indices; hence, this supply effect was not reflected in recorded movements in U.S. import prices. When a supply proxy for foreign production is included in the U.S. import demand function along with the normal arguments, the estimated income elasticity of demand drops from above two to somewhere between 1.3 and 1.7. This still leaves the income elasticity for U.S. nonoil imports above that for U.S. nonagricultural exports (1.2) but the difference is no longer substantial. Similar views that the high estimated income elasticity for Japanese

---

[59] If income elasticities for imports and exports are the same, then conventional trade models of course yields the implication that a country which grows faster than its trading partners will suffer a deterioration in its trade balance. Indeed, such nonsynchronization of growth rates is typically at the root of most explanations for large switches in current account positions; e.g. see Truman (1978), Lawrence (1978), Wallich (1978).

[60] An exception is the recent study by Balassa (1979). This study however uses a constant-market-shares approach to export modelling and this renders the "apparent" income elasticities derived from it noncomparable in a strict sense with income elasticities from traditional export demand equations.

exports may really be picking up the influence of some collinear omitted variable have often been put forward but less success has been achieved in identifying just what that omitted variable could be.

A second challenge to the Houthakker–Magee thesis is that it neither differentiates between the trade balance effects of secular versus cyclical income movements nor does it account for the (positive) effect of secular income movements on export supply. Bazdarich (1979), for example, has noted that cyclical increases in U.S. GNP have generally been associated with deterioration in the U.S. trade balance and dollar depreciation whereas increases in potential or trend GNP have had the opposite effect. Perhaps more interesting, Geraci and Prewo (1980) found that while the long-run income elasticity of demand for U.S. imports was high (1.5), it was low relative to the long-run export *supply* elasticity with respect to trend real income (2.5). Similarly, the trend-income demand elasticity for imports was low relative to the trend-income supply elasticity for exports for Japan, whereas the two elasticities were quite close together for France, Germany, and the United Kingdom. Although Geraci and Prewo (1980) interpret their findings as consistent with persistent trade surpluses by the United States (1958–1974) and Japan, their results could still be compatible with the Houthakker–Magee thesis if it was export demand rather than export supply that was the constraint on actual exports during the sample period.

A final criticism of the Houthakker–Magee hypothesis, and indeed of all income-based trade models, is that the analysis is too partial-equilibrium in nature. One branch of the criticism, as represented in recent papers by McKinnon (1978), Artus (1979), and Sachs (1981), reminds us of Alexander's (1952) fundamental insight that the current account surplus must be equal to the difference between income and expenditure or, to what is the same thing, to the difference between savings and investment.[61] Application of this "absorption view" to the observed current account imbalances of the 1970s yields the conclusion that the observed imbalances reflected inter-country differences in the incentives to savings and investment [Artus (1979)] and inter-country differences in shifts in investment induced in turn by inter-country differences in permanent income [Sachs (1981)]. Note that the two approaches (income and absorption) need not be incompatible if, as suggested in Section 2, conventional import and export demand equations use permanent or life-cycle income as the scale variable rather than current income.

Our fourth broad conclusion is based on the estimates shown in Table 4.4. There are significant differences in both price and income elasticities of demand across commodity groups. More particularly, the price elasticity of demand for manufactures is significantly larger than that for nonmanufactures.[62] Within

---

[61]Another branch of criticism comes from the monetary approach [Frenkel and Johnson (1976)] which predicts that countries with high growth rates of real income will run balance-of-payments surpluses because of the positive effect of higher real income on the demand for real money balances.

[62]We have restricted Table 4.4 to imports because most export demand equations for nonmanufac-

nonmanufactures, price elasticities for raw materials and fuels appear to be larger than those for food and beverages, but the differences do not seem large. In the case of the activity elasticities, the comparisons are clouded by the use of different activity variables across commodity groups but, on balance, we again see a higher elasticity for manufactures (especially if estimates of the activity elasticity for fuels do not reflect recent conservation efforts). The chief implication of these inter-commodity differences in income and price elasticities is that differences in the commodity structure of trade can lead both to differences across countries in price and income elasticities for their total imports and exports and to differences in elasticities as between the exports and imports of a single country.

But differences in the commodity composition of trade are not the only explanation for the observed inter-country differences in price elasticities of demand. In fact, two other explanations have already been alluded to in Section 2, namely differences in the share of imports in total domestic demand and supply, as in eq. (2.17) of the perfect substitutes model, and differences in the share of imports in total domestic demand, as derived from eq. (2.20) of the Armington model. Yet another explanation, which is highlighted in an interesting recent study by Goldsbrough (1981), is that price elasticities are much smaller for intra-firm trade (trade among affiliates of the same firm) than for conventional trade, and that the share of intra-firm trade in total trade differs across countries.[63] Given the resources that have been devoted to estimating price elasticities and the implications of inter-country differences in these elasticities for, say, the required change in exchange rates needed to remove existing trade imbalances, a strong case can be made for doing more research on competing explanations for inter-country differences in price elasticities.[64]

---

tures omit any relative price term, implying that the price elasticity for these goods is either zero or infinite.

[63]Still a fourth explanation is Vernon's (1966) "product cycle" which implies that the size of a country's price elasticities will depend on its stage in the product cycle, i.e. on whether it is exporting new and technologically-intensive manufactured goods (early stage) or exporting or importing these goods once their production has become standardized (later stage). Price elasticities are expected to be low in the early stage of the product cycle and high in the later stages. The same theory also implies differences in price elasticities as between a single country's exports and imports [Magee (1975)].

[64]As an initial modest step in this direction, we performed some simple rank correlations between the ordinal rankings of countries by size of price elasticity, as indicated by the studies in Table 4.1, and the ordinal rankings that emerge alternatively from differences in the commodity structure of imports and from differences in the share of imports in total domestic demand and supply. For the commodity structure model, we assigned each country the same import price elasticity of demand for each of the four broad commodity groups listed in Table 4.4. In this way, cross-country differences in the price elasticity of demand for total imports reflect solely cross-country differences in the structure (value shares) of imports across commodities. Similarly, by using eq. (2.17) of the perfect substitutes model, and by assigning each country the same price elasticities of demand (l_1) and supply (n_1) for importables, we were able to generate cross-country differences in the price elasticity of demand for total imports (ε_f^d) that reflect solely cross-country differences in the shares of imports in domestic demand (I_i/D_i) and in domestic supply (I_i/S_i). The commodity structure model yielded considerably higher correlation with the econometric results than did the perfect substitutes (or the Armington) model.

Table 4.4

Long-run price and activity elasticities for disaggregated import categories: Some representative estimates

Commodity categories	Deppler–Ripley (1978)[a]	Taplin (1973)[b]	Basevi (1973)[c]	Clark (1977)[c]	Ball–Marwah (1962)[d]	Houthakker–Magee (1969)[d]	Barker (1976)[e]	Stern et al. (1976)[f]	Theil and Clements (1978)[g]
					Price elasticities				
Foods and beverages (SITC0 + 1)	−0.34	−0.57	−0.55	−1.14	−0.47	−0.18 to −1.28	−0.13 to −0.18	−0.78	−0.58
Raw materials (SITC2 + 4)	—	−0.63	−0.13	−1.25	−0.83	−1.8[h]	−0.44[h]	−0.50	−0.95
Fuels (SITC3)	—	−0.63	−0.04	—	n.a.			−0.96	n.a.
Manufactures and misc. goods (SITC5-9)	−0.97	−1.23	−0.71	−4.72	−1.98	−1.8 to −4.0	−1.37	−1.34	−1.16 to −1.4
					Activity elasticities				
Foods and beverages (SITC0 + 1)	2.83	0.84	1.08	0.38	0.96	0.30 to 1.28	1.12 1.16	n.a.	0.14
Raw materials (SITC2 + 4)	0.32	0.75	0.83	0.96	1.15	0.61[h]	1.91[h]	n.a.	0.25
Fuels (SITC3)	1.22	0.96	1.40	—	n.a.	—	1.99	n.a.	n.a.
Manufactures and misc. goods (SITC5-9)	1.27	1.44	1.46	2.60	2.07	1.11		n.a.	0.28 to 0.32

[a] Unweighted average, 14 industrial countries.
[b] Unweighted average, 25 industrial or semi-industrial countries.
[c] Unweighted average, 10 industrial countries.
[d] United States.
[e] United Kingdom.
[f] Median estimate, all industrial countries.
[g] Pooled, cross-section for 13 industrial countries.
[h] Raw materials plus fuels.

4.2. Supply elasticities, import and export pass-throughs, and export price determination

Despite over thirty years of econometric work on trade equations, it does not take a very large table to present a reasonably comprehensive list of existing estimates of the price elasticity of supply for exports.[65] Table 4.5 presents those estimates, most of which come from export supply functions similar to those presented in the imperfect substitutes model of Section 2 [eq. (2.4)].

Although the supply-elasticity estimates show somewhat more variation across studies than did the demand-price elasticities, the following conclusions emerge from Table 4.5. First, excluding the United States, the supply-price elasticity for the total exports of a representative industrial country appears to be in the range of one to four. The supply elasticity for U.S. exports is probably considerably higher than that, perhaps even reaching ten to twelve. Second, there is a tendency in the empirical results for the estimated export supply elasticity to vary *positively* with the size of the exporting country (as measured say by its real GNP) and *negatively* with the ratio of export openness. Gylfason (1978), for example, reports a rank correlation of 0.66 between his estimates of export supply elasticities and the real GNP of the sample countries, and one of −0.43 between the supply elasticities and the ratios of exports to GNP.[66] The relatively high degrees of export openness of Germany and the United Kingdom may explain why their estimated supply-price elasticities are smaller than might be expected on the basis of their size alone. A third conclusion is that supply-price elasticities for disaggregated exports are higher than those for total exports. This is consistent with a priori reasoning, as resources for expanding production of total exports can come only from the import-competing or nontradable sector, whereas resources for expanding exports of one industry can come from other export industries as well. The fourth but more tentative conclusion is that time lags in the adjustment of export supply to price changes are longer than those on the demand side [Geraci and Prewo (1980)]. This may reflect the larger start-up costs associated with export production, different skill requirements in export production than in the rest of the economy, or the greater degree of uncertainty associated with selling abroad rather than domestically.

Because the evidence on export supply elasticities is so meagre, the policy implications that one can draw from this evidence are likewise thin. The observation that export supply elasticities differ significantly across countries does

---

[65]As regards estimates of supply-price elasticities for imports, even a table is unnecessary. In the recent literature, we know only of Magee's (1970) estimate for U.S. imports of finished manufactures and Gylfason's (1978) estimates of imports supply for some industrial countries.

[66]In a similar vein, Magee (1970) suggests that a back-of-the-envelope method for estimating a country's supply-price elasticity for total exports is to multiply the ratio of GNP to exports by two. He derives this formula from the observation that his estimated supply-price elasticity for U.S. exports is roughly twice the ratio of U.S. GNP to exports.

Table 4.5
Estimates of long-run supply-price elasticity for exports

Investigator	Supply-price elasticity	Level of aggregation	Country
(1) Magee (1970)	11.5	Total exports	United States
(2) Goldstein and Khan (1978)	6.6	Total exports	United States
	4.6	Total exports	Germany
	2.5	Total exports	Netherlands
	1.9	Total exports	France
	1.4	Total exports	United Kingdom
	1.2	Total exports	Belgium
	1.1	Total exports	Italy
(3) Dunlevy (1979)	2.1	Exports of manufactures	United States
	0.7	Total exports	United Kingdom
(4) Basevi (1973)	3.8	Exports of chemicals and fertilizers to U.S.A.	Canada
	4.9	Exports of minerals and metals to world (less U.S.A.)	Canada
(5) Artus and Sosa (1978)	4.6	Exports of nonelectrical machinery	Germany
	4.2	Exports of nonelectrical machinery	United Kingdom
	3.1	Exports of nonelectrical machinery	United States
(6) Gylfason (1978)	2.4	Total exports	United States
	1.7	Total exports	Japan
	1.4	Total exports	Netherlands
	0.8	Total exports	Germany
	0.8	Total exports	United Kingdom
	0.5	Total exports	Italy
(7) Geraci and Prewo (1980)	12.2	Total exports	United States
	6.7	Total exports	Japan
	4.6	Total exports	Germany
	1.4	Total exports	United Kingdom

suggest, however, that export subsidies and other incentives to exporting will not yield the same export supply responses across countries. In other words, even if comprehensive codes could be legislated and enforced that would equalize export subsidies across countries, some countries (most likely the larger, less open ones) would still get more export-supply response than others.

Another implication, and one that relies only on the conclusion that export supply elasticities are less than infinite, is that export prices in domestic currency will move to offset some (or even all) of the effect of a change in the exchange rate on the foreign-currency price of exports. In other words, the "pass-through" of exchange rate changes into export price changes (in foreign currency terms) will be less than complete.[67] The consequence for the trade balance effect of an exchange rate change, however, depends on the size of the price elasticity of demand for exports.[68] If the demand elasticity is greater than or equal to unity, a lower supply elasticity reduces the effect of an exchange rate change on the value of the trade balance; alternatively, when demand is inelastic, a lower supply elasticity enlarges the effects of an exchange rate change. The often-cited conclusion that devaluation can still be effective when the sum of the demand elasticities is less than unity so long as supply elasticities are less than infinite [e.g. Gylfason (1978)], is just an implication of this general result. The reasoning for this result is no different than in domestic applications of price theory: an inelastic supply curve produces a larger price increase for a given rightward shift of the demand curve than an elastic one, and the impact of that price increase on the *value* of sales depends on whether demand is elastic or not. Since the weight of the evidence in Table 4.1 is that demand price elasticities are greater than unity in the long run, we interpret the lower-than-infinite export supply elasticities as a factor that will *diminish* the trade balance effects of exchange rate changes.

An alternative to inferring the size of export and import-price pass-throughs from estimates of demand and supply price elasticities is to estimate these pass-throughs directly by regressing import or export prices on exchange rates. One strong advantage of this latter approach is that if high-frequency data (monthly, quarterly) are used, the results can tell us something useful about the *timing* of the response of import and export prices to exchange rate changes.

Table 4.6 presents some representative estimates of import and export-price responses (pass-throughs) to a hypothetical 10 percent devaluation in the country's currency. Three features of the evidence in Table 4.6 merit explicit mention. First, there is a marked tendency for import prices to rise more quickly (in domestic currency) than export prices in response to devaluation; the contrast is particularly evident in the short run (six months) but still holds, albeit to a lesser degree, in the medium run (two years). As suggested earlier, this type of price behavior, in combination with low short-run price elasticities of demand, are what accounts for the "*J*-curve" response of the trade balance to a devaluation. Second, time lags in the import-price pass-through are short; typically the effect is complete in

---

[67]Branson (1972, p. 21) shows that the percentage change in export prices in foreign currency terms $(\mathrm{d}PX/PX)$ associated with a percentage change in the exchange rate $(\mathrm{d}e/e)$, call it k, can be expressed as:

$$k = (\mathrm{d}PX/PX)/(\mathrm{d}e/e) = \left(1 - \left(\varepsilon_x^{\mathrm{d}}/\varepsilon_x^{\mathrm{s}}\right)\right)^{-1},$$

where $\varepsilon_x^{\mathrm{d}}$ and $\varepsilon_x^{\mathrm{s}}$ are the demand-price and supply-elasticities for exports, respectively. Note that since $-\infty \le \varepsilon_x^{\mathrm{d}} \le 0$ and $\infty \le \varepsilon_x^{\mathrm{s}} \le 0$, an infinite supply elasticity for exports implies full "pass-through" $(k = 1)$ of exchange rate changes into export price changes, whereas a zero export supply elasticity implies no pass through $(k = 0)$; by analogy, note also that when the demand elasticity is infinite, $k = 0$, whereas $k = 1$ when the demand elasticity is zero.

[68]The case for imports is symmetrical to that for exports.

Table 4.6
Estimates of import and export price changes (in domestic
currency terms) in response to a 10 percent devaluation

| | Spitaeller (1980) | | | | Kreinin (1977) | Robinson et al. (1979) | |
| | Import prices | | Export prices | | Import prices | Export prices | |
	6 months	2 years	6 months	2 years	2 years	6 months	2 years
Belgium	10.2	10.2	6.8	6.8	9.0	13.8	13.8
Canada	10.1	10.1	6.7	9.5	n.a.	4.5	8.9
France	8.3	10.3	5.3	5.9	n.a.	7.1	7.1
Germany	7.3	7.3	1.7	2.6	6.0	7.7	9.3
Italy	10.9	10.9	8.7	10.5	10.0	9.9	9.9
Japan	11.5	11.5	5.9	5.9	8.0	12.1	6.5
Netherlands	6.6	11.6	6.8	6.8	n.a.	5.7	6.0
Sweden	10.2	10.2	2.3	4.8	n.a.	10.1	10.1
United Kingdom	9.3	10.6	3.5	5.6	n.a.	7.9	7.9
United States	7.1	10.2	3.2	3.2	5.0	5.8	5.8

six months, except perhaps for the largest industrial countries which have significant buying power on the international market. Thus, Spitaeller (1980) finds that import prices rise by the full extent of the devaluation in all countries except Germany, whereas Kreinin (1977) finds significant departure from full pass-through only for the United States and Germany. Recalling our preceding discussion of supply elasticities, the finding of full import price pass-through is consistent with the proposition that import supply elasticities are large relative to both import demand elasticities and export-supply elasticities, particularly over the short term. Full import price pass-through also implies that countries cannot count on much slippage between exchange rate changes and import price changes as a moderating factor in the domestic price feedback effects of exchange rate changes. A third feature of the evidence in Table 4.6 is the larger degree of export price pass-through in the smaller more-open industrial countries than in the larger less-open ones. For example, Robinson et al.'s (1979) estimates suggest that within two years of a devaluation, the domestic currency price of total exports will rise so as to offset nearly 100 percent of the devaluation for small open economies (e.g. Sweden, Austria, Belgium), 70–90 percent for medium-sized economies (e.g. France, Germany, Italy, the United Kingdom), and roughly 60 percent for large, relatively-closed economies (Japan, the United States). Spitaeller's (1980) export pass-through estimates are lower but convey a similar cross-country pattern.[69] The clear message is that the larger less-open countries

[69]Other empirical work on export price pass-throughs also shows that the size of the pass-through falls with the share of manufactures in total exports, implying that those countries with high shares of manufactures in total exports will be able to retain the competitive price advantage from devaluation longer than those with relatively high shares of primary commodities in total exports.

Table 4.7

Elasticity of export prices of manufactures with respect to domestic prices or wage costs and competitors' export prices

Country	Deppler–Ripley (1978)		Artus (1974)		Samuelson (1973)	
	Unit labor costs	Competitors' prices	Wage rates	Competitors' prices	Domestic prices	Competitors' prices
Austria	...	1.02	n.a.	n.a.	...	0.21
Belgium	0.51	0.44	n.a.	n.a.	...	0.78
Canada	0.49	0.46	n.a.	n.a.	0.67	...
Denmark	0.26	0.66	n.a.	n.a.	0.36	0.46
France	0.56	0.40	0.71	0.41	0.42	0.59
Germany	0.57	0.40	0.58	0.36	0.38	...
Italy	0.19	0.44			...	0.80
Japan	0.58	0.58	0.42	0.54	...	0.60
Netherlands	...	0.24	n.a.	n.a.	0.15	0.56
Norway	...	1.31	n.a.	n.a.	...	0.96
Sweden	...	0.99	n.a.	n.a.	0.39	0.83
Switzerland	...	0.32	n.a.	n.a.	1.05	...
United Kingdom	0.42	0.51	0.62	0.11	0.82	0.27
United States	1.53	...	0.85	0.09	0.99	0.19

will, ceteris paribus, be able to hold the initial competitive export-price advantage obtained by devaluation longer than the smaller more-open industrial countries [Goldstein (1980)].

Table 4.7 provides some complementary evidence on export price determination but this time drawing on empirical studies where imperfect competition is the maintained hypothesis. In these studies, the "mark-up" export price equation [e.g. eq. (2.4')] replaces the export supply model [e.g. eq. (2.4)]. The two determinants of export price that are accorded major importance in Table 4.7 are competitors' export prices and domestic factor costs. The interesting thing about the estimated elasticities of export price with respect to these two determinants is not so much their absolute size as their relative size across different groups of countries.[70] Here, we find a consistent pattern. The smaller more-open countries apparently base their export prices on competitors' export prices; conversely, the larger less-open countries apparently use domestic factor costs or prices as the prime mover of export prices. Theoretical justifications for this finding are presented in Deppler and Ripley (1978) and Beenstock and Minford (1976), among others. The basic idea is that the relative weight given to competitors' export prices (PX_c) in export price determination will vary positively with the price elasticity of

---

[70] The reader may note that the elasticity of export price with respect to competitors' export prices often differs from the elasticity with respect to the exchange rate, even though in theory they should be equal. Spitaeller (1980) provides a case for unequal elasticities in terms of the shares of different currencies used in invoicing exports and imports. More general implications of alternative mixes of invoice currencies are analyzed in Magee (1973) and Magee and Rao (1980).

demand for the country's exports and with the slope of the marginal cost curve for producing exportables. Small countries, so the argument goes, with their small shares of world trade and limited domestic factor supplies, face both nearly perfect competition for their exports and sharply rising marginal costs in export production; hence, export prices follow competitors' prices with an elasticity close to one. At the other end of the spectrum are the large countries with their higher trade shares (and assumed higher degree of monopoly power) and larger production bases that together mean lower demand price elasticities for their exports and flatter marginal cost curves; this translates in turn into export price formation that is dominated by domestic factor cost behavior. Other factors that can influence the relative contributions of competitors' prices and domestic costs are the degree of specialization of exports (more specialization reduces the weight of PX_c), the degree of capacity utilization (higher utilization increases the weight of PX_c), and the share of exportables in total production (a higher export share increases the weight of PX_c).

In sum, the imperfect-competition export price models imply that countries can be classified as either "price makers" (price-transmitters) or "price takers" (price-receivers) on the basis of the structural characteristics that govern the demand and supply elasticities for their exports. While these characteristics need not be fully captured by size and degree of openness, the empirical results do identify the larger less-open industrial countries as the ones with the most latitude in export pricing and hence, also with the greatest potential for holding on longest to the export price advantage conferred by devaluation. These models also highlight the importance of the domestic cost and price feedback effects of exchange rate changes for relative traded goods prices. It is to this latter topic that we now turn.

4.3. Domestic price feedback effects of import price changes

Table 4.8 presents some representative estimates of the effect of import price changes on the three most widely-used aggregate domestic price indices (i.e. the consumer price index, the wholesale price index, and the GDP deflator). The tale told by Table 4.8 and the associated empirical literature can be summarized as follows.[71] First, import price changes do have a sizeable effect on the domestic price level in industrial countries. A consensus estimate would be that a 10 percent change in import prices leads eventually to a change in domestic prices of

---

[71] In addition to the studies listed in Table 4.8, estimates of the effect of import price changes on domestic prices can be found in Goldstein (1977), and Hooper and Lowry (1979).

Table 4.8
Estimates of the elasticity of domestic
prices with respect to changes in import prices

	Consumer prices		Wholesale prices	GDP deflator
	Dornbusch and Krugman (1976)	Spitaeller (1980)	Beenstock and Minford (1976)	Artus and McGuirk (1981)
Canada	0.20	0.24	0.28	0.17
France	0.16	0.32	0.28	0.23
Germany	0.03	0.08	0.23	0.22
Italy	0.28	0.36	—	0.16
Japan	0.24	n.a.	0.20	0.14
United Kingdom	0.19	0.20	—	0.27
United States	0.14	0.16	0.05	0.14

anywhere from 1.5 to 4.0 percent for a "representative" industrial country.[72] In this regard, Bruno (1978) in a pooled cross-section time-series regression for 16 OECD countries over the 1972–1976 period, found that each 10 percent change in import prices was associated with a 1.8 percent change in consumer prices. Second, time lags in the pass-through of import price changes onto domestic price changes are longer than those associated with the pass-through of exchange rate changes into import price changes, but most studies find that roughly half of the final domestic price effect takes place within one year. Where long lags are apparent, they are usually explainable in terms of institutional arrangements that limit the frequency with which wages can be renegotiated to take account of unexpected developments in the cost of living, exchange rate-induced or otherwise. Third, there are large differences across countries in the effect of import price changes on domestic prices, with the United States clearly being at the low end of the spectrum among the seven major industrial countries, and with the United Kingdom, France, and Italy at the upper end. Furthermore, if some of the smaller more-open industrial countries (e.g. Belgium, the Netherlands) were included in Table 4.8, it is possible that they would show even larger domestic price feedbacks. The very low estimated feedback elasticity for Germany's consumer prices is surprising in view of Germany's size and openness; in this respect, the feedback estimates for Germany's wholesale prices and its GDP deflator are probably more reliable.

---

[72] From time to time the argument has been made that positive changes in import prices have a greater proportionate effect on domestic prices than negative ones, thereby leading to a progressive "ratcheting-up" of domestic prices in the face of exchange rate fluctuations. The arguments and empirical evidence for such a "ratchet effect" have been examined by Goldstein (1977), who finds little support for it. A somewhat more sympathetic verdict is offered by Kenen and Pack (1979).

If the domestic price effect of import price changes is significant and varies across countries, we can next ask what determines the size of that effect? Theory and empirical work suggest four principal factors: (i) the substitutability between imported and domestic goods in consumption and production; (ii) the share of imports in final expenditure or total output; (iii) the elasticity of factor prices, particularly money wages, with respect to actual (or expected) domestic price changes; and (iv) the elasticity of domestic prices with respect to changes in factor prices (again, principally money wages). The higher are each of these parameters, the greater will be the elasticity of domestic prices with respect to import price changes.[73]

If imports were perfect substitutes for domestic goods, then the domestic price equation would be a simple one; the only explanatory variable would be import prices and it would carry an estimated coefficient of unity [Isard (1977b)]. As indicated earlier, however, in our discussion of the "law of one price", the empirical literature has rejected the perfect substitutes hypothesis. This means that import price increases and decreases can still generate "sympathetic" and "disciplinary" effects respectively on domestic prices of similar goods, but that these effects are likely to be much smaller than unity [Kravis and Lipsey (1978)].[74]

Where imports represent inputs to production, standard production theory predicts that the elasticity of domestic prices with respect to import prices should be approximated by the (value) share of imports in total output, at least in the case of a Cobb–Douglas production function; [Ball et al. (1977)].[75] Thus, ceteris paribus, the more "import-open" the economy, the greater should be the domestic price effects of import price changes. Further, since countries differ much more with regard to the sizes of their import shares [Salant (1977)] than to either labor's share in total output or the response of money wages to domestic inflation, it is likely that this first factor is the dominant source of the inter-country variation in the elasticity of domestic prices with respect to import prices that we observe in the empirical studies.[76]

If there was some money illusion in the 1950s and 1960s, there does not seem to be any left in the 1970s and 1980s, to judge from the unitary coefficient on expected inflation rates now commonly found in aggregate wage equations [Santomero and Seater (1978)]. But this does not mean that the money wage response to domestic price changes is the same in all countries. In some countries

---

[73] See Goldstein (1974), Ball et al. (1977) and Bruno (1978).

[74] de Melo and Robinson (1981) show how the degrees of demand and supply substitution also affect the domestic price effects of changes in tariff and (export) subsidy rates.

[75] Note that substitutability still counts here, but it is the substitution in production between imports and other factor inputs (labor, capital) that matters, not that between similar final goods in expenditure.

[76] Bruno (1978) dissents on this point. He finds small inter-country differences in the effect of *PI* on *P* within a pooled time-series cross-section framework, and explains this by arguing that countries are more similar in the share of tradables in production and consumption than import or export data suggest.

money wages are formally indexed to the cost of living on practically a one-for-one basis; in other countries indexation is used but with a price index that specifically omits changes in the terms of trade; in other countries recourse has sometimes been made to incomes policies that guarantee labor an increased real wage; and in still others, indexation itself is prohibited.[77] All of this, plus differences across countries in the basic bargaining power of unions vis-à-vis employers, leads to differences in what Sachs (1980) calls the degree of "real wage resistance" among countries. Where indexation is widespread and where downward real wage resistance is strong, the domestic price effects of import price changes will likewise be strong.

What then are the policy implications of this feedback effect of import price changes on domestic prices? In our view, there are two major ones. The first is that the feedback effects can sharply diminish the *real* exchange rate changes that result from nominal exchange rate changes, and thereby sharply reduce the expenditure-switching effects of such exchange rate changes even in the face of both reasonably high demand and supply elasticities for imports and exports and of supporting macroeconomic policies that keep a firm handle on the level of demand. Artus and McGuirk (1981) use the Fund's multilateral exchange rate model to contrast the trade balance effects of a 10 percent devaluation under low and high domestic price feedbacks. For the low feedback simulation, the elasticities of wages and the cost of capital with respect to the cost-of-living index are 0.5 and 0.3, respectively; in the high feedback simulation, these two elasticities jump to 0.85 and 0.70, respectively. Holding everything else constant, the trade balance effects with high domestic price feedback turn out to be only 60 percent as large as those with low feedback. In short, high domestic price feedback makes exchange rate changes less effective.[78,79]

The second implication of domestic price feedbacks arises out of their timing. Because the domestic price effects of exchange rate changes typically appear much before the resource allocation effects (due to low short-run price elasticities of demand and supply), there is a sense in which the "costs" of devaluation come before the "benefits".[80] This timing problem can act as a serious obstacle to devaluation itself.

---

[77] A good review of inter-country differences in indexation practices can be found in Braun (1976).

[78] Indeed, some observers [e.g. Lewis (1976)] have gone farther. They argue that with floating rates the domestic price feedback effects of exchange rate changes induce further depreciation of the exchange rate, thereby drawing high inflation countries into a "vicious circle" of high inflation and exchange rate depreciation, and low-inflation countries into a "virtuous circle" of price stability and exchange rate appreciation. This argument however neglects the role of excess money balances in driving both the inflation rate and the exchange rate, as well as other factors that help to put a check on the circle; see Bilson (1979), and Goldstein (1980).

[79] We speak here only of the expenditure-switching role of exchange rate changes. Even if domestic prices to rise by the full extent of the devaluation, the current account may improve as economic agents reduce expenditure to restore their desired level of real money balances.

[80] Of course, the same argument implies that benefits precede the costs in the case of revaluation.

4.4. *Overview of the effectiveness of exchange rate changes*

Since so much of the empirical trade literature over the past thirty years has focused on estimating price elasticities to determine whether devaluation "works" (i.e. improves the current account), it could seem appropriate to conclude this section with some broad generalizations on the effectiveness of exchange rate changes.

(1) Relative prices matter. There is nothing in the empirical evidence on price elasticities themselves to indicate that their magnitude would be a barrier to successful devaluation over a time period of two to three years. Recent efforts to isolate the medium-term expenditure-switching effects of exchange rate changes [e.g. Artus and McGuirk (1981)] suggest that a 10 percent devaluation, along with low domestic price feedback, would improve the trade balance of a representative industrial country by somewhere between 4 and 10 percent of the initial value of trade; the corresponding figure for high domestic feedback would be roughly half that large. In this sense, we interpret the existing empirical evidence as endorsing Harberger's (1957) conclusion that " ··· the price mechanism works powerfully and pervasively in international trade".

(2) The short run is not, however, the same as the medium or long run. For time periods up to six months or perhaps even a year, the low trade volume response combined with the more rapid rise in local currency import prices than in export prices can quite commonly produce a deterioration in the trade balance of the depreciating country. In a similar vein, the domestic price feedback effects of exchange rate changes will appear before the resource allocation effects. In small, relatively open, highly-indexed economies, a 10 percent devaluation might well yield a 5 percent rise in the cost of living within a year.

(3) Relative prices are not the only things that matter. Whatever the price elasticities of demand and supply for imports, exports, tradables, and nontradables, it is worth remembering the lesson of the absorption approach that an improvement in the current account requires a reduction in expenditure relative to income; likewise, the monetary approach reminds us that there is a capital account as well as a current account, and that an exchange rate-induced excess demand for real money balances, if permitted to arise, can be satisfied from either channel. Both of these lessons are relevant for interpreting case histories of exchange rate changes [Laffer (1977), Miles (1979)]. In our view, before/after trade balance comparisons that indicate that devaluation does not work are typically instead examples of: lack of supporting expenditure-reducing policies (usually the offsetting of the positive effect of devaluation on the demand for real money balances by expansions in the money supply), of longer-term incentive patterns that favor expenditure over saving, of faster adjustment speeds in asset than in goods markets that cause devaluation to work via the capital rather than the current account, or of accompanying trade policies that swamp the goods

market effect of devaluation. In such circumstances, it is easy for the association between nominal exchange rate changes and current account imbalances to look weak even in the long run.

(4) Countries are different. While we read the empirical evidence as supportive of the effectiveness of exchange rate changes, we do not read it as supportive of *equal* effectiveness across countries. Differences in the commodity composition of trade, in degrees of import and export openness, in the degree of capacity utilization, in the degree of real wage resistance, and in the efficacy of monetary and fiscal policies all count. Although it is difficult to generalize on the basis of just one or two characteristics, it is our impression that the larger, less-open industrial countries face smaller domestic price feedbacks and can hold on to more of the initial competitive price advantage conferred by exchange rate changes than the smaller, more-open countries. Consistent with this, world trade models typically show a higher trade balance elasticity with respect to the exchange rate for the former group than for the latter.[81] These inter-country differences in the effectiveness of devaluation may also explain why countries often hold different views on the optimal degree of exchange rate flexibility.

5. Concluding observations

In some respects, empirical work on the time-series behavior of foreign trade flows has changed little over the past thirty years. The major thrust of this literature is still by and large single-equation studies that regress import or export volumes on the level of real economic activity at home or abroad and on relative traded goods' prices, with attention closely focused on the estimated income and price elasticities of demand. Despite the dramatic improvement in estimation techniques and capabilities, our review of the empirical evidence also did not uncover any indication that there have been dramatic changes in the sizes of these elasticities themselves over this period. While harder to document, we likewise suspect that the uses to which these elasticities are put are still pretty much the same, with forecasts of trade balances under alternative growth and inflation paths and simulations of the expenditure-switching effects of exchange rate changes leading the way. Finally, most of the major methodological pitfalls in the specification and estimation of trade models that currently preoccupy researchers had already been identified by the early 1950s.

But all of this should not convey the impression that we have learned little of late about income and price effects in foreign trade. As illustrated in the previous three sections, noteworthy advances have been registered in understanding, inter alia, the determinants of export supply and export prices, the role of nonprice

---

[81] See Artus and McGuirk (1981).

rationing in both import demand and export supply, the domestic price feedback effects of exchange rate changes, differences between short-run and long-run price elasticities of demand and between secular and cyclical income elasticities, the theoretical framework appropriate for computing all the own and cross-price elasticities of demand associated with a set of multilateral relative price changes for traded goods, the practical consequences for estimated price and income elasticities of measurement error in the price data, improper aggregation across commodity groups, ignoring the simultaneity between trade volumes and trade prices, and of the possibility of instability in the basic relationships.

At the same time, it is also apparent from our survey of the literature that existing empirical work is subject to some serious criticisms and that significant gaps remain to be filled by future research. To be more specific, there is in our view still a tendency for empirical trade work to be isolated from what is happening in macroeconomic theory. Two prominent examples of this isolation are the neglect of "permanent" or "life-cycle" income constructs in aggregate import and export demand functions and the absence of "expected" prices from export supply functions. Given the maintained hypothesis that imports and exports are (imperfect) substitutes for domestic goods, it does not make sense to have one theory of consumption or of aggregate supply for domestically-produced goods and another quite different one for imports and exports. Also, application of these concepts to trade models would help to remedy another shortcoming of this literature, namely the tendency for intertemporal considerations to be almost exclusively backward-looking rather than forward-looking.

A second broad area in which existing trade models come up short is in the integration of the real and financial sectors, i.e. in the interaction of goods and asset markets. Such integration would not be necessary if partial-equilibrium trade models were used only to answer partial-equilibrium questions. These trade models, however, are frequently employed to answer general-equilibrium questions that impinge on asset markets as well as goods markets, such as what would be the current account repercussions of exchange rate changes or of across-the-board tariff reductions. Such questions can be restricted by assumption to expenditure-switching effects in the goods market (i.e. one can assume that the authorities act to hold the overall level of final domestic demand constant), but it would be useful to know more about the implications for other macro variables, even under a constant-expenditure policy. This need not mean that trade models, if they are to be useful, should be appendages of large-scale economy-wide macro models; but it does suggest that we need to know more about to how the scale and relative price variables in trade equations are influenced by traditional macro policy instruments (monetary and fiscal policy) and how slower speeds of adjustment in goods than in asset markets will affect the short- and medium-run response of trade flows to internal and external price and income shocks.

Closer to the traditional pastures of trade modelling, we still see a significant pay-off to additional econometric work on time lags in export and import volume equations. As discussed in Sections 3 and 4, the existing literature has not yet produced anything approaching a consensus on the mean lag in the response of trade volumes to relative price changes despite, many studies on just that subject. More concretely, we have suggested ways in which the better qualities of geometric and polynomial distributed lags might be combined for this purpose; similarly, it would be worthwhile applying recent advances in time-series estimation to get a better handle on these lags. But better econometric methods alone are not likely to be sufficient. We will simultaneously need to learn more about the institutional factors (currency invoicing, lags between orders and deliveries, productions lags, etc.) that give rise to these lags so that we can have some solid priors to rely on in the estimation. Econometric advances in recent years can also be fruitfully applied in dealing with the issues of simultaneity and stability that still arise in the area of applied trade. We would certainly recommend that such techniques, discussed at length in Section 3, be utilized in future research on foreign trade relationships.

Our final priority area for future research is in the area of inter-country differences in price and income elasticities of demand and supply for traded goods. As suggested in Sections 2 and 4, there are many potential explanations for such observed inter-country differences (some relating to the commodity structure of trade, others to shares of imports and exports in domestic consumption and production or in world imports and exports, others to product cycles for new products, etc.), but very little has yet been done on testing these competing explanations. Since differences in elasticities across countries are often as crucial for assessing the trade impacts of income and price changes as the absolute sizes of the elasticities themselves, research on the former topic strikes us as important for understanding these impacts.

References

Adams, F.G., et al. (1969), An econometric analysis of international trade (Organization for Economic Cooperation and Development, Paris).

Aghevli, B. and M.S. Khan (1980), "Credit policy and the balance of payments in developing countries", in: W.L. Coats and D.R. Khatkhate, eds., Money and monetary policy in less-developed countries (Pergamon Press, Oxford) 685–711.

Ahluwalia, I. and E. Hernandez-Cata (1975), "An econometric model of U.S. merchandise imports under fixed and fluctuating exchange rates, 1959–73", IMF Staff Papers, 22:791–824.

Aigner, D.J. and S.M. Goldfeld (1973), "Simulation and aggregation: A reconsideration", Review of Economics and Statistics, 55:114–118.

Aigner, D.J. and S.M. Goldfeld (1974), "Estimation and prediction from aggregate data when aggregates are measured more accurately than their components", Econometrica, 42:113–134.

Alexander, S.S. (1952), "Effects of devaluation on a trade balance", IMF Staff Papers, 2:263–278.

Amano, A. (1974), Export price behavior in selected industrial countries, unpublished (Kobe University, Japan).

Amano, A., A. Muruyama and M. Yoshitomi (1981), A three-country linkage model (Economic Planning Agency, Tokyo).

Armington, P.S. (1969), "A theory of demand for products distinguished by place of production", IMF Staff Papers, 26:159–178.

Armington, P.S. (1970), "Adjustment of trade balances: Some experiments with a model of trade among many countries", IMF Staff Papers, 27:488–526.

Artus, J.R. (1973), "The short-run effects of domestic demand pressure on export delivery delays for machinery", Journal of International Economics, 3:21–36.

Artus, J.R. (1977), "The behavior of export prices for manufactures", in: P.B. Clark, D.E. Logue and R.J. Sweeney, eds., The effects of exchange rate adjustments (U.S. Treasury, Washington, D.C.), 319–340.

Artus, J.R., (1979), Persistent surpluses and deficits on current account among major industrial countries, unpublished (IMF, Washington, D.C.).

Artus, J.R. and A.K. McGuirk (1981), "A revised version of the multilateral exchange rate model", IMF Staff Papers, 28:275–309.

Artus, J.R. and R.R. Rhomberg (1973), "A multilateral exchange rate model, IMF Staff Papers", 20:591–611.

Artus, J.R. and S.C. Sosa (1978) "Relative price effects on export performance: The case of nonelectrical machinery", IMF Staff Papers, 25:25–47.

Balassa, B. (1979), "Export composition and export performance in the industrial countries, 1953-71", Review of Economics and Statistics, 61:604–607.

Ball, R.J. and K. Marwah (1962), "The U.S. demand for imports, 1948-1958", Review of Economics and Statistics, 44:395–401.

Ball, R.J., J.R. Eaton and M.D. Steuer (1966), "The relationship between United Kingdom export performance in manufactures and the internal pressure of demand", Economic Journal, 76:501–518.

Ball, R.J., T. Burns and J. Laury (1977), "The role of exchange rate changes in balance of payments adjustment: The United Kingdom case", Economic Journal, 87:1–29.

Barker, T.S. (1970), "Aggregation error and estimates of the U.K. import demand function", in: K. Hilton and D.E. Heathfield, eds., The econometric study of the United Kingdom (London) 115–145.

Barker, T.S. (1976), "Imports", in: T.S. Barker, ed., Economic structure and policy (Chapman and Hall, London) 162–176.

Basevi, G. (1973), "Commodity trade equations in project LINK", in: R. Ball, ed., The international linkage of national economic models (North-Holland, Amsterdam) 227–281.

Bazdarich, M. (1979), "Has a strong U.S. economy meant a weak dollar"? Federal Reserve Bank of San Francisco Economic Review, Spring: 35–46.

Beenstock, M. and P. Minford (1976), A quarterly econometric model of trade and prices 1955-72, in: M. Parkin and G. Zis, eds., Inflation in open economies (Manchester University Press, Manchester).

Bilson, J.F.O. (1979), "The 'vicious circle' hypothesis", IMF Staff Papers, 26:1–37.

Bond, M.E. (1980), "The world trade model: invisibles", IMF Staff Papers, 26:257–333.

Boylan, T.A., M.P. Cuddy and J. O'Muircheartaigh (1980), "The functional form of the aggregate import demand equation: A comparison of three European economies", Journal of International Economics, 10:561–566.

Box, G.E.P. and D.R. Cox (1964), "An analysis of transformations", Journal of the Royal Statistical Society, 26, Series B:211–243.

Box, G.E.P. and G.M. Jenkins (1970), Time series analysis: Forecasting and control (Holden-Day, San Francisco).

Branson, W.H. (1968), A Disaggregated model of the U.S. balance of trade, Staff Economic Studies No. 44, Board of Governors of the Federal Reserve System, February.

Branson, W.H. (1972), "The trade effects of the 1971 currency realignments", Brookings Papers on Economic Activity, 15–69.

Branson, W.H. (1980), "Trends in United States international trade and investment since World War II", in: M. Feldstein, ed., The American economy in transition (National Bureau of Economic Research, Chicago) 183–257.

Braun, A. (1976), "Indexation of wages and salaries in developed economies", IMF Staff Papers, 23:226–271.

Brillembourg, A. (1975), "Specification bias in the demand for imports: The case of the Grancolombian countries", April, unpublished (IMF, Washington, D.C.).

Brown, R.L., J. Durbin and J.M. Evans (1975), "Techniques for testing the constancy of regression relationships over time", Journal of the Royal Statistical Society, 37, Series B:149–163.

Bruno, M. (1978), "Exchange rates, import costs, and wage-price dynamics", Journal of Political Economy, 86:379–404.

Buckler, M. and C. Almon (1972), Imports and exports in an input-output model, Research Memorandum No. 38, Maryland Inter-Industry Forecasting Project.

Bureau of Labor Statistics (1980), Comparisons of United States, German and Japanese export price indexes (Washington, D.C.).

Burgess, D.F. (1974), "Production theory and the derived demand for imports", Journal of International Economics, 4:103–117.

Cagan, P. (1956), "The monetary dynamics of hyperinflation", in: M. Friedman, ed., Studies in the quantity theory of money (University of Chicago Press, Chicago) 25–117.

Cheng, H.S. (1959), "Statistical estimates of elasticities and propensities in international trade – a survey of published studies", IMF Staff Papers, 7:107–158.

Chow, G.C. (1960), "Tests of equality between subsets of coefficients in two linear regressions", Econometrica, 28:591–605.

Clark, P.B. (1977), "The effects of recent exchange rate changes on the U.S. trade balance", in: P.B. Clark, D.E. Logue and R.J. Sweeney, eds., The effects of exchange rate adjustments (U.S. Treasury, Washington, D.C.) 201–236.

Clements, K.W. and H. Theil (1978), "A simple method of estimating price elasticities in international trade", Economic Letters, 1:133–137.

Deardorff, A.V. and R.M. Stern (1977), "International economic interdependence: Evidence from econometric models", unpublished (University of Michigan, Ann Arbor, Mich.).

de Melo, J. and S. Robinson (1981), "Trade policy and resource allocation in the presence of product differentiation", Review of Economics and Statistics, 63:169–177.

Deppler, M.C. and D.M. Ripley (1978), "The world trade model: Merchandise trade", IMF Staff Papers, 25:147–206.

Dornbusch, R. and S. Fischer (1978), Macroeconomics (McGraw-Hill, New York).

Dornbusch, R. and D.M. Jaffee (1978), "Purchasing power parity and exchange rate problems: Introduction", Journal of International Economics, 8:157–162.

Dornbusch, R. and P. Krugman (1976), "Flexible exchange rates in the short run", Brookings Papers on Economic Activity, 1:143–185.

Dunlevy, J.A. (1979), "Export demand, export supply, and capacity pressure: A simultaneous equations study of American and British export performance", unpublished (Auburn University).

Eckstein, O. and G. Fromm (1968), "The price equation", American Economic Review, 68:1159–1183.

Edwards, J.B. and G.H. Orcutt (1969), "Should aggregation prior to estimation be the rule?", Review of Economics and Statistics, 51:409–420.

Fair, R.C. (1979), "On modelling the economic linkages among countries", in: R. Dornbusch and J.A. Frenkel, eds., International economic policy – Theory and evidence (The Johns Hopkins University Press, Baltimore) 209–238.

Fair, R.C. and H.H. Kelejian (1974), "Methods of estimation for markets in disequilibrium: A further study", Econometrica, 52:177–190.

Frenkel, J.A. and H.G. Johnson eds. (1976), The monetary approach to the balance of payments (Allen and Unwin, London).

Geraci, V.J. and W. Prewo (1980), "An empirical demand and supply model of multilateral trade", March, unpublished (University of Texas, Texas).

Goldsbrough, D.J. (1981), "International trade of multinational corporations and its responsiveness to changes in aggregate demand and relative prices", IMF Staff Papers, 28:573–599.

Goldstein, M. (1974), "The effect of exchange rate changes on wages and prices in the United Kingdom", IMF Staff Papers, 21:694–739.

Goldstein, M. (1977), "Downward price inflexibility, ratchet effects and the inflationary impact of import price changes", IMF Staff Papers, 24:569–612.

Goldstein, M. (1980), "Have flexible exchange rates handicapped macroeconomic policy?", Special Papers in International Economics, No. 14 (Princeton University).

Goldstein, M. and M.S. Khan (1976), "Large versus small price changes and the demand for imports", IMF Staff Papers, 23:200–225.

Goldstein, M. and M.S. Khan (1978), "The supply and demand for exports: A simultaneous approach", Review of Economics and Statistics, 60:275–286.

Goldstein, M. and L.H. Officer (1979), "New measures of prices and productivity for tradable and nontradable goods", Review of Income and Wealth, 25:413–427.

Goldstein, M., M.S. Khan and L.H. Officer (1980), "Prices of tradable and nontradable goods in the demand for total imports", Review of Economics and Statistics, 62:190–199.

Granger, C.W.J. (1969), "Investigating causal relations by econometric models and cross-spectral methods", Econometrica, 37:424–438.

Gregory, R. (1971), "United States imports and internal pressure of demand", American Economic Review, 61:28–47.

Grossman, G.M. (1981), "Import competition from developed and developing countries", unpublished (Princeton University, Princeton, N.J.).

Grunfeld, Y. and Z. Griliches (1960), "Is aggregation necessarily bad?", Review of Economics and Statistics, 42:1–13.

Gylfason, T. (1978), "The effect of exchange rate changes on the balance of trade in ten industrial countries", October, unpublished (IMF, Washington D.C.).

Hall, R.E. (1978), "Stochastic implications of the life cycle-permanent income hypothesis: Theory and evidence", Journal of Political Economy, 86:971–988.

Hall, R.E. and R.C. Sutch (1967), "A flexible infinite distributed lag", paper presented at The Econometric Society Meetings.

Harberger, A.C. (1953), "A structural approach to the problem of import demand", American Economic Review, 43:148–159.

Harberger, A.C. (1957), "Some evidence on the international price mechanism", Journal of Political Economy, 65:506–521.

Hausman, J.A. (1978), "Specification tests in econometrics", Econometrica, 46:1251–1272.

Hay, G. (1970), "Production, prices, and inventory theory, American Economic Review", 60:531–545.

Heien, D.M. (1968), "Structural stability and the estimation of international import price elasticities", Kyklos, 21:695–712.

Hemphill, W.L. (1974), "The effect of foreign exchange receipts on imports of less developed countries", IMF Staff Papers, 21:637–677.

Hickman, B. and L. Lau (1973), "Elasticities of substitution and export demand in a world trade model", European Economic Review, 4:347–380.

Honda, Y. and K. Ohtani, (1980), "The joint specification of functional form and relative price restriction in the aggregate import demand equation", unpublished (Kobe University, Japan).

Hooper, P. (1976), "Forecasting U.S. export and import prices and volumes in a changing world economy", International Finance Discussion Paper No. 99, Board of Governors of the Federal Reserve System, December.

Hooper, P. (1978), "The stability of income and price elasticities in U.S. trade, 1957-1977", International Finance Discussion Paper No. 119, Board of Governors of the Federal Reserve System, June.

Hooper, P. and S. Kohlhagen (1978), "The effect of exchange rate uncertainty on the prices and volume of international trade", Journal of International Economics, 8:438–511.

Hooper, P. and B. Lowry (1979), "The impact of dollar depreciation on the U.S. price level: An analytical survey of empirical estimates", International Finance Discussion Paper No. 128, Board of Governors of the Federal Reserve System.

Houthakker, H.S. and S.P. Magee (1969), "Income and price elasticities in world trade", Review of Economics and Statistics, 51:111–125.

Houthakker, H.S. and L.D. Taylor (1970), Consumer demand in the United States: Analyses and projections (Harvard University Press, Cambridge).

International Bank for Reconstruction and Development (1981), World Development Report 1981 (Washington, D.C.).

Isard, P. (1977a), "The price effects of exchange-rate changes", in: P.B. Clark, D.E. Logue and R.J.

Sweeney, eds., The effects of exchange rate adjustments (U.S. Treasury, Washington, D.C.) 369–388.

Isard, P. (1977b), "How far can we push the 'law of one price'?", American Economic Review, 67:942–948.

Johnson, H.G. (1958), International trade and economic growth; Studies in pure theory (Allen and Unwin, London).

Junz, H.B. and R.R. Rhomberg (1965), "Prices and export performance of industrial countries, 1953–63", IMF Staff Papers, 12:224–269.

Junz, H.B. and R.R. Rhomberg (1973), "Price competitiveness in export trade among industrial countries", American Economic Review, 63:412–418.

Kemp, M.C. (1962a), "Errors of measurement and bias in estimates of import demand parameters", Economic Record, September:369–372.

Kemp, M.C. (1962b), "The demand for Canadian imports: 1926–55" (University of Toronto Press, Toronto).

Kenen, P.B. and C. Pack (1979), "Exchange rates and domestic prices: A survey of the evidence", Research Memorandum, International Finance Section, (Princeton University, Princeton).

Khan, M.S. (1974), "Import and export demand in developing countries, IMF Staff Papers", 21:678–693.

Khan, M.S. (1975), "The structure and behavior of imports of Venezuela", Review of Economic and Statistics, 57:221–224.

Khan, M.S. and K.Z. Ross (1975), "Cyclical and secular income elasticities of the demand for imports", Review of Economics and Statistics, 57:357–361.

Khan, M.S. and K.Z. Ross (1977), "The functional form of the aggregate import equation", Journal of International Economics, 7:149–160.

Kohli, U.R. (1982), "Relative price effects and the demand for imports", Canadian Journal of Economics, May:205–219.

Kmenta, J. (1971), Elements of econometrics (Macmillan, New York).

Kravis, I.B. and R.E. Lipsey (1971), Price competitiveness in world trade (NBER, New York).

Kravis, I.B. and R.E. Lipsey (1974), "International trade prices and price proxies", in: N. Ruggles, ed., The role of the computer in economic and social research in Latin America (NBER, New York) 253–268.

Kravis, I.B. and R.E. Lipsey (1978), "Price behavior in the light of balance of payments theories", Journal of International Economics, 8:193–246.

Kreinin, M.E. (1961), "Effects of tariff changes on the prices and volume of imports", American Economic Review, 51:297–329.

Kreinin, M.E. (1967), "Price elasticities in international trade", Review of Economics and Statistics, 49:510–516.

Kreinin, M.E. (1977), "The effect of exchange rate changes on the prices and volume of foreign trade", IMF Staff Papers, 24:207–329.

Kreinin, M.E. (1979), International economics (Harcourt Brace Jovanich, New York).

Kreinin, M. and L.H. Officer (1978), "The monetary approach to the balance of payments: A survey", Studies in International Finance No. 43 (Princeton University).

Laffer, A.B. (1977), "Exchange rates, the terms of trade, and the trade balance", in: P.B. Clark, D.E. Logue, and R.J. Sweeney, eds., The effects of exchange rate adjustments (U.S. Treasury, Washington, D.C.) 32–44.

Lawrence, R. (1978), "An analysis of the 1977 U.S. trade deficit", Brookings Papers on Economic Activity, 1:159–190.

Leamer, E.E. (1981), "Is it a demand curve, or is it a supply curve? Partial identification through inequality constraints", Review of Economics and Statistics, 63:319–327.

Leamer, E.E. and R.M. Stern (1970), Quantitative international economics (Allyn and Bacon, Boston).

Lewis, P. (1976), "The weak get weaker with floating rates", New York Times, October 10.

Liu, T.C. (1954), "The elasticity of U.S. import demand: A theoretical and empirical reappraisal", IMF Staff Papers, 3:416–441.

Lucas, R.E. (1973), "Some international evidence on output-inflation trade-offs", American Economic Review, 63:326–334.

Lucas, R.E. (1976), "Econometric policy evaluation", in: K. Brunner and A. Meltzer, eds., The

Phillips curve and labor market (North-Holland, Amsterdam).

Maddala, G.S. (1977), Econometrics (McGraw-Hill, New York).

Magee, S.P. (1970), "A theoretical and empirical examination of supply and demand relationships in U.S. international trade", unpublished, (Council of Economic Advisers, Washington, D.C.).

Magee, S.P. (1972), "Tariffs and U.S. trade", unpublished (Council of Economic Advisers, Washington, D.C.).

Magee, S.P. (1973), "Currency contracts, pass-through, and devaluation", Brookings Papers on Economic Activity, 1:303-323.

Magee, S.P. (1975), "Prices, income and foreign trade: A survey of recent economic studies", in: P.B. Kenen, ed., International trade and finance: Frontiers for research (Cambridge University Press, Cambridge).

Magee, S.P. and R. Rao (1980), "Vehicle and nonvehicle currencies in international trade", American Economic Review, 70:368-373.

McCloskey, D.N. and J.R. Zecher (1976), "How the gold standard worked, 1980-1913", in: J.A. Frenkel and H.G. Johnson, eds., The monetary approach to the balance of payments (Allen and Unwin, London) 357-385.

McKinnon, R. (1978), "Exchange rate instability, trade imbalances, and monetary policies in Japan and the United States", unpublished (Stanford University, Stanford, CA.).

Miles, M.A. (1979), "The effects of devaluation on the trade balance and the balance of payments: Some new results", Journal of Political Economy 87:600-620.

Minford, P. (1978), Substitution effects, speculation and exchange rate stability (North-Holland, Amsterdam).

Mintz, I. (1967), Cyclical fluctuations in the exports of the United States since 1879, Studies in Business Cycles No. 15 (NBER, New York).

Morgan, D.I. and W.J. Corlett (1951), "The influence of price in international trade: A study in method", Journal of the Royal Statistical Society 114, Series A:307-358.

Murray, T. and P. Ginman, (1976), "An empirical examination of the traditional aggregate import demand model", Review of Economics and Statistics, 58:75-80.

Mutti, J.H. (1977), "The specification of demand equations for imports and domestic substitutes", Southern Economic Journal, 44:68-73.

Okun, A. (1975), "Inflation: Its mechanics and welfare costs", Brookings Papers on Economic Activity, 2:351-501.

Orcutt, G. (1950), "Measurement of price elasticities in international trade", Review of Economics and Statistics, 32:117-132.

Prais, S.J. (1962), "Econometric research in international trade: A review", Kyklos, 15:560-577.

Ramsey, J.B. (1969), "Tests for specification errors in classical least-squares regression analysis", Journal of the Royal Statistical Society, 31, Series B:350-371.

Rhomberg, R.R. (1973), "Towards a general trade model", in: R.J. Ball, ed., The international linkage of national economic models (North-Holland, Amsterdam), 9-20.

Rhomberg, R.R. and L. Boissonneault (1965), "The foreign sector", in: The Brookings quarterly econometric model of the United States, (Rand McNally, Chicago) 375-406.

Richardson, J.D. 1973, "Beyond (but back to?) the elasticity of substitution in international trade", European Economic Review, 4:381-392.

Robinson, P., T. Webb and M. Townsend (1979), "The influence of exchange rate changes on prices: A study of 18 industrial countries", Economica, 46:27-50.

Sachs, J. (1980), "Wage indexation, flexible exchange rates, and macroeconomic policy", Quarterly Journal of Economics, 94:731-748.

Sachs, J. (1981), "The current account and macroeconomic adjustment in the 1970s", Brookings Papers on Economic Activity, 1:201-268.

Salant, W. (1977), "International transmission of inflation", in: L. Krause and W. Salant, eds., Worldwide inflation (Brookings Institution, Washington), 167-226.

Samuelson, L. (1973), "A new model of world trade", OECD Occasional Studies (Organization for Economic Cooperation and Development, Paris).

Sargent, T.J. (1976), "The observational equivalence of natural and unnatural rate theories of macroeconomics", Journal of Political Economy, 84:631-640.

Santomero, A. and J. Seater (1978), "The inflation-unemployment trade-off: A critique of the literature", Journal of Economic Literature, 16:499–544.

Sims, C. (1971), "Discrete approximations to continuous time distributed lags in econometrics", Econometrica, 39:545–564.

Sims, C. (1972), "Money, income, and causality", American Economic Review, 62:540–552.

Spitaeller, E. (1978), "A model of inflation and its performance in the seven main industrial countries, 1958–76", IMF Staff papers, 25:254–277.

Spitaeller, E. (1980), "Short-run effects of exchange rate changes on terms of trade and trade balance", IMF Staff Papers, 27:320–348.

Stern, R.M., J. Francis and B. Schumacher (1976), Price elasticities in international trade – An annotated bibliography (Macmillan, London).

Stern, R.M., C.F. Baum and M.N. Greene (1979), "Evidence on structural change in the demand for aggregate U.S. imports and exports", Journal of Political Economy, 87:179–192.

Stone, Joe A. (1979), "Price elasticities of demand for imports and exports: Industry estimates for the U.S., the E.E.C. and Japan", Review of Economics and Statistics, 61:117–123.

Taplin, G.B. (1973), "A model of world trade", in: R.J. Ball, ed., The international linkage of national economic models (North-Holland, Amsterdam) 177–223.

Theil, H. (1954), Linear aggregation of economic relations (North-Holland, Amsterdam).

Theil, H. and K.W. Clements (1978), "A Differential Approach to U.S. Import Demand", Economics Letters, 1:249–254.

Truman, E. (1978), "Balance-of-payments adjustment from a U.S. perspective: The lessons of the 1970's", unpublished (Board of Governors of the Federal Reserve System, Washington, D.C.).

Vernon, R. (1966), "International Investment and International Trade in the Product Cycle", Quarterly Journal of Economics, 80:191–207.

Wallich, H. (1978), "Reflections on the U.S. balance of payments", Challenge March/April, 34–40.

Weisskoff, R. (1979), "Trade, protection and import elasticities for Brazil", Review of Economics and Statistics, 51:58–66.

Wilson, J.F. and W. Takacs (1979), "Differential responses to price and exchange rate influences in the foreign trade of selected industrial countries", Review of Economics and Statistics, 51:267–279.

Winters, L.A. (1976), "Exports", in: T.S. Barker, ed., Economic structure and policy (Chapman and Hall, London) 131–161.

Wymer, C.E. (1972), "Econometric estimation of stochastic differential equation systems", Econometrica, 40:565–577.

Chapter 21

EMPIRICAL STUDIES OF MACROECONOMIC INTERDEPENDENCE

JOHN F. HELLIWELL AND TIM PADMORE

University of British Columbia

Contents

Handbook of International Economics, vol. II, edited by R.W. Jones and P.B. Kenen
© *Elsevier Science Publishers B.V., 1985*

1. Introduction

In this chapter we present and compare some empirical results from studies of macroeconomic interdependence. We concentrate on studies that involve linked macroeconometric models of two or more countries. This restricts our attention to about a dozen research projects, and means bypassing studies based on partial models, general equilibrium trade models, and single economy models. We have chosen to specialize in this way so that we can focus in some detail on a few key issues. We have been fortunate in having the collaboration of many of the modellers in running and helping to interpret experiments that expose some of the main channels of international transmission. Since most of the models are continually changing, our survey can be only a partial snapshot that is bound to be outdated soon. This is a discouraging but inevitable feature of surveys of empirical work. To keep the rate of obsolescence as low as possible, we limit the amount of detail we present about specific versions of the models, and concentrate the analysis on broad questions of continuing importance, with special attention to the role of exchange rates in international transmission. We have also attempted, so far as possible, to collect results relevant to the 1970s and 1980s rather than the 1950s and 1960s.

In the next section, we classify the main linkage projects, paying special attention to those features of the models that have important bearing on the international transmission of disturbances under fixed and flexible exchange rates. In the three subsequent sections we discuss the international repercussions of fiscal policy, monetary policy, and changes in world oil prices. After that, we provide some evaluation of the empirical results available to us and make some conjectures about the likely future course of research.

2. An overview of linkage models

While not complete, our selection of models covers most of the projects for which model specifications and simulation results were published during the 1970s and early 1980s. We limit our attention to linked macroeconometric models.[1] In this section we outline the main features of the models, with special attention to those that provided the simulation results assessed in subsequent sections.

---

[1] Hickman (1982) surveys a broad range of model types that were presented at a 1980 conference, with an emphasis on models with global coverage. Courbis (1981) surveys some of the multinational econometric models and general equilibrium trade models presented at a 1976 conference. Whalley and Shoven are in the process of surveying the general equilibrium world trade models.

Table 2.1 divides the models into four groups. The first group includes Project LINK and the Eurolink Project,[2] both of which are based on national models that are regularly used for independent forecasting within the national economies. In the case of Project LINK, however, some of the newer models, especially those of the Eastern European Comecon countries, have been built and operated in international agencies, or at the Project LINK central office. The national models vary greatly in size, in theoretical conception, and especially in their treatment of international financial linkages. Project LINK has been producing world trade forecasts for more than ten years but, until very recently, there has been no mechanism for determining international capital flows and exchange rates.[3]

In the more recent Eurolink, initial efforts have also been directed to consistent explanation of bilateral trade flows, with the modelling of exchange rates and capital flows being developed subsequently.

Thus, for the purposes of our survey, the Project LINK and Eurolink results illuminate trade and price linkages under the assumptions of fixed exchange rates and full sterilization of reserve flows. Since Project LINK, among all the linkage models, contains the most detailed analysis of world trade, it is of especial use in the analysis of world-level shocks, such as changes in the world price of crude oil.

The second group comprises structural models designed with monetary and exchange-rate linkages in mind, and therefore able to cast light on the nature of international transmission under alternative exchange rate systems. Although they all make use of aggregate quarterly models of substantial scale, the three projects are nevertheless quite different in scope.

The Japanese Economic Planning Agency (EPA) world econometric model is the most comprehensive, as it includes nine country models and six regional trade models. The U.S. Federal Reserve Board's Multi-Country Model (MCM) contains five country models, completed by trading links with the rest of the world. The national models in both projects were constructed at the research centers in Tokyo and Washington, respectively. The Japanese group also made use of foreign country specialists seconded to Tokyo to assist with particular national models.

---

[2] The main strategy and results of Project LINK are recorded in three North-Holland volumes, respectively edited by R.J. Ball (1973), J.L. Waelbroeck (1976) and J.A. Sawyer (1979). The main simulation results we shall refer to in this chapter are from Hickman (1974), Johnson and Klein (1974), Hickman and Schleicher (1978), Klein (1978), Filatov, Hickman and Klein (1982), and Klein, Simes and Voisin (1981).

The Eurolink model, which is run by the Commission of the European Communities in Brussels, joins quarterly models of the United Kingdom, France, Italy, and Germany, with the system being closed by a "Rest of the World" model. The trade linkages are described in Ranuzzi (1981) and some alternative exchange rate and capital market linkages by Ranuzzi and Anthemus (1981). It is intended to add models for the other EEC countries, for Canada, and for the United States.

[3] Hickman (1981) describes the current and planned treatment of exchange rates within Project LINK.

Table 2.1
Classification of linkage models

Model and reference	Trade linkage[a]	Monetary linkage	Exchange rates	Country coverage
Group I: Linkage of available national models.				
1. Project LINK [Ball (1973), Waelbroeck (1976), Sawyer (1979)]	Klein–Van Peterssen	Capital flows among developed countries, but only in short term simulations	Fixed in long term simulations. Floating according to reaction functions or PPP	18 OECD countries, seven Comecon countries, and four developing regions
2. Eurolink [Ranuzzi (1981)]	Bilateral imports determined by total imports and competing export prices	Total inflows set by portfolio balance	Fixed or managed float with structural balance of payments approach	Germany, Italy, France U.K and ROW
Group II: Linkage of structural models built with monetary and exchange rate linkages in mind.				
1. EPA World Econometric Model [Amano et al. (1982)]	Hickman–Lau	Incomes, assets, and interest rates	Fixed or managed float with exchange-rate bands and reserve flow target	Major seven OECD countries plus Australia, S, Korea, and six trading regions
2. MCM Howe et al. (1981)]	Bilateral imports determined by income, and importer, exporter and competitor prices	Multilateral service account and direct investment flows	Fixed or flexible with inverted capital-account portfolio-balance equation	U.S, Canada, Japan, U.K., Germany and ROW
3. RDX2-MPS [Helliwell (1974)]	Bilateral	Interest rates and portfolio balance	Fixed, Bretton Woods, flexible and crawling peg.	Canada and U.S.

Models with a common structure, main focus on trade linkages and no monetary linkages.

1. INTERLINK [OECD (1982)]	Modified Samuelson–Kurihara	None	Fixed	23 OECD countries plus eight regions
2. COMET [Barten et al. (1976)]	d'Alcantara–Barten–Italianer	None	Fixed	11 European countries, U.S., Japan and 5 regions
3. DESMOS [Waelbroeck and Dramais (1976) and Dramais (1981)]	Hickman–Lau with income and capacity utilization adjustments	None	Fixed	8 EEC countries and U.S. with trade links to Japan and three regions
4. METEOR [Kooyman (1982)]	Modified Samuelson–Kurihara	None	Fixed	6 EEC countries plus U.S., Japan, Canada and 5 regions

Group IV:

Groupings of small national models with common structure focussed on monetary and exchange-rate linkages.

1. Fair (1981a)	Export share equations	Capital flow equations interest rate reaction functions	Exchange rate reaction functions	64 countries plus ROW
2. Darby et al. (1982)	Indirect	Interest rates and reserve flows	Fixed and flexible rates from inverted import demand equation	Seven major OECD countries plus Netherlands
3. Minford et al. (1981)	Indirect	Interest rates and reserve flows	Real interest parity condition on real exchange rate.	Seven major OECD plus Netherlands, Belgium and three regions (with trade links only)

[a]See Appendix for a detailed discussion of trade linkages.

Another notable feature of the EPA project is that it has provided what appears to be the most methodical comparative test of the various methods for consistent estimation of international trade flows.[4] The Appendix is adapted from the EPA summary of the relative price and activity elasticities of the alternative linkage methods applied to aggregate real exports of the fifteen EPA countries and trading regions. Seven methods are compared, and, for six of them, long-run price elasticities are calculated for each country and region. Even though the elasticities are long run, and are based on export prices, rather than on the less closely linked national output prices, only seven of the 90 estimated price elasticities are greater than 1.0 in absolute value. The preferred Hickman–Lau approach gives price elasticities for export shares of −0.38 for the United States, −0.63 for Japan, and −0.59 for Germany, the three countries involved in the initial linkage experiments. Long-term price elasticities for imports of goods are −0.76 for the United States, −0.40 for Germany, and −1.18 for Japan. The lags are such that there are substantial *J*-curve effects for the United States and Germany, but not for Japan. A structural approach is adopted for the explanation of exchange rates, with exchange rates determined so as to equilibrate continually the market for foreign exchange. A combination of official intervention and exchange-rate-stabilizing private capital flows provides exchange market stability.

The U.S.-based MCM model has bilateral trade flows and endogenous international capital movements. The model explains bilateral exchange rates between the United States and each of the other four country models. Exchange rates are determined as one set of a number of market clearing prices in the MCM's general equilibrium system. Since exchange rates have their greatest direct impact on trade and capital flows, it is convenient to view them as being determined primarily by clearing the model's balance of payments equations [see Berner et al. (1976) and Stevens et al. (1983)].

In the first version of the MCM, capital account equations in the balance of payments were estimated directly. For two reasons [as described in Hooper et al. (1982)], in the present version of the model these equations have been inverted and estimated as exchange rate equations. First, the exchange rate changes associated with monetary and fiscal policy shocks were very large and, in some cases unstable under a freely floating regime when the estimated intervention functions were dropped from the model. Second, in attempting to reestimate the model's capital flow equations over a sample period extended to include data for the period 1976–1980, it was found that the coefficients on interest rate and exchange rate terms were often insignificant or had the wrong sign and that, by

---

[4]Gana, Hickman, Lau and Jacobson (1979) report a comparison of results from application of the Klein–Van Peeterssen and the Hickman–Lau methods to a four-commodity-class disaggregation of world trade. They find the Hickman–Lau method better for imports of commodity group SITC 5–9, and the Klein–Van Peeterssen method better for total world trade, GDP, and total exports and trade balances of individual countries. They also found that both methods generally dominated the assumptions of constant export shares in terms of either value or volume, although the latter provided the best estimates of SITC 5–9 exports.

conventional statistical tests, the equation structure had shifted. Also, instability in some simulations was traced to longer-term *J*-curve effects, which the MCM researchers found could be eliminated by forcing domestic prices, foreign prices and exchange rates to have symmetrical effects on trade flows. The MCM simulation results analyzed in subsequent sections are based on the revised version of the model with directly estimated exchange rate equations. The effect of using directly estimated exchange rate equations is to make the capital account an automatic buffer for changes in the current account. In the presence of short-term *J*-curve effects, this is not only necessary for exchange market stability but is justifiably based on speculative arbitrage across the *J*-curve.

The third group II project involves only Canada and the United States. The two national models were built at about the same time, but all of the linkage was established from the Canadian side. The bilateral linkages were embedded in the Canadian RDX2 model, making use of variables explained by the U.S. MPS model. Both models were provided with trade linkages to the rest of the world. In addition, RDX2 contains bilateral capital account and migration linkages between the two countries and between Canada and the rest of the world. The endogenous exchange rate is the bilateral rate between Canada and the United States, with the exchange rates between the United States and the rest of the world treated as exogenous and the triangular arbitrage condition used to determine the effective exchange rate between Canada and all third countries.

Several exchange rate regimes have been used to link RDX2 and MPS, including rigidly fixed rates, the Bretton Woods pegged-rate system with behaviorally-estimated official intervention within the 1 percent margins, a crawling peg, and a floating exchange rate without official intervention. Even though there were *J*-curve effects in the current account linkages between the two models, there were sufficient exchange-rate-stabilizing capital flows to ensure exchange market stability. As noted earlier in connection with the MCM results, this result may have to do with the fact that one of the capital account portfolio equations was renormalized and directly estimated as an exchange rate equation.

The projects in the third group all involve sets of country models with a common structure. They are all linked by trade and trade-price equations, with exogenous exchange rates and no monetary or capital account linkages. The OECD INTERLINK model started as a consistent explanation of trade flows, but has since been expanded to include domestic activity and price equations, and plans are underway to develop a more complete modelling of aggregate supply and to endogenize eventually capital movements and exchange rates. The COMET, DESMOS, and METEOR models are all primarily models of the major EEC countries and the trade linkages between them.

Most of the group IV models use very small national models, based on quarterly data, with primary emphasis on monetary and exchange rate linkages. The Fair multicountry model contains 64 separate national models, many more than any other linkage project. The model of the United States is large, but all of the other national models contain estimated equations only for imports, consumption, investment, output, GNP deflator, export price index, demand for money, long-term interest rate, and forward exchange rate, and estimated reaction functions for the short-term interest rate and the exchange rate. As in most of the linkage models in the first three groups, each national model determines imports and the price of output, with a trade share matrix being used to distribute world trade among competing suppliers, and to determine import prices as functions of exchange rates and suppliers' export prices. In some of the reported results [Fair (1981b)], the real export shares matrix is treated as exogenous, while in subsequent work [Fair (1981c, 1982)] it is made endogenous by direct estimation of the export quantity shares as functions of relative export prices. In subsequent unpublished work, Fair has moved to direct estimation of export flows from each country to each other country. The results confirm the relatively low price elasticities found by the Japanese EPA researchers (and reported in our Appendix). Like the Fair model, the Japanese EPA project uses data for aggregate exports and export prices, although from a much smaller sample of countries. Fair (1981c, p.11) reports elasticities that in only one or two cases are greater than 1.0 in absolute value, although they are negative for all but three countries, and significantly different from zero for more than three-quarters of the 64 countries. For the seven largest OECD countries, the elasticities of export shares range from -0.231 (for Germany) to -0.333 (for Canada), with an average value of -0.29 and an average t-ratio of 6.0.

The elasticities of national imports with respect to import prices are not constrained to be equal to the elasticities with respect to output prices, and they are significantly negative for only 6 of the 64 countries outside the United States, and for none of the larger OECD economies [Fair (1981a, p. 20)]. The import price elasticities in the Fair model are substantially less than in any of the linkage models described above, and his combination of import and export price elasticities, along with the method for determining export prices, are such that the Marshall–Lerner conditions are not met for most country models even in the long term. This means that the current account responses to exchange rate changes are destabilizing even with export shares endogenous. [Fair (1981c, pp. 18–19) shows this result for depreciation of the DM and the pound sterling.] Under these circumstances, there would be little incentive for exchange-rate-stabilizing private capital flows. Instead of invoking such flows, Fair endogenizes the exchange rate by means of an exchange-rate reaction functions for 22 countries; these depend on the lagged exchange rate and some subset of the following variables: the DM/$ exchange rate, relative prices, relative interest rates, demand pressure, and net foreign assets. Given this officially-set exchange rate, the current account balance is matched by some combination of private capital movements and changes in official reserves. The latter combination is never disentangled, since the private and government sectors are aggregated in Fair's model, and net foreign assets are defined by accumulating current account surpluses.

The second model in this group is the International Transmission Model of Darby et al. (1982). The model is applied to the seven major OECD countries plus the Netherlands. In scale, the national models are about the size of Fair's non-U.S. models, with an equation for the price level (based on an inverted demand-for-money equation), an equation for the unemployment rate, a policy-reaction equation for the money supply, a real interest rate equation intended to equilibrate savings and investment, an import demand equation, an export equation, an import price equation, a net capital outflows equation, and an exchange-market intervention equation (for use when the exchange rate is endogenous). Under floating exchange rates, the import demand equation is renormalized (for estimation as well as simulation) to make the exchange rate the dependent variable. The renormalization has very significant effects on the parameter estimates, and hence on the properties of the resulting model.

The international linkages in the Darby model are not as completely specified as in the other linkage models described earlier. There are no consistency checks forcing world exports to equal world imports, so the sum of the balances of payments for the eight linked countries is assumed to be passively financed by the rest of the world. The foreign real income and price variables are weighted averages of the income and price variables in the eight modelled countries.

The final project in this group is the Liverpool-based multilateral model of Patrick Minford and associates. There are nine country models (the OECD major seven plus Belgium and the Netherlands) and trade equations for three other trading regions. The special focus of the model is on the use of forward simulations to generate expected future values of variables. The structure and estimation of this model are still at a very preliminary stage. The only estimated equations reported to date (in Minford, Ioannidis, and Marwaha, 1981) are for stock demands for fixed assets in eight countries, consumption functions for five countries, portfolio demand-for-money equations for seven countries, and trade equations for the three trading blocks.

All of the three models in the fourth group are at a more experimental stage than the other linkage models, and their parameter estimates and structure may be too preliminary to permit useful empirical inferences about the nature of international transmission. The Fair model is the most complete and empirically informative of the three, and so it will get correspondingly more attention in the subsequent sections.

3. Transmission of fiscal policy

What can be learned from a comparison of the various estimates of the cross-country effects of fiscal policies? Deardorff and Stern (1979) asked this question when they reviewed various estimates of cross-country government expenditure multipliers under fixed exchange rates. They began by constructing a simple expenditure multiplier for each of eight major OECD countries using marginal propensities to consume and to import equal to historical averages. Then they linked these country multipliers, using fixed bilateral trade weights to spread each country's imports across supplying countries. A fiscal shock in country i thus influences country j according to the size of country i's multiplier, the size of country i's marginal propensity to import from country j, and the size of country j's multiplier in response to the induced change in its exports.

Deardorff and Stern then computed static "elasticity multipliers" defined as the percentage change in a country's GNP or GDP resulting from a spending shock equal to 1 percent of GNP in the initiating country; for an own-country shock, the elasticity multiplier is the conventional GNP multiplier. They compared their "naive model" to values obtained from fiscal simulations under fixed exchange rates from five linkage projects: LINK, DESMOS, COMET, METEOR and RDX2-MPS (see Table 3.1). They found that their naive estimate often fell within the range of results from the linked model simulations, and they concluded that the information contributed by the linked models was quite limited.

We think that divergence of linked model results from simple linkage calculations is not a good guide to the information content of the models. After all, there are some reasons why the Deardorff/Stern multipliers are too small (for example, they ignore induced investment and feedback effects from the second country back to the first country) and there are other reasons why they are too large (they ignore the expenditure-reducing effects of induced inflation, induced higher interest rates, and other forms of supply constraint). Since there is, a priori, no way of deciding whether the "true" dynamic multipliers, either on average or in any particular year, should be above or below the simple static multipliers calculated by Deardorff and Stern, it is not appropriate to use the extent of divergence as a measure of the information provided by the linkage projects.

Although the Deardorff and Stern calculations do not provide grounds for telling whether anything can be learned from the linked simulations, they do provide useful benchmark data on the strength of bilateral trade linkages. Fair (1979) compares fiscal multipliers for an overlapping but somewhat different set of linkage projects. In both surveys, only the RDX2-MPS results involve capital movements and alternative exchange rate systems, and neither of the surveys deal with the importance of feedback effects. We have attempted to supplement these earlier surveys of linkage results. Our survey of expenditure linkages is based on a larger set of linkage models, and it also attempts to show the effects of linkage feedbacks, of fixed and flexible exchange rates, and of the financing used for the government expenditures.

Table 3.1 shows the own-country and cross-country real income effects of bond-financed government spending in each of the seven major OECD countries. The models include all of those surveyed by Deardorff and Stern (COMET, DESMOS, LINK, METEOR, and RDX2-MPS) supplemented by results from a

Table 3.1

Impacts of fiscal shocks with the LINK, OECD INTERLINK, EPA World Econometric Model, mini-METEOR, DESMOS, Fair, COMET, RDX2-MPS, Deardorff-Stern Naive, and MCM models. [a] Impacts are presented as percentage change in income for a shock of 1 percent of income in the initiating country.

Income shock in	Model	Simulation year[b]	Impact on income in						
			US	JA	GE	FR	UK	IT	CA
US	LINK(a)	1	1.18	0.13	0.04	0.02	0.08	0.08	0.31
US	LINK(a)	2	1.87	0.27	0.08	0.04	0.21	0.17	0.56
US	LINK(a)	3	2.58	0.40	0.14	d0.06	0.35	0.31	0.86
US	LINK(b)	1	1.60	0.13	0.13	0.05	0.08	0.14	0.53
US	LINK(b)	2	2.39	0.20	0.21	0.06	0.12	0.21	0.63
US	LINK(b)	3	2.73	0.22	0.33	0.07	0.13	0.26	0.63
US	INTERLINK	2	1.52	0.18	0.20	0.16	0.21	0.19	0.59
US	INTERLINK	3	2.06	0.34	0.43	0.34	0.39	0.39	0.93
US	EPA	1	1.59	0.11	0.09	0.07	0.22	0.06	0.46
US	EPA	2	2.60	0.33	0.25	0.27	0.56	0.20	0.83
US	EPA	3	3.29	0.53	0.37	0.44	0.70	0.34	1.41
US	METEOR	1	2.46	0.22	0.19	0.12	0.19	0.15	0.65
US	METEOR	2	2.86	0.45	0.43	0.30	0.45	0.34	1.29
US	RDX2-MPS	2	2.03						−0.15
US	RDX2-MPS	4	0.93						0.28
US	Naive	Any	2.24	1.12	0.07	0.03	0.10	0.07	0.65
US	MCM	1	1.98	0.14	0.16		0.10		0.34
US	MCM	2	1.90	0.21	0.32		0.16v		0.54
US	MCM	3	1.43	0.20	0.38		0.08		0.61
US	Fair	1	1.43	0.06	0.05	0.03	0.07	0.04	0.18
US	Fair	2	1.39	0.18	0.19	0.01	0.21	0.19	0.55
JA	LINK(a)	1	0.02	1.18	0.01	0.00	0.02	0.01	0.02
JA	LINK(a)	2	0.04	1.50	0.01	0.01	0.04	0.02	0.04
JA	LINK(a)	3	0.06	1.50	0.02	0.01	0.06	0.03	0.04
JA	LINK(b)	1	0.01	1.08	0.03	0.01	0.01	0.02	0.02
JA	LINK(b)	2	0.03	1.15	0.04	0.01	0.02	0.04	0.03
JA	LINK(b)	3	0.04	1.22	0.06	0.02	0.03	0.05	0.04
JA	INTERLINK	2	0.04	1.41	0.05	0.04	0.06	0.04	0.06
JA	INTERLINK	3	0.08	1.97	0.13	0.10	0.13	0.13	0.12
JA	EPA	1	0.02	1.45	0.04	0.02	0.05	0.02	0.05
JA	EPA	2	0.02	2.17	0.11	0.11	0.15	0.08	0.12
JA	EPA	3	0.03	2.38	0.16	0.18	0.17	0.11	0.18
JA	Naive	Any	0.03	1.69	0.01	0.01	0.01	0.01	0.05
JA	MCM	1	0.08	1.21	0.02		0.02		0.02
JA	MCM	2	0.10	1.50	0.03		0.04		0.04
JA	MCM	3	0.03	1.63	0.02		0.07		0.03
GE	LINK(a)	1	0.04	0.04	0.98	0.08	0.10	0.19	0.05
GE	LINK(a)	2	0.11	0.09	1.38	0.16	0.25	0.42	0.10
GE	LINK(a)	3	0.26	0.18	1.20	0.21	0.53	0.81	0.35
GE	LINK(b)	1	0.04	0.06	1.83	0.11	0.09	0.28	0.06
GE	LINK(b)	2	0.10	0.11	1.87	0.12	0.12	0.35	0.09
GE	LINK(b)	3	0.16	0.17	2.91	0.17	0.19	0.52	0.13
GE	INTERLINK	2	0.11	0.13	1.96	0.40	0.34	0.46	0.07
GE	INTERLINK	3	0.11	0.13	1.96	0.40	0.34	0.46	0.14
GE	EPA	1	0.01	0.04	1.44	0.19	0.12	0.14	0.04

Table 3.1 (continued)

Income shock in	Model	Simulation year[b]	Impact on income in						
			US	JA	GE	FR	UK	IT	CA
GE	EPA	2	0.02	0.14	1.98	0.66	0.34	0.42	0.12
GE	EPA	3	−0.00	0.24	1.77	0.84	0.33	0.56	0.18
GE	METEOR	1	0.05	0.04	1.75	0.16	0.09	0.17	0.04
GE	METEOR	2	0.13	0.09	1.06	0.29	0.20	0.27	0.13
GE	DESMOS	1			1.25	0.08	0.04	0.08	
GE	DESMOS	3			1.56	0.14	0.08	0.16	
GE	COMET	1			1.29	0.16	0.08	0.24	
GE	COMET	8			0.87	0.44	0.24	0.40	
GE	Naive	Any	0.02	0.01	1.50	0.10	0.03	0.13	0.02
GE	MCM	1	0.06	0.02	1.45		0.04		0.01
GE	MCM	2	0.07	0.05	1.95		0.10		0.02
GE	MCM	3	−0.03	0.10	2.20		0.16		0.01
GE	Fair	1	0.02	0.02	2.36	0.25	0.12	0.20	0.01
GE	Fair	2	0.02	0.06	2.36	0.46	0.17	0.48	0.03
FR	LINK(a)	1	0.01	0.01	0.04	1.21	0.04	0.07	0.02
FR	LINK(a)	2	0.02	0.01	0.05	1.19	0.05	0.08	0.01
FR	LINK(a)	3	0.01	0.00	0.06	1.22	0.04	0.11	0.00
FR	LINK(b)	1	0.02	0.03	0.09	1.07	0.03	0.09	0.03
FR	LINK(b)	2	0.03	0.04	0.12	1.07	0.04	0.11	0.04
FR	LINK(b)	3	0.04	0.05	0.19	1.07	0.06	0.14	0.05
FR	INTERLINK	2	0.04	0.04	0.19	1.31	0.13	0.18	0.05
FR	INTERLINK	3	0.08	0.09	0.40	1.82	0.25	0.35	0.10
FR	EPA	1	0.01	0.01	0.07	1.85	0.06	0.06	0.01
FR	EPA	2	0.01	0.05	0.24	3.02	0.21	0.19	0.05
FR	EPA	3	0.03	0.11	0.32	2.63	0.23	0.30	0.09
FR	METEOR	1	0.04	0.03	0.14	1.78	0.07	0.11	0.03
FR	METEOR	2	0.09	0.06	0.23	1.16	0.15	0.18	0.08
FR	DESMOS	1			0.07	1.46	0.03	0.05	
FR	DESMOS	3			0.09	1.61	0.04	0.08	
FR	Naive	Any	0.01	0.01	0.08	1.72	0.03	0.09	0.01
UK	LINK(a)	1	0.01	0.01	0.02	0.01	1.24	0.03	0.03
UK	LINK(a)	2	0.04	0.03	0.03	0.02	1.69	0.06	0.06
UK	LINK(a)	3	0.05	0.03	0.04	0.02	1.51	0.08	0.05
UK	LINK(b)	1	0.02	0.03	0.08	0.03	1.07	0.08	0.05
UK	LINK(b)	2	0.04	0.05	0.11	0.04	1.14	0.11	0.07
UK	LINK(b)	3	0.06	0.05	0.17	0.05	1.16	0.13	0.08
UK	INTERLINK	2	0.03	0.04	0.11	0.09	1.16	0.09	0.07
UK	INTERLINK	3	0.06	0.08	0.23	0.19	1.43	0.19	0.12
UK	EPA	1	0.01	0.03	0.08	0.10	1.31	0.05	0.04
UK	EPA	2	0.02	0.09	0.23	0.30	0.78	0.15	0.11
UK	EPA	3	0.01	0.14	0.26	0.38	0.65	0.22	0.15
UK	METEOR	1	0.04	0.03	0.07	0.06	1.55	0.05	0.08
UK	METEOR	2	0.11	0.07	0.15	0.12	1.23	0.11	0.16
UK	DESMOS	1			0.02	0.02	1.19	0.02	
UK	DESMOS	3			0.04	0.03	1.29	0.04	
UK	Naive	Any	0.01	0.01	0.03	0.03	1.57	0.03	0.04
UK	MCM	1	0.05	0.01	0.02		1.15		0.02
UK	MCM	2	0.07	0.03	0.03		1.20		0.03
UK	MCM	3	0.03	0.03	0.03		1.15		0.02

Table 3.1 (continued)

Income shock in	Model	Simulation year[b]	US	JA	GE	FR	UK	IT	CA
IT	LINK(a)	1	0.01	0.01	0.02	0.02	0.03	1.30	0.02
IT	LINK(a)	2	0.03	0.02	0.03	0.03	0.06	1.51	0.02
IT	LINK(a)	3	0.05	0 03	0.05	0.04	0.08	1.80	0.03
IT	LINK(b)	1	0.01	0.02	0.07	0.03	0.02	1.61	0.02
IT	LINK(b)	2	0.04	0.05	0.16	0.06	0.06	1.83	0.05
IT	LINK(b)	3	0.06	0.05	0.20	0.06	0.06	1.94	0.05
IT	INTERLINK	2	0.02	0.02	0.08	0.08	0.05	1.16	0.02
IT	INTERLINK	3	0.04	0.04	0.18	0.16	0.11	1.54	0.05
IT	EPA	1	0.02	0.02	0.14	0.19	0.09	1.18	0.03
IT	EPA	2	−0.02	0.08	0.30	0.43	0.15	1.39	0.08
IT	EPA	3	0.00	0.12	0.34	0.53	0.17	1.68	0.12
IT	DESMOS	1			0.05	0.04	0.03	1.69	
IT	DESMOS	3			0.09	0.08	0.05	2.37	
IT	Naive	Any	0.01	0.00	0.05	0.06	0.02	1.70	0.01
CA	LINK(a)	1	0.08	0.02	0.02	0.01	0.05	0.03	1.15
CA	LINK(a)	2	0.12	0.05	0.03	0.01	0.09	0.05	1.15
CA	LINK(a)	3	0.13	0.04	0.03	0.01	0.08	0.06	0.79
CA	LINK(b)	1	0.02	0.01	0.01	0.00	0.01	0.01	1.38
CA	LINK(b)	2	0.04	0.01	0.02	0.00	0.01	0.02	1.36
CA	LINK(b)	3	0.05	0.01	0.02	0.01	0.01	0.02	1.37
CA	INTERLINK	2	0.05	0.01	0.02	0.01	0.03	0.02	1.27
CA	INTERLINK	3	0.07	0.03	0.04	0.03	0.05	0.03	1.49
CA	EPA	1	0.02	0.01	0.01	0.01	0.02	0.01	1.52
CA	EPA	2	0.06	0.06	0.06	0.06	0.07	0.05	1.97
CA	EPA	3	0.09	0.11	0.11	0.12	0.09	0.07	1.84
CA	RDX2-MPS	2	−0.04						0.89
CA	RDX2-MPS	4	−0.09						0.80
CA	Naive	Any	0.05	0.01	0.01	0.00	0.02	0.01	1.50
CA	MCM	1	0.12	0.02	0.02		0.00		1.04
CA	MCM	2	0.17	0.03	0.03		−0.01		1.00
CA	MCM	3	0.12	0.01	0.03		−0.02		1.00

[a]Sources for the results are as follows: for METEOR and Naive, Deardorff and Stern (1979); for LINK(a), Hickman (1974); for LINK(b), Filatov, Hickman and Klein (1982); for RDX2-MPS, Helliwell (1974); for DESMOS, Waelbroeck and Dramais (1974); for Fair, Fair (1982); for COMET, Barten et al. (1976); for INTERLINK, OECD (1980); for EPA, Amano, et al. (1982). The MCM results were produced for this survey.
[b]Simulation period for LINK(a) was 1973–75; for LINK(b) 1979–82; for DESMOS, 1970–74; for COMET, 1973–80; for RDX2-MPS, 1963–70; for MCM, 1975–78; for Fair, 1976I–77IV; for INTERLINK, 1978–80; for EPA, 1974–77.

newer version of LINK, the EPA World Econometric model, INTERLINK, the Fair model, and the MCM model. The expenditure shock is generally a bond-financed increase in government spending equal to 1 percent of GNP, although there is an implicit combination of bond and money finance employed in those cases where the interest rate is held fixed.

Each of the seven panels of Table 3.1 shows the results for all countries of an expenditure increase in one of the countries. To find the own-country multipliers for Germany, for example, look in the GE column (where the effects on Germany are shown) of the third panel (where the effects of the German fiscal policy are shown). This method of presentation makes it very easy to compare results from the different models. Anywhere from one to three years of dynamic multipliers are reported for each of the models.

The OECD results reflect accelerator effects but no changes in prices, interest rates, or exchange rates. All of the other models have endogenous prices, although the results reported in the table are all (except for MCM) obtained from fixed-exchange-rate versions of the respective models. In most of the models, the assumed monetary policy is an unchanged interest rate. The money supply is therefore altered by enough to keep the interest rate constant, implying that the increase in government expenditure, and any induced changes in the stock of foreign exchange reserves, is financed by some mix of money, debt, and induced taxes.

The assumed monetary policy differs from model to model in Project LINK, but in general involves unchanged interest rates (and hence some degree of monetary expansion) in response to increases in government expenditure. In the Japanese EPA world model, the official discount rate is the key monetary policy variable in each model, and these interest rates are held constant in the fiscal policy experiments.

The MCM results involve a flexible exchange rate and generally fixed money supplies. The results for Canada and the United States are therefore more comparable to the RDX2-MPS results in the top panel of Table 3.5 than to the fixed-exchange-rate results shown elsewhere in Table 3.1. The U.K. model used in MCM has an interest-rate reaction function instead of a fixed money supply. The U.K. interest rate rises with the Canadian rate, and the resulting negative effects on GNP outweigh the positive effects from the U.K. share of induced Canadian imports.

The EPA and INTERLINK results are useful for giving some idea of the feedback effects running from the indirectly affected countries back to the country initiating the policy. The evidence on this is obtained by comparing own-country multipliers from unlinked and fully linked fiscal policy simulations. The INTER-LINK model in its 1980 form is likely to provide relatively high estimates of these feedbacks, since it has a complete trade matrix, a fairly complete set of country models, and has no monetary or price effects, no exchange rate flexibility, and no supply constraints to limit the passing of aggregate demand among the trading partners.

Table 3.2 shows the ratios of the linked to the unlinked fiscal multipliers for both the OECD and EPA models. The ratio rises with the size of the country, with the degree of its openness to trade, and with the ratio of other-country to own-country multipliers. The last factor is more likely to vary with the structure of the country models. Both the OECD and the EPA results show linked multipliers to be generally 5–15 percent higher than the unlinked multipliers for the five largest OECD economies. The linked and unlinked multipliers are almost the same for Canada, reflecting its relatively small size. The EPA results for Italy, and most of the other intercountry differences reveal the importance of model structure in determining the results. The very large effects of linkage on the Italian multiplier and on the second-year U.K. multiplier in the EPA results appear to be a consequence of a very low own-country multiplier coupled with fairly high multipliers in the EPA models of the main trading partners.

Tables 3.3–3.5 help to show the effects of alternative exchange rate and monetary policies. Table 3.3 shows the effects of exchange rate flexibility in the EPA model by reporting the ratio of the flexible-exchange-rate to the fixed-exchange-rate own-country and cross-country multipliers. With key interest rates held fixed, as in the EPA simulations in Tables 3.3 and 3.4, and in one set of RDX2-MPS results in Table 3.5, an expansion of government spending leads to an induced trade deficit, a loss of foreign exchange reserves under fixed exchange rates, and a depreciation of the currency under flexible exchange rates. (The tabulated exchange rate impacts refer to bilateral exchange rates, in units of currency per U.S. dollar, except for the U.S. rate, which is an effective rate.) The depreciation of the domestic currency typically increases the size of the own-country multiplier and lowers the cross-country multipliers. The domestic price effects of the fiscal policy are greater under flexible rates than under fixed exchange rates, given a monetary policy that holds key interest rates constant. As shown by the EPA results in Table 3.4, the effects on foreign inflation (still assuming fixed interest rates) are substantially greater under fixed than under flexible exchange rates.

The chief exception to these generalizations is provided by the United States, but only in the current version of the EPA model [Amano et al. (1982)]. In this case, expansionary fiscal policy, even with unchanged U.S. interest rates, leads to

Table 3.2
Ratio of linked to unlinked government spending multipliers[a]

Country	OECD		EPA	
	1st year	2nd year	1st year	2nd year
US	1.05	1.08	1.02	1.08
JA	1.01	1.04	1.12	1.13
GE	1.11	1.20	1.05	1.10
FR	1.07	1.12	1.01	1.03
UK	1.06	1 12	1.03	1.40
IT	1.05	1.08	1.26	1.70
CA	1.01	1.01	1.00	1.00

[a] Calculated from data in OECD (1980), and Amano et al. (1982).

a strengthening of the U.S. dollar, which then increases the expansionary effects on other countries. This result was not evident in the earlier EPA trilateral linkage results [Amano et al. (1981)]; it appears to be a consequence of an implausibly large induced devaluation of the DM, which in turn appears to be due to an implausibly large outflow of capital from Germany.

When countries hold their money supplies rather than their interest rates fixed, the effect of exchange rate flexibility is rather different, as shown by comparing

Table 3.3

Effect of endogenizing exchange rates in the EPA World Econometric Model.[a] Displayed are the ratios of the fiscal multiplier with exchange rates endogenous to the multiplier when the exchange rate is exogenous. Actual values of the multipliers with exogenous exchange rates are given in Table 3.1. Impacts on prices and exchange rates are given in Table 3.4.

Increase in expenditure in	Year	Multiplier ratio for						
		US	JA	GE	FR	UK	IT	CA
US	1974	1.016	1.000	4.000	1.000	1.225	1.197	0.842
US	1975	1.042	0.964	4.102	0.952	1.195	1.689	0.882
US	1976	1.063	0.879	5.444	2.030	1.111	1.346	0.807
US	1977	1.135	0.902	6.361	3.165	1.364	1.374	1.019
JA	1974	0.474	0.987	0.757	1.000	1.000	1.474	1.000
JA	1975	0.474	1.013	0.504	0.920	0.874	1.000	0.919
JA	1976	−0.333	1.084	0.312	0.944	0.882	1.000	0.722
JA	1977	Small	1.198	0.216	0.721	1.050	0.847	0.469
GE	1974	Small	1.000	0.923	0.927	0.937	1.106	1.216
GE	1975	−1.467	0.789	1.139	0.762	0.781	0.964	0.874
GE	1976	Large	0.613	1.584	0.773	0.952	1.150	0.707
GE	1977	−2.500	0.513	2.485	0.778	1.968	1.405	0.682
FR	1974	1.000	1.000	0.373	1.014	1.000	0.712	1.000
FR	1975	2.941	0.680	0.357	1.083	0.919	0.953	0.680
FR	1976	1.692	0.667	0.378	1.083	0.771	0.882	0.805
FR	1977	2.056	0.458	0.315	1.157	0.626	0.667	0.696
UK	1974	1.100	1.032	0.631	0.884	1.024	1.189	1.000
UK	1975	0.476	0.667	0.319	0.725	1.381	0.935	0.726
UK	1976	2.000	0.462	0.292	0.587	1.475	0.900	0.214
UK	1977	3.095	0.436	0.502	0.421	0.926	1.089	0.212
IT	1974	1.000	1.000	0.496	0.729	0.800	1.130	1.000
IT	1975	1.000	0.602	0.332	0.614	0.779	1.215	0.795
IT	1976	Large	0.575	0.350	0.581	0.702	1.173	0.575
IT	1977	Large	0.449	0.295	0.507	0.817	1.257	0.504
CA	1974	1.000	1.000	1.000	1.000	0.500	1.000	1.030
CA	1975	1.386	0.596	0.596	0.596	0.838	0.756	1.109
CA	1976	1.000	0.443	0.670	0.602	0.711	0.831	1.321
CA	1977	1.134	0.276	1.000	0.545	0.381	0.505	1.740

[a]From Amano et al. (1982). See footnote to Table 3.4.

Table 3.4

Impact of increased autonomous expenditure in the Japanese EPA World Economic Model.[a] Impacts are presented[b] as percent difference from control for a 1 percent increase in expenditure

Increase in expenditure in	Year	Impact on absorption price in						
		US	JA	GE	FR	UK	IT	CA
		Endogenous exchange rates						
US	1974	0.024	0.061	0.024	0.024	0.085	0.085	0.024
US	1975	−0.098	0.245	0.257	−0.000	0.527	0.747	0.208
US	1976	−0.116	0.541	0.812	0.606	0.877	1.676	0.593
US	1977	0.121	1.172	1.751	1.131	0.391	3.341	0.943
JA	1974	0.019	−0.065	0.000	−0.000	0.019	0.019	0.009
JA	1975	0.057	0.085	0.009	−0.019	0.132	0.066	0.057
JA	1976	0.070	0.609	0.010	−0.030	0.220	0.040	0.110
JA	1977	0.032	1.710	0.011	−0.053	0.095	0.021	0.116
GE	1974	0.037	0.007	0.060	−0.060	0.060	0.037	0.022
GE	1975	0.067	−0.097	0.425	−0.231	0.209	0.052	0.060
GE	1976	0.084	−0.353	1.089	−0.261	0.115	0.353	0.092
GE	1977	0.080	−0.689	1.868	−0.240	−0.248	0.890	0.088
FR	1974	−0.008	−0.008	−0.000	−0.134	0.008	−0.034	−0.008
FR	1975	−0.008	−0.034	−0.017	−0.252	0.017	−0.008	−0.008
FR	1976	0.026	−0.052	−0.026	−0.428	0.035	0.122	0.026
FR	1977	0.037	−0.147	−0.028	−0.111	−0.000	0.046	0.046
UK	1974	0.021	−0.000	0.000	−0.032	0.368	0.032	0.011
UK	1975	0.021	−0.072	−0.000	−0.113	1.471	0.021	0.021
UK	1976	−0.022	−0.209	−0.022	−0.110	3.824	0.044	0.022
UK	1977	0.000	−0.258	−0.032	−0.043	6.794	0.333	0.022
IT	1974	0.017	−0.000	−0.000	−0.085	0.017	0.734	0.000
IT	1975	0.016	−0.050	−0.016	−0.149	0.066	2.116	0.017
IT	1976	0.034	−0.154	−0.034	−0.120	0.051	3.498	0.034
IT	1977	0.035	−0.278	−0.052	−0.122	0.000	4.814	0.035
CA	1974	−0.011	−0.000	0.000	−0.000	0.000	0.000	0.528
CA	1975	0.000	−0.011	0.000	−0.011	0.023	0.045	1.662
CA	1976	0.023	−0.035	0.024	0.000	0.083	0.106	2.842
CA	1977	0.012	−0.085	0.049	0.012	0.085	0.146	3.994
		Exogenous exchange rates						
US	1974	0.073	0.012	0.000	−0.000	0.049	0.024	0.109
US	1975	0.000	0.037	0.037	−0.025	0.319	0.061	0.417
US	1976	0.206	0.103	0.166	−0.064	0.748	0.103	0.864
US	1977	0.795	0.148	0.216	−0.054	1.266	0.175	1.320
JA	1974	0.009	0.084	0.000	0.000	0.009	0.009	0.009
JA	1975	0.047	0.236	0.019	−0.000	0.094	0.047	0.076
JA	1976	0.070	0.120	0.060	−0.010	0.240	0.070	0.160
JA	1977	0.084	−0.275	0.095	−0.021	0.370	0.063	0.211
GE	1974	0.015	0.015	0.082	−0.015	0.037	0.030	0.015
GE	1975	0.052	0.045	0.462	−0.082	0.223	0.097	0.074
GE	1976	0.100	0.084	0.889	−0.130	0.491	0.138	0.169
GE	1977	0.120	0.112	1.138	−0.088	0.705	0.153	0.248
FR	1974	0.000	0.000	0.000	−0.243	0.008	−0.000	0.000
FR	1975	0.017	0.008	0.025	−0.562	0.092	0.000	0.017
FR	1976	0.035	0.026	0.079	−0.586	0.245	0.017	0.061

Table 3.4 (continued)

Increase in expenditure in	Year	Impact on absorption price in						
		US	JA	GE	FR	UK	IT	CA
FR	1977	0.046	0.034	0.138	−0.332	0.359	0.018	0.101
UK	1974	0.011	0.011	0.000	−0.011	0.378	0.011	0.011
UK	1975	0.031	0.021	0.031	−0.041	1.029	0.041	0.062
UK	1976	0.055	0.055	0.088	−0.066	1.278	0.055	0.132
UK	1977	0.075	0.065	0.129	−0.043	1.688	0.065	0.172
IT	1974	0.017	0.017	0.000	−0.017	0.017	0.085	0.017
IT	1975	0.033	0.033	0.050	−0.066	0.116	0.182	0.050
IT	1976	0.051	0.051	0.120	−0.086	0.240	0.326	0.103
IT	1977	0.070	0.070	0.174	−0.070	0.365	0.556	0.156
CA	1974	0.011	0.000	0.000	0.000	0.011	0.000	0.404
CA	1975	0.045	0.023	0.011	0.000	0.057	0.034	1.243
CA	1976	0.094	0.047	0.035	−0.000	0.142	0.059	1.757
CA	1977	0.122	0.061	0.061	−0.000	0.244	0.073	1.863

Increase in expenditure in	Year	Impact on endogenous exchange rate in						
		US	JA	GE	FR	UK	IT	CA
US	1974	−0.776	0.412	2.596	0.898	0.946	0.995	−0.340
US	1975	−1.997	1.176	6.960	1.703	1.715	4.607	−0.417
US	1976	−5.620	2.655	15.636	12.684	0.825	10.389	1.353
US	1977	−8.998	6.021	29.755	17.390	−0.687	18.993	0.674
JA	1974	0.205	−0.626	−0.168	−0.093	0.065	0.000	−0.075
JA	1975	0.274	−0.245	−0.557	−0.330	−0.057	−0.085	−0.142
JA	1976	−0.359	2.805	−0.399	−0.190	−0.699	−0.190	−0.120
JA	1977	−1.710	8.573	0.348	−0.021	−0.940	0.053	−0.148
GE	1974	0.328	−0.112	−0.887	−0.813	0.007	−0.224	−0.052
GE	1975	−0.037	−0.700	2.287	−1.281	−0.655	−0.074	−0.142
GE	1976	−0.598	−1.633	6.387	−0.337	−2.063	1.809	−0.153
GE	1977	−1.339	−2.389	10.525	0.128	−1.683	4.361	−0.200
FR	1974	−0.126	−0.017	−0.160	1.528	−0.000	0.025	−0.025
FR	1975	−0.151	−0.084	−0.386	2.717	−0.361	0.403	−0.034
FR	1976	0.262	−0.280	−0.787	0.723	−0.691	0.411	−0.026
FR	1977	0.046	−0.617	−0.166	1.814	−0.507	0.322	−0.018
UK	1974	0.147	−0.074	−0.347	−0.378	0.126	−0.032	−0.074
UK	1975	−0.422	−0.391	−0.689	−0.535	5.567	0.021	−0.123
UK	1976	−1.752	−0.771	−0.154	0.231	15.186	0.683	−0.066
UK	1977	−1.290	−0.774	−0.172	0.151	11.105	1.398	−0.043
IT	1974	0.222	−0.051	−0.495	−0.632	−0.051	2.835	−0.051
IT	1975	0.397	−0.281	−0.942	−0.512	−0.248	7.620	−0.083
IT	1976	0.429	−0.669	−0.840	0.000	−0.583	10.718	−0.069
IT	1977	0.556	−1.043	−0.904	−0.348	−0.382	13.364	−0.104
CA	1974	−0.326	−0.011	0.011	−0.011	0.000	0.011	0.943
CA	1975	−0.746	−0.079	0.023	−0.045	0.000	0.147	2.238
CA	1976	−1.415	−0.259	0.142	0.130	−0.047	0.318	4.328
CA	1977	−2.484	−0.390	0.560	0.280	−0.134	0.499	7.330

[a]Calculated from data in Amano et al. (1982).
[b]Actual shocks were a sustained increase in real government non-wage expenditure in the U.S. of $10 billion, a sustained increase in real government expenditure in West Germany of 10 billion DM, a sustained increase in real government gross fixed investment in Japan of 1 trillion yen, an increase in the U.K. of general gross fixed capital formation by 1 billion pounds, increases in Italy of government expenditure and the constant term of the fixed investment equation by 700 billion lire, and an increase in Canada of government fixed investment by $1 billion

Table 3.5

Impact of fiscal policy in linked RDX2-MPS system.[a] Sustained cut equal to 1 percent of 1963 GNP. Impacts given as percent difference from control. Shock starts in 1963

Decreased expenditure in	Year	Impact on GNP[b] in		Impact on price of GNP in		Impact on short interest rate[c] in		Impact on exchange rate
		US	CA	US	CA	US	CA	
		Flexible exchange rate, fixed money supplies						
US	1964	1.97	−0.16	−0.21	0.01	−0.29	−0.02	−0.37
US	1966	0.88	0.22	−1.08	−0.20	−0.32	−0.03	−0.35
CA	1964	−0.06	0.83	−0.00	−0.61	−0.01	−0.55	1.23
CA	1966	−0.10	0.58	−0.04	−1.06	−0.02	−0.60	1.27

Decreased expenditure in	Year	Impact on GNP in		Impact on price of GNP in		Impact on short interest rate in		
		US	CA	US	CA	US	CA	
		Fixed exchange rate, fixed money supplies						
US	1964	2.03	−0.15	−0.21	0.02	−0.29	−0.02	
US	1966	0.93	0.28	−1.08	−0.11	−0.32	−0.01	
CA	1964	−0.04	0.89	0.00	−0.66	−0.01	−0.52	
CA	1966	−0.09	0.80	−0.02	−1.37	−0.02	−0.69	

Decreased expenditure in	Year	Impact on GNP in		Impact on price of GNP in		Impact on money supply (M1) in		Impact on exchange rate
		US	CA	US	CA	US	CA	
		Flexible exchange rate, fixed short-term interest rates						
US	1964	2.47	−0.27	−0.21	−0.00	−1.62	−0.18	0.05
US	1966	2.43	−0.11	−1.28	−0.19	−2.70	−0.31	0.20
CA	1964	−0.13	2.02	−0.00	−0.99	−0.07	−2.99	−0.31
CA	1966	−0.16	2.69	−0.07	−2.00	−0.16	−4.47	−0.88

[a] From Helliwell (1974, pp. 259–261) and Helliwell and McRae (1977, pp. 174–175).
[b] Percent of 1963 GNP
[c] Percentage points.

the various cases in Table 3.5. If the domestic balance of payments moves into incipient surplus, leading to an appreciation of the domestic currency, the domestic output effects of an expansive fiscal policy will generally be smaller, and the foreign effects larger, under flexible exchange rates. In terms of the familiar IS–LM diagram with a balance-of-payments or exchange-rate equilibrium curve added, this will happen if the BP curve is flatter than the LM curve. The RDX2-MPS results shown in Table 3.5 reveal that this condition is met in the Canadian–United States case, so that fiscal contraction weakens (and fiscal expansion strengthens) the domestic currency under flexible exchange rates. Thus exchange-rate flexibility slightly reduces the domestic GNP effects, and increases the foreign effects, of changes in bond-financed government expenditure under flexible exchange rates. This result is what follows if money supplies are held equal to their control values in both countries, and reverses the effects of exchange rate flexibility derived from the case where nominal interest rates are pegged while the fiscal shock takes place.

Having emphasized that the international transmission of fiscal shocks depends heavily on the nature of the accompanying monetary and exchange market policies, we turn now to consider the available evidence on the international effects of monetary changes on their own.

4. Transmission of monetary policy

Many of the linkage models primarily emphasize trade linkages and have not paid equivalent attention to the mechanisms whereby monetary impulses are transmitted. The EPA model is one that does, and Table 4.1 shows its own-country and cross-country effects of separate increases in the official discount rates of each of the seven major OECD countries. For all of these countries except the United States, flexible exchange rates lead to greater negative effects of the contractionary monetary policy on own GNP, and lesser (and frequently positive) effects on others' GNP, compared to the situation with fixed exchange rates. Furthermore, the decrease in own-country effects for the United States is very small. The increase in own-country GNP effects among the other countries tends to be greater for the more open economies, although the pattern is not very clear. In all cases, the changes in the cross-country effects are fairly small in absolute terms, but large relative to their values under fixed exchange rates.

The RDX2-MPS results support the EPA finding that the effects of exchange rate flexibility on the domestic impacts of monetary policy are much greater for the more open economies. For example, after two years of tighter monetary policy in Canada, sufficient to appreciate the Canadian dollar by 3 percent, the real output effects are two and a half times as great under flexible exchange rates as under the Bretton Woods system [Helliwell and Maxwell (1974, p. 95)]. The

Table 4.1

Impact of a one percentage point increase in discount rate in the Japanese EPA World Economic Model.[a] Impacts are presented as per cent difference from control solution.

Increase in interest rate in	Year	Impact on GNP in						
		US	JA	GE	FR	UK	IT	CA
		Endogenous exchange rates						
US	1974	−0.36	−0.03	0.24	−0.02	−0.01	−0.01	−0.13
US	1975	−0.68	−0.10	0.22	−0.11	−0.15	−0.00	−0.38
US	1976	−0.51	−0.14	0.06	−0.04	−0.17	−0.14	−0.43
US	1977	−0.14	−0.13	−0.15	−0.12	−0.06	−0.21	−0.40
JA	1974	0.01	−0.08	0.01	0.00	−0.01	0.01	0.01
JA	1975	0.01	−0.20	0.02	0.02	−0.01	0.01	0.02
JA	1976	0.01	−0.31	0.03	0.03	−0.01	0.02	0.03
JA	1977	0.02	−0.39	0.04	0.06	−0.01	0.03	0.05
GE	1974	−0.00	0.00	−0.54	−0.11	−0.03	−0.02	0.01
GE	1975	−0.03	−0.04	−1.29	−0.42	−0.22	−0.22	−0.03
GE	1976	−0.04	−0.09	−2.01	−0.77	−0.30	−0.42	−0.07
GE	1977	−0.05	−0.11	−2.31	−0.72	−0.40	−0.61	−0.08
FR	1974	−0.00	0.00	0.01	−0.21	−0.01	0.01	0.01
FR	1975	−0.01	−0.00	−0.01	−0.48	−0.03	−0.02	0.00
FR	1976	−0.01	0.01	0.01	−0.69	−0.03	−0.01	0.01
FR	1977	0.00	−0.01	−0.01	−0.52	−0.03	−0.03	0.01
UK	1974	0.01	0.01	0.02	0.01	−0.14	0.03	0.01
UK	1975	0.00	0.01	0.01	0.02	−0.08	0.01	0.02
UK	1976	0.01	0.02	0.02	0.05	0.08	0.00	0.04
UK	1977	0.03	0.01	0.02	0.05	−0.07	0.03	0.04
IT	1974	−0.01	0.00	0.01	0.01	−0.00	−0.16	0.00
IT	1975	−0.03	0.01	−0.00	0.03	−0.02	−0.41	0.01
IT	1976	−0.05	0.01	−0.02	0.04	−0.03	−0.40	0.01
IT	1977	−0.05	−0.01	−0.02.	0.03	−0.02	−0.24	0.02
CA	1974	0.00	0.00	0.00	0.00	0.00	0.00	0.00
CA	1975	0.01	0.00	0.01	0.00	0.00	0.01	−0.05
CA	1976	−0.00	0.01	0.02	0.01	0.01	0.02	−0.49
CA	1977	0.01	0.01	0.02	0.01	−0.01	0.01	−0.87
		Exogenous exchange rates						
US	1974	−0.39	−0.03	−0.02	−0.02	−0.06	−0.02	−0.09
US	1975	−0.75	−0.11	−0.07	−0.09	−0.19	−0.06	−0.40
US	1976	−0.60	−0.16	−0.11	−0.13	−0.17	−0.09	−0.37
US	1977	−0.20	−0.17	−0.10	−0.11	−0.09	−0.10	−0.33
JA	1974	0.01	−0.04	−0.00	−0.00	−0.00	−0.00	0.00
JA	1975	0.02	−0.12	−0.01	−0.01	−0.01	−0.00	−0.00
JA	1976	0.02	−0.19	−0.01	−0.01	−0.01	−0.01	−0.00
JA	1977	0.02	−0.24	−0.01	−0.01	−0.02	−0.01	−0.01
GE	1974	0.01	−0.01	−0.27	−0.11	−0.03	−0.03	−0.01
GE	1975	0.02	−0.05	−0.81	−0.47	−0.16	−0.19	−0.04
GE	1976	0.04	−0.12	−1.14	−0.78	−0.25	−0.36	−0.09
GE	1977	0.05	−0.18	−1.14	−0.76	−0.26	−0.46	−0.12
FR	1974	0.01	−0.00	−0.01	−0.16	−0.01	−0.01	0.00

Table 4.1 (continued)

Increase in interest rate in	Year	Impact on GNP in						
		US	JA	GE	FR	UK	IT	CA
FR	1975	0.01	−0.01	−0.03	−0.41	−0.02	−0.02	−0.00
FR	1976	0.02	−0.01	−0.05	−0.52	−0.04	−0.04	−0.01
FR	1977	0.02	−0.02	−0.05	−0.44	−0.04	−0.05	−0.01
UK	1974	0.01	0.00	−0.00	−0.00	−0.06	−0.00	0.00
UK	1975	0.02	−0.00	−0.01	−0.02	−0.04	−0.01	0.00
UK	1976	0.03	−0.00	−0.01	−0.01	0.03	−0.01	0.01
UK	1977	0.03	0.00	0.00	−0.00	−0.03	−0.00	0.02
IT	1974	−0.00	−0.00	−0.01	−0.01	−0.01	−0.06	−0.00
IT	1975	−0.00	−0.01	−0.04	−0.05	−0.02	−0.18	−0.01
IT	1976	−0.00	−0.02	−0.06	−0.08	−0.03	−0.24	−0.02
IT	1977	−0.00	−0.02	−0.06	−0.08	−0.03	−0.14	−0.02
CA	1974	0.00	0.00	0.00	0.00	0.00	0.00	0.00
CA	1975	0.00	0.00	−0.00	−0.00	−0.00	0.00	−0.01
CA	1976	0.01	−0.01	−0.01	−0.01	−0.01	−0.01	−0.45
CA	1977	0.01	−0.02	−0.02	−0.02	−0.02	−0.02	−0.35

Increase in interest rate in	Year	Impact on absorption price in						
		US	JA	GE	FR	UK	IT	CA
		Endogenous exchange rates						
US	1974	−0.08	0.13	0.04	0.05	0.01	0.12	−0.02
US	1975	−0.12	0.38	0.18	0.04	0.06	0.55	−0.16
US	1976	−0.31	0.61	0.28	0.18	−0.09	0.54	−0.37
US	1977	−0.47	0.84	0.26	0.01	−0.29	0.39	−0.48
JA	1974	0.01	−0.28	0.00	0.01	0.01	0.01	0.01
JA	1975	0.02	−0.76	0.00	0.01	0.03	0.02	0.01
JA	1976	0.03	−1.27	−0.00	0.01	0.08	0.01	0.02
JA	1977	0.04	−1.74	−0.01	0.02	0.12	0.00	0.02
GE	1974	0.03	0.02	−0.05	0.01	0.03	0.02	0.02
GE	1975	0.02	0.02	−0.39	0.12	0.05	−0.13	0.02
GE	1976	0.03	0.08	−0.79	0.18	0.08	−0.25	0.01
GE	1977	0.06	0.23	−1.31	0.31	0.25	−0.57	0.00
FR	1974	0.01	0.01	0.00	−0.09	0.01	0.03	0.01
FR	1975	0.01	−0.01	0.01	−0.04	0.03	−0.03	0.01
FR	1976	0.03	−0.01	0.01	−0.11	0.04	0.00	0.02
FR	1977	0.04	−0.02	0.01	−0.01	0.07	−0.07	0.03
UK	1974	0.02	0.01	0.00	0.01	−0.13	0.08	0.01
UK	1975	0.03	−0.00	0.01	0.02	−0.70	0.12	0.03
UK	1976	0.04	−0.05	0.01	0.01	−1.21	0.06	0.03
UK	1977	0.03	−0.10	0.01	−0.01	−1.33	0.05	0.04
IT	1974	0.01	0.01	0.00	0.01	0.01	−0.36	0.01
IT	1975	0.02	0.02	0.01	0.03	0.04	−1.26	0.02
IT	1976	0.05	−0.01	0.01	0.02	0.08	−1.89	0.04
IT	1977	0.06	−0.07	0.01	0.02	0.08	−1.91	0.04
CA	1974	0.00	0.00	0.00	0.00	0.00	0.00	0.00
CA	1975	0.01	0.00	0.00	0.00	0.00	0.01	−0.06
CA	1976	0.04	−0.01	0.00	−0.00	0.02	0.06	−0.41
CA	1977	0.03	−0.03	0.01	0.00	0.05	0.06	−0.96

Table 4.1 (continued)

Increase in expenditure in	Year	Impact on absorption price in						
		US	JA	GE	FR	UK	IT	CA
		Exogenous exchange rates						
US	1974	−0.02	−0.01	−0.00	0.00	−0.02	−0.01	−0.02
US	1975	−0.05	−0.01	−0.01	0.01	−0.10	−0.02	−0.14
US	1976	−0.22	−0.04	−0.03	0.01	−0.23	−0.05	−0.31
US	1977	−0.37	−0.06	−0.06	−0.00	−0.33	−0.08	−0.39
JA	1974	−0.00	−0.01	−0.00	−0.00	−0.00	−0.00	0.00
JA	1975	−0.00	−0.02	−0.00	−0.00	−0.00	−0.00	−0.00
JA	1976	0.00	−0.03	−0.00	0.00	−0.01	−0.01	−0.01
JA	1977	0.01	−0.04	−0.01	0.00	−0.02	−0.01	−0.01
GE	1974	−0.00	−0.00	−0.02	0.01	−0.01	−0.01	−0.00
GE	1975	−0.02	−0.02	−0.15	0.05	−0.07	−0.04	−0.02
GE	1976	−0.05	−0.04	−0.36	0.12	−0.23	−0.07	−0.07
GE	1977	−0.06	−0.06	−0.55	0.13	−0.40	−0.09	−0.12
FR	1974	0.00	−0.00	−0.00	0.01	−0.00	−0.00	0.00
FR	1975	−0.00	−0.00	−0.00	0.05	−0.01	−0.00	−0.00
FR	1976	−0.00	−0.01	−0.01	0.08	−0.03	−0.01	−0.01
FR	1977	−0.00	−0.01	−0.02	0.07	−0.05	−0.01	−0.01
UK	1974	0.00	0.00	−0.00	0.00	−0.01	−0.00	0.00
UK	1975	0.00	−0.00	−0.00	0.00	−0.05	−0.00	0.00
UK	1976	0.01	−0.00	−0.01	0.01	−0.04	−0.00	0.00
UK	1977	0.01	−0.00	−0.01	0.00	−0.04	0.00	0.01
IT	1974	−0.00	−0.00	−0.00	0.00	−0.00	−0.01	−0.00
IT	1975	−0.01	−0.00	−0.01	0.01	−0.01	−0.02	−0.01
IT	1976	−0.01	−0.01	−0.01	0.02	−0.03	−0.03	−0.01
IT	1977	−0.01	−0.01	−0.03	0.02	−0.05	−0.04	−0.02
CA	1974	0.00	0.00	0.00	0.00	0.00	0.00	0.00
CA	1975	0.00	0.00	0.00	0.00	−0.00	0.00	0.01
CA	1976	−0.01	−0.00	−0.00	−0.00	−0.01	−0.00	−0.10
CA	1977	−0.01	−0.01	−0.01	−0.00	−0.02	−0.01	−0.27

Increase in interst rate in	Year	Impact on endogenous exchange rate in						
		US	JA	GE	FR	UK	IT	CA
US	1974	−1.03	0.75	2.63	1.10	0.85	1.25	0.19
US	1975	−1.08	1.63	2.49	0.63	0.82	2.80	0.03
US	1976	−1.23	2.38	2.19	2.34	0.05	2.24	−0.06
US	1977	−0.74	2.90	0.94	0.69	0.23	0.84	−0.10
JA	1974	0.28	−1.18	−0.10	0.03	0.03	0.01	−0.01
JA	1975	0.66	−2.71	−0.22	−0.06	0.13	−0.05	−0.02
JA	1976	0.97	−4.00	−0.30	−0.03	0.20	−0.10	−0.02
JA	1977	1.31	−5.09	−0.47	−0.03	0.12	−0.15	−0.03
GE	1974	0.51	−0.02	−2.08	−0.36	0.08	−0.29	−0.00
GE	1975	0.60	0.01	−3.17	0.39	0.38	−0.80	0.06
GE	1976	1.01	0.33	−5.34	−0.33	1.28	−1.49	0.09
GE	1977	1.45	0.83	−7.79	0.56	1.19	−2.93	0.09
FR	1974	0.15	−0.01	−0.10	−1.08	0.02	−0.09	−0.00

Table 4.1 (continued)

Increase in interest rate in	Year	Impact on endogenous exchange rate in						
		US	JA	GE	FR	UK	IT	CA
FR	1975	0.08	−0.06	−0.04	−0.46	0.01	−0.22	−0.01
FR	1976	0.26	−0.12	−0.16	−1.79	0.11	−0.29	0.01
FR	1977	0.03	−0.20	0.02	−0.02	0.08	−0.34	0.02
UK	1974	0.27	−0.01	−0.11	−0.01	−1.63	0.20	−0.01
UK	1975	0.55	−0.11	−0.22	−0.06	−3.12	0.12	−0.02
UK	1976	0.54	−0.27	−0.18	−0.12	−2.76	−0.13	−0.04
UK	1977	0.30	−0.41	−0.04	0.04	−1.28	0.06	−0.05
IT	1974	0.01	0.02	−0.04	0.02	0.01	−1.64	0.00
IT	1975	0.05	−0.03	−0.19	−0.06	0.03	−5.00	−0.00
IT	1976	0.14	−0.19	−0.30	−0.23	−0.01	−5.94	−0.01
IT	1977	0.18	−0.41	−0.26	−0.10	−0.05	−4.90	−0.04
CA	1974	0.00	0.00	0.00	0.00	0.00	0.00	0.00
CA	1975	0.18	−0.00	0.01	−0.01	−0.01	0.05	−0.50
CA	1976	0.75	−0.06	−0.01	−0.03	0.08	0.20	−2.08
CA	1977	0.86	−0.12	0.08	0.04	0.03	0.18	−2.38

[a] Calculated from data in Amano et al. (1982).
[b] For the U.S., U.K., Germany and Japan, the discount rates were increased, in France, the call money rate, in Italy, the treasury bill rate. In Canada, M1 was reduced appropriately.

effects of exchange rate flexibility on the United States were not material in these experiments, in part because all of the other U.S. bilateral exchange rates were held constant.

The RDX2-MPS linkage experiments also indicated that tighter U.S. monetary policy would lower Canadian GNP much less under flexible than under fixed exchange rates [Helliwell and Maxwell (1974, p. 97)], but lower it nonetheless. This contradicts the well-known result from the Meade–Fleming–Mundell model [e.g. Mundell (1963)] that tighter monetary policy should lower GNP at home and raise it abroad. The Mundell result comes about if capital flows are responsive only to interest-rate differentials. In order to balance the capital account inflow to the tight-money home country, there has to be an offsetting current account deficit, induced by the higher value of the domestic currency, leading to a higher demand for the real output of the foreign country. The RDX2-MPS results for U.S. monetary policy (but not for Canadian monetary policy) reversed this result. The essential reason was that exchange-rate-stabilizing capital flows broke the tight link between the current account and the interest-induced capital flows, permitting there to be simultaneously a strengthening of the current account of the home country *and* interest-induced capital inflows, with the sum of these two net inflows offset by speculative outflows. The argument was made that the same exchange-rate-stabilizing speculative capital movements that are required to "look through" the widely prevalent *J*-curve effects also permit international transmission of tight-money-induced drops in GNP.

The EPA model shows some positive and some negative GNP cross-effects in response to monetary policy under flexible exchange rates. Amano et al. (1981) describes how the capital flow equations of the EPA models are equipped with exchange-rate-stabilizing features that would permit them, in principle, to have positive cross-country GNP effects. In addition, the exchange rate mechanism used in solving the models involves a considerable amount of active official exchange market intervention. This official intervention also raises the possibility of regaining the fixed-exchange-rate result, that tighter monetary policy lowers GNP both at home and abroad. It is interesting to note that even with private and official stabilizing intervention, some of the EPA results show own-country and cross-country income effects of opposite sign. This illustrates, as do the RDX2-

Table 4.2

Impacts of a coordinated 1 percent cut in interest rates as simulated by LINK[a] and the Multi-Country Model.[b] Impacts are presented as percent difference from control solution

| Model | Year | Impact on income in | | | | |
		US	JA	GE	UK	CA
LINK	1980	0.3	0.4	0.5	0.1	0.2
	1981	0.6	0.4	1.0	0.3	0.4
	1982	0.7	0.6	1.2	0.2	0.8
	1983	0.7	0.6	1.5	0.1	0.7
MCM	1975	0.2	0.2	0.2	0.1	0.1
	1976	0.7	0.5	0.5	0.2	0.5
	1977	0.6	0.6	0.7	0.2	0.7
	1978	0.4	0.6	0.6	0.1	0.7

| | | Impact on price level in | | | | |
		US	JA	GE	UK	CA
LINK	1980	0.0	0.0	0.0	0.0	0.0
	1981	−0.3	0.1	0.0	0.0	0.0
	1982	−0.3	0.3	0.1	0.1	0.2
	1983	−0.6	0.3	0.1	0.2	0.4
MCM	1975	0.0	0.0	0.0	0.0	0.0
	1976	0.0	0.1	0.1	0 0	0.1
	1977	0.0	0.1	0.2	0.1	0.4
	1978	0.1	0.2	0.4	0.2	0.6

[a]From data in Klein, Simes and Voisin (1981). Simulated shock was a 2 percent cut, so we have scaled the impacts by 0.5. Exchange rates are exogenous, and in the case of Japan and some other countries not shown, investment was shocked directly by 1 percent in the first year, 2 percent in the second and 3 percent in the last two years.

[b]From a simulation provided for this study. Exchange rates are endogenous. The shock was a monetary contraction, so we have reversed the signs of the impacts. The shock was administered through the central bank discount rate and standardized across countries to yield approximately one percentage point change in short term interest rates at the outset.

MPS results, that the transmission process need not be symmetric when countries of different size and structure are linked together.

Tables 4.2 and 4.3 show the effects of coordinated and uncoordinated monetary expansion in the LINK and MCM models. For the five countries that appear in both models, Table 4.2 shows the real income and price level consequences of initial 1 percent reductions in the key interest rates in all of the countries. The LINK and MCM results for real income are fairly similar, and both models show proportionate increases in real income that are greater than the proportionate increases in the price level for each of the first three years. However, LINK is more optimistic with respect to prices; the US Wharton model used in LINK even suggests a lower domestic price level after four years of an expansionary monetary policy starting in 1980.

Table 4.3 contrasts the effects of coordinated monetary expansion with the consequences of isolated policies. The table shows the amount of price increase per percentage point increase in output for the fourth years of isolated and coordinated monetary expansions. For Project LINK, which is operated with fixed exchange rates in these experiments, the coordination does not make much difference. For the MCM models, however, with their flexible exchange rates, the coordination avoids the currency depreciation and resulting additional inflation that would arise if a country were alone in adopting an expansionary monetary policy. Thus the coordinated expansion provides a given increase in real income with a smaller amount of induced inflation, although the effect differs substantially from one country to another.

Table 4.3

Comparison of the effects of isolated and coordinated monetary policy as simulated by LINK[a] and MCM[b]. The tabulated figures are ratios of the percent change in price level to the percent change in income in the fourth year of the shock, a measure of the inflation cost of the induced output (In no case did output decrease)

	Price/output ratio in				
	US	JA	GE	UK	CA
LINK (isolated)	−0.9	0.4	−0.0	0.1	0.5
LINK (coordinated)	−0.9	0.5	0.0	0.4	0.5
MCM (isolated)	1.0	0.3	0.9	LARGE	1.1
MCM (coordinated)	0.3	0.3	0.7	2.0	0.9

[a] Calculated from data in Klein, Simes and Voisin (1981). See notes to Table 4.2.

[b] Calculated from data in a simulation provided for this study. See notes to Table 4.2.

5. The impact of changes in world oil prices

One of the most interesting and as yet unsettled issues is how changes in world oil prices influence real output, national prices, and exchange rates throughout the world. It is an issue that almost demands the use of international linkage models, since the indirect effects coming through changes in the volume and prices of non-oil world trade are often more important for any individual country than the direct effects of higher oil prices. For example, simulations of the Bank of Japan model reported by Yomo (1982) show that a 10 percent increase in the world oil price lowers real GNP by 0.05 percent if other foreign variables are unchanged, but lowers it by 0.28 percent if the real GNP of partner countries is assumed to drop by 0.5 percent as a consequence of higher oil prices. Thus most of the likely real GNP effects (but not the price effects) flow from assumed effects on other countries. In these circumstances, it is important to obtain more information about the direct impacts on other countries, and on the transmission mechanisms between countries.

Many of the established national and multinational econometric models were designed before the price of oil changed so dramatically as to force a re-thinking of the aggregation, pricing, production, and factor utilization assumptions in econometric models. Thus, many of the linkage models are not ideally suited to depict the national effects of changes in world energy prices. They are likely to feed imperfect information back into the system of international prices, trade flows, capital movements, and exchange rates. There is a further complication at the national level, posed by the complex and diverse taxing and pricing arrangements that link world oil prices to the prices paid by final energy users in various countries. Since the prices to final users, especially of transportation fuels, are often several times as high as the price of the crude oil content, and the proportionate changes in crude oil and final energy prices are often very different, the modelling of these margins becomes very important.

At the international level, it is clearly important to work with a group of models large enough to encompass a substantial share of the output of the trading world and to close the system by realistic assumptions about the amount and nature of increased OPEC spending, as well as the likely investment pattern for OPEC current-account surpluses caused by the higher oil prices. Hooper and Tryon (1982) have reported alternative simulations of the MCM model showing that, even in their five-country-plus-OPEC model, raising OPEC's induced imports has substantial impact on the real GNP effects of the 1979–80 increase in world oil prices. For example, they estimate that raising OPEC imports by 50 percent (or US$ 50 billion) in 1982, and by similar proportions in 1979, 1980 and 1981, would have eliminated the loss of GNP in Japan due to the oil price shock and would have turned the German loss into a gain. The figures: Without the

Table 5.1

Impact of an oil price shock according to four models. Impacts are presented as percent difference from control, in the second year of the shock

10% oil price increase modelled by	Year	Impact of GNP in							Impact on price of GNP in						
		US	JA	GE	FR	UK	IT	CA	US	JA	GE	FR	UK	IT	CA
Fair[a]	1977	-0.23	0.08	-0.10	0.19	-0.14	0.10	-0.22	0.59	0.58	0.02	0.38	0.26	1.01	0.22
EPA[b]	1975	-0.64	-0.62	-0.19	-0.29	-0.47	-0.44	-0.06	0.32	2.59	.10	0.36	0.84	1.56	0.31
EPA[c]	1975	-0.66	-0.78	-0.07	-0.21	-0.49	-0.44	-0.02	0.37	1.35	0.13	0.39	0.60	0.99	0.34
MCM[d]	1980	-0.21	-0.56	-0.09		-0.18		-0.05	0.39	1.32	0.43		0.24		0.15
Eurolink[e]	1981I			-1.46	-0.17	-0.46	-0.33				0.20	0.03	1.00	-0.38	

10% oil price increase modelled by	Year	Impact on exchange rate in						
		US	JA	GE	FR	UK	IT	CA
EPA	1975	-1.20	5.08	-0.07	-0.43	1.33	1.89	0.00
MCM	1980	-0.91	2.62	0.41		-0.20		0.04

[a] Calculated from data in Fair (1982, Table 10). A 50 percent price shock was simulated, so we have scaled down Fair's impacts by 5.

[b] From Amano et al. (1982), with endogenous exchange rate.

[c] From Amano et al. (1982), with exogenous exchange rate.

[d] Calculated from data in Hooper and Tryon (1982, tables 7 to 11). Estimated historical patterns for OPEC absorption and investment. Their price shock was 100 percent of the base, so we have scaled their impacts down by 10.

[e] Simulation provided for this survey. The shock was a 25 percent price increase, so impacts have been scaled down by 2.5.

increased OPEC spending, the price shock reduces real Japanese GNP by 2.2 percent; with the extra spending, GNP is virtually unchanged. Without the spending, German GNP drops 0.5 percent; with it, GNP rises by 1.6 percent.

We have thus far been unable to develop easily comparable oil price results from the various linkage projects, and the models continue to differ importantly in coverage and in the likely accuracy and completeness of their modelling of the impacts of oil prices on the various national economies. We have nevertheless tried to draw together in Table 5.1 some of the estimates of the second-year real GNP and price effects of a hypothetical 10 percent increase in world oil prices. Since we have often had to scale results down, and to draw approximate second-year results from a longer and more complicated set of responses, we also reproduce some of the primary material in subsequent tables.

A rough summary of the results, putting greater weight on the more complete models, is that a 10 percent increase in world oil prices lowers real GNP in a typical industrial country by between 0.5 and 1 percent in the second year and increases the consumer price by somewhat more. The results pertaining to pre-1979 increases need to be scaled up somewhat to apply to the early 1980s, because the world oil price doubled between 1979 and 1981, and oil spending has become a larger share of total costs, and because most models estimate the price elasticity of the demand for crude oil to be substantially less than 1.0 in absolute value.

The Japanese EPA results in Tables 5.1 and 5.2 are especially useful in showing how exchange rate flexibility alters the nature of the transmission process.[5] In the Japanese case, the oil price increase triggers a substantial depreciation of the yen, which reduces the real GDP losses but induces much higher domestic inflation. Given the significant export dependence of the German and Japanese economies and the significant swings in their current accounts after the two oil price shocks of the 1970s, it is not surprising that the EPA linkage results for oil price increases were significantly altered (and became more stagflationary on average) when the original three-country system was expanded. Indeed, the GNP cuts in Table 5.1 are 0.1–0.4 percent deeper than those calculated with the three-country version [Amano et al. (1981)], and the price impacts are slightly greater. The current EPA trade linkage model for OPEC imports involves a 0.21 propensity to import from current increases in export revenues plus a 0.52 propensity to spend the previous period's foreign exchange reserves. Since the EPA model is quarterly, this implies a substantial re-spending of OPEC oil revenues, although apparently about one

---

[5] Table 5.1 also shows the exchange rate changes for the MCM and Fair models. However, there are no comparable results run under fixed exchange rates. McGuirk (1982) uses the International Monetary Fund's multilateral exchange rate model [MERM, Artus and McGuirk (1981)] to estimate the real exchange rate changes required to eliminate the trade imbalances caused by the OPEC price increases. The summary discussion in that volume contains an attempt to compare and reconcile the MCM and MERM results.

Table 5.2

Impact of a 10 percent oil price increase with the Japanese EPA model. The impacts are presented as percent difference from control solution

Year	US	JA	GE	FR	UK	IT	CA
			Impact on GNP in				
			Endogenous exchange rates				
1974	−0.22	−0.23	0.01	−0.09	−0.17	0.03	0.05
1975	−0.64	−0.62	−0.19	−0.29	−0.47	−0.44	−0.06
1976	−0.85	−0.69	−0.39	−0.53	−0.50	−0.85	−0.27
1977	−0.85	−0.60	−0.55	−0.54	−0.39	−1.03	−0.42
			Exogenous exchange rates				
1974	−0.23	−0.27	0.05	−0.10	−0.23	−0.03	0.07
1975	−0.66	−0.78	−0.07	−0.21	−0.49	−0.44	−0.02
1976	−0.81	−1.03	−0.22	−0.25	−0.46	−0.70	−0.16
1977	−0.79	−1.08	−0.23	−0.22	−0.43	−0.82	−0.24

Year	US	JA	GE	FR	UK	IT	CA
			Impact on absorption price in				
			Endogenous exchange rates				
1974	0.26	1.36	0.03	0.31	0.26	1.06	0.19
1975	0.32	2.59	0.10	0.36	0.84	1.56	0.31
1976	0.33	3.95	0.12	0.33	1.04	1.45	0.30
1977	0.32	5.42	0.07	0.37	1.06	1.17	0.21
			Exogenous exchange rates				
1974	0.29	1.08	0.03	0.27	0.25	0.77	0.20
1975	0.37	1.35	0.13	0.34	0.60	0.99	0.34
1976	0.38	1.30	0.18	0.41	0.63	1.09	0.37
1977	0.45	1.31	0.17	0.41	0.55	1.18	0.36

Year	US	JA	GE	FR	UK	IT	CA
			Impact on exchange rate in				
			Endogenous exchange rates				
1974	−0.53	1.41	0.21	0.54	0.81	1.51	0.01
1975	−1.20	5.08	−0.07	−0.43	1.33	1.89	0.00
1976	−1.95	9.65	−0.07	−1.20	1.10	0.32	−0.15
1977	−2.58	13.67	−0.86	−0.80	1.18	−1.11	−0.30

From Amano et al. (1982).

Table 5.3

Impacts of oil price shocks calculated by LINK.[a] Impacts[b,c] are presented as percent shock minus control over control, or, where indicated, in billions of $US.

	Impact on GDP in								Impact on price of GDP in						
Year	US	JA	GE	FR	UK	IT	CA	OECD	US	JA	GE	FR	UK	IT	CA
1978	-0.4	-2.3	-0.8	-0.6	-0.4	-0.6	0.0	$-10b	0.0	1.0	-0.3	1.6	0.4	-0.1	0.5
1979	-0.5	-4.0	-1.1	-0.9	-0.5	-0.8	-0.1	$-32b	0.0	1.1	-0.7	1.9	1.2	-0.1	0.9
1979								-0.5							
1980								-0.9							
1981								-1.4							
1982								-1.9							

	Impact on consumption price in								Impact on trade balance in							Impact on world price
Year	US	JA	GE	FR	UK	IT	CA	OECD	US	JA	GE	FR	UK	IT	CA	
1978	0.2	6.6	—	1.9	0.6	0.4	0.3	1.1	-6.7	-6.0	-1.6	-1.9	-0.2	-1.2	0.2	4.4
1979	0.2	6.0	—	2.3	1.2	0.6	0.7	1.1	-15.5	-13.0	-4.2	-4.3	0.1	-2.3	0.1	2.1
1979								0.3								1.8
1980								0.6								2.7
1981								1.1								4.4
1982								1.5								4.4

[a] The 1978–79 simulation is from Klein (1978, table 2) and the 1979–82 simulation is from Filatov, Hickman and Klein (1982, table 6).
[b] In the 1978–79 simulation, the shock is an oil price increase of $2 per barrel over control in the first year and $4 per barrel over control in the second year.
[c] In the 1979–82 simulation, the shock is an oil price increase over control of 8.5 percent in the first year, an additional 3.2 percent in the second year, an additional 6.5 percent in the third, and an additional 5.2 percent in the fourth.

Table 5.4
Impact of an oil price shock in the Fair model.[a]
Impacts are presented as percent difference from control

Year	Impact on GNP							Impact on price of GNP						
	US	JA	GE	FR	UK	IT	CA	US	JA	GE	FR	UK	IT	CA
1976II	-0.30	0.03	-0.40	0.47	-0.30	-0.24	-0.19	1.22	0.81	0.10	0.46	0.32	1.33	0.33
1977II	-1.16	0.41	-0.51	0.94	-0.71	0.51	-1.12	2.96	2.91	0.08	1.89	1.30	5.06	1.10

Year	Impact on short interest rate							Impact on exchange rate						
	US	JA	GE	FR	UK	IT	CA	US	JA	GE	FR	UK	IT	CA
1976II	0.25	1.91	-0.02	0.91	-0.01	2.44	0.44	–	1.47	-1.47	-1.69	-0.94	-0.40	-0.16
1977II	0.02	2.39	-0.21	0.79	-0.12	2.31	0.80	–	5.05	-6.30	-5.26	-5.51	-1.60	-0.71

[a]From Fair (1982, table 10). The shock is a sustained 50 percent increase in the price of exports from the oil exporting countries, beginning in 1976I.

Table 5.5
Impact of an oil price shock in the Eurolink model.[a]
Impacts are presented as percent difference from control

Year	Impact on GNP in				Impact on price of GNP in			
	GE	FR	UK	IT	GE	FR	UK	IT
1980	− 2.03	0.07	− 0.19	0.33	0.18	− 0.83	0.73	− 1.34
1981	− 3.66	− 0.43	− 1.14	− 0.83	0.49	0.08	2.50	− 0.95
1982	− 3.41	− 0.99	− 1.36	− 1.13	0.27	1.21	3.72	− 0.01
1983	− 1.75	− 0.85	− 1.20	− 1.14	0.18	2.04	4.41	0.12

Year	Impact on consumption price in				Impact on short interest rate in			
	GE	FR	UK	IT	GE	FR	UK	IT
1980	0.63	0.54	0.61	− 0.50	...	3.07	...	0.78
1981	1.35	1.64	1.80	− 0.13	...	6.13	...	0.84
1982	1.52	2.49	2.45	0.73	...	6.92	...	2.76
1983	1.66	3.18	2.83	0.86	...	8.78	...	1.84

[a]Simulation provided for this survey. In the simulation, Rest of World is exogenous, and in the shock mode, the Rest of World oil price (SITC 3) is increased by 25 percent throughout the period of the simulation.

quarter of the incremental oil revenues are invested abroad in some more permanent form.[6]

The two sets of Project LINK results reported in Table 5.3 suggest that model revisions between 1978 and 1980 have somewhat increased the GNP responses of the system to world oil prices. If we compare the 1980 responses from the 1979–85 simulation with the 1979 responses from the 1978–79 simulation, we see GNP and consumer price level responses that are about as large, although the size of the shock is much smaller – a 12 percent oil price increase relative to control in the second year of the 1979–85 simulation, compared to a 28 percent increase in the second year of the 1978–79 simulation. In the earlier simulation, despite the larger shock, eight of 13 countries had relative GDP drops that were smaller than that for the 13 LINK countries in the second year of the later simulation. If we make a linearity assumption to standardize the shocks, the second-year GDP response for the 13 countries in the later simulation is 1.75 times as big as in the earlier one, and the response of the consumption price deflation is 1.30 times as big. To better understand the reasons for these disparities, it would be useful to run comparable oil price shocks with successive versions of the LINK system, as well as with alternative linkage systems.

[6]Amano et al. (1982, p. 376). While 21 percent of oil export revenues are spend on current imports, only 56 percent ultimately goes into foreign exchange reserves. This implies that the remaining 23 percent is invested abroad in some form other than official foreign exchange reserves.

In the linkage results reported in Table 5.1, the stagflationary effects of higher oil prices tend to lead to higher nominal and lower real interest rates in most countries. Marion and Svensson (1982) emphasize that the lower real interest rates are a natural counterpart of the higher OPEC savings, and they act to partially offset the income effects of the terms-of-trade loss for countries that are net debtors as well as net oil importers.

6. Summary and implications for further research

In this section we summarize our preliminary conclusions and suggest promising directions for further empirical research.

Our review of the effects of fiscal shocks shows that it is very important to consider jointly the exchange-rate and monetary linkages. The amount of evidence available on this score is still fairly limited, as only the Japanese and RDX2-MPS results compare the international effects of fiscal shocks under fixed and flexible exchange rates, and only the latter do so under alternative monetary policy assumptions. The experiments suggest that if policy-set interest rates are held at their control values and exchange rates are fixed, uncoordinated increases in government spending will usually lead to current account deficits for the initiating country. Under flexible exchange rates, the induced current account deficits are smaller, and hence the fiscal policy's effects on GNP in other countries are likewise less. However, with exchange rates to some extent policy-determined, as in the EPA model, the fixed and flexible exchange rate results are not very different. The RDX2-MPS results with fixed money supplies show even less difference between fixed and flexible exchange rates; in the Canadian case, the fiscal policy does not induce much change in the balance of payments under fixed exchange rates, and hence little change in the exchange rate under flexible exchange rates. Other countries will differ to some extent, but in general it would not be surprising if the short-term international effects of fiscal policy turn out to be fairly similar under fixed and flexible exchange rates. Much depends, of course, on how exchange rates are modelled. The pervasiveness of *J*-curve effects among the linkage models, and the modest size of estimated long-term elasticities of substitution among exports from different countries, mean that either official intervention or exchange-rate-stabilizing private capital movements are a necessary condition for exchange market stability.

Exchange rate flexibility becomes more important when one considers the international effects of monetary policy. Even with substantial amounts of exchange-rate smoothing by official intervention or private sector capital flows, the reported international effects of monetary policy are markedly different under fixed and flexible exchange rates. This difference does not show up, of course, in the models that concentrate on trade linkage, but it does appear wherever there are capital account and exchange rate linkages. The flexible exchange rate does serve to increase the domestic income and price effects of domestic monetary policy, and it reduces the foreign effects, but only sometimes does it produce the Mundell (1963) result in which real income moves in opposite directions at home and abroad.

The available evidence on the multinational effects of changes in world oil prices is still fairly limited, and still somewhat preliminary in nature. This is in part because the induced OPEC spending and saving behavior are not well and easily modelled, and in part because the supply sides of many of the national models, especially the role of energy in the production process, are still rather rudimentary. As the models develop, they continue to show substantial stagflationary effects from higher world oil prices. Conversely, substantial drops in world oil prices can be expected to produce less inflation and more growth, although relatively few tests have been run of the symmetry of the responses of world trade, output, and inflation with respect to fluctuations in the world price of oil.

Our judgment is that many of the past and current empirical studies of macroeconomic interdependence have produced useful results. These studies have served to put likely signs on some of the uncertain theoretical propositions, and to reduce somewhat the range of uncertainty about the strength of key linkages. However, despite the sometimes heroic efforts of the researchers, and despite the assistance of a few interpretive surveys, many linkage models still have too much the reputation of black boxes. This reputation is largely unjustified for the linkage models reported here, because they are models for which the equation structures and parameter estimates are generally available. To some extent, the reputation reflects the unwillingness of those only peripherally interested in quantitative results to make the required investment in knowledge about macroeconomic facts and models. However, it is also the case that the models themselves are seldom presented in a way that makes it feasible, even for their operators, to assess the relative quantitative importance of the various channels of international linkage. Such information is in short supply, even for national models, so it is not surprising that still less is available for the linkage projects, most of which are of fairly recent origin.

Empirical studies of macroeconomic interdependence have been producing useful results for over a decade. The earliest studies were mainly of two types: large multilateral projects based mainly on linkage through trade flows and trade prices, and bilateral or few-country models with a more complete and consistent modelling of trade, capital, exchange rate, and, occasionally, migration linkages. More recently, the availability of better multi-country data sets has made possible the construction of many-country models based on consistent aggregate theoretical structures and emphasizing monetary and exchange rate linkages. At the same time, forecasting models such as Project LINK, the OECD INTERLINK, and the EEC Eurolink models have moved some way towards a complete specification of monetary and capital account linkages, and modellers have been examining and ironing out unnecessary differences among the structures of the individual country models.

The use of structural econometric models for policy analysis has been criticized for not taking explicit account of the possible effects of such policy actions on private sector expectations. To the extent that this criticism is valid, it applies as much to the international linkage models assessed here as to national econometric models. The ability of the linkage models to depict accurately the international repercussions of national policy changes depends on the policies being not much more or less predictable or exploitable than previous ones. The sensitivity of model results to changes in the formation of expectations is especially great under flexible exchange rates. Increasing attention is likely to be paid to these issues as flexible exchange rates become a more general feature of linkage models.

There has arisen a distinction, emphasized in the linkage context by Fair (1979), between small and large national models as building blocks for empirical studies of macroeconomic interdependence. From our survey of model structures and results, we conclude that the actual size of the models in question is much less important, from the point of view of the user of results, than the ease with which the properties of the models can be fully understood and described. Thus we have found it easier to interpret and assess the reliability of results from some of the larger models (e.g. those of the Japanese EPA project) than from the constellation of smaller models in our group IV projects. Of course, this is partly because some of the latter projects are at a very early stage of development and hence not very well tested, corrected, and understood.

What is needed, in our view, for all of the models, are clearer explanations of the comparative properties of the component national models, as well as a clearer analytical and empirical decomposition of the strength and nature of the links between countries. Hickman and Filatov (1982), in their decomposition of international trade multipliers, provide a useful move in this direction, but there is much more in the way of comparative macroeconomics that can usefully be done within the context of linked econometric models.[7] Indeed, this comparative analysis is probably a necessary element in understanding the reasons for many of the particular linkage results and an important aid to the design of better empirical models.

---

[7]De Bever et al. (1979) provide an example of the quantitative decomposition and comparison of model properties that we think could usefully be applied to whole sets of country models.

References

Amano, A. (1982), "Exchange rate modelling in the EPA world econometric model", prepared for International Workshop on Exchange Rates in Multi–country Econometric Models, University of Leuven, Belgium, 26–28 November 1981.

Amano, A., S. Akira and T. Sasaki (1981), "Structure and application of the EPA world econometric model", Discussion Paper No. 22, (Economic Research Institute, Japan).

Amano, A., E. Kurihara and L. Samuelson (1980), "Trade Linkage Sub-Models in the EPA World Economic Model", Economic Bulletin No. 19, (Economic Research Institute, Japan).

Amano, A., A. Maruyama and M. Yoshitomi, eds. (1981), A three-country linkage model (Economic Planning Agency, Tokyo).

Amano, A., A. Maruyama and M. Yoshitomi, eds. (1982), EPA world economic model, Vols. I and II (Economic Planning Agency, Tokyo).

Artus, J.R. and A.K. McGuirk (1981), "A revised version of the Multilateral Exchange Rate Model", I.M.F. Staff Papers, 28:275–309.

Ball, R.J., ed. (1973), The international linkage of national economic models (North-Holland, Amsterdam).

Barten, A.P., G. d'Alcantara and G.J. Carrin (1976), "COMET: A medium-term macroeconomic model for the European Economic Community", European Economic Review, 7:63–115.

Barten, A.P. and G. d'Alcantara (1977), "Models of Bilateral Trade Flows", in: H. Albach, E. Helmstadter and R. Henn, eds., Quantitative Wirtschaftsforschung. Wilhelm Krelle zum 60. Geburtstag (J.C.B. Mohr, Tubingen) 43–57.

Berner R., P. Clark, H. Howe, S. Kwack, and G. Stevens (1976), "Modeling the international influences on the U.S. economy: A multi-country approach", International Finance Discussion Papers, No. 93 (Board of Governors of the Federal Reserve System: Washington, D.C.).

Corden, W.M. and J.P. Neary (1982), "Booming sector and deindustrialisation in a small open economy", Economic Journal, 92:825–848.

Courbis, R., ed. (1981), International trade and multicountry models (Economica, Paris).

d'Alcantara, G. and A. Italianer (1981), "Bilateral trade flows in the COMET model", prepared for the LINK Conference, La Hulpe, Belgium, 30 August–4 September 1981.

Darby, M.R. (1980), "International transmission under pegged and floating exchange rates: An empirical comparison", N.B.E.R. Working Paper No. 585.

Darby, M.R., J.R. Lothian, A.E. Gandolfi, A.J. Schwartz, and A.C. Stockman (1982), "The international transmission of inflation", Vol. 1 (N.B.E.R., Cambridge, Mass.).

De Bever, L., D.K. Foot, J.F. Helliwell, G.V. Jump, T. Maxwell, J.A. Sawyer and H.E.L. Waslander (1979), "Dynamic properties of four Canadian macroeconomic models: A collaborative research project", Canadian Journal of Economics, 12:133–194.

Deardorff, A.V. and R.M. Stern (1978), "Modeling the effects of foreign prices on domestic price determination: Some econometric evidence and implications for theoretical analysis", Banca Nazionale del Lavoro Quarterly Review, 127:333–353.

Deardorff, A.V. and R.M. Stern (1979) "What have we learned from linked econometric models? A comparison of fiscal-policy simulations", Banca Nazionale del Lavoro, 130:415–432.

Dramais, A. (1981), "The DESMOS model", in: R. Courbis, ed., International trade and multicountry models (Economica, Paris) 221–234.

Fair, R.C. (1979), "On modelling the economic linkages among countries", in: R. Dornbusch and S. Fischer, eds., International economic policy, theory and evidence (The Johns Hopkins University Press, Baltimore and London) 209–245.

Fair, R.C. (1981a), "A multicountry econometric model", N.B.E.R. Working Paper No. 414R.

Fair, R.C. (1981b), "Estimated output, price, interest rate, and exchange rate linkages among countries", N.B.E.R. Working Paper No. 677.

Fair, R.C. (1981c),"Estimated effects of relative prices on trade shares", N.B.E.R. Working Paper No. 696.

Fair, R.C. (1982), "Estimated output, price, interest rate, and exchange rate linkages among countries," Journal of Political Economy, 90:507–535.

Filatov, V.B., B.G. Hickman, and L.R. Klein (1982), "Long-term simulations with the Project Link System, 1978–1985," in: B.G. Hickman, ed., Global international economic models (Proceedings of the 8th IIASA Symposium on Global Modeling).

Gana, J.L., B.G. Hickman, L.J. Lau, and L.R. Jacobson (1979), "Alternative approaches to the linkage of national econometric models," in: J.A. Sawyer, ed., Modelling the international transmission mechanism. (North-Holland, Amsterdam).

Helliwell, J.F. (1974), "Trade capital flows, and migration as channels for international transmission of stabilization policies", in: International aspects of stabilization policies, (Federal Reserve Bank, Boston) 241–278.

Helliwell, J.F. (1975), "Adjustment under fixed and flexible exchange rates", in: P.B. Kenen, ed., International trade and finance (Cambridge University Press, Cambridge) 379–410.

Helliwell, J.F. and T. Maxwell (1974), "Monetary interdependence of Canada and the United States under alternative exchange rate systems", in: R.Z. Aliber, ed., National monetary policies and the international system (University of Chicago Press, Chicago) 82–108.

Helliwell, J.F. and R. McRae (1977), "The interdependence of monetary, debt and fiscal policies in an international setting", in: R.Z. Aliber, ed., The political economy of monetary reform (The Macmillan Press Ltd., London) 157–178.

Hickman, B.G. (1974), "International transmission of economic fluctuations and inflation", in: A. Ando, R. Herring and R. Marston, eds., International aspects of stabilization policies (Federal Reserve Bank, Boston) 201–231.

Hickman, B.G. (1981), "Exchange rates in Project LINK", prepared for the International Workshop on Exchange Rates in Multicountry Econometric Models, University of Leuven, Belgium, 26–28 November 1981.

Hickman, B.G. (1982), "A cross section of global international economic models", in: B.G. Hickman, ed., Global international economic models (Proceedings of the 8th IIASA Symposium on Global Modeling).

Hickman, B.G. and V. Filatov (1982), "On a decomposition of international income multipliers", Center for Research in Economic Growth, Stanford University, Research Memoranda Series No. 250. To be published in: B. Hickman and F.G. Adams, eds., Global econometrics, essays in honor of L.R. Klein, (MIT Press, Cambridge, 1983).

Hickman, B.G. and L.J. Lau (1973), "Elasticities of Substitution and Export Demands in a World Trade Model", European Economic Review, 4:347–380.

Hickman, B.G. and S. Schleicher (1978), "The interdependence of national economies and the synchronization of economic fluctuations: Evidence from the LINK Project", Weltwirtschaftliches Archiv. 114:642–708.

Hooper, P., R.D. Haas, S.A. Symansky, and L. Steckler (1982), "Alternative approaches to general equilibrium modeling of exchange rates and capital flows: The MCM experience", paper presented at special session of Project LINK, (Bundesbank, Bonn, September 1982).

Hooper, P. and R. Tryon (1982), "Macroeconomic and exchange rate effects of an oil price shock under alternative OPEC investment scenarios", in: K. Clinton, ed., Proceedings of the Fifth Pacific Basin Central Bank Economists' Conference: Supply side Shocks, the balance of payments and monetary policy (Bank of Canada, Ottawa).

Howe, H., E. Hernandez-Cata, G. Stevens, R. Berner, P. Clark, and S.Y. Kwack (1981), "Assessing international interdependence with a multi-country model", Journal of Econometrics 15:65–92.

Italianer, A. (1982), "An evaluation of the bilateral trade flows in the COMET model", Katholieke Universiteit Leuven.

Johnson, K.N. (1978), "Balance of payments equilibrium and equilibrating exchange rates in a world econometric model", unpublished Ph.D. Dissertation, University of Pennsylvania.

Johnson, K.N. and L.R. Klein (1974), "Stability in the international economy: The LINK experience", in: A. Ando, R. Herring and R. Marston, eds., International aspects of stabilization policies (Federal Reserve Bank, Boston) 147–188.

Klein, L.R. (1978), "Disturbances to the international economy", in: After the Phillips curve: Persistence of high inflation and high unemployment (Federal Reserve Bank, Boston) 84–103.

Klein, L.R. and A. Van Peeterssen (1973) "Forecasting world trade within Project LINK", in: R.J. Ball, ed., The international linkage of national economic models (North-Holland Amsterdam).

Klein, L.R., R. Simes, and P. Voisin (1981), "Coordinated monetary policy and the world economy", Prevision et Analyse Economique, 2:75–105.

Kooyman, J. (1982), "The METEOR model", in: R. Courbis, ed., International trade and multicountry models (Economica, Paris) 235–242.

McGuirk, A.K. (1982), "The oil price increases and real exchange rate changes among industrial countries", in: K. Clinton, ed., Proceedings of the Fifth Pacific Basin Central Bank Economists' Conference: Supply side shocks, the balance of payments and monetary policy (Bank of Canada, Ottawa).

Marion, N.P. and L.E.O. Svensson (1982), "Structural differences and macroeconomic adjustment to oil price increases in a three-country model", N.B.E.R. Working Paper No. 839.

Minford, P., C. Ioannidis and S. Marwaha (1981), "Floating exchange rates in a multilateral macro model", prepared for International Workshop on Exchange Rates in Multi-country Econometric Models, University of Leuven, Belgium, 26–28 November 1981.

Moriguchi, C. (1973), "Forecasting and Simulation Analysis of the World Economy", American Economic Review, 63: No. 2.

Mundell, R.A. (1963), "Capital mobility and stabilization policy under fixed and flexible exchange rates", Canadian Journal of Economics and Political Science 29:475–485.

OECD (1979), "The OECD international linkage model", OECD Economic Outlook, Occasional Studies (OECD, Paris).

OECD (1980), Fiscal policy simulations with the OECD international linkage model: Incomes policy in theory and practice (OECD, Paris).

OECD (1982), OECD Interlink System: Structure and operation, Vol. 1 (OECD, Paris).

Ranuzzi, P. (1981), "The experience of the E.E.C. Eurolink Project in modeling bilateral trade linkage equations", Journal of Policy Modeling, 3:153–173.

Ranuzzi, P. and P. Anthemus (1981), "Eurolink model: Monetary linkages", prepared for International Workshop on Exchange Rates in Multi-country Econometric Models (University of Leuven, Belgium), 26–28 November 1981.

Sachs, J. (1980), "Energy and growth under flexible exchange rates: A simulation study", N.B.E.R. Working Paper No. 582.

Samuelson, L. and E. Kurihara (1980), "OECD trade linkage methods applied to the EPA world econometric model", Economic Bulletin No. 18 (Economic Research Institute, Japan).

Sawyer, J.A., ed. (1979), Modelling the international transmission mechanism (North-Holland, Amsterdam).

Shishido, S., M. Aiso, H. Fujiwara and T. Fukuchi (1981), "Revised version of Tsukuba–Fais world econometric model (T-FAIS V)", prepared for the LINK Conference, La Hulpe, Belgium, 30 August–4 September.

Stevens, G., R. Berner, P. Clark, E. Hernandez-Cata, H. Howe and S. Kwack (1983), "The U.S. economy in an interdependent world: A multi-currency model (Board of Governors of the Federal Reserve System, Washington).

Waelbroeck, J.L., ed. (1976), The models of Project LINK (North-Holland, Amsterdam).

Waelbroeck, J. and A. Dramais (1974), "DESMOS: A model for the coordination of economic policies in the E.E.C. countries", in: A. Ando, R. Herring and R. Marston, eds., International aspects of stabilization policies (Federal Reserve Bank, Boston) 285–347.

Yomo, Hiroshi (1982), "The macroeconomic impact of increased energy prices for Japan", in: K. Clinton, ed., Proceedings of the Fifth Pacific Basin Central Bank Economists' Conference: Supply side shocks, the balance of payments and monetary policy (Bank of Canada, Ottawa).

Appendix[8]

The basic idea of trade linkage models may be summarized as follows. Suppose that there are n countries and that the jth country model can determine its total real imports, M_j, and its export price to each country, PX_{jk} ($j, k = 1, 2, \ldots, n$). Suppose also that a trade linkage sub-model can determine the export share of

[8]Adapted, with permission, from Amano et al. (1981).

each country in the jth import market, $a_{ij} = X_{ij}/M_j$, where X_{ij} denotes real exports of country i to country j. Then, total exports of each country, X_i, is determined as $X_i = \sum_{j=1}^{n} a_{ij} M_j$, and total world exports $\sum_{i=1}^{n} X_i$ is necessarily identical to total world imports $\sum_{j=1}^{n} M_j$. Moreover, a similar consistency condition also holds with respect to total value of world trade, since

$$\sum_{i=1}^{n} \sum_{j=1}^{n} PX_{ij} X_{ij} = \sum_{j=1}^{n} \sum_{i=1}^{n} PX_{ij} X_{ij}.$$

The aggregate export price of country i, PX_i, is determined as $PX_i = \sum_{j=1}^{n} (X_{ij}/X_i) PX_{ij}$ and the aggregate import price of country j, PM_j, as $PM_j = \sum_{i=1}^{n} a_{ij} PX_{ij}$. Similar argument applies when the trade-linkage sub-model can determine, instead of a_{ij}, any one of the following: (a) bilateral real trade, X_{ij}, (b) bilateral nominal trade, XV_{ij} ($= PX_{ij} X_{ij}$), or (c) the nominal trade share, v_{ij} ($= XV_{ij}/\sum_{i=1}^{n} XV_{ij}$). The consistent determination of bilateral trade flows is thus an essential role of any trade-linkage sub-model.

After reviewing over a dozen of the existing linkage models, we selected the following five approaches as candidates for our own model: Moriguchi (1973), Klein and van Peeterssen (1973), Hickman and Lau (1973), Johnson (1978), and Samuelson and Kurihara (1980).[9]

The Moriguchi approach assumes that the real export share of an exporting country in a particular import market depends on relative export prices and the ratio of export capacity to the size of the import market. A real export share function is estimated from pooled data for each exporting country.

The Klein–van Peeterssen approach is what has been used in the Project LINK. It estimates the value of exports by each country as a linear function of its export price, the export prices of competing countries, the sum of nominal imports of importing countries or regions multiplied by the respective nominal export shares of the country concerned in these import markets, and a time trend.

---

[9] The present authors have extended the Amano analysis by including comparative data from Italianer (1982) on a method developed by d'Alcantara, Barten and Italianer. [See also Barten and d'Alcantara (1977) and d'Alcantara and Italianer (1981).]

In the d'Alcantara–Barten–Italianer approach, an import value matrix is estimated in a supply and demand framework determining the matrix elements as functions of domestic prices, export supply capacity and total import demand. A scaling factor is applied to the matrix elements for each country to ensure consistent adding up of import volume and value.

The most important difference in Italianer's simulation exercise is the use of annual data where Amano uses quarterly data, with quarterly dummy variables. Estimation periods are comparable. The results of the exercise have been added to Tables A.3 and A.4.

It can be seen that this approach performs respectably compared to the approaches reviewed by Amano's group. For nominal and real exports, it is almost as accurate as Hickman–Lau and for import prices it is better, although the comparison of nominal export shares in Table A.4, from which the prices are derived, is probably a better measure of the relative merits of the method.

Consistent world trade flows are then estimated by applying the RAS method to adjust the nominal trade share matrix.

The Hickman–Lau approach is based on an assumption that imports from various countries are imperfect substitutes and that for any importing country the elasticity of substitution between any pair of exports is common and constant. A real bilateral trade flow equation is estimated for each importing country from pooled data, and parameters are estimated in such a way that aggregate export functions constructed from these parameters automatically satisfy the world trade consistency requirement.

The Johnson approach is an extension of the Klein–van Peeterssen approach, applying the framework of linear expenditure system to the process whereby total nominal imports of an importing country are allocated to imports from various countries. A bilateral nominal trade flow equation is estimated from pooled data

Table A.1
Major characteristics of the alternative trade linkage models[a]

Trade linkage model	Variables to be given by country or regional models	Determination of endogenous variables — Estimated equations	Determination of endogenous variables — Definitional equations			Presence of partial adjustment process	Stage in which the consistency is assured
Moriguchi approach		a_{ij}	X_{ij}, X_i, PCM_{ij}			no	Simulation
Hickman–Lau approach	$M_j,$ PX_i	X_{ij}	a_{ij}, X_i, PM_j	$\nu_{ij},$ $XV_{ij},$ $XV_i,$ MV_j	$PM_j,$ $TW,$ $TWV,$ PTW	yes	Estimation
Samuelson–Kurihara approach		X_i	a_{ij}, X_{ij}, PXC_i			no	Simulation (RAS method)
Klein–van Peeterssen approach	$MV_j,$ PX_i	XV_i	$XV_{ij}, PCOM_i$	$\nu_{ij},$ $a_{ij},$ $X_{ij},$ X_i, M_j		no	Estimation
Johnson approach		XV_{ij}	XV_i			yes	
d'Alcantara–Barten–Italianer approach	$PB_i,$ $XP_i,$ M_j	MV_{ij} PX_i	$MV_j, M_{ij},$ XV_i			yes	Simulation

[a] The table refers to a number of new variables: PCM_{ij}, competitors' export price of country i on market j; PXC_i, competitor's export price for country i; $PCOM_i$, competitive export price for country i; TW, real world trade; TWV, nominal world trade; PTW, world export price; PB_i, domestic price index; XP_i, export capacity of country i.

Table A.2
Comparison of long-run price and activity elasticities

Country or region	Moriguchi approach	Klein–van Peeterssen approach	Hickman–Lau approach	Johnson approach	Samuelson–Kurihara approach(I)	Samuelson–Kurihara approach(II)
			Price elasticities			
US	−0.23	−0.35	−0.38	−0.46	−0.31	−0.19
UK	0.18	0.31	−0.58	−0.25	−0.13	0.01
FR	−0.26	−0.20	−0.60	−0.35	−0.28	−0.36
GE	−0.26	−0.19	−0.59	−0.38	−0.11	−0.20
IT	0.01	0.59	−0.59	−0.28	−0.75	−0.75
CA	0.05	−0.39	−0.77	−0.35	—	−0.17
JA	−1.16	−0.81	−0.63	−0.43	−1.00	−0.80
			Activity elasticities			
US	1.17	0.81	1.0	1.04	0.99	1.02
UK	0.70	0.95	1.0	0.85	0.91	0.93
FR	0.70	0.74	1.0	1.15	1.28	1.14
GE	1.08	1.25	1.0	1.04	1.22	1.12
IT	0.74	1.37	1.0	1.00	0.78	0.73
CA	1.13	0.62	1.0	0.86	0.76	0.96
JA	1.02	2.03	1.0	1.36	1.01	1.06

for each importing country, as in the Hickman–Lau approach, by an iterative OLS procedure. The parameter estimates thus obtained are then used to construct aggregate export functions that meet the world trade consistency condition.

Finally, the Samuelson–Kurihara approach is based on aggregate export functions of the ordinary type. Total real exports of each country is estimated as a log-linear function of relative prices and an activity variable (the sum of total real imports of importing countries multiplied by the respective shares of the country concerned in these import markets). The real trade share matrix is then adjusted by the RAS method to obtain consistent world trade flows. In what follows we report two versions for this approach: versions (I) and (II). The difference between then lies in the lag-distribution of relative price terms. That is, version (II) uses the Shiller-method for estimating lag-distributions, while version (I) simply assumes a uniform lag-distribution.

Major characteristics of each approach are summarized in Table A.1.

We applied these approaches to a common set of data carefully compiled from IMF data tape (*Direction of Trade* and *International Financial Statistics*).

Table A.2 shows two types of elasticities for each approach: the relative price elasticity (the elasticity of real exports with respect to the export price relative to competitors' export prices) and the activity elasticity (the elasticity of real exports with respect to total real world trade). These elasticities are calculated from the parameter estimates, and are all long-run elasticities. In the case of linear functions, the elasticities are evaluated around the sample means.

As can be seen from the table, price elasticities are mostly in the range of -0.3 to -1.0 and activity elasticities cluster around unity. (Note that we are working with aggregate trade data with no commodity breakdown, while most of the above approaches were originally applied to SITC 5–9 group. Relatively low price elasticities on our part may largely be due to this difference.) There are, however, some deviants both in price and activity elasticity estimates, depending on the approaches, which are probably due to the existence of multi-collinearities. The Hickman–Lau and Johnson approaches do not suffer from these anomalies.

Table A.3 compares the results of dynamic simulation tests performed for each approach within the relevant estimation periods. In these simulations export prices and total imports (real or nominal depending on the approach) are treated as exogenous variables, and hence, percentage errors for total exports are the same in nominal and real terms. In Table A.3 the Samuelson–Kurihara approach exhibits relatively smaller errors for total exports compared with other approaches, followed by the Klein–van Peeterssen and Hickman–Lau approaches. As to import prices, the Hickman–Lau approach is obviously superior to all others.

Table A.3
Root mean square percentage errors of in-sample dynamic simulations (percent)[a]

Country or region	Moriguchi approach	Klein–van Peeterssen approach	Hickman–Lau approach	Johnson approach	Samuelson–Kurihara approach(I)	Samuelson–Kurihara approach(II)	d'Alcantara–Barten–Italianer approach
			Nominal and real exports				
US	6.6	4.4	5.6	5.3	4.0	2.6	2.2
UK	5.4	4.8	5.6	5.3	4.5	3.3	5.5
FR	5 7	2.9	5.0	4.8	2.6	2.3	3.6
GE	3.3	2.3	2.9	3.0	2.6	2.3	6.7
IT	6.4	5.8	6.8	6.6	5.3	5.1	6.7
CA	5.5	3.0	4.9	5.6	3.0	2.9	
JA	10.5	5.1	6.6	6.5	4.2	4.1	3.9
			Import price				
US	2.5	2.1	0.5	3.6	2.3	2.2	0.3
UK	2.4	2.4	0.6	1.5	2.0	2.1	0.2
FR	0.9	1.1	0.7	1.0	0.7	0.8	0.2
GE	0.9	0.9	0.4	0.4	0.7	0.7	0.2
IT	1.7	1.7	0.8	1.2	1.2	1.4	0.1
CA	1.5	1.6	0.4	0.6	1.8	1.7	
JA	2.7	2.7	1.0	2.3	2.5	2.4	0.3

[a]The simulation period is the same for all approaches: 1971:II–1977:IV, except d'Alcantara: 1970–76.

Error measures for bilateral trade flows are not easy to summarize, but we report in Table A.4 root mean square errors of export shares, averaged for each import market. That is, we computed the root mean square error of every exporting country or region in each import market, and took simple averages of the RMSE's with respect to the import markets. Table A.4 shows that in almost all markets, the Hickman–Lau approach gives smallest prediction errors both in nominal and real terms.

Finally, Table A.5 presents the results of post-sample dynamic simulation tests. Since the data on bilateral trade flows were not available at the time of simulation exercises, we could compute prediction errors only for individual countries. Here the performance of different approaches become much closer with each other. The Johnson and Samuelson–Kurihara approaches appear to have small advantages in predicting exports, as does the Hickman–Lau approach in the case of import prices.

The results of these comparisons are somewhat mixed, and there is no single approach that outperforms in every respect. Our synthetic judgment is that the Hickman–Lau approach has many desirable properties such as theoretical clarity in the share determination process, reasonable parameter estimates, and reliability

Table A.4
Root mean square errors of nominal and real export shares averaged for each
import market in in-sample dynamic simulations (percentage points)

Country or region	Moriguchi approach	Klein–van Peeterssen approach	Hickman–Lau approach	Johnson approach	Samuelson–Kurihara approach(I)	Samuelson–Kurihara approach(II)	d'Alcantara-Barten-Italianer approach
US	1.25	1.00	0.70	1.00	1.04	1.02	0.73
	1.27	1.00	0.69	1.22	1.07	1.04	
	1.04	1.00	0.59	0.91	0.95	0.98	0.67
UK	1.08	1.04	0.58	0.90	0.98	1.01	
	0.54	0.49	0.43	0.53	0.50	0.51	0.54
FR	0.53	0.50	0.44	0.55	0.48	0.50	
	0.56	0.53	0.38	0.52	0.52	0.53	0.40
GE	0.59	0.55	0.38	0.50	0.53	0.54	
	0.72	0.65	0.49	0.58	0.62	0.65	0.36
IT	0.74	0.68	0.50	0.60	0.62	0.66	
	0.64	0.59	0.54	0.57	0.60	0.58	
CA	0.68	0.66	0.54	0.56	0.68	0.66	
	0.91	0.87	0.77	0.88	0.88	0.84	0.45
JA	0.98	0.93	0.75	0.92	0.92	0.87	

Note:
Simulation periods are the same as in Table A.3. Upper figures are for nominal shares and lower figures for real shares.

in predictions. Our world econometric model has therefore been based primarily on this linkage method.

However, parallel use has occasionally been made of the Samuelson–Kurihara approach [version (II)], in view of its better prediction records for the Japanese trade.

Table A.5
Root mean square percentage errors of post-sample dynamic simulations (percent)

Country	Moriguchi approach	Klein–van Peeterssen approach	Hickman–Lau approach	Johnson approach	Samuelson–Kurihara approach(I)	Samuelson–Kurihara approach(II)
			Nominal and real exports			
US	3.4	4.7	5.0	3.5	4.7	4.9
UK	6.4	4.8	8.7	5.5	5.0	5.3
FR	5.4	6.5	4.7	4.7	2.9	1.9
GE	4.5	2.8	1.8	2.0	3.0	2.8
IT	11.8	9.4	11.3	11.5	13.2	14.0
CA	4.9	4.5	4.8	4.4	5.6	4.9
JA	12.1	13.8	9.8	9.7	6.2	6.1
			Import price			
US	7.4	4.4	3.3	4.8	5.1	4.7
UK	8.2	8.8	9.5	8.9	8.7	8.8
FR	1.0	0.8	0.9	0.9	0.8	0.8
GE	1.3	1.3	1.4	1.3	1.3	1.3
IT	4.2	3.7	3.5	3.9	3.7	3.6
CA	3.9	3.2	3.3	3.6	3.3	3.2
JA	6.8	7.0	7.1	7.1	7.0	7.1

Note:
The simulation period is the same for all approaches: 1978:I–1979:IV. For other notes see Table A.3. Figures in parentheses are corresponding averages for in-sample simulations.

Chapter 22

INTERNATIONAL MONEY AND INTERNATIONAL MONETARY ARRANGEMENTS

STANLEY W. BLACK*

University of North Carolina, Chapel Hill

Contents

*Helpful comments were received from Alec Chrystal, Richard Cooper, Dale Henderson, Peter Kenen, Michael Mussa, Douglas Purvis, John Williamson and other participants at the May 1982 Conference at Princeton University.

Handbook of International Economics, vol. II, edited by R.W. Jones and P.B. Kenen
© *Elsevier Science Publishers B.V., 1985*

1. Introduction

Since the excellent surveys of this subject by Williamson (1973) and Cohen (1975), much evidence has accumulated on the operation of international monetary arrangements in a world in which exchange rates among major currencies are floating. In general terms, the major issue has been whether the analysis developed under the Bretton Woods system continues to be valid with floating rates or whether entirely new concepts must be adopted. More specific research issues have included changes in the working of the mechanism of adjustment of payments imbalances, changes in the availability of financing of payments imbalances, changes in the demand for international reserves, the effects of demonetization of gold, the development of new international reserve assets, the controllability of the stock of reserve assets, diversification in the demand for reserve assets, and the relative role of markets and institutions in international monetary relations. The literature has tended to move away from narrow discussion of international reserves and the international monetary system to broader concepts of international money and international monetary arrangements as defined below. This survey will attempt to reflect both the broadening of concepts and the results of research examining changes in behavior.

It should perhaps be noted at the outset that the broadening of concepts can be interpreted as reflecting a change in the role of international monetary institutions as compared with market forces as determining factors in the international monetary arena. Max Corden (1981b) has gone so far as to describe this as a change to "international *laissez-faire*", while John Williamson has referred to the "non-system" [in Bernstein (1976)]. However, the broadening of concepts should not be allowed to obscure essential normative questions relating to the functioning of the international monetary system.

Let us now consider the extent to which the analysis of international monetary arrangements can be related to conventional monetary theory, taken in a broad sense. Domestic money and the arrangements for its use are commonly conceived of as a social contrivance to facilitate transactions in the marketplace, to provide a temporary store of value, and to provide a standard unit of account for contracts. A successful money requires both trust in the reliability of its issuer and a reasonable degree of stability in its value. International monetary arrangements are needed whenever transactions involve residents of countries with different currencies, since assets must usually be converted from one currency into another in the process of payment. Such arrangements are designed to guarantee convertibility of assets denominated in different currencies, much as domestic banking arrangements are designed to guarantee convertibility of deposits issued by different banks. Convertible or "international" monetary assets are described as international "reserves" when held in liquid form by official monetary institutions for purposes such as insuring convertibility of their own currencies. As it turns out, official holdings of reserve assets are usually denominated in one or more "key" currencies. The concept of international "liquidity" includes both reserves and access to unconditional borrowing facilities. An international monetary "system" may then be established involving a more or less formal set of rules for international monetary arrangements. The Bretton Woods Agreement of 1944 on the charter of the International Monetary Fund is one such set of arrangements.

This chapter first examines current research on the basic purpose and functions of international monetary arrangements. The terms and conditions under which assets denominated in different currencies may be exchanged for each other are related both to the intrinsic worth or "purchasing power" of the different currencies and to restrictions imposed by the issuers of currencies, as influenced by the agreed rules of the system. At the heart of such a system are the rules for financing and adjusting payments imbalances in order to insure continued convertibility.

The chapter next turns to research on the demand for reserve assets, which is in principle dependent on the design of the system, since it depends upon the chosen mix between adjustment and financing of payments imbalances. Thus one must consider the effects of floating exchange rates, the degree of capital mobility, central bank intervention in exchange markets, and the use of private bank financing of payments imbalances on the demand for reserve assets.

The supply of reserve assets as shown in Tables 1.1 and 1.2 is even more heavily influenced by the design of the system. The Jamaica Agreement of 1976 amended the IMF charter to ratify the adoption of floating exchange rates and

Table 1.1
Official holdings of reserve assets (billions of SDRs, end of period)

	1970[a]	1973	1981
All countries:			
Total reserves excluding gold	56.2	117.7	342.4
IMF reserve positions	7.7	6.2	21.3
Special drawing rights	3.1	8.8	16.4
Foreign exchange	45.4	102.7	304.7
Gold			
Quantity (millions of ounces)	1057	1022	952[b]
Value at London market price	39.6	95.0	324.6[b]

[a] Excluding People's Republic of China.
[b] Excluding 86 million ounces valued at SDR 29 billion held with the European Monetary Cooperation Fund as partial backing for its ECU liabilities, which are included in Foreign Exchange Holdings.
Source: International Monetary Fund, *Annual Report 1978, Annual Report 1982, International Financial Statistics Yearbook,* 1982.

Table 1.2
Composition of Reserve Assets (in percent)

	1973-I	1981-IV
U.S. dollar	78.4	58.4[a]
Pound sterling	6.5	2.0
Deutsche mark	5.5	11.2
French franc	0.9	1.0
Swiss franc	1.1	2.5
Netherlands guilder	0.3	0.9
Japanese yen	---	3.6
ECU	---	15.4[a]
Unspecified currencies	7.3	5.6
	100.0	100.0

[a] If the SDR value of ECUs which were issued against U.S. dollars swapped with the European Monetary System were included instead of ECU, the U.S. dollar share would be 70.6 percent.
Source: International Monetary Fund, Annual Report 1982.

de-emphasize gold as a basis for the system. Important issues remain, however, including the future role of gold as well as international reserve assets such as the IMF's Special Drawing Rights (SDRs). The de facto result of Jamaica was to increase the role of key currencies such as the dollar in the international monetary system, but it is clear from Table 1.2 that a multi-reserve currency system is developing. The European Economic Community has sought to create a new international reserve asset, the European Currency Unit (ECU), in order to strengthen the ongoing process of European monetary integration. A basic issue not resolved at Jamaica is whether the supply of any or all of these reserve assets can or should be controlled by some international body or agreed rules of behavior.

The final topic addressed by this chapter is the optimal design of international monetary arrangements. There is a potentially wide choice of degree of flexibility of exchange rates and degree of reliance on markets as opposed to institutions. Much evidence has now accumulated on the behavior of national governments under different types of arrangements in the 1970s. Given national preferences and behavior, recent analysis has asked how national policies will interact under different sets of international monetary arrangements. Such analysis leads to proposals for changes in the design of the system to improve the international distribution of income, to improve control over the growth of international reserve assets, and to improve the macroeconomic performance of the world economy as it is affected by the interaction of national economic policies.

2. Purpose and functions of international monetary arrangements

2.1. Exchange arrangements: Convertibility and flexibility

Recently McKinnon (1979) has clarified the role of international monetary arrangements in a multi-currency world. The most important aspect of a currency with respect to transactions involving other currencies is its convertibility. A currency is convertible if:

> Domestic [residents] wishing to buy foreign goods and services, not specifically restricted, can freely sell domestic for foreign currency in a unified market at a single but possibly variable exchange rate covering all current transactions inclusive of normal trade credit, whereas [non-residents] with balances in domestic currency arising from current transactions can sell them at the same foreign exchange rate or purchase domestic goods freely at prevailing domestic-currency prices [McKinnon (1979, p. 6)].

This definition does *not* require convertibility at a fixed parity with gold or some other currency, nor does it require convertibility for all capital account transactions. Nevertheless, it requires that both residents and non-residents have free access to the foreign exchange market for virtually all income-account transactions. Of the 141 members of the International Monetary Fund in 1981, only 43 could be said to maintain convertibility in the sense defined. All of the other members, as well as virtually all non-member countries, restrict the ability of residents and non-residents to use domestic currency to purchase foreign exchange for current account transactions.

These restrictions effectively limit the quality of the domestic currency and lead to a host of well-known inefficiencies in the allocation of resources [Bhagwati (1978)]. A major purpose of the establishment of the International Monetary Fund was "to assist in the establishment of a multilateral system of payments in respect of current transactions among members and in the elimination of foreign exchange restrictions which hamper the growth of world trade" (IMF Articles of Agreement, Art. I).

It should, of course, be understood that convertibility is not the only criterion for well-functioning international monetary arrangements. Indeed another major purpose of the IMF is "to facilitate the expansion and balanced growth of international trade, and to contribute thereby to the promotion and maintenance of high levels of employment and real income and to the development of the productive resources of all members as primary objectives of economic policy" (Art. I). The difficult problems come in balancing the objectives of convertibility and high employment, as has been found in the design of domestic monetary policy as well. Thus the basic objectives in designing international monetary arrangements can be taken as the maintenance of convertibility in a system that promotes high employment and the growth of real incomes.

The degree of flexibility in the terms on which currencies are to be convertible was deliberately left open in the discussion above, even as it was in the Second Amendment to the IMF Articles agreed at Jamaica, because it is clear that different countries wish to adopt different degrees of flexibility in their exchange rates (see Section 5.1 below). The tabulation of exchange arrangements in the IMF's *International Financial Statistics* indicates that of 145 IMF members reporting at end-1982, 94 had pegged either to a convertible currency or composite basket of currencies, 5 operated a crawling peg, 8 were engaged in a joint float, and 38 had other arrangements, including independent floating. This diversity of behavior alone can justify Corden's description of international laissez-faire cited earlier.

2.2. Vehicle currencies and reserve assets

The demand for a vehicle currency arises out of economies of scale conferred by the use of a single currency rather than multiple currencies in certain international transactions. Here it is useful to distinguish between international transactions in goods markets, which are arranged (invoiced) between exporters and importers, and international transactions in the foreign exchange markets (payments), which are primarily intermediated through commercial banks. It was originally thought that importers invoicing in a group of foreign currencies would have an incentive to hold foreign exchange balances and arrange their payments in a single vehicle currency [Swoboda (1968)]. Recent studies have shown that exporters from industrial countries tend to invoice their products in the domestic currency [Grassman (1973), Page (1977), Carse, Williamson, and Wood (1980), and Scharrer (1979)]. Table 2.1 confirms this pattern, but shows that exports of developing countries and Japan are generally denominated in dollars.

McKinnon explains the difference between the industrialized country pattern of invoicing and the LDC pattern of invoicing by distinguishing between "Tradables I," heterogeneous manufactured products exported primarily by developed countries for which the producer has control in the short-run over his own price, and "Tradables II," homogeneous products exported mainly by developing countries whose prices are quoted in international commodity markets on a standardized basis. Lack of convertibility of the domestic currency must also be a relevant factor for many LDC's, while Japan can only be explained as a "former LDC."

As McKinnon has noted, the actual markets for convertible foreign *currencies* are almost entirely intermediated through commercial banks. Chrystal (1980) has applied the theory of media of exchange [Jones (1976)] to the choice of a vehicle

Table 2.1
Proportions of domestic and foreign currency denominations in trade contracts:
1976 (percent of the total)

	Own currency		US $	
	X	M	X	M
U.S.A.	90	–	90	–
Germany	87	42	5	31
Switzerland (1977)	83	41	7	–
U.K. (1977)	69	–	17	–
France	68	32	9	29
Sweden	67	26	14	22
Austria	55	25	10	16
Denmark	54	25	12	23
Netherlands	50	31	13	23
Belgium	47	26	12	25
Italy	39	16	31	43
Finland	16	–	22	–
Japan	30	1–2	68	90
New Zealand	20–30	–	75	70–80
Latin America	0	0	85	–
OPEC	0	0	95	–
Others	0	0	70	–
World, total			52	52

X = exports.
M = imports.
– = not available.
Source: Hans–Eckhart Scharrar, "Die Wahrungsstruktur im Welthandel",
Wirtschafts Dienst, September 1979, cited in Heller (1981a).

currency in the interbank market for foreign exchange. Assume there are n
currencies and a large number of individual dealers.

To accomplish any given exchange, say of currency i for j, a dealer searches
randomly for another dealer who wishes to exchange currency j for currency i.
The transactions cost to the individual dealer is assumed to be proportional to
the time spent searching for a complementary trade. The dealer will seek to
structure his trades so as to minimize this cost. His trading strategy will be
chosen prior to entering the market (i.e., before picking up the phone) on the
basis of his belief about the probabilities of finding takers for various deals.
These beliefs are derived from his previous experience in the market, whereas
the true probabilities are the fractions of traders offering to buy or sell each
currency. It is assumed that the subjective probability, P_i, that any randomly
encountered dealer will wish to sell currency i is the same as the probability
that he will want to buy currency i... Each dealer also assumes that the
currency supplied by each other dealer is independent of the currency de-

manded... This allows us to state the subjective probability of another dealer wishing to trade currency i for currency j as $P_i P_j$. The objective of each dealer is to achieve a given ultimate exchange in minimum time, i.e., with a minimum number of phone calls. If he does this by *direct* exchange, the expected number of phone calls is

$$\frac{1}{P_i P_j}.$$

If he does this by *indirect* exchange, whereby i is traded for k and k for j, the expected number of phone calls is

$$\frac{1}{P_i P_k} + \frac{1}{P_k P_j}.$$

The optimizing dealer will obviously choose the currency with the highest expected probability of being bought and sold as his intermediary currency.... If $P_n > P_i + P_j$ for any pair (i, j), indirect trade using currency n will be adopted. This will raise P_n and lower all other $P_i (i \neq n)$ [Chrystal (1980)].

Chrystal goes on to show, using a simple model due to Jones, that the vector of subjective probabilities $P = (P_1, \ldots, P_n)$ and actual proportions of dealers supplying currencies $q = (q_1, \ldots, q_n)$ will converge to an equilibrium level in which a fraction s of all ultimate exchanges of currencies will be conducted via the intermediary or vehicle currency n. The system can in fact have multiple locally stable equilibria with different values of s, depending on the pattern of ultimate demands u_i for the different currencies. One possible equilibrium is where $s = 1 - u_n$ in which *all* trades involve currency n either directly (u_n) or indirectly (s).

This argument makes it easy to see why the demand for a vehicle currency will arise in the interbank market, even in the absence of direct use of the vehicle currency by exporters and importers. As noted by Chrystal, gradual shifts in the pattern of dollar versus non-dollar denominated trade and capital flows can change the extent of use of the dollar as a vehicle currency in the interbank market. Shifts in the techniques of government intervention in the exchange market, either in the extent of intervention or the currency of intervention, can also change the pattern of ultimate demands for currencies. Oil has been a major factor raising the share of dollar denominated trade and investment in the 1970s, although OPEC's demand for non-dollar-denominated goods and investments must also be allowed for [Krugman (1980)]. Another factor which may change the role of the dollar as a vehicle currency in interbank trade is the availability to dealers on CRT screens of quotations on a range of major currencies from any major bank in the world. Thus direct exchanges of major currencies can be effected more easily, although not without a phone call to establish a firm price and quantity.

Some evidence on the role of dollars in international financial markets is available from the Bank of International Settlements' data on Euro-currency markets [Heller (1981a), Kenen (1982)]. As noted by Heller (1981a), the dollar share of Euro-markets in total has apparently dropped only slightly in the 1970s, from 81 percent in 1970 to 76 percent in 1980. In the foreign currency positions of *non-American* commercial banks, the share of dollars in European banks' foreign assets has dropped from 78 percent in 1970 to 69 percent in 1980, as the Deutschemark share especially has risen from 11 to 16 percent. In particular countries, the dollar share of foreign currency assets in 1979 ranged from a high of 90 percent in Canada to between 40 and 70 percent in most European countries. Kenen points out, however, that data on shares measured in terms of dollars include valuation effects, during a period in which the dollar declined in value. In terms of domestic currency values, dollar assets have apparently kept up with non-dollar assets through 1980.

Of course non-banks that participate in Euromarkets also have substantial vehicle currency assets and liabilities. The reasons for the development of this phenomenon are four-fold: the economies of scale originally discussed by Swoboda (1968), escape from the regulations setting interest rates and reserve requirements on assets and liabilities in domestic financial markets, more competitive conditions in the international Euro-market than in protected national banking systems in many countries, and currency diversification to reduce exchange rate risk. [McKinnon (1979, ch. 9)]. While McKinnon argues that exporters and importers will have "preferred monetary habitats" in their own local currencies, this is not necessarily the case for multi-national firms which produce and sell in dozens of countries. This issue is related to the question of the appropriate measure of purchasing power for the stockholders of the firm and their needs for currency diversification [see Adler and Dumas (1981)].

The factors which have led the interbank currency market to be primarily intermediated in dollars (sterling before the Second World War) make it almost inevitable that central banks' exchange market intervention will involve purchases or sales of the vehicle currency or currencies. Central banks intervene in exchange markets either to peg their currencies or to manage exchange rate movements (see Section 5.1). In the days of the gold standard, this could be done by formally pegging the domestic currency to gold and buying and selling gold at the fixed price. However, during the period of the pre-First World War gold standard, sterling was the primary vehicle currency in international financial markets and a substantial proportion of world trade was denominated in and financed in sterling. Thus it is no surprise that Lindert (1969) found that in 1913 holdings of reserve *currencies* were a third as large as reported holdings of gold reserves.

Gold reserves were "officially demonetized" by the Jamaica Agreement of 1976, but according to Table 1.1 they are still being held in substantial quantity as a "store of value" and perhaps for "precautionary" reasons by governments and central banks. The "means of payment" functions involving exchange market intervention has been taken over entirely by reserve currencies. Special Drawing Rights (SDRs) must also be regarded as serving the precautionary and store of value functions, since they cannot be used directly in market transactions. The "unit of account" function involves both denomination of contracts, public and private, and the collection and presentation of data. In this field the SDR is beginning to compete with the dollar in public international agreements and in data produced by the International Monetary Fund, but has not yet been widely adopted elsewhere.

2.3. Adjustment mechanisms

An individual country's demand to hold reserve assets depends on the expected costs of adjustment to external imbalances compared to the costs of holding reserves, as will be shown more explicitly in Section 3.1. The availability of different types of adjustment mechanisms and their associated costs will thus be a key ingredient in any particular set of international monetary arrangements. But why need there be any mechanisms of adjustment at all? If international capital markets were perfect and if investors were risk neutral so that assets denominated in different currencies were perfect substitutes for one another in individual portfolios, there would then be in practice a single world real interest rate for short-term borrowing. Countries could presumably *finance* balance of payments deficits or surpluses of any size in this international capital market, since there would be no real distinction between the convertibility characteristics of the official liabilities of different borrowers. In fact, of course, nonreserve currency countries quickly run into limits on their ability to finance deficits by borrowing abroad in their *own* currencies because of exchange risk. Potential creditors will also eventually become concerned about *default* risk if a country has a payments imbalance that has no appearance of being reversed in the future.

Thus it is essential for countries to have access to and utilize mechanisms of adjustment of payments imbalances. Earlier chapters of this Handbook, including Chapters 13, 14, 17, and 20, discuss some of these mechanisms of adjustment more completely. The main mechanisms are adjustments in income via monetary and fiscal policy, adjustments in relative prices via exchange rates and/or tariffs, taxes and subsidies, quantitative restrictions (QRs) on current account or capital account items in the balance of payments, and general exchange controls over the allocation of foreign exchange. The use of tariffs, taxes, subsidies, QRs, and exchange controls involve, of course, a loss of convertibility of the domestic currency together with resulting allocational inefficiencies [Bhagwati (1978)].

Some work has been done on the cost of alternative means of adjustment to external disturbances. Most approaches to date have used a partial equilibrium approach, estimating the income loss required by various specific adjustment policies to produce a given improvement in the balance of payments. For example, Kreinin and Heller (1973) use the Marshall–Lerner condition to evaluate the terms-of-trade cost of adjustment via devaluation and the marginal propensity to import to evaluate the cost of a Keynesian income adjustment. Frenkel (1974), on the other hand, uses the average propensity to import to measure the effect of a change in the terms of trade on the demand for money and hence reserves in a monetarist model of adjustment. Finally, Cooper (1968) and Hipple (1974) argue that the average propensity to import measures vulnerability to external disturbances.

The use of intertemporal optimization models permits these cost calculations to be integrated in a general equilibrium approach, taking account of random disturbances [Iyoha (1971)]. Assume the existence of an econometric model that describes the economic structure of a country, including its external relationships and access to private international capital markets. The authorities are assumed to have an intertemporal welfare function including the rates of inflation and unemployment and real income per head. Holding reserves or acquiring them via foreign borrowing reduces current income per head as measured by the opportunity cost of capital but leads to lower expected costs of future adjustment to payments imbalances. Given initial reserves and a terminal or transversality condition on the stock of reserves, a policy-maker may calculate the optimal "adjustment" policy for various types of specific disturbances or distributions of random disturbances. He may then evaluate the change in the present value of the welfare function allowed by a unit increase in initial reserves. Such models have been applied rather narrowly to the demand for reserves and are discussed in Section 3.1 below, but they could also be applied to the optimal adjustment problem. A step in this direction has been taken by Branson and deMacedo (1980), reviewed in Section 5.1 below.

The constraints placed on the adjustment mechanism by the structure of the economy and by international rules about the use of techniques of adjustment will definitely affect both the cost of adjustment and the demand for reserves. In addition, the terms on which financing is available will also be an important determinant.

2.4. Financing

Several major developments have shaped recent debates over the availability and terms of financing for payments imbalances: private financing via the Euromarkets, the changing real rate of interest, and the conditionality of official financing from the IMF. Much of the OPEC surplus due to the oil price rises of 1974 and 1979–80 was intermediated through the Euro-currency markets. The OPEC deposits corresponding to oil importers' debts add to the world total of international liquidity, in a process known as "liability settlement", since the borrowing countries effectively created Euro-dollar liabilities with which to settle their payments imbalances. As this type of settlement was formerly restricted to reserve center countries, which created liabilities in reserve currencies to foreign central banks, it has drawn wide comment as a change in the availability and form of financing. The increased availability of financing was of course welcome in the context of the oil deficits, but the shift to private bank financing of balance of payments deficits with counterpart reserve creation has been criticized on several grounds [OECD (1977), Cohen (1982)]. First, the conditional lending of the IMF has been undermined by the availability of an unconditional alternative (see Section 5.3). Secondly, the large scale of Euro-market lending has been associated with an increase in the number of countries with arrears and reschedulings, as in the recent cases of Poland, Mexico, Argentina, Brazil, and Turkey [Heller (1981)]. Thirdly, the creation of international reserves "on demand" has undermined control over the long-run rate of growth of reserves (see Section 4.4).

While changes in the availability of financing have certainly been significant, changes in the real rate of interest on such borrowing are no doubt even more important in affecting the willingness of countries to finance instead of adjust. The lengthy period of low or negative real rates of interest during the 1970s must have been a powerful factor in favor of borrowing, thus demonstrating the importance of the conduct of monetary policy in the dominant reserve center country on the overall behavior of the system.

3. The demand for reserve assets

3.1. Theory of adjustment versus financing

The theory of the demand for reserve assets is a precautionary theory which depends on balancing the costs of holding the assets against the benefits provided. In the case of reserve assets, the benefit is a reduced probability of incurring costs of adjustment to a payments imbalance, via either expenditure-reducing policies such as restriction of income or via expenditure-switching policies such as exchange rate changes or controls on foreign transactions. Here we have a rudimentary form of the theory discussed in Section 2.3 of the optimal division between adjustment and financing of payments imbalances via use of reserves or borrowing.

Two branches of the literature have developed, depending on whether the marginal cost of adjustment is assumed to be constant or increasing with the amount of adjustment. Heller's original (1966) analysis of the problem of optimal reserve holdings assumes constant marginal cost, so that adjustment is postponed to the last minute. The surplus or deficit in the balance of payments at a given (fixed) exchange rate is assumed to be a discrete random variable which can take on the value $\pm h$ with equal probabilities. Thus except when an adjustment is taking place the level of reserves will follow a random walk with step size h. Given initial reserves R, the probability of running out of reserves in R/h steps is $(1/2)^{R/h}$. The cost of a unit adjustment at that time by means of a reduction in income is assumed to be $1/m$, where m is the marginal propensity to import. The expected cost of a unit adjustment is then $(1/2)^{R/h}/m$. Equating this expected marginal cost to the opportunity cost of holding a unit of reserves r, the optimal holding is then derived as

$$R^* = \frac{\log(rm)}{\log(0.5)} h.$$

Hamada and Ueda (1977) point out that Heller's formula ignores the possibility of arriving at zero reserves by other than a straight run of R/h steps. They use the theory of Markov processes with absorbing barriers at $(R,0)$ to calculate the long run steady-state probability of arriving at zero reserves via any possible path with equal-sized steps as $1/2(R-1)$. They also criticize his use of the single period interest rate r as the opportunity cost of holding reserves until exhaustion. Their analysis minimizes the average cost of holding reserves until exhaustion $(rR/2)$ plus the expected cost of adjustment $1/2m(R-1)$. The optimal holding turns out to be

$$R^* = \left[1 + \frac{1}{\sqrt{rm}} \right] h.$$

This formula leads to higher optimal reserves, since the probability of running out from an initial level is seen to be higher than in Heller's analysis. Hamada and Ueda go on to consider fundamental disequilibrium (i.e. a larger probability for either decreases or alternatively increases in reserves), a fixed cost for converting liquid assets into illiquid assets at the ceiling, time lags in adjustment, serial correlation in the stochastic process of reserve changes, and speculative movements in the balance of payments.

   Frenkel and Jovanovic (1981) generalize the analysis by assuming an adjustment from zero to R in one step, in an intertemporal optimizing framework that also considers the cost of holding reserves until exhaustion. They assume a continuous time stochastic process for changes in reserves analogous to a random walk with drift in the mean, namely $dR(t) = -\mu \, dt + \sigma \, dW(t)$, where $W(t)$ is a Wiener process. Instead of analyzing the steady-state costs as do Hamada and Ueda, they calculate the expected cost of adjustment and opportunity cost of holding reserves from a dynamic programming recursion relationship, which yields a total expected cost

$$\frac{R}{1-\alpha} - \frac{\mu}{r} + \frac{\alpha}{1-\alpha} C,$$

where C is the marginal cost of adjustment and α is the Laplace transform of the first passage of reserves through the boundary point zero. They derive a formula

$$R^* = \left[\frac{2C\sigma}{\left(\mu^2 + 2r\sigma^2\right)^{1/2} - \mu} \right]^{1/2},$$

which has economies of scale with respect to the measure of variability σ, in contrast to the linearity of the previous formulas with respect to h.

In the other branch of the literature, the marginal cost of adjustment is assumed to increase with the size of the adjustment, so that it pays not to postpone the adjustment until reserves drop to zero. Clark (1970) and Kelly (1970) set up welfare functions involving the mean and variance of income, while Nyberg and Viotti (1974) consider welfare to be a nonlinear function of income. Britto and Heller (1973) assume a nonlinear cost of adjustment function and prove the optimality of a gradual adjustment policy.

The Kelly–Clark analysis can be summarized in Figure 3.1, taken from Williamson (1973). Both the rate of adjustment of reserves γ and the optimal level towards which they adjust R^* are to be optimized in order to maximize a utility function depending on the mean and variance of income. In the northeast quadrant, mean income declines along EE due to the opportunity cost of holding larger reserves, as long as the rate of interest paid on reserve holdings is less than the rate of return on alternative investments. In the southeast quadrant, Tchebychev's inequality is used to relate the proability of *not* running out of reserves $P(R \geq 0)$ to the speed of adjustment and the optimal level R^*. A constant probability of not exhausting reserves along curve PQ can be maintained *either* by means of rapid adjustment *or* by means of large reserve holdings. The southwest quadrant shows that the standard deviation of income will increase nonlinearly along OS with the speed of adjustment to payments imbalances.[1] These three curves then combine to produce the tradeoff OT between mean income and the standard deviation of income in the northwest quadrant. The analysis is completed with the mean-standard deviation indifference curve UU and the optimal choice at point A.

---

[1] The following model for Figure 3.1 is based on Kelley (1970) and Clark (1970):

(i)	$\Delta R = \gamma[R^* - R_{-1}] + u,$		$u \sim N(0, \sigma_u^2),$
(ii)	$\sigma_R = [\gamma(2-\gamma)]^{-1/2}\sigma_u$		from (i),
(iii)	$P(R \geq 0) = \sigma_R^2/2R^{*2} = \sigma_u^2/2\gamma(2-\gamma)R^{*2},$		(SE quadrant),
(iv)	$\sigma_y = \gamma\sigma_R/m = \gamma\sigma_u/m[\gamma(2-\gamma)]^{1/2},$		(SW quadrant),
(v)	$E_y = Y_0 - rR^*.$		

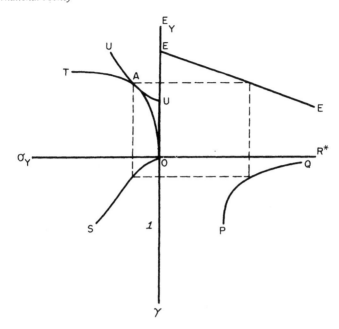

Figure 3.1 Optimal reserves and adjustment.

It is clear from this diagram that a decrease in the opportunity cost of holding reserves will lead to a flattening of *EE* in the northeast quadrant, an upward shift of the opportunity locus *OT* in the northwest quadrant, an increase in the optimal holding of reserves, and a decrease in the speed of adjustment. A reduction in the assumed probability of not running out of reserves will shift the curve *PQ* in towards the origin and reduce both the speed of adjustment and the level of reserve holdings. Thus adjustment and reserve holdings are jointly determined.

3.2. Effects of floating exchange rates

It was generally expected that the adoption of floating exchange rates would reduce the demand to hold reserves by allowing greater reliance on adjustment via changes in the exchange rate [Haberler (1977)]. For example, Makin (1974) attempted to estimate how much the variance of the distribution of reserve losses would fall with widening of the bands around parity in the Bretton Woods system. For the case of Canada, he suggested an elasticity of demand for precautionary reserve balances with respect to increased exchange rate flexibility of between -0.50 and -0.333. Actual experience under floating rates has seen no apparent reduction in reserve use [Williamson (1976a)], perhaps because of increased payments imbalances. An alternative suggested explanation is that central banks have engaged in unprofitable destabilizing intervention [Taylor (1982)]. While the empirical studies reviewed below have found only minor changes in the demand to hold reserves, theoretical reasons for such results are still being sought.

One suggestion, due to Williamson (1976a), is that in the absence of stabilizing capital flows a J-curve in the current account may result in short-run instability of the exchange market. In that case, reduced intervention by central banks may perversely be associated with increased volatility in reserves. Williamson's model includes a current account with a J-curve:

$$c_t = -\alpha_0 e_t + \alpha_1 e_{t-1} + u_t,$$

where u_t is a random disturbance term with variance σ_u^2. In the absence of capital flows, this must equal central bank purchases of foreign currency, assumed to respond to deviations from a "target" rate $\tilde{e}$:

$$\Delta x_t = -\delta(e_t - \tilde{e}).$$

In this simple model, the variance of the exchange rate is $\sigma_u^2/[(\delta - \alpha_0)^2 - \alpha_1^2]$ and the variance of reserve flows $\sigma_{\Delta x}^2$ is just δ^2 times this variance. It can then be verified that $\partial \sigma_{\Delta x}^2/\partial \delta < 0$ since $\alpha_1 > \alpha_0$.

A more intriguing possibility is what may be called the "Harrod effect". Long ago, Sir Roy Harrod (1965) suggested that increased flexibility of exchange rates would raise the level of exchange risk perceived by risk-averse private speculators and thereby reduce their willingness to assume positions in foreign currency. The result, he predicted, would be increased volatility of both reserves and exchange rates. This is an example of an inter-relationship between government policy rules and the behavior of the public of the type envisaged by Lucas (1976). Black (1983) has analyzed this problem in a simple stochastic model previously discussed by Black (1973), Williamson (1976a), and Driskill and McCafferty (1980). Suppose the current account responds normally to the exchange rate with a random term u_t:

$$c_t = \alpha e_t + u_t,$$

while the flow of capital responds to movements in the expected change in the exchange rate with a random term v_t:

$$\Delta f_t = \Delta \beta (E_t e_{t+1} - e_t) + v_t.$$

With the same intervention policy as above, the rational expectations solution of this model gives the one-period conditional variance in the exchange rate [Driskill and McCafferty (1980)] as

$$\sigma_{e,1}^2 = \left(\sigma_u^2 + \sigma_v^2 \right) / \left[\alpha + \delta + \beta (1 - \lambda) \right]^2,$$

where

$$\lambda = 1 + \frac{\alpha + \delta}{2\beta} - \frac{\alpha + \delta}{2\beta} \sqrt{1 + \frac{4\beta}{\alpha + \beta}}$$

is the stable characteristic root. As noted by Driskill and McCafferty, speculators who are maximizing expected utility with constant absolute risk aversion in the face of this type of uncertainty would choose $\beta = 1/\phi\sigma_{e,1}^2$, where ϕ is the measure of risk aversion. Black (1983) shows that these two relationships can be solved uniquely for β and λ, yielding:

$$\beta = \frac{(\alpha + \delta)^2 \phi \left(\sigma_u^2 + \sigma_v^2 \right)}{\left[\phi \left(\sigma_u^2 + \sigma_v^2 \right) - (\alpha + \delta) \right]^2}.$$

Assuming the bracketed term in the denominator to be positive, one can easily see that β depends positively on δ, whence the "Harrod" effect.

Williamson (1976b) also pointed out that intervention by peripheral countries pegged to a floating currency will suffer increased variability simply due to exchange rate fluctuations between the floaters. He showed that if the peripheral country's overall balance of payments measured in dollars (x) is the sum of a dollar component (y) and a non-dollar component which is the product (rz) of the dollar exchange rate of the non-dollar area (r) and the component measured in non-dollar currency (z), then $\sigma_x^2 = \sigma_y^2 + \sigma_z^2 + \sigma_r^2(\sigma_z + \bar{z}^2)$, on plausible simplifying assumptions. The last of the three additive components is the additional effect of floating on the variability of the peripheral country's balance of payments.

3.3. The composition of reserve asset portfolios

Given the availability of a range of reserve assets, including gold, dollars, deutschemarks, sterling, Japanese yen, and SDRs, countries face a problem of choice in the management of their reserve asset portfolios. The existence of this choice problem was at the heart of Triffin's analysis of weaknesses of the key-currency system, discussed in Section 4.2 below. The literature of the 1960s, beginning with Kenen (1960) and coming up to Makin (1971), considered the choice between gold and dollars within the Tobin–Markowitz portfolio framework, finding that relative rates of return do indeed seem to matter to central banks.

More recently, with the demonetization of gold and the development of alternative reserve currencies, attention has turned to choices *among* reserve currencies, within the same portfolio framework (see Table 1.2). For example, Ben–Basset (1980) and Macedo (1980) calculate "optimal" portfolio proportions based on historical rates of return and variance–covariance matrices. Ben–Basset compares these with actual portfolio shares and finds that industrialized countries hold larger shares of dollars than would be "optimal", implying that other factors besides risk and return must play a role. Heller and Knight (1978), however, took a different approach, arguing that central banks have broader objectives than portfolio optimization. They were able to study the actual currency composition of reserve asset portfolios, using confidential IMF data. They showed that the vehicle-currency phenomenon discussed in Section 2.2 was a key factor, along with trade shares, in explaining the composition of reserve asset holdings, since countries tend to hold larger balances of the currency of intervention.

Another criticism of the portfolio approach is that it ignores the interdependent nature of the international monetary system, analyzed in Section 5.2 below. Williamson (1973) reviews various "signalling" theories, according to which movements in reserve-asset proportions constitute a "signal" to the United States concerning the asset-holders' desires for either different U.S. monetary policies within a U.S.-dominated but interdependent system [Mundell (1968, ch. 20)] or else different degrees of monetary independence from the United States [Cohen (1970)]. Officer and Willett's (1974) analysis showed that political "distance" from the United States was an important factor in determining the share of dollars held. More recently, the development of the European Monetary System has been interpreted as evidence of a desire for increased monetary independence in Europe [Cohen (1979)].

Macedo's calculations of optimal portfolios (1982) take the point of view of an "international" investor, whose consumption basket is given by international trade patterns. The resulting price indexes are used to define expected real rates of return and the covariance matrices required for portfolio analysis. As in the usual portfolio analysis, two-fund separation permits the optimal portfolio to be written as the sum of a minimum variance portfolio and a zero net worth speculative portfolio (or any other pair of portfolios on the opportunity locus). The calculations in Macedo (1983) show that the resulting optimal portfolios fluctuate significantly over time because of changing rates of return. The basic assumption underlying this analysis is that both domestic and foreign prices follow stationary Itô processes; that is, inflation rates are random variables with known means and variances. As a result, there is no riskless asset, and the minimum variance portfolio is approximately a trade-weighted basket. This analysis seems to explain some of the diversification away from the dollar during 1979–80 due to a low rate of return during 1977–78.

Adler and Dumas (1981) argue on the other hand that the appropriate price index for residents of a given country is its own consumer price index, rather than a trade-weighted average of national price indexes. Since deviations from purchasing power parity are extensive and primarily due to exchange rate movements, the domestic price level is "relatively" stable for domestic investors, and they will have the domestic currency as their "preferred monetary habitat". The minimum variance portfolio is then domestic. This argument does not appear applicable to central banks, and indeed Heller and Knight found trade shares to be important explanatory variables in their regressions.

3.4. Empirical studies

The major empirical issue of the 1970s has been the effect of floating rates on the demand for reserves. Heller and Khan (1978) estimated aggregate time series relationships of the form $R = f(M/Y, M, \sigma_R^2)$ for various groups of countries over the period 1964–76, where σ_R^2 is the variability of percentage changes in reserves. The average propensity to import M/Y had a negative sign, consistent with the Keynesian income-cost-of-adjustment interpretation rather than the monetary model or vulnerability interpretation of its role. Stability tests indicated a shift in the demand functions, significant at the 10 percent level, occurring in the fourth quarter of 1973 for industrial countries and in mid-1972 for non-oil-developing countries. The commodity price boom of 1972–73 is taken to be the reason for the LDC result. Forecasts of the 1973–76 period from equations estimated over the sample period 1960–72 show an overprediction of reserve holdings for industrialized countries and an underprediction for developing countries, suggesting a decline in the demand for reserves by the former group and an increase for the latter. These results are consistent with the fact that industrialized countries are more likely to float, while developing countries usually peg.

Frenkel (1980) estimated cross-sectional relationships for two groups of 22 developed and 32 developing countries, annually from 1963 to 1977. His results give the average propensity to import a positive sign, consistent with the monetary or vulnerability interpretation and with previous cross-section results. Pooling the cross-sections over the periods 1963–72 and 1973–77, Frenkel finds there was a structural change at the end of 1972, with the two groups of countries becoming more alike, but that the 1963–72 equations still do rather well in forecasting over the floating rate period. These results appear to contradict the time-series evidence that suggests an increase in demand by developing countries and a fall in demand by industrial countries. As do Heller and Khan, he finds that developing countries have a lower elasticity of demand with respect to the variability of payments imbalances than developed countries, attributing this to their greater willingness to use balance of payments restrictions instead of reserves.

One problem with the annual cross-section estimates is the implicit assumption that countries are on their demand functions for reserves every year. Bilson and Frenkel (1979) use annual average data for the same groups of countries over the periods 1964–72 and 1973–77 to estimate demand functions, finding similar results to those obtained from annual data with respect to the influence of variability but higher elasticities for other variables. They also find much less difference between the pegged and floating rate periods. The estimated demand functions are then used to predict *desired* reserve holdings for each country over time, including the country-specific average residual from the overall demand function. The next step estimates time-series partial adjustment equations, which show relatively rapid adjustment toward desired levels, with a speed of adjustment parameter of about one-half. Tests for nonlinearity in the adjustment mechanism produce evidence for the existence of the tradeoff between the average reserve holding and the speed of adjustment shown in the southeast quadrant of Figure 1. Countries hold larger reserves in order to be able to adjust more gradually. There is also some evidence for a "Mrs. Machlup's wardrobe" effect [Machlup (1966)] during the pegged rate period for industrial countries, according to which central bankers have a higher tolerance for increases in reserves above the desired level than for decreases below it.

In none of these studies has the opportunity cost of holding reserves been found to be significant, perhaps because of inadequate variation across countries or over time in the measures of opportunity cost. Frenkel and Jovanovic (1981) pooled cross-section and time series data for developed countries and found a marginally significant negative coefficient on the government bond yield in an equation that omitted the cost of adjustment term.

The main conclusion from these post-1973 studies is that the same framework still appears to be appropriate for estimating the demand for reserves. There does, however, appear to have been a shift in demand after 1973.

4. The supply of reserve assets

According to Table 1.1, the supply of reserve assets is composed of gold, foreign exchange reserves, IMF reserve positions, and Special Drawing Rights. Table 1.2 gives further details on the composition of foreign exchange reserves, which include key currencies such as the dollar and other reserve currencies, as well as European Currency Units (ECUs). Since 1970, several important changes in the international monetary system have altered the conditions under which these reserve assets are supplied.

The unilateral suspension of convertibility between gold and the U.S. dollar at the fixed price of $35 an ounce in August 1971 set off the first of these changes, leading to the Smithsonian Agreement of December 1971, an attempt to stave off the collapse of the Bretton Woods system. At the Smithsonian, a complex package was agreed to, including a wider margin or band for fluctuations of exchange rates about their declared parities in terms of the dollar, as well as a devaluation of the dollar relative to gold and revaluations of other currencies against the dollar. In early 1972, members of the European Economic Community formed the EC Narrow Margins Agreement or "Snake" in order to prevent wider dollar margins from allowing even wider fluctuations in cross-rates among member currencies.

These evidences of growing pressures on the Bretton Woods edifice led to the creation in 1972 within the framework of the International Monetary Fund of a twenty-member Committee on the Reform of the International Monetary System, soon to become known as the "Committee of Twenty," or "C-20" for short. This group labored long and hard over the issues, within a framework whose purpose was to revitalize the Bretton Woods system of adjustably pegged rates, a goal strongly supported especially by the French and many developing countries. But the floating of the British pound in June 1972, the Swiss franc and then the Italian lira in January and February 1973 quickly proved that the system of pegged exchange rates, even as mended at the Smithsonian, could not cope with the fatal combination of independent monetary policies and highly mobile capital.

In early March 1973, following a second devaluation of the dollar, exchange markets closed for two weeks, to reopen in April with major currencies, including the EC Snake as a single currency bloc, floating against each other. During 1973 and 1974 floating exchange rates, accompanied by ever-increasing flows of private capital through the Euro-currency system, proved capable of handling the enormous changes in payments flows that were generated by the increase in oil prices administered by the OPEC cartel. Furthermore, the United States government quickly became a strong proponent of floating rates. Given this *fait accompli*, the C-20 gave up on full-fledged reform of Bretton Woods, published the results of its studies [IMF (1974)], and in effect recommended regularization of floating rates, which were in violation of the IMF Articles of Agreement. The C-20 also recommended creation of a 20-member Interim Committee of the Board of Governors to oversee further development of the system. The issues before the C-20 and the reasons why it was unable to reach agreement on real reform have been thoroughly explored by Williamson (1977, revised view in 1981b), who blames the failure on inadequate staff work, lack of political will and, more recently, on U.S. insistence on complete freedom for its monetary policy.

The major issues incorporated but not resolved in the C-20's Outline of Reform cover the gamut of problems with the Bretton Woods system of adjustable pegged rates. Since most of these problems will inevitably face any new effort at reform, it is useful to examine the issues briefly, prior to discussing specific issues in more detail. The Outline of Reform [reprinted in IMF (1974)] discusses ways and means of achieving greater symmetry in the obligations of deficit and surplus countries to adjust to payments imbalances. This problem has been resurrected under floating rates in the discussion over "vicious" and "virtuous" circles of exchange rate adjustment, which arise from the fact that depreciation adds to inflation while appreciation subtracts from it [Basevi and deGrauwe (1977)]. The possibility of using "objective indicators" such as reserve levels or flows to initiate adjustment was discussed at length.

Various types of symmetric intervention schemes such as multi-currency intervention and SDR intervention were considered as means of replacing the asymmetry of a dollar-based intervention system, in which the U.S. government has no obligation to intervene in the dollar's behalf. The de facto adoption of floating rates led to discussion of guidelines for the use of floating rates, including acceptable forms of intervention and proposals for IMF surveillance of the process (see Sections 5.2 and 5.3 below).

The problem of control over the growth in the quantity of reserves was debated without being resolved. Proponents of control advocated various forms of asset settlement of payments imbalance to avoid the creation of reserves through the uncontrolled issuance of liabilities (recall Section 2.4). Opponents argued that such control was neither necessary nor feasible (Section 4.4). At the same time, the C-20 debated how to achieve greater symmetry in the supply of reserve assets—this was referred to as dealing with the "dollar overhang". The French government insisted on the restoration of gold convertibility, while the United States sought to maintain the status quo. The major compromise proposal was the "substitution account" (see Section 4.2). Finally, the problems of the SDR were discussed, including methods of allocation and valuation and whether to tie allocation of SDRs to development objectives (the SDR-aid "Link").

Following the C-20's deliberations and recognizing the continuation of floating exchange rates, the IMF in July 1974 decided to value the SDR as a basket of 16 currencies, rather than leaving it tied solely to the floating U.S. dollar. Subsequently, at the first "Economic Summit" meeting of the leaders of six of the largest industrial countries at Rambouillet, France in November 1975 the U.S. and French governments agreed to compromise their divergent views on the future of the international monetary system. The result was the Jamaica Agreement of January 1976 leading to the Second Amendment to the IMF Articles of Agreement.

At Jamaica the Interim Committee of the IMF Board of Governors agreed on a number of steps to regularize floating rates and implement the compromise of Rambouillet [see Bernstein et al. (1976) for commentary]. First, it was agreed that countries could legally float their exchange rates and that stability in those rates, while a desirable object, should be sought through underlying monetary and fiscal policies rather than pegging. Second, the process of floating should be subject to "firm surveillance" by the International Monetary Fund, including the institution of guidelines for intervention by central banks and regular consultations with member countries. These provisions recognized the concerns of the United States and French governments, respectively, as agreed at Rambouillet. Third, the SDR was to "become the principal reserve asset and the role of gold and reserve currencies will be reduced". The SDR was to replace the dollar as *numeraire* for Fund transactions and SDRs were made more freely transferable among a wider range of eligible holders. However, a substitution account to promote the exchange of gold or dollar reserves for SDRs was not established. Fourth, the official price of gold was abolished, one-sixth of the Fund's gold was to be restored to members and one-sixth to be sold at auction for the benefit of a Trust Fund for developing countries, and gold was not to be further used in Fund transactions. Thus was the status quo accepted, with gestures in the direction of appeasing various groups of countries that were unhappy with it.

Since the ratification of the Second Amendment to the IMF Articles of Agreement, two other significant developments have altered the institutional arrangements for the supply of reserve assets. In 1978 the European Communities agreed to enlarge and strengthen the mechanism of the EC "Snake", in the process renaming it as the European Monetary System and creating the European Currency Unit (ECU), discussed in Section 4.3 below. Finally, in January 1981 the IMF simplified the valuation of the SDR by reducing to five the number of currencies in the weighted basket, in an effort to improve its attractiveness.

4.1. The role of gold

According to Table 1.1, gold remains a "store of value" component in the international reserves of most countries, despite the Jamaica Agreement to demonetize it officially. At market prices, 49 percent of reserves of IMF member countries were in the form of gold at the end of 1981. This represents a very substantial amount of capital tied up in precautionary assets. A large social saving could theoretically be achieved by using a key currency or international reserve asset instead of gold. This social saving can be measured by the flow of seignorage that would accrue to the issuer of such a reserve asset. The aggregate demand for reserve assets, derived from the theories discussed in Section 3.1, can be graphed as a function of the opportunity cost of holding reserves. The area under this demand function measures the aggregate social benefit from holding reserves. The social cost of holding reserves is measured by the opportunity cost of the capital tied up on reserve assets. Assume that the existing stock of monetary gold and the resources used to augment the gold stock could be gradually transferred to other uses yielding a market rate of return. Then the net social benefit of a pure international gold standard would be the area between the demand curve and the market opportunity cost of capital. Substitution of a fiduciary reserve asset such as SDRs or dollars would yield a social benefit in the form of seignorage equal to the excess of the opportunity cost of capital over the costs of provision of the fiduciary asset, including any interest paid on such an asset by the issuer. Thus substitution of a reserve currency or international reserve asset for gold holdings would generate a large saving in the use of resources, which the key-currency system has already in part accomplished. The savings already achieved have been divided between seignorage gains to the issuer and interest paid to the holders [see Williamson (1973) for some quantitative estimates for the 1960s]. The failure to complete this substitution and reap further gains must be counted as one cost of the failure of the effort to reform the Bretton Woods system.

Under present conditions, prices in the gold market are heavily dominated by speculative anticipations of changes in the gold supply (e.g. IMF and/or government auctions during the period 1976–80, Soviet sales, and Arab purchases or sales) and by changes in the carrying cost of gold (the interest rate) [Salant and Henderson (1978)]. While central banks are free since Jamaica to trade gold at mutually agreed prices, evidently none have actually done so. However, the European Monetary System has used a portion of members' gold stocks valued at near market prices as backing for the issuance of European Currency Units (see Section 4.3). Thus gold remains a part of the international monetary system, albeit an inactive part.

4.2. Key currencies

The basic dilemma of a key currency system of reserve asset supply is the confidence problem identified in Robert Triffin's *Gold and the Dollar Crisis* (1960). A key currency country cannot increase the supply of its official liabilities to serve as others' reserves without facing a deteriorating gold/liabilities ratio, which calls into question its ability to maintain convertibility into gold at a fixed price. Among the solutions proposed for the "Triffin dilemma" were an increase in the price of gold, replacement of the gold exchange standard by flexible exchange rates, and the creation of "international" reserve assets such as SDRs. Triffin thought the system would run into difficulty because of an inadequate supply of reserves and advocated the third solution. In fact, breakdown of the Bretton Woods system ended gold convertibility, achieved flexibility in exchange rates, ended the reserve supply problem via creation of reserve assets "on demand", and also led to a sharp rise in the price of gold.

Indeed the collapse of Bretton Woods was accompanied by a vast increase in the supply of dollar reserves during the period 1970–72, amounting to a 57 percent increase in the supply of reserve assets from that one source alone, as central banks bought dollars in a vain attempt to forestall the inevitable. It is possible to interpret the subsequent general rise in prices, including the price of gold, as at least in part a response to the resulting monetary imbalance (see Section 4.4). This monetary disturbance was not however a feature of the floating exchange rate regime, but rather of the disorderly transition period.

Under floating rates, the process of creation of dollar reserve assets has two endogenous channels. The first is the creation and destruction of dollar reserves via central bank intervention in exchange markets. The second is the creation of Euro-dollars via "liability settlement". When the price of oil quintupled in 1974, a substantial portion of the increased oil bill was paid by means of Euro-currency borrowing which had as its counterpart the accumulation of Euro-currency deposits by OPEC countries. Thus oil importers settled their payments imbalances with reserves created by borrowing [Black (1977), McKinnon (1979)]. More recently, this process has ebbed and flowed with fluctuations in the exchange rate of the dollar and with fluctuations in the real dollar interest rate, pointing to a systemic difficulty that has not been generally recognized. When real interest rates have been low, as during the inflationary episodes 1973–74 and 1978–80, creation of dollar liabilities has been high, but the demand to hold them has been depressed. In such periods, seignorage earnings of the United States have been substantial, and vice versa when real rates have been high. The resulting swings in the real cost of borrowing have been a root cause of some of the serious financial difficulties into which many unwary LDC borrowers have fallen. It is hard to escape the conclusion that the functioning of the international monetary system under *laissez-faire* is in fact heavily dependent on the conduct of monetary policy in the reserve center country.

Central bankers have reported in Roosa et al. (1982) and Group of Thirty (1982) that the diversification into non-dollar reserve currencies noted in Section 2.2 has occurred partly in response to perceived instability in the dollar and partly in response to the increased attractiveness of alternative reserve currencies arising from changes in their own characteristics. It should be noted, however, that Heller and Knight found *larger* than average dollar holdings among members of the EEC Snake agreement, since the members agreed to limit their holdings of partners' currencies to working balances.

The recurrent pressures for diversification away from dollar assets led during 1979–80 to discussions within the IMF and elsewhere of proposals to establish a "substitution account" [Sobol (1979), Kenen (1981), Bernstein (1982)]. The basic idea was to provide an institutional means for diversification into an SDR-denominated asset, to relieve exchange market pressure on the dollar, and to reduce the drift towards a multi-currency reserve system. Because of unwillingness to amend the IMF's Articles of Agreement, such a fund would have to stand on its own resources, although administered by the IMF. Therefore the exchange risk associated with the account would have to be shared among the participants.

With assets denominated in U.S. dollars and liabilities denominated in SDRs, any substantial movement in the SDR value of the dollar would generate large profits or losses for the account. As Kenen's simulations of such an account over the 1970s show, there are potential problems both in financing current interest payments and in guaranteeing the long-term solvency of the account. If the United States were to assume the entire risk associated with movements in the SDR value of the dollar assets of the account, it would amount to a U.S. guarantee of the SDR value of the dollar balances in the account. Other risk-sharing arrangements, including the controversial suggestion that IMF gold holdings be used to guarantee the account's solvency, proved impossible to negotiate.

The de facto development of a multiple reserve currency system has generated argument over the potential for instability in such a system. Under pegged exchange rates, the destabilizing possibilities are obvious and follow from Gresham's law. But under floating exchange rates it is unclear whether diversified reserve holdings entail any serious difficulties for the system. The Group of Thirty (1982) survey of central bankers found little concern over the issue.

4.3. International reserve assets

The Special Drawing Right (SDR) was agreed to in the First Amendment to the Articles of the International Monetary Fund in 1967 in an effort to resolve the problems pointed out by Triffin. The Second Amendment, agreed to at Jamaica, expressed a hoped-for objective that the SDR eventually should become the "principal reserve asset". What was created is a revolving credit facility, which is regarded as an international reserve asset because its use via transfer to a designated country provides convertible foreign currencies to the user, at a cost represented by the interest rate on SDRs. However, its use is limited by various conditions, some of which were relaxed following the Second Amendment. For political reasons, the SDR was valued after the adoption of floating exchange rates as a basket of 16 currencies, again limiting its appeal. This unwieldy grouping was drastically simplified in an effort to make it more attractive by the move to a five-currency basket in 1981 [Polak (1981)]. The interest rate charged on SDR use and paid to those accepting SDRs was originally set at a low 1.5 percent, raised in steps to 80 percent of a weighted average of interest rates in five leading currencies in 1979, and raised to the full weighted average rate in 1981.

The new, five-currency SDR is practically as good as the original basket from the point of view of diversification of exchange risk (IMF Survey, 26 January, 1981) and is much easier to hedge through purchases or sales of the five currencies, which have large, active spot and forward markets. The difference between the opportunity cost of capital and the interest rate paid on SDRs represents the seignorage generated by net use of SDRs. As Harry Johnson (1969) explained, this seignorage was initially distributed to the members of the IMF by allocating the new SDRs free of charge. The distribution of the seignorage in proportion to IMF quotas of members was resisted unsuccessfully by the poorer member countries, who sought a "link" between SDR allocation and aid to developing countries. [For discussion of this and other LDC issues, see Cline (1976).] More recently, the increase of the rate of interest on SDRs to the full market rate of interest on the five-currency basket has greatly reduced the seignorage available and therefore interest in the "link" proposal. The increase in the rate of interest on the SDR also makes it a more attractive reserve asset to hold and thereby a less attractive asset to use, as shown by Murphy and Von Furstenberg (1981) in an analysis of SDR use by non-oil-developing countries. Nevertheless, the SDR still does not appear to be very popular among central bankers [Group of Thirty (1982)].

A rival international drawing right, the European Currency Unit (ECU), was established with the creation of the European Monetary System (EMS) in 1979 [see Trezise (1980) and De Vries (1980)]. Two major factors motivated West German Chancellor Helmut Schmidt and French President Valery Giscard d'Estaing to propose the enlargement of the Snake; first, a desire to reduce intra-European exchange rate fluctuations and promote convergence of macroeconomic policies within Europe, and second, a desire to reduce the dependence of European monetary policy on the policies of the United States. There are three main components of the EMS: (1) an enlargement of the EC Snake with its bilateral intervention points to narrow fluctuations among members to include as additional members France, Italy, and Ireland; (2) a "divergence indicator" to signal the need for changes in underlying monetary or fiscal policies whenever one individual country's exchange rate deviates too far from its parity in terms of the ECU, which itself is defined as a weighted average of the nine member currencies; and (3) an enlarged access to short and medium-term financing for intra-EMS exchange market intervention through a system of ECU-denominated transferable deposits in the European Monetary Cooperation Fund (EMCF). These deposits were created on the basis of three-month revolving swaps of 20 percent of the gold and dollar reserves of member central banks with the EMCF. It was proposed that the EMCF be transformed into a European Monetary Fund by making these swaps into a permanent pooling of reserves, but German resistance to reserve-pooling together with a stronger dollar have postponed this development indefinitely. The valuation of the ECU as a nine-currency basket appears to limit its usefulness to the function of a unit of account and revolving credit fund among EMS central banks [see the appendix to Roosa et al. (1982)]. On the other hand, the deposit of gold and dollar reserves of members against the issuance of

ECU again enables gold reserves to be utilized, albeit on an indirect basis for short-term purposes only.

4.4. Effects of disequilibrium in reserves

What has been called "global monetarism" or the "international quantity theory" [Whitman (1975), Williamson (1973)] postulates a direct relationship between increases in total world holdings of international reserves, the world money supply, and worldwide inflation [Johnson (1972), Mundell (1971)]. This theory follows from a Hume's Law response by national monetary authorities to reserve flows. Statistical tests on aggregate time series data by Heller (1976), Genberg and Swoboda (1977), and Khan (1979) appear to confirm the existence of this relationship over periods including the early 1970s. Rabin and Pratt (1981) show that Heller's (1976) results were strongly affected by the inclusion of the 1970–72 period when, as noted above, the breakdown of the Bretton Woods system gave rise to a 57 percent increase in international reserve holdings. Nevertheless, Bilson and Frenkel's (1979) partial adjustment equations also imply an expansionary response to an excess supply of reserves.

There is no question that the explosion of reserves from 1970 to 1972 coincided with rapid growth in monetary base and money supplies in major industrialized countries [Black (1978)]. The only exceptions were the United States, Italy, and the United Kingdom, where monetary growth was rapid during the period either without reserve growth (Italy and the United States) or without growth in the monetary base (United Kingdom). This experience suggests that control over the growth of international reserves may indeed by a crucial element missing from the current international monetary system.

Haberler (1977), Fleming (1961, 1975), Polak (1970) and Sohmen (1978) argue that the national monetary policy reaction functions implied by Hume's Law ignore the importance of other, mainly domestic, objectives of monetary policy such as inflation and unemployment. For evidence on the importance of both internal and external objectives see Black (1983). Willett (1979) uses sterilization coefficients and reaction functions to estimate that most of the monetary expansion of the early 1970s was due to domestic objectives. Williamson (1982a) makes several additional points. First, the payment of market interest rates on reserve holdings eliminates not only the seignorage but also the reluctance of countries to hold excess reserves. Second, the continued existence of well-defined demand functions for reserves under floating rates does not imply that countries must necessarily inflate to adjust to increases in the supply of reserves, since they may instead allow their currencies to appreciate. Third, the widespread availability of liability settlement through the creation of Euro-dollars (Section 4.2 above) makes it impossible to control reserves without controlling the Euro-markets.

The desirability and feasibility of controlling the Euro-markets has been widely discussed [see, for example, the papers by Wallich and McKinnon in Dreyer, Haberler, and Willett (1982), Aliber (1980), and Swoboda (1980)]. Proponents of regulation cite problems such as uncontrolled creation of credit, undermining of domestic monetary policy due to increased capital mobility, facilitation of destabilizing capital flows, excessive lending to insufficiently credit-worthy borrowers, and excessive risk-taking in foreign-exchange trading. These problems were discussed in the Cooke Committee, established by the central banks of the Group of Ten, the industrial countries who participate in the IMF's General Arrangements to Borrow.

The basic problem uncovered by the Cooke Committee was that foreign branches of banks were frequently not supervised either by the home country authorities or the authorities of the host country, especially with regard to their "offshore" business or their foreign exchange transactions. A concordat among the Group of Ten central banks was thus reached in 1975 [published in an Annex to IMF (1981)], agreeing that the home country central bank would be responsible for supervising the lending and foreign exchange practices of "offshore" banks and further setting up an exchange of information among central banks, as well as improved reporting of offshore lending. This approach avoids the difficulty that host country supervision would simply induce offshore banks to seek another, less restrictive, haven.

These actions did not address the control of credit creation, but rather the so-called "prudential" issues of traditional bank supervision. On the broader issue of credit control, academic opinion has concluded that the amount of credit creation involved is actually relatively modest, and that most credit flowing through the Euro-markets has merely been diverted there by the attraction of an unregulated market [Aliber (1980), Swoboda (1980), McKinnon (1979)]. While not removing the effects of the Euro-markets on domestic monetary policy and capital flows, this argument suggests that harmonization of regulations and reduction in the inflation tax on money holdings will go a long way to reducing the impact of the problem.

5. Optimal international monetary arrangements

The normative theory of international monetary arrangements begins with discussion of the objective function, which may be called a world welfare function [Williamson (1973)]. As noted in Section 2.1, this is generally agreed to include the usual objectives of high employment and economic growth, as well as price stability. Growth of international trade, and hence reduction of trade barriers and restrictions on currency convertibility, is generally agreed to be instrumental in achieving these ends, at least in the world as a whole, on the basis of the usual theorems of international trade.

The constraints under which such an objective function might be optimized include the behavior of national governments suboptimizing under the constraints faced by individual countries. Section 5.1 discusses some of the growing literature on national policy behavior, while Section 5.2 moves on to consider the problems of the system as a whole.

5.1. National policy choices

Optimal national policy choices between adjustment and financing of payments imbalances can be derived in the context of optimizing analyses such as those of Clark and Kelly (Figure 3.1 above), Britto and Heller (1973), Buiter (1977), Henderson (1979), or Roper and Turnovsky (1980). Each of these papers attempts to derive a policy response function consisting of a mixture of reserve use and adjustment measures to optimize some objective function, usually the variance of output or the mean and variance of output. Further progress along this line can be expected from the application of optimal control techniques using more general objective functions and a wider mix of policy responses. [For an early example, see Iyoha (1971).] There is also a developing empirical literature on the study of national policy reaction functions. Black (1983a) examines the response of the instruments of monetary policy in ten industrial countries to internal and external targets. Using monthly data on discount rates, credit controls, reserve requirements, and open market operations, he concludes that "the measured instruments of monetary policy respond significantly in predictable ways to customary measures of internal and external imbalance". Other conclusions relate to the relative importance attached to inflation or unemployment in different countries and the relative importance attached to internal versus external objectives. Countries with greater flexibility in their exchange rates tend to put more emphasis on internal objectives than countries with pegged exchange rates.

Kenen's (1975) simulation study of the effect of alternative rules for exchange rate adjustment used stability of export volume as a rough guide to optimality in a single equation model of exchange rate determination. Various specific rules of thumb or "objective indicators" for changes in exchange rates were tested against a range of types of exchange rate regime – free float, fixed rate with intervention, temporary float, adjustable peg, and crawling peg; the "objective indicators" according to which exchange rates were adjusted included the level of reserves, the change in reserves, and the "basic" balance of payments. While the study ruled out several indicators as unstable, it did not attempt a full optimization, since the objective function omitted measures of the cost of holding reserves and the effects of adjustment on income. Branson and Macedo (1980) use more sophisticated optimal control techniques to analyze the same problem of rules of adjustment, with an objective function including the variance of the current account, the level of reserves, and changes in the exchange rate. Their results generalize Kenen's, but again fall short of full optimization, since the objective function omits internal balance.

The factors that can lead an individual country to choose a particular degree of flexibility have been analyzed in the literature on optimal currency areas and the choice of exchange rate regime [Artus and Young (1979), Tower and Willett (1976), Argy (1981)]. These factors include the resource allocation effects caused by fluctuations in real exchange rates, the insulation of the domestic economy from different types of disturbances, and the effectiveness of domestic policy instruments under different exchange rate regimes. (See Chapter 20 in this Handbook.)

Resource allocation effects can be *caused* by the exchange rate regime whenever delayed adjustment of a pegged rate leads to exaggerated corrective movements in the relative prices of traded and non-traded goods *or* when a flexible exchange rate overshoots its equilibrium value for a substantial period of time. Both types of variability in real exchange rates can increase the degree of risk associated with international trade and investment activities. (See Chapter 9 in this Handbook.) The resource allocation effects of the adjustable peg were long ago pointed out by Johnson (1966) and Hause (1966) and confirmed empirically by Kouri (1979) and Coes (1981) in the contexts of Finland and Brazil. Efforts to test for the effects of exchange risk due to floating rates have found either small effects or no effects. Studies by Clark and Haulk (1972) for Canada and by Hooper and Kohlhagen (1978) for industrialized countries defined exchange risk in terms of variability of the nominal exchange rate and found no evidence of any effect on trade flows. Studies by Rana (1981) for a group of Asian LDCs and by Cushman (1982) for a group of industrialized countries defined exchange risk in terms of the variability of the real exchange rate and found small but significant negative effects of risk on trade flows. Thursby (1980) evaluated the Canadian experience with different regimes, finding lower resource allocation costs under floating than under pegged rates.

Several authors, including Itagaki (1982) and Cushman (1980), have pointed out that trade and direct investment flows may be either complements or substitutes. Itagaki's theoretical analysis compares firms which may produce final goods at home for export or produce them abroad (substitute relationship) with firms which produce intermediate goods at home for export and final processing abroad (complementary relationship). Cushman (1980) examined the effect of real exchange rate risk on direct investment flows among a group of industrialized countries and found a weak, but significant *positive* relationship with exchange risk, suggesting a substitution of direct investment for trade. Nevertheless, none of these effects of risk due to floating rates appear to be very large, in contrast to findings of sizeable effects arising from the adjustable peg.

A second factor affecting a country's choice of regime is the degree to which the domestic economy is insulated from various types of shocks. Henderson (1979) has elegantly generalized Poole's analysis of the optimal monetary instrument under different shocks to the financially developed open economy with imperfect substitutability between domestic and foreign assets. Henderson shows that the best reaction to real shocks is a flexible exchange rate, while the best reaction to financial shocks is a pegged rate, concluding that a managed float is the optimal policy for such an economy.

If a decision has been made to peg the exchange rate, a further question arises as to which currency or basket of currencies should a country peg. Black (1976) concluded that a developing country faced with a combination of real shocks and differential inflation rates should adopt a crawling peg vis-à-vis a trade-weighted basket, in order to stabilize the real exchange rate, defined as the relative price of traded to non-traded goods. Branson and Papaefstratiou (1980) ask whether developing countries can affect their terms of trade by choice of weights in the basket, but find little ability to do so. Lipschitz and Sundararajan (1980) have further developed the criterion of minimization of the variance of the real exchange rate by using exchange rate changes as predictors of price changes, which are only observed with a lag. For a recent review of this literature, see Williamson (1982c). Heller (1978) and Holden, Holden, and Suss (1979) have demonstrated empirically that the actual choices of exchange arrangements made by different countries do indeed reflect many of the factors indicated here.

Optimal government exchange market intervention policies have been analyzed in a macroeconomic context by Buiter (1977), Boyer (1978), Henderson (1979, 1982), Roper and Turnovsky (1980), Frenkel (1980), and Canzoneri (1981). When disturbances come from different sources, these papers show that governments interested in stabilizing output will generally be interested in intervening to some extent, as long as assets denominated in different currencies are not perfect substitutes. When they are perfect substitutes, intervention is not distinguishable from domestic monetary policy operations, and sterilized intervention is useless [Mussa (1980), Genberg (1981)]. A recent argument has it that sterilized intervention might nevertheless signal the authorities' willingness to adopt domestic monetary policy targets even in the case of perfect substitutability [Obstfeld (1980)]. This literature has recently been surveyed by Argy (1982).

One objective of national policy omitted by all of the studies cited above is the maintenance of employment or output in some specific sector following an external or internal disturbance, either temporary or permanent. This is the motive for what Corden (1982) has called "exchange rate protection", in which the real exchange rate is deliberately undervalued to protect output of the tradable goods sector. A perverse form of exchange rate protection may involve deliberate *over*-valuation in order to protect foreign investors [Diaz-Alejandro (1981)].

5.2. Optimal design of the system

The welfare maximization approach to the optimal provision of international reserves has been described by Williamson (1973): "The optimum rate of reserve growth is characterized by beneficial effects in the form of higher employment and fewer restrictions being equal at the margin to the untoward effects of inflation and the resource misallocation implied by larger reserve flows." Similar statements could be constructed for the optimum degree of exchange rate flexibility and the optimum provision of international lending facilities. Such an approach in principle lay behind the C-20's unsuccessful efforts to reform the Bretton Woods system, which was finally entombed in the Jamaica Agreement leading to the Second Amendment to the IMF Charter. [Bernstein et al. (1976), but see the debate in Parts Four and Five of Dreyer, Haberler and Willett (1978).] The question remains, however, whether present conditions in the international monetary "non-system", as Williamson dubs it, are susceptible of improvement and how one might design an "optimal" system. Willett (1979) appears to believe the present system is close enough to optimality, while the central bankers surveyed by the Group of Thirty (1982) agree it is not optimal, but see little chance of improvement. Corden (1981) suggests that the appropriate model for present arrangements is *laissez-faire*, since he argues they depend entirely on decentralized decision-making in individual countries with no international rules of behavior, at best weakly coordinated by international institutions such as the OECD, IMF, and the Economic Summits. The "surveillance" of adjustment policies incorporated in the Second Amendment to the Fund charter has not constrained wide variations in exchange rate policies and monetary policies in major countries recently. Corden suggests that suboptimal behavior taking the form of inconsistent targets in different countries and a poor balance between adjustment and financing will lead to excessive costs, followed by modifications of the suboptimal behavior. If excessive costs quickly lead to modifications in the adjustment process, such a system could be close to optimal.

The "market" solution to the balance between adjustment and financing is in this case provided by movements in the rate of interest paid on owned or borrowed reserves, which determines the trade-off between present and future costs of adjustment. When real interest rates fluctuate as widely as in the late 1970s and early 1980s, the "market" terms of trade between adjustment and financing also fluctuate widely, leading to cycles of over-expansion and contraction in the world economy. As noted earlier, this system is heavily dependent on the conduct of monetary policy in the reserve center country.

Suboptimal behavior can be defined in terms of the spillover effects by which one country's policies affect another's outcomes, leading to conflict of interest. The literature on interdependence, surveyed in Chapter 21 of this Handbook, deals with this problem. The main issue that is relevant here is the so-called "$n - 1$" or "redundancy" problem [Mundell (1968, ch. 13)]. In a pegged exchange rate world, the sum of payments imbalances must equal the (exogenous) growth of world reserves. Only $n - 1$ countries can independently choose balance of payments targets. To avoid policy conflicts, Mundell suggested that the extra degree of freedom, policy in the n-th country, should be used to control the world price level, leaving its balance of payments to be determined by "benign neglect". Hamada (1974, 1979) generalized this analysis, using game theory to suggest cooperative solutions involving coordination among the policy instruments of the n countries. In a managed floating exchange rate world, the problem changes form. There are only $n - 1$ relative prices (exchange rates) to be determined, requiring the n-th country to refrain from intervening to solve the redundancy problem, another form of "benign neglect".

McKinnon (1974, 1982) argues that the appropriate solution to the problem of policy conflicts in both pegged and flexible exchange rate regimes is for monetary authorities to coordinate growth targets for the monetary base in each country and then refrain from sterilizing the effects of exchange market interventions, if any. This would prevent episodes of rapid growth in world reserves such as those generated during 1970–72 or 1977–78, by assuring cooperative outcomes and the working of the monetary adjustment mechanism. It is not clear how this proposal would reduce widely fluctuating real interest rates.

At a higher level of abstraction, Jones (1983) has tried to find the optimal balance between adjustment and financing in a two-country fixed-price model of the Fleming–Mundell type. The idea is to consider parametric variations in the relative weight given to reserve changes and output fluctuations in a country's welfare function. For a given value of that weight, each country has a reaction function for monetary policy, which leads to an overall equilibrium for the system. In cooperative equilibrium, the optimal weight is zero and unlimited financing is allowed, while non-cooperative behavior requires some degree of reserve stringency to avoid undesirable outcomes.

5.3. The role of the International Monetary Fund

The International Monetary Fund has at least two major functions to perform in the international monetary system. First, if national policy choices turn out ex post to be suboptimal, the IMF is ready to come in with a conditional lending program to help the national government to establish a more viable set of policies. This function, akin to the "lender of last resort" role of national central banks, also partakes of the "Dutch uncle" model of credit advisor. The second major role of the IMF is to supervise the overall functioning of the international monetary system, promoting a proper balance between adjustment and financing, with due allowance for the overall state of world aggregate demand, supply and inflation.

The IMF has been frequently charged with imposing excessively rigid and unnecessarily stringent terms in its conditional lending, particularly to developing countries [Dell and Lawrence (1980)]. The argument is made that many of the financial difficulties of such countries during the 1970s were due to factors beyond their control, such as the oil price increases and the slowdown in growth of the industrialized countries. However Black (1981) has shown by discriminant analysis that domestic policies and individual country characteristics were at least as important as external factors in the balance of payments problems of non-oil-developing countries during this period, implying that conditional lending has an important role to play.

The Fund itself has produced a very detailed set of analyses describing the impacts of its conditional lending policies in a variety of areas [Reichmann and Stillson (1978), Johnson and Salop (1980), Beveridge and Kelly (1980), Donovan (1982)]. For example, Reichmann and Stillson (1978) examined 79 cases of standby agreements over the period 1963–72, comparing the results of the programs to their stated objectives. A remarkable 73 percent of the programs examined appeared to achieve their objectives. A later study covering the 1970s was less favorable, however, and the Donovan (1982) study adopted a different standard for the analysis of 78 programs during the period 1971–80. On the basis of a comparison with pre-program performance in the same country, 72 percent of the cases showed improvement in one or more measures of external balance in the first year of the program. Compared with the average behavior of all non-oil-producing developing countries, 80 percent of the cases did better on one or more measures of external balance. Less impressive results were obtained for measures of inflation and economic growth, but the main point is to note the relaxation in the standard of performance that is implied. Further debate and analysis on this problem can be found in Williamson (1982b) and Killick (1982).

Under the Second Amendment to the Fund charter, the primary technique for the IMF to supervise the overall functioning of the system appears to have shifted to the "surveillance" of floating exchange rates, since there is no pretense of control over the rate of creation of international reserves and no consensus on the importance of such control. In practice, the surveillance process appears to be a regularized series of consultations with each member country, leading to few if any observable effects on either individual country behavior or the overall functioning of the system. This justifies Corden's use of the term *laissez-faire*.

References

Adler, M. and B. Dumas (1981), International portfolio choice and corporation finance: A survey (Centre d'Enseignement Superieur des Affaires, Jouy-en-Josas, France).
Aliber, R.Z. (1980), "The integration of the offshore and domestic banking system", Journal of Monetary Economics, 6:509–526.
Argy, V. (1981), The postwar international monetary crisis (Allen & Unwin, London).
Argy, V. (1982), "Exchange rate management in theory and practice", Princeton Studies in International Finance No. 50.
Artus, J.R. and J.H. Young (1979), "Fixed and flexible exchange rates: A renewal of the debate", IMF Staff Papers, 26:654–698.
Basevi, G. and P. de Grauwe (1977), "Vicious and virtuous circles: A theoretical analysis and a policy proposal for managing exchange rates", European Economic Review 10:277–301
Ben–Basset, A. (1980), "The optimal composition of foreign exchange reserves", Journal of International Economics, 10:285–295.
Bernstein, E.M., et al. (1976), "Reflections on Jamaica", Princeton Essays in International Finance 115.
Bernstein, E.M. (1982), "The future of the dollar and other reserve assets", in: J.S. Dreyer, G. Haberler and T.D. Willett, eds., The international monetary system: A time of turbulence (American Enterprise Institute for Public Policy Research, Washington) 410–429.
Beveridge, W.A. and M.R. Kelly (1980), "Fiscal content of financial programs supported by stand-by arrangements in the upper credit tranches, 1969–78", IMF Staff Papers, 27:205–249.
Bhagwati, J. (1978), Anatomy and Consequences of Exchange Control Regimes (Ballinger, Cambridge).
Bilson, J.F.O. and J.A. Frenkel (1979), "Dynamic Adjustment and the demand for international reserves", NBER Working Paper No. 407 (National Bureau of Economic Research, Cambridge).
Black, S.W. (1976), "Comment on J. Williamson, 'Exchange rate flexibility and reserve use'," Scandinavian Journal of Economics, 78:340–345.
Black, S.W. (1977), Floating exchange rates and national economic policy (Yale University Press, New Haven).
Black, S.W. (1978), "Policy responses to major disturbances of the 1970s and their transmission through international goods and capital markets", Weltwirtschaftliches Archiv, 114:614–641.
Black, S.W. (1981), "The impact of changes in the world economy on stabilization policies in the 1970s", in: W.R. Cline and S. Weintraub, eds., Economic stabilization in developing countries (Brookings, Washington) 43–77.
Black, S.W. (1983a), "The use of monetary policy for internal and external balance in ten industrial countries", in: J.A. Frenkel, ed., Exchange rates and international macroeconomics (University of Chicago Press, Chicago), forthcoming.
Black, S.W. (1983b), "The effect of alternative intervention policies on the variability of exchange rates: The 'Harrod' effect", Working paper 83-W06, Vanderbilt University.
Boyer, R.S. (1978), "Optimal foreign exchange market intervention", Journal of Political Economy, 86:1045–1056.
Branson, W.H. and J.B. de Macedo (1980), "The optimal weighting of indicators for a crawling peg", NBER Working Paper No. 527 (National Bureau of Economic Research, Cambridge).
Branson, W.H. and L.T. Papaefstratiou (1980), "Income instability, terms of trade, and the choice of exchange rate regime", Journal of Development Economics 7:49–69.
Britto, R. and H.R. Heller (1973), "International adjustment and optimal reserves", International Economic Review 14:182–195.
Buiter, W. (1979), "Optimal foreign exchange market intervention with rational expectations", in: J. Martin and A. Smith, eds., Trade and payments adjustment under flexible exchange rates (Macmillan, London).

Canzoneri, M.B. (1981), "Exchange intervention in a multiple currency world", International Finance Discussion Papers No. 174 (Board of Governors of the Federal Reserve System, Washington).

Carse, S., J. Williamson, and G. Wood (1980), The financing procedures of british foreign trade (Cambridge University Press, London).

Chow, G.C. (1981), Econometric analysis by control methods. (J. Wiley & Sons, New York).

Chrystal, K.A. (1980), "On the theory of international money", Department of Economics Working Paper Series No. 147 (University of California, Davis).

Clark, P.B. (1970), "Optimum international reserves and the speed of adjustment", Journal of Political Economy 75, 356–376.

Clark, P.B. and C.J. Haulk (1972), "Flexible exchange rates and the level of trade: A preliminary analysis of the canadian experience", unpublished paper (Federal Reserve Board, Washington).

Cline, W.R. (1976), International monetary reform and the developing countries (Brookings, Washington).

Coes, D. (1979), The impact of price uncertainty: A study of brazilian exchange rate policy (Garland, New York).

Cohen, B.J. (1975), "International reserves and liquidity", in: p.B. Kenen, ed., International trade and finance (Cambridge University Press, Cambridge) 411–452.

Cohen, B.J. (1979), "Europe's money, america's problem", Foreign Policy 35:31–47.

Cohen, B.J. (1982), "Balance of payments financing: Evolution of a regime", International Organization 36.

Cohen, S.D. (1970), International monetary reform, 1964–69: The political dimension (Praeger, New York).

Cooper, R.N. (1968), "The relevance of international liquidity to developed countries", American Economic Review 58:625–636.

Corden, W.M. (1981a), "Exchange rate protection", in: R.N. Cooper et al., eds., The international monetary system under flexible exchange rates, Essays in Honor of Robert Triffin (Ballinger, Cambridge) 17–34.

Corden, W.M. (1981b), "The logic of the international monetary non-system", Centre for Economic Policy Research Discussion Papers No. 24 (Australian National University, Canberra).

Cushman, D.B. (1980), The effects of exchange rate risk on international trade and investment, unpublished dissertation (Vanderbilt University, Nashville).

Cushman, D.B. (1983), "The effects of exchange rate risk on international trade", Journal of International Economics 13, forthcoming.

Dell, S. and R. Lawrence (1980), The balance of payments adjustment process in developing countries (Pergamon, New York).

DeVries, T. (1980), "On the meaning and future of the european monetary system", Princeton Essays in International Finance No. 138.

Diaz–Alejandro, C.F. (1981), "Southern cone stabilization plans", in: W.R. Cline and S. Weintraub, eds., Economic stabilization in developing countries (Brookings, Washington) 119–141.

Donovan, D.J. (1981), "Real responses associated with exchange rate action in selected upper credit tranche stabilization programs", IMF Staff Papers 28: 698–727.

Donovan D.J. (1982), "Macroeconomic performance and Adjustment under fund-supported programs: The experience of the seventies", IMF Staff Papers 29:171–203.

Dornbusch, R. (1981), "Exchange risk and the macroeconomics of exchange rate determination", in: R. Levich, R. Hawkins and C. Wihlborg, eds., Internationalization of financial markets and national economic policy (JAI Press, New York).

Dreyer, J.S., G. Haberler, and T.D. Willett (eds.) (1978), Exchange rate flexibility. (American Enterprise Institute for Public Policy, Washington).

Dreyer, J.S., G. Haberler, and T.D. Willett (eds.) (1982), The international monetary system: A time of turbulence (American Enterprise Institute for Public Policy, Washington).

Driskill, R. and S. McCafferty (1980), "Speculation, rational expectations, and stability of the foreign exchange market", Journal of International Economics 10:91–102.

Fleming, J.M. (1971), "International liquidity: Ends and means", IMF Staff Papers 8:439–463.

Fleming, J.M. (1975), "Floating Exchange rates, asymmetrical intervention, and the management of international liquidity", IMF Staff Papers 22:263–283.

Frenkel, J.A. (1974), "Openness and the demand for reserves", in: R.Z. Aliber, ed., National monetary policies and the international financial system (University of Chicago Press, Chicago) 289–298.

Frenkel, J.A. (1980), "The demand for international reserves under pegged and flexible exchange rate regimes and aspects of the economics of managed float", in: D. Bigman and T. Taya, eds., The functioning of floating exchange rates: Theory, evidence, and policy implications (Ballinger, Cambridge) 169–195.

Frenkel, J.A. and B. Jovanovic (1981), "Optimal international reserves: A stochastic framework", Economic Journal 91:507–514.

Genberg, H. and A.K. Swoboda (1977), "Worldwide inflation under the dollar standard", Discussion Paper No. 12 (Graduate Institute of International Studies, Geneva).

Genberg, H. (1981), "Effects of central bank intervention in the foreign exchange market", iMF Staff Papers 28:451–476.

Gold, J. (1970), Special drawing rights: Character and use (International Monetary Fund, Washington).

Grassman, S. (1973), "A fundamental symmetry in international payments patterns", Journal of International Economics 3:195–106.

Group of Thirty (1982), How central banks manage their reserves (Group of Thirty, New York).

Haberler, G. (1977), "How important is control over international reserves"? in: R.A. Mundell and J.J. Polak, eds., The new international monetary system (Columbia University Press, New York) 111–132.

Hamada, K. (1974), "Alternative exchange rate systems and the interdependence of monetary policies", in: R.Z. Aliber, ed., National monetary policies and the international financial system (University of Chicago Press, Chicago) 13–333.

Hamada, K. (1979), "Macroeconomic strategy and coordination under alternative exchange rates", in: R. Dornbusch and J.A. Frenkel, eds., International economic policy (Johns Hopkins University Press, Baltimore) 292–324.

Hamada, K. and K. Ueda (1979), "Random walks and the theory of the optimal international reserves", Economic Journal 87:722–742.

Harrod, R. (1964), Reforming the world's money (Macmillan, London) 45–47.

Hause, J. (1966), "The welfare cost of disequilibrium exchange rates", Journal of Political Economy 74:333–352.

Heller, H.R. (1966), "Optimal international reserves", Economic Journal, 74:296–311.

Heller, H.R. (1976), "International reserves and world-wide inflation", IMF Staff Papers 23:61–87.

Heller, H.R. (1978), "Determinants of exchange rate practices", Journal of Money, Credit, and Banking 10:308–321.

Heller, H.R. (1981a), "The dollar in the international monetary system", presented at the Conference on the Political Economy of the United States (Bank of America, San Francisco).

Heller, H.R. (1981b), "International lending, risk, and portfolio quality", presented at the Conference on the Conditions for International Monetary Stability (Bank of America, San Francisco).

Heller, H.R. and M.S. Khan (1978), "The demand for rreserves under fixed and floating exchange rates", IMF Staff Papers 25:623–649.

Heller, H.R. and M. Knight (1978), "Reserve-currency preferences of central banks", Princeton Essays in International Finance No. 131.

Henderson, D.W. (1979), "Financial policies in open economies", American Economic Review 67:537–548.

Henderson, D.W. (1983), "Exchange market intervention operations: Their effects and their role in financial policy", in: J.A. Frenkel, ed., exchange rates and international macroeconomics (University of Chicago Press, Chicago), forthcoming.

Hipple, F.S. (1974), "The disturbances approach to the demand for international reserves", Princeton Studies in International Finance No. 35.

Holden, P., Holden, M. and E.C. Suss (1979), "The determinants of exchange rate flexibility: An empirical investigation", Review of Economics and Statistics, 61:327–33.

Hooper, P. and S.W. Kohlhagen (1978), "The effect of exchange rate uncertainty on the prices and volume of international trade", Journal of International Economics 8:483–511.

International Monetary Fund (1974), International monetary reform: Documents of the committee of twenty (Washington, D.C.).

International Monetary Fund (1981), International capital markets, recent developments and short-term prospects (Washington, D.C.).

Iyoha, M. (1971), "Optimal balance of payment strategy by stochastic dynamic programming", Western Economic Journal 9:700–11.

Itagaki, T. (1982), "Systems of taxation of multinational firms under exchange risk", Southern Economic Journal 48:708–723.

Johnson, H.G. (1966), "The welfare costs of exchange rate stabilization", Journal of Political Economy 74:512–518.

Johnson, H.G. (1967), "Theoretical problems of the international monetary system", Pakistan Development Review 7:1–28; reprinted in: R.N. Cooper, ed., International finance (Penguin, Baltimore, 1969).

Johnson, H.G. (1972), Inflation and the monetarist controversy (North-Holland, Amsterdam).

Johnson, O. and J. Salop (1980), "Distributional aspects of stabilization programs in developing countries", IMF Staff Papers 27:1–23.

Jones, M. (1983), "International liquidity: A welfare analysis", Quarterly Journal of Economics 98:1–23.

Jones, R.A. (1976), "The origin and development of media of exchange", Journal of Political Economy 84:757–775.

Kelly, M.G. (1970), "The demand for international reserves", American Economic Review 60:655–667.

Kenen, P.B. (1960), "International liquidity and the balance of payments of a reserve currency country", Quarterly Journal of Economics 74:572–86.

Kenen, P.B. (1975), "Floats, guides and indicators", Journal of International Economics 5:107–151.

Kenen, P.B. (1981), "The analytics of a substitution account", Banca Nazionale del Lavoro Quarterly Review No. 139:403–426.

Kenen, P.B. (1982), "The role of the U.S. dollar as a store of value in international financial markets", Research Memorandum, Princeton University.

Khan, M.S. (1979), "Inflation and international reserves: A time series analysis", IMF Staff Papers 26:699–724.

Kouri, P.J.K. (1979), "Profitability and growth in a small open economy", in: A. Lindbeck, ed., Inflation and employment in open economies (North-Holland, Amsterdam) 129–142.

Kreinin, M.E. and H.R. Heller (1974), "Adjustment costs, optimal currency areas, and international reserves", in: W. Sellekaerts, ed., International trade and finance, essays in honour of Jan Tinbergen (Macmillan, London) 127–140.

Krugman, P. (1983), "Oil and the dollar", in: J.A. Frenkel, ed., Exchange rates and international macroeconomics (University of Chicago Press, Chicago), forthcoming.

Lindert, P.B. (1969), "Key currencies and gold", Princeton Studies in International Finance No. 24.

Lipschitz, L. and V. Sundararajan (1980), "The optimal basket in a world of generalized floating", IMF Staff Papers 27:80–100.

Lucas, R.E., Jr. (1976), "Econometric policy evaluation: A critique", in: K. Brunner and A.H. Meltzer, eds., The Phillips curve and labor markets (North-Holland, Amsterdam) 19–46.

Macedo, J.B. (1982), "Portfolio diversification across currencies", in: R.N. Cooper et al, eds., The international monetary system under flexible exchange rates, Essays in Honor of Robert Triffin (Ballinger, Cambridge).

Macedo, J.B. (1983), "International portfolio diversification: Short-term financial assets and gold", in: J.A. Frenkel, ed., Exchange rates and international macroeconomics (University of Chicago Press, Chicago), forthcoming.

Machlup, F. (1966), "The need for monetary reserves", Banca Nazionale del Lavoro Quarterly Review No. 78:3–50.

Makin, J.H. (1971), "The composition of international reserve holdings: A problem of choice involving risk", American Economic Review 61:818–832.

Makin, J.H. (1974), "Exchange rate flexibility and the demand for reserves", Weltwirtschaftliches Archiv 110:229–243.

McKinnon, R.I. (1974), "A new tripartite monetary agreement of a limping dollar standard"? Princeton Essays in International Finance No. 106.

McKinnon, R.I. (1979), Money in international exchange: The convertible currency system (Oxford University Press, New York).

McKinnon, R.I. (1982), "Currency substitution and instability in the world dollar standard", American Economic Review 72.

Mundell, R.A. (1968), International economics (Macmillan, New York).

Mundell, R.A. (1971), Monetary theory (Goodyear, Pacific Palisades, California).

Murphy, R.G. and G.M. von Furstenberg (1981), "An analysis of factors influencing the level of SDR holdings in non-oil developing countries", IMF Staff Papers 28:310–337.

Mussa, M. (1980), The role of Official intervention (Group of Thirty, New York).

Nyberg, L. and S. Viotti (1974), "The policy conflict between internal and external balance under fixed exchange rates: An optimizing approach", Swedish Journal of Economics 76:415–433.

Obstfeld, M. (1980), "Imperfect asset substitutability and monetary policy under fixed exchange rates", Journal of International Economics 10:177–200.

OECD (1977), Towards full employment and price stability (Organization for Economic Cooperation and Developement, Paris).

Officer, L.H. and T.D. Willett (1974), "Reserve-asset preferences in the crisis zone, 1958–67", Journal of Money, Credit, and Banking 6:191–211.

Page, S.A.B. (1977), "Currency invoicing in merchandise trade", National Institute Economic Review.

Polak, J.J. (1970), "Money: National and international", in: International reserves: Needs and availability (International Monetary Fund, Washington).

Polak, J.J. (1979), "The SDR as a basket of currencies", IMF Staff Papers 26:627–563.

Poole, W. (1970), "Optimal choice of monetary policy instruments in a simple stochastic macro model", Quarterly Journal of Economics 84:197–216.

Rabin, A. and L.J. Pratt (1981), "A note on heller's use of regression analysis", IMF Staff Papers 28:225–229.

Rana, P. (1981), The impact of generalized floating on trade flows and reserve needs: Selected asian developing countries (Garland Publishing Co., New York).

Reichmann, T.M. and R.T. Stillson (1978), "Experience with programs of balance of payments adjustment: Stand-by arrangements in the higher credit tranches, 1963–72", IMF Staff Papers 25:293–309.

Roper, D.E. and S.J. Turnovsky (1980), "Optimal exchange market intervention in a simple stochastic macro model", Canadian Journal of Economics 13:269–309.

Roosa, R.V., et al. (1982), Reserve currencies in transition (Group of Thirty, New York).

Salant, S.W. and D.W. Henderson (1978), "Market anticipations of government policies and the price of gold", Journal of Political Economy 86:627–648.

Scharrer, H.E. (1974), Die Wahrungsstruktur im Welthandel, Wirtschafts Dienst, cited in Heller 1981a.

Sobol, D.M. (1979), "A substitution account: precedents and issues", Federal Reserve Bank of New York Quarterly Review 4:40–48.

Sohemn, E. (1978), International liquidity issues under flexible exchange rates, in: J. Dreyer, G. Haberler and T.W. Willett, eds., Exchange rate flexibility (American Enterprise Institute, Washington) 255–263.

Swoboda, A.K. (1968), "The Euro-dollar market: An interpretation", Princeton Essays in International Finance No. 64.

Swoboda, A.K. (1980), Credit creation in the Euromarket: Alternatives theories and implications for control (Group of Thirty, New York).

Taylor, D. (1982), "Official intervention in the foreign exchange market, or bet against the central bank", Journal of Political Economy 90: 356–368.

Thursby, M.C. (1980), "The resource reallocation costs of fixed and flexible exchange rates: A counterexample", Journal of International Economics 10:79–90.

Tower, E. and T.W. Willett (1976), "The theory of Optimum currency areas and exchange rate flexibility", Princeton Special Papers in International Economics No. 11.

Trezise, P.H., ed. (1979), The European monetary system: Its promise and prospects (Brookings, Washington).

Triffin, R. (1960), Gold and the dollar crisis (Yale University Press, New Haven).

Whitman, M. v.N. (1975), "Global monetarism and the monetary approach to the balance of payments", Brookings Papers on Economic Activity: 531–555.

Willett, T.D. (1980), International liquidity issues (American Enterprise Institute for Public Policy Research, Washington).

Williamson, J.H. (1973), "International liquidity: A survey", Economic Journal 83:685–746.

Williamson, J.H. (1976a), "Exchange rate flexibility and reserve use", Scandinavian Journal of Economics 78:327–339.

Williamson, J.H. (1976b), "Generalized floating and the reserve needs of developing countries", in: D.M. Leipziger, ed., The international monetary system and the developing nations (Agency for International Development, Washington) 75–92.

Williamson, J.H. (1977), The failure of world monetary reform, 1971–1974 (New York University Press, New York).

Williamson, J.H. (1980), "Economic theory and international monetary fund policies", Carnegie Rochester Conference Series on Public Policy 13:255–278.

Williamson, J.H. (1981a), "The crawling peg in historical perspective", in: J.H. Williamson, ed., Exchange Rate Rules: The theory, performance, and prospects of the crawling peg (Macmillan, London) 3–30.

Williamson, J.H. (1981b), "The failure of world monetary reform: A reassessment", in: R.N. Cooper et al. eds., The international monetary system under flexible exchange rates, Essays in Honor of Robert Triffin (Ballinger, Cambridge) 297–307.

Williamson, J.H. (1982a), "The growth of official reserves and the issues of world monetary control", in J.S. Dreyer, G. Haberler and T.D. Willett, eds., The international monetary system: A time of turbulence (American Enterprise Institute for Public Policy Research, Washington).

Williamson, J.H. (1982b), IMF conditionality (Institute for International Economics, Washington).

Williamson, J.H. (1982c), "A survey of the literature on the optimal peg", Journal of Development Economics 11:39–61.

Chapter 23

ECONOMIC INTERDEPENDENCE AND COORDINATION OF ECONOMIC POLICIES

RICHARD N. COOPER*

Harvard University

Contents

*I am grateful to Ralph Bryant and Peter Kenen for detailed comments on an earlier version of this chapter.

Handbook of International Economics, vol. II, edited by R.W. Jones and P.B. Kenen
© *Elsevier Science Publishers B.V., 1985*

0. Introduction

The term "economic interdependence" has come into widespread use during the past decade. This chapter addresses the various meanings of this term, the possible reasons for increased economic interdependence on some of its meanings, and the implications of that increased economic interdependence for the functioning of national economies, including national economic policy. Except in passing, it does not cover the rapid growth of empirical work on interdependence.

1. Definition of terms

The OED defines "interdependence" as "the fact or condition of depending each upon the other; mutual dependence", and cites Coleridge as having used the term as early as 1822, followed by Huxley and Spencer, who used the term in connection with nature and social institutions, respectively. I have not done an exhaustive survey of use of the term by economists, but it was used in a meaning similar to that developed here as early as 1940 by W.A. Brown, Jr. in his *The International Gold Standard Re-interpreted, 1914–1934* (1940, p. 77).[1]

The first serious examination of "interdependence" by economists arose, not in the literature on the international economy, but in discussion of the philosophical underpinnings of econometric analysis, during the 1950s. The question there was whether in reality economies were truly simultaneous, or "interdependent", in a *causal* sense, or whether causation did not run clearly and unambiguously from one variable to another, such that any properly specified model should be "recursive" in nature.[2] This distinction is important for econometric estimation, since "interdependence" among endogenous variables introduces biases into ordinary least squares and other estimation techniques that were in almost universal use at that time. Whatever the merits of the underlying philosophical debate on the nature of causality, it is prudent to assume that endogenous variables in many models of economic behavior influence one another within the time periods covered by our observations, and estimation techniques designed to correct for simultaneous equation bias have now come into almost routine use.

[1] The term "interdependence" was used once by Albert Hirschman in his *National Power and the Structure of Foreign Trade* (1945, p. 10). Baldwin (1980) adopts the dubious procedure of imputing to Hirschman's casual use of the term a meaning based on the content of his entire book to argue that economists used this term to apply to power relationships among countries. Brown's use, which parallels that adopted below, antedates Hirschman's. More on this issue below, because there has been some divergence between economists and political scientists on the meaning and importance of economic interdependence.

[2] See, for example, Bentzel and Hansen (1954–55).

In ordinary usage, "economic interdependence" typically refers to some measure of the value of economic transactions between two countries, or between a country and the rest of the world, perhaps scaled to total national output or to some measure of total financial assets. But these measures are not satisfactory from an analytical point of view. On close inspection, there are really two quite different phenomena that are commingled in the term interdependence, each of which in turn is multi-dimensional.

The first concerns how costly it would be to do without the transactions in question, perhaps after a period of adjustment. Costly losses tend to be highly correlated with transactions levels, but it is possible to imagine instances in which a particular product is imported in small amounts but is such a crucial input into important productive processes, with no close substitutes, that its loss would entail large losses to the economy. This situation can be characterized as high dependence on another part of the world; if the dependence is reciprocal, it could be called high interdependence, although for reasons given below I prefer to call it high mutual dependence, or reciprocal dependence. This kind of dependence is obviously multidimensional, since it concerns specific commodities. In the context of a total cessation of trade between two countries, e.g. due to a war or a trade embargo, the many dimensions can be collapsed into the "loss of GNP" resulting from cessation. The measurement should contain a time dimension to reflect the fact that optimal adjustments to the loss of critical materials typically take time. This concept is of special interest to political scientists, who are concerned with the use and the threatened use of power as sources of influence. It has been called "vulnerability interdependence" by Keohane and Nye (1977).[3]

The second phenomenon concerns how much adjustment a country has to make to "foreign" events under conditions of normal economic activity, where frequency as well as cost is taken into account. When the requirements to adjust run both ways between two countries, Keohane and Nye call this "sensitivity interdependence". It involves marginal (as opposed to average) relationships, along with the magnitude and frequency of disturbances normally emanating from the foreign economies. The measures of sensitivity involve such factors congenial to economists as marginal propensities to spend on foreign products or assets, elasticities of substitution between foreign and domestic products or assets, elasticities of substitution in production, and relative size of the economies in question. This notion of interdependence is in harmony with the methodological discussion of interdependent systems of the 1950s, which also focussed on marginal relationships between the variables under examination.

---

[3]An example of vulnerability interdependence would be the dependence of Iran on the United States for spare parts for its military and telecommunications equipment, which became evident following the invasion of Iran by Iraq in 1980 while Iran was under a U.S. embargo, combined with the dependence of the United States on Iran for oil and for intelligence stations crucial to monitoring Soviet missile tests and other strategic military activity.

Some political scientists do not like this use of the term interdependence, on the grounds that it creates terminological confusion with the other concept, more relevant to them.[4] The difficulty is worse than that: sensitivity interdependence may be rising even when vulnerability interdependence is falling, and even for the same reasons. For example, as substitution possibilities increase due to technical changes that reduce cost differentials between home and foreign production of certain goods, the impact of normal foreign disturbances will rise while the cost (in a given time period) of a trade embargo will fall.

Each discipline must specify concepts and define terms in ways that are most suitable for its purposes. Economists do not focus on the threatened use of force so avidly as political scientists do, and they are more concerned professionally with the relatively humdrum problems of analyzing and managing economies under conditions of normal economic intercourse. I would therefore suggest that we use the term "mutual dependence" when two countries are dependent on (i.e. vulnerable to) one another, and, OED notwithstanding, that we use the term "interdependence" to refer to the degree of two-way influence of one economy on another at the margin. The key point, whatever the labels, is that the concepts are different, and each is useful in its own context. The political scientist may be more interested in a flow chart of economic transactions between two countries and in statistics concerning the share of its total supply of a crucial product that a country imports from potential adversaries (although even those can merely represent starting points for his analysis). The economist will be more interested in the matrix of partial derivatives linking a set of interesting variables, plus normal variation in the disturbances exogenous to his model, although when it comes to the impact of foreign disturbances on the domestic price level he too will be interested in import shares. Because of its implications for the framework of policy-making, however, political scientists should also take an interest in the economist's notion of interdependence.

Interdependence defined in this way must be distinguished from "openness," which refers simply to the exposure which a country has to the rest of the world.[5] It is only if the openness and size of the economy are such that the economy is itself affected by the impact of its own actions on the rest of the world that the openness becomes "interdependent". Nonetheless, because of its comparative simplicity, a small, open economy is frequently a useful point of departure for the analysis of interdependence, as is done later in this chapter.

[4] See Waltz (1970) and Baldwin (1980).
[5] Bryant (1980, pp. 156–159), uses the term openness and interdependence more or less interchangably.Certainly in reality there will be a close correspondence between them. But it is worth maintaining the distinction for two reasons: (1) "openness" refers to average relationships, such as the ratio of imports to GNP, whereas interdependence as used here refers mainly to marginal relationships, such as the marginal propensity to import; and (2) a single country can be open (in marginal as well as average terms) yet not *inter*dependent because it is too small to influence conditions in the rest of the world appreciably.

Interdependence must also be distinguished from the integration of markets across national boundaries. We can take August Cournot's definition of a market, cited with approval by Alfred Marshall, as "the whole of any region in which buyers and sellers are in such free intercourse with one another that the prices of the same goods tend to equality easily and quickly" – after allowing for transfer costs. We can speak of international economic integration to the extent that markets so defined cross national boundaries, the limiting case of course being the entire globe. However, markets here refer to single commodities and securities; a worldwide market implies that the law of one price obtains *for each of those goods and securities*. It is difficult to imagine a high degree of interdependence among nations in the presence of a low degree of market integration.[6] Nevertheless, a high degree of market integration can certainly exist without producing high interdependence, even when the countries involved are not so small that the impact of economic events in the rest of the world can be neglected. For instance, the elasticities of substitution between home and foreign goods or securities might be very low, despite highly integrated markets, or the marginal propensities to import goods or securities out of additional income or wealth might be very low.[7] Integration thus refers to a single product over space; interdependence typically refers to high substitutability between many products over space. In practice, high integration of markets, one by one, is necessary for high interdependence, but does not assure it.

Finally, it will be useful in this discussion of concepts and definitions to distinguish between several types of interdependence, the exact meaning of which will become clearer with the examples in later sections. There is first of all *structural* interdependence, whereby two or more economies are highly open (at the margin) with respect to one another, so that economic events in one strongly influence economic events in the other. It is this sort of interdependence which has been implicit in the discussion above. Its presence implies that each country will have a strong interest in information about both the structure of the other economy and likely events there. Detailed knowledge about developments in the German economy may be just as important for framing Dutch economic policies, for instance, as knowledge about the structure of the Dutch economy.

Second, there may be interdependence among the *objectives* of economic policy; that is, one country will be concerned about the attainment of policy targets in the other country. This would be trivially so when the targets are the same, such as the exchange rate between them; or, less obviously, when they are

---

[6]But not completely impossible. Because of natural endowments, for example, each of two countries might produce goods that were demanded *only* in the other country.

[7]Allen and Kenen (1980, p. 377 and passim), identify integrated markets with high elasticities of substitution between home and foreign goods and securities. This usage is somewhat confusing, since markets that are "perfect" in the sense that the law of one price prevails could, on this definition, be poorly integrated. It seems preferable to use high substitution elasticities as one measure of openness and, when the magnitudes are appropriate, of interdependence.

both subject to some overall constraint, such as that the current account positions of the world must add up to zero. Less trivial cases involve direct concern for developments elsewhere. Such concern has been clearly manifested in non-economic realms, as when country A's demand for defense expenditures depends directly on defense expenditures outside the country (positively when the foreigner is an adversary, negatively when he is an ally, unless institutional arrangements for burden-sharing are present), or when the residents of country A feel strongly about human rights conditions in foreign countries. There are beginnings of this cross-targeting in the economic realm as well, especially with respect to the distribution of income and wealth between and within countries.

Third, there may be low or high interdependence among the *exogenous disturbances* to two or more countries. As we will see, high structural interdependence implies that events in one country will cause disturbances in others (perhaps welcome ones), and vice versa. But here we are speaking of disturbances exogenous to both countries. If these disturbances are poorly (or inversely) correlated, high structural interdependence may actually on balance reduce their impact on economic variables of interest, such as national incomes or price levels [see Cooper (1974)]. If they are highly correlated, however, they will reinforce one another and this diversifying effect will be diminished or lost. Unfortunately, the same tendencies which increase structural interdependence may also increase the correlations among the exogenous shocks to which economies are subjected.

Fourth, there may be a high degree of *policy interdependence* between countries, in the sense that the optimal course of action for one country depends decisively on the action taken by another country, and vice versa. Such policy interdependence arises directly from structural interdependence or the interdependence of objectives already mentioned. Here we stress the game-theoretic or strategic aspects of policy interdependence: actions by country A will influence actions by country B, and vice versa, and each "player" should in general take these anticipated responses into account in framing his own actions. Moreover, the manner in which they are taken into account can influence strongly the extent to which countries may attain their national objectives. This type of interdependence will be discussed more fully in Section 5.

Most of the discussion that follows, under all of the categories above, will concern macroeconomic interdependence. But similar issues and problems arise if one's principal concern is microeconomic issues of regulation or taxation. These will be discussed briefly in the final section of this chapter.

2. Macroeconomic interdependence: A simple illustration

To fix ideas concerning the economist's approach to interdependence, consider first a small economy that exchanges goods and securities with the rest of the world. Here "small" is taken to mean that events in our country cannot appreciably influence the level of income, prices, or interest rates in the rest of the world; these are taken as given, exogenous, beyond our country's influence. We can then ask how much influence our country can have on its *own* level of income, prices, and interest rates through bond-financed government spending (fiscal policy) or through central bank open-market operations in domestic bonds (monetary policy). After examining the small, open economy we can turn to an economy that is large enough to influence conditions in the rest of the world, to ascertain what difference that makes. For concreteness, the economy (and, when we introduce it, the rest of the world) will be assumed to have well-defined aggregate demand schedules for their composite goods, for money, for the interest-bearing, one-period domestic security, and for the interest-bearing, one-period foreign security. The prices of the composite goods will be assumed to be fixed, as is the exchange rate. The nominal interest rate and the real interest rate are thus identical. The analysis will be shortrun in nature, assuming changes in stocks (e.g. of fixed capital or of outstanding government debt) to be negligible during the period under consideration. These assumptions are strong and tenable only for short-period analysis – and in any case are merely designed to introduce the key issues in simplified but concrete manner, by way of illustration. They follow the early tradition of open-economy macroeconomic analysis pioneered by Meade (1951), Fleming (1962), and Mundell (1968).

For the single country we can write:

$$Y = E(Y, r) + T(Y, Y') + G, \tag{2.1}$$

$$M = H + R = L(Y, r), \tag{2.2}$$

$$B = \Delta R = T(Y, Y') - \Delta F, \tag{2.3}$$

where

Y = national output,

E = national private expenditure,

G = government expenditure,

T = exports less imports,

M = high-powered money supply,

H = central bank holdings of domestic bonds,

R = central bank holdings of international reserves,

L = public demand for high-powered money,

B = balance of international payments,

F = private domestic holdings of foreign securities,

r = rate of interest on domestic bonds,

r' = rate of interest on foreign bonds.

A prime indicates that the variable is for the rest of the world.

We assume that the country is initially in short-run equilibrium in that the variables are unchanging and $B = 0$ by choice of an appropriate exchange rate. We then want to examine the impact of small changes in G and in H on the endogenous variables, Y and r, in the case of the small economy. Differentiate (2.1) and (2.2) totally with $dY' = dr' = 0$, let dx stand for the deviation of x from its initial value x_0 and re-arrange terms:

$$(s + m)\, dY - E_r\, dr = dG,$$ (2.4)

$$L_y\, dY + L_r\, dr = dM,$$ (2.5)

or in matrix terms:

$$\begin{pmatrix} s + m & -E_r \\ L_y & L_r \end{pmatrix} \begin{pmatrix} dY \\ dr \end{pmatrix} = \begin{pmatrix} dG \\ dM \end{pmatrix}.$$ (2.6)

Here $m = -T_y$, $s = 1 - E_y$, both assumed to be positive, and subscripts indicate the variable of differentiation: $L_y > 0$, $L_r < 0$, $E_r < 0$. The balance of payments poses a problem in this model of fixed exchange rates, for so long as $B \neq 0$ reserves will be changing and so will the money supply in the absence of offsetting action. We will therefore assume that, during the period under examination, sterilization of balance-of-payments flows takes place. Thus, we assume $dM = dR + dS + dH$, so that for $dS = -dR$, $dM = dH$, where dS is the purchase or sale of domestic securities designed to offset the change in reserves (sterilization), and dH is the purchase or sale of domestic securities over and above that.

This formulation, while satisfactory in the short run, has the undesirable consequence of excluding transactions in international securities from having any influence on domestic variables. We will therefore make one further adjustment. Suppose that home demand for foreign securities depends on the interest rate differential between our country and the rest of the world, $r' - r$. Suppose also that there is no foreign demand for home securities and that monies are not held by non-residents. Then a change in this differential will lead to a once-for-all change $\Delta F = F_r(dr' - dr)$ in domestic holdings of foreign securities, $F_r > 0$. Since the central bank fixes the exchange rate, this change in desired holdings by the public can be satisfied instantaneously. We will assume that this rapid adjustment occurs, and that the resulting change in reserves is *not* sterilized. That is, sterilization only applies to subsequent flow imbalances, arising through the trade account. (Alternatively, we can interpret our results as pertaining to very short-run equilibrium, before trade flows have influenced reserves enough to have discernable impact.) So the central bank account is revised to read

$$dM = dR_f + dR_t + dS + dH = dR_f + dH,$$

where f signifies reserve changes arising from (instantaneous) capital account transactions, t signifies reserve changes arising from imbalances in trade, and

$dS = -dR_f$. The reasons for this somewhat artificial distinction will become clear below.

Since $dR_f = -F_r(dr' - dr)$, (2.5) can now be rewritten for $dr' = 0$ as:

$$L_y \, dY + (L_r - F_r) \, dr = dH \tag{2.5'}$$

and (2.6) becomes:

$$\begin{pmatrix} s + m & -E_r \\ L_y & L_r - F_r \end{pmatrix} \begin{pmatrix} dy \\ dr \end{pmatrix} = \begin{pmatrix} dG \\ dH \end{pmatrix}, \tag{2.6'}$$

or $Ay = x$ for short, where A represents the "structure" of the economy around its equilibrium position. The economy's linkages with the rest of the world are captured in the coefficients m and F_r.

It is easy to show how the policy variables, G and H, affect the target variables:

$$\frac{dY}{dG} = \frac{L_r - F_r}{\Lambda} > 0, \tag{2.7}$$

$$\frac{dY}{dH} = \frac{E_r}{\Lambda} > 0, \tag{2.8}$$

$$\frac{dr}{dG} = \frac{-L_y}{\Lambda} > 0, \tag{2.9}$$

$$\frac{dr}{dH} = \frac{s + m}{\Lambda} < 0, \tag{2.10}$$

where $\Lambda = (s + m)(L_r - F_r) + E_r L_y < 0$. That is to say, expansionary fiscal policy ($dG > 0$) or monetary policy ($dH > 0$) will raise output, and fiscal expansion will raise the interest rate but expansionary monetary policy will lower it, in each case by amounts that depend on *all* the structural coefficients of the economy.

How are these policy coefficients (2.7)–(2.10) influenced by the international linkages? This can be seen by differentiating them with respect to m and F_r, respectively. By doing so, we discover that increased linkages with the rest of the world (larger m and F_r) generally weaken the impact of a given increase in G or H on the target variables Y and r.[8] There are, however, two exceptions.

(1) Higher F_r (a stronger response in holdings of foreign securities to a given change in the interest differential) strengthens the impact of G on Y, by leading to a sale of foreign securities which augments reserves and hence the money supply and thus weakens the drag on output of what otherwise would be higher domestic interest rates. This stimulative influence would of course be nullified if the capital movements were subject to sterilization.

(2) Higher m increases the magnitude of the (negative) effect of higher H on r, by reducing the stimulus to output and hence reducing the income-induced

---

[8]We assume that the remaining structural coefficients are unchanged, an assumption that needs to be questioned for large changes in m and F_r.

increase in demand for money. But in the six remaining combinations *higher foreign linkages reduce the impact of domestic policy variables on target variables.*

Is this general effect altered by allowing for interdependence – i.e. by dropping the assumption that our country is small? We can incorporate the rest of the world explicitly into the analysis by writing down equations analogous to (2.1) and (2.2) above for the rest of the world, treating its policy actions as exogenous, but allowing its income Y' and interest rate r' to respond to income and interest rates in the home country. Differentiating as before and putting the entire world system together yields:

$$
\begin{bmatrix}
s+m & -E_r & 0 & -m' \\
L_y & L_r - F_r & F_r & 0 \\
\hline
0 & F_r & L'_r - F_r & L'_y \\
-m & 0 & -E'_r & s'+m'
\end{bmatrix}
\begin{bmatrix}
dY \\
dr \\
\hline
dr' \\
dY'
\end{bmatrix}
=
\begin{bmatrix}
dG \\
dH \\
\hline
dH' \\
dG'
\end{bmatrix},
\tag{2.11}
$$

or $Ay = x$ for short. Here the variables are defined as before, except that primes are neglected on the subscripts to L'_r, L'_y and E'_r to avoid unduly complicated notation, and F_r must be interpreted as the change in holdings of foreign securities in response to a change in the interest differential, not in r alone. Now both countries are assumed to sterilize imbalances in payments (trade), except for those reflecting the instantaneous adjustments in portfolios that occur whenever the interest differential is altered.

The structural matrix A in (2.11) has been partitioned into two "domestic" blocks along the main diagonal, in the northwest and southwest corners – although they include some linkage coefficients – and two "international" blocks in the northeast and southeast corners. This will offer a convenient format for generalization to many countries.

As before, it is possible to calculate the policy multipliers on the target variables. We will focus on the influence of fiscal and monetary policy on national output; the interest rate is typically only an intermediate target or is not targeted at all.

It can readily be shown that in this larger system $dY/dG > 0$ and $dY/dH > 0$, as before, although the expressions are much more complex than (2.7) and (2.8).[9]

[9]Here

$$
\frac{dY}{dG} = \frac{1}{\Lambda}\left\{ (s'+m')\left[L_r L'_r - F_r(L_r + L'_r)\right] + (L_r - F_r) E'_r L'_y \right\} > 0,
$$

where

$$
\Lambda = (ss' + m's + ms')\left[L_r L'_r - F_r(L_r + L'_r)\right] + (s+m)(L_r - F_r)E'_r L'_y
$$
$$
+ (s+m')(L'_r - F_r)E_r L_y + E_r L_y E'_r L'_y - F_r\left(mE_r L'_y + m'E'_r L_y \right) > 0.
$$

What happens to these policy coefficients as international interdependence, as we may now call it, increases? In order to avoid unwanted compositional effects, we suppose that m and m' increase in the same proportion k; F_r can also increase, independently.

It can be shown that dY/dG declines unambiguously as k increases. dY/dH also declines as k increases so long as the two economies are identical in their (marginal) structural coefficients, and in any case for sufficiently small values of F_r or, equivalently, if capital flows are sterilized. For large F_r and economies that are sufficiently different, however, it is possible for an increase in openness as measured by m and m' to enhance the impact of open market operations on national output. For instance, if E_r'/s' is greater than E_r/s, then monetary expansion at home will stimulate investment in the rest of the world sufficiently to increase the impact on home income through higher exports (due to higher values of m'), despite the higher leakages through m.

dY/dH declines unambiguously as F_r increases if the two economies are similar in the sense that $E_r/L_r = E_r'/L_r'$, and will often decline even if this condition is not met.

dY/dG responds ambiguously to increases in F_r. For identical economies, increases in small values of F_r (values below $-L_r$) lead to an increase in dY/dG, as the enhanced demand for money with higher output is satisfied by sales of foreign securities and conversion of the proceeds into domestic money at the central bank.[10] For values of F_r sufficiently above L_r, however, further increases in F_r will reduce dY/dG, whether the economies are identical or not. This result stands in contrast to the small open economy, where the higher F_r, the greater the impact of fiscal policy on home output. Once the influence on income abroad is taken into account, higher capital mobility can reduce the effectiveness of fiscal policy via its depressing effects on foreign output (so long as $m, m' > 0$).

In summary, increased openness in terms either of goods or of securities generally weakens the effectiveness of the traditional instruments of macroeconomic policy on national output (substitution of tax reduction for increases in government expenditure would not fundamentally alter this analysis), although some exceptions can be found, arising mainly from consequential differences in the structures of the two economies.[11]

While the effectiveness of fiscal policy on output is reduced with increased trade linkages, by the same token its impact on income in the rest of the world is increased. Thus with increased interdependence policy actions in one country become larger "disturbances" in the other country. It does not follow, however, that the impact of a given dG on *world* output, $dY + dY'$, will remain unchanged.

---

[10] For $dr' = 0$, $F_r < -L_r$ implies that domestic bonds and domestic money are closer substitutes than are foreign and domestic bonds.

[11] Bryant (1980, ch. 12), has a lucid discussion of the influence of openness on policy multipliers, emphasizing the difficulties in making strong generalizations about them.

This will be so, in general, only if the two economies are identical in their structure. If they are not, redistributing the policy impact between the two economies, as any international linkages do, will alter the total impact on world output because of differences in response in the two economies. These compositional effects are also present within national economies, but we suppress them with the conventional assumptions of a single aggregate investment function, savings function, demand for money function, etc.

This two-country model is presented here merely to introduce the notion of economic interdependence, in the form of trade flows and capital movements, and to indicate how changes in international linkages will alter the effectiveness of some traditional instruments of macroeconomic policy. The simplification brings out the main elements, but it does so only by ignoring other elements and complexities that attend actual linkages among economies. It will perhaps be helpful to suggest directions in which the simplified model might be extended in the macro-economic realm. Discussion of international linkages that affect other aspects of policy is reserved until the final section.

First, this model has assumed a constant price level – an assumption that is perhaps plausible for an under-employed economy but not for a fully employed one. It is relatively straightforward to allow demand stimulus to affect prices and output in different proportions in a closed economy [see Tobin and Buiter (1980)], but here we are dealing with two economies. If the two national price levels respond differently to a given disturbance or policy action, substitution between the (composite) goods of the two countries will presumably take place, so relative prices must be introduced as a factor affecting demand for each country's output. The magnitude of this substitution effect represents another linkage between the two countries.[12] With many traded goods, there will of course be correspondingly many price relationships.

Second, the model could allow explicitly for response lags in the key variables – income, interest rates, trade, and capital movements – instead of assuming, as above, that the key variables move to their new (short-run) equilibrium values at once. In other words, time could be introduced explicitly into the model.

Third, once time is introduced explicitly allowance could and should be made for the cumulative influence of flow variables on stocks – of payments imbalances on reserves and (dropping the assumption of sterilization) money supply, of government deficits on outstanding bonds, of investment on capital stock, of savings on wealth.

---

[12] It has lately become fashionable to study international trade on the assumption of a single internationally traded good competing for national expenditure with non-traded goods in each country. On this more complex formulation (since two relative prices are involved), the elasticities of substitution between traded and non-traded goods within each country measure the degree of linkage.

Fourth, the assumption of a fixed exchange rate can be relaxed. Going to the other extreme of a fully flexible exchange rate has the advantage of assuring continuous balance in international payments and thus no influence of reserve changes on the money supply. But it has the disadvantage of altering radically the expectational environment concerning the future, for which credibly fixed exchange rates provide a firm point of reference. Allowance must be made for expectations regarding the durability or reversibility of any change in exchange rates, and therefore also for the influence of exchange rates on rates of return on and the domestic-currency value of foreign-currency assets.[13]

Fifth, allowance could be made explicitly for the policy reactions in the rest of the world to "disturbances" that arise from policy actions in the home country, and then in turn for the new responses of the home country. The dynamics of policy interaction between interdependent economies and the possible gains from coordination of policies will be taken up below.

3. Reasons for greater economic interdependence

Why might interdependence have risen in recent years? The roots lie in improvements in international transportation and communication. These in turn have diffused both production and management techniques and have reduced the dependence of exports on distinctive locational advantages. The result has probably been a sharp reduction in differences in comparative costs, giving rise to greater substitution possibilities in production [see Cooper (1968, ch. 3) and Lindbeck (1973)]. In addition, knowledge about the possibilities of producing or buying abroad has greatly improved, giving rise to much greater integration of markets. Official barriers to trade have also been reduced, especially among industrialized countries, although they remain high in many developing countries. The "foreignness" in foreign transactions is diminishing. Greater familiarity with foreign financial markets, the emergence of the euro-currency market, and the lowering of barriers to capital movements have all increased the interdependence among national financial markets. The move to flexible exchange rates, in contrast, has probably reduced interdependence, ceteris paribus, by introducing a modest barrier of (short-run) uncertainty for both trade and international financial transactions.

---

[13] Tobin and Braga de Macedo (1980) formulate a two-country instantaneous model under flexible exchange rates approached from the perspective of portfolio holdings of foreign and domestic assets and money; the goods market is suppressed but implicit. They do not discuss the influence of greater interdependence on policy coefficients, but they do demonstrate that a consistent balance sheet approach casts doubt on some of the strong generalizations about policy coefficients that were made in the Meade–Fleming–Mundell tradition, basically because of the possible effects, even in the short run, of changes in stocks.

4. Macroeconomic interdependence: A general dynamic formulation

The formulation of structural interdependence introduced in Section 2 can be generalized by considering the relationships between some set of target variables, y, determined within the economic system subject to analysis, and another set of variables, z, which are exogenous to that system but influence it. z can be considered either as disturbance variables, which are shocks from outside the system subject to analysis, or as policy variables, which are assumed to be under control of the policy-makers. More precisely, we will consider y to be deviations of target variables from their desired target values y^*, and z to be the outside influences that create non-zero values of y. It will sometimes be convenient to designate as x the subset of z that are policy instruments subject to control.

By linearizing in the neighborhood of y^*, we can describe the time path of the economic system for specified values of z as:

$$\delta y/\delta t = Ay + Bz(t). \tag{4.1}$$

The matrices A and B describe the influences of the variables y and z, respectively, on the rate of change of y. (In a steady state, $\delta y/\delta t = 0$.) If both A and B are diagonal matrices, the variables y are independent of one another and each one depends on a single element of z. If A and B are triangular matrices, there is a "recursive" system involving hierarchical dependence, with the first element of y depending only on a single element of z, the second element of y depending on the first element of y and the first two elements of z, and so forth through the y and z vectors. If A and B are both full matrices, all the elements of y depend on one another and on all the elements of z. This system is called an interdependent economic system. A captures the structural interdependence defined in Section 1, and B offers one way to capture the degree of interdependence among disturbances.

If now the elements of y and z are ordered so that the variables from different countries are grouped together, we can use eq. (4.1) to characterize the world economy made up of different countries, as eq. (2.11) did for two countries. If A and B are *block* diagonal, the individual national economies will be independent of one another. But if A and B are full matrices, all of the national economies will be structurally interdependent. Obviously many combinations of interdependence are possible. More interesting from our point of view, however, is the degree of interdependence, which in this formulation is measured by the magnitude of off-diagonal (or off-block diagonal) elements in the A and B matrices. Such an element in the B matrix indicates that a disturbance in country i, say, *directly* affects a variable in country j. Such an element in the A matrix indicates that a disturbance in country i indirectly affects a variable in county j, via the influence of a variable in country i. It is clear from this formulation that "interdependence" is multidimensional, since in principle there are hundreds of off-diagonal elements, and while some are rising (in absolute value) over time, implying higher interdependence, others may be falling. Talk of "greater economic interdependence" among countries thus must refer to some unspecified average characterization of these off-diagonal elements.

The potential linkages among economies are numerous, but the most obvious channels involve direct shifts in demand for a country's products or securities, price linkages, interest rate linkages, and direct links in the formation of expectations on the basis of universally available news. As interdependence rises, "disturbances" in one economy diffuse rapidly and widely to other economies. The meaning of "disturbance" of course depends very much on the analytical framework within which one is operating. What is a disturbance in one framework is an endogenous response in another. In particular, political science has taken on the fundamentally difficult task of attempting to endogenize a number of actions – especially policy responses – which economists typically assume to be exogenous within their analytical framework.

If the original disturbances are not perfectly correlated, higher interdependence may actually reduce the disturbances which a national economy experiences in an interval of time by diffusing them widely and leading to some cancelling out of effects [see Kenen (1969) and Cooper (1974)]. The same forces that have increased interdependence, however, are also likely to increase the correlation among disturbances. Consumption fads in one country are more likely to be emulated in other countries; labor unions are more conscious of what their companion institutions are doing in neighboring countries; inflationary expectations are likely to be influenced by world-wide events; and so on. In that case, the rapid diffusion of disturbances may not, on balance, diminish much the total impact of disturbances, since the scope for cancelling out will be reduced. Moreover, greater interdependence may actually create disturbances on a global scale. For example, the smooth functioning of financial markets depends on the law of large numbers – on the mutual offsetting of numerous individual judgments and transactions. Where bandwagon effect become global in character, fostered by instant communication, this essential cancelling out may be diminished or lost.

Just as disturbances spread more quickly and more widely under high interdependence, so do the policy actions of individual countries (recall that x, policy actions, is a subset of z). This in turn has two consequences. First, policy actions in one country become "disturbances" in others, perhaps welcome, perhaps unwelcome. Second, as we saw in Section 2, policy actions may become less efficacious at home with respect to the objectives they seek; as the leakages abroad increase, the impact at home declines, so the instruments of policy generally have to be worked harder to achieve a given effect. Most policy instruments have multiple effects, and the costs associated with their side effects (e.g. the unwanted allocational effects of a general tax increase) typically rise with the extent to which the instrument is used. As a result, increased leakages will lead to greater side effects, domestic as well as foreign, in relation to the original intended effect.

The economic system characterized by eq. (2.11) is a particular example of the more general formulation in eq. (4.1) once we specify desired values y^* for the income and interest rate variables, and on the assumption that the system has settled down so that $\delta y / \delta t = 0$. Extension of the system (2.11) from two to many countries does not alter the general findings about the policy multipliers so long as all the countries are identical in structure (implying that bilateral relations between any pair of countries are the same for all possible pairs). But once allowance is made for important differences in size and structure, compositional effects become much more important, and simple, strong generalizations break down.[14]

The dynamic economic system (4.1) is stable around the desired values of y^* so long as the matrix A of structural coefficients is stable, that is, so long as its characteristic roots are negative. Under these circumstances, the role of macroeconomic stabilization policy is not literally to stabilize, but to accelerate the return of target variables to their target values. This role will be the more important, the longer are the lags with which the economic system "rights itself" after having been pitched away from its targets by outside disturbances. Stabilization policy becomes necessary if the economic system is not inherently stable around its targeted values, as is the case with some Keynesian systems with their under-employment equilibria. Policy variables then become crucial not merely for speeding up adjustment, but for attaining the targets at all. As Tinbergen showed many years ago, attainment of n targets y^* in a linear system such as (4.1) will in general require an equal number of policy instruments.[15]

Sufficient instruments will assure attainment of targets in this kind of system if there are no constraints on the use of instruments. But the instruments and targets are here assigned to different countries, and a natural question is whether the nationally autonomous pursuit of national targets will in fact converge to those targets in an interdependent system. Mundell (1968) proposed his "principle of effective market classification" to match targets with instruments in a decentralized system of policy making: each instrument should be used in pursuit of that target for which it has comparative advantage. Mundell was mainly interested in the roles to be assigned to monetary and fiscal policy within a single economy, but the appropriate assignment of instruments to targets is a more

---

[14]See Aoki (1981, chs. 13 and 15) for a discussion of these compositional effects and a method for analyzing them

[15]For a variety of reasons, including uncertain knowledge of the structural coefficients and constraints on wide use of some instruments, it is desirable to have more instruments than objectives. In the optimizing approach taken up in Section 5 below, the equation between numbers of instruments and targets is also avoided by expressing a national objective function explicitly. On the influence of uncertainty on the use of policy instruments, see Brainard (1967).

general issue and is of greater interest when two or more countries are involved.[16] An assignment of instruments to targets on the basis of comparative impact will always assure stability of a decentralized system if there are only two targets and two instruments, but the notion of "comparative advantage" becomes less clear in systems with a large number of instruments and targets, and no easy generalization is possible [see Patrick (1973)]. Even with stability assured, moreover, convergence to targets may be slow.

The problem can be formulated more formally. Suppose the instruments of policy are adjusted according to the rule:

$$\delta x / \delta t = Cy, \tag{4.2}$$

where y is the deviation of the targets variables from their target values y^*, and C can be considered a coordination matrix, since it indicates which target variables are guiding which instruments. The question then arises, if national governments target only their own national objectives in a system like (4.1), can they be assured of achieving their objectives? Or is it possible that actions by one country in pursuit of its targets will so dislodge the target variables of other countries that their policy responses in pursuit of their targets have the consequence of driving the first country further away from its target, evoking further destabilizing action by the first country, and so on?

The policy adjustment rule in (4.2) may be combined with the dynamic economic structure in (4.1) to produce:

$$Dx = C(D - A)^{-1} Bx,$$

which with reorganization becomes:

$$D(D - A)x - BCx = 0, \tag{4.3}$$

where D is a diagonal matrix of differential operators. This is a second-order system of differential equations, and it will converge to y^* only if the real parts of all roots are negative. The question concerning the workability of decentralized policy-making can then be posed as: Can a block diagonal matrix C be found that will assure the convergence of equation (4.3)?

Aoki (1976) addresses this question for the special case in which the B matrix is structured so that policy actions in each country do not affect *directly* the target variables in the other countries, except where the targets are common to two or more countries (e.g. the exchange rate) that is, B is block diagonal except with respect to the common targets. He supposes further that the coordination matrix

---

[16]Mundell (1971) later addressed the appropriate assignments of national monetary policies in a closed, interdependent world economy with fixed exchange rates. He suggested that all countries except for the United States should use their monetary instruments to assure balance in their international payments, and the United States should use its monetary instrument to target the world price level.

C takes the special form:

$$C = \begin{bmatrix} C_{11} & C_{12} & 0 \\ 0 & C_{22} & C_{23} \end{bmatrix} = \begin{bmatrix} g_1 & (w_1, w_2, 0) \\ g_2 & (0, w_3, w_4) \end{bmatrix}, \tag{4.4}$$

where the w's are the weights which the national authorities attach to their respective objectives (the middle column reflecting the common objective), and g_i is the "gain" or strength which they apply to their instrument variables in response to deviations from target. Under these circumstances, Aoki shows that for two countries, each with one instrument (but many possible targets, some held in common between the countries), values for g_1 and g_2 can be found that will assure the stability of eq. (4.3) provided A is stable. He suggests that this result can be generalized to many countries, but does not demonstrate it. Moreover, even in the two-country case, g_1 and g_2 must be chosen cooperatively if stability is to be assured (that is, if policy is not to destabilize a basically stable system); or at a minimum one of them must be chosen taking into account knowledge of the other.

The task of stabilization in a decentralized system can be eased if there is a direct feedback of policy variables on their own rates of change, that is, if instead of (4.2) the policy adjustment rule takes the form:

$$\delta x / \delta t = Cy + Ex. \tag{4.5}$$

This converts the total system, after substitution and re-arrangement, to

$$D^2 x - (A + C^{-1}EC)Dx - (BC - AC^{-1}EC)x = 0. \tag{4.6}$$

For E (block) diagonal, sufficiently large negative elements can be chosen to assure that the decentralized system is stable if A itself is stable, i.e. if stabilization policy is necessary only to speed up the process of adjustment. If A is not stable, a suitable E can be found to stabilize the entire system in the 3×3 case, but E must be chosen cooperatively, not with each country acting on its own.

In general, then, it does not seem possible to assure stability for decentralized policy-making,[17] although in most practical instances it is likely that an astute choice of policy adjustment rule will permit decentralized policy-making to proceed successfully if there are sufficient instruments.[18]

---

[17]Aoki, an engineer by training, takes for granted that instability is possible. See Aoki (1981, p. 273).

[18]A generalization of Mundell's principle of market classification to many targets and instruments has been attempted by Patrick (1973) and Aoki (1976, appendix 8). Aoki states the conditions required for instruments to have comparative advantage with respect to target in a system given by eqs (4 1) and (4.5), on the assumption that this system is stable. Successful decentralization on this principle is not assured when these conditions are not satisfied, or, even if they are, if the appropriate pairing of instrument to target crosses a national boundary, such that country A controls the instrument appropriate for pursuit of one of country B's targets.

Even if convergence to target were assured, however, the path back to the targets following some disturbance might oscillate, involving much overshooting and delay in the attainment of targets. The longer a country is away from its targets, moreover, the larger the loss in its welfare, ceteris paribus. In these circumstances, there is a strong case for international coordination of policy actions to assure a minimum of working at cross purposes and a speedy return of target variables to their target values. This issue has been explored through simulation of two-country systems by Cooper (1969) and Roper (1971).

The questions addressed in this section are of interest because nations in an interdependent world economy do in fact pursue their domestic policy targets without explicit regard for the actions other countries are taking, except insofar as they impinge directly and visibly on each national economy. It is useful to know, therefore, whether decentralized policy-making of this type, with imperfect information about the prospective actions of others, is likely to achieve the desired results even in the absence of conflicting objectives, which pose a different set of problems.

5. Macroeconomic interdependence: Conflict among objectives

The preceding section was profoundly non-economic in one respect – it assumed that all targets can be reached. With nations, as with individuals, aspiration generally exceeds attainment. We must allow for the likelihood that all targets cannot be achieved simultaneously, that choices must be made among them at the margin, and that national targets for jointly determined variables may even be in direct conflict.

To handle trade-offs and direct conflicts among targets requires an optimizing approach based on some national welfare (or loss) function, introduced to analysis of government policy by Theil (1964) and extended to the international context by Niehans (1968) and by Hamada in a series of pioneering articles.[19] Hamada addresses the general question whether the behavior of nations, each pursuing its own national objectives in an interdependent world, will lead to a result that is optimal from the viewpoint of the community of nations. The general answer is that it will not. He therefore goes on to ask whether this general

---

[19]See, especially, Hamada (1979) and the references there cited; also Bryant (1980, pp. 464–470). A direct conflict among objectives arises when one party desires $\hat{y}$ and another party desires (not $\hat{y}$). A generalized conflict among objectives, calling for choice, arises when a party wants both $\hat{x}$ and $\hat{y}$, but circumstances (the opportunity set) do not permit him to get arbitrarily close to both objectives at the same time; he must choose one or the other, or some compromise between them. The use of a national welfare function allows both kinds of conflict to be handled when more than one objective is involved by introducing the possibility of an opportunity cost to the attainment of objectives.

answer can be altered through institutional "rules of the game" within which nations pursue their objectives.

These questions are exceedingly important, and implicitly have engaged the attention of statesmen over the years. But they have not been addressed in their full generality by economists, in part because of their difficulty. Hamada explores some of the key elements in a simple two-country framework, briefly extended to three, in which each country is assumed to target its rate of inflation and its balance-of-payments position in a regime of fixed exchange rates. Each controls a single policy instrument, the level of domestic credit creation. In this framework, neither country can attain both its objectives by acting alone, except by coincidence; and of course the objectives of the two countries will typically conflict, again except by coincidence. Hamada then addresses how successful the countries might be if they cooperated in pursuit of their objectives, and compares this with two alternative approaches to policy: (1) each country pursues its pair of objectives independently, taking actions by the other country as given and not anticipating how the other country will respond to its actions; and (2) each country pursues its pair of objectives independently, but one country (the "leader") anticipates how the other country will react to its actions. This format gives rise to three different kinds of solution, well known from duopoly theory: a cooperative, joint solution which will be Pareto optimal; a Cournot–Nash solution which in general will not be Pareto optimal; and a Stackelberg–Nash solution which in general will also not be Pareto optimal but will leave the leading country better off than the Cournot–Nash solution, and which may leave the other country either better or worse off.

The structure of this approach can be illustrated with a simple model in which two countries under flexible exchange rates are concerned with two targets, the rate of change in output and the rate of inflation, and each disposes of a single instrument of policy, the rate of monetary expansion.[20] (We will return to Hamada's fixed exchange rate example below.) For simplicity, we will assume that the two countries are identical in their economic structure and their preferences with respect to these targets. Concretely, suppose that each country desires to minimize the loss function:

$$U = -\left(q^2 + wp_c^2\right), \tag{5.1}$$

where q is the percentage rate of change in national output, p_c is the rate of inflation, and w is the weight that is accorded to inflation as opposed to output changes. Note that the function U is symmetric for increases and decreases, so changes in either direction cause disutility.

---

[20] This illustration is a variant, suggested by Jeffrey Sachs, of an analysis found in Canzoneri and Gray (1983).

The common structure of the economies in the neighborhood of equilibrium is given by the following relationships:

$$q = \gamma(e + p^* - p) - \lambda i, \tag{5.2}$$

$$m - p = \alpha q - \beta i, \tag{5.3}$$

$$p_c = \mu(p^* + e) + (1 - \mu)p, \tag{5.4}$$

$$i = i^*. \tag{5.5}$$

Here e is the percentage change in the exchange rate (domestic currency price of a unit of foreign currency), m is the percentage change in the supply of money, p is the percentage change in prices of domestic output, i is the instantaneous change in the interest rate, and an asterisk ($*$) designates the variables for the foreign country. Greek letters are structural coefficients, assumed constant and positive. Eq. (5.2) represents the demand for output as a function of relative prices and the interest rate. Eq. (5.3) is the demand for real money balances as a function of output and the interest rate. Eq. (5.4) gives the consumer price index as a weighted average of the prices of domestic output and of imported goods. Eq. (5.5) is an interest arbitrage condition, valid because of our assumption of symmetry between the two countries, implying no expected change in the exchange rate. We will assume that in the relatively short run under consideration, the rate of change of domestic output prices is fixed and is identical in the two countries at $\bar{p} > 0$. This assumption implies that changes in nominal interest rates are the same as changes in real interest rates.

Equations (5.2)–(5.5) can be solved to yield reduced form relationships in terms of the two policy variables, m and m^*, and the exogenous rate of change of output prices,

$$q = am - bm^* + c\bar{p}, \tag{5.6}$$

$$e = (m - m^*)/2\alpha\gamma, \tag{5.7}$$

$$p_c = \bar{p} + \mu e = \bar{p} + \mu(m - m^*)/2\alpha\gamma, \tag{5.8}$$

where $a > b > 0$ and $c = b - a < 0$.[21] Comparable expressions hold for the starred country.

Because of the underlying symmetry, e must equal zero. But in that case $p_c = p_c^* = \bar{p}$, and the loss function (5.1) is minimized by setting $q = q^* = 0$. From (5.6) and its counterpart for the starred country, this result will be achieved when

[21]

$$a = (\beta + 2\alpha\lambda)/2\alpha(\beta + \alpha\lambda),$$

$$b = \beta/2\alpha(\beta + \alpha\lambda),$$

$$c = -\lambda/(\beta + \alpha\lambda).$$

$m = m^* = \bar{p}$. This then represents the optimal, cooperative solution for these two economies, the best they can do under the postulated circumstances.

However, if the two countries act independently, each will believe that it can do better. The unstarred country, for example, can reduce its rate of inflation p_c by appreciating its currency, and will believe that it can do that by reducing the rate of growth of its money supply, m, if it assumes that m^* remains unchanged. Specifically, if it assumes that $m^* = \bar{p}$, the unstarred country can minimize U by setting $dU/dm = 0$, which yields:

$$m = gm^* - h\bar{p} < \bar{p}, \qquad (5.9)$$

where $g < 1$.[22] Eq. (5.9) specifies the m that the unstarred country desires as a function of m^*; it is the country's reaction function.

Because of the underlying symmetry, however, the starred country will reason in precisely the same way: for a given m, it can minimize its loss function U^* by choosing m^* such that:

$$m^* = gm - h\bar{p}. \qquad (5.10)$$

Eq. (5.10) is the starred country's reaction function. Taken together with (5.9), it yields the non-cooperative, Cournot–Nash solution to this policy game:

$$m = m^* = [-h/(1 - g)]\,\bar{p}, \qquad (5.11)$$

which is unambiguously less than $\bar{p}$. Thus the non-cooperative solution leads each country to contract monetary conditions in an effort to appreciate its currency in order to reduce inflation. In policy equilibrium, however, the exchange rate remains unchanged, as does the rate of inflation in each country, but by (5.6) output has fallen, so both countries are clearly worse off than they would be with the cooperative solution.

The contrast between the two solutions is illustrated graphically in Figure 5.1. The two reaction functions, (5.9) and (5.10), are plotted in the $m - m^*$ plane; their intersection at N shows the non-cooperative solution. The loss function (5.1) would be a family of ellipses in the $g - p_c$ plane, and since both of these variables are linear in m and m^*, it is also a family of ellipses in the $m - m^*$ plane. Its

[22] Here

$$g = \frac{ab + wk^2}{a^2 + wk^2},$$

and

$$h = \frac{ac + k}{a^2 + wk^2},$$

where $k = \mu/2\alpha\gamma$. It can be shown that $m > 0$ for $\bar{p} > 0$ unless α, the elasticity of demand for real money balances with respect to output, is well under $1/4$, an unlikely possibility. In this example, e becomes an intermediate target for both countries, which have conflicting objectives.

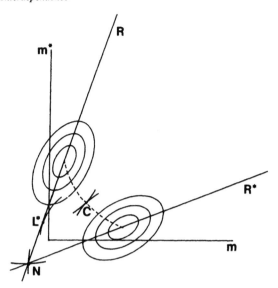

Figure 5.1

orientation depends upon the structural coefficients as well as upon $\bar{p}$. A similar, mirror image utility map can be drawn for the starred country, with the 45° line providing the mirror. These are also sketched in Figure 5.1. Pareto efficient combinations of policies lie along the locus of tangencies between the two utility maps, and the cooperative solution C is the symmetric point on this locus, i.e. the one where $e = 0$ and therefore $m = m^*$. Note that the values for $m(= m^*)$ are higher at C than they are at N, the intersection of the two reaction functions, as demonstrated above. (The reaction function R of the unstarred country is obtained by treating m^* as a parameter and is the locus of points on that country's utility map that have horizontal tangents. The reaction function R^* is the locus of vertical tangencies on the starred country's utility map.)

It can be seen in Figure 5.1 that if a country takes into account the other country's reaction to its own actions, it can do better than it will do at N, the non-cooperative solution. Thus the starred country can maximize its utility non-cooperatively by choosing an m^* at which its utility map is tangent to the other country's reaction function, shown as L^* in Figure 1. The starred country, acting as a "leader" in the Stackelberg sense, over-expands in the knowledge that the follower will try to appreciate its currency and thereby induce global contraction. In this framework, the "leader" improves its position compared with N, but the gains of the follower are even greater in this particular example, leading to the possibility that each country will wait for the other to take the first step (after you, Alphonse) while they both linger at N. L^* is clearly inferior to C for the starred country, although not, as drawn, for the unstarred one. In any case, $e \neq 0$ at L^*, so the interest arbitrage condition (5.5) would have to be revised and the model solved under those new conditions.

Are there institutional arrangements that will lead both countries to the cooperative arrangement C? If the exchange rate is fixed by agreement, as under the Bretton Woods Agreement, C will be assured, since the temptation to appreciate to reduce home inflation will be removed. Under these circumstances, the starred country (say) will choose m^* to minimize U^* on the assumption that $e = 0$, i.e. that $dm = dm^*$. It can be shown that this will lead to the cooperative solution C, where the utility surfaces are tangent to one another.[23]

Even this simple formulation of policy interdependence is very complicated. The cooperative solution $m = m^* = \bar{p}$, which clearly maximizes mutual advantage in the short run, will also sustain the initial rate of change of output prices, $\bar{p}$, and thus the rate of inflation. The non-cooperative solution, in contrast, has $m = m^* < \bar{p}$, which will not sustain the initial rate of inflation. It will subside gradually at rates depending on factors that have not been specified, linking the decline in output to the price level. Thus, in this example the non-cooperative solution may lead to higher utility in the long run, while the one period cooperative solution leads to higher utility in the short run. A total assessment thus also involves an intertemporal choice.[24] But in the short run, in this model, flexible exchange rates and decentralized decision-making will lead to excessive contraction in response to, say, an exogenous world supply shock that raises p and p^*. Arguably, this kind of analysis captures an important element of what actually happened to the world economy in 1980–82.

The Bretton Woods system was designed specifically to avoid manipulation of exchange rates in the pursuit of national macroeconomic objectives. Historically, this manipulation involved competitive depreciation for the purpose of stimulating employment, but the rules would also have prohibited competitive appreciation in pursuit of anti-inflationary objectives. A system of fixed exchange rates has its own problems, however, even when the rates themselves are equilibrium exchange rates. Most of Hamada's discussion of policy interdependence takes place within a regime of fixed exchange rates, in which countries target the rate of inflation and the rate of increase in their international reserves. He shows that the non-cooperative solution is sub-optimal, as it is in the flexible exchange rate illustration given above. In particular, if both countries desire increases in reserves

---

[23] $dU^*/dm^* = \partial U^*/\partial m^* + (\partial U^*/\partial m)(dm/dm^*) = 0$ implies, for $dm = dm^*$, that $\partial U^*/\partial m^* = -\partial U^*/\partial m$. By symmetry in the model, therefore, $(\partial U^*/\partial m^*)/(\partial U^*/\partial m) = (\partial U/\partial m^*)/(\partial U/\partial m)$, i.e. a tangency between the utility surfaces. This condition plus $e = 0$ establishes the cooperative solution.

[24] Sachs (1983) has shown that non-cooperative solutions are inferior to multi-period cooperative ones in an extended model involving many periods.

and manipulate their monetary policies to assure balance-of-payments surpluses, the "world" will be subjected to economic contraction, and inflation rates will be below the desired level [see Hamada (1974)].

If the sum of targets for payments balance exceeds the growth in world reserves in Hamada's models, monetary policy will be more contractionary and inflation rates will be lower than desired in a non-cooperative regime, whereas some of these contractionary influences would be avoided in a cooperative regime. If, in contrast, the sum of desired payments balances falls short of world reserve growth, inflation in a non-cooperative regime will be greater than desired.

Here is an instance in which the targets of the two countries are inconsistent, and the attempt to achieve the inconsistent targets, while leading to a stable solution, as in the illustration with floating exchange rates given above, results in a general loss in welfare compared with what is possible. The natural "systemic" solution in this instance is for the international regime to create enough international reserves to satisfy the growing demand for them, so that both countries can run payments surpluses. Special Drawing Rights created by the International Monetary Fund can be viewed in this light – as an outside source of international reserves for a world in which national demands for reserves are growing over time and nations are willing if necessary to conduct their policies so as to assure some growth in their owned reserves.

This method for reconciling conflicting national goals would not work where the goals involved trade or current account surpluses, rather than increases in international reserves. In the former cases, there is a global consistency requirement summing the national balances to zero. Reconciliation in this case must involve changing the targets themselves (or, more generally, the way in which the targets enter national preferences), possibly by inducing a major country to adopt a position of indifference toward its trade or current account balance and thus to act as a residual for the world as a whole.

Of course, if the countries participating in a policy "game" make up a substantial part of the world economy (as they do in a two-country model), it is unlikely that each government will ignore foreign response to its own actions. Taking these reactions into account, a Stackelberg leader can improve its position, compared with the Cournot–Nash non-cooperative solution, by choosing the point on the foreigner's reaction curve that maximizes its welfare (like the point L^* in Figure 5.1). The effect on the welfare of the followers may range from deterioration to improvement much greater than that of the leader, compared with the Nash non-cooperative equilibrium, depending upon the exact assumptions of the "game" being played.

The analysis so far of policy interdependence has been somewhat artificial or contrived, as is duopoly theory in general. Outcomes depend critically on the details of structure, preferences, and information, and on the degree of anticipatory or strategic behavior by the actors. But these efforts capture an important point about the real world. National objectives may conflict, and countries – especially since there are many rather than only two – may fail to take adequately into account the behavior of other countries: they engage in partial rather than general equilibrium analysis with respect to the consequences of their actions. This phenomenon is especially likely in a world of roughly 160 nations, most of them small relative to the world as a whole, such that each can plausibly take events elsewhere as beyond its influence. The United States, the European Community, and Japan, in contrast, are all oligops in that they should recognize the consequences of their own actions for the system as a whole as well as for themselves. That realization has come only recently and incompletely to Japan, however, and the European Community is still made up of ten not fully harmonized national parts, especially with regard to macroeconomic policy. The situation is further complicated by the fact that national policy actions in democratic societies are the resultant of diverse and usually conflicting domestic pressures, so even when interdependence with the rest of the world is clearly present and intellectually recognized, it will not be fully reflected in national policy actions.

Allusions have been made from time to time to competition among nations in the pursuit of their objectives, to the matching of instruments to targets along the lines of comparative advantages, and so on. These allusions are drawn from economic analysis of private markets and agents. Yet we know that under certain general conditions "competition" among private agents, while thwarting their individual objectives to some extent, conduces to the social good; and we know that even though all objectives cannot be attained, the operation of a price system under competition will reconcile competing claims to output in a way that is efficient and even often harmonious. Might not the same line of reasoning apply to nations? Might not non-cooperative behavior among them nonetheless lead to an overall optimum outcome?

This is a profound question, yet it has received little analysis.[25] It will not be attempted here. But two general remarks about the analogy can be made. First, private competitive markets are known to "fail" – that is, produce sub-optimal results – in the presence of externalities of all kinds. In particular, they produce too few public goods – goods with pervasive externalities, in the sense that once produced they can be enjoyed by many at little or no extra cost. Are there international public goods (or bads)? The clearest example, periodically preoccupying to many people around the world, is national expenditure on strategic nuclear weapons. Their existence raises the possibility of a truly global devastation, clearly a public bad. Control of contagious disease (e.g. the elimination of smallpox) falls clearly into the category of international public goods. Economic stabilization in the major industrial countries of the world, most notably the

---

[25] For partial attempts along these lines, see Cooper (1974) and Corden (1983).

United States, arguably also falls in this category. Although what exactly is meant by stabilization is subject to disagreement, there is little doubt that economic management in the United States (and Europe and Japan) has strong externalities for the rest of the world, externalities which the major countries have not typically taken into account when framing their economic policies.

Second, the structure of the world of nations lies far from what would be required to meet the conditions of perfect competition. There are only about 160 members to the community of nations, many of which are large enough to influence *some* of the markets in which they operate, a few of which are large enough to influence all of the markets in which they operate. In short, the community of nations exists in the presence of extensive monopoly power–although, as with private monopoly power, it is limited by the alternative opportunities that other nations have. The attempt to exercise this limited monopoly in the pursuit of national objectives – to improve the terms of trade or to draw resources from the rest of the world – violates the conditions of "competition" and gives rise to the pervasive possibility of pushing economic policies toward global suboptimality. That in turn gives rise to possible gains from collusion, or, as it is more politely called in the context of economic policy, cooperation and coordination in order to enhance attainment of national economic objectives.

6. Possible responses to economic interdependence

The responses to increased economic interdependence have varied in character and direction. One response involves steps toward *dis*integration, to reduce the interdependence and restore some freedom of action to national policy-makers. A second response involves attempts to coordinate national policy actions in one fashion or another, sometimes through conscious collaboration among nations, sometimes by one nation attempting to impose its preferred course of action on others. A third response involves the search for new policy instruments not subject to the same degree of erosion as the traditional instruments, or even choosing instruments that capitalize on the increased economic openness and mobility.

New barriers to foreign trade and international movement of capital would be examples of dis-integration, of efforts to reduce interdependence by providing for increased separation between national markets. We have experienced some of that during the past decade or two. Many countries have maintained some control over inward or outward movements of capital. Even the United States, with its relative commitment to free markets, attempted to limit outward movements of capital from 1963 to 1973, with its interest equalization tax and directives to banks. There have also been periodic revivals of protectionism. On the whole, however, dis-integrative responses to increased interdependence have been limited, partly in recognition of the great gains from interdependence and, what is not quite the same thing, the great costs associated with trying to restore effective national insulation from the world economy.

The most significant step toward less interdependence has been the movement to flexible exchange rates which took place among the major currencies in 1973. That move was complicated in its effects. It may have sustained interdependence by helping to preserve relative freedom of trade and capital movements, which would have been restricted much more severely under the pressures of the 1970s if countries had tried to maintain fixed exchange rates. But one interpretation of the movement to flexible exchange rates is that it reflected the unwillingness of countries to accept the restraints on national monetary policies entailed by a commitment to maintain fixed exchange rates in a world of high capital mobility. It therefore represented an effort to restore some monetary autonomy in a world of high interdependence. It also increases the impact of monetary actions, via the exchange rate, on real economic activity. Yet flexible exchange rates do not insulate national economies completely from the rest of the world.[26]

I will touch later on the search for new instruments of policy. But the main response to greater interdependence has been to call for greater coordination of national economic policies. Since "coordination" is always difficult, especially among independent nations, we must try to distinguish among various kinds of coordination and indicate why and under what circumstances each might be necessary.

6.1. What is to be coordinated?

Several aspects of economic policy can be coordinated. First, goals might be coordinated; these in turn may be common goals, competitive goals, or goals that relate to one another only through general economic interdependence. Second, information might be "coordinated", or exchanged, on goals, forecasts, economic structure, and intended actions. Third, the choice, magnitude, and timing of policy actions might be coordinated.

Sometimes countries will share an objective that requires costly actions for its attainment. Under these circumstances, attainment of the goal will require the interested countries to coordinate, that is, assign, their respective contributions toward that common goal. Without such coordination, or "burden-sharing",

---

[26]See Bryant (1980, ch. 23), for a discussion of the extent to which flexible exchange rates may be expected to permit autonomy in the national use of monetary policy and to insulate a national economy from disturbances originating in the rest of the world. (For the improved effectiveness of monetary policy under flexible as compared with fixed exchange rates, and some qualifications, see p. 423 ff.)

countries will be tempted to try to enjoy the benefits without paying the costs, by letting other countries take the necessary actions. And if all countries thus try to become free riders, the goal will not be achieved. There is a natural analogy with domestic public goods, where compulsory taxation may be necessary to finance them. With countries of unequal size, the larger ones may purchase some of the international public good even without contributions by the smaller countries, but the purchase will be sub-optimal except under special conditions. [27] Examples of these international public goods would be a military alliance, the encouragement of economic development through foreign aid (e.g. contributions to the International Development Association), or the attempt to limit world demand (or supply) of oil. The International Energy Agency attempted in 1979 to assign targets for reductions in oil imports among industrialized consumer countries during a period of world oil shortage; OPEC's members attempted in 1982 to restrict output during a period of world oil surplus. In each of these instances, setting the overall target and the assignment of shares were in practice inseparable.

Another example of a common goal with the necessity for assigning roles is recovery from a world recession, where each country would prefer to experience export-led recovery engineered by other countries. Under these circumstances the recovery is likely to be delayed, to the disadvantage of all.[28]

Because of the problem of distributing costs, a common goal is often converted into a competitive game, with each country manuevering to incur as low a cost as possible without jeopardizing the goal – including use of the tactic of suggesting that the goal may not be all that important, i.e. concealing the country's true preferences. In this competitive negotiating environment, the common goal is often lost to view.

Sometimes goals are directly competitive, in the sense that they are arithmetically related. The currencies of two countries have a common exchange rate, the payments or trade positions of all countries must sum to zero, and so on. As in the examples cited above, countries may set inconsistent target values for these variables, and they will be non-realizable no matter how policy measures are manipulated. For concreteness, consider overall balance-of-payments targets. Ex post, and apart from recording errors, payments positions must add to zero for the world as a whole unless there is some outside source of international reserves, i.e. some reserve asset that is not the liability of any country. Consistency must be achieved, however, even if targeted reserve changes do not add to zero; if they do not, the costs of attaining their targets will eventually reach the

[27] The particular case of financing a military alliance has been examined by Olson and Zeckhauser (1966) and by van Ypersele (1967). For a general discussion of the problem of public goods, not focussing on the international aspects, see Olson (1971).

[28] For a discussion of the "locomotive" proposal for coordinated expansionist actions by the United States, Japan, and West Germany in 1977, see Cooper (1982).

point at which countries choose to adjust them, and the ex post condition is met. In the end, the targets will be reconciled. But the outcome of this process, as we saw in Section 5, may be socially sub-optimal. This result can be avoided in several ways. One is to coordinate the targets at the outset so they are consistent; a second is to adjust the total quantity of outside reserves (such as through the issuance of Special Drawing Rights by the International Monetary Fund) so that it accommodates the ex ante target; a third (really a special variant of the first) is to persuade one country to abandon its target and act as a residual for the rest of the world.

As was noted earlier, the second solution could be made to work for reserve increases, but not for current account or trade balances. There was some attempt to "allocate" current account deficits among OECD countries after the sharp increase in oil prices and the emergence of a huge surplus by the oil-exporting nations in 1974. The attempt did not succeed formally, but it probably served the purpose of helping to avoid a self-defeating race among countries to reduce deficits that were irreducible so long as oil-exporting countries had large surpluses.

The third solution – designating a residual country to solve the so-called nth country problem, whether one is dealing with exchange rates or payments balances – is technically workable, but it may be unacceptable both to the nth country and to other countries.[29] The perception that the United States could run large payments deficits in the 1960s and its "benign neglect" of the exchange rate in the 1970s and early 1980s were both sources of great resentment abroad. In the early 1970s, in turn, the United States resented the fact that it could not effectively control its exchange rate. And for the United States to have run the "residual" current account deficit that corresponded to the OPEC surpluses of 1974–75 or 1980–81 surely would have evoked strong protectionist reactions from Americans.

Suppose that consistency of targets is assured through one solution or another. Can coordination stop here? Unfortunately not. The resulting outcome of independent national pursuit of targets may still lead to less than optimal results if countries are proceeding on different assumptions regarding the magnitude of their (non-competitive) targets, their forecasts of exogenous variables, their views of the structure of the interdependent world economy (including in particular the policy multipliers), or their forecasts of the actions by other countries. The question of information is complex, since in reality no one has perfect information and the result of action based on diverse, independent views of what will happen might conceivably be superior to the result of action taken on the basis of agreed but erroneous views concerning forecasts and economic structure.

---

[29] For a rigorous examination of optimal exchange rate arrangements to assure output stability, and the necessity for a residual country or for the imposition of a consistency rule on all countries, see Jones (1982).

Nonetheless, pooling information is likely to improve performance of the world economy as a whole. One may presume that with respect to its own targets and prospective actions each country has superior information that can be usefully shared with others. Exchanging views on forecasts and on economic structure is also likely to improve comprehension of where the greatest uncertainties lie, even if no consensus is reached on the information pool.

With consistent goals and with full information on forecasts, structure, and prospective action by others, there is a basis for successful, independent pursuit of objectives. Even then, however, the results may be inferior to those that could be achieved through close coordination of *actions*. The prospective actions reported to others will in general be contingent on the actions to be taken by others. A single iteration may be insufficient for the contingent prospective actions to converge to actions that are actually desired all around. If countries take the actions they have reported to others, they will generally discover that they have not reached their objectives because of actions taken simultaneously by others. A series of iterations through time may be necessary for convergence on the policy targets, but this process of iteration will lead to avoidable divergences from targets while it occurs, i.e. to welfare losses as compared with full coordination of actions [see Cooper (1969) and Roper (1971)]. In other words, even with consistent targets and exchange of information, the magnitude, mix, and timing of policy actions may lead to over- or under-shooting of targets. Arguably this was the principal characteristic of the world boom in 1972 and of the severity of the world recession in 1975 as countries in each case undertook macroeconomic actions without making full allowance for the actions being taken by other countries.

Of course, in principle countries could act independently if they knew fully not only the structure of foreign economies but also their policy responses under all likely contingencies. Each country could then "solve the entire system" for its own optimal policy responses and move directly to the appropriate result. Since the same (correct) information base would be shared by all countries, convergence to the desired results would be rapid.

However, the information requirements for this kind of solution would be enormous. Information about structure is not typically correct. Moreover, most governments do not know their likely reactions until confronted with actual choices. In practice, the exchange of information on policy responses under all likely contingencies would hardly be distinguishable from coordination of policy actions as the contingencies arise.

The European Community – whose very creation can be interpreted as a response to growing economic interdependence – has on occasion attempted to coordinate not only macroeconomic targets of members of the Community, but also the use of instruments. McKinnon (1982) has suggested that monetary actions in the United States, Japan, and West Germany, at a minimum, must be closely coordinated to achieve smooth global macroeconomic performance, including avoidance of inflation, because of the high substitutability among the financial assets of these countries.

6.2. Decentralized action within agreed regimes

Coordination of policy targets and actions on a continuous basis is difficult under the best of circumstances, and among democratic nations it could never be more than a very imperfect process. These difficulties raise the important question whether it is possible to establish rule-bound regimes – constitutions, as it were – which would permit decentralized national pursuit of national objectives within the rules of the regime to lead to socially optimal outcomes, or at least to avoid the worst of the unregulated, decentralized solutions. Such a framework has been successfully achieved in such areas as containment of contagious diseases, the nuclear test ban treaty (for those who signed), and the nuclear non-proliferation treaty. In the economic arena, it has been attempted with some success in the General Agreement on Tariffs and Trade (GATT) and in the Bretton Woods Agreement concerning international monetary relations.

A simple, damage-limiting view of the GATT is that it was designed to avoid the mutually disadvantageous Nash solution of countries seeking to maximize their national welfare through trade restrictions without allowing for retaliation by others, described years ago by Scitovsky (1941). Actually it was more ambitious than that. Not only did it prohibit new restrictions on trade, except under carefully controlled circumstances (and it allowed for controlled retaliation when this prohibition was violated), but it also called for non-discrimination in trade restrictions[30] (thereby reducing greatly opportunities for tariff-induced improvements in terms of trade), and it called for trade liberalization under conditions of reciprocity. Over the entire thirty-five years the GATT has been in operation, it must be reckoned a great success in accomplishing its objectives.

The Bretton Woods arrangements, with their call for fixed exchange rates, adjustable only by international agreement, was established in part to avoid the sub-optimal practices of competitive depreciation and exchange controls for purposes of generating employment and assuring payments equilibrium or even surplus. But implicit in fixed exchange rates with high capital mobility (the implications of which were not fully comprehended in the 1940s) is coordination of national monetary policies. Exchange market intervention (to maintain the

---

[30]Except for customs unions and free trade areas, an exception that preserved the purpose of limiting opportunities for tariff-induced improvements in the terms of trade. And the new common tariff of customs unions could be no more restrictive against imports from non-members, on average, than the national tariffs they replaced.

agreed exchange rate) is monetary policy; and monetary policy governed by the need to fix the exchange rate assures coordination among national monetary policies, although it leaves open the question of how world monetary policy is determined.[31]

In 1970 the International Monetary Fund began to issue SDRs, on the assumption that countries' targets for increases in owned reserves exceeded the amount of additional gold that was available for increments to monetary reserves, and that an increase in outside reserves was preferable to a scramble for payments surpluses, or to continued deficits by the United States as other countries added to their dollar holdings. Implicit in this novel arrangement was the assumption that the demand was for *owned* reserves, and not for *earned* reserves, i.e. that countries really wanted to add to their reserves, and were not merely or mainly interested in the employment and growth effects of payments surpluses.

Rule-based regimes have considerable merit if the rules are widely accepted, and this constitutional approach to international economic coordination has demonstrated some success during the past three decades. If appropriate rules can be found, rule-based regimes have the advantage over non-cooperative regimes of leading to superior outcomes, while at the same time preserving the reality of national autonomy and decentralization in economic decision-making. The nation-state and the forms of decision-making that have been developed within it are predicated on the assumption of efficacy of decisions taken at the national level. Through infrequent international negotiations of treaties or less formal agreements, a framework can perhaps be found that will preserve these forms while reducing their costs in an interdependent world.

Decision-taking at the supra-national level, or its analytical near equivalent, continuous international coordination of national policy actions, can always in principle lead to results that are superior to those produced by rule-based regimes (since when appropriate they encompass those regimes); but they do so only by threatening existing decision-making arrangements at the national level, and constitutional change at the national level entails costs as well. The search for rule-based international regimes is designed to compromise between these conflicting considerations.

Of course, in practice rule-based regimes go beyond simply laying down rules once and for all. They establish procedures for enforcing the rules, for adjudicating disputes, and for modifying the rules as necessary. They thus encourage continual consultations, if not formal decision-making, among their member states. Indeed, while it is difficult to separate the two, the consultative process may sometimes be even more important than the rules themselves. But the rules

---

[31]As noted above, Mundell (1971) suggested that that was the proper role for monetary policy in the United States, another manifestation of the nth country solution.

from a useful psychological and legal bulwark against domestic pressures for short-run, national optimizing behavior predicated, often unrealistically, on the assumption that other nations will not respond in similar manner and the regime will survive.[32]

Rule-based regimes do not usually solve the problem of conflicts in timing of economic actions, however. Moreover, a constitutional regime is typically not highly adaptable in the face of evolutionary change in economic conditions. Constitutional rules tend to be rigid – they derive much of their usefulness, while they are useful, from their inflexibility – and are not easily changed except under strong provocation. Hence there is a danger that rule-base regimes will collapse sooner or later, or erode into irrelevance as they are increasingly ignored.

6.3. Obstacles to economic coordination

The coordination of policy actions among countries is rare. There is, perhaps paradoxically, a somewhat better record at creation and maintenance of rule-based regimes, but it has proven extremely difficult to alter them in an orderly way. The reasons for lack of coordination lie in different perspectives and different interests among nations, even in settings in which all recognize the potential gains from coordination.

First, countries may not agree on the objectives. Among like-minded countries (e.g. excluding those committed to a completely different system of economic or political organization, such as communist countries), there are not likely to be radical differences of view; they operate within the same general conceptual framework. But they still may differ on such matters as the balance to be struck in macro-economic management between combating inflation and protecting employment. (Assertions that there is no trade-off between inflation and employment is a pious wish, clearly at variance with experience in the short to medium run, and untested in the long run, which is a series of short runs.) Such differences inhibit coordinated macro-economic action. Also, even with commonly agreed ultimate objectives, the distribution among nations of benefits and costs will differ depending on the exact measures undertaken, and these divergent distributional objectives may inhibit collective action.

Second, even if countries have compatible objectives and similar circumstances, they may differ on their forecasts of future events, either with respect to the course of events without changes in policy or with respect to the influence of policy actions on the targetted variables. In short, they may disagree on the

---

[32] For a skeptical discussion of the merits of rule-based regimes as compared with continual coordination, see Bryant (1980, pp. 470–475). For a skeptical discussion of continuous coordination, see Polak (1981).

structure of the economy and hence on the relationship of means to ends. This factor seemed to be part of the problem (although disagreement on objectives may also have lain beneath the surface) between the United States and West Germany in 1977, when the German government thought that a given fiscal stimulus would have a greater influence on the price level, relative to employment and output, than American officials did.[33]

Third, there may be lack of trust between nations. This factor can be important even for single episode of coordination, since heads of government typically do not take final action; they merely set in motion a political process which with luck and skill will lead to the desired action. If some leaders are thought to be unable to "deliver" on their commitments, that will inhibit cooperation by others.

Trust is even more important in a rule-based regime if it is to have durability over time. The rules of a regime cannot cover all contingencies, and few are so air-tight that they are self-enforcing in the sense that deviation from the rules leads automatically to penalties sufficiently severe to deter those deviations. Thus rule-based regimes depend for their effectiveness on adherence to the spirit as well as to the letter of the agreed rules. Decision-makers may have an incentive to deviate from previously agreed paths in new circumstances or – most importantly in this context – if they believe that *other* governments will follow the rules. Where such deviations would work to the disadvantage of the other countries, their lack of trust will inhibit the conclusion of otherwise mutually beneficial schemes of cooperation which they fear will prove to be one-sided.[34]

Fourth, public sentiment for preserving national freedom of action still runs sufficiently strong in many countries to make coordination of economic policy – especially agreement on restraints on future action – politically difficult. The illusion of national autonomy is still widespread and is widely confused with national sovereignty. The latter concerns the formal ability of a nation to act on its own rather than under the instruction of another nation. That remains undiminished. National autonomy, in contrast, is the ability of a nation to attain its objectives through unilateral action. That is heavily constrained, as we have seen, in an environment of high interdependence. Economic cooperation may

---

[33] It is possible that both were right – with respect to their own economies. That is, they found themselves in different circumstances. Sachs (1979) has argued that a high fraction of the unemployment in Germany, in contrast to the United States, was due to excessive real wages in the wake of the 1974 oil price increase rather than to deficient aggregate demand. The German government at this time encouraged increased export sales, however, which suggests that German officials did not consistently hold the Sachs view.

[34] The entire verification issue in arms-control agreements reflects deep lack of trust among the participants. In some formal economic literature, this question of trust – or lack of it – has been labelled "time inconsistency", a misleading and inappropriate term, since the "inconsistency" refers only to a particular analytical framework for choosing optimal policy over a finite period of time, and in any case the problem of forward-looking expectations has been exaggerated within that framework. On the last points, see Kydland and Prescott (1977) and the critique by Chow (1980).

restore some effectiveness in pursuit of objectives. Far from undermining national sovereignty, such cooperation often represents wise exercise of that sovereignty.

Finally, cooperation may be inhibited by the fact that no nation is willing to take the lead to achieve it. In view of the difficulties and inhibitions enumerated above, building a coalition within and among nations for effective international cooperation requires a clear view of the objective and constant effort and persuasion to achieve it. The importance of this kind of leadership, as opposed simply to taking the first move in the static games of Section 5, has been emphasized by Kindleberger (1973) who sees faltering world leadership a major cause of the Great Depression of the 1930s, by Cooper (1972), and by Whitman (1979).

6.4. The search for new instruments of policy

Two directions for economic policy created by higher interdependence have been addressed: disintegrative steps to reduce interdependence, and attempts to coordinate policies. A third involves the search for new instruments of policy that have not been subject to erosion or have actually been enhanced in their effectiveness by higher interdependence. The introduction of new instruments of policy is often neglected by economists because it falls outside their usual framework for analysis, with its relatively fixed structure. But it has undeniably occurred. In particular, as the general instruments of macroeconomic policy – overall government spending and taxation, and monetary policy – diminish in efficacy as tools for economic stabilization and growth, governments have turned elsewhere to restore some control. "Fiscal" policy has for some countries increasingly become "industrial" policy, that is, provision of industry-specific tax breaks and government expenditures designed to stimulate both domestic and foreign investment in the desired activity. To the extent that mobile foreign capital and firms can be attracted into the country, employment and growth will be stimulated. In effect, residents are willing (via the tax/expenditure system) to reduce their real after-tax rewards per unit of effort for the sake of greater employment or growth.

This process has proceeded farthest in small, highly open countries, where the leakages from overall monetary or fiscal actions are most obvious, and where the possible gains (relative to the size of the economy) from attracting internationally mobile firms are also obvious. The process can also be seen among states or provinces within the United States and Canada.[35]

---

[35]Some evidence for this shift in emphasis to attracting mobile firms is found in Cooper (1968, 1974) and Lindbeck (1973).

7. Other areas of interdependence

National economic policy in the modern economy goes well beyond macroeconomic stabilization and growth; it tries to inform and protect consumers and investors, to encourage specific forms of investment, to provide public goods and services, and to redistribute income. In each case successful policy action requires that the jurisdiction of government have a span of control that covers the domain of geographical mobility of those economic agents that are the objects of regulation or redistribution. Otherwise, those agents can escape the regulation or taxation by moving beyond the government's jurisdictional reach.

As the domain of mobility increases with improved information and communication – as international interdependence increases – the capacity of national governments to regulate and to tax economic activity is eroded.[36] Of course, the increased mobility of firms, capital, or individuals makes it attractive for some countries to provide tax or regulatory incentives to relocate, as noted in the previous section. Thus, tax havens, flags of convenience, and havens from bank regulation have sprung up around the world. Countries compete with one another in the reduction of onerous conditions imposed on desired, mobile economic agents, of which U.S. passage of the International Banking Act in 1981 to permit "offshore" banking in the United States is only one recent example.

In some cases this mobility beyond the regulating jurisdiction may improve the world's allocation of resources. Consider as an example air pollution which is relatively localized in it effects. If country A finds its air polluted to an unacceptable degree, it may impose anti-pollution regulations on its firms. Some of these firms may then find it economical to shift their activities to country B, which has no anti-pollution regulations. If the residents of country B are prepared in full knowledge to accept the additional pollution (perhaps because they have much less to start with), and if the air pollution has only local effects, both countries will be made better off in the long run by the move.

For pollution which is pervasive or global in its effects, in contrast, competition in regulatory laxity will leave the world worse off than would a coordinated approach to regulation. As in some cases of macro-economic management, international coordination of policy actions could avoid mutually damaging competition to reduce regulations; and coordination is necessary to assure Pareto-optimal results.

---

[36]Two qualifying distinctions must be made here. First, to the extent that taxation finances desired public goods and these are available only within the tax jurisdiction, taxation does not induce the departure of mobile firms, capital, or individuals. Taxation for redistribution or to finance public goods that are available outside the tax jurisdiction, e.g. general foreign or defense policies, will encourage movement. Second, to the extent that regulation applies to products rather than production processes, governmental jurisdictions can apply the regulations to imports and thus can preserve their efficacy.

This chapter is already too long to undertake a detailed analysis of these other dimensions of interdependence and their implications for economic policy and for cooperation among nations. Some further discussion can be found in Vernon (1971) and in Cooper (1968, 1974).

References

Aliber, R.Z., ed. (1974), National monetary policies and the international financial system (University of Chicago Press, Chicago).
Aliber, R.Z., ed. (1977), The political economy of monetary reform (Macmillan, London).
Allen, P.R. and P.B. Kenen (1980), Asset markets, exchange rates, and economic integration: A synthesis (Cambridge University Press, New York).
Ando, A., E.C. Brown, and A.F. Friedlaender, eds. (1968), Studies in economic stabilization (The Brookings Institution, Washington).
Aoki, M. (1976), "On decentralized stabilization policies and dynamic assignment problems", Journal of International Economics, 6:143-171.
Aoki, M. (1981), Dynamic analysis of open economies (Academic Press, New York).
Baldwin, D.A. (1980), "Interdependence and power: A conceptual analysis," International Organization, Autumn, 34:471-506.
Bentzel, R. and B. Hansen (1954), "On recursiveness and interdependency in economic models", Review of Economic Studies, 22:153-168.
Brainard, W.C. (1967), "Uncertainty and the effectiveness of policy," American Economic Review, Papers and Proceedings, 57:411-425.
Brown, W.A., Jr. (1940), The international gold standard reinterpreted, 1914-1934, (National Bureau of Economic Research, New York).
Bryant, R.C. (1980), Money and monetary policy in interdependent nations (The Brookings Institution, Washington).
Buiter, W. and J. Eaton (1985), "Policy decentralization and exchange rate management in interdependent economies", in: J.S. Bhandari, ed., Exchange rate management under uncertainty (MIT Press, Cambridge, Mass.).
Canzoneri, M.B., and J.A. Gray (1983), "Two essays on monetary policy in an interdependent world", International Finance Discussion Paper, No. 219 (Federal Reserve Board, Washington, February).
Chow, G.C. (1980), "Econometric policy evaluation and optimization under rational expectations", Journal of Economic Dynamics and Control, 2:47-60.
Cooper, R.N. (1968), The economics of interdependence (McGraw-Hill, New York).
Cooper, R.N. (1969), "Macroeconomic policy adjustments in interdependent economies", Quarterly Journal of Economics, 83:1-24.
Cooper, R.N. (1972), "Trade policy is foreign policy", Foreign Policy, 9:18-36.
Cooper, R.N. (1974), Economic mobility and national economic policy (Alquist and Wiksell, Stockholm).
Cooper, R.N. (1975), "Prolegomena to the choice of an international monetary system", International Organization, 29:63-97.
Cooper, R.N. (1982), "Global economic policy in a world of energy shortage", in: Joseph Pechman and James Simler, eds., Economics in the public service (Norton, New York).
Corden, W.M. (1983), "The logic of the international monetary non-system", in: F. Machlup et al., eds., Reflections on a troubled world economy: Essays in honor of Herbert Giersch (MacMillan, London).
Dornbusch, R. and J.A. Frenkel, eds. (1979), International economic policy (The John Hopkins University Press, Baltimore).
Fleming, J.M. (1962), "Domestic financial policies under fixed and flexible exchange rates", International Monetary Fund Staff Papers, 9:369-79.
Hamada, K. (1974), "Alternative exchange rate systems and the interdependence of monetary policies", in: Aliber.

Hamada, K. (1976), "A strategic analysis on monetary interdependence", Journal of Political Economy, 84:677–700.

Hamada, K. (1979), "Macroeconomic strategy and coordination under alternative exchange rates", in: Dornbusch and Frenkel.

Hirschman, A.O. (1945), National power and the structure of foreign trade, (University of California Press, Berkeley).

Johnson, H.G. (1958), "Optimum tariffs and retaliation", in: International trade and economic growth (George Allen and Unwin, London).

Jones, M. (1982), "Automatic output stability and the exchange arrangement: A multi-country analysis", Review of Economic Studies, 49:91–107.

Kenen, P.B. (1969), "The theory of optimum currency areas: An eclectic view", in: Mundell and Swoboda.

Keohane, R.O. and J.S. Nye (1977), Power and interdependence: World politics in transition (Little Brown, Boston).

Kindleberger, C.P. (1973), The world in depression, 1929–1939 (University of California Press, Berkeley).

Kydland, F.E. and E.C. Prescott (1977), "Rules rather than discretion: The inconsistency of optimal plans", Journal of Political Economy, 85:473–491.

Lindbeck, A. (1973), The national state in an internationalized world economy, Rio de Janeiro Conjunto Univsitario Candido Mendes.

McKinnon, R.I. (1982), "Currency substitution and instability in the world dollar market", American Economic Review, 72:320–333.

Meade, J.E. (1951), The theory of international economic policy, Vol. 1, The balance of payments (Royal Institute for International Affairs, London).

Mundell, R.A. (1968), International economics (Macmillan, New York).

Mundell, R.A. and A.K. Swoboda eds., (1969) Monetary problems of the international economy (University of Chicago Press, Chicago).

Mundell, R.A. (1971), Monetary theory: Inflation, interest, and growth in the world economy (Goodyear Publishing Co., Pacific Palisades, Calif.).

Mussa, M. (1979), "Macroeconomic interdependence and the exchange rate regime", in: Dornbusch and Frenkel.

Niehans, J. (1968), "Monetary and fiscal policies in open economies under fixed exchange rates: An optimizing approach", Journal of Political Economy, 76:893–920.

Olsen, M., Jr. (1971), The logic of collective action, 2nd edn. (Harvard University Press, Cambridge, Mass.).

Olsen, M., Jr. and R. Zeckhauser (1966), "An economic theory of alliances", Review of Economics and Statistics, 48:266–279.

Patrick, J.D. (1973), "Establishing convergent decentralized policy assignment", Journal of International Economics, 3:37–51.

Polak, J.J. (1981), Coordination of national economic policies (Group of Thirty, New York).

Resnick, S. (1968), "An empirical study of economic policy in the common market", in: Ando et al. (1968).

Roper, D.E., 1971, "Macroeconomic policies and the distribution of the world money supply", Quarterly Journal of Economics, 85:119–146.

Sachs, J. (1983), "International policy coordination in a dynamic macroeconomic model", NBER Working Paper No. 1166.

Sachs, J. (1979), "Wages, profits, and macroeconomic adjustment: A comparative study", Brookings Papers on Economic Activity, 269–319.

Scitovsky, T. (1942), "A reconsideration of the theory of tariffs", Review of Economic Studies, 9:89–110; reprinted in A.E.A.: Readings in the theory of international trade (Blakiston, Philadelphia, 1949).

Swoboda, A.K., and R. Dornbusch (1973), "Adjustment, policy, and monetary equilibrium in a two-country model", in: M.B. Connolly and Alexander K. Swoboda, eds., International trade and money (George Allen and Unwin, London).

Theil, H. (1964), Optimal decision rules for government and industry (North-Holland, Amsterdam).

Tinbergen, J. (1952), On the theory of economic policy (North-Holland, Amsterdam).

Tobin, J. and W. Buiter (1980), "Fiscal and monetary policies, capital formation, and economic activity", in: George von Furstenberg ed., The government and capital formation (Ballinger, Cambridge, Mass.).

Tobin, J. and J.B. de Macedo (1980), "The short-run macroeconomics of floating exchange rates: An exposition", in: J.S. Chipman and C.P. Kindleberger, eds., Flexible exchange rates and the balance of payments (North-Holland, Amsterdam).

Van Ypersele, J. (1967), "Sharing the defense burden among western allies", Review of economics and statistics, 49:527–536.

Vernon, R. (1971), Sovereignty at bay (Basic Books, New York).

Waltz, K. (1970), "The myth of interdependence", in: C.P. Kindleberger, ed., The multinational corporation.

Whitman, M.v.N. (1979), Reflections of interdependence (University of Pittsburgh Press, Pittsburgh).

INDEX

HANDBOOKS IN ECONOMICS

1. HANDBOOK OF MATHEMATICAL ECONOMICS (in 4 volumes)
    Volumes 1, 2 and 3 edited by Kenneth J. Arrow and Michael D. Intriligator
    Volume 4 edited by Werner Hildenbrand and Hugo Sonnenschein

2. HANDBOOK OF ECONOMETRICS (in 6 volumes)
    Volumes 1, 2 and 3 edited by Zvi Griliches and Michael D. Intriligator
    Volume 4 edited by Robert F. Engle and Daniel L. McFadden
    Volume 5 edited by James J. Heckman and Edward Leamer
    Volume 6 is in preparation (editors James J. Heckman and Edward Leamer)

3. HANDBOOK OF INTERNATIONAL ECONOMICS (in 3 volumes)
    Volumes 1 and 2 edited by Ronald W. Jones and Peter B. Kenen
    Volume 3 edited by Gene M. Grossman and Kenneth Rogoff

4. HANDBOOK OF PUBLIC ECONOMICS (in 4 volumes)
    Edited by Alan J. Auerbach and Martin Feldstein

5. HANDBOOK OF LABOR ECONOMICS (in 5 volumes)
    Volumes 1 and 2 edited by Orley C. Ashenfelter and Richard Layard
    Volumes 3A, 3B and 3C edited by Orley C. Ashenfelter and David Card

6. HANDBOOK OF NATURAL RESOURCE AND ENERGY ECONOMICS
    (in 3 volumes). Edited by Allen V. Kneese and James L. Sweeney

7. HANDBOOK OF REGIONAL AND URBAN ECONOMICS (in 4 volumes)
    Volume 1 edited by Peter Nijkamp
    Volume 2 edited by Edwin S. Mills
    Volume 3 edited by Paul C. Cheshire and Edwin S. Mills
    Volume 4 is in preparation (editors J. Vernon Henderson and Jacques-François Thisse)

8. HANDBOOK OF MONETARY ECONOMICS (in 2 volumes)
    Edited by Benjamin Friedman and Frank Hahn

9. HANDBOOK OF DEVELOPMENT ECONOMICS (in 4 volumes)
    Volumes 1 and 2 edited by Hollis B. Chenery and T.N. Srinivasan
    Volumes 3A and 3B edited by Jere Behrman and T.N. Srinivasan

10. HANDBOOK OF INDUSTRIAL ORGANIZATION (in 3 volumes)
    Volumes 1 and 2 edited by Richard Schmalensee and Robert R. Willig
    Volume 3 is in preparation (editors Mark Armstrong and Robert H. Porter)

11. HANDBOOK OF GAME THEORY with Economic Applications (in 3 volumes)
    Edited by Robert J. Aumann and Sergiu Hart

12. HANDBOOK OF DEFENSE ECONOMICS (in 1 volume)
    Edited by Keith Hartley and Todd Sandler

13. HANDBOOK OF COMPUTATIONAL ECONOMICS (in 2 volumes)
    Volume 1 edited by Hans M. Amman, David A. Kendrick and John Rust
    Volume 2 is in preparation (editors Kenneth L. Judd and Leigh Tesfatsion)

14. HANDBOOK OF POPULATION AND FAMILY ECONOMICS (in 2 volumes)
    Edited by Mark R. Rosenzweig and Oded Stark

15. HANDBOOK OF MACROECONOMICS (in 3 volumes)
    Edited by John B. Taylor and Michael Woodford

16. HANDBOOK OF INCOME DISTRIBUTION (in 1 volume)
    Edited by Anthony B. Atkinson and François Bourguignon

17. HANDBOOK OF HEALTH ECONOMICS (in 2 volumes)
    Edited by Anthony J. Culyer and Joseph P. Newhouse

18. HANDBOOK OF AGRICULTURAL ECONOMICS (in 4 volumes)
    Edited by Bruce L. Gardner and Gordon C. Rausser

19. HANDBOOK OF SOCIAL CHOICE AND WELFARE (in 2 volumes)
    Volume 1 edited by Kenneth J. Arrow, Amartya K. Sen and Kotaro Suzumura
    Volume 2 is in preparation (editors Kenneth J. Arrow, Amartya K. Sen and Kotaro Suz

20. HANDBOOK OF ENVIRONMENTAL ECONOMICS (in 3 volumes)
    Volume 1 is edited by Karl-Goran Mäler and Jeff Vincent
    Volumes 2 and 3 are in preparation (editors Karl-Goran Mäler and Jeff Vincent)

FORTHCOMING TITLES

HANDBOOK OF EXPERIMENTAL RESULTS ECONOMICS
Editors Charles Plott and Vernon L. Smith

HANDBOOK OF THE ECONOMICS OF FINANCE
Editors George M. Constantinides, Milton Harris and René M. Stulz

HANDBOOK ON THE ECONOMICS OF GIVING, RECIPROCITY AND ALTRUISM
Editors Serge-Christophe Kolm and Jean Mercier Ythier

HANDBOOK ON THE ECONOMICS OF ART AND CULTURE
Editors Victor Ginsburgh and David Throsby

HANDBOOK OF ECONOMIC GROWTH
Editors Philippe Aghion and Steven N. Durlauf

HANDBOOK OF LAW AND ECONOMICS
Editors A. Mitchell Polinsky and Steven Shavell

All published volumes available

Printed and bound by CPI Group (UK) Ltd, Croydon, CR0 4YY

08/05/2025

01864967-0001